An Introduction to English Sentence Structure

This outstanding resource for students offers a step-by-step, practical introduction to English syntax and syntactic principles, as developed by Chomsky over the past 15 years. Assuming little or no prior background in syntax, Andrew Radford outlines the core concepts and how they can be used to describe various aspects of English sentence structure. This is an abridged version of Radford's major new textbook *Analysing English Sentences* (also published by Cambridge University Press), and will be welcomed as a handy introduction to current syntactic theory.

ANDREW RADFORD is Professor & Head of the Department of Language and Linguistics at the University of Essex. His recent publications include *Minimalist Syntax: Exploring the Structure of English* (Cambridge, 2004) and *English Syntax: An Introduction* (Cambridge, 2004).

An Introduction to English Sentence Structure

ANDREW RADFORD

University of Essex

CAMBRIDGE UNIVERSITY PRESS
Cambridge, New York, Melbourne, Madrid, Cape Town, Singapore, São Paulo, Delhi

Cambridge University Press
The Edinburgh Building, Cambridge CB2 8RU, UK

Published in the United States of America by Cambridge University Press, New York

www.cambridge.org
Information on this title: www.cambridge.org/9780521731904

First published 2009

Printed in the United Kingdom at the University Press, Cambridge

A catalogue record for this publication is available from the British Library

Library of Congress Cataloguing in Publication data
Radford, Andrew.
An introduction to English sentence structure / Andrew Radford.
  p. cm.
Includes bibliographical references and index.
ISBN 978-0-521-51693-8 – ISBN 978-0-521-73190-4 (pbk.)   1. English language – Sentence –
Problems, exercises, etc.   2. English language – Syntax – Problems, exercises, etc.   3. English
language – Rhetoric – Problems, exercises, etc.   4. English language – Grammar.   I. Title.

PE1441.R36   2009
428.2 – dc22   2008040106

ISBN 978-0-521-51693-8 hardback
ISBN 978-0-521-73190-4 paperback

Contents

Preface

Aims

This book supercedes my *English Syntax* book, published in 2004. Although there is much in common between the two books, it should be noted that this book contains new material and new analyses (particularly in later chapters). It has two main aims. The first is to provide an intensive introduction to recent work in syntactic theory (more particularly to how the *syntactic component* operates within the model of grammar assumed in recent work within the framework of Chomsky's *Minimalist Program*). The second is to provide a description of a range of phenomena in English syntax, making use of Minimalist concepts and assumptions wherever possible.

Key features

The book is intended to be suitable both for people with only minimal grammatical knowledge, and for those who have already done quite a bit of syntax but want to know something (more) about Minimalism. It is not historicist or comparative in orientation, and does not presuppose knowledge of earlier or alternative models of grammar. It is written in an approachable style, avoiding unnecessary complexity and unexplained jargon. Each chapter contains:

- a core text (divided up into eight sections or so) focusing on a specific topic
- a summary recapitulating the main points in the chapter
- a list of key concepts/principles introduced in the chapter
- a bibliographical section providing extensive references to original source material
- a workbook section containing two different kinds of exercise
- a set of *model answers* accompanying the exercises, together with extensive *helpful hints* designed to eliminate common errors students make and to help students whose native language is not English
- an extensive glossary and integral list of abbreviations

The bibliographical background section often contains references to primary research works which are highly technical in nature, and so it would not be appropriate for students to tackle them until they have read the whole book: they are intended to provide a useful source of bibliographical information for extended essays or research projects in particular areas, rather than being essential back-up reading: indeed, the exercises in the book are designed in such a way that they can be tackled on the basis of the coursebook material alone. The *glossary* at the end of the book provides simple illustrations of how key technical terms are used (both theory-specific terms like **EPP** and traditional terms like **subject**): technical terms are written in **bold** print when they are mentioned for the first time in the main text (*italics* being used for highlighting particular expressions – e.g. a key word appearing in an example sentence). The glossary also contains an integrated list of *abbreviations*.

The book is intensive and progressive in nature, which means that it starts at an elementary level but gets progressively harder as you delve further into the book. A group of students I taught an earlier version of the book to gave the following degree-of-difficulty score to each chapter on a 5-point scale ranging from $1 = very\ easy$ to $5 = very\ hard$: ch.1 = 1.7; ch.2 = 2.2; ch.3 = 2.7; ch.4 = 2.9; ch.5 = 3.2; ch.6 = 3.4; ch.7 = 3.7; ch.8 = 4.2; ch.9 = 4.4.

Successive chapters become cumulatively more complex, in that each chapter presupposes material covered in previous chapters as well as introducing new material: hence it is helpful to go back and read material from earlier chapters every so often. In some cases, analyses presented in earlier chapters are subsequently refined or revised in the light of new assumptions made in later chapters.

Teaching materials

For teachers adopting the book, I have developed a series of web materials (in the form of Powerpoint transparencies) designed to provide two hours' worth of teaching material for each chapter. The relevant materials present detailed step-by-step analyses of those exercise examples which have the symbol **(w)** after them in the coursebook. They can be accessed at www.cambridge.org/radford

Companion volume

This book is being produced in parallel with a longer version entitled *Analysing English Sentences: A Minimalist Approach.* In this shorter version, the main text (particularly in the later chapters) is generally about a third shorter than the main text in the longer version (with the exception of chapters 1 and 6). This shorter version is aimed primarily at students whose native language is not English, and who are taking (English) syntax as a minor rather than a major course. The two books have an essentially parallel organisation into chapters and sections (though additional sections, technical discussion and bibliographial references are included in the longer version), and contain much the same exercise material.

In keeping the two books parallel in structure and organisation as far as possible, I am mindful of the comment made in a review of two earlier books which I produced in parallel longer and shorter versions (Radford 1997a and Radford 1997b) that some readers may wish to read the short version of a given chapter first, and then look at the longer version afterwards, and that this is 'not facilitated' if there is 'an annoyingly large number of non-correspondences' between the two (Ten Hacken 2001, p. 2). Accordingly, I have tried to maximise correspondence between the 'long' and 'short' versions of these two new books.

Acknowledgments

I am grateful to Neil Smith (of University College London) for his forebearance in patiently wading through an earlier draft of the manuscript and pointing out some of the imperfections in it, while managing to make his comments challenging and good-humoured at the same time. Thanks also go to my Essex colleague Bob Borsley for helpful comments, and to Michèle Vincent for preparing the index.

Dedication

This book is dedicated to my long-suffering wife Khadija (who has had to put up with extended periods of authorial autism) and to her family, who have always spoiled me shamefully (and done their best to indulge my every whim) whenever we visit Morocco.

1 Grammar

1.1 Overview

In broad terms, this book is concerned with aspects of grammar. Grammar is traditionally subdivided into two different but interrelated areas of study – **morphology** and **syntax**. Morphology is the study of how words are formed out of smaller units (called **morphemes**), and so addresses questions such as 'What are the component morphemes of a word like *antidisestablishmentarianism*, and what is the nature of the morphological operations by which they are combined together to form the overall word?' Syntax is the study of the way in which phrases and sentences are structured out of words, and so addresses questions like 'What is the structure of a sentence like *What's the president doing?* and what is the nature of the grammatical operations by which its component words are combined together to form the overall sentence structure?' In this chapter, we begin (in §1.2) by taking a brief look at the approach to the study of syntax taken in **traditional grammar**: this also provides an opportunity to introduce some useful grammatical terminology. In the remainder of the chapter, we look at the approach to syntax adopted within the theory of **Universal Grammar** developed by Chomsky.

1.2 Traditional grammar: Categories and functions

Within traditional grammar, the syntax of a language is described in terms of a taxonomy (i.e. classificatory list) of the range of different types of syntactic structures found in the language. The central assumption underpinning syntactic analysis in traditional grammar is that phrases and sentences are built up of a series of **constituents** (i.e. syntactic units), each of which belongs to a specific **grammatical category** and serves a specific **grammatical function**. Given this assumption, the task of the linguist in analysing the syntactic structure of any given type of sentence is to identify each of the constituents in the sentence, and (for each constituent) to say what category it belongs to and what function it serves. For example, in relation to the syntax of a simple sentence like:

(1)   Students protested

it would traditionally be said that the sentence consists of two constituents (the word *students* and the word *protested*), that each of these constituents belongs to a specific grammatical category (*students* being a plural **noun** and *protested* a past tense **verb**) and that each serves a specific grammatical function (*students* being the **subject** of the sentence, and *protested* being the **predicate**). The overall sentence *Students protested* has the categorial status of a **clause** which is **finite** in nature (by virtue of denoting an event taking place at a specific time), and has the semantic function of expressing a **proposition** which is **declarative** in **force** (in that it is used to make a statement rather than e.g. ask a question). Accordingly, a traditional grammar of English would tell us that the simplest type of finite declarative clause found in English is a sentence like (1), in which a nominal subject is followed by a verbal predicate. Let's briefly look at some of the terminology used here.

In traditional grammar, words are assigned to grammatical categories (called **parts of speech**) on the basis of their **semantic** properties (i.e. meaning), **morphological** properties (i.e. the range of different forms they have) and **syntactic** properties (i.e. word-order properties relating to the positions they can occupy within sentences): a set of words which belong to the same category thus have a number of semantic, morphological and syntactic properties in common. There are traditionally said to be two different types of word, namely **content words/contentives** (= words which have substantive lexical content) on the one hand, and **function words/functors** (= words which essentially serve to mark grammatical properties) on the other. The differences between the two can be illustrated by comparing a contentive like *car* with a functor like *they*. A noun like *car* has substantive lexical content in that it denotes an object which typically has four wheels and an engine, and it would be easy enough to draw a picture of a typical *car*; by contrast, a pronoun such as *they* has no descriptive content (e.g. you can't draw a picture of *they*), but rather is a functor which simply marks grammatical (more specifically, person, number and case) properties in that it is a third person plural nominative pronoun. Because they have lexical semantic content, content words often (though not always) have antonyms (i.e. 'opposites') – e.g. the adjective *tall* has the antonym *short*, the verb *increase* has the antonym *decrease*, and the preposition *inside* has the antonym *outside*: by contrast, a typical function word like e.g. the pronoun *me* has no obvious antonym. Corresponding to these two different types of (content and function) word are two different kinds of grammatical category – namely **lexical/substantive categories** (= categories whose members are content words) on the one hand, and **functional categories** (= categories whose members are function words) on the other.

Let's begin by looking at the main **lexical/substantive categories** found in English – namely **noun, verb, adjective, adverb** and **preposition** (conventionally abbreviated to N, V, A, ADV and P in order to save space). **Nouns** (= N) are traditionally said to have the semantic property that they denote entities: so, *bottle* is a noun (since it denotes a type of object used to contain liquids), *water* is a noun (since it denotes a type of liquid) and *John* is a noun (since it denotes a specific person). There are a number of distinct subtypes of noun: for example, a noun like *chair* is a **count noun** in that it can be counted (cf. *one chair, two chairs . . .*), whereas a noun like *furniture* is a **mass noun** in that it denotes an uncountable mass (hence the ungrammaticality of *one furniture, *two furnitures* – a prefixed star/asterisk being used to indicate that an expression is ungrammatical). Likewise, a distinction is traditionally drawn between a **common noun** like *boy* (which can be modified by a determiner like *the* – as in *The boy is lying*) and a **proper noun** like *Andrew* (which cannot be used in the same way in English, as we see from the ungrammaticality of *The Andrew is lying*). Count nouns generally have the morphological property that they have two different forms: a **singular** form (like *horse* in *one horse*) used to denote a single entity, and a **plural** form (like *horses* in *two horses*) used to denote more than one entity. Common nouns have the syntactic property that only (an appropriate kind of) noun can be used to end a sentence such as *They have no . . .* In place of the dots here we could insert a singular count noun like *car*, or a plural count noun like *friends* or a mass noun like *money*, but not other types of word (e.g. not *see* or *slowly* or *up*, as these are not nouns).

A second lexical/substantive category is that of **verb** (= V). These are traditionally said to have the semantic property that they denote actions or events: so, *eat*, *sing*, *pull* and *resign* are all (action-denoting) verbs. From a syntactic point of view, verbs have the property that only an appropriate kind of verb (in its uninflected **infinitive** form) can be used to complete a sentence such as *They/It can . . .* So, words like *stay*, *leave*, *hide*, *die*, *starve* and *cry* are all verbs and hence can be used in place of the dots here (but words like *apple*, *under*, *pink* and *if* aren't). From a morphological point of view, regular verbs like *cry* in English have the property that they have four distinct forms: e.g. alongside the **bare** (i.e. uninflected) **form** *cry* we find the **present tense** form *cries*, the **past tense/perfect participle/passive participle** form *cried* and the **progressive participle** form *crying*. (See the Glossary of terminology at the end of this book if you are not familiar with these terms.)

A third lexical/substantive category is that of **adjective** (= A). These are traditionally said to have the semantic property of denoting states or attributes (cf. *ill*, *happy*, *tired*, *conscientious*, *red*, *cruel*, *old* etc.). They have the syntactic property that they can occur after *be* to complete a sentence like *They may be . . .* (as with *They may be tired/ill/happy* etc.), and the further syntactic property that (if they denote a **gradable** property which can exist in varying degrees) they can be modified by a degree word like *very/rather/somewhat* (cf. *She is very happy*). Many (but not all) adjectives have the morphological property that they have **comparative** forms ending in -*er* and **superlative** forms ending in -*est* (cf. *big/bigger/biggest*).

A fourth lexical/substantive category is that of **adverb** (= ADV). These often have the semantic property that they denote the manner in which an action is performed (as with *well* in *She sings well*). Regular adverbs have the morphological property that they are formed from adjectives by the addition of the suffix *-ly* (so that corresponding to the adjective *sad* we have the adverb *sadly*). A syntactic property of adverbs is that an adverb (like e.g. *badly*) is the only kind of word which could be used to end sentences such as *She behaved . . ., He treats her . . .* or *He worded the statement . . .*

The fifth and final lexical/substantive category found in English is that of **preposition** (= P). Many of these have the semantic property of marking location (cf. *in/on/off/inside/outside/under/above/below*). They have the syntactic property that a preposition (with the appropriate kind of meaning) can be modified by *right* in the sense of 'completely', or by *straight* in the sense of 'directly' (as with the preposition *down* in *He fell right down the stairs* and the preposition *to* in *He went straight to bed*). Prepositions have the morphological property that they are invariable/uninflected forms (e.g. the preposition *off* has no past tense form **offed*, no superlative form **offest* and so on).

In addition to the five lexical/substantive categories identified above, English also has a number of functional categories. One such functional category is that of **determiner** (= D) – a category whose members are traditionally said to include the definite article *the* and the demonstrative determiners *this/that/these/those*. They are called determiners because they have the semantic property that they determine specific semantic properties of the noun expression that they introduce, marking it as a definite referring expression: for example, an expression like *the car* in a sentence such as *Shall we take the car?* is a definite referring expression in the sense that it refers to a definite (specific) car which is assumed to be familiar to the hearer/addressee. A related class of words are those which belong to the functional category **quantifier** (= Q), denoting expressions of quantity, such as *some/all/no/any/each/every/most/much/many*. (We shall also take the indefinite article *a* to be a quantifier – one which quantifies over a single entity.)

A further type of functional category found in English is that of **pronoun** (= PRN). Pronouns are items which are said to 'stand in place of' (the meaning of the prefix *pro-*) or 'refer back to' noun expressions. However, there are reasons to think that there are a number of different types of pronoun found in English and other languages. For example, in sentences such as *John has a red car and Jim has a blue one*, the word *one* is traditionally said to be a pronoun because it has no lexical semantic content of its own, but rather takes its content from its **antecedent** (i.e. *one* refers back to the noun *car* and so *one* is interpreted as having the same meaning as *car*). However, from a morphological perspective, the pronoun *one* behaves like a regular count noun in that it has a plural form ending in *-s* (as in *I'll take the green apples if you haven't got any red ones*). So, more accurately, we could say that *one* is an N-pronoun (or pronominal noun). By contrast, in a sentence like *Many miners were rescued, but some died*, the word *some* seems to function as a Q-pronoun (i.e. a pronominal quantifier). And in a sentence like *These apples are ripe, but those aren't*, the word *those* seems to be a D-pronoun (i.e. a pronominal determiner). Indeed, some linguists have argued that so-called **personal pronouns** like *I/me/we/us/you/he/him/she/her/it/they/them* are also

D-pronouns: the rationale for this is that some such pronouns can be used as determiners which modify a following noun (as in *We republicans don't trust you democrats*, where *we* could be argued to be a determiner modifying the noun *republicans*, and *you* could be seen as a determiner modifying the noun *democrats*). While, as noted here, pronouns can be argued to belong to a number of distinct types of category, in order to simplify discussion I shall simply refer to them as belonging to the category PRN throughout this book. (Because there are a number of different types of pronoun, some linguists prefer to refer to them by using the more general term **proform**.)

Another type of functional category found in English is that of **auxiliary (verb)**. They have the semantic property of marking grammatical properties such as **tense**, **aspect**, **voice** or **mood** (see the Glossary of terminology at the end of the book if you are not sure what these terms mean). Auxiliaries have the syntactic property that (unlike lexical/main verbs) they can be inverted with their subject in questions (so that corresponding to a statement like *It is raining* we have the question *Is it raining?* where the auxiliary *is* has moved in front of the subject *it* and is said to have been *inverted*). The items italicised in (2) below (in the use illustrated there) are traditionally categorised as auxiliaries taking a [bracketed] complement containing a bold-printed verb:

(2) (a)   He *has/had* [**gone**]
    (b)   She *is/was* [**staying** at home]
    (c)   They *are/were* [**taken** away for questioning]
    (d)   He really *does/did* [**say** a lot]
    (e)   You *can/could* [**help** us]
    (f)   They *may/might* [**come** back]
    (g)   He *will/would* [**get** upset]
    (h)   I *shall/should* [**return**]

In the uses illustrated here, *have/be* in (2a,b) are (**perfect/progressive**) **aspect** auxiliaries, *be* in (2c) is a (**passive**) **voice** auxiliary, *do* in (2d) is an **expletive** or **dummy** auxiliary (i.e. one with no intrinsic lexical semantic content), and *can/could/may/might/will/would/shall/should* in (2e–h) are **modal** auxiliaries. What auxiliaries in sentences like those above have in common is the fact that they inflect for present/past tense. Hence, in work in syntax over the past ten years or so, they have been said to belong to the category T (= tense-marked auxiliary).

An interesting word which has been argued to be related to tense-marking auxiliaries in work over the past thirty years or so is the infinitive particle *to*, in sentences such as:

(3)   They are now expecting the president *to* be impeached tomorrow

In a sentence like (3), infinitival *to* seems to have future time-reference (in that the act of impeachment will take place at some time in the future), and this is why we can use the word *tomorrow* in the *to*-clause. In this respect, infinitival *to* seems to have much the same function as the auxiliary *will* in *They are now expecting that the president will be impeached tomorrow*, suggesting that infinitival *to* is an **infinitival tense marker**, and so belongs to the same category T as present/past tense auxiliaries such as *is/was*. The difference between auxiliaries and infinitival *to* is that most auxiliaries overtly inflect for present/past tense (though this is not true of the invariable auxiliaries *must* and *ought*), whereas infinitival *to* is invariable in form. We can thus say that an auxiliary like *will* is a finite T constituent, whereas infinitival *to* is a nonfinite T.

The last type of functional category which we will look at is a kind of word (like each of the words italicised in the examples below) which is traditionally termed a (subordinating) **conjunction**:

(4) (a)   I think [*that* you may be right]
   (b)   I doubt [*if* you can help me]
   (c)   I'm anxious [*for* you to receive the best treatment possible]

Each of the bracketed clauses in (4) is a complement clause, in that it is the complement of the word immediately preceding it (*think/doubt/anxious*); for this reason, the italicised word which introduces each clause is known in work since the 1960s as a **complementiser** (= C), and this is the terminology which will be adopted throughout this book. Complementisers are functors in the sense that they encode particular sets of grammatical properties. For example, complementisers encode (non)finiteness by virtue of the fact that they are intrinsically finite or nonfinite. More specifically, the complementisers *that* and *if* are inherently finite in the sense that they can only be used to introduce a finite clause (i.e. a clause containing a present or past tense auxiliary or verb, like the present tense auxiliaries *may* and *can* in 4a and 4b); by contrast, *for* is an inherently infinitival complementiser, and so can be used to introduce a clause containing infinitival *to* (as in 4c). Moreover, *that* introduces a **declarative** clause (i.e. one which has the **force** of a statement), *if* introduces an **interrogative** clause (i.e. one which has the force of a question) and *for* introduces an **irrealis** clause (i.e. one relating to a hypothetical event which hasn't yet taken place and may or may not take place at some stage in the future). Hence, we can say *that* is a finite declarative complementiser, *if* is a finite interrogative complementiser and *for* is an infinitival irrealis complementiser.

Using the set of syntactic categories outlined above, we can employ the traditional **labelled bracketing** technique to *categorise* words (i.e. assign them to grammatical categories) in a way which describes how they are being used in a particular sentence. Using this technique, the words in sentence (5a) below can be categorised as in (5b):

(5) (a)   The president is clearly feeling angry that Congress has refused to negotiate with him
   (b)   [D The] [N president] [T is] [ADV clearly] [V feeling] [A angry] [C that]
          [N Congress] [T has] [V refused] [T to] [V negotiate] [P with] [PRN him]

The labelled bracketing in (5b) tells us that *the* is a D/determiner, *president* a N/noun, *is* a T/present tense auxiliary, *clearly* an ADV/adverb, *feeling* a V/verb, *angry* an A/adjective, *that* a C/complementiser, *Congress* a N/noun, *has* a T/present tense auxiliary, *refused* a V/verb, *to* a T/infinitival tense particle, *negotiate* a V/verb, *with* a P/preposition and *him* a PRN/pronoun.

The discussion of grammatical categories presented above is merely a brief sketch: however, it suffices to illustrate the point that when traditional grammarians analyse the syntax of sentences, they begin by assigning each of the words in the sentence to a grammatical category which describes how it is being used in the sentence concerned. Grammatical differences between individual words belonging to the same category are traditionally described in terms of sets of **grammatical features**, and these features (by convention) are enclosed in square brackets. For example, both *she* and *us* are pronouns, but they differ in that *she* is a **third person** pronoun which is **feminine** in **gender**, **singular** in **number** and **nominative** in **case**, whereas *us* is a first person pronoun which is **plural** in number and **accusative** in case. Accordingly, we can describe the differences between these two pronouns by saying that the pronoun *she* carries the features [third-person, singular-number, feminine-gender, nominative-case], whereas *us* carries the features [first-person, plural-number, accusative-case].

As noted at the beginning of this section, traditional grammarians are also concerned to describe the **grammatical functions** which words and other expressions fulfil within the sentences containing them. We can illustrate this point in terms of the following set of sentences:

(6) (a)   *John* smokes
    (b)   *The president* smokes
    (c)   *The president of Utopia* smokes
    (d)   *The former president of the island paradise of Utopia* smokes

Sentence (6a) comprises the noun *John* which serves the function of being the **subject** of the sentence (and denotes the person performing the act of smoking), and the verb *smokes* which serves the function of being the **predicate** of the sentence (and describes the act being performed). In (6a), the subject is the single noun *John*; but as the examples in (6b,c,d) show, the subject of a sentence can also be an (italicised) phrase like *the president*, or *the president of Utopia* or *the former president of the island paradise of Utopia*.

Now consider the following set of sentences:

(7) (a)   John smokes *cigars*
    (b)   John smokes *Cuban cigars*
    (c)   John smokes *Cuban cigars imported from Havana*
    (d)   John smokes *a specific brand of Cuban cigars imported by a friend of his from Havana*

Sentence (7a) comprises the **subject** *John*, the **predicate** *smokes* and the **complement** (or **direct object**) *cigars*. (The complement *cigars* describes the entity on which the act of smoking is being performed; as this example illustrates, subjects normally precede the verb with which they are associated in English, whereas complements typically follow the verb.) The complement in (7a) is the single noun *cigars*; but a complement can also be a **phrase**: in (7b), the complement of *smokes* is the phrase *Cuban cigars*; in (7c) the complement is the phrase *Cuban cigars imported from Havana*; and in (7d) the complement is the phrase *a specific brand of Cuban cigars imported by a friend of his from Havana*. A verb which has a noun or pronoun expression as its direct object complement is traditionally said to be **transitive**.

From a semantic perspective, subjects and complements share in common the fact that they generally represent entities directly involved in the particular action or event described by the predicate: to use the relevant semantic terminology, we can say that subjects and complements are **arguments** of the predicate with which they are associated. Predicates may have one or more arguments, as we see from sentences such as (8) below, where each of the bracketed nouns is a different argument of the italicised predicate:

(8) (a)   [John] *resigned*
   (b)   [John] *felt* [remorse]
   (c)   [John] *sent* [Mary] [flowers]

A predicate like *resign* in (8a) which has a single argument is said to function as a **one-place predicate** (in the relevant use); one like *feel* in (8b) which has two arguments is a **two-place predicate**; and one like *send* in (8c) which has three arguments is a **three-place predicate**.

In addition to predicates and arguments, sentences can also contain **adjuncts**, as we can illustrate in relation to (9) below:

(9) (a)   The president smokes a cigar *after dinner*
   (b)   The president smokes a cigar *in his office*

In both sentences in (9), *smokes* functions as a two-place predicate whose two arguments are its subject *the president* and its complement *a cigar*. But what is the function of the phrase *after dinner* which also occurs in (9a)? Since *after dinner* isn't one of the entities directly involved in the act of smoking (i.e. it isn't consuming or being consumed), it isn't an argument of the predicate *smoke*. On the contrary, *after dinner* simply serves to provide additional information about the time when the smoking activity takes place. In much the same way, the italicised expression *in his office* in (9b) provides additional information about the location of the smoking activity. An expression which serves to provide (optional) additional information about the time or place (or manner, or purpose etc.) of an activity or event is said to serve as an **adjunct**. So, *after dinner* and *in his office* in (9a,b) are both **adjuncts**.

So far, all the sentences we have looked at in (6–9) have been **simple sentences** which contain a single **clause**. However, alongside these we also find **complex sentences** which contain more than one clause, like (10) below:

(10)   Mary knows John smokes

If we take the traditional definition of a clause as a predication structure (more precisely, a structure containing a predicate which has a subject, and which may or may not also contain one or more complements and adjuncts), it follows that since there are two predicates (*knows* and *smokes*) in (10), there are correspondingly two clauses – the *smokes* clause on the one hand, and the *knows* clause on the other. The *smokes* clause comprises the subject *John* and the predicate *smokes*; the *knows* clause comprises the subject *Mary*, the predicate *knows* and the complement *John smokes*. So, the complement of *knows* here is itself a clause – namely the clause *John smokes*. More precisely, the *smokes* clause is a **complement clause** (because it serves as the complement of *knows*), while the *knows* clause is the **main clause** (or **principal clause** or **independent clause** or **root clause**). The overall sentence (10) *Mary knows John smokes* is a **complex sentence** because it contains more than one clause. In much the same way, (11) below is also a complex sentence:

(11)   The press clearly think the president deliberately lied to Congress

Once again, it comprises two clauses – one containing the predicate *think*, the other containing the predicate *lie*. The main clause comprises the subject *the press*, the adjunct *clearly*, the predicate *think* and the complement clause *the president deliberately lied to Congress*. The complement clause in turn comprises the subject *the president*, the adjunct *deliberately*, the predicate *lie* and the complement *to Congress*.

As was implicit in our earlier classification of (1) as a **finite** clause, traditional grammars draw a distinction between **finite** and **nonfinite** clauses. In this connection, consider the contrast between the italicised clauses below (all of which function as the complement of an underlined adjective or verb):

(12) (a)   She was <u>glad</u> *that he apologised*
      (b)   She <u>demanded</u> *that he apologise*
      (c)   I can't <u>imagine</u> *him apologising*
      (d)   It would be <u>sensible</u> *for him to apologise*
      (e)   It's important to <u>know</u> *when to apologise*

The italicised clauses in (12a,b) are finite, and it is characteristic of finite clauses in English that they contain an (auxiliary or main) verb marked for tense/mood, and can have a nominative pronoun like *he* as their subject. In (12a), the verb *apologised* is finite by virtue of being inflected for past tense and **indicative mood**, and by virtue of having a nominative subject (*he*); in (12b), the verb *apologise* is finite by virtue of being inflected for **subjunctive mood** (and perhaps present tense, though this is far from clear), and by virtue of having a nominative subject (*he*). A clause containing a verb in the indicative mood denotes a real (or **realis**, to use the relevant grammatical term) event or state occurring at a specific point in time; a subjunctive clause by contrast denotes a hypotheti-cal or unreal (= **irrealis**) event or state which has not yet occurred and which may never occur. In contrast to the italicised clauses in (12a,b), the clauses ital-icised in (12c–e) are nonfinite, in that they contain no verb marked for tense or mood, and do not allow a nominative subject. For example, the verb *apologis-ing* in (12c) is nonfinite because it is a tenseless and moodless **gerund** form, and has an **accusative** subject *him*. Likewise, the verb *apologise* in (12d,e) is a tenseless and moodless **infinitive** form (as we see from the fact that it fol-lows the infinitive particle *to*), and has an accusative subject *him* in (12d), and a 'silent' (implicit) subject in (12e). (Excluded from our discussion here are gerund structures with genitive subjects like the italicised in 'I can't stand *his perpetual(ly) whining about syntax*', since these are more nominal than clausal in nature.)

As the examples in (12) illustrate, whether or not a clause is finite in turn determines the kind of subject it can have, in that finite clauses can have a **nomi-native** pronoun like *he* as their subject, but nonfinite clauses cannot. Accordingly, one way of telling whether a particular clause is finite or not is to see whether it can have a nominative pronoun (like *I/we/he/she/they*) as its subject. In this connection, consider whether the italicised clauses in the dialogues in (13a,b) below are finite or nonfinite:

(13) (a)   SPEAKER A: I know you cheat on me
             SPEAKER B: OK, I admit it. *I cheat on you*. But not with any of your friends
     (b)   SPEAKER A: I know you cheat on me
             SPEAKER B: *Me cheat on you?* No way! I never would!

The fact that the italicised clause in speaker B's reply in (13a) has the nominative subject *I* suggests that it is finite, and hence that the verb *cheat* (as used in the italicised sentence in 13a) is a first person singular present tense form. By contrast, the fact that the italicised clause in speaker B's reply (13b) has the accusative subject *me* suggests that it is nonfinite, and that the verb *cheat* (as used in the italicised sentence in 13b) is an infinitive form (and indeed this is clear from sentences like *Me be a cheat? No way!* where we find the infinitive form *be*).

In addition to being finite or nonfinite, each clause within a sentence has a specific **force**. In this connection, consider the following simple (single-clause) sentences:

(14) (a)   He went home
     (b)   Are you feeling OK?
     (c)   You be quiet!
     (d)   What a great idea that is!

A sentence like (14a) is traditionally said to be **declarative** in force, in that it is used to make a statement. (14b) is **interrogative** in force in that it is used to ask a question. (14c) is **imperative** in force, by virtue of being used to issue an order or command. (14d) is **exclamative** in force, in that it is used to exclaim surprise or delight. In complex sentences, each clause has its own force, as we can see in relation to (15) below:

(15) (a)   He asked where she had gone
    (b)   Did you know that he has retired?
    (c)   Tell her what a great time we had!

In (15a), the main (*asked*) clause is declarative, whereas the complement (*gone*) clause is interrogative; in (15b) the main (*know*) clause is interrogative, whereas the complement (*retired*) clause is declarative; and in (15c), the main (*tell*) clause is imperative, whereas the complement (*had*) clause is exclamative.

We can summarise this section as follows. From the perspective of traditional grammar, the syntax of a language is described in terms of a **taxonomy** (i.e. a classificatory list) of the range of different phrase-, clause- and sentence-types found in the language. So, for example, a typical traditional grammar of (say) English will include chapters on the syntax of negatives, interrogatives, exclamatives, imperatives and so on. The chapter on interrogatives will note (e.g.) that in main-clause questions in English like 'Is he winning?' the present tense **auxiliary** *is* **inverts** with (i.e. moves in front of) the subject *he*, but not in complement clause questions like the *if*-clause in 'I wonder if he *is* winning', and will typically not be concerned with trying to explain *why* **auxiliary inversion** applies in main clauses but not complement clauses: this reflects the fact that the primary goal of traditional grammar is *description* rather than *explanation*.

1.3   Universal Grammar

In contrast to the **taxonomic** approach adopted in traditional grammar, Chomsky takes a **cognitive** approach to the study of grammar. For Chomsky, the goal of the linguist is to determine what it is that native speakers *know* about their native language which enables them to speak and understand the language, and how this linguistic knowledge might be represented in the mind/brain: hence, in studying language, we are studying a specific kind of cognition (i.e. human knowledge). In a fairly obvious sense, any native speaker of a language can be said to *know* the grammar of his or her native language. For example, any native speaker of English can tell you that the negative counterpart of *I like syntax* is *I don't like syntax*, and not e.g. **I no like syntax*: in other words, native speakers know how to combine words together to form expressions (e.g. negative sentences) in their language. Likewise, any native speaker of English can tell you that a sentence like *She loves me more than you* is ambiguous and has two **interpretations** which can be paraphrased as 'She loves me more than she loves you' and 'She loves me more than you love me': in other words, native speakers also know how to **interpret** (i.e. assign meaning to) expressions in their language.

However, it is important to emphasise that this grammatical knowledge of how to form and interpret expressions in your native language is **tacit** (i.e. subconscious) rather than **explicit** (i.e. conscious): so, it's no good asking a native speaker of English a question such as 'How do you form negative sentences in English?' since human beings have no conscious awareness of the processes involved in speaking and understanding their native language. To introduce a technical term devised by Chomsky, we can say that native speakers have grammatical **competence** in their native language: by this, we mean that they have tacit knowledge of the grammar of their language – i.e. of how to form and interpret words, phrases and sentences in the language.

In work in the 1960s, Chomsky drew a distinction between **competence** (the native speaker's tacit knowledge of his or her language) and **performance** (what people actually say or understand by what someone else says on a given occasion). Competence is 'the speaker-hearer's knowledge of his language', while performance is 'the actual use of language in concrete situations' (Chomsky 1965, p. 4). Very often, performance is an imperfect reflection of competence: we all make occasional slips of the tongue, or occasionally misinterpret something which someone else says to us. However, this doesn't mean that we don't know our native language or that we don't have *competence* in it. Misproductions and misinterpretations are **performance errors**, attributable to a variety of performance factors like tiredness, boredom, drunkenness, drugs, external distractions and so forth. A grammar of a language tells you what you need to know in order to have native-like competence in the language (i.e. to be able to speak the language like a fluent native speaker): hence, it is clear that grammar is concerned with competence rather than performance. This is not to deny the interest of performance as a field of study, but merely to assert that performance is more properly studied within the different – though related – discipline of psycholinguistics, which studies the psychological processes underlying speech production and comprehension.

Thus, when we study the grammatical competence of a native speaker of a language like English we're studying a cognitive system internalised within the brain/mind of native speakers of English which is the product of a 'cognitive organ' which is 'shared among human beings and in crucial respects unique to them' (Chomsky 2006, p. 1). In the terminology adopted by Chomsky (1986a, pp. 19–56), our ultimate goal in studying competence is to characterise the nature of the internalised linguistic system (or **I-language**, as Chomsky terms it) which makes native speakers proficient in English. Such an approach has obvious implications for the descriptive linguist who is concerned to develop a grammar of a particular language like English. According to Chomsky (1986a, p. 22) a grammar of a language is 'a theory of the I-language . . . under investigation'. This means that in devising a grammar of English, we are attempting to uncover the internalised linguistic system (= I-language) possessed by native speakers of English – i.e. we are attempting to characterise a mental state (a state of competence, and thus linguistic knowledge).

Chomsky's ultimate goal is to devise a theory of **Universal Grammar/UG** which generalises from the grammars of particular I-languages to the grammars of all possible natural (i.e. human) I-languages. He defines UG (1986a, p. 23) as 'the theory of human I-languages . . . that identifies the I-languages that are humanly accessible under normal conditions'. (The expression 'are humanly accessible' means 'can be acquired by human beings'.) In other words, UG is a theory about the nature of possible grammars of human languages: hence, a theory of Universal Grammar answers the question: 'What are the defining characteristics of the grammars of human I-languages?'

There are a number of **criteria of adequacy** which a theory of Universal Grammar must satisfy. One such criterion (which is implicit in the use of the term *Universal Grammar*) is **universality**, in the sense that a theory of UG must provide us with the tools needed to provide a **descriptively adequate** grammar for any and every human I-language (i.e. a grammar which correctly describes how to form and interpret expressions in the relevant language). After all, a theory of UG would be of little interest if it enabled us to describe the grammar of English and French, but not that of Swahili or Chinese.

However, since the ultimate goal of any theory is explanation, it is not enough for a theory of Universal Grammar simply to list sets of universal properties of natural language grammars; on the contrary, a theory of UG must seek to *explain* the relevant properties. So, a key question for any adequate theory of UG to answer is: 'Why do grammars of human I-languages have the properties they do?' The requirement that a theory should explain why grammars have the properties they do is conventionally referred to as the criterion of **explanatory adequacy**.

Since the theory of Universal Grammar is concerned with characterising the properties of natural (i.e. human) I-language grammars, an important question which we want our theory of UG to answer is: 'What are the defining characteristics of human I-languages which differentiate them from, for example, artificial languages like those used in mathematics and computing (e.g. Java, Prolog, C etc.), or from animal communication systems (e.g. the tail-wagging dance performed by bees to communicate the location of a food source to other bees)?' It therefore follows that the descriptive apparatus which our theory of Universal Grammar allows us to make use of in devising natural language grammars must not be so powerful that it can be used to describe not only natural languages, but also computer languages or animal communication systems (since any such excessively powerful theory wouldn't be able to pinpoint the criterial properties of natural languages which differentiate them from other types of communication system). In other words, a third condition which we have to impose on our theory of language is that it be maximally *constrained*: that is, we want our theory to provide us with technical devices which are so limited in their expressive power that they can only be used to describe natural languages, and are not appropriate for the description of other communication systems. A theory which is constrained in appropriate ways should enable us to provide a principled explanation for why certain types of syntactic structure and syntactic operation simply aren't found in natural languages. One way of constraining grammars is to suppose that grammatical operations obey certain linguistic principles, and that any operation which violates the relevant principles leads to ungrammaticality: see the discussion in §1.5 below for a concrete example.

A related requirement is that linguistic theory should provide grammars which make use of the minimal theoretical apparatus required: in other words, grammars should be as simple as possible. Some earlier work in syntax involved the postulation of complex structures and principles: as a reaction to the excessive complexity of this kind of work, Chomsky in work over the past two decades has made the requirement to minimise the theoretical and descriptive apparatus used to describe language the cornerstone of the *Minimalist Program for Linguistic Theory* which he has been developing. He has suggested that language is a *perfect* system of *optimal design* in the sense that natural language grammars create structures which are designed to **interface** perfectly with other components of the mind – more specifically with speech and thought systems, so that (in the words of Chomsky 2005b, p. 2) 'Language is an optimal way to link sound and meaning.'

To make this discussion rather more concrete, let's look at the internal organisation of the grammar of a language. One component of a grammar is a **lexicon** (= dictionary = list of all the **lexical items/**words in the language and their linguistic properties), and in forming a given sentence out of a set of words, we first have to take the relevant words out of the lexicon. Our chosen words are then combined together by a series of syntactic computations in the **syntax** (i.e. in the **syntactic/computational component** of the grammar), thereby forming a **syntactic structure**. This syntactic structure serves as input into two other components of the grammar. One is the **semantic component** which **maps** (i.e. 'converts') the syntactic structure into a corresponding **semantic representation** (i.e. into a representation of linguistic aspects of its meaning): the other is a **PF component**, so called because it maps the syntactic structure into a **PF representation** (i.e. a representation of its **Phonetic Form**, giving us a phonetic **spellout** for each word, telling us how it is pronounced). The semantic representation interfaces with systems of thought, and the PF representation with systems of speech – as shown in diagrammatic form below:

(16)

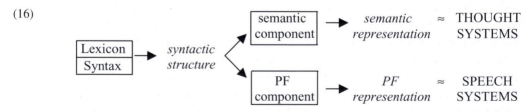

Chomsky (2005b, p. 3) refers to the interface with thought systems as the 'conceptual-intentional interface (CI)', and to the interface with speech systems as the 'sensory-motor interface (SM)'. In terms of the model in (16), an important consideration is that the (semantic and PF) representations which are 'handed over' to the (thought and speech) interface systems should contain only elements which are **legible** by the appropriate interface system – so that the semantic representations handed over to thought systems contain only elements contributing to meaning, and the PF representations handed over to speech systems contain only elements which contribute to phonetic form (i.e. to determining how the sentence is pronounced).

The neurophysiological mechanisms which underlie linguistic competence make it possible for young children to acquire language in a remarkably short period of time. Accordingly, a fourth condition which a linguistic theory must meet is that of **learnability**: it must provide grammars which are learnable by young children in a short period of time. The desire to maximise the **learnability** of natural language grammars provides an additional argument for minimising the theoretical apparatus used to describe languages, in the sense that the simpler grammars are, the simpler it is for children to acquire them.

1.4 The Language Faculty

Mention of *learnability* leads us to consider the related goal of developing a **theory of language acquisition**. An acquisition theory is concerned with the question of how children acquire grammars of their native languages. Children generally produce their first recognisable word (e.g. *Mama* or *Dada*) by around the age of twelve months (with considerable variation between individual children, however). For the next six months or so, there is little apparent evidence of grammatical development in their speech production, although the child's productive vocabulary typically increases by about five words a month until it reaches around thirty words at age eighteen months. Throughout this single-word stage, children's utterances comprise single words spoken in isolation: e.g. a child may say *Apple* when reaching for an apple, or *Up* when wanting to climb up onto someone's knee. During the single-word stage, it is difficult to find any immediately visible evidence of the acquisition of grammar, in that children do not make productive use of inflections (e.g. they don't productively add the plural *-s* ending to nouns, or the past tense *-d* ending to verbs), and don't productively combine words together to form two- and three-word utterances. (However, it should be noted that perception experiments have suggested that infants may acquire some syntactic knowledge even before one year of age.)

At around the age of eighteen months (though with considerable variation from one child to another), we find the first visible signs of the acquisition of grammar: children start to make productive use of inflections (e.g. using plural nouns like *doggies* alongside the singular form *doggy*, and inflected verb forms like *going/gone* alongside the uninflected verb form *go*), and similarly start to produce elementary two- and three-word utterances such as *Want Teddy*, *Eating cookie*, *Daddy gone office* etc. From this point on, there is a rapid expansion in their grammatical development, until by the age of around thirty months they have typically acquired a wide variety of the inflections and core grammatical constructions used in English, and are able to produce adult-like sentences such as *Where's Mummy gone? What's Daddy doing? Can we go to the zoo, Daddy?* etc. (though occasional morphological and syntactic errors persist until the age of four years or so – e.g. *We goed there with Daddy, What we can do?* etc.).

So, the central phenomenon which any theory of language acquisition must seek to explain is this: how is it that after a long-drawn-out period of many months in which there is no obvious sign of grammatical development, at around the age of eighteen months there is a sudden spurt as multiword speech starts to emerge, and a phenomenal growth in grammatical development then takes place over the next twelve months? This *uniformity* and (once the spurt has started) *rapidity* in the pattern of children's linguistic development are the central facts which a theory of language acquisition must seek to explain. But how?

Chomsky maintains that the most plausible explanation for the uniformity and rapidity of first language acquisition is to posit that the course of acquisition is determined by a biologically endowed innate **Faculty of Language/FL** (or *language acquisition program*, to borrow a computer software metaphor) within the brain, which provides children with a genetically transmitted algorithm (i.e. set of procedures) for developing a grammar, on the basis of their linguistic **experience** (i.e. on the basis of the speech input they receive). The way in which Chomsky visualises the acquisition process can be represented schematically as in (17) below (where L is the language being acquired):

(17)

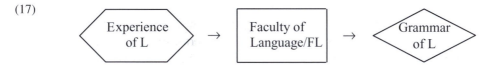

Children acquiring a language will observe people around them using the language, and the set of expressions in the language which a child hears (and the contexts in which they are used) in the course of acquiring the language constitute the child's linguistic **experience** of the language. This experience serves as input to the child's Faculty of Language/FL, which incorporates a set of UG principles (i.e. principles of Universal Grammar) which enable the child to use the experience to devise a grammar of the language being acquired. Thus, the input to the language faculty is the child's experience, and the output of the language faculty is a grammar of the language being acquired.

The claim that the course of language acquisition is determined by an innate language faculty is known popularly as the **innateness hypothesis**. Chomsky maintains that the ability to speak and acquire languages is unique to human beings, and that natural languages incorporate principles which are also unique to humans and which reflect the nature of the human mind:

> Whatever evidence we do have seems to me to support the view that the ability to acquire and use language is a species-specific human capacity, that there are very deep and restrictive principles that determine the nature of human language and are rooted in the specific character of the human mind.   (Chomsky 1972, p. 102)

Moreover, he notes, language acquisition is an ability which all humans possess, entirely independently of their general intelligence:

> Even at low levels of intelligence, at pathological levels, we find a command of language that is totally unattainable by an ape that may, in other respects, surpass a human imbecile in problem-solving activity and other adaptive behaviour.   (Chomsky 1972, p. 10)

In addition, the apparent uniformity in the types of grammars developed by different speakers of the same language suggests that children have genetic guidance in the task of constructing a grammar of their native language:

> We know that the grammars that are in fact constructed vary only slightly among speakers of the same language, despite wide variations not only in intelligence but also in the conditions under which language is acquired.   (Chomsky 1972, p. 79)

Furthermore, the rapidity of acquisition (once the grammar spurt has started) also points to genetic guidance in grammar construction:

> Otherwise it is impossible to explain how children come to construct grammars ... under the given conditions of time and access to data.   (Chomsky 1972, p. 113)

(The sequence 'under ... data' means simply 'in so short a time, and on the basis of such limited linguistic experience'.) What makes the uniformity and rapidity of acquisition even more remarkable is the fact that the child's linguistic experience is often degenerate (i.e. imperfect), since it is based on the linguistic performance of adult speakers, and this may be a poor reflection of their competence:

> A good deal of normal speech consists of false starts, disconnected phrases, and other deviations from idealised competence.   (Chomsky 1972, p. 158)

If much of the speech input which children receive is ungrammatical (because of performance errors), how is it that they can use this degenerate experience to develop a (competence) grammar which specifies how to form grammatical sentences? Chomsky's answer is to draw the following analogy:

> Descartes asks: how is it when we see a sort of irregular figure drawn in front of us we see it as a triangle? He observes, quite correctly, that there's a disparity between the data presented to us and the percept that we construct. And he argues, I think quite plausibly, that we see the figure as a triangle because there's something about the nature of our minds which makes the image of a triangle easily constructible by the mind.   (Chomsky 1968, p. 687)

The obvious implication is that in much the same way as we are genetically predisposed to analyse shapes (however irregular) as having specific geometric properties, so too we are genetically predisposed to analyse sentences (however ungrammatical) as having specific grammatical properties.

A further argument Chomsky uses in support of the innateness hypothesis relates to the fact that language acquisition is an entirely subconscious and involuntary activity (in the sense that you can't consciously choose whether or not to acquire your native language – though you can choose whether or not you wish to learn chess); it is also an activity which is largely unguided (in the sense that parents don't teach children to talk):

> Children acquire . . . languages quite successfully even though no special care is taken to teach them and no special attention is given to their progress.   (Chomsky 1965, pp. 200–1)

The implication is that we don't learn to have a native language, any more than we learn to have arms or legs; the ability to acquire a native language is part of our genetic endowment – just like the ability to learn to walk.

Studies of language acquisition lend empirical support to the innateness hypothesis. Research has suggested that there is a **critical period** for the acquisition of syntax, in the sense that children who learn a given language before puberty generally achieve native competence in it, whereas those who acquire a (first or second) language after the age of nine or ten years rarely manage to achieve native-like syntactic competence. A particularly poignant example of this is a child called Genie, who was deprived of speech input and kept locked up on her own in a room until age thirteen. When eventually taken into care and exposed to intensive language input, her vocabulary grew enormously, but her syntax never developed. This suggests that the acquisition of syntax is determined by an innate 'language acquisition program' which is in effect switched off (or gradually atrophies) around the onset of puberty.

Further support for the key claim in the *innateness hypothesis* that the human Language Faculty comprises a modular cognitive system autonomous of non-linguistic cognitive systems such as vision, hearing, reasoning or memory comes from the study of language disorders. Some disorders (such as *Specific Language Impairment*) involve impairment of linguistic abilities without concomitant impairment of other cognitive systems. By contrast, other types of disorder (such as *Williams Syndrome*) involve impairment of cognitive abilities in the absence of any major impairment of linguistic abilities. This double dissociation between linguistic and cognitive abilities lends additional plausibility to the claim that linguistic competence is the product of an autonomous Language Faculty.

Given the assumption that human beings are endowed with an innate language faculty, the overall goal of linguistic theory is to attempt to uncover:

> the properties that are specific to human language, that is, to the 'faculty of language' FL. To borrow Jespersen's formulation eighty years ago, the goal is to unearth 'the great principles underlying the grammars of all languages' with the goal of 'gaining a deeper insight into the innermost nature of human language and of human thought.' The biolinguistic perspective views FL as an 'organ of the body,' one of many subcomponents of an organism that interact in its normal life.   (Chomsky 2005b, p. 1)

However, Chomsky (2006, p. 1) notes that some properties of human language may reflect 'principles of biology more generally, and perhaps even more fundamental principles about the natural world'. Accordingly:

> development of language in the individual must involve three factors: (1) genetic endowment, which sets limits on the attainable languages, thereby making language acquisition possible; (2) external data, converted to the experience that selects one or another language within a narrow range; (3) principles not specific to FL.   (Chomsky 2006, p. 2: FL = Faculty of Language)

The 'third factor principles' referred to under (3) 'enter into all facets of growth and evolution' and include 'principles of efficient computation' (Chomsky 2006, p. 2) and – more generally – 'properties of the human brain that determine what cognitive systems can exist, though too little is yet known about these to draw specific conclusions about the design of FL' (Chomsky 2006, fn. 6)

1.5   Principles of Universal Grammar

If (as Chomsky claims) human beings are biologically endowed with an innate language faculty, an obvious question to ask is what the nature of the language faculty is. An important point to note in this regard is that children can in principle acquire *any* natural language as their native language (e.g. Afghan orphans brought up by English-speaking foster parents in an English-speaking community acquire English as their first language). It therefore follows that the language faculty must incorporate a theory of **Universal Grammar/UG** which enables the child to develop a grammar of *any* natural language on the basis of suitable linguistic experience of the language (i.e. sufficient speech input). Experience of a particular language L (examples of words, phrases and sentences in L which the child hears produced by native speakers of L in particular contexts) serves as input to the child's language faculty which incorporates a theory of Universal Grammar providing the child with a procedure for developing a grammar of L.

If the acquisition of grammatical competence is indeed controlled by a genetically endowed language faculty incorporating a theory of UG, then it follows that certain aspects of child (and adult) competence are known without experience, and hence must be part of the genetic information about language with which we are biologically endowed at birth. Such aspects of language would not have to be learned, precisely because they form part of the child's genetic inheritance. If we make the (plausible) assumption that the language faculty does not vary significantly from one (normal) human being to another, those aspects of language which are innately determined will also be universal. Thus, in seeking to determine the nature of the language faculty, we are in effect looking for **UG principles** (i.e. principles of Universal Grammar) which determine the very nature of language.

But how can we uncover such principles? The answer is that since the relevant principles are posited to be universal, it follows that they will affect the application of every relevant type of grammatical operation in every language. Thus, detailed analysis of one grammatical construction in one language could reveal evidence of the operation of principles of Universal Grammar. By way of illustration, let's look at question-formation in English. In this connection, consider the following dialogue:

(18)   SPEAKER A: He had said someone would do something
            SPEAKER B: He had said who would do what?

In (18), speaker B largely echoes what speaker A says, except for replacing *someone* by *who* and *something* by *what*. For obvious reasons, the type of question produced by speaker B in (18) is called an **echo question**. However, speaker B could alternatively have replied with a **non-echo question** like that below:

(19)   Who had he said would do what?

If we compare the echo question *He had said who would do what?* in (18) with the corresponding non-echo question *Who had he said would do what?* in (19), we find that (19) involves two movement operations which are not found in (18). One is an **auxiliary inversion** operation by which the past tense auxiliary *had* is moved in front of its subject *he*. The other is a **wh-movement** operation by which the **wh-word** *who* is moved to the front of the overall sentence, and positioned in front of *had*. (A wh-word is a question word like *who/what/where/when* etc. beginning with *wh*.)

A closer look at questions like (19) provides evidence that there are UG principles which constrain the way in which movement operations may apply. An interesting property of the questions in (18B, 19) is that they contain two auxiliaries (*had* and *would*) and two wh-words (*who* and *what*). Now, if we compare (19) with the corresponding echo-question in (18), we find that the *first* of the two auxiliaries (*had*) and the *first* of the wh-words (*who*) is moved to the front of the sentence in (19). If we try inverting the second auxiliary (*would*) and fronting the second wh-word (*what*), we end up with ungrammatical sentences, as we see from (20c–e) below (key items are bold-printed/italicised, and the corresponding echo question is given in parentheses; 20a is repeated from the echo question in 18B, and 20b from 19):

(20) (a)   He **had** said *who* **would** do *what*? (= echo question)

  (b)   *Who* **had** he said would do what? (cf. He **had** said *who* would do what?)

  (c)   **Who* **would** he had said do what? (cf. He had said *who* **would** do what?)

  (d)   **What* **had** he said who would do? (cf. He **had** said who would do *what*?)

  (e)   **What* **would** he had said who do? (cf. He had said who **would** do *what*?)

If we compare (20b) with its echo-question counterpart (20a) *He had said who would do what?* we see that (20b) involves preposing the first wh-word *who* and the first auxiliary *had*, and that this results in a grammatical sentence. By contrast, (20c) involves preposing the first wh-word *who* and the second auxiliary *would*; (20d) involves preposing the second wh-word *what* and the first auxiliary *had*; and (20e) involves preposing the second wh-word *what* and the second auxiliary *would*. The generalisation which emerges from the data in (20) is that auxiliary inversion preposes the *closest* auxiliary *had* (i.e. the one nearest the beginning of the sentence in (20a) above) and likewise wh-fronting preposes the *closest* wh-expression *who*. The fact that two quite distinct movement operations (auxiliary inversion and wh-movement) are subject to the same locality condition (which requires preposing of the *most local* – i.e. closest – expression of the relevant type) suggests that one of the principles of Universal Grammar incorporated into the language faculty is a **Locality Principle** which can be outlined informally as:

(21)   **Locality Principle**
   Grammatical operations are local

In consequence of (21), auxiliary inversion preposes the closest auxiliary, and wh-movement preposes the closest wh-expression. It seems reasonable to suppose that (21) is a principle of Universal Grammar (rather than an idiosyncratic property of question-formation in English). In fact, the strongest possible hypothesis we could put forward is that (21) holds of all grammatical operations in all natural languages, not just of movement operations; and indeed we shall see in later chapters that other types of grammatical operation (including **agreement** and **case assignment**) are subject to a similar locality condition. If so, and if we assume that abstract grammatical principles which are universal are part of our biological endowment, then the natural conclusion to reach is that (21) is a principle which is biologically wired into the language faculty, and which thus forms part of our genetic make-up.

 A theory of grammar which posits that grammatical operations are constrained by innate principles of UG offers the important advantage that it minimises the burden of grammatical learning imposed on the child (in the sense that children do not have to learn e.g. that auxiliary inversion affects the first auxiliary in a sentence, or that wh-movement likewise affects the first wh-expression). This is an important consideration, since we saw earlier that learnability is a criterion of adequacy for any theory of grammar – i.e. any adequate theory of grammar must be able to explain how children come to learn the grammar of their native language(s) in such a rapid and uniform fashion. The UG theory developed by Chomsky provides a straightforward account of the rapidity of the child's grammatical development, since it posits that there is a universal set of innately endowed grammatical principles which determine how grammatical operations apply in natural language grammars. Since UG principles which are innately endowed are wired into the language faculty and so do not have to be learned by the child, this minimises the learning load placed on the child, and thereby maximises the learnability of natural language grammars. It also (correctly) predicts that there are certain types of error which children will not make – e.g. producing sentences such as (20c–e).

1.6   Parameters

Thus far, we have argued that the language faculty incorporates a set of universal principles which guide the child in acquiring a grammar. However, it clearly cannot be the case that all aspects of the grammar of languages are universal; if this were so, all natural languages would have the same grammar and there would be no **grammatical learning** involved in language acquisition (i.e. no need for children to learn anything about the grammar of the language they are acquiring), only **lexical learning** (viz. learning the lexical items/words in the language and their idiosyncratic linguistic properties, e.g. whether a given item has an irregular plural or past tense form). But although there are universal principles which determine the broad outlines of the grammar of natural languages, there also seem to be language-particular aspects of grammar which children have to learn as part of the task of acquiring their native language. Thus, language acquisition involves not only lexical learning but also some grammatical learning. Let's take a closer look at the grammatical learning involved, and what it tells us about the language acquisition process.

Clearly, grammatical learning is not going to involve learning those aspects of grammar which are determined by universal (hence innate) grammatical operations and principles. Rather, grammatical learning will be limited to those **parameters** (i.e. dimensions or aspects) of grammar which are subject to language-particular variation (and hence vary from one language to another). In other words, grammatical learning will be limited to parametrised aspects of grammar (i.e. those aspects of grammar which are subject to parametric variation from one language to another). The obvious way to determine just what aspects of the grammar of their native language children have to learn is to examine the range of **parametric variation** found in the grammars of different (adult) natural languages.

We can illustrate one type of parametric variation across languages in terms of the following contrast between the English example in (22a) below and its Italian counterpart in (22b):

(22) (a)   Maria thinks that *(they) speak French
      (b)   Maria pensa che parlano francese
              'Maria thinks that speak French'

(The notation *(*they*) in 22a means that the sentence is ungrammatical if *they* is omitted – i.e. that the sentence *Maria thinks that speak French* is ungrammatical.) The finite (present tense) verb *speak* in the English sentence (22a) requires an overt subject like *they*, but its Italian counterpart *parlano*$_{speak}$ in (22b) has no overt subject. However, there are two pieces of evidence suggesting that the Italian verb *parlano*$_{speak}$ must have a 'silent' subject of some kind. One is *semantic* in nature, in that the verb *parlano*$_{speak}$ is understood as having a third person plural subject, and this understood subject is translated into English as *they*; in more technical terms, this amounts to saying that in the relevant use, the verb *parlano*$_{speak}$ is a two-place predicate which requires both a subject argument and an object argument, and so it must have an 'understood' silent subject of some kind in (22b). The second piece of evidence is grammatical in nature. Finite verbs agree with their subjects in Italian: hence, in order to account for the fact that the verb *parlano*$_{speak}$ is in the third person plural form in (22b), we need to posit that it has a third person plural subject to agree with. Since the verb *parlano*$_{speak}$ has no overt subject, it must have a **null subject** which can be thought of as a silent or invisible counterpart of the pronoun *they* which appears in the corresponding English sentence (22a). This null subject is conventionally designated as **pro**, so that (22b) has the fuller structure *Maria pensa che **pro** parlano francese* 'Maria thinks that *pro* speak French,' where *pro* is a null subject pronoun.

The more general conclusion to be drawn from our discussion here is that in languages like Italian, any finite verb can have either an overt subject like *Maria* or a null *pro* subject. But things are very different in English. Although finite verbs can have an overt subject like *Maria* in English, they cannot normally have a null *pro* subject – hence the ungrammaticality of *Maria thinks that speak French* (where the verb *speak* has a null subject). So, finite verbs in a language like Italian can have either overt or null subjects, but in a language like English, finite verbs can generally have only overt subjects, not null subjects. We can describe the differences between the two types of language by saying that Italian is a **null-subject language**, whereas English is a **non-null-subject language**. More generally, there appears to be parametric variation between languages as to whether or not they allow finite verbs to have null subjects. The relevant parameter (termed the **Null Subject Parameter**) would appear to be a binary one, with only two possible settings for any given language L, viz. *L either does or doesn't allow any finite verb to have a null subject.* There appears to be no language which allows the subjects of some finite verbs to be null, but not others – e.g. no language in which it is OK to say *Drinks wine* (meaning 'He/she drinks wine') but not OK to say *Eats pasta* (meaning 'He/she eats pasta'). The range of grammatical variation found across languages appears to be strictly limited to just two possibilities – languages either do or don't systematically allow finite verbs to have null subjects.

A more familiar aspect of grammar which appears to be parametrised relates to word order, in that different types of language have different word orders in specific types of construction. One type of word-order variation can be illustrated in relation to the following contrast between English and Chinese questions:

(23) (a)   What do you think he will say?
    (b)

Ni	xiang	ta	hui	shuo	shenme
You	think	he	will	say	what?

In simple wh-questions in English (i.e. questions containing a single word beginning with *wh-* like *what/where/when/why*) the wh-expression is moved to the beginning of the sentence, as is the case with *what* in (23a). By contrast, in Chinese, the wh-word does not move to the front of the sentence, but rather remains **in situ** (i.e. in the same place as would be occupied by a corresponding non-interrogative expression), so that *shenme* 'what' is positioned after the verb *shuo* 'say' because it is the (direct object) complement of the verb, and complements of the relevant type are normally positioned after their verbs in Chinese. Thus, another parameter of variation between languages is the **Wh-Parameter** – a parameter which determines whether wh-expressions are fronted (i.e. moved to the front of the overall interrogative structure containing them) or not. Significantly, this parameter again appears to be one which is binary in nature, in that it allows for only two possibilities – viz. a language either does or doesn't allow **wh-movement** (i.e. movement of wh-expressions to the front of the sentence). Many other possibilities for wh-movement just don't seem to occur in natural language: for example, there is no language in which the counterpart of *who* undergoes wh-fronting but not the counterpart of *what* (e.g. no language in which it is OK to say *Who did you see?* but not *What did you see?*). Likewise, there is no language in which wh-complements of some verbs can undergo fronting, but not wh-complements of other verbs (e.g. no language in which it is OK to say *What did he drink?* but not *What did he eat?*). It would seem that the range of parametric variation found with respect to wh-fronting is limited to just two possibilities: viz. a language either does or doesn't allow wh-expressions to be systematically fronted.

Let's now turn to look at a rather different type of word-order variation, concerning the relative position of **heads** and **complements** within phrases. It is a general (indeed, universal) property of phrases that every phrase has a head word which determines the nature of the overall phrase. For example, an expression such as *students of philosophy* is a plural Noun Phrase because its head word (i.e. the key word in the phrase whose nature determines the properties of the overall phrase) is the plural noun *students*: the noun *students* (and not the noun *philosophy*) is the head word because the phrase *students of philosophy* denotes kinds of student, not kinds of philosophy. The following expression *of philosophy* which combines with the head noun *students* to form the Noun Phrase *students of philosophy* functions as the **complement** of the noun *students*. In much the same way, an expression such as *in the kitchen* is a Prepositional Phrase which comprises the head preposition *in* and its complement *the kitchen*. Likewise, an expression such as *stay with me* is a Verb Phrase which comprises the head verb *stay* and its complement *with me*. And similarly, an expression such as *fond of fast food* is an Adjectival Phrase formed by combining the head adjective *fond* with its complement *of fast food*.

In English all heads (whether nouns, verbs, prepositions or adjectives etc.) immediately precede their complements; however, there are also languages like Korean in which all heads immediately follow their complements. In informal terms, we can say that English is a **head-first language**, whereas Korean is a **head-last language**. The differences between the two languages can be illustrated by comparing the English examples in (24) below with their Korean counterparts in (25):

(24) (a)   Close the door   (b) desire for change

(25) (a)   Muneul dadara   (b) byunhwa-edaehan galmang
           Door   close   change-for   desire

In the English Verb Phrase *close the door* in (24a), the head verb *close* immediately precedes its complement *the door*; if we suppose that *the door* is a Determiner Phrase, then the head of the phrase (= the determiner *the*) immediately precedes its complement (= the noun *door*). Likewise, in the English Noun Phrase *desire for change* in (24b), the head noun *desire* immediately precedes its complement *for change*; the complement *for change* is in turn a Prepositional Phrase in which the head preposition *for* likewise immediately precedes its complement *change*. Since English consistently positions heads before complements, it is a head-first language. By contrast, we find precisely the opposite ordering in Korean. In the Verb Phrase *muneul dadara* (literally 'door close') in (25a), the head verb *dadara* 'close' immediately follows its complement *muneul* 'door'; likewise, in the Noun Phrase *byunhwa-edaehan galmang* (literally 'change-for desire') in (25b) the head noun *galmang* 'desire' immediately follows its complement *byunhwa-edaehan* 'change-for'; the expression *byunhwa-edaehan* 'change-for' is in turn a Prepositional Phrase whose head preposition *edaehan* 'for/about' immediately follows its complement *byunhwa* 'change' (so that *edaehan* might more appropriately be called a **postposition**; prepositions and postpositions are differents kinds of **adposition**). Since Korean consistently positions heads immediately after their complements, it is a head-last language. Given that English is head-first and Korean head-last, it is clear that the relative positioning of heads with respect to their complements is one word-order parameter along which languages differ; the relevant parameter is termed the **Head Position Parameter**.

It should be noted, however, that word-order variation in respect of the relative positioning of heads and complements falls within narrowly circumscribed limits. There are many logically possible types of word-order variation which just don't seem to occur in natural languages. For example, we might imagine that in a given language some verbs would precede and others follow their complements, so that (e.g.) if two new hypothetical verbs like *scrunge* and *plurg* were coined in English, then *scrunge* might take a following complement, and *plurg* a preceding complement. And yet, this doesn't ever seem to happen: rather, all verbs typically occupy the same position in a given language with respect to a given type of complement.

What this suggests is that there are universal **constraints** (i.e. restrictions) on the range of parametric variation found across languages in respect of the relative ordering of heads and complements. It would seem that there are only two different possibilities which the theory of Universal Grammar allows for: a given type of structure in a given language must either be **head-first** (with the relevant heads positioned immediately before their complements), or **head-last** (with the relevant heads positioned immediately after their complements). Many other logically possible orderings of heads with respect to complements appear not to be found in natural language grammars. The obvious question to ask is why this should be. The answer given by the theory of parameters is that the language faculty imposes genetic constraints on the range of parametric variation permitted in natural language grammars. In the case of the **Head Position Parameter** (i.e. the parameter which determines the relative positioning of heads with respect to their complements), the language faculty allows only a binary set of possibilities – namely that a given kind of structure in a given language is either consistently head-first or consistently head-last.

We can generalise our discussion in this section in the following terms. If the **Head Position Parameter** reduces to a simple binary choice, and if the **Wh-Parameter** and the **Null Subject Parameter** also involve binary choices, it seems implausible that **binarity** could be an accidental property of these particular parameters. Rather, it seems much more likely that it is an inherent property of parameters that they constrain the range of structural variation between languages, and limit it to a simple binary choice. Generalising still further, it seems possible that all grammatical variation between languages can be characterised in terms of a set of parameters, and that for each parameter, the language faculty specifies a binary choice of possible values for the parameter.

1.7   Parameter-setting

The theory of parameters outlined in the previous section has important implications for a theory of language acquisition. If all grammatical variation can be characterised in terms of a series of parameters with binary settings, it follows that the only grammatical learning which children have to undertake in relation to the syntactic properties of the relevant class of constructions is to determine (on the basis of their linguistic experience) which of the two alternative settings for each parameter is the appropriate one for the language being acquired. So, for example, children have to learn whether the native language they are acquiring is a null subject language or not, whether it is a wh-movement language or not, and whether it is a head-first language or not . . . and so on for all the other parameters along which languages vary. Of course, children also face the formidable task of **lexical learning** – i.e. building up their vocabulary in the relevant language, learning what words mean and what range of forms they have (e.g. whether they are regular or irregular in respect of their morphology), what kinds of structures they can be used in and so on. On this view, the acquisition of grammar involves the twin tasks of **lexical learning** and **structural learning** (with the latter involving **parameter-setting**).

This leads us to the following view of the language acquisition process. The central task which the child faces in acquiring a language is to construct a grammar of the language. The innate Language Faculty incorporates (i) a set of universal grammatical principles, and (ii) a set of grammatical parameters which impose severe constraints on the range of grammatical variation permitted in natural languages (perhaps limiting variation to binary choices). Since universal principles don't have to be learned, the child's syntactic learning task is limited to that of **parameter-setting** (i.e. determining an appropriate setting for each of the relevant grammatical parameters). For obvious reasons, the theory outlined here (developed by Chomsky at the beginning of the 1980s) is known as **Principles-and-Parameters Theory/PPT**.

The PPT model clearly has important implications for the nature of the language acquisition process, since it vastly reduces the complexity of the acquisition task which children face. PPT hypothesises that grammatical properties which are universal will not have to be learned by the child, since they are wired into the language faculty and hence part of the child's genetic endowment: on the contrary, all the child has to learn are those grammatical properties which are subject to parametric variation across languages. Moreover, the child's learning task will be further simplified if it turns out (as research since 1980 has suggested) that the values which a parameter can have fall within a narrowly specified range, perhaps characterisable in terms of a series of binary choices. This simplified **parameter-setting model** of the acquisition of grammar has given rise to a metaphorical acquisition model in which the child is visualised as having to set a series of switches in one of two positions (*up/down*) – each such switch representing a different parameter. In the case of the **Head Position Parameter**, we can imagine that if the switch is set in the *up* position (for particular types of head), the language will show head-first word order in relevant kinds of structure, whereas if it is set in the *down* position, the order will be head-last. Of course, an obvious implication of the switch metaphor is that the switch must be set in either one position or the other, and cannot be set in both positions. (This would preclude e.g. the possibility of a language having both head-first and head-last word order in a given type of structure.)

The assumption that acquiring the grammar of a language involves the relatively simple task of setting a number of grammatical parameters provides a natural way of accounting for the fact that the acquisition of specific parameters appears to be a remarkably rapid and error-free process in young children. For example, young children acquiring English as their native language seem to set the Head Position Parameter at its appropriate head-first setting from the very earliest multiword utterances they produce (at around eighteen months of age), and seem to know (tacitly, not explicitly, of course) that English is a head-first language. Accordingly, the earliest verb phrases and Prepositional Phrases produced by young children acquiring English consistently show verbs and prepositions positioned before their complements, as structures such as the following indicate (produced by a young boy called Jem/James at age twenty months; head verbs are italicised in (26a) and head prepositions in (26b), and their complements are in non-italic print):

(26) (a)   *Touch* heads. *Cuddle* book. *Want* crayons. *Want* malteser. *Open* door. *Want* biscuit. *Bang* bottom. *See* cats. *Sit* down

   (b)   *On* Mummy. *To* lady. *Without* shoe. *With* potty. *In* keyhole. *In* school. *On* carpet. *On* box. *With* crayons. *To* mummy

The obvious conclusion to be drawn from structures like (26) is that children like Jem consistently position heads before their complements from the very earliest multiword utterances they produce. They do not use different orders for different words of the same type (e.g. they don't position the verb *see* after its complement but the verb *want* before its complement), or for different types of words (e.g. they don't position verbs before and prepositions after their complements).

A natural question to ask at this point is how we can provide a principled explanation for the fact that from the very onset of multiword speech we find English children correctly positioning heads before their complements. The **Principles-and-Parameters** model enables us to provide an explanation for why children manage to learn the relative ordering of heads and complements in such a rapid and error-free fashion. The answer provided by the model is that learning this aspect of word order involves the comparatively simple task of setting a binary parameter at its appropriate value. This task will be a relatively straightforward one if the language faculty tells the child that the only possible choice is for a given type of structure in a given language to be uniformly head-first or uniformly head-last. Given such an assumption, the child could set the parameter correctly on the basis of minimal linguistic experience. For example, once the child is able to analyse the structure of an adult utterance such as *Help Daddy* and knows that it contains a Verb Phrase comprising the head verb *help* and its complement *Daddy*, then (on the assumption that the language faculty specifies that all heads of a given type behave uniformly with regard to whether they are positioned before or after their complements), the child will automatically know that all verbs in English are canonically (i.e. normally) positioned before their complements.

One of the questions posed by the parameter-setting model of acquisition outlined here is just how children come to arrive at the appropriate setting for a given parameter, and what kind(s) of evidence they make use of in setting parameters. There are two types of evidence which we might expect to be available to the language learner in principle, namely **positive evidence** and **negative evidence**. Positive evidence comprises a set of observed expressions illustrating a particular phenomenon: for example, if children's speech input is made up of structures in which heads precede their complements, this provides them with positive evidence which enables them to set the Head Position Parameter at the head-first setting appropriate to English. Negative evidence might be of two kinds – **direct** or **indirect**. Direct negative evidence could come from the correction of children's errors by other speakers of the language. However, (contrary to what is often imagined) correction plays a fairly insignificant role in language acquisition, for two reasons. Firstly, correction is relatively infrequent: adults simply don't correct all the errors children make (if they did, children would soon become inhibited and discouraged from speaking). Secondly, children are notoriously unresponsive to correction, as the following dialogue (from McNeill 1966, p. 69) illustrates:

(27)   CHILD: Nobody don't like me
          ADULT: No, say: 'Nobody likes me'
          CHILD: Nobody don't like me
          (*8 repetitions of this dialogue*)
          ADULT: No, now listen carefully. Say 'Nobody likes me'
          CHILD: Oh, nobody don't likes me

As Hyams (1986, p. 91) notes: 'Negative evidence in the form of parental disapproval or overt corrections has no discernible effect on the child's developing syntactic ability.'

Direct negative evidence might also take the form of self-correction by other speakers. Such self-corrections tend to have a characteristic intonation and rhythm of their own, and may be signalled by a variety of fillers (such as those italicised in (28) below):

(28) (a)   The picture was hanged . . . *or rather* hung . . . in the Tate Gallery
     (b)   The picture was hanged . . . *sorry* hung . . . in the Tate Gallery
     (c)   The picture was hanged . . . *I mean* hung . . . in the Tate Gallery

However, self-correction is arguably too infrequent a phenomenon to play a major role in the acquisition process.

Rather than say that children rely on direct negative evidence, we might instead imagine that they learn from **indirect negative evidence** (i.e. evidence relating to the non-occurrence of certain types of structure). Suppose that a child's experience includes no examples of structures in which heads follow their complements (e.g. no Prepositional Phrases like *dinner after in which the head preposition *after* follows its complement *dinner*, and no Verb Phrases such as *cake eat in which the head verb *eat* follows its complement *cake*). On the basis of such indirect negative evidence (i.e. observing that such structures never occur in English), the child might infer that English is not a head-last language.

Although it might seem natural to suppose that indirect negative evidence plays some role in the acquisition process, there are potential **learnability** problems posed by any such claim. After all, the fact that a given construction does not occur in a given chunk of the child's experience does not provide conclusive evidence that the structure is ungrammatical, since it may well be that the non-occurrence of the relevant structure in the relevant chunk of experience is an accidental (rather than a systematic) gap. Thus, the child would need to process a very large (in principle, infinite) chunk of experience in order to be sure that non-occurrence reflects ungrammaticality. It is implausible that young children process massive chunks of experience in this way and search through it for negative evidence about the non-occurrence of certain types of structure, since this would impose an unrealistic memory load on them. In any case, given the assumption that parameters are binary and single-valued, negative evidence becomes entirely unnecessary: after all, once the child hears a Prepositional Phrase like *with Daddy* in which the head preposition *with* precedes its complement *Daddy*, the child will have positive evidence that English allows head-first order in prepositional phrases; and given the assumption that the Head Position Parameter is a binary one and the further assumption that each parameter allows only a single setting, then it follows (as a matter of logical necessity) that if English allows head-first Prepositional Phrases, it will not allow head-last Prepositional Phrases. Thus, in order for the child to know that English doesn't allow head-last Prepositional Phrases, the child does not need negative evidence from the non-occurrence of such structures, but rather can rely on positive evidence from the occurrence of the converse order in head-first structures (on the assumption that if a given structure is head-first, UG specifies that it cannot be head-last). And, as we have already noted, a minimal amount of positive evidence is required in order to identify English as a uniformly head-first language (i.e. a language in which *all* heads precede their complements). Learnability considerations such as these have led Chomsky (1986a, p. 55) to conclude that 'There is good reason to believe that children learn language from positive evidence only.' The claim that children do not make use of negative evidence in setting parameters is known as the **No-Negative-Evidence Hypothesis**; it is a hypothesis which is widely assumed in current acquisition research.

1.8   Summary

We began this chapter in §1.2 with a brief look at traditional grammar, noting that this is a **taxonomic** (i.e. classificatory) system in which the syntax of a given sentence is described by assigning each of the constituents in the sentence to a grammatical category, and saying what grammatical function it has. In §1.3, we noted that Chomsky takes a very different **cognitive** approach to the study of language in which a grammar of a language is a model of the grammatical knowledge (or **competence**) internalised in the mind/brain of a native speaker (hence a model of the speaker's **I-language**). We saw that Chomsky's ultimate goal is to develop a theory of **Universal Grammar/UG** which characterises the defining properties of the grammars of natural languages – a theory which is universal, explanatory and constrained, and which provides descriptively adequate grammars that are minimally complex and hence learnable. In §1.4, we went on to look at the nature of language acquisition, and argued that the most fundamental question for a theory of language acquisition to answer is why it should be that after a period of a year and a half during which there is little evidence of grammatical development visible in the child's speech output, most of the grammar of the language is acquired by children during the course of the following year. We outlined the **Innateness Hypothesis** put forward by Chomsky, under which the course of language acquisition is genetically predetermined by an innate **Language Faculty**. In §1.5, we noted Chomsky's claim that the Language Faculty incorporates a theory of **Universal Grammar/UG** which embodies a set of universal grammatical principles that determine the ways in which grammatical operations work; and we saw that the syntax of questions in English provides evidence for postulating that syntactic operations are constrained by the following principle:

Locality Principle: Every grammatical operation is *local* in the sense that it affects the closest constituent of the relevant type

In §1.6, we went on to argue that the grammars of natural languages vary along a number of **parameters**. We looked at three such parameters, namely:

Wh-Parameter: Some languages (like English) require movement of an interrogative wh-expression to the front of an interrogative clause, whereas others (like Chinese) leave interrogative wh-expressions in situ

Null Subject Parameter: Some languages (like Italian) allow a null pronoun (= *pro*) to be used as the subject of any finite (auxiliary or main) verb, whereas other languages (like English) do not

Head Position Parameter: Some languages (like English) position head words immediately before their complements, whereas others (like Korean) position them immediately after their complements.

We hypothesised that each such parameter has a binary choice of settings. In §1.7, we argued that the syntactic learning task which children face involves **parameter-setting** – i.e. determining which of two possible settings is the appropriate one for each parameter in the language being acquired. We further argued that if parameters have binary settings (e.g. so that a given kind of structure in a given language is either head-first or head-last), we should expect to find evidence that children correctly set parameters from the very onset of multiword speech: and we presented evidence to suggest that from their very earliest multiword utterances, children acquiring English as their mother tongue correctly set the Head Position Parameter at the head-first value appropriate for English. We concluded that the acquisition of grammar involves the twin tasks of lexical learning (i.e. acquiring a **lexicon**/vocabulary) and parameter-setting. We went on to ask what kind of evidence children use in setting parameters, and concluded that they use **positive evidence** from their experience of the occurrence of specific types of structure (e.g. head-first structures, or null subject structures or wh-movement structures).

1.9   Bibliographical background

For a fuller account of the grammatical categories discussed in §1.2, see chapter 2 of Radford (2004a) or (2004b). On the nature of determiners, see Giusti (1997), Spinillo (2004) and Isac (2006). On different types of pronoun, see Cardinaletti and Starke (1999), Wiltschko (2001) and Déchaine and Wiltschko (2002). On the claim that personal pronouns are D constituents, see Postal (1966) and Abney (1987). On the claim that infinitival *to* is a tense particle, see Freidin (2004, p. 117, fn. 32). For a technical discussion of tense, see Julien (2001) and Ishii (2006a). The term *complementiser* dates back to Rosenbaum (1965, 1967) and Bresnan (1970). For more extensive discussion of the notion of I-language introduced in §1.3, see Smith (2004). Chomsky's *Minimalist Program* is developed in Chomsky (1993, 1995, 1998, 1999, 2001, 2002, 2005a, 2005b, 2006). For discussion of Chomsky's idea that language is a perfect system of optimal design, see Lappin, Levine and Johnson (2000a, 2000b, 2001), Holmberg (2000a), Piattelli-Palmarini (2000), Reuland (2000, 2001b), Roberts (2000, 2001a), Uriagereka (2000, 2001) and Freidin and Vergnaud (2001). For further discussion of the innateness hypothesis outlined in §1.4, see Lightfoot (1999), Anderson and Lightfoot (2002), Antony and Hornstein (2003), Givón (2002), Hauser, Chomsky and Fitch (2002) and Fitch, Hauser and Chomsky (2005); for a more critical view, see Everett (2005, 2006) and Sampson (2005), and for a reply to such criticism, see Chomsky's contributions to Antony and Hornstein (2003). For a textbook summary of perceptual evidence that very young infants may be sensitive to syntactic structure, see Lust (2006, §9.2.1). For evaluation of the idea that children learn languages in spite of receiving *degenerate input*, see Pullum and Scholz (2002), Thomas (2002), Sampson (2002), Fodor and Crowther (2002), Lasnik and Uriagereka (2002), Legate and Yang (2002), Crain and Pietroski (2002), Scholz and Pullum (2002), Lewis and Elman (2002) and Gualmini and Crain (2005). For discussion of the *critical period* in language acquisition, see Lenneberg (1967), Hurford (1991) and Smith (1998, 2004); on Genie, see Curtiss (1977) and Rymer (1993). On evidence of a double dissociation between linguistic and cognitive abilities, see Clahsen (2008). The idea outlined in §1.5 that grammars incorporate a set of UG principles is developed in Chomsky (1981). The Locality Principle sketched in the same section has its historical roots in a number of related principles, including the *Relativised Minimality Principle* of Rizzi (1990), the *Shortest Move* principle of Chomsky (1995) and the *Attract Closest Principle* of Richards (1997). The idea that grammatical differences between languages can be reduced to a small number of parameters is developed in Chomsky (1981). A complication glossed over in the text discussion of the Null Subject Parameter is posed by languages in which only some finite verb forms can have null subjects: see Vainikka and Levy (1999) and the collection of papers in Jaeggli and Safir (1989) for illustration and discussion. The discussion of the Wh-Parameter in the main text is simplified by ignoring the complication that some languages allow more than one wh-expression to be fronted in wh-questions (see Bošković 2002a, Grohmann 2006 and Surányi 2006), and the additional complication that wh-movement appears to be optional in some languages, either in main clauses, or in main and complement clauses alike (see Denham 2000, and Cheng and Rooryck 2000); on *wh-in-situ* structures, see Pesetsky (1987), Cheng (1997), Cole and Hermon (1998), Reinhart (1998) and Bruening (2007). The claim made in the outline of the Head Position Parameter that all heads of a given type occupy a uniform position with respect to their complements is called into question by the behaviour of prepositions in German, most of which precede their complements, but a few of which (e.g. *entlang* 'along') follow them. Although we assumed in the text that parameters have binary settings, it should be noted that some researchers have assumed that parameters can have more than two alternative settings (e.g. Manzini and Wexler 1987). For discussion of a wide range of parametric variation between languages, see Cinque and Kayne (2005). For a critique of the idea that cross-linguistic variation is reducible to a small number of structural *parameters*, see Culicover and Nowak (2003), Newmeyer (2004, 2006) and Abeillé and Borsley (2006): for a defence of parameters, see Roberts and Holmberg (2006). For a defence of the claim made in §1.7 that parameters are correctly set by children at a very early stage in their development, see Wexler (1998). The claim that no negative evidence is used in setting parameters is made in Chomsky (1981, pp. 8–9); supporting evidence can be found in McNeill (1966), Brown, Cazden and Bellugi (1968), Brown and Hanlon (1970), Braine (1971), Bowerman (1988), Morgan and Travis (1989) and Marcus (1993) – but for potential counterevidence, see Lappin and Shieber (2007). On how children set parameters, see Fodor (2001) and Fodor and Sakas (2005). For a technical account of language acquisition within the framework used here, see Guasti (2002) and Lust (2006).

Workbook section

Exercise 1.1

Word-order parameters like the **Head Position Parameter** determine the canonical (i.e. 'basic', 'normal' or 'underlying') word order found in particular types of structure in a given language. However (as we will see in subsequent chapters), languages may have a variety of movement operations which allow particular types of expression to be fronted (i.e. preposed) and thereby be moved out of their canonical position into some new position at the front of a particular phrase, clause or sentence. For example, in a head-first language like English, both main and auxiliary verbs immediately precede their complements. Accordingly, in a sentence like *John has gone home*, the verb *gone* immediately precedes its complement *home*, and the auxiliary *has* immediately precedes its complement *gone home*. But in a question like *Where has John gone?* wh-movement means that the complement *where* of the verb *gone* is moved to the front of the overall sentence, and so the verb *gone* no longer immediately precedes its complement *where*. Likewise, the auxiliary *has* undergoes auxiliary inversion (thereby moving in front of its subject

John) and consequently no longer immediately precedes its complement *gone where*.

Below are a number of sentences taken from various plays written by Shakespeare, representing a variety of English sometimes referred to as *Elizabethan English* (because it was spoken during the reign of Queen Elizabeth the First). Elizabethan English (like present-day English) was a head-first language in which heads were canonically positioned in front of their complements. In relation to the sentences below, show how movement operations which fronted various types of expression could mask the underlying head-first setting of the Head Position Parameter in Elizabethan English.

1   Seawater shalt thou drink (Prospero, *The Tempest*, I.ii)
2   That letter hath she delivered (Speed, *Two Gentlemen of Verona*, II.i)
3   Friend hast thou none (Duke, *Measure for Measure*, III.i)
4   True is it that we have seen better days (Duke Senior, *As You Like It*, II.vii) **(w)**
5   She may more suitors have (Tranio, *The Taming of the Shrew*, I.ii)
6   Run you to the citadel! (Iago, *Othello*, V.i)
7   Came you from the church? (Tranio, *Taming of the Shrew*, III.ii)
8   What think you he hath confessed? (First Lord, *All's Well That Ends Well*, IV.iii) **(w)**
9   What will this come to? (Flavius, *Timon of Athens*, I.ii)
10   What visions have I seen! (Titania, *Midsummer Night's Dream*, V.i)

Helpful hints

Take *none* in 3, *more* in 5 and *what* in 10 to be quantifiers with a noun as their complement (and assume that the negative quantifier is spelled out as *no* if immediately followed by its complement, but as *none* otherwise). Note that 1–5 are declarative sentences (used to make a statement), 6 is an imperative sentence (used to issue an order), 7–9 are interrogative sentences (used to ask a question) and 10 is an exclamative sentence (used to exclaim amazement).

Model answer for 1

The auxiliary verb *shalt* 'shall' has the subject *thou* 'you$_{singular}$' and the complement *drink seawater*.

The main verb *drink* has the complement *seawater*. If no movement operations took place in the relevant sentence, we should expect to find the word order *Thou shalt drink seawater*, with the auxiliary *shalt* immediately preceding its complement *drink seawater*, and the verb *drink* immediately preceding its complement *seawater*, in keeping with the assumption that Elizabethan English has a head-first setting for the Head Position Parameter. However, the noun *seawater* undergoes a fronting/preposing operation in order to highlight it, and this means that instead of occupying its canonical position immediately after the verb *drink*, it is instead moved to a new position at the front of the overall sentence. Likewise, the auxiliary *shalt* undergoes a separate (subject–auxiliary) inversion operation which means that instead of occupying its canonical position immediately preceding its complement *drink seawater*, it is instead moved to a new position immediately preceding its subject *thou*. The effect of these two movement operations is shown schematically below:

UNDERLYING ORDER: Thou <u>shalt</u> drink *seawater*
SUPERFICIAL ORDER: *Seawater* <u>shalt</u> thou drink

In the underlying order, the auxiliary *shalt* immediately precedes its complement *drink seawater*, and the verb *drink* immediately precedes its complement *seawater*. But preposing *seawater* and inverting *shalt* means that the verb *drink* no longer immediately precedes its complement *seawater*, and likewise that the auxiliary *shalt* no longer immediately precedes its complement *drink seawater*. The main theoretical point which our discussion here illustrates is that word-order parameters determine the *underlying* order of constituents rather than their superficial order (which may be disrupted by movement operations). A point of incidental interest to note in relation to sentence 1 is that inversion was not just restricted to interrogative sentences in Elizabethan English, but could also take place in declaratives and other types of sentence. Moreover (as you will see from other examples in this exercise), it could affect main verbs as well as auxiliary verbs.

Exercise 1.2

Below are examples of utterances produced by a girl called Lucy at age twenty-four months. Comment on whether Lucy has correctly set the three parameters discussed in the text (the Head Position Parameter, the Wh-Parameter and the Null Subject Parameter). Discuss the significance of the relevant examples for the parameter-setting model of acquisition.

	CHILD SENTENCE	ADULT COUNTERPART
1	What doing?	'What are you doing?'
2	Want bye-byes	'I want to go to sleep'
3	Daddy play with me (**w**)	'Daddy played with me'; this was in reply to 'What did Daddy do in the park yesterday?'
4	Mummy go shops	'Mummy went to the shops'; this was in reply to 'Where did Mummy go?'
5	Where Daddy gone? (**w**)	'Where's Daddy gone?'
6	Gone office	'He's gone to the office'
7	Me have yoghurt?	'Can I have a yoghurt?'
8	Daddy doing? (**w**)	'What's Daddy doing?'
9	Cry (**w**)	'(I) cry'; this was in reply to 'What do you do when Daddy gets cross with you?'
10	I play (**w**)	'I play'; this was in reply to 'What do you do in the park?'
11	What me having?	'What am I having?'; this followed her mother saying 'Mummy's having fish for dinner'
12	No me have fish	'I'm not going to have fish'
13	Want bickies	'She wants some biscuits'; this was her reply to 'What does Dolly want?'
14	What Teddy have?	'What can Teddy have?'
15	Where going?	'Where are you going?'
16	What Nana eating?	'What's Grandma eating?'
17	Dolly gone?	'Where's Dolly gone?'
18	Watch te'vision	'I'm going to watch television'
19	Me have more	'I want to have some more'
20	Open door	'Open the door!'

Helpful hints

If Lucy has correctly set the Wh-Parameter, we should expect to find that she systematically preposes wh-expressions and positions them sentence-initially. If she has correctly set the Head

Position Parameter, we should expect to find (e.g.) that she correctly positions the complement of a verb after the verb, and the complement of a preposition after the preposition; however, where the complement is a wh-expression, we expect to find that the complement is moved into sentence-initial position in order to satisfy the requirements of the Wh-Parameter (if the Wh-Parameter in some sense overrides the Head Position Parameter). If Lucy has correctly set the Null Subject Parameter, we should expect to find that she does not use null subjects in finite clauses: however, it seems clear that many of the sentences produced by two-year old English children like Lucy do indeed have null subjects – and this led Nina Hyams in influential research (1986, 1992) to conclude that English children go through a *null subject stage* in which they use Italian-style null (*pro*) subjects in finite clauses. If Hyams is right, this implies that children may sometimes start out with incorrect settings for a given parameter, and then later have to *reset* the parameter – a conclusion which (if true) would provide an obvious challenge to the simple parameter-setting model of acquisition outlined in the main text.

However, the picture relating to the use of null subjects is complicated by the fact that although English does not have **finite null subjects** (i.e. the kind of null *pro* subject found in finite clauses in languages like Italian), it has three other types of null subject. One is the kind of **imperative null subject** found in imperatives such as *Shut up!* and *Don't say anything!* (Imperatives are sentences used to issue orders; they are the kind of sentences you can put *please* in front of – as in *Please don't say anything!*) Another is the kind of **nonfinite null subject** found in a range of nonfinite clauses in English (i.e. clauses containing a verb which is not marked for tense and agreement), including main clauses like *Why worry?* and complement clauses like those bracketed in *I want* [*to go home*] and *I like* [*playing tennis*]: the kind of null subject found in nonfinite clauses in English is usually designated as *PRO* and called 'big PRO' (whereas the kind of null subject found in a finite clause in a null-subject language like Italian is designated as *pro* and called 'little pro'. The terms *big* and *little* here simply reflect the fact that PRO is written in 'big' capital letters, and *pro* in 'small' lower-case letters). A third type of null subject found in English can be called a **truncated null subject**, because English has a process of **truncation** which allows one or more words at the beginning of a sentence to be truncated (i.e. omitted) in certain types of style (e.g. diary styles of written English and informal styles of spoken English). Hence in colloquial English, a question like *Are you doing anything tonight?* can be reduced (by truncation) to *You doing anything tonight?* and further reduced (again by truncation) to *Doing anything tonight?* Truncation is also found in abbreviated written styles of English: for example, a diary entry might read *Went to a party. Had a great time. Got totally smashed* (with the subject *I* being truncated in each of the three sentences). An important constraint on truncation is that it can only affect words at the beginning of a sentence, not e.g. words in the middle of a sentence: hence, although we can truncate *are* and *you* in *Are you doing anything tonight?*, we can't truncate them in *What are you doing tonight?* (as we see from the ungrammaticality of *What doing tonight?*) since here *are* and *you* are preceded by *what* and hence occur in the middle of the sentence.

What all of this means is that in determining whether Lucy has mis-set the Null Subject Parameter and has misanalysed English as a null subject language (i.e. a language which allows the kind of finite null 'little *pro*' subjects found in Italian), you have to bear in mind the alternative possibility that the null subjects used by Lucy may represent one or more of the three kinds of null subject permitted in adult English (viz. imperative null subjects, truncated null subjects and nonfinite null subjects).

Since truncation occurs only sentence-initially (at the beginning of a sentence), but finite null (little *pro*) subjects in a genuine null subject language like Italian can occur in any subject position in a sentence, one way of telling the difference between a finite null subject and a truncated null subject is to see whether children omit subjects only when they are the first word in a sentence (which could be the result of *truncation*), or whether they also omit subjects in the middle of sentences (as is the case in a genuine null-subject language like Italian). Another way of differentiating the two is that in null subject languages like Italian with null finite *pro* subjects, we find that overt pronoun subjects are only used for emphasis, so that in an Italian sentence like *L'ho fatto io* (literally 'It have done I') the subject pronoun *io* 'I' has a contrastive interpretation, and the relevant sentence is paraphraseable in English as '*I* was the one who did it' (where italics indicate contrastive stress): by contrast, in a non-null-subject language like English, subject pronouns are not intrinsically emphatic – e.g. *he* doesn't necessarily have a contrastive interpretation in an English diary-style sentence such as *Went to see Jim. Thought he might help*. A third way of telling whether truncation is operative in Lucy's grammar or not is to see whether expressions other than subjects can be truncated, as can happen in adult English (e.g. *What time is it?* can be reduced to *Time is it?* via truncation in rapid spoken English).

At first sight, it might seem unlikely that (some of) Lucy's null subjects could be nonfinite ('big PRO') null subjects, since all the clauses she produces in the data given above occur in finite contexts (i.e. in contexts where adults would use a finite clause). Note, however, that two-year-old children typically go through a stage which Wexler (1994) calls the *Optional Infinitives/OI* stage, during which (in finite contexts) they sometimes produce finite clauses, and sometimes nonfinite clauses (the relevant nonfinite clauses typically containing an infinitive form like *go* or a participle like *going/gone*). Hence, an additional possibility to bear in mind is that some of Lucy's clauses may be nonfinite and have nonfinite ('big PRO') null subjects.

In relation to the sentences in 1–20, make the following assumptions. In 1 *doing* is a verb which has a null subject and the complement *what*. In 2 *want* is a verb which has a null subject and the complement *bye-byes*. In 3 *play* is a verb which has the subject *Daddy* and the complement *with me* (and in turn *me* is the complement of the preposition *with*). In 4 *go* is a verb which has the subject *Mummy* and the complement *shops*. In 5 *gone* is a verb which has the subject *Daddy* and the complement *where*. In 6 *gone* is a verb which has a null subject and the complement *office*. In 7 *have* is a verb which has the subject *me* and the complement *yoghurt*. In 8 *doing* is a verb which has the subject *Daddy*, and its complement is a null counterpart of *what*. In 9 *cry* is a verb with a null subject. In 10, *play* is a verb and *I* is its subject. In 11, *having* is a verb which has the subject *me* and the complement *what*. In 12 *no* is a negative particle which has the complement *me have fish* (assume that *no* is the kind of word which doesn't have a subject), and *have* is a verb which has the subject *me* and the complement *fish*. In 13 *want* is a verb which has a null subject and the complement *bickies*. In 14 *have* is a verb which has the subject *Teddy* and the complement *what*. In 15 *going* is a verb which has a null subject and the complement *where*. In 16 *eating* is a verb which has the subject *Nana* and the complement *what*. In 17 *gone* is a verb which has the subject *Dolly* and its complement is a null counterpart of *where*. In 18 *watch* is a verb which has a null subject and the complement *te'vision*. In 19 *have* is a verb which has the subject *me* and the complement *more*. In 20 *open* is a verb whose subject is null and whose complement is *door*.

Model answer for 1

In *What doing?* the verb *doing* has an overt object *what* and a null subject of some kind. Since the object *what* does not occupy the normal postverbal position associated with objects in English (cf. the position of the object *something* in *Do something!*), *what* has clearly undergone wh-movement: this suggests that Lucy has correctly set the Wh-Parameter at the 'requires wh-movement' value appropriate for English. Because the object complement *what* has undergone wh-movement, we cannot tell (from this sentence) whether Lucy generally positions (unmoved) complements after their heads: in other words, this particular sentence provides us with no evidence of whether Lucy has correctly set the Head Position Parameter or not (though other examples in the exercise do). Much more difficult to answer is the question of whether Lucy has correctly set the Null Subject Parameter at the value appropriate to English, and hence (tacitly) 'knows' that finite clauses do not allow a null finite *pro* subject in English. At first sight, it might seem as if Lucy has wrongly analysed English as a null subject language (and hence mis-set the Null Subject Parameter), since *What doing?* has a null subject of some kind. But the crucial question here is: What kind of null subject does the verb *doing* have? It clearly cannot be an imperative null subject, since the sentence is interrogative in force, not imperative. Nor can it be a truncated null subject, since truncated subjects only occur in sentence-initial position (i.e. as the first word in a sentence), and *what* is the first word in the sentence in *What doing?* (since preposed wh-words occupy sentence-initial position in questions). This leaves two other possibilities. One is that the null subject in *What doing?* is the 'little *pro*' subject found in finite clauses in genuine null subject languages like Italian: since the verb *doing* is nonfinite, this would entail positing that the sentence *What doing?* contains a null counterpart of the finite auxiliary *are* (raising questions about why the auxiliary is null rather than overt); this in turn would mean that Lucy has indeed mis-set the Null Subject Parameter (raising questions about how she comes to do so, and why she doesn't mis-set the other two parameters we are concerned with here). However, an alternative possibility is that the structure *What doing?* is a nonfinite clause (like adult questions such as *Why worry?*) and has the kind of nonfinite ('big PRO') null subject found in nonfinite clauses in many languages (English included). If so (i.e. if *What doing* is a nonfinite clause which has the structure *What PRO doing?*), there would be no evidence that Lucy has mis-set the Null Subject Parameter – i.e. no evidence that she ever produces finite clauses with a 'little *pro*' subject. This in turn would mean that we can maintain the hypothesis put forward in the main text that children correctly set parameters at their appropriate value from the very earliest stages of the acquisition of syntax. The error Lucy makes in producing sentences like *What doing?* would be in not knowing that main clauses generally have to be finite in English, and that main clause questions generally have to contain a finite auxiliary.

2 Structure

2.1 Overview

In this chapter, we introduce the notion of **syntactic structure**, looking at how words are combined together to form phrases and sentences. We shall see that phrases and sentences are built up by a series of **merger** operations, each of which combines a pair of constituents together to form a larger constituent. We show how the resulting structure can be represented in terms of a **tree diagram**. We look at some of the principles which underlie sentence formation, and we explore ways of testing the structure of phrases and sentences.

2.2 Phrases

To put our discussion on a concrete footing, let's consider how an elementary two-word phrase such as the italicised response produced by speaker B in the following mini-dialogue is formed:

(1)   SPEAKER A: What are you trying to do?
        SPEAKER B: *Help you*

As speaker B's utterance illustrates, the simplest way of forming a phrase is by **merging** (a technical term meaning 'combining') two words together: for example, by merging the word *help* with the word *you* in (1), we form the phrase *help you*. The resulting phrase *help you* seems to have verb-like rather than pronoun-like properties, as we see from the fact that it can occupy the same range of positions as the simple verb *help*, and hence e.g. occur after the infinitive particle *to*: cf.

(2) (a)   We are trying to *help*
    (b)   We are trying to *help you*

By contrast, the phrase *help you* cannot occupy the same kind of position as a pronoun such as *you*, as we see from (3) below:

(3) (a)   *You* are very difficult
    (b)   **Help you* are very difficult

So, it seems clear that the grammatical properties of a phrase like *help you* are determined by the verb *help*, and not by the pronoun *you*. Much the same can be said about the semantic properties of the expression, since the phrase *help you* describes an act of help, not a kind of person. Using the appropriate technical terminology, we can say that the verb *help* is the **head** of the phrase *help you*, and hence that *help you* is a **Verb Phrase**: and in the same way as we abbreviate category labels like **verb** to **V**, so too we can abbreviate the category label **Verb Phrase** to **VP**. If we use the traditional labelled bracketing technique to represent the category of the overall verb phrase *help you* and of its constituent words (the verb *help* and the pronoun *you*), we can represent the structure of the resulting phrase as in (4) below:

(4)   [vp [v help] [prn you]]

An alternative (equivalent) way of representing the structure of phrases like *help you* is via a **labelled tree diagram** such as (5) below (which is a bit like a family tree diagram – albeit for a small family):

(5)

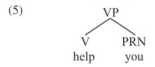

What the tree diagram in (5) tells us is that the overall phrase *help you* is a Verb Phrase (VP), and that its two **constituents** are the verb (V) *help* and the pronoun (PRN) *you*. The verb *help* is the **head** of the overall phrase (and so is the key word which determines the grammatical and semantic properties of the phrase *help you*). Introducing another technical term at this point, we can say that, conversely, the VP *help you* is a **projection** of the verb *help*, in the sense that the verb *help* is projected into a larger structure by merging it with another constituent of an appropriate kind. In this case, the constituent which is merged with the verb *help* is the pronoun *you*, which has the grammatical function of being the (**direct object**) **complement** of the verb *help*. The head of a projection/phrase determines grammatical properties of its complement: in this instance, since *help* is a **transitive** verb, it requires a complement with accusative case (e.g. a pronoun like *me/us/him/them*), and this requirement is satisfied here since *you* can function as an accusative form (as you can see from the table of pronouns listed under the entry for **Case** in the Glossary at the end of the book). The tree diagram in (5) is entirely equivalent to the labelled bracketing in (4), in the sense that the two provide us with precisely the same information about the structure of the phrase *help you*. The differences between a labelled bracketing like (4) and a tree diagram like (5) are purely notational: each category is represented by a single labelled **node** in a tree diagram (i.e. by a point in the tree which carries a category label like VP, V or PRN), but by a pair of labelled brackets in a labelled bracketing.

Since our goal in developing a theory of Universal Grammar is to uncover general structural principles governing the formation of phrases and sentences, let's generalise our discussion of (5) at this point and hypothesise that all phrases are formed in essentially the same way as the phrase in (5), namely by a **binary** (i.e. pairwise) merger operation which combines two constituents together to form a larger constituent. In the case of (5), the resulting phrase *help you* is formed by merging two words. However, not all phrases contain only two words – as we see if we look at the structure of the italicised phrase produced by speaker B in (6) below:

(6)   SPEAKER A: What was your intention?
         SPEAKER B: *To help you*

The phrase in (6B) is formed by merging the infinitive particle *to* with the Verb Phrase *help you*. What's the head of the resulting phrase *to help you*? A reasonable guess would be that the head is the infinitival tense particle/T *to*, so that the resulting expression *to help you* is an infinitival **TP** (= infinitival tense projection = infinitival tense phrase). This being so, we'd expect to find that TPs containing infinitival *to* occur in a different range of positions from VPs/Verb Phrases – and this is indeed the case, as we see from the contrast below:

(7) (a)   They **ought** *to help you* (= **ought** + TP *to help you*)
    (b)   *They **ought** *help you* (= **ought** + VP *help you*)

(8) (a)   They **should** *help you* (= **should** + VP *help you*)
    (b)   *They **should** *to help you* (= **should** + TP *to help you*)

If we assume that *help you* is a VP whereas *to help you* is a TP, we can account for the contrasts in (7) and (8) by saying that *ought* is the kind of word which **selects** (i.e. 'takes') an infinitival TP as its complement, whereas *should* is the kind of word which selects an infinitival VP as its complement. Implicit in this claim is the assumption that different words like *ought* and *should* have different **selectional properties** which determine the range of complements which they can take.

The infinitive phrase *to help you* is formed by merging the infinitive particle *to* with the Verb Phrase *help you*. If (as we argued in the previous chapter) infinitival *to* is an **infinitival tense particle** (belonging to the category T) and if *to* is the head of the phrase *to help you*, the structure formed by merging *to* with the Verb Phrase/VP *help you* in (5) will be the TP in (9) below:

(9)

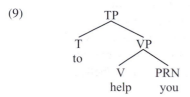

The **head** of the resulting infinitival tense projection *to help you* is the infinitive particle *to*, and the Verb Phrase *help you* is the **complement** of *to*; conversely, *to help you* is a **projection** of *to*. In keeping with our earlier observation that 'The head of a projection/phrase determines grammatical properties of its complement,' the infinitival tense particle *to* requires an infinitival Verb Phrase as its complement: more specifically, *to* requires the head V of its VP complement to be a verb in its **infinitive** form, so that we require the (bare/uninflected) infinitive form *help* after infinitival *to* (and not an inflected form like *helping/helped/helps*). Refining our earlier observation somewhat, we can therefore say that 'The head of a projection/phrase determines grammatical properties of the *head word of* its complement.' In (9), *to* is the head of the TP *to help you*, and the complement of *to* is the VP *help you*; the head of this VP is the V *help*, so that *to* determines the form of the V *help* (requiring it to be in the infinitive form *help*).

More generally, our discussion here suggests that we can build up phrases by a series of binary merger operations which combine successive pairs of constituents to form ever larger structures. For example, by merging the infinitive phrase *to help you* with the verb *trying*, we can form the even larger italicised phrase *trying to help you* produced by speaker B in (10) below:

(10)   SPEAKER A: What are you doing?
          SPEAKER B: *Trying to help you*

The resulting phrase *trying to help you* is headed by the verb *trying*, as we see from the fact that it can be used after words like *be*, *start* or *keep*, which select a complement headed by a verb in the *-ing* form (cf. *They were/started/kept trying to help you*). This being so, the italicised phrase produced by speaker B in (10) is a VP (= Verb Phrase) which has the structure (11) below:

(11)

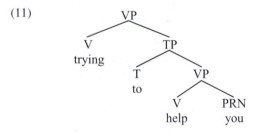

(11) tells us (amongst other things) that the overall expression *trying to help you* is a Verb Phrase/VP; its **head** is the verb/V *trying*, and the **complement** of *trying* is the TP/infinitival tense phrase *to help you*: conversely, the VP *trying to help you* is a **projection** of the V *trying*. An interesting property of syntactic structures which is illustrated in (11) is that of **recursion** – that is, the property of allowing a given structure to contain more than one instance of a given category (in this case, more than one Verb Phrase/VP – one VP headed by the verb *help* and another VP headed by the verb *trying*).

Since our goal in developing a theory of Universal Grammar/UG is to attempt to establish universal principles governing the nature of linguistic structure, an important question to ask is whether there are any general principles of constituent structure which we can abstract from structures like (5, 9, 11). If we look closely at the relevant structures, we can see that they obey the following two (putatively universal) constituent structure principles:

(12)   **Headedness Principle**
        Every nonterminal node in a syntactic structure is a projection of a head word

(13)   **Binarity Principle**
        Every nonterminal node in a syntactic structure is binary-branching

(A *terminal* node is one at the foot/bottom of a tree, whereas a nonterminal node is one which branches down into other nodes: consequently, the V-*trying*, T-*to*, V-*help* and PRN-*you* in (11) are terminal nodes because they do not branch down into any other node; by contrast, the VP and TP constituents are *nonterminal* because they branch down into other nodes.) For example, the structure (11) obeys the Headedness Principle (12) in that the VP *help you* is headed by the V *help*, the TP *to help you* is headed by the T *to*, and the VP *trying to help you* is headed by the V *trying*. Likewise, (11) obeys the Binarity Principle (13) in that the VP *help you* branches into two **immediate constituents** (in the sense that it has two constituents immediately beneath it, namely the V *help* and the PRN *you*), the TP *to help you* branches into two immediate constituents (the nonfinite tense particle T *to* and the VP *help you*) and the VP *trying to help you* likewise branches into two immediate constituents (the V *trying* and the TP *to help you*). Our discussion thus leads us towards a *principled* account of constituent structure – i.e. one based on a set of principles of Universal Grammar.

There are several reasons for trying to uncover constituent structure principles like (12) and (13). From a learnability perspective, such principles reduce the range of alternatives which children have to choose between when trying to determine the structure of a given kind of expression: they therefore help us develop a more constrained theory of syntax. Moreover, additional support for the Binarity Principle comes from evidence that phonological structure is also binary, in that (e.g.) a syllable like *bat* has a binary structure, consisting of the **onset** |b| and the **rhyme** |at|, and the rhyme in turn has a binary structure, consisting of the **nucleus** |a| and the **coda** |t| – vertical bars being used to enclose sounds or sequences of sounds. Likewise, there is evidence that morphological structure is also binary, and hence (e.g.) that the noun *indecipherability* is formed by adding the prefix *de-* to the noun *cipher* to form the verb *decipher*; then adding the suffix *-able* to this verb to form the adjective *decipherable*; then adding the prefix *in-* to this adjective to form the adjective *indecipherable*; and then adding the suffix *-ity* to the resulting adjective to form the noun *indecipherability*. It would thus seem that *binarity* is an inherent characteristic of the phonological, morphological and syntactic structure of natural languages: as our discussion develops below, we shall uncover empirical evidence in support of the claim that syntactic structure is indeed binary.

2.3   Clauses

Having considered how phrases are formed, let's now turn to look at how **clauses** and **sentences** are formed. By way of illustration, suppose that speaker B had used the simple (single-clause) sentence italicised in (14) below to reply to speaker A, rather than the phrase used by speaker B in (10):

(14)   SPEAKER A: What are you doing?
          SPEAKER B: *We are trying to help you*

What's the structure of the italicised clause produced by speaker B in (14)?

In work in the 1960s, clauses were generally taken to belong to the category **S** (*Sentence/Clause*), and the sentence produced by B in (14) would have been taken to have a structure along the following lines:

(15)

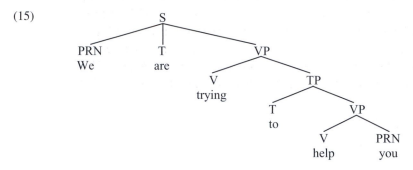

However, a structure such as (15) violates the two constituent structure principles which we posited in (12) and (13) above. More particularly, the S analysis of clauses in (15) violates the **Headedness Principle** (12) in that the S *We are trying to help you* is a structure which has no head of any kind. Likewise, the S analysis in (15) also violates the **Binarity Principle** (13) in that the S constituent *We are trying to help you* is not binary-branching but rather ternary-branching, because it branches into three immediate constituents, namely the PRN *we*, the T *are* and the VP *trying to help you*. If our theory of Universal Grammar requires every syntactic structure to be a binary-branching projection of a head word, it is clear that we have to reject the S analysis of clause structure in (15) as one which is not in keeping with UG principles.

Let's therefore explore an alternative analysis of the structure of clauses which is consistent with the *headedness* and *binarity* requirements in (12) and (13). More specifically, let's make the unifying assumption that clauses are formed by the same binary merger operation as phrases. This in turn will mean that the italicised clause in (14B) is formed by merging the (present) tense auxiliary *are* with the Verb Phrase *trying to help you,* and then subsequently merging the resulting expression *are trying to help you* with the pronoun *we*. Since *are* belongs to the category T of tense auxiliary, it might at first sight seem as if merging *are* with the Verb Phrase *trying to help you* will derive (i.e. form) the

tense projection/tense phrase/TP *are trying to help you.* But this can't be right, since it would provide us with no obvious account of why speaker B's reply in (16) below is ungrammatical:

(16)   SPEAKER A: What are you doing?
              SPEAKER B: *Are trying to help you*

If *Are trying to help you* is a complete TP, how come it can't be used to answer A's question in (16), since we see from sentences like (6B) that TP constituents like *to help you* can be used to answer questions.

An informal answer we can give is to say that the expression *Are trying to help you* is somehow 'incomplete', and that only 'complete' expressions can be used to answer questions. In what sense is *Are trying to help you* incomplete? The answer is that finite (e.g. present/past tense) T constituents require a subject, and the finite auxiliary *are* doesn't have a subject in (16). More specifically, let's assume that when we merge a tense auxiliary (= T) with a Verb Phrase (= VP), we form an **intermediate projection** which we shall here denote as T′ (pronounced 'tee-bar'); and that only when we merge the relevant T-bar constituent with a subject like *we* do we form a **maximal projection** – or, more informally a 'complete TP'. Given these assumptions, the italicised clause in (14B) will have the structure (17) below:

(17)

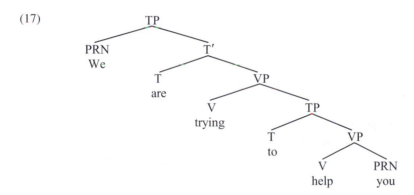

What this means is that a tense auxiliary like *are* has two projections: a smaller **intermediate projection** (T′) formed by merging *are* with its complement *trying to help you* to form the T-bar (intermediate tense projection) *are trying to help you*; and a larger **maximal projection** (TP) formed by merging the resulting T′ *are trying to help you* with its subject *we* to form the TP *We are trying to help you.* Saying that TP is the **maximal projection** of *are* in (17) means it is the largest constituent headed by the auxiliary *are*.

Why should tense auxiliaries require *two* different projections, one in which they merge with a following complement to form a T-bar, and another in which the resulting T-bar merges with a preceding subject to form a TP? The requirement for tense auxiliaries to have two projections (as in (17) above) was taken by Chomsky in earlier work to be a consequence of a principle of Universal Grammar known as the **Extended Projection Principle** (conventionally abbreviated to **EPP**), which specified that a finite tense constituent T must be extended into a TP projection containing a subject.

However, comparative evidence suggests that there are other languages in which a tense auxiliary does not require a preceding subject of its own – as illustrated by an Italian sentence such as:

(18)   È stata arrestata una vecchia signora
         Is been arrested an old lady
         'An old lady has been arrested'

The absence of any subject preceding the present tense auxiliary *è* 'is' in (18) suggests that it cannot be a principle of Universal Grammar that every tense auxiliary in every finite clause in every language has a subject. Rather, it seems more likely that this is a property of tense auxiliaries in particular languages like English, but not of their counterparts in some other languages. Recall that we noted in §1.2 that the grammatical properties of categories of word are traditionally described in terms of sets of **features**, and by convention these are enclosed in square brackets. So, for example, in order to describe the grammatical properties of the auxiliary *are* (in a sentence like *They are lying*) as a third person plural present progressive auxiliary, we could say that it carries the features [third-person, plural-number, present-tense, progressive-aspect]. Using this convention, Chomsky suggested in later work that English tense auxiliaries like *are* carry an **EPP feature** which requires them to have an extended projection into a TP containing a subject. If all finite auxiliaries in English carry an EPP feature, it follows that any English clause structure (like that produced by speaker B in (16) above) containing a tense auxiliary which does not have a subject will be ungrammatical.

The EPP requirement (for a finite auxiliary in English to have a subject) would seem to be essentially *syntactic* (rather than semantic) in nature, as we can see from sentences such as (19) below:

(19) (a)   *It* was alleged that he lied under oath
     (b)   *There* has been no trouble

In structures like (19), the italicised subject pronouns *it/there* seem to have no semantic content (in particular, no referential properties) of their own, as we see from the fact that neither can be questioned by the corresponding interrogative words *what?/where?* (cf. the ungrammaticality of **What was alleged that he lied under oath?* and **Where has been no trouble?*), and neither can receive contrastive focus (hence *it/there* cannot be contrastively stressed in sentences like 19 above). Rather, they function as **expletive pronouns** – i.e. pronouns with no intrinsic meaning which are used to satisfy the syntactic requirement for a finite auxiliary like *was/has* to have a subject.

It is interesting to note that theoretical considerations also favour a binary-branching TP analysis of clause structure like (17) over a ternary-branching S analysis like (15). The essential spirit of Minimalism is to reduce the theoretical apparatus which we use to describe syntactic structure to a minimum. Within this spirit, it has generally been assumed that tree diagrams should only contain information about hierarchical structure (i.e. containment/constituent structure relations), not about linear structure (i.e. left-to-right word order), because linear information is redundant (in the sense that it can be predicted from hierarchical structure by simple word-order rules) if we use binary-branching trees. Suppose, for example, that we have a word-order rule for English to the effect that 'Any constituent of a phrase which is directly merged with the head word of the phrase is positioned to the right of the head, but any other constituent of the phrase is positioned to the left of the head.' This word-order rule will correctly predict (inter alia) that the VP *trying to help you* in (17) must be positioned to the right of the tense auxiliary/T *are* (because the relevant VP is directly merged with the T-head *are*), and that the pronoun *we* must be positioned to the left of *are* (because *we* is not merged with T-*are* but rather with the T-bar *are trying to help you*). As you can see for yourself, it's not clear how we can achieve the same result (of eliminating redundant word-order information from trees) under a ternary-branching analysis like (15), since both the pronoun *we* and the Verb Phrase *trying to help you* are merged with T-*are* in (15). It should be noted in passing that an important consequence of assuming that linear order is not a *syntactic* relation is that it entails that syntactic operations cannot be sensitive to word order (e.g. we can't handle subject–auxiliary agreement by saying that a finite auxiliary agrees with a *preceding* noun or pronoun expression): rather, all syntactic operations must be sensitive to hierarchical rather than linear structure. On this view (and assuming the overall structure of a grammar in diagram 16 of §1.3), word order is a PF property (i.e. a property assigned to constituents in the PF component on the basis of linearisation rules like that sketched informally above).

An interesting implication of the analysis of clause structure we have presented here is that heads can have more than one kind of projection: e.g. the tense auxiliary *are* in (17) above has an intermediate (T-bar) projection into *are trying to help you* and a maximal (TP) projection into *We are trying to help you*. The same is true of other types of head, as can be illustrated by the italicised expressions below:

(20) (a)   *American intervention in Iraq* has caused considerable controversy
     (b)   She arrived at the solution *quite independently of me*
     (c)   He must go *straight to bed*
     (d)   Nobody expected the film to have *so dramatic an ending*

In (20a) the noun *intervention* merges with its complement *in Iraq* to form the intermediate projection (N-bar) *intervention in Iraq*, and the resulting N-bar in turn merges with the adjective *American* to form the maximal projection (NP) *American intervention in Iraq*. In (20b) the adverb *independently* merges with its complement *of me* to form the intermediate projection (ADV-bar) *independently of me*, and this in turn merges with the adverb *quite* to form the maximal projection

(ADVP) *quite independently of me*. In (20c) the preposition *to* merges with its complement *bed* to form the intermediate (P-bar) projection *to bed*, and this in turn merges with the adverb *straight* to form the maximal (PP) projection *straight to bed*. In (20d), the quantifier (indefinite article) *an* merges with its complement *ending* to form the intermediate (Q-bar) projection *an ending* which in turn merges with the expression *so dramatic* to form the maximal projection (QP) *so dramatic an ending*.

In clause structures like (17) above, the pronoun *we* which merges with the intermediate T-bar projection *are trying to help you* to form the maximal TP projection *We are trying to help you* has the function of being the **subject** of the TP. However, the expressions which merge with the relevant intermediate projections to form maximal projections in (20) don't always have the function of being subjects. If we take a fairly flexible view of what a subject is, we could perhaps say that the adjective *American* is the 'subject' of the expression *intervention in Iraq* in (20a) by virtue of denoting the entity perpetrating the act of intervention. But we certainly wouldn't want to say that *quite* is the subject of *independently of me* in (20b), or that *straight* is the subject of *to bed* in (20c), or that *so dramatic* is the subject of *an ending* in (20d). Rather, the expressions which precede the head word in the examples in (20b-d) seem to have the function of being **modifiers** of the expression that follows them – so that *quite* modifies *independently of me*, *straight* modifies *to bed* and *so dramatic* modifies *an ending* (and perhaps *American* modifies *intervention in Iraq* in 20a).

What our discussion here illustrates is that it is important to draw a distinction between the *position* occupied by an expression in a given structure, and its *function*. In order to get a clearer view of the distinction, let's take a closer look at the derivation of (20c) *He must go straight to bed*. As we noted earlier, the preposition *to* merges with its noun complement *bed* to form the P-bar *to bed* which in turn is merged with the adverb *straight* to form the PP *straight to bed*. The resulting PP is then merged with the verb *go* to form the VP *go straight to bed*. This in turn is merged with the present tense auxiliary *must* to form the T-bar *must go straight to bed*. This T-bar merges with the pronoun *he* to form the TP below:

(21)

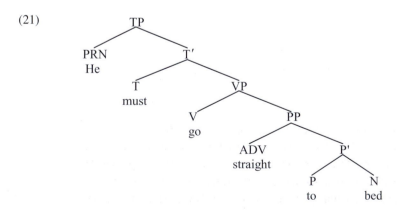

In a fairly obvious sense, the pronoun *he* occupies the same kind of position within TP as the adverb *straight* does within PP: more specifically, *he* merges with an intermediate T-bar projection to form a maximal TP projection in the same way as *straight* merges with an intermediate P-bar projection to form a maximal PP projection. Since it's useful to have a term to designate the position they both occupy, let's say that they both occupy the **specifier** position within the expression containing them. More specifically, let's say that *he* occupies the specifier position within the T-projection (conventionally abbreviated to **spec-T** or **spec-TP**) and that *straight* occupies the specifier position within PP (= **spec-P** or **spec-PP**). However, although *he* and *straight* occupy the same specifier position within the expressions containing them, they have different functions: *he* is the **subject** of the T-bar expression *has gone to bed*, whereas *straight* is a **modifier** of the P-bar expression *to bed*. In much the same way, we can say that *American* occupies the specifier position within the Noun Phrase *American intervention in Iraq* in (20a), *quite* occupies the specifier position within the Adverbial Phrase *quite independently of me* in (20b) and *so dramatic* occupies the specifier position within the Quantifier Phrase *so dramatic an ending* in (20d).

2.4   Clauses containing complementisers

A question which we have not so far asked about the structure of clauses concerns what role is played by complementisers like *that*, *for* and *if*, e.g. in speaker B's reply in (22) below:

(22)   SPEAKER A: What are you saying?
              SPEAKER B: *That we are trying to help you*

Where does the C/complementiser *that* fit into the structure of the sentence? The answer suggested in work in the 1970s was that a complementiser merges with an S constituent like that in (15) above to form an **S′/S-bar** (pronounced 'ess-bar') constituent like that shown below (simplified by not showing the internal structure of the VP *trying to help you*, which is as in (11) above):

(23)

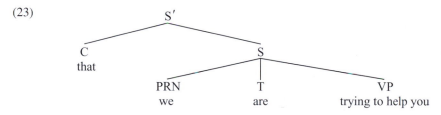

However, the claim that a clause introduced by a complementiser has the status of an S-bar constituent falls foul of the **Headedness Principle** (12), which requires every nonterminal node in a tree to be a projection of a *head word*. The principle is violated because S-bar in (23) is analysed as a projection of the S constituent *we are trying to help you*, and S is clearly not a word (but rather a string of words).

An interesting way round the *headedness* problem is to suppose that the head of a clausal structure introduced by a complementiser is the complementiser itself: since this is a single word, there would then be no violation of the Headedness Principle (12) requiring every syntactic structure to be a projection of a head word. Let's therefore assume that the complementiser *that* merges with the TP *we are trying to help you* (whose structure is shown in (17) above) to form the **CP/complementiser projection/complementiser phrase** in (24) below:

(24)

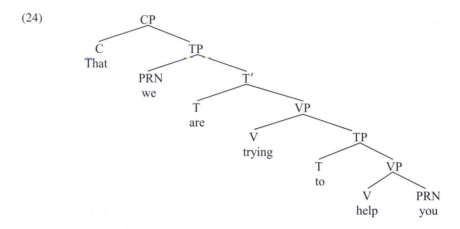

(24) tells us that the complementiser *that* is the **head** of the overall clause *that we are trying to help you* (and conversely, the overall clause is a **projection** of the complementiser *that*) – and indeed this is implicit in the traditional description of such structures as *that*-clauses. (24) also tells us that the complement of *that* is the TP/tense phrase *we are trying to help you*. Clauses introduced by complementisers have been taken to have the status of CP/complementiser phrase constituents since the early 1980s.

An interesting aspect of the analyses in (17) and (24) above is that clauses and sentences are analysed as **headed** structures – i.e. as projections of head words (in conformity with the Headedness Principle). In other words, just as phrases are projections of a head word (e.g. a verb phrase like *help you* is a projection of the verb *help*), so too a sentence like *We will help you* is a projection of the auxiliary *will*, and a complement clause like the bracketed *that*-clause in *I can't promise [that we will help you]* is a projection of the complementiser *that*. This enables us to arrive at a unitary analysis of the structure of phrases, clauses and sentences, in that clauses and sentences (like phrases) are projections of head words. More generally, it leads us to the conclusion that clauses/sentences are simply particular kinds of phrase (e.g. a *that*-clause is a complementiser phrase).

An assumption which is implicit in the analyses which we have presented here is that phrases and sentences are **derived** (i.e. formed) in a **bottom-up** fashion (i.e. they are built up from bottom to top). For example, the clause in (24) involves the following sequence of **merger** operations: (i) the verb *help* is merged with the pronoun *you* to form the VP *help you*; (ii) the resulting VP is merged with the nonfinite T/tense particle *to* to form the TP *to help you*; (iii) this TP is in turn merged with the verb *trying* to form the VP *trying to help you*; (iv) the resulting VP is merged with the T/tense auxiliary *are* to form the T-bar *are trying to help you*; (v) this T-bar is merged with its subject *we* to form the TP *we are trying to help you*; and (vi) the resulting TP is in turn merged with the C/complementiser *that* to form the CP structure (24) *that we are trying to help you*. By saying that the structure (24) is derived in a **bottom-up** fashion, we mean that lower parts of the structure nearer the bottom of the tree are formed before higher parts of the structure nearer the top of the tree.

As those of you familiar with earlier work will have noticed, the kind of structures we are proposing here are very different from those assumed in traditional grammar and in work in linguistics in the 1960s and 1970s. Earlier work implicitly assumed that only items belonging to **substantive/lexical categories** could project into phrases, not words belonging to **functional categories**. More specifically, earlier work assumed that there were Noun Phrases headed by nouns, Verb Phrases headed by verbs, Adjectival Phrases headed by adjectives, Adverbial Phrases headed by adverbs and Prepositional Phrases headed by prepositions. However, more recent work has argued that not only content words but also function words can project into phrases, so that we have Tense Phrases headed by a tense-marker, Complementiser Phrases headed by a complementiser, Determiner Phrases headed by a determiner – and so on. More generally, the assumption made in work over the last three decades is that in principle *all* word-level categories can project into phrases. This means that some of the structures we make use of here may seem (at best) rather strange to those of you with a more traditional background, or (at worst) just plain *wrong*. However, the structure of a given phrase or sentence cannot be determined on the basis of personal prejudice or pedagogical precepts inculcated into you at secondary school, but rather has to be determined on the basis of syntactic evidence of the kind discussed in the next section below. I would therefore ask traditionalists to be open to new ideas and new analyses (a prerequisite for understanding in any discipline).

2.5   Testing structure

Thus far, we have argued that phrases and sentences are built up by merging successive pairs of constituents into larger and larger structures, and that the resulting structure can be represented in terms of a labelled tree diagram. The tree diagrams which we use to represent syntactic structure make specific claims about how sentences are built up out of various different kinds of **constituent** (i.e. syntactic unit): hence, trees can be said to represent the **constituent structure** of sentences. But this raises the question of how we know (and how we can test) whether the claims made about syntactic structure in tree diagrams are true. So far, we have relied mainly on *intuition* in analysing the structure of sentences – we have in effect *guessed* at the structure. However, it is unwise to rely on intuition in attempting to determine the structure of a given expression in a given language. For, while experienced linguists over a period of years tend to acquire fairly strong intuitions about structure, novices by contrast tend to have relatively weak, uncertain and unreliable intuitions; moreover, even the intuitions of supposed experts may ultimately turn out to be based on little more than personal preference.

For this reason, it is more satisfactory (and more accurate) to regard constituent structure as having the status of a *theoretical construct*. That is to say, it is part of the theoretical apparatus which linguists find they need to make use of in order to explain certain observations about language (just as molecules, atoms and subatomic particles are constructs which physicists find they need to make use of in order to explain the nature of matter in the universe). It is no more reasonable to rely wholly on intuition to determine syntactic structure than it would be to rely on intuition to determine molecular structure. Inevitably, then, much of the evidence for syntactic structure is of an essentially empirical character, based on the observed grammatical properties of particular types of expression. The evidence typically takes the form 'If we posit that such-and-such an expression has such-and-such a constituent structure, we can provide a principled account of the observed grammatical properties of the expression.' Thus, structural representations ultimately have to be justified in empirical terms, i.e. in terms of whether or not they provide a principled account of the grammatical properties of phrases and sentences.

In order to make our discussion more concrete, we'll look at how we can test the structure of the following sentence:

(25)   The chairman has resigned from the board

Let's suppose that (25) is derived as follows. The determiner *the* is merged with the noun *board* to form the DP *the board*. This DP is merged with the preposition *from* to form the PP *from the board*. The resulting PP is merged with the verb *resigned* to form the VP *resigned from the board*. This VP is then merged with the auxiliary *has* to form the T-bar *has resigned from the board*. This T-bar is in turn merged with its subject/specifier *the chairman* (which is a DP formed by merging the determiner *the* with the noun *chairman*), thereby forming the TP shown in (26) below:

(26)

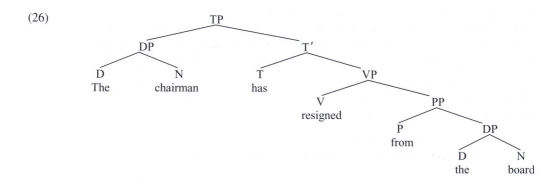

The tree diagram in (26) is a representation of (what we take to be) the structure of (25) *The chairman has resigned from the board.*

However, a tree diagram like (26) has the status of a hypothesis (i.e. untested and unproven assumption) about the structure of the relevant sentence. How can we test our hypothesis and determine whether (26) is or isn't an appropriate representation of the structure of the sentence? The answer is that there are a number of standard heuristics (i.e. 'tests') which we can use to determine structure: we shall discuss just three of these here. The first relates to the phenomenon of **co-ordination**. English and other languages have a variety of **co-ordinating conjunctions** like *and/but/or* which can be used to **co-ordinate** (= **conjoin** = join together) expressions such as those bracketed below:

(27) (a)   [fond of cats] *and* [afraid of dogs]
    (b)   [slowly] *but* [surely]
    (c)   [to go] *or* [to stay]

In each of the expressions in (27), an italicised co-ordinating conjunction has been used to conjoin the bracketed pairs of expressions. Clearly, any adequate grammar of English will have to provide a principled answer to the question: 'What kinds of strings (i.e. sequences of words) can and cannot be co-ordinated?'

Now, it turns out that we can't just co-ordinate any random set of strings, as we see by comparing the grammatical reply produced by speaker B in (28) below:

(28)   SPEAKER A: What does he do to keep fit?
            SPEAKER B: Run *up the hill* and *up the mountain*

with the ungrammatical reply produced by speaker B in (29) below:

(29)   SPEAKER A: What did he do about his bills?
            SPEAKER B: *Ring *up the phone company* and *up the electricity company*

Why should it be possible to co-ordinate the string *up the hill* with the string *up the mountain* in (28), but not possible to co-ordinate the string *up the phone company* with the string *up the electricity company* in (29)? We can provide a principled answer to this question in terms of constituent structure: the italicised string *up the hill* in (28) is a constituent of the phrase *run up the hill* (*up the hill* is a Prepositional Phrase, in fact), and so can be co-ordinated with another similar type of Prepositional Phrase (e.g. a PP such as *up the mountain*, or *down the hill* or *along the path* etc.). Conversely, however, the string *up the phone company* in (29) is not a constituent of the phrase *ring up the phone company*, and so cannot be co-ordinated with another similar string like *up the electricity company*. (Traditional grammarians say that *up* is associated with *ring* in expressions like *ring up someone*, and that the expression *ring up* forms a kind of complex verb which carries the sense of 'telephone'.) On the basis of contrasts such as these, we can formulate the following generalisation:

(30)   **Co-ordination Condition**
            Only constituents of the same type can be co-ordinated

A **constraint** (i.e. principle imposing restrictions on certain types of grammatical operation) along the lines of (30) is assumed in much work in traditional grammar.

Having established the condition (30), we can now make use of it as a way of testing the tree diagram in (26) above. In this connection, consider the data in (31) below (in which the bracketed strings have been co-ordinated by *and*):

(31) (a)   The chairman has resigned from [*the board*] and [*the company*]
     (b)   The chairman has resigned [*from the board*] and [*from the company*]
     (c)   The chairman has [*resigned from the board*] and [*gone abroad*]
     (d)   The chairman [*has resigned from the board*] and [*is living in Utopia*]
     (e)   *The [*chairman has resigned from the board*] and [*company has replaced him*]
     (f)   [*The chairman has resigned from the board*] and [*the company has replaced him*]

(31a) provides us with evidence in support of the claim in (26) that *the board* is a Determiner Phrase constituent, since it can be co-ordinated with another DP like *the company*; similarly, (31b) provides us with evidence that *from the board* is a Prepositional Phrase constituent, since it can be co-ordinated with another PP like *from the company*; likewise, (31c) provides evidence that *resigned from the board* is a Verb Phrase constituent, since it can be co-ordinated with another VP like *gone abroad*; in much the same way, (31d) provides evidence that *has resigned from the board* is a T-bar constituent, since it can be co-ordinated with another T′ like *is living in Utopia* (thereby providing interesting evidence in support of the *binary-branching* structure assumed in the TP analysis of clauses, and against the ternary-branching analysis assumed in the S analysis of clauses); and in addition, (31f) provides evidence that *the chairman has resigned from the board* is a TP constituent, since it can be co-ordinated with another TP like *the company has replaced him*. Conversely, however, the fact that (31e) is ungrammatical suggests that (precisely as (26) claims) the string *chairman has resigned from the board* is not a constituent, since it cannot be co-ordinated with a parallel string like *company has replaced him* (and the constraint in (30) tells us that two strings of words can only be co-ordinated if both are constituents – and, more precisely, if both are constituents of the same type). Overall, then, the co-ordination data in (31) provide empirical evidence in support of the analysis in (26).

A second way of testing structure is to use a **substitution** test. The assumption underlying this test is that a string of words is a constituent if it can be substituted by a single word. In this connection, consider:

(32) (a)   *The chairman* has resigned from the board, and **he** is now living in Utopia
     (b)   The press say that the chairman has *resigned from the board*, and **so** he has
     (c)   %If the Managing Director says the chairman has *resigned from the board*, he must have **done**
     (d)   If the chairman has *resigned from the board* (**which** you say he has), how come his car is still in the company car park?

(The percentage sign in front of 32c indicates that this type of structure is only found in certain varieties of English – notably, British English.) In each of the above sentences, the italicised string can be replaced (or referred back to) by a particular kind of **proform**. (Recall that a proform is a function word that can stand 'in place of' some other expression.) The fact that the expression *the chairman* in (32a) can be substituted by a single word (in this case, the proform/pronoun *he*) provides evidence in support of the claim in (26) that *the chairman* is a single constituent (a DP/determiner phrase, to be precise). Likewise, the fact that the expression *resigned from the board* in (32b,c,d) can serve as the antecedent of the proforms *so/done/which* provides evidence in support of the claim in (26) that *resigned from the board* is a constituent (more precisely, a VP/verb phrase). Unfortunately, since English has a very limited inventory of proforms, this test is of limited usefulness.

A third way of testing structure is to use a **preposing** test. The core assumption underlying this test is that only a string of words forming a constituent can be preposed (and thereby moved to the front of the structure containing it) in order to highlight it in some way (e.g. in order to mark it out as a topic containing familiar/old information, or as a focused constituent containing unfamiliar/new information). However, there are restrictions on the kind of constituent which can be highlighted by preposing – as can be illustrated by the following contrast:

(33) (a)   *Straight to bed* he must go
     (b)   **To bed* he must go straight

As we see from the structure in (21) above, both *straight to bed* and *to bed* are constituents of sentence (20c) *He must go straight to bed*. So how come only the larger of these two constituents can be preposed? The answer would appear to be that *straight to bed* is a PP and hence a maximal projection, whereas *to bed* (when modified by *straight*) is a P-bar constituent, and hence an intermediate projection. And it would seem (from contasts like that in 33) that only a maximal projection can undergo the relevant kind of preposing operation. This being so, one way we can test whether a given expression is a maximal projection or not is by seeing whether it can be preposed. In this connection, consider the following sentence:

(34)   The press said that the chairman would resign from the board, and *resigned from the board* he has

The fact that the italicised expression *resigned from the board* can be preposed in (34) indicates that it must be a maximal projection: this is consistent with the analysis in (26) which tells us that *resigned from the board* is a Verb Phrase which is the maximal projection of the verb *resigned*.

However, an important caveat which should be noted in relation to the preposing test is that particular expressions can sometimes be difficult (or even impossible) to prepose even though they are maximal projections. This is because there are **constraints** (i.e. restrictions) on such movement operations. One such constraint can be illustrated by the following contrast:

(35) (a)   He resolutely refused to surrender to the enemy
   (b)   *Surrender to the enemy*, he resolutely refused to
   (c)   **To surrender to the enemy*, he resolutely refused

Here, the VP/Verb Phrase *surrender to the enemy* can be highlighted by being pre-posed, but the TP/infinitival tense phrase *to surrender to the enemy* cannot – even though it is a maximal projection (by virtue of being the largest expression headed by infinitival *to*). What is the nature of the restriction on preposing *to+infinitive* expressions illustrated by the ungrammaticality of (35c)? The answer is not clear, but may be semantic in nature. When an expression is preposed, this is in order to highlight its semantic content in some way (e.g. for purposes of contrast – as in e.g. '*Syntax*, I don't like but *phonology* I do'). It may be that infinitival *to* has no intrinsic lexical semantic content, and that this makes an infinitival *to*-phrase an unsuitable candidate for highlighting. If so, this suggests that when preposing material for highlighting purposes, we should prepose *as few words as possible.* This requirement would seem to be related to Grice's (1975) 'Be concise' maxim (which amounts to 'Use as few words as possible'), and we can conflate the two together in terms of the following more general condition:

(36)   **Economy Condition**
       Syntactic structures should contain as few words as possible, and syntactic operations should affect as few words as possible

Given that only a maximal projection can be preposed for highlighting purposes, it follows from the Economy Condition that the following (more specific) condition will hold on preposing:

(37)   **Preposing Condition**
       When material is preposed in order to highlight it, what is preposed is the smallest possible maximal projection containing the highlighted material

So, if we want to highlight the semantic content of the VP *surrender to the enemy*, we prepose the VP *surrender to the enemy* rather than the TP *to surrender to the enemy* because the VP is smaller than the TP containing it.

However, this is by no means the only constraint on preposing, as we see from (38) below (where *FBA* is an abbreviation for the *Federal Bureau of Assassinations* – a purely fictitious body, of course):

(38) (a)   Nobody had expected that the FBA would assassinate the king of Ruritania
   (b)   **King of Ruritania*, nobody had expected that the FBA would assassinate the
   (c)   *The king of Ruritania*, nobody had expected that the FBA would assassinate
   (d)   **The FBA would assassinate the king of Ruritania*, nobody had expected that (NB *that* = |ðət|)
   (e)   *That the FBA would assassinate the king of Ruritania*, nobody had expected

The ungrammaticality of (38b,d) tells us that we can't prepose the NP *King of Ruritania* or the TP *the FBA would assassinate the King of Ruritania*. Why should this be? One possibility is that there is a constraint on movement operations to the effect that a DP can be preposed but not an NP contained within a DP, and likewise that a CP can be preposed but not a TP contained within a CP. One implementation of this idea would be to posit a constraint like (39) below:

(39)   **Functional Head Constraint/FHC**
         The complement of a certain type of functional head F (such as a determiner or complementiser) cannot be moved on its own (without also moving F)

Suppose, then, that we want to highlight the NP *king of Ruritania* in (38a) by preposing. (37) tells us to move *the smallest possible maximal projection containing the highlighted material*, and hence we first try to move this NP on its own: but the Functional Head Constraint tells us that it is not possible to prepose this NP on its own, because it is the complement of the determiner *the*. We therefore prepose the next smallest maximal projection containing the hightlighted NP *king of Ruritania* – namely the DP *the king of Ruritania*; and as the grammaticality of (38c) shows, the resulting sentence is grammatical.

Now suppose that we want to highlight the TP *the FBA would assassinate the king of Ruritania*. (37) tells us to move the smallest maximal projection containing the highlighted material – but the FHC (39) tells us that we cannot prepose a constituent which is the complement of a complementiser. Hence, we prepose the *next smallest* maximal projection containing the TP which we want to highlight, namely the CP *that the FBA would assassinate the King of Ruritania* – as in (38e).

However, an apparent problem for the **Functional Head Constraint** (39) is posed by examples like:

(40) (a)   *Surrender to the enemy*, I never **will**
     (b)   *Surrender to the enemy*, he resolutely refused **to**

The preposed Verb Phrase *surrender to the enemy* is the complement of *will* in (40a), and the complement of *to* in (40b). Given the analysis in §1.2, *will* is a finite T/tense auxiliary and *to* is a nonfinite T/tense particle. If (as we have assumed so far) T is a functional category, we would expect the Functional Head Constraint (39) to block preposing of the VP *surrender to the enemy* because this VP is the complement of the functional T constituent *will/to*. The fact that the resulting sentences (40a,b) are grammatical might lead us to follow Chomsky (1999) in concluding that T is a **substantive** category rather than a **functional category**, and hence does not block preposing of its complement. Alternatively, it may be that the constraint only applies to certain types of functional category (as hinted at in 39) – e.g. D and C but not T (perhaps because D and C are the 'highest' heads within nominal and clausal structures respectively – and indeed in chapter 9 we shall reformulate this constraint along such lines).

It is interesting to note that alongside sentences like (40) above in which a phrase has been highlighted by being preposed, we also find sentences like (41) below in which a single word has been preposed:

(41) (a)   *Surrender*, I never will
     (b)   *Surrender*, he resolutely refused to

In (41) the verb *surrender* has been preposed on its own. At first sight, this might seem to contradict our earlier statement that only **maximal projections** can undergo preposing. However, more careful reflection shows that there is no contradiction here: after all, the maximal projection of a head H is *the largest expression headed by H*; and in a sentence like *I never will surrender*, the largest expression headed by the verb *surrender* is the verb *surrender* itself – hence, *surrender* in (41) is indeed a maximal projection. This provides another illustration of a point noted earlier – namely that an individual word can itself be a maximal projection, if it has no complement or specifier of its own.

The overall conclusion to be drawn from our discussion here is that the preposing test has to be used with care. If an expression can be preposed in order to highlight it, it is a maximal projection; if it cannot, this may either be because it is not a maximal projection, or because (even though it *is* a maximal projection) a syntactic **constraint** of some kind prevents it from being preposed, or because its head word has insufficient semantic content to make it a suitable candidate for highlighting.

2.6   Structural relations and the syntax of polarity items

Throughout this chapter, we have argued that phrases and sentences are formed by a series of binary merger operations, and that the resulting structures can be represented in the form of tree diagrams. Because they mark the way that words are combined together to form phrases of various types, tree diagrams are referred to in earlier technical work as **phrase-markers** (abbreviated to **P-markers**). They show us how a phrase or sentence is built up out of **constituents** of various types: hence, a tree diagram provides a visual representation of the **constituent structure** of the corresponding expression. Each **node** in the tree (i.e. each point in the tree which carries a category label like N, V, A′, T′, PP, CP etc.) represents a different constituent of the sentence; hence, there are as many different constituents in any given phrase-marker as there are nodes carrying category labels. As we saw earlier, nodes at the very bottom of the tree are called **terminal nodes**, and other nodes are **nonterminal nodes**: so, for example, all the D, N, T, V and P nodes in (26) are terminal nodes, and all the DP, PP, VP, T′ and TP nodes are nonterminal nodes. The topmost node in any tree structure (i.e. TP in the case of (26) above) is said to be its **root**. Each terminal node in the tree carries a single **lexical item** (i.e. an item from the **lexicon**/dictionary, like *dog* or *go* etc.): lexical items are sets of phonological, semantic and grammatical properties/features (with category labels like N, V, T,

C etc. being used as shorthand abbreviations for the set of grammatical features carried by the relevant items).

It is useful to develop some terminology to describe the syntactic relations between constituents, since these relations turn out to be central to syntactic description. Essentially, a P-marker is a graph comprising a set of points (= labelled nodes), connected by branches (= solid lines) representing **containment** relations (i.e. telling us which constituents contain or are contained within which other constituents). We can illustrate what this means in terms of the following abstract tree structure (where A, B, C, D, E, F, G, H and J are different nodes in the tree, representing different constituents):

(42)

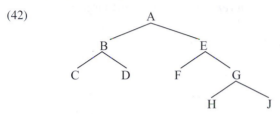

In (42), G **immediately contains** H and J (and conversely H and J are the two constituents immediately contained within G, and hence are the two **immediate constituents** of G): this is shown by the fact that H and J are the two nodes immediately beneath G which are connected to G by a **branch** (solid line). Likewise, E immediately contains F and G; B immediately contains C and D; and A immediately contains B and E. We can also say that E **contains** F, G, H and J; and that A contains B, C, D, E, F, G, H and J (and likewise that G contains H and J; and B contains C and D). Using equivalent kinship terminology, we can say that A is the **mother** of B and E (and conversely B and E are the two **daughters** of A); B is the mother of C and D; E is the mother of F and G; and G is the mother of H and J. Likewise, B and E are **sisters** (by virtue of both being daughters of A) – as are C and D; F and G; and H and J.

A particularly important syntactic relation is **c-command** (a conventional abbreviation of **constituent-command**), which provides us with a useful way of determining the relative position of two different constituents within the same tree (in particular, whether one is lower in the tree than the other or not). We can define this relation informally as follows (where X, Y and Z are three different nodes):

(43)   **c-command**
            A constituent X c-commands its sister constituent Y and any constituent Z
            which is contained within Y

For those of you who find it difficult to conceptualise such abstractions, a more concrete way of visualising this is to think of a tree diagram as representing a network of train stations, with each of the labelled nodes representing the name of a different station in the network, and the branches representing the rail tracks linking the stations. We can then say that one node X c-commands another node Y if you can get from X to Y on the network by taking a northbound train, getting off at the first station, changing trains there and then travelling one or more stops south *on a different line*.

In the light of the definition of **c-command** given above, let's consider which constituents each of the nodes in (42) c-commands. A doesn't c-command any of the other nodes, since A has no sister. B c-commands E, F, G, H and J because B's sister is E, and E contains F, G, H and J. C c-commands only D, because C's sister is D, and D does not contain any other constituent; likewise, D c-commands only C. E c-commands B, C and D because B is the sister of E and B contains C and D. F c-commands G, H and J, because G is the sister of F and G contains H and J. G c-commands only F, because G's sister is F, and F does not contain any other constituents. H and J likewise c-command only each other because they are sisters which have no daughters of their own.

We can illustrate the importance of the c-command relation in syntactic description by looking at the distribution of a class of expressions which are known as **polarity items**. These are items which have an inherent 'polarity' in the sense that they are restricted to occurring in certain types of sentence. In this connection, consider the quantifier *any* in English (and its compounds like *anyone, anything, anywhere* etc.). It has two different uses. One is as a **universal** (or **free choice**) **quantifier** with a meaning similar to *every* (as in *You can have any cake you like*): in this use, the initial *a* of *any* is stressed, and the relevant word is not a polarity item. The second use of *any* is as a **partitive** (or **existential**) **quantifier**: in this use, it has a meaning similar to *some* and can be unstressed (with its initial vowel reduced to schwa or even being truncated in rapid colloquial speech styles – e.g. *He wouldn't do 'nything to help me*), and in this second use it is indeed a polarity item. As the sentences in (44) below illustrate, partitive *any* (and its compounds) can occur in a clause containing a (bold-printed) interrogative expression like *how often* in (44a), a negative expression like *no student* in (44b) or a conditional expression like *if* in (44c) – but not in a positive declarative clause like (44d):

(44) (a)   I wonder **how often** we find *any* morality in business
    (b)   **No student** will complain about *anything*
    (c)   **If** *anyone* should ask for me, say I've gone to lunch
    (d)   *I'd like *any* coffee, please

Klima (1964, p. 313) conjectured that negative, interrogative and conditional expressions share 'a common grammatico-semantic feature to be referred to as *affective*'. In his terms, expressions like *how often, no student* and *if* are all 'affective' constituents (by which he seems to mean that they are non-assertive – or *nonveridical*, to employ the alternative term used by Giannikidou (1997, 1998, 1999)). Using Klima's terminology, we can suppose that a polarity item such as (partitive) *any* is restricted to occurring in a structure containing an affective constituent. It turns out that numerous other expressions (italicised below) are similarly restricted to occurring in a structure containing a (bold-printed) affective constituent:

(45) (a)   I **didn't** think I would *ever* pass the exam
     (b)   *I thought I would *ever* pass the exam

(46) (a)   **Nobody** *dare* contradict him
     (b)   *Everybody *dare* contradict him

(47) (a)   I **don't** think he *need* apologise
     (b)   *He *need* apologise

Curiously, the items *need* and *dare* are polarity items when they function as auxiliaries (and so do not take the third person singular present tense *s*-affix, and are not followed by infinitival *to*), but not when they function as main verbs (e.g. in sentences like *Professor Knutter needs to see a psychiatrist*).

It might at first sight seem as if we can characterise the relevant restriction on the use of polarity items by saying that they can only be used after (i.e. when they follow) an affective constituent. However, any such claim is falsified by contrasts such as the following:

(48) (a)   The fact that he has resigned **won't** change *anything*
     (b)   *The fact that he **won't** resign will change *anything*

In both (48a) and (48b), the polarity item *anything* follows a bold-printed affective item (the negative auxiliary *won't*), and yet only (48a) is grammatical. Why should this be? The answer is that (as originally noted by Klima), polarity items like partitive *any* are subject to a structural condition on their use which can be characterised in the following terms:

(49)   **Polarity Condition**
        A polarity item must be c-commanded by an affective (e.g. negative, interrogative or conditional) constituent

To see how this works, consider whether the polarity item *anything* satisfies the Polarity Condition (49) in a structure such as the following:

(50)

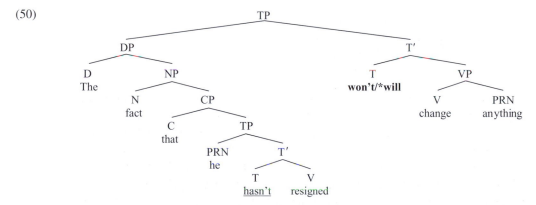

Consider first of all whether the pronoun *anything* is c-commanded by the bold-printed T-auxiliary *will/won't*. Since the sister of [T *will/won't*] is the VP *change anything*, and since *anything* is one of the constituents of this VP, it follows that

[T *will/won't*] does indeed c-command [PRN *anything*] under the definition of c-command given in (43) above. What this means is that using the negative auxiliary *won't* in (50) will satisfy the Polarity Condition (49), so correctly predicting that the corresponding sentence (51) below is grammatical:

(51)   The fact that he hasn't resigned won't change anything

But now consider whether [PRN *anything*] is c-commanded by the underlined T-auxiliary *hasn't* in (50). The sister of [T *hasn't*] is the V-constituent *resigned*, and it is clear that *anything* is not a constituent of the verb *resigned*, and hence that [T *hasn't*] does not c-command *anything* in (50). The Polarity Condition (49) therefore (correctly) predicts the ungrammaticality of a sentence such as the following:

(52)   *The fact that he hasn't resigned will change anything

The overall conclusion which our discussion here leads us to is thus that restrictions on the use of polarity items can be given a structural characterisation in terms of the relation **c-command**.

2.7   The c-command condition on binding

A second class of expressions whose distribution can be given a principled characterisation in tems of the relation c-command are so-called **anaphors**. These include **reflexives** (i.e. *self/selves* forms like *myself/yourself/themselves* etc.), and **reciprocals** like *each other* and *one another*. Such anaphors have the property that they cannot be used to refer directly to an entity in the outside world, but rather must by **bound** by (i.e. take their reference from) an **antecedent** elsewhere in the same phrase or sentence. Where an anaphor has no (suitable) antecedent to bind it, the resulting structure is ungrammatical – as we see from contrasts such as that in (53) below:

(53) (a)   **He** must feel proud of *himself*
     (b)   ***She** must feel proud of *himself*
     (c)   **Himself* must feel proud of you

In (53a), the third person masculine singular anaphor *himself* is bound by a suitable third person masculine singular antecedent (*he*), with the result that (53a) is grammatical. But in (53b), *himself* has no suitable antecedent (the feminine pronoun *she* is not a suitable antecedent for the masculine anaphor *himself*), and so is **unbound** (with the result that (53b) is ill-formed). In (53c), there is no antecedent of any kind for the anaphor *himself*, with the result that the anaphor is again unbound and the sentence ill-formed.

There are structural restrictions on the binding of anaphors by antecedents, as we see from:

(54) (a)   **The president** may blame *himself*
     (b)   **Supporters of **the president** may blame *himself*

(55) (a)   **They** may implicate *each other*
    (b)   *The evidence against **them** may implicate *each other*

As a third person masculine singular anaphor, *himself* must be bound by a third person masculine singular antecedent like *the president*; similarly, as a plural anaphor, *each other* must be bound by a plural antecedent like *they/them*. However, it would seem from the contrasts above that the antecedent must occupy the right kind of position within the structure in order to bind the anaphor or else the resulting sentence will be ungrammatical. The question of what is the right position for the antecedent can be answered in terms of the following structural condition:

(56)   **Binding Condition**
           A bound constituent must be c-commanded by an appropriate antecedent

The relevant bound constituent is the reflexive anaphor *himself* in (54), and its antecedent is *the president*; the bound constituent in (55) is the reciprocal anaphor *each other*, and its antecedent is *they/them*. Sentence (54a) has the structure (57) below:

(57)

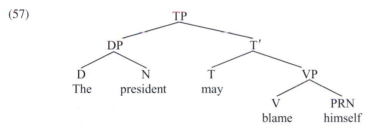

The reflexive pronoun *himself* can be bound by the DP *the president* in (57) because the sister of the DP node is the T-bar node, and the pronoun *himself* is one of the constituents of the relevant T-bar node: consequently, the DP *the president* c-commands the anaphor *himself* and the Binding Condition (56) is satisfied. We therefore correctly specify that (54a) *The president may blame himself* is grammatical, with *the president* interpreted as the antecedent of *himself*.

But now consider why a structure like (58) below is ungrammatical (cf. (54b) above):

(58)

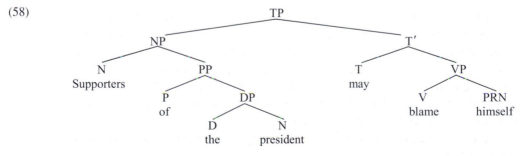

The answer is that the DP node containing *the president* doesn't c-command the PRN node containing *himself*, because the sister of the DP node is the P node *of*, and *himself* is clearly not a constituent of the preposition *of*. Since there is no other appropriate antecedent for *himself* within the sentence (e.g. although the NP *supporters of the president* c-commands *himself*, it is not a suitable antecedent because it is a plural expression, and *himself* requires a singular antecedent), the anaphor *himself* remains unbound – in violation of the Binding Condition on anaphors. This is the reason why (54b) **Supporters of the president may blame himself* is ungrammatical.

Our brief discussion of polarity items and anaphors in this section and the last underlines the importance of the relation **c-command** in syntax. It also provides further evidence for positing that sentences have a hierarchical constituent structure, in that the Polarity Condition (49) and the Binding Condition (56) are both characterised in structural terms.

2.8   Bare phrase structure

In this chapter, we have used a system of category labels based on the **bar notation** which has been widely adopted since the 1970s. Within this framework, a sentence like (the title of Gloria Gaynor's immortal song) *I will survive* has the structure shown below:

(59)

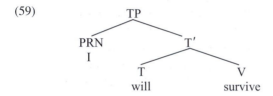

The bar notation used in (59) posits that there are three different **levels** of projection (i.e. types of expression): (i) **heads** (also called **minimal projections**) like the T/tense auxiliary *will*; (ii) **intermediate projections** like the T-bar *will survive*; and (iii) **maximal projections** like the TP *I will survive*. However, Chomsky (1999, p. 2) argues that a system which posits three different types of category label for projections of a given head H (viz. H, H-bar and HP) violates a UG principle called the Inclusiveness Condition which specifies that no new information can be introduced in the course of the syntactic computation – a principle which Chomsky (2006, p. 4) claims to be 'a natural principle of efficient computation'. The reason why the bar notation used in trees like (59) violates Inclusiveness is as follows. When the word *will* is taken out of the lexicon, its lexical entry specifies that it has a set of properties which include the grammatical properties represented by the category label T in (59). But the tree in (59) tells us that when *will* is merged with its complement *survive*, the resulting string *will survive* belongs to the category T-bar – in other words, it is an **intermediate projection** of *will*. Likewise, the tree in (59) also tells us that the larger string *I will survive* is a TP – in other words, it is the **maximal projection** of *will*. But this information about intermediate and maximal projections is not part of the lexical entry for *will*, and hence has seemingly been added in the course of the syntactic computation. However, adding such information about projection levels violates the Inclusiveness Condition.

One way of avoiding violation of Inclusiveness is to remove all information about projection levels from trees, and hence replace a tree like (59) above by one like (60) below:

(60)

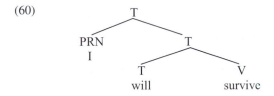

What our revised tree (60) says is that *will*, *will survive* and *I will survive* are all projections of the tense auxiliary *will* and hence are all **tense expressions**. Information about projection levels is omitted in (60) because it is redundant, since it is predictable from looking at the relative positions of constituents within a given structure. Simply by looking at the positions they occupy in the tree (60), we can tell that *will* is the minimal projection of *will* (i.e. it is the smallest expression headed by *will*), that *will survive* is an intermediate projection of *will* (by virtue of being neither the smallest nor the largest expression headed by *will*) and that *I will survive* is the maximal projection of *will* (by virtue of being the largest expression headed by *will*). Similarly, we can tell that the V *survive* is both a minimal and a maximal projection, in that it is both the smallest and the largest expression headed by *survive*: hence (e.g.) it can behave like a maximal projection and undergo preposing (as in *Survive, I will*). In much the same way, we know from looking at the structure in (60) that the pronoun *I* is likewise both a minimal and a maximal projection: given their status as maximal projections, it follows that pronouns can undergo preposing (as with the pronoun *him* in *Him, I would never trust*). Since the information about projection levels in the bar notation is redundant, Chomsky reasons, such information should not be represented in the system of category labels used in tree diagrams: after all, the goal of **Minimalism** is to reduce theoretical apparatus to the minimum that is conceptually necessary.

Chomsky goes even further and argues in favour of a theory of **bare** (i.e. category-free) **phrase structure** in which the nodes in trees do not carry category labels. We can illustrate the kind of reasoning behind his thinking in the following terms. In a category-based theory of syntax, the grammatical properties of a pronoun like *he* are described by assigning it to the category PRN of pronoun. But simply telling us that *he* belongs to the category PRN does not characterise its other grammatical properties – e.g. the fact that it is a third person expression, it is singular in number, masculine in gender and nominative in case. The traditional way of describing grammatical properties like these is in terms of a set of features like [third-person], [singular-number], [masculine-gender], [nominative-case], with grammatical features conventionally enclosed within square brackets. But Chomsky (1965, 1970) argued that the categorial properties of words can also be described in terms of sets of grammatical features: one such feature might indicate that *he* is nominal (rather than verbal) in nature, and another might indicate that it is a function word (rather than a content word). If all the grammatical properties of words (including their categorial properties) can be described in terms of sets of grammatical features, the possibility arises that category labels can be entirely replaced by sets of features, so opening up the possibility of developing a theory of **bare phrase structure** – i.e. a theory in which there are no category labels in syntactic trees. A radical possibility along these lines would be for the structure of *I will survive* to be represented in terms of an **unlabelled tree diagram** like (61) below (i.e. a tree containing no category labels):

(61)

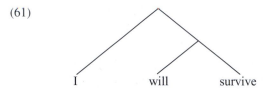

An unlabelled tree diagram like (61) tells us that the constituents of (61) are *I*, *will*, *survive*, *will survive* and *I will survive*. The lexical entries for the items *I*, *will* and *survive* comprise sets of features which include information about their grammatical and selectional properties: e.g. the entry for *will* tells us that it is a finite auxiliary which selects an infinitival complement. The fact that *will* selects an infinitive complement (and that *survive* is an infinitive form and is the sister of *will*) means that *survive* must be the complement of *will* and hence that *will survive* is a projection of *will*. Likewise, the fact that *will* has an EPP feature requiring it to project a subject means that the nominative pronoun *I* must be the subject of *will*, and hence that *I will survive* is an extended projection of *will*. As before, the relative position of the relevant constituents within the overall structure tells us that *will* is a minimal projection (of itself), *will survive* is an intermediate projection of *will*, and *I will survive* is the maximal projection of *will*. The overall conclusion we arrive at is that the information about category labels and projection levels in a conventional labelled tree diagram like (59) above may well be redundant.

Given that **bare phrase structure** is more of a leading idea than a fully developed theory and that it has not been widely adopted in descriptive work, we shall continue to use traditional labelled trees and the bar notation to represent structure, category membership and projection levels throughout the rest of this book, because this remains the notation most widely used in contemporary work in syntax.

2.9   Summary

In this chapter, we have looked at how words are combined together to form phrases and sentences. In §2.2 we showed how more and more complex phrases can be built up by successive binary **merger** operations, each of which combines a pair of constituents to form a larger constituent. In §2.3 we argued that clauses containing a finite tense auxiliary are formed by merging the tense auxiliary with a verbal complement to form an intermediate T-bar projection which is then merged with a subject to form an extended TP/tense phrase projection. On this view, a sentence like *It may rain* would be formed by merging the present tense auxiliary *may* with the verb *rain* to form the T-bar constituent *may rain*, and then merging the resulting T-bar with the pronoun *it* to derive the TP *It may rain*. We also noted that the requirement for English tense auxiliaries to have a subject can be described by saying that a T-auxiliary in English has an **EPP feature** requiring it to have an extended phrasal projection containing a subject. Introducing a new term, we said that the subject occupies the **specifier** position within TP, and that specifiers are constituents which merge with an intermediate projection to form a maximal projection. We noted that other kinds of constituent can also have specifiers, so that (e.g.) *straight* occupies the specifier position within a Prepositional Phrase like *straight to bed*. In §2.4 we argued that clauses introduced by a complementiser/C are formed by merging C with a TP complement to form a CP/complementiser phrase. In §2.5, we looked at ways of testing constituent structure, outlining tests relating to co-ordination, substitution and preposing. We noted that a variety of factors can sometimes prevent constituents from being preposed in order to highlight them; for example, only maximal projections can be highlighted via preposing, and phrases headed by items with little or no substantive lexical semantic content generally cannot be preposed: moreover, there are also syntactic restrictions on preposing, in that the **Functional Head Constraint** bars the complement of a determiner or complementiser from being moved on its own. In §2.6, we looked at the structural relations between constituents within tree diagrams, noting that the relation **c-command** plays a central role in accounting for the syntax of polarity items. In §2.7, we went on to show that the relation c-command is also central to any account of the binding properties of anaphors. In §2.8 we discussed the potential redundancy in the system of labels used to represent categories and projection levels in traditional phrase structure trees, and noted that Chomsky has been seeking to develop a theory of **bare phrase structure** in recent work.

For those of you familiar with work in traditional grammar, it will be clear that the assumptions made about syntactic structure within the Minimalist framework are somewhat different from those made in traditional grammar. Of course, there are some similarities: within both types of framework, it is assumed that lexical categories project into phrases, so that by combining a noun with one or more other constituents we can form a Noun Phrase, and likewise by combining a verb/preposition/adjective/adverb with one or more other constituents we can form a Verb Phrase/Prepositional Phrase/Adjectival Phrase/Adverbial Phrase. But there are two major differences between the two types of framework. One is that Minimalism (unlike traditional grammar) assumes that function words also project into phrases (so that by combining a determiner/D with a noun expression we form a Determiner Phrase/DP, by combining a (present or past tense) auxiliary/T with a complement and a subject we form a Tense Projection/TP, and by combining a complementiser with a TP we form a Complementiser Projection/CP). This in some cases results in an analysis which is rather different from that found in traditional grammar, so that (for example) *the nose* would be considered a Noun Phrase in traditional grammar, but is taken to be a Determiner Phrase within the framework adopted here. A further difference between the two frameworks is that Minimalism assumes that all syntactic structure is binary-branching, whereas traditional grammar (implicitly) does not.

Key principles/conditions introduced in this chapter include the following:

(12)   **Headedness Principle**
        Every nonterminal constituent in a syntactic structure is a projection of a head word

(13)   **Binarity Principle**
        Every nonterminal constituent in a syntactic structure is binary-branching

(30)   **Co-ordination Condition**
        Only constituents of the same type can be co-ordinated

(36)   **Economy Condition**
        Syntactic structures should contain as few words as possible, and syntactic operations should affect as few words as possible

(37)   **Preposing Condition**
        When material is preposed in order to highlight it, what is preposed is the smallest possible maximal projection containing the highlighted material

(39)   **Functional Head Constraint/FHC**
        The complement of a certain type of functional head F (such as a determiner or complementiser) cannot be moved on its own (without also moving F)

(49)   **Polarity Condition**
        A polarity item must be c-commanded by an affective (e.g. negative, interrogative or conditional) constituent

(56)   **Binding Condition**
        A bound constituent must be c-commanded by an appropriate antecedent

An important relation introduced in the chapter is the following:

(43)   **c-command**
        A constituent X c-commands its sister constituent Y and any constituent Z which is contained within Y

Recall that – using a train metaphor which treats the nodes in a tree as stations on a train network – we characterised *c-command* rather more informally by saying that a node X c-commands another node Y if you can get from X to Y by taking a northbound train, getting off at the first station/node, changing trains there and then travelling one or more stops/nodes south *on a different line.*

2.10   Bibliographical background

The claim made in §2.2 that syntactic structures are headed dates back in spirit to Bloomfield (1935) – but with the difference that Bloomfield assumed that some structures are headless. The idea that all syntactic structure is binary goes back to Kayne (1984). On the claim that syllable structure and morphological structure are binary, see Radford *et al.* (1999, pp. 88ff. and p. 164 respectively). The traditional S analysis of clauses outlined in §2.3 dates back to Chomsky (1955, 1957, 1975), and the S-bar analysis to Bresnan (1970, 1972, 1979). Chomsky (1981, 1986b) argued for an alternative analysis of S constituents as projections of a head I/INFL/Inflection constituent and hence as IP constituents; when INFL was supplanted by T/tense in later work, S was reanalysed as a TP projection. Likewise, Chomsky (1981, 1986b) and Stowell (1981) reanalysed S-bar as CP. For a range of views on the nature of the EPP property of T, see Chomsky (1982, 1995, 1998), Rothstein (1983), Alexiadou and Anagnostopoulou (1998), Déprez (2000), Grohmann, Drury and Castillo (2000), Holmberg (2000b), Kiss (2001), Bošković (2002b), Roberts and Roussou (2002), Rosengren (2002), Haeberli (2003), van Craenenbroeck and den Dicken (2006) and Landau (2007). On the claim that syntactic structure contains information about hierarchical structure but not linear structure (i.e. word order), see Kayne (1994), Yang (1999), Chomsky (2001) and Kural (2005). An alternative to Chomsky's bottom-up model of syntax is the top-down model presented in Phillips (2003): but see Chomsky (2006, p. 4) for a suggestion that the bottom-up/top-down dichotomy may be a false one. The claim made in §2.4 that phrases are formed by combining heads with complements and specifiers dates back to the model of *X-bar Syntax* developed in Jackendoff (1974, 1977a, 1977b): for a textbook introduction to X-bar Syntax, see Radford (1981, 1988). In earlier work (e.g. Chomsky 1957, 1965) nominal expressions like *the nose* were taken to have the status of NP/Noun Phrase; however, in much work since Abney (1987) they have been analysed as having the status DP/Determiner Phrase constituents – though it should be pointed out that the DP analysis is not without posing problems (see e.g. Pollard and Sag 1994, Sadler and Arnold 1994, van Langendonck 1994, Escribano 2004 and van Eynde 2006). The DEGP analysis of phrases such as *quite so rapid* also derives from Abney (1987). On the syntax of nominal expressions like *the government ban on imports*, see Radford (1993). The Functional Head Constraint is inspired by a similar suggestion made in Chomsky (1999). For a more detailed discussion of the co-ordination criterion used to test structure in §2.5, see Radford (1988, pp. 75–78). The c-command condition on polarity items discussed in §2.6 dates back in spirit to Klima (1964): fuller discussion of the syntactic and semantic conditions governing the distribution of polarity items can be found in Fauconnier (1975, 1978), Ladusaw (1979), Linebarger (1987), Giannikidou (1997, 1998, 1999), Lahiri (1998), von Fintel (1999), Acquaviva (2002), Watanabe (2004), Benmamoun (2006), Borroff (2006), Chierchia (2006) and Herdan and Sharvit

(2006). The c-command condition on binding outlined in §2.7 (and the binding principles discussed in exercise §2.2) date back to Chomsky (1980): more recent technical accounts of binding can be found in Reuland (2001a), Reuland and Everaert (2001), Büring (2005), Lasnik (2006) and Giorgi (2007). A technical defence of the primitive nature of c-command can be found in Frank and Vijay-Shanker (2001). The theory of Bare Phrase Structure sketched in §2.8 has its origins in Chomsky (1995, p. 249): see Uriagereka (1998) for a textbook account. The *Inclusiveness Condition* is outlined in Chomsky (1999, p. 2), and is an outgrowth of the earlier *No Tampering Condition* proposed in Chomsky (2005b, p. 5) to the effect that 'Merge of X and Y . . . cannot break up X or Y, or add new features to them.' (By saying that merge cannot 'break up' an existing structure, Chomsky means that merge cannot e.g. add a constituent in the middle of an existing structure, only at its edge, so that 'Merge is invariably "to the edge".')

Workbook section

Exercise 2.1

Discuss the derivation of the following sentences, showing how their structure is built up in a pairwise fashion by successive binary merger operations.

1   He has become very fond of Mary
2   She must be quite pleased to see you
3   He will need to ask for help **(w)**
4   They are expecting to hear from you
5   You should try to talk to the president of Utopia
6   Inflation has undermined some parts of the economy **(w)**
7   He won't admit that he was defrauding the company **(w)**
8   Nobody could believe that Sam was working for the government

Show how evidence from co-ordination and proforms can be used in support of your analysis. In addition, say which constituents can (and cannot) be preposed – and why.

Helpful hints

Assume that the sentences are derived in a **bottom-up** fashion by first merging the last two words in the sentence to form a constituent, then merging the constituent thereby formed with the third-from-last word to form an even larger constituent, then merging this even larger constituent with the fourth-from-last word . . . and so on. (It should be noted, however, that while this simple procedure will work for most of the sentences in the two exercises in this chapter, it requires modification to handle sentences with more complex specifiers, like sentences 10 and 12 in exercise 2.2.) Take *very* and *quite* to be adverbs which function as the specifiers of the adjectival expressions *fond of Mary* and *pleased to see you* respectively in 1 and 2. In 7, take *won't* (for the purposes of this exercise) to be a negative auxiliary occupying the head T position of TP.

Model answer for 1

Merging the preposition *of* with the noun *Mary* which serves as its complement derives the PP (Prepositional Phrase) in (i) below:

(i)

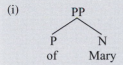

Merging the adjective *fond* with the resulting PP (which is the complement of *fond*) forms the intermediate adjectival projection (A-bar) *fond of Mary* in (ii) below:

(ii)

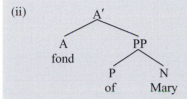

Merging the A-bar in (ii) with the adverb *very* which serves as its specifier (in that it modifies *fond of Mary*) forms the AP/Adjectival Phrase in (iii) below:

(iii)

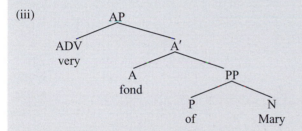

Merging the verb *become* with the AP *very fond of Mary* which serves as the complement of *become* forms the VP/Verb Phrase in (iv) below:

(iv)

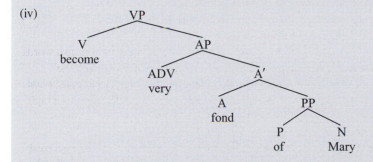

Merging the tense auxiliary (T constituent) *has* with its Verb Phrase complement *become very fond of Mary* forms the intermediate T-bar projection (v) below:

(v)

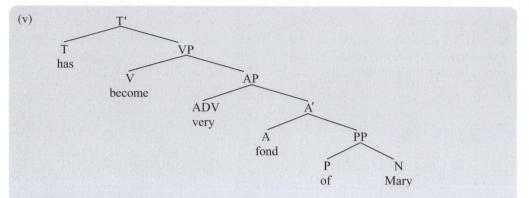

Merging the T-bar in (v) with the pronoun *he* which serves as its subject/specifier will derive the TP:

(vi)

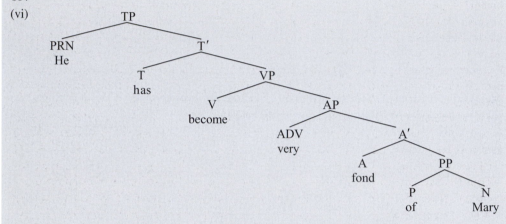

Evidence in support of the analysis in (vi) comes from co-ordination data in relation to sentences such as:

(vii) (a)   He has become very fond [*of Mary*] and [**of her sister**]
  (b)   He has become very [*fond of Mary*] and [**proud of her achievements**]
  (c)   He has become [*very fond of Mary*] but [**less fond of her sister**]
  (d)   He has [*become very fond of Mary*] and [**grown used to her mother**]
  (e)   He [*has become very fond of Mary*] and [**is hoping to marry her**]

The fact that each of the italicised strings can be co-ordinated with another similar (bold-printed) string is consistent with the claim made in (vi) that *of Mary* is a PP, *fond of Mary* is an A-bar, *very fond of Mary* is an AP, *become very fond of Mary* is a VP and *has become very fond of Mary* is a T-bar.

Additional evidence in support of the analysis in (vi) comes from the use of the proforms *so/which* in:

(viii)(a) He is apparently *very fond of Mary*, though nobody expected him to become **so**
   (b) If he has *become very fond of Mary* (**which** he has), why doesn't he ask her out?

The fact that *very fond of Mary* is the antecedent of *so* in (viiia) is consistent with the claim made in (vi) that *very fond of Mary* is an AP; likewise, the fact that *become very fond of Mary* is the antecedent of *which* in (viiib) is consistent with the claim made in (vi) that *become very fond of Mary* is a VP.

If we look at the question of which expressions in the sentence can and cannot be preposed in order to highlight them, we find the following picture (*?* indicates questionable grammaticality):

(ix) (a) *Mary*, he (certainly) has become very fond of
    (b) ?*Of Mary*, he (certainly) has become very fond
    (c) **Fond of Mary*, he (certainly) has become very
    (d) *Very fond of Mary*, he (certainly) has become
    (e) *Become very fond of Mary*, he (certainly) has
    (f) **Has become very fond of Mary*, he (certainly)

(Adding the adverb *certainly* improves the acceptability of some of the relevant sentences, for discourse reasons which need not concern us.) In (37) in the main text, we suggested that highlighting involves preposing the smallest possible maximal projection containing the highlighted material. Suppose that we want to highlight *Mary* via preposing. Since *Mary* is a maximal projection in (vi) by virtue of being the largest expression headed by the word *Mary*, preposing *Mary* in (ixa) yields a grammatical outcome, as expected. By contrast, preposing the Prepositional Phrase *of Mary* yields a somewhat degraded sentence, as we see from (ixb): this may be because if we want to highlight *Mary* alone, we prepose the *smallest* maximal projection containing *Mary*, and this is clearly the N *Mary* not the PP *of Mary*. There would only be some point in preposing *of Mary* if we wanted to highlight *of* as well as *Mary*; but since the preposition *of* (rather like infinitival *to*) has little or no semantic content (some linguists suggesting that it is a **genitive case particle** in this kind of use and hence a functor), an *of*-phrase is not a good candidate for highlighting. The string *fond of Mary* cannot be preposed in (ixc) because it is an intermediate (A-bar) projection of the adjective *fond*, not its maximal projection (the maximal projection of the adjective *fond* being the AP *very fond of Mary*). By contrast, the string *very fond of Mary* can be preposed in (ixd) by virtue of its status as the maximal projection of *fond* (i.e. the largest expression headed by *fond*). In (ixe) we see that *become very fond of Mary* can also be preposed by virtue of being the maximal projection of the verb *become* – even though it is the complement of the T constituent *has*; hence, either T is not a functional category (as suggested in Chomsky 1999), or else the Functional Head Constraint applies only to some functional categories (e.g. those like D and C which are the highest heads in nominal/clausal structures respectively). By contrast, the string *has become very fond of Mary* cannot be preposed in (ixf) because of its status as an intermediate (T-bar) projection of *has* – the corresponding maximal projection of *has* being the TP *He has become very fond of Mary*.

Helpful hints for sentences 2–7

Discuss whether the analysis you propose accounts for the (un)grammaticality of the sentences below (which represent intuitions about grammaticality in my own British English variety). To help you, I have italicised parts of the sentences of particular interest.

Example 2

(a)   She must be quite pleased to *see you* and *meet your mother*
(b)   She must be quite pleased *to see you* and *to meet your mother*
(c)   She must be quite *pleased to see you* and *glad that you are OK*
(d)   She must be *quite pleased to see you* and *very glad that you are OK*

  (e)   She must *be quite pleased to see you* and *feel relieved that you're OK*

  (f)   She *must be quite pleased to see you* but *will not admit it*

  (g)   She must be *quite pleased to see you*, even if she doesn't seem *so*.

  (h)   *You* she must be quite pleased to see (though not your sister)

  (i)   ?*See you*, she (certainly) must be quite pleased to

  (j)   **To see you*, she (certainly) must be quite pleased

  (k)   **Pleased to see you*, she (certainly) must be quite

  (l)   *Quite pleased to see you*, she (certainly) must be

  (m)   ?*Be quite pleased to see you*, she (certainly) must

  (n)   **Must be quite pleased to see you*, she (certainly)

Example 3

  (a)   He will need to ask *for help* and *for advice*

  (b)   He will need to *ask for help* and *seek advice*

  (c)   He will need *to ask for help* and *to accept it*

  (d)   He will *need to ask for help*, and *expect to get it*

  (e)   He *will need to ask for help*, but *can't count on it*

  (f)   A lot of people think he will *need to ask for help*, and *so* he will

  (g)   If he has to *ask for help* (*as* he will need to), will he get any?

  (h)   *Help*, he will (certainly) need to ask for (though not money)

  (i)   ?*For help* he will (certainly) need to ask (though not for money)

  (j)   *Ask for help*, he will (certainly) need to

  (k)   **To ask for help*, he will (certainly) need

  (l)   *Need to ask for help*, he (certainly) will

  (m)   **Will need to ask for help*, he (certainly)

Example 4

  (a)   They are expecting to hear *from you* and *from her*

  (b)   They are expecting to *hear from you* and *meet you*

  (c)   They are expecting *to hear from you* and *to meet you*

  (d)   They are *expecting to hear from you* and *longing to meet you*

  (e)   They *are expecting to hear from you* and *are longing to meet you*

  (f)   They said they were *expecting to hear from you*, and *so* they are

  (g)   *You*, they are (certainly) expecting to hear from (though not your sister)

  (h)   ?*From you*, they (certainly) are expecting to hear (though not from your sister)

  (i)   *Hear from you*, they (certainly) are expecting to

  (j)   **To hear from you*, they (certainly) are expecting

  (k)   *Expecting to hear from you*, they (certainly) are

  (l)   **Are expecting to hear from you*, they

Example 5

  (a)   You should try to talk to the president *of Utopia* and *of Ruritania*

  (b)   You should try to talk to the *president of Utopia* and *head of the government*

  (c)   You should try to talk to *the president of Utopia* and *the leader of the opposition*

  (d)   You should try to talk *to the president of Utopia* and *to the leader of the opposition*

(e)   You should try to *talk to the president of Utopia* and *convince him*

(f)   You should try *to talk to the president of Utopia* and *to convince him*

(g)   You should *try to talk to the president of Utopia* and *contact his aides*

(h)   You *should try to talk to the president* but *may not succeed*

(i)   You *should try to talk to the president of Utopia* and *should contact his aides*

(j)   He said you should *try to talk to the president of Utopia*, and *so* you should

(k)   ?*Utopia,* you should certainly try to talk to the president of

(l)   **Of Utopia*, you should certainly try to talk to the president

(m)   **President of Utopia*, you should (certainly) try to talk to the

(n)   *The president of Utopia*, you should (certainly) try to talk to

(o)   ?*To the president of Utopia*, you should (certainly) try to talk (though not to his aides)

(p)   *Talk to the president of Utopia*, you should (certainly) try to

(q)   **To talk to the president of Utopia*, you should certainly try

(r)   *Try to talk to the president of Utopia*, you (certainly) should

(s)   **Should try to talk to the president of Utopia*, you (certainly)

Example 6

(a)   Inflation has undermined some parts of *the economy* and *the stockmarket*

(b)   Inflation has undermined some parts *of the economy* and *of the stockmarket*

(c)   Inflation has undermined some *parts of the economy* and *sectors of the stockmarket*

(d)   Inflation has undermined *some parts of the economy* and *many sectors of the stockmarket*

(e)   Inflation has *undermined some parts of the economy* and *jeopardised growth*

(f)   Inflation *has undermined some parts of the economy* and *is spiralling out of control*

(g)   If inflation has *undermined some parts of the economy* (*as* it has), why doesn't the government act?

(h)   The president said that inflation has *undermined some parts of the economy*, and *so* it has.

(i)   **Economy*, inflation (certainly) has undermined some parts of the

(j)   *The economy*, inflation (certainly) has undermined some parts of

(k)   **Of the economy*, inflation (certainly) has undermined some parts

(l)   **Parts of the economy*, inflation (certainly) has undermined some

(m)   *Some parts of the economy*, inflation (certainly) has undermined

(n)   *Undermined some parts of the economy*, inflation (certainly) has

(o)   **Has undermined some parts of the economy*, inflation (certainly)

Example 7

(a)   He won't admit that he was defrauding *the company* and *the workforce*

(b)   He won't admit that he was *defrauding the company* and *bankrupting it*

(c)   He won't admit that he *was defrauding the company* and *had bankrupted it*

(d)   He won't admit that *he was defrauding the company* and *it was being bankrupted*

(e)   He won't admit *that he was defrauding the company* or *that he was bankrupting it*

(f)   He won't *admit that he was defrauding the company* or *concede that he lied*

(g)   He *won't admit that he was defrauding the company* and *doesn't accept that he has bankrupted it*

(h)   If he won't *admit that he was defrauding the company* (*which* he won't), what can we do about it?

(i)   He won't admit *that he was defrauding the company*, even though everybody knows *it*
(j)   *Company*, he (certainly) won't admit that he was defrauding the
(k)   *The company*, he (certainly) won't admit that he was defrauding
(l)   *Defrauding the company*, he (certainly) won't admit that he was
(m)   *Was defrauding the company*, he (certainly) won't admit that he
(n)   *He was defrauding the company*, he (certainly) won't admit that (= |ðət|)
(o)   *That he was defrauding the company*, he (certainly) won't admit
(p)   *Admit that he was defrauding the company*, he (certainly) won't
(q)   *Won't admit that he was defrauding the company*, he (certainly)

Example 8

(a)   Nobody could believe that Sam was working for *the government* and *the opposition*
(b)   Nobody could believe that Sam was working *for the government* and *for the opposition*
(c)   Nobody could believe that Sam was *working for the government* and *siding with the opposition*
(d)   Nobody could believe that Sam *was working for the government* and *was siding with the opposition*
(e)   Nobody could believe that *Sam was working for the government* and *his wife was working for the opposition*
(f)   Nobody could believe *that Sam was working for the government* and *that his wife was working for the opposition*
(g)   Nobody could *believe that Sam was working for the government* or *imagine that his wife was working for the opposition*
(h)   Nobody *could believe that Sam was working for the government* or *would admit that his wife was working for the opposition*
(i)   If people couldn't *believe that Sam was working for the government* (*which* nobody could), why didn't they ask him whether it was true?
(j)   If nobody could believe than Sam was *working for the government* (*as* he was), why didn't they ask him whether it was true?
(k)   *Government*, nobody could believe that Sam was working for the
(l)   *The government*, nobody could believe that Sam was working for
(m)   ??*For the government*, nobody could believe that Sam was working
(n)   *Working for the government*, nobody could believe that Sam (really) was
(o)   *Was working for the government*, nobody could believe that Sam
(p)   *Sam was working for the government*, nobody could believe that (= |ðət|)
(q)   *That Sam was working for the government*, nobody could believe
(r)   *Believe that Sam was working for the government*, nobody (really) could
(s)   *Could believe that Sam was working for the government*, nobody

Exercise 2.2

We saw in §2.7 that the relation c-command plays an important role in accounting for the syntax of **polarity expressions** which are restricted to occurring in a position where they are c-commanded by an 'affective' (e.g. negative, interrogative or conditional) constituent. Show how the c-command condition on the use of polarity items accounts for the (un)grammaticality of the following:

1   You mustn't talk to anyone
2   Nobody need do anything
3   Who dare blame anyone?
4   She has refused to sign anything
5   She should know if anyone has made any changes
6   I don't think that anyone dare lift a finger
7   He may have no desire to change anything (**w**)
8   Nobody will think that anything has changed
9   He may feel unable to do anything
10   No politician dare offend anyone (**w**)
11   *Anyone isn't helping me (**w**)
12   *The fact that nothing has happened will change anything
13   John will deny that anything has happened
14   *John has denied anything
15   John has denied any involvement
16   John has denied any involvement in any fraud

In relation to 11 (intended to be synonymous with *There isn't anyone helping me*) show how the traditional ternary-branching analysis of clauses as S constituents (whereby 11 would be analysed as an S constituent comprising the pronoun/PRN *anyone*, the present tense auxiliary/T *isn't* and the Verb Phrase/VP *helping me*) would be unable to provide a principled account of the ungrammaticality of 11 in terms of the c-command condition on polarity items. In relation to 13 and 14, consider why some linguists (e.g. Landau 2002) have claimed that it is not the verb *deny* which is negative in 13, 14, but rather the complementiser *that*, and say why sentences like 15 and 16 cast doubt on this. Consider an alternative account of data like 13–16 under which we assume that a polarity item must be **asymmetrically c-commanded** by an affective item, and we define asymmetric c-command as follows:

(i)   X asymmetrically c-commands Y if X c-commands Y but Y does not c-command X

In §2.7, we also showed how the relation *c-command* plays an important role in accounting for the syntax of reflexive and reciprocal anaphors. The same can be argued to be true of two other types of expression, namely non-anaphoric pronominals like *he/him/her/it/them* etc. and referential noun expressions like *John* or *the president*. Chomsky (1980, 1981) developed a *Theory of Binding* which incorporated the three binding principles outlined in a slightly revised form below:

(ii)   **Binding Principles**

   Principle A: An anaphor must be bound within its local domain
   Principle B: A (non-anaphoric) pronominal (expression) must be free within its local domain
   Principle C: An R-expression (i.e. referring noun expression) must be free within the overall structure containing it

Although there is controversy about how best to define the notion of *local domain* in relation to binding, for present purposes assume that this corresponds to the notion of TP, and that the three binding principles in (ii) thus amount to the following:

(iii) A: An anaphor (like *himself*) must be bound by (i.e. must refer to) a c-commanding constituent within the closest TP immediately containing it

   B: A pronominal (like *him*) must not be bound by (i.e. must not refer to) any c-commanding constituent within the closest TP immediately containing it

   C: An R-expression (i.e. a referring noun expression like *John/the president*) must not be coreferential to (i.e. must not refer to the same entity as) any c-commanding expression within the overall structure containing it

In the light of the Binding Principles outlined informally in (ii), discuss the binding properties of the expressions *Fred*, *John*, *he/him* and *himself* in sentences 17–22 below, drawing trees to represent the structure of the sentences.

17 a   John must feel that Fred has disgraced himself **(w)**
   b   *John must feel that himself has disgraced Fred

18 a   John must feel that Fred has disgraced him **(w)**
   b   John must feel that he has disgraced Fred

19 a   John may suspect that Fred has taken some pictures of him
   b   John may suspect that Fred has taken some pictures of himself

20 a   The rumours about Fred have upset him
   b   *The rumours about Fred have upset himself

21 a   The rumours about him have upset Fred **(w)**
   b   *The rumours about himself have upset Fred

22 a   John may wonder if the rumours about Fred will affect him
   b   John may wonder if the rumours about him will affect Fred

Helpful hints

Make the following assumptions about examples 1–16. When *need/dare* take a bare *to*-less infinitive complement, they are modal auxiliaries which occupy the head T position of TP and take a VP complement, and they are polarity items in this use. Assume that *no* in 7 and 10 is a quantifier (= Q) which heads a quantifier phrase (= QP) constituent and has a noun or Noun Phrase as its complement: assume that when the head Q of QP is negative, the overall QP is negative as well (because a phrase carries the same features as its head by virtue of being a projection of the relevant head). In addition, assume that *mustn't/don't/isn't* are (inherently negative) T/tense auxiliaries. Finally, assume that *anyone/anything/nobody/nothing* are pronouns (more specifically, they are Q-pronouns, i.e. pronominal quantifiers). In addition, assume that in the examples in 1–16 above, *any* and its compounds are partitive in use, and hence polarity items. In relation to examples 17–22, assume (when drawing your trees) that *him* and *himself* belong to the category PRN/pronoun – even though they have different binding properties (*himself* being an anaphoric pronoun, and *him* being a non-anaphoric pronoun).

Model answer for 1

Given the assumptions made in the text, 1 will have the structure (iv) below:

(iv)

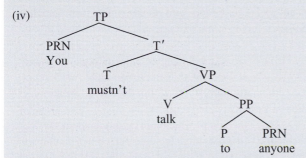

The T node containing the negative auxiliary *mustn't* here c-commands the PRN node containing the polarity item *anyone* because the sister of [T *mustn't*] is [VP *talk to anyone*], and *anyone* is contained within this VP, since the PRN node is one of the grandchildren of the VP node. If you prefer to use the alternative train metaphor suggested in §2.7 (under which X c-commands Y if you can get from X to Y on a train by going one stop north, then taking a southbound train on a different line and travelling as many stops south as you choose), you can say that [T *mustn't*] c-commands [PRN *anyone*] because if you travel one stop north from the T station you arrive at the T-bar station, and if you then change trains at the T-bar station you can get a southbound train on a different line which will take you to the PRN station containing *anyone* (at the end of the line) via the VP and PP stations. Since the polarity item *anyone* is c-commanded by the negative auxiliary *mustn't*, the c-command condition on the use of polarity items is satisfied, and sentence 1 is therefore grammatical.

Model answer for 20a

Although we will not attempt to argue this here, there are good reasons for thinking that sentence 20a has the structure (v) below:

(v)

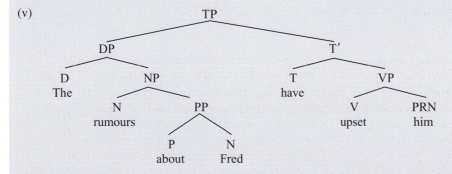

Him is a pronominal (i.e. a non-anaphoric pronoun), and hence subject to Principle B of Binding Theory. This specifies that a pronominal like *him* cannot refer to any expression c-commanding it within the closest TP containing it; and from this it follows that such a pronominal can (a) refer to an expression contained in a different TP within the same sentence, or (b) refer to an expression within the same TP as long as that expression does not c-command *him*, or (c) refer to some entity in the domain of discourse (e.g. some person not mentioned in the relevant sentence, but present in the discourse context). The second of these possibilities (b) allows for *him* to refer to *Fred* in (i), since although *him* and *Fred* are contained within the same TP, *Fred* does not c-command *him* (the only constituent which *Fred* c-commands being the preposition *about*) so that principle B is satisfied if *him* refers to *Fred* (or if indeed *him* refers to some other person not mentioned in the sentence).

The noun *Fred* is an R-expression by virtue of being a referring noun expression, and hence is subject to Principle C of Binding Theory. This specifies that an R-expression like *Fred* cannot be coreferential to any expression which c-commands it anywhere within the overall structure containing it. However, there is no violation of Principle C in (i) if *Fred* and *him* are coreferential, since *Fred* is not c-commanded by *him*. (The only constituent which *him* c-commands is the V *upset*.) There is likewise no violation of Principle C if *Fred* refers to some person not mentioned within the sentence. Overall, then, principles B and C allow for the twin possibilities that *him* can either refer to *Fred* or refer to someone other than Fred who is not directly mentioned in the sentence.

3 Null constituents

3.1 Overview

So far, our discussion of syntactic structure has tacitly assumed that all constituents in a given structure are **overt** (in the sense that they have audible phonetic features, as well as grammatical and semantic features). However, in this chapter we argue that syntactic structures may also contain **null constituents** (also known as **empty categories**) – i.e. constituents which have grammatical and semantic features but lack audible phonetic features (and so are 'silent' or 'inaudible').

3.2 Null subjects

We are already familiar with one kind of null constituent from the discussion of the **Null Subject Parameter** in §1.6. There, we saw that alongside finite clauses like that produced by speaker A in the dialogue in (1) below with an overt subject like *Maria*, Italian also has finite clauses like that produced by speaker B, with a null subject pronoun conventionally designated as *pro* (and referred to affectionately as 'little *pro*'):

(1)   SPEAKER A: Maria è tornata?
                   Maria is returned?
                   'Has Maria returned?'
      SPEAKER B: Sì, *pro* è tornata
                   Yes, *pro* is returned
                   'Yes, she has returned'

One reason for positing *pro* in (1B) is that it captures the intuition that the sentence has an 'understood' subject (as is clear from the fact that its English translation contains the subject pronoun *she*). A second reason relates to the agreement morphology carried by the auxiliary *è* 'is' and the participle *tornata* 'returned' in (1). Just as the form of the (third person singular) auxiliary *è* 'is' and the (feminine singular) participle *tornata* is determined via agreement with the overt (third person feminine singular) subject *Maria* in (1A), so too the auxiliary and participle agree in exactly the same way with the null *pro* subject in (1B), which (as used here) is third person feminine singular by virtue of referring to *Maria*.

If the sentence in (1B) were subjectless, it is not obvious how we would account for the relevant agreement facts. Since all finite clauses in Italian allow a null *pro* subject, we can refer to *pro* as a **finite null subject**.

Although English is not an Italian-style null subject language (in the sense that it is not a language which allows any and every kind of finite clause to have a null *pro* subject), it does have three different types of null subject (briefly discussed in exercise 1.2). As the examples in (2) below illustrate, an imperative sentence in English can have an overt subject which is either a second person expression like *you*, or a third person expression like *anyone*:

(2) (a)   Don't *you* lose your nerve!
   (b)   Don't *anyone* lose their nerve!

However, English also allows an **imperative null subject** in imperative sentences like (3a) below, and these are intrinsically second person – as the contrast with (3b) illustrates:

(3) (a)   Don't lose your nerve!
   (b)   *Don't lose their nerve!

In other words, imperative null subjects seem to be a silent counterpart of *you*. One way of describing this is to say that the pronoun *you* can have a **null spellout** (and thereby have its phonetic features not spelled out – i.e. deleted/omitted) when it is the subject of an imperative sentence.

English also has a second kind of null subject which we will call a **truncated null subject**. In informal styles of spoken English (and also in diary styles of written English) a sentence can be **truncated** (i.e. shortened) by giving a subject pronoun like *I/you/he/we/they* a null spellout if it is the first word in a sentence, and if it is weak (i.e. unstressed/non-contrastive). So, in sentences like those in (4) below:

(4) (a)   *I* can't find my pen
   (b)   *I* think I left it at home
   (c)   Why do I always lose things?

the two italicised occurrences of the subject pronoun *I* can be given a null spellout because in each case *I* is the first word in the sentence, but not other occurrences of *I* – as we see from (5) below:

(5) (a)   Can't find my pen
   (b)   Think I left it at home/*Think left it at home
   (c)   *Why do always lose things?

However, not all sentence-initial subjects can be truncated (e.g. we can't readily truncate *He* in a sentence like *He is tired*, giving **Is tired*): the precise nature of the constraints on **truncation** are unclear.

A third type of null subject found in English is a **nonfinite null subject**, found in nonfinite clauses which don't have an overt subject. In this connection, compare the structure of the bracketed infinitive clauses in the (a) and (b) examples below:

(6) (a)   We would like [*you* to stay]
    (b)   We would like [to stay]

(7) (a)   We don't want [*anyone* to upset them]
    (b)   We don't want [to upset them]

Each of the bracketed infinitive complement clauses in the (a) examples in (6) and (7) contains an overt (italicised) subject. By contrast, the bracketed complement clauses in the (b) examples appear to be subjectless. However, we shall argue that apparently subjectless infinitive clauses contain a **null subject**. The particular kind of null subject found in the bracketed clauses in the (b) examples has the same grammatical and referential properties as a pronoun, and hence appears to be a null pronoun. In order to differentiate it from the null ('little *pro*') subject found in finite clauses in null subject languages like Italian, it is conventionally designated as **PRO** and referred to as 'big PRO'. Given this assumption, a sentence such as (6b) will have a parallel structure to (6a), except that the bracketed TP has an overt pronoun *you* as its subject in (6a), but a null pronoun PRO as its subject in (6b) – as shown below:

(8)

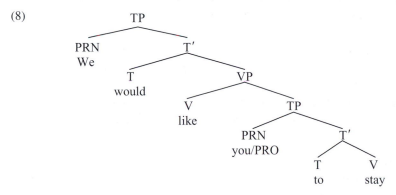

Using the relevant technical terminology, we can say that the null PRO subject in (8) is **controlled** by (i.e. refers back to) the subject *we* of the **matrix** (= containing = next highest) clause – or, equivalently, that *we* is the **controller** or **antecedent** of PRO: hence, a structure like 'We would like PRO to stay' has an interpretation akin to that of 'We would like *ourselves* to stay.' Verbs (such as *like*) which allow an infinitive complement with a PRO subject are said to function (in the relevant use) as **control verbs**; likewise, a complement clause with a null PRO subject is known as a **control clause**.

An obvious question to ask at this juncture is why we should posit that apparently subjectless infinitive complements like those bracketed in (6b) and (7b) above have a null PRO subject. Part of the motivation comes from the intuition that the verb *stay* in (6b) above has an understood subject – and positing a PRO subject for the *stay* clause captures this intuition. The null PRO subject of a control infinitive becomes overt if the infinitive clause is substituted by a finite clause, as we see from the paraphrase for (9a) below given in (9b):

(9) (a)   Jim promised [*PRO* to come to my party]
   (b)   Jim promised [*he* would come to my party]

The fact that the bracketed clause in the (b) example contains an overt (italicised) subject makes it plausible to suppose that the bracketed clause in the synonymous (a) example has a null PRO subject.

Further evidence in support of positing a null PRO subject in such clauses comes from the syntax of **reflexive anaphors** (i.e. *self/selves* forms such as *myself/yourself/himself/themselves* etc.). As examples such as the following indicate, reflexives generally require a local **antecedent** (the reflexive being italicised and its antecedent bold printed):

(10) (a)   They want [**John** to help *himself*]
    (b)   ***They** want [John to help *themselves*]

In the case of structures like (10), a local antecedent means 'a *clausemate* antecedent' – i.e. an antecedent contained within the same [bracketed] clause/TP as the reflexive. (10a) is grammatical because it satisfies this clausemate condition: the antecedent of the reflexive *himself* is the noun *John*, and *John* is contained within the same (bracketed) *help*-clause as *himself*. By contrast, (10b) is ungrammatical because the reflexive *themselves* does not have a clausemate antecedent (i.e. it does not have an antecedent within the bracketed clause containing it); its antecedent is the pronoun *they*, and *they* is contained within the *want* clause, not within the [bracketed] *help* clause. In the light of the requirement for reflexives to have a local antecedent, consider now how we account for the grammaticality of the following kind of structure:

(11)   John wants [to prove himself]

It follows from the clausemate condition on reflexives that *himself* must have an antecedent within the clause/TP immediately containing it. This clausemate condition is satisfied if we assume that the complement clause in (11) has a PRO subject of its own, as shown in simplified form in (12) below:

(12)   John wants [$_{TP}$ PRO [$_T$ to] prove himself]

We can then say that PRO serves as a clausemate antecedent for *himself* (i.e. PRO is the antecedent of *himself*, and is immediately contained within the same bracketed TP as *himself*). Since PRO in turn is controlled by *John* (i.e. *John* is the antecedent of PRO), this means that *himself* is **coreferential** to (i.e. refers to the same individual as) *John*.

However, it might be objected that we can account for sentences like (11) without the need for positing a PRO subject for the bracketed *to*-clause if we posit that a reflexive contained within a subjectless clause can have an antecedent in a higher clause. We could then suppose that the bracketed TP in (11) is subjectless, and that the antecedent of *himself* is the main-clause subject *John*. However, the assumption that infinitival TPs like that bracketed in (11) don't have a subject of their own but rather the main-clause subject serves as the subject of both the main and the complement clause proves problematic in respect of structures such as those below:

(13) (a)   It's vital [to prepare *myself* properly for the exam]
  (b)   It's important [not to take *oneself* too seriously]
  (c)   John didn't want [to get *themselves* into trouble]
  (d)   John proposed [to become *partners*]
  (e)   John wanted [to work *together*]

If the bracketed infinitive clause were subjectless in (13a,b), the reflexive *myself/yourself* would have to refer to the main-clause subject *it*, so we would wrongly predict that *itself* has to be used and that sentences like (13a,b) are ungrammatical. Likewise, if the bracketed infinitive clause in (13c) were subject-less, the only possible antecedent for the reflexive *themselves* within the sentence would be the main-clause subject *John* – and yet it is clear that the two don't match (in that *he* is singular and *themselves* plural): so once again, we would wrongly predict that sentences like (13c) are ungrammatical. A similar mismatch would arise if the bracketed infinitive clause in (13d) were subjectless, since there would then be a mismatch between the plural noun *partners* and the sin-gular subject *John* with which it is associated – the same kind of mismatch that we find in **John became partners*. And since the adverb *together* as used in sentences like (13e) must be associated with a plural expression (cf. *They/*He worked together*), it is clear that saying that the bracketed infinitive clause in (13e) is subjectless would wrongly predict that (13e) should be ungrammatical, because of the number mismatch between (singular) *John* and (plural) *together*.

By contrast, we can overcome these problems if we suppose that seemingly subjectless clauses have a null subject, and that sentences like those in (13) have the structure shown in simplified form below:

(14) (a)   It's vital [PRO to prepare *myself* properly for the exam]
  (b)   It's important [PRO not to take *oneself* too seriously]
  (c)   John didn't want [PRO to get *themselves* into trouble]
  (d)   John proposed [PRO to become *partners*]
  (e)   John wanted [PRO to work *together*]

We could then say that PRO in (14a) refers to the speaker who uttered the sentence, so that PRO is a first person singular subject (like *I*), and hence can serve as the antecedent of *myself*: when PRO refers to some entity within the domain of discourse but not directly mentioned in the sentence, we can say that PRO has a **discourse controller**. In (14b), PRO has **arbitrary reference**, and so denotes 'any arbitrary person you care to mention' and hence has essentially the same interpretation as arbitrary *one* in sentences like '*One* can't be too careful these days': consequently, PRO can serve as the antecedent of *oneself*.

In (14c–e), PRO is a third person plural subject (like *they*), and it is **partially controlled** by the main clause subject *John* (in the sense that the antecedent of PRO is a plural expression which denotes a set of individuals including *John* – i.e. referring to John and one or more other people): since PRO is a plural subject, it is compatible in number with expressions like *themselves/partners/together*.

A different kind of argument in support of positing that control clauses have a silent PRO subject can be formulated in theoretical terms. In the previous chapter, we noted that T-auxiliaries like *will* have an EPP feature which requires them to project a subject on the edge of TP. However, since we argued in chapter 1 that infinitival *to* also belongs to the category T (by virtue of its status as an infinitival tense particle), we can suggest the broader generalisation that all T constituents have an EPP feature requiring them to project a subject on the edge of TP – not only T-auxiliaries like *will* but also the infinitival T constituent *to*. The analysis in (8) above is consistent with this generalisation, since it posits that the *stay* clause either has an overt *you* subject or a null PRO subject, with either type of subject satisfying the EPP feature of *to*. This leads us to the more general conclusion that just as infinitive complements like *you to stay* in (6a) have an overt subject (*you*), so too seemingly subjectless infinitive complements like *to stay* in (6b) have a null PRO subject – as shown in (8) above.

3.3   Null auxiliaries

So far, all the clauses we have looked at in this chapter and the last have contained a TP projection headed by a finite auxiliary or infinitival *to*. The obvious generalisation suggested by this is that all clauses contain TP. An important question begged by this assumption, however, is how we are to analyse finite clauses which contain no overt auxiliary. In this connection, consider the structure below:

(15)   He could have helped her, or [she have helped him]

Both clauses here (viz. the *he* clause and the bracketed *she* clause) appear to be finite, since both have nominative subjects (*he/she*). If all finite clauses contain a TP projection headed by a finite T constituent, it follows that both clauses in (15) must be TPs containing a finite T. This is clearly true of the *he* clause, since this contains the finite modal auxiliary *could*; however, the *she* clause doesn't seem to contain any finite auxiliary constituent, since *have* is an infinitive form in (15) (the corresponding finite form which would be required with a third person subject like *she* being *has*). How can we analyse finite clauses as projections of a finite T constituent when clauses like that bracketed in (15) contain no finite auxiliary?

A plausible answer is to suppose that the string *she have helped him* in (15) is an **elliptical** (i.e. abbreviated) variant of *she could have helped him*, and that the

T constituent *could* in the second clause undergoes a particular form of ellipsis called **gapping**. (Gapping is a grammatical operation which allows the head of a phrase to be given a **null spellout** – and so be 'silent' – when the same item occurs elsewhere within the sentence, and is so called because it leaves an apparent 'gap' in the phrase where the head would otherwise have been.) If so, the second clause will have the structure shown below (where ~~could~~ marks an ellipsed counterpart of *could*, and we assume that a nonfinite auxiliary like *have* occupies the head AUX/Auxiliary position of an AUXP/Auxiliary Phrase: see §4.6 on AUXP):

(16)

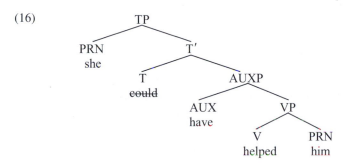

The head T position of TP in a structure like (16) is filled by the ellipsed auxiliary ~~could~~. Although an ellipsed item loses its phonetic features, it retains its grammatical and semantic features, so that ~~could~~ in (16) is a silent counterpart of *could*. The **null T** analysis in (16) provides a principled account of three observations. Firstly, the bracketed clause in (15) is interpreted as an elliptical form of *she could have helped him*: this can be straightforwardly accounted for under the analysis in (16) since T contains a null counterpart of *could*. Secondly, the subject is in the nominative case form *she*: this can be attributed to the fact that the T position in (16) is filled by a 'silent' counterpart of the finite auxiliary *could*, which (like other finite auxiliaries) requires a nominative subject. Thirdly, the perfect auxiliary *have* is in the infinitive form: this is because ~~could~~ (being a null copy of *could*) has the same selectional properties as *could*, and so (like *could*) selects a complement headed by an item (like *have*) in the infinitive form.

A further argument in support of the null T analysis in (16) comes from facts relating to **cliticisation** (a process by which one word attaches itself in a leech-like fashion to another). The perfect auxiliary *have* has a range of variant forms in the spoken language. When unstressed, it can lose its initial /h/ segment and have its vowel reduced to schwa /ə/, and so be pronounced as /əv/ e.g. in sentences such as *You should have been there*. (Because *of* is also pronounced /əv/ when unstressed, some people mistakenly write this as *You should of been there* – not *you*, of course!) However, when *have* is used with a pronominal subject ending in a vowel or diphthong (e.g. a pronoun like *I/we/you/they*), it can lose its vowel entirely and be contracted down to /v/; in this weak form, it is phonetically too insubstantial to survive as an independent word and **encliticises** onto (i.e. attaches to the end of) its subject, resulting in structures such as:

(17) (a)   *You've* done your duty
     (b)   *They've* retired General Gaga
     (c)   *I've* forgotten to lock the door
     (d)   *We've* saved you a place

However, note that *have* cannot cliticise onto *she* in (18) below:

(18)   *He could have helped her or *she've* helped him

so that *she've* is not homophonous with the word *sheave*. Why should cliticisation of *have* onto *she* be blocked here? Let's suppose that *have*-cliticisation is subject to the following structural conditions:

(19)   ***Have*-cliticisation**
        Have can encliticise onto a word W ending in a vowel or diphthong provided that
     (i)   W c-commands *have* and
     (ii)   W is immediately adjacent to *have*

(W is immediately adjacent to *have* if there is no constituent between the two – i.e. no constituent which c-commands *have* and which in turn is c-commanded by W. A descriptive detail which we set aside here is that (19) applies specifically to encliticisation of *have*: encliticisation of the *'s* variant of *has* and of other contracted auxiliary forms is subject to far less restrictive conditions on its use – but this will not be pursued here.)

To see how (19) works, consider the structure below:

(20)

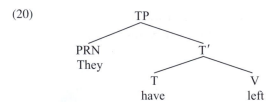

Here, the pronoun *they* ends in a diphthong and so is the kind of pronoun that *have* can cliticise onto. The c-command condition (19i) is met in that *they* c-commands *have*, and the adjacency condition (19ii) is also met in that there is no constituent intervening between *they* and *have*. Since both its structural conditions are met, (19) correctly predicts that *have* can encliticise onto *they*, so deriving *They've left*. The kind of cliticisation involved here is essentially phonological (rather than syntactic), so that *they* and *have* remain separate words in the syntax, but are fused together in the PF component (i.e. the component responsible for determining Phonetic Form) once the structure **generated** (i.e. formed) by the syntax has been handed over to the PF component for morphological and phonological processing.

In the light of our discussion of *have*-cliticisation, now consider why cliticisation of *have* onto *she* is not possible in (18) **He could have helped her or* *she've helped him*. Under the *null T* analysis suggested above, the second clause in (18) contains a null variant of *could* and has the structure shown in (16) above. Although the c-command condition (19i) is met in (16) in that *she* c-commands *have*, the adjacency condition (19ii) is not met in that *she* is not immediately adjacent to *have* because the null auxiliary ~~could~~ intervenes between the two (in that ~~could~~ c-commands *have*, and ~~could~~ is in turn c-commanded by *she*). Thus, the presence of the intervening null auxiliary ~~could~~ blocks cliticisation of *have* onto *she* in (16), thereby accounting for the ungrammaticality of (18) **He could have helped her or she've helped him*. Turning this conclusion on its head, we can say that the ungrammaticality of (18) provides us with empirical evidence that the bracketed clause in (15) contains a null counterpart of *could* intervening between *she* and *have* – as claimed in the analysis in (16) above.

3.4   Null T in finite clauses

Our analysis of the kind of auxiliariless clauses discussed in §3.3 as TPs headed by a T which has a null phonetic spellout suggests the more general hypothesis that:

(21)   All finite clauses are TPs headed by an (overt or null) T constituent

Such a hypothesis has interesting implications for finite clauses such as the following which contain a finite verb, but no auxiliary:

(22) (a)   He enjoys syntax
     (b)   He enjoyed syntax

It implies that we should analyse auxiliariless indicative clauses like those in (22a,b) above as TP constituents which have the respective structures shown in (23a,b) below:

(23)

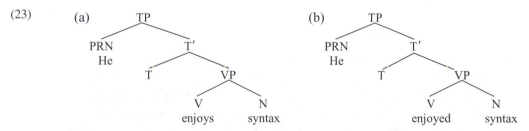

Structures like those in (23) would differ from null-auxiliary structures like (15) *He could have helped her or she ~~could~~ have helped him* in that they don't contain a silent counterpart of a specific auxiliary like *could* or *is*, but rather simply don't contain any auxiliary at all.

However, there's clearly something very odd about a *null T* analysis like (23) if we say that the relevant clauses are TPs which are headed by a T constituent which contains *absolutely nothing*. For one thing, a category label like T is an abbreviation for a set of features (i.e. grammatical properties) carried by a lexical item – hence, if we posit that structures like (23) are TPs, the head T position of TP has to be occupied by some kind of lexical item. Moreover, the structures which are generated by the syntactic component of the grammar are eventually handed over to the semantic component to be assigned a semantic interpretation, and it seems reasonable to follow Chomsky (1995) in requiring all heads in a syntactic structure to play a role in determining the meaning of the overall structure. If so, it clearly has to be the case that the head T of TP contains some item which contributes in some way to the semantic interpretation of the sentence. But what kind of item could T contain?

In order to try and answer this question, it's instructive to contrast auxiliariless structures like those in (23) above with auxiliary-containing structures like those in (24) below:

(24)

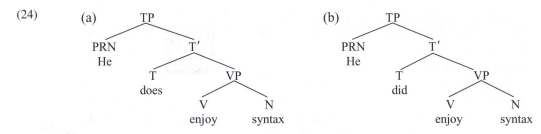

The head T position in TP is occupied by the present tense auxiliary *does* in (24a), and by the past tense auxiliary *did* in (24b). If we examine the internal morphological structure of these two words, we see that *does* contains the present tense affix *-s*, and that *did* contains the past tense affix *-d* (each of these affixes being attached to an irregular stem form of the auxiliary DO). In schematic terms, then, we can say that the head T constituent of TP in structures like (24) is of the form *auxiliary stem+tense affix*.

If we now look back at the auxiliariless structures in (23), we see that the head V position of VP in these structures is occupied by the verbs *enjoys* and *enjoyed*, and that these have a parallel morphological structure, in that they are of the form *verb stem+tense affix*. So, what finite clauses like (23) and (24) share in common is that in both cases they contain an (auxiliary or main) verb carrying a tense affix. In structures like (24) which contain an auxiliary like DO, the tense affix is attached to the auxiliary; in structures like (23) which contain no auxiliary, the tense affix attaches instead to the main verb *enjoy*. If we make the reasonable assumption that (as its label suggests) T is the **locus** of the tense properties of a finite clause (in the sense that T is the constituent which carries its tense features), an interesting possibility to consider is that the relevant tense affix (in both types of clause structure) originates in the head T position of TP. Since tensed verbs agree with their subjects in person and number, let us suppose that the tense affix (below abbreviated to *Af*) also carries person and number features. On this view, sentences like *He does enjoy syntax* and *He enjoys syntax* would have the respective syntactic structures indicated in (25a,b) below, where [*3SgPr*] is an abbreviation for the features [third-person, singular-number, present-tense]:

(25)

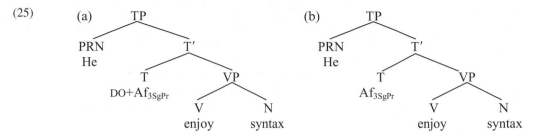

The two structures share in common the fact that they both contain a tense affix (*Af*) in T; they differ in that the tense affix is attached to the auxiliary DO in (25a), but is unattached in (25b) because there is no auxiliary in T for the affix to attach to. (An interesting implication of the analysis in (25b) is that it requires us to make a minor revision to the assumption we made in the previous chapter that all nonterminal nodes in a tree are projections of a head *word*, since a tense affix is clearly not a *word*.)

Under the analysis in (25), it is clear that T in auxiliariless clauses like (25b) would not be empty, but rather would contain a tense/agreement affix whose semantic contribution to the meaning of the overall sentence is that it marks tense. But what about the phonetic spellout of the tense affix? In a structure like (25a), it is easy to see why the (third person singular present) tense affix is ultimately spelled out as an *s*-inflection on the end of the auxiliary *does*, because the affix is directly attached to the auxiliary DO in T. But how come the affix ends up spelled out as an *s*-inflection on the main verb *enjoys* in a structure like (25b)? We can answer this question in the following terms. Once the syntax has formed a clause structure like (25), the relevant syntactic structure is then sent to the **semantic component** to be assigned a semantic interpretation, and to the **PF component** to be assigned a phonetic form. In the PF component, a number of morphological and phonological operations apply. One of these morphological operations is traditionally referred to as *Affix Hopping*, and can be characterised informally as follows:

(26)   **Affix Hopping**
         When some constituent C contains an unattached affix *Af*, in the PF component *Af* is lowered onto the head H of the complement of C (provided H is an appropriate **host** for the affix to attach to)

Since the Affix is in T in (25b), and since the complement of T is the VP *enjoy syntax*, (26) means that the affix in T will be lowered onto the head V *enjoy* of the relevant VP – provided that V is an appropriate kind of host for the affix. But since the affix in T is a tense affix which needs to attach to a verbal host, it is clear that the verb *enjoy* is indeed an appropriate host for the tense affix. Accordingly, in the PF component the unattached affix in T in (25b) will be lowered onto the verb *enjoy* via the morphological operation of Affix Hopping (26), in the manner shown by the arrow in (27) below:

(27)

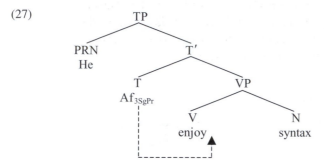

Since inflections in English are **suffixes**, we can assume that the tense affix will be lowered onto the *end* of the verb *enjoy*, to derive the structure [*enjoy*+*Af$_{3SgPr}$*]. Given that *enjoy* is a regular verb, the resulting structure will ultimately be spelled out in the phonology as the form *enjoys*.

What we have done so far in this section is sketch out an analysis of auxiliariless finite clauses as TPs headed by a T constituent containing an abstract tense affix which is subsequently lowered onto the verb by an **Affix Hopping** operation in the PF component (so resulting in a clause structure which looks as if it contains no T constituent). However, an important question to ask at this juncture is why we should claim that auxiliariless clauses contain an abstract T constituent. From a theoretical point of view, one advantage of the abstract T analysis is that it provides a unitary characterisation of the syntax of clauses, since it allows us to say that all clauses contain a TP projection, that the subject of a clause is always in **spec-T** (i.e. always serves as the specifier of T), that a finite clause always contains an (auxiliary or main) verb carrying a tense affix, and so on. Lending further weight to theory-internal considerations such as these is a substantial body of empirical evidence, as we shall see.

One argument in support of the **tense affix** analysis comes from co-ordination facts in relation to sentences such as:

(28)　(a)　He *enjoys syntax*, and **has learned a lot**
　　　 (b)　He *enjoyed syntax*, and **is taking a follow-up course**

In both sentences, the italicised string *enjoys syntax/enjoyed syntax* has been co-ordinated with a bold-printed constituent which is clearly a T-bar in that it comprises a present tense auxiliary (*has/is*) with a Verb Phrase complement (*learned a lot/taking a follow-up course*). On the assumption that only the same kinds of constituent can be conjoined by *and*, it follows that the italicised (seemingly T-less) strings *enjoys syntax/enjoyed syntax* must also be T-bar constituents; and since they contain no overt auxiliary, this means they must contain an abstract T constituent of some kind – precisely as the tense affix analysis in (27) claims.

A direct consequence of the tense affix analysis (27) of auxiliariless finite clauses is that finite auxiliaries and finite main verbs occupy different positions within the clause: finite auxiliaries occupy the head T position of TP, whereas finite main verbs occupy the head V position of VP. An interesting way of testing this hypothesis is in relation to the behaviour of items which have the status of auxiliaries in some uses, but of verbs in others. One such word is HAVE. In the kind of uses illustrated in (29) below, HAVE is a **perfect** auxiliary (and so requires the main verb to be in the perfect participle form *seen/been*):

(29) (a)   They *have* seen the ghost
     (b)   They *had* been warned about the ghost

However, in the uses illustrated in (30) below, HAVE is causative or experiential in sense, and so has much the same meaning as *cause* in (30a,b) and as *experience* in (30c,d):

(30) (a)   The doctor *had* an eye-specialist examine the patient
     (b)   The doctor *had* the patient examined by an eye-specialist
     (c)   The teacher *had* three students walk out on her
     (d)   I've never *had* anyone send me flowers

By traditional tests of auxiliarihood, perfect *have* is an auxiliary, and causative/experiential *have* is a main verb: e.g. perfect HAVE can undergo inversion (*Has she gone to Paris?*) whereas causative/experiential HAVE cannot (**Had the doctor an eye specialist examine the patient?*). In terms of the assumptions we are making here, this means that finite forms of HAVE are positioned in the head T position of TP in their perfect use, but in the head V position of VP in their causative or experiential use.

Evidence in support of this claim comes from cliticisation. We noted earlier in (19) above that the form *have* can cliticise onto an immediately adjacent pronoun ending in a vowel/diphthong which c-commands *have*. In the light of this, consider contrasts such as the following:

(31) (a)   *They've* seen a ghost (= perfect *have*)
     (b)   **They've* their car serviced regularly (= causative *have*)
     (c)   **They've* students walk out on them sometimes (= experiential *have*)

How can we account for this contrast? If we assume that perfect *have* in (31a) is a finite (present tense) auxiliary which occupies the head T position of TP, but that causative *have* in (31b) and experiential *have* in (31c) are main verbs occupying the head V position of a VP complement of a null T, then prior to cliticisation the three clauses will have the respective simplified structures indicated by the partial labeled bracketings in (32a–c) below (where *Af* is an abstract tense affix):

(32) (a)   [$_{TP}$ They [$_T$ *have*+*Af*] [$_{VP}$ [$_V$ seen] a ghost]]
     (b)   [$_{TP}$ They [$_T$ *Af*] [$_{VP}$ [$_V$ *have*] their car serviced regularly]]
     (c)   [$_{TP}$ They [$_T$ *Af*] [$_{VP}$ [$_V$ *have*] students walk out on them sometimes]]

(Here and throughout the rest of the book, *partial* labelled bracketings are used to show those parts of the structure most relevant to the discussion at hand, omitting other parts. In such cases, we generally show relevant heads and their maximal projections but omit intermediate projections, as in (32) above where we show e.g. T and TP but not T-bar.) Since we claimed in (19) above that cliticisation of *have* onto a pronoun is blocked by the presence of an intervening constituent, it should be obvious why *have* can cliticise onto *they* in (32a) but not in (32b,c): after all, there is no intervening constituent separating the pronoun *they* from *have* in (32a), but *they* is separated from the verb *have* in (32b,c) by an intervening T constituent containing a tense affix (*Af*), so blocking contraction. It goes without saying that a crucial premise of this account is the assumption that *have* is positioned in the head T position of TP in its use as a finite perfect auxiliary, but in the head V position of VP in its use as a causative or experiential verb. In other words, *have*-cliticisation data suggest that finite clauses which lack a finite auxiliary are TPs headed by an abstract T constituent containing a tense affix.

In this section, we have argued that T in a finite clause always contains a tense affix. In clauses containing an auxiliary, the auxiliary is directly merged with the tense affix to form an *auxiliary+affix* structure; in auxiliariless clauses, the tense affix is lowered onto the main verb by an **Affix Hopping** operation in the PF component, so forming a *verb+affix* structure. When an affix is stranded with no verbal stem to attach to, it is spelled out as an inflected form of DO (as we shall see in more detail later).

3.5   Null T in infinitive clauses

In the previous section, we argued that auxiliariless finite clauses are TP constituents headed by an abstract T containing a tense affix. Given that clauses containing a finite auxiliary are also TPs, a plausible conclusion to draw is that all finite clauses are TPs. Since clauses containing infinitival *to* are also TPs (with *to* serving as a nonfinite tense particle) we can generalise still further and say that all finite and infinitival clauses are TPs. This in turn has implications for how we analyse **bare** (i.e. *to*-less) infinitive complement clauses such as those bracketed below (where the italicised verb is infinitival in form):

(33) (a)   I have never known [Tom *criticise* anyone]
     (b)   A reporter saw [Senator Sleaze *leave* Benny's Bunny Bar]
     (c)   You mustn't let [the pressure *get* to you]

If (as we are suggesting) all finite and infinitival clauses are indeed TPs, bare infinitive clauses like those bracketed in (33) will be TPs headed by a null T constituent. Since the relevant null T constituent resembles infinitival *to* in requiring the (italicised) verb in the bracketed complement clause to be in the infinitive form, we can take it to be a null counterpart of infinitival *to* (below symbolised as *to̶*). This in turn will mean that the bracketed infinitive clause in (33a) has the structure (34) below:

(34)

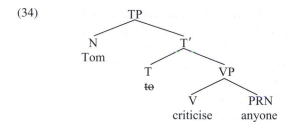

We could then say that verbs like *know*, *see* and *let* (as used in (33) above) take an infinitival TP complement headed by an infinitive particle with a null spellout, whereas verbs like *expect*, *judge*, *report*, *believe* etc. take a TP complement headed by an infinitive particle which is overtly spelled out as *to* in structures like those below:

(35) (a)   I expect [him *to* win]
      (b)   I judged [him *to* be lying]
      (c)   They reported [him *to* be missing]
      (d)   I believe [him *to* be innocent]

This means that all infinitive clauses are TPs headed by an infinitival T which is overtly spelled out as *to* in infinitive clauses like those bracketed in (35), but which has a null spellout in infinitive clauses like those bracketed in (33).

From a historical perspective, the null infinitive particle analysis is far from implausible since bare infinitive clauses in present-day English had *to* infinitive counterparts in earlier varieties of English – as illustrated by the following Shakespearean examples:

(36)(a)   I saw [her coral lips *to* move] (Lucentio, *Taming of the Shrew*, I.i)
      (b)   My lord your son made [me *to* think of this] (Helena, *All's Well That Ends Well*, I.iii)
      (c)   What would you have [me *to* do]? (Lafeu, *All's Well That Ends Well*, V.ii)
      (d)   I had rather hear [you *to* solicit that] (Olivia, *All's Well That Ends Well*, III.i)

Moreover, some bare infinitive clauses have *to*-infinitive counterparts in present-day English: cf.

(37) (a)   I've never known [Tom (to) criticise anyone]
      (b)   Tom has never been known [*to* criticise anyone]

(38) (a)   A reporter saw [Senator Sleaze leave Benny's Bunny Bar]
      (b)   Senator Sleaze was seen [*to* leave Benny's Bunny Bar]

The infinitive particle which heads the bracketed infinitival TP in sentences like (37, 38) must be overtly spelled out as *to* when the relevant TP is used as the complement of a passive participle like *known* in (37b) or *seen* in (38b), but can have a null spellout when the relevant TP is the complement of an active transitive verb like the perfect participle *known* in (37a) or the past tense form *saw* in (38a) – a key difference (in my British variety of English) being that a null spellout for the infinitive particle is optional in structures like (37a) but obligatory in structures like (37b). However, occasional 'slips of the tongue' can result in the infinitive particle sometimes being overt even in active structures like (38a) – as we see from the following sentences recorded from TV programmes:

(39) (a) The Mayor of New Orleans would like to see parts of the city which were devastated in the hurricane *to* get back to normal (BBC TV newsreader)

   (b) Arsenal's back five are making Essien and Frank Lampard *to* work very hard across the pitch (Sky TV sports commentator)

Although data like (36–39) are suggestive rather than conclusive, they make it plausible to suppose that bare infinitive clauses are TPs headed by a null variant of infinitival *to*.

Additional support for the *null infinitive particle* analysis of bare infinitive clauses comes from cliticisation facts in relation to sentences such as the following:

(40) (a) I can't let [*you have* my password]

   (b) *I can't let [*you've* my password]

If we suppose that the bracketed infinitive complement in (40b) is a TP headed by a null variant of infinitival *to* as in:

(41) I can't let [$_{TP}$ you [$_T$ *t̶o̶*] have my password]

we can account for the fact that *have* cannot cliticise onto *you* by positing that the presence of the null infinitive particle *t̶o̶* intervening between *you* and *have* blocks cliticisation of *have* onto *you*.

Our discussion here leads us to the wider conclusion that both *to*-infinitive clauses and bare (*to*-less) infinitive clauses are TP constituents headed by an infinitive particle which has the overt spellout *to* in most types of infinitive clause, but has a null spellout in bare infinitive clauses. Given that we earlier argued that all finite clauses contain a TP projection (headed by a T which contains a tense affix, and may or may not also contain an auxiliary), the overall conclusion which we reach is that all finite and infinitival clauses contain a TP, and that T is overt in clauses containing a finite auxiliary or infinitival *to*, but is null elsewhere (because *to* in bare infinitive clauses has a null spellout, and the tense affix in auxiliariless finite clauses is lowered onto the main verb in the PF component). One advantage of this analysis is that it enables us to attain a uniform characterisation of the syntax of (finite and infinitival) clauses as TP structures headed by a T with a V or VP complement.

3.6   Null C in finite clauses

The overall conclusion to be drawn from our discussion in §§3.3–3.5 is that all finite and infinitive clauses contain an overt or null T constituent which projects into TP (with the subject of the clause occupying the specifier position within TP). However, given that clauses can be introduced by complementisers such as *if/that/for*, a natural question to ask is whether apparently complementiserless clauses can likewise be argued to be CPs headed by a null complementiser. In this connection, consider the following:

(42) (a)   We didn't know [*if* he had resigned]
    (b)   We didn't know [*that* he had resigned]
    (c)   We didn't know [he had resigned]

The bracketed complement clause is interpreted as interrogative in force in (42a) and declarative in force in (42b), and it is plausible to suppose that the force of the clause is determined by a force feature carried by the italicised complementiser introducing the clause: in other words, the bracketed clause is interrogative in force in (42a) because it is introduced by the interrogative complementiser *if*, and is declarative in force in (42b) because it is introduced by the declarative complementiser *that*.

But now consider the bare (i.e. seemingly complementiserless) clause in (42c): this can only be interpreted as declarative in force (not as interrogative), so that (42c) is synonymous with (42b) and not with (42a). Why should this be? One answer is to suppose that the bracketed bare clause in (42c) is a CP headed by a null variant of the declarative complementiser *that* (below symbolised as *t̶h̶a̶t̶*), and that the bracketed complement clauses in (42a,b,c) have the structure (43) below:

(43)

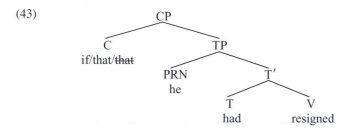

Given the analysis in (43), we could then say that the force of each of the bracketed complement clauses in (42) is determined by the force feature carried by the head C of the overall CP; in (42a) the clause is a CP headed by the interrogative complementiser *if* and so is interrogative in force; in (42b) it is a CP headed by the declarative complementiser *that* and so is declarative in force; and in (42c) it is a CP headed by a null variant of the declarative complementiser *that* and so is likewise declarative in force. More generally, the **null complementiser** analysis would enable us to arrive at a uniform characterisation of all finite clauses as CPs in which the force of a clause is indicated by the force feature carried by an (overt or null) complementiser introducing the clause.

Empirical evidence in support of the null complementiser analysis of bare complement clauses like that bracketed in (42c) comes from co-ordination data in relation to sentences such as:

(44)   We didn't know [*he had resigned*] or [**that he had been accused of corruption**]

In (44), the italicised bare clause has been co-ordinated with a bold-printed clause which is clearly a CP since it is introduced by the overt complementiser *that*. If we make the traditional assumption that only constituents of the same type can be co-ordinated, it follows that the italicised clause *he had resigned* in (44) must be a CP headed by a null counterpart of *that* because it has been co-ordinated with a bold-printed clause headed by the overt complementiser *that* – as shown in simplified form in (45) below:

(45)   We didn't know [~~that~~ *he had resigned*] or [**that he had been accused of corruption**]

What such an analysis implies is that the complementiser *that* can optionally be given a null phonetic spellout by having its phonetic features deleted in the PF component under certain circumstances.

So far in this section, we have argued that seemingly complementiserless finite declarative complement clauses are introduced by a null C constituent (here analysed as a null counterpart of the complementiser *that*). However, the null C analysis can be extended from finite embedded clauses to **main (= root = principal = independent) clauses** like those produced by speakers A and B in (46) below:

(46)   SPEAKER A: I am feeling thirsty
           SPEAKER B: Do you feel like a Coke?

The sentence produced by speaker A is declarative in force (by virtue of being a statement). If force is marked by a force feature carried by the head C of CP, this suggests that such declarative main clauses are CPs headed by a null complementiser carrying a declarative force feature. And indeed, theoretical considerations require us to assume this, if we suppose that the set of UG principles wired into the Language Faculty include a **Categorial Uniformity Principle** to the effect that all expressions of the same type belong to the same category (and, more specifically, all clauses with the same force belong to the same category): since declarative *that*-clauses are clearly CPs, it follows from the Categorial Uniformity Principle that all other declarative clauses (including declarative main clauses) must be CPs. This leads to the conclusion that a declarative main clause like that produced by speaker A in (46) is a CP headed by a null declarative complementiser. But what is the nature of the relevant null complementiser?

It seems unlikely that the null complementiser introducing declarative main clauses is a null counterpart of *that*, since *that* in English is only used to introduce embedded clauses, not main clauses. Let's therefore suppose that declarative main clauses in English are introduced by an inherently null complementiser (below symbolised as ∅), and hence that the sentence produced by speaker A in (46) has the structure shown in (47) below:

(47)

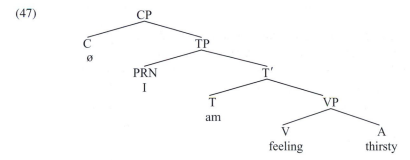

Under the CP analysis of main clauses in (47), the declarative force of the overall sentence is attributed to the sentence being a CP headed by a null complementiser ∅ carrying a declarative force feature which we can represent as [Dec-Force]. (The purists among you may object that it's not appropriate to call a null declarative particle introducing a main clause a *complementiser* when it doesn't introduce a complement clause: however, in keeping with work over the past four decades, we'll use the term complementiser/C in a more general sense here, to designate a category of word which can introduce both complement clauses and other clauses, and which serves to mark properties such as force and finiteness.)

From a cross-linguistic perspective, an analysis such as (47) which posits that main clauses are CPs headed by a force-marking complementiser is by no means implausible in that we find languages like Arabic in which both declarative and interrogative main clauses can be introduced by an overt complementiser, as the examples below illustrate:

(48) (a)   *?inna* l-walada taraka l-bayta (adapted from Ross 1970, p. 245)
            That the-boy left the-house
            'The boy left the house' (declarative)

    (b)   *Hal* taraka l-waladu l-bayta?
            If left the-boy the-house
            'Did the boy leave the house?' (interrogative)

Moreover (as we will see in more detail in §4.2), there is some evidence from sentences like (49) below that inverted auxiliaries in main-clause yes-no questions occupy the head C position of CP in English:

(49)   SPEAKER A: What were you going to ask me?
            SPEAKER B: (a) *If* **you** feel like a Coke
                       (b) *Do* **you** feel like a Coke?
                       (c) **If do* **you** feel like a Coke?

The fact that the inverted auxiliary *do* in (49b) occupies the same pre-subject position (in front of the bold-printed subject **you**) as the complementiser *if* in (49a), and the fact that *if* and *do* are mutually exclusive (as we see from the fact that structures like (49c) are ungrammatical) suggests that inverted auxiliaries (like complementisers) occupy the head C position of CP. This in turn means that main-clause questions are CPs headed by a C which is interrogative in force by virtue of containing an interrogative force feature which can be represented as [Int-Force].

Interestingly, an interrogative main clause can be co-ordinated with a declarative main clause, as we see from sentences like (50) below:

(50)   [I am feeling thirsty], but [*should I save my last Coke till later*]?

In (50) we have two (bracketed) main clauses joined together by the co-ordinating conjunction *but*. The second (italicised) conjunct *should I save my last Coke till later?* is an interrogative CP containing an inverted auxiliary in the head C position of CP. Given the traditional assumption that only constituents which belong to the same category can be co-ordinated, it follows that the first conjunct *I am feeling thirsty* must also be a CP; and since it contains no overt complementiser, it must be headed by a null complementiser – precisely as assumed in (47) above.

The assumption that all complete clauses contain an (overt or null) complementiser has important implications for the analysis of the case-marking of subjects – as we can illustrate in relation to the case-marking of the italicised pronouns in a sentence like (51a) below, with the structure in (51b):

(51) (a)   *They* may feel that/~~that~~ *She* can't help *him*
     (b)

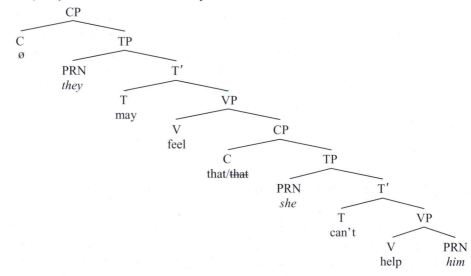

We've already seen that the relation **c-command** plays a central role in the syntax of a wide range of phenomena, including the binding of anaphors, morphological operations like Affix Hopping, phonological operations like *have*-cliticisation, and so on. It therefore seems plausible to hypothesise that c-command is also central to case assignment. Reasoning along these lines, let's suppose that case assignment is subject to the following condition:

(52)   **Case Condition**
         A pronoun or noun expression is assigned case by the closest
         case-assigning head which c-commands it

The requirement that a (pro)noun expression be assigned case by the *closest* case assigner c-commanding it is arguably a consequence of the Locality Principle which we posited in §1.5. Let's look at what (52) implies for the case-marking of the italicised pronouns in (51b).

Given the traditional assumption that transitive verbs like *help* are accusative case assigners, it follows that the closest case assigner c-commanding the pronoun *him* will be the transitive verb *help*, and that this will assign accusative case to *him* in accordance with (52). If we suppose that finite complementisers are nominative case assigners in English, we can also account for why *she* and *they* are assigned nominative case in (51b). The closest case assigner c-commanding *she* in (51b) is the finite complementiser *that/that*, and this therefore assigns nominative case to the pronoun *she* in conformity with (52). Similarly, the closest case assigner c-commanding the pronoun *they* in (51b) is the null complementiser introducing the main clause, and this assigns nominative case to *they* in accordance with (52). Note that a consequence of the c-command analysis of case-marking outlined in (52) is that we need to assume that seemingly complementiserless finite clauses contain a null complementiser in order to account for how the subjects of such clauses come to be assigned nominative case.

The conclusion that our discussion in this section leads us to is that all finite clauses have the status of CPs introduced by a complementiser. Finite complement clauses are CPs headed either by an overt complementiser like *that* or *if* or by a null complementiser (e.g. a null variant of *that* in the case of declarative complement clauses). Finite main clauses are likewise CPs headed by a C which contains an inverted auxiliary if the clause is interrogative, and an inherently null complementiser otherwise. A finite C constituent (whether overt or null) assigns nominative case to the subject of its clause under c-command.

3.7   Null C in infinitive clauses

The overall conclusion to be drawn from our discussion in §3.6 is that all finite clauses (whether main clauses or complement clauses) are CPs headed by an (overt or null) complementiser which marks the force of the clause and case-marks its subject. But what about nonfinite clauses? It seems clear that a *for-to* infinitive clause such as that bracketed in (53a) below is a CP with the structure shown in (53b) since it is introduced by the infinitival complementiser *for*:

(53) (a)   I will arrange [*for* him to see a specialist]

(b)

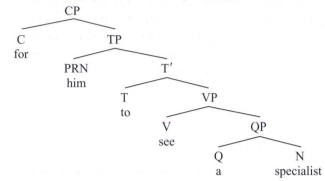

If we assume that the complementiser *for* (like the preposition *for*) is an accusative case assigner, it will then follow that the infinitive subject *him* will be assigned accusative case by the complementiser *for*, since *for* is the closest case assigner c-commanding *him*.

But what is the status of the type of (bracketed) infinitive complement clause found after verbs like *want* in sentences such as (54) below?

(54)   She wanted [*him* to apologise]

At first sight, it might seem as if the bracketed complement clause in a sentence like (54) can't be a CP, since it isn't introduced by the infinitival complementiser *for*. However, the type of infinitive complement bracketed in (54) can be co-ordinated with a CP introduced by *for* in sentences such as the following – as noted by Sawada (1995, p. 406, fn. 5) and Nomura (2006, p. 78):

(55)   I want [Mary to come to Japan] and [for her to see my parents]

This suggests that the infinitive complement of *want* is always a CP, and that the head C of the relevant CP sometimes has an overt spellout as *for* and sometimes has a null spellout. This in turn would mean that the complement of *want* in structures like (54) is a CP headed by a variant of *for* which ultimately receives a null spellout in the PF component (below symbolised as *f̶o̶r̶*), so that (54) has the skeletal structure (56) below (simplified by showing only those parts of the structure directly relevant to the discussion at hand):

(56)   She wanted [CP [C *f̶o̶r̶*] [TP him [T to] apologise]]

We can then say that the infinitive subject *him* is assigned accusative case by the complementiser *f̶o̶r̶* in structures like (56) in exactly the same way as the accusative subject *him* is assigned accusative case by the complementiser *for* in the complement clause in (53). One way of accounting for why the complementiser isn't overtly spelled out as *for* in structures like (56) is to suppose that it is given a null spellout (and thereby has its phonetic features deleted) when introducing the complement of a verb like *want*: we can accordingly refer to verbs like *want* as *for*-deletion verbs.

For speakers of varieties of English like my own (British) variety, *for*-deletion with verbs like *want* is obligatory when the *for*-clause immediately follows a verb like *want*, but cannot apply when the *for*-clause is separated from *want* in some way – e.g. when the two are separated by an intervening adverbial expression such as *more than anything*, as the examples below illustrate:

(57) (a)   *More than anything, she **wanted** *for him to apologise*
     (b)   More than anything, she **wanted** *him to apologise*
     (c)   She **wanted** more than anything *for him to apologise*
     (d)   *She **wanted** more than anything *him to apologise*

Likewise, when the complement of *want* is in **focus position** in a **pseudo-cleft sentence** as in (58) below, it is obligatory for the complementiser to have an overt spellout as *for* (because it does not immediately follow the verb *want*, but rather follows the copula *was*):

(58) (a)   What she **wanted** was *for him to apologise*
     (b)   *What she **wanted** was *him to apologise*

(Pseudo-cleft structures are sentences such as 'What John bought was *a car*', where the italicised expression is said to be **focused** and to occupy **focus** position within the sentence.)

Interestingly, not all *for*-deletion verbs behave exactly like *want*: for example, in my own (British) variety of English the verb *prefer* optionally (rather than obligatorily) allows deletion of *for* when it immediately follows *prefer* – cf.:

(59) (a)   We would very much **prefer** *for you to be there*
     (b)   We would very much **prefer** *you to be there*

The precise set of verbs which optionally allow (or obligatorily require) deletion of *for* when it immediately follows the verb seems to vary from one variety to another, and even from one speaker to another.

Having looked at *for*-deletion verbs which select an infinitival complement with an accusative subject, we now turn to look at **control** infinitive clauses with a null PRO subject like that bracketed in (60) below:

(60)   I will arrange [PRO to see a specialist]

What we shall argue here is that control clauses which have a null PRO subject are introduced by a null infinitival complementiser. However, the null complementiser introducing control clauses differs from the null complementiser found in structures like *want/prefer someone to do something* in that it never surfaces as an overt form like *for*, and hence is inherently null. There is, however, parallelism between the structure of a *for*-infinitive clause like that bracketed in (53a) above, and that of a control infinitive clause like that bracketed in (60), in that they are both CPs and they have a parallel internal structure, as shown in (61a,b) below (simplified by not showing the internal structure of the Verb Phrase *see a specialist*):

(61)

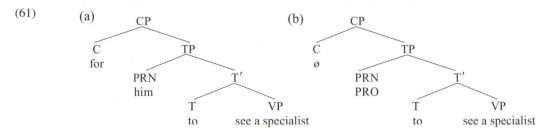

The two types of clause thus have essentially the same CP+TP+VP structure, and differ only in that a *for*-infinitive clause like (61a) has an overt *for* complementiser and an overt accusative subject like *him*, whereas a control infinitive clause like (61b) has a null ø complementiser and a null PRO subject.

Some evidence in support of claiming that a control clause with a null PRO subject is introduced by a null complementiser comes from co-ordination data in relation to sentences such as the following:

(62)   I will arrange [*to see a specialist*] and [**for my wife to see one at the same time**]

The fact that the italicised control infinitive can be conjoined with the bold-printed CP headed by *for* suggests that control infinitives must be CPs (if only the same types of constituent can be conjoined).

Further evidence in support of the CP status of control infinitives comes from the fact that they can be focused in **pseudo-cleft sentences**. In this connection, consider the contrast below:

(63) (a)   What I'll try and arrange is [*for you to see a specialist*]
     (b)   *What I'll try and arrange for is [*you to see a specialist*]
     (c)   What I'll try and arrange is [*PRO to see a specialist*]

The grammaticality of (63a) suggests that a CP like *for you to see a specialist* can occupy focus position in a pseudo-cleft sentence, whereas conversely the ungrammaticality of (63b) suggests that a TP like *you to see a specialist* cannot. If CP can be focused in pseudo-clefts but TP cannot, then the fact that a control infinitive like *PRO to see a specialist* can be focused in a pseudo-cleft like (63c) suggests that it must have the same CP status as (63a) – precisely as the analysis in (61b) above claims.

An interesting issue which arises in relation to control infinitives concerns the morphological properties of the null PRO subject which they contain. It is clear from a structure like:

(64)   Mary promised [cp [c ø] [tp PRO [t to] take care of herself]]

that PRO must carry the same person, number and gender properties as other pronouns (in that PRO must be third person feminine singular in order to be able to serve as the antecedent of *herself*). It is therefore plausible to suppose that PRO carries the same morphological properties as overt personal pronouns like *she*. But if this is so, then PRO must also carry case of some kind. But what case? The morphological effect of case is to determine how a noun or pronoun expression is spelled out (e.g. as *he*, *him* or *his*). Since PRO has a null spellout, we can therefore suppose that PRO carries *null case*. The effect of null case is to ensure that a pronoun is unpronounced – just as the morphological effect of nominative case is to ensure that (e.g.) a third person masculine singular pronoun is pronounced as *he*. Given the assumption we have made in this section and the last that the subject of a CP clause is case-marked by the head C of CP, it follows that PRO must be assigned null case by the inherently null complementiser introducing a control clause. This means that an (overt or null) finite complementiser in English is a nominative case assigner, that the infinitival complementiser *for* (and its null counterpart *f͟o͟r͟*) is an accusative case assigner, and that the inherently null infinitival complementiser ∅ introducing a control clause is a null case assigner.

Overall, the conclusion which our analysis in this section leads us to is that infinitive complements containing the complementiser *for* (or its null counterpart *f͟o͟r͟*) are CPs, and so are control infinitives (which contain a null complementiser ∅ as well as a null *PRO* subject). In each case, the subject of the infinitive is case-marked by the head C of CP, with *for/f͟o͟r͟* assigning accusative case to the subject, and the null complementiser ∅ in control clauses assigning null case to its PRO subject.

3.8   Defective clauses

In §3.6, we argued that all finite clauses are CPs, and in §3.7 we went on to argue that *for*-infinitives with accusative subjects and control infinitives with null PRO subjects are likewise CPs. These two assumptions lead us to the more general conclusion that:

(65)   All complete clauses are CPs

And indeed this is an assumption widely held in recent work. However, there is one particular type of clause which is exceptional (and incomplete) in that it lacks the CP layer found in complete clauses – namely infinitival complement clauses like those bracketed in (66) below which have (italicised) accusative subjects:

(66) (a)   They believe [*him* to be innocent]
    (b)   We didn't intend [*you* to hurt anyone]

Complement clauses like those bracketed in (66) are exceptional in that their subjects are assigned accusative case by the transitive verb (*believe/intend*) immediately preceding them: what's exceptional about this is that the verb is in a different clause from the subject which it assigns accusative case to. For this reason, such clauses are known as **exceptional case-marking clauses** (or **ECM clauses**); and verbs (like *believe*) when used with an ECM clause as their complement are known as **ECM verbs**.

ECM complement clauses seem to be TPs which lack the CP layer found in complete clauses, and for this reason they can be considered **defective clauses**. One reason for thinking that the bracketed ECM clauses in sentences like (66) are not complete CPs is that they cannot readily be co-ordinated with *for*-infinitives, as we see from the ungrammaticality of (67) below:

(67)   *We didn't intend [*you to hurt him*] or [**for him to hurt you**]

Although (for speakers like me) the verb *intend* can take either a bare ECM infinitive complement or a *for*-infinitive complement, the fact that the two cannot be conjoined suggests that the bare ECM infinitive clauses have the status of TPs while *for-to* infinitive clauses have the status of CPs. (Speakers who, unlike me, accept sentences like (67), seem to have the additional possibility of using *intend* as a verb taking an infinitival CP complement headed by the null complementiser *for*.) By contrast, co-ordination is indeed possible in sentences like:

(68)   We didn't intend [*you to hurt him*] or [**him to hurt you**]

and this is because both bracketed clauses in (68) are infinitival TPs.

Further evidence that ECM infinitive clauses like those bracketed in (66) are TPs rather than CPs comes from the fact that they cannot occur in focus position in pseudo-clefts, as we see from the ungrammaticality of the sentences below:

(69) (a)   *What they believe is [*him to be innocent*]
     (b)   *What we hadn't intended was [*you to hurt anyone*]

If ECM clauses are TPs, this follows from the restriction noted in (63) that only a CP (not a TP) can occur in focus position in a pseudo-cleft sentence. Moreover, a further property of sentences like (66), which would be difficult to account for if the bracketed complement clause were a CP, is the fact that its (italicised) subject can be **passivised** and thereby made into the subject of the main clause, as in (70) below:

(70) (a)   *He* is believed to be innocent
     (b)   *You* weren't intended to hurt anyone

This is because it is a property of the subject of an infinitival CP complement clause like that bracketed in (71a) below that its subject cannot be passivised – as we see from the ungrammaticality of (71b):

(71) (a)   We didn't intend [for *you* to hurt anyone]
     (b)   **You* weren't intended [for to hurt anyone]

Why should the subject of a CP be unable to passivise? The answer lies in a constraint which we will return to look at in greater detail in chapter 9 (where we will see that it subsumes the Functional Head Constraint discussed in §2.5), but which we can formulate for the time being as follows:

(72)   **Impenetrability Condition**
A constituent in the domain of (i.e. c-commanded by) a complementiser is impenetrable to (and so cannot be attracted by) a higher head c-commanding the complementiser

Anticipating the analysis of passivisation to be presented in chapter 6, let's suppose that what happens in a passive structure like (71b) is that the main-clause T constituent *weren't* **attracts** the pronoun *you* to move out of its original position (as the subject of the infinitival T constituent *to*) into a new position where it becomes the subject of *weren't* – as shown by the arrow below:

(73)   [CP [C ø] [TP *You* [T weren't] intended [CP [C **for**] [TP ~~you~~ [T to] hurt anyone]]]]

Because the pronoun *you* originates within the domain of the complementiser *for* (i.e. in a position where it is c-commanded by *for*), and the T-auxiliary *weren't* c-commands the complementiser *for*, it follows from the Impenetrability Condition (72) that *you* is impenetrable to the T-auxiliary *weren't* and so *you* cannot become the subject of *weren't* via passivisation. For analogous reasons, the subject of the infinitival CP complement of a *for*-deletion verb like *want* cannot be passivised either: cf.

(74)   (a)   She wanted [~~for~~ *John* to apologise]
        (b)   *John* was wanted [~~for~~ to apologise]

and indeed this is precisely what we expect if the Impenetrability Condition prevents the subjects of CPs from passivising, and if the bracketed complement clauses in (74) are CPs headed by a null counterpart of *for*, as claimed in §3.7. However, the fact that the passive sentences in (70) are grammatical suggests that the bracketed complement clauses in (66) are TPs rather than CPs (since the Impenetrability Condition allows the subject of an infinitival TP to be passivised, but not the subject of an infinitival CP). Hence, complement clauses like those bracketed in (66) above are defective clauses which have no CP layer, and (66a) *They believe him to be innocent* accordingly has the structure (75) below (with *Af* representing a present tense affix):

(75)

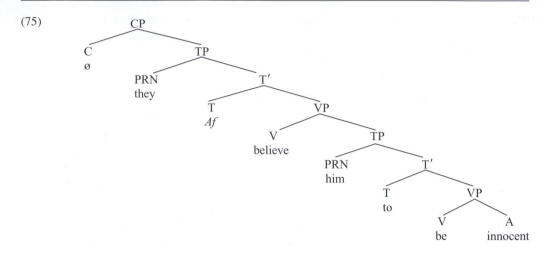

The particular aspect of the analysis in (75) most relevant to our discussion in this section is the claim that the complement clause *him to be innocent* is an infinitival TP headed by *to*, and its subject *him* is assigned accusative case by the closest case assigner c-commanding it (namely the transitive verb *believe*), in accordance with the Case Condition (52) above.

3.9   Null determiners and quantifiers

Thus far, we have argued that empty categories play an important role in the syntax of clauses in that clauses may contain a null subject, a null T constituent and a null C constituent. We now turn to argue that the same is true of the syntax of **nominals** (i.e. noun expressions), and that **bare nominals** (i.e. noun expressions which contain no overt determiner or quantifier) are generally headed by a null determiner or null quantifier.

In this connection, consider the syntax of the italicised bare nominals in (76) below:

(76)   *John* admires *Mary*

As we see from (77a) below, the Greek counterparts of the bare nouns in (76) are DPs headed by a definite determiner:

(77)   O Gianis thavmazi tin Maria
         The John admires the Mary
         'John admires Mary'

This raises the possibility that bare nouns like those italicised in (76) above are DPs headed by a null definite determiner, so that the overall sentence in (76) has the structure (78) below:

(78)

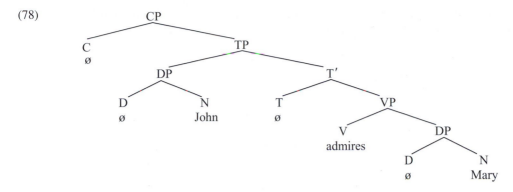

The assumption that all definite noun expressions are DPs (including those not containing an overt determiner) is known as the **DP hypothesis**. A DP analysis of bare definite noun expressions is plausible from a semantic perspective in that a name like *John* is a referring expression which denotes a specific/definite individual in precisely the same way as a DP such as *this/that/the boy* does.

One piece of empirical evidence in support of analysing bare nouns as DPs comes from sentences like:

(79)   *John* and [**the chairman**] are attending a meeting

The fact that a bare noun like *John* can be co-ordinated with a determiner phrase/DP like *the chairman* provides us with empirical evidence that bare nouns must be DPs, given the assumption that expressions can only be co-ordinated if they belong to the same category.

If (as we are suggesting here) English has a null D constituent, we should expect this not only to have identifiable semantic properties (viz. in marking definiteness/specificity) but also to have identifiable grammatical properties. And indeed there is evidence that (like definite determiners such as *this/these*) the null D constituent carries person properties. In this respect, consider sentences such as:

(80) (a)   We linguists take **ourselves/*yourselves/*themselves** too seriously, don't
           *we/*you/*they*?

    (b)   You linguists take **yourselves/*ourselves/*themselves** too seriously, don't
           *you/*we/*they*?

    (c)   John takes **himself/*ourselves/*yourselves** too seriously, doesn't *he/*don't
           we/*don't you*?

(80a) shows that a first person expression such as *we linguists* can only bind (i.e. serve as the antecedent of) a first person reflexive like *ourselves*, and can only be tagged by a first person pronoun like *we*. (80b) shows that a second person expression like *you linguists* can only bind a second person reflexive like *yourselves*, and can only be tagged by a second person pronoun like *you*. (80c) shows that a bare noun like *John* can only bind a third person reflexive like *himself* and can only be tagged by a third person pronoun like *he*. One way to account for the relevant facts is to suppose that the nominals *we linguists/you linguists/John* in (80a,b,c) are DPs with the respective structures shown in (81a,b,c) below:

(81)

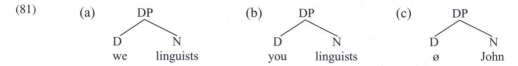

(a) DP — D *we*, N linguists
(b) DP — D *you*, N linguists
(c) DP — D ø, N John

and that the person properties of a DP are determined by the person features carried by its head determiner. If *we* is a first person determiner, *you* is a second person determiner and ø is a third person determiner, the grammaticality judgments in (80a,b,c) above are precisely as the analysis in (81a,b,c) would lead us to expect. More generally, we can conclude that all definite referring expressions are D-expressions: thus, an expression such as *the chairman* is a DP headed by the overt determiner *the*; a name/proper noun such as *John* is a DP headed by a null determiner; and a definite pronoun such as *he* is a pronominal D constituent (or a D-pronoun).

In addition to having a null definite determiner, English can also be argued to have a null (indefinite) quantifier. In this connection, consider the following sentences:

(82) (a)   *Eggs* and <u>many dairy products</u> cause cholesterol
     (b)   I'd like *toast* and <u>some coffee</u> please

The fact that the bare plural noun *eggs* is co-ordinated with the QP/quantifier phrase *many dairy products* in (82a) suggests that *eggs* is a QP headed by a null quantifier. Likewise, the fact that the bare singular noun *toast* is co-ordinated with the QP *some coffee* in (82b) suggests that *toast* is also a QP headed by a null quantifier, so that the italicised nouns in (82) have the structure shown below:

(83)

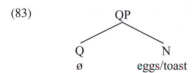

QP — Q ø, N eggs/toast

The null quantifier has the semantic property of being generic or partitive in interpretation: thus, *eggs* in (82a) has a generic interpretation which can be paraphrased as 'eggs in general', while *toast* in (82b) has a partitive interpretation paraphraseable as 'some toast'.

In addition to having its own semantic properties, the null quantifier found in 'bare' indefinite noun expressions in English has its own *selectional* properties – as illustrated by the following examples:

(84) (a)   I wrote *poems*
     (b)   I wrote *poetry*
     (c)   *I wrote *poem*

If each of the italicised bare nouns in (84) is the complement of a null quantifier ∅, the relevant examples show that ∅ can select as its complement an expression headed by a plural count noun like *poems*, or by a singular mass noun like *poetry* – but not by a singular count noun like *poem*. The complement-selection properties of the null quantifier ∅ mirror those of the overt quantifier *enough*: cf.

(85) (a)   I've read **enough** *poetry*
      (b)   I've read **enough** *poems*
      (c)   *I've read **enough** *poem*

The fact that ∅ has the same selectional properties as a typical overt quantifier such as *enough* strengthens the case for positing the existence of a null quantifier ∅, and for analysing bare indefinite noun expressions as QPs headed by a null quantifier.

We have argued that bare definite noun expressions (like *John*) are DPs headed by a null determiner which is definite in interpretation, and that bare indefinite noun expressions (like *toast* or *eggs*) are QPs headed by a null quantifier which is generic or partitive in interpretation. The claim that null determiners and quantifiers have specific semantic properties is an important one from a theoretical perspective in the light of the principle suggested in Chomsky (1995) that all heads must be **interpretable** at the **semantics interface** (i.e. must be able to be assigned a semantic interpretation by the semantic component of the grammar, and hence must contribute something to the meaning of the sentence containing them). This principle holds of null constituents as well as overt constituents, so that e.g. a null T constituent contains an abstract affix carrying an interpretable tense feature, and a null C constituent contains an abstract morpheme carrying an interpretable force feature. If the null D constituent found in a structure like (81c) is definite in interpretation and the null Q found in a structure like (83) is generic or partitive in interpretation, the requirement for heads to have identifiable semantic properties will be met.

The overall conclusion to be drawn from this section is that definite expressions (like *the president* and *John*) are DPs headed by an overt or null determiner, whereas indefinite expressions (like *an apple* or *cheese*) are QPs headed by an overt or null quantifier.

3.10   Summary

In this chapter, we have seen that null constituents (i.e. constituents which have no overt phonetic form but have specific grammatical and semantic properties) play a central role in syntax. We began by looking at null (finite, imperative, truncated and nonfinite) subjects in §3.2, arguing in particular that control infinitive clauses have a null PRO subject which can refer to some expression within a higher clause, or refer to some entity in the domain of discourse, or have arbitrary reference. In §3.3 we showed that elliptical clauses like that bracketed in *He could have helped her or* [*she have helped him*] are TPs headed by a null (ellipsed) tense auxiliary. In §3.4 we extended this **null T** analysis to auxiliariless finite clauses like *He enjoys syntax*, arguing that they contain a TP headed by an abstract tense affix which is lowered onto the main verb by the morphological operation of *Affix Hopping* in the PF component. In §3.5 we argued that bare (*to*-less) infinitive clauses like that bracketed in *I can't let* [*you have my password*] are TPs headed by a null variant of infinitival *to*. We concluded that all finite and infinitive clauses contain a TP headed by an overt or null T constituent carrying finite or nonfinite tense. In §3.6, we argued that all finite clauses are CPs, and that those which are not introduced by an overt complementiser are CPs headed by a null complementiser which encodes the force of the clause and assigns nominative case to its subject (so that a sentence like *He enjoys syntax* is declarative in force by virtue of being a CP headed by a null declarative C which is finite and so assigns nominative case to the subject *he*). In §3.7 we saw that *for*-infinitives are also CPs, and that the subject of the infinitive is assigned accusative case by the complementiser *for*. We went on to argue that the complement of *want*-class verbs in structures like *We want him to stay* is a CP headed by a null counterpart of *for* which assigns accusative case to the subject. We also argued that the infinitive complement of a control verb like *promise* in *He promised to stay* is a CP headed by an inherently null complementiser which assigns null case to the PRO subject of the infinitive. In §3.9 we argued that ECM (Exceptional Case Marking) clauses with accusative subjects like that bracketed in *I believe* [*him to be innocent*] are defective clauses which have the status of TPs rather than CPs, and that the subject of the infinitive clause is assigned accusative case by the verb in the matrix/containing clause (*believe* in this case). In §3.9, we looked briefly at the syntax of nominals (i.e. noun expressions), maintaining that bare definite nominals are DPs headed by a null determiner, and bare indefinite nominals are QPs headed by a null quantifier; consequently, in a sentence such as *John wanted eggs for breakfast*, the bare noun *John* is a DP headed by a null definite determiner, whereas the bare noun *eggs* is a QP headed by a null indefinite quantifier.

Key assumptions made in this chapter are recapitulated below:

(19)   **Have-cliticisation**
         Have can encliticise onto a W ending in a vowel or diphthong provided
         that
   (i)   W c-commands *have* and
   (ii)   W immediately adjacent *to have*

(26)   **Affix Hopping**
         When some constituent C contains an unattached affix *Af*, in the PF
         component *Af* is lowered onto the head H of the complement of C (provided
         H is an appropriate **host** for the affix to attach to)

(52)   **Case Condition**
         A pronoun or noun expression is assigned case by the closest
         case-assigning head which c-commands it

(Recall in relation to 52 that we argued that a finite complementiser in English assigns nominative case, the infinitival complementisers *for/~~for~~* assign accusative case and the inherently null complementiser ∅ introducing a control clause assigns null case)

(72)   **Impenetrability Condition**
         A constituent in the domain of (i.e. c-commanded by) a complementiser is
         impenetrable to (and so cannot be attracted by) a higher head
         c-commanding the complementiser

3.11 Bibliographical background

For a range of accounts of the null *pro* subjects discussed in §3.2, see Chomsky (1981), Rizzi (1982, 1986, 1997), Jaeggli (1982, 1984), Huang (1984), Montalbetti (1984), Safir (1984), Suñer (1984), Hyams (1986), Jaeggli and Safir (1989), Roberts (1993), Barbosa (1995, 2000, 2007), Barbosa, Duarte and Kato (2005), Kato (1999, 2000), Alexiadou and Anagnostopoulou (1998), Holmberg (2005), Neeleman and Szendrői (2005) and Tamburelli (2006, 2007). On truncated null subjects in English, see Haegeman (1990) and Rizzi (2000). On imperatives in English, see Potsdam (1998) and Rupp (2003). The idea that control infinitives have a null PRO subject dates back to Chomsky (1977): for more recent discussion of control infinitives, see Landau (1999, 2001, 2003, 2004, 2006a). Although the discussion in §3.2 focuses on null subjects, it should be noted that many languages (though not English) productively allow null *objects* (see Rizzi 1986; Raposo 1986; Authier 1989; Farrell 1990; Huang 1991; Groefsema 1995; Cummins and Roberge 2004, 2005). The idea in §3.3 that null constituents can arise via gapping and other forms of ellipsis has a long history, dating back to Hankamer (1971), Hankamer and Sag (1976), Sag (1980), Kuno (1981), Pesetsky (1982), Hardt (1993), McCawley (1993), Lobeck (1995), Schwarz (1999, 2000), Johnson (2000), Merchant (2001, 2005), Coppock (2002), Kennedy (2002, 2003), Carlson, Dickey and Kennedy (2005) and Frazier and Clifton (2005). The *Affix Hopping* account of verb morphology outlined in §3.4 dates back in spirit to Chomsky (1955, 1957). For alternative analyses of the type of infinitive clause structures discussed in §3.5, see Felser (1999a,b) and Basilico (2003). On the historical development of *to*-infinitives, see Los (2005). The claim in §3.6 that apparently complementiserless clauses contain a null complementiser dates back in spirit more than four decades (see e.g. Stockwell, Schachter and Partee 1973, p. 599): for evidence of null complementisers in Japanese, see Kishimoto (2006). For discussion of factors governing the null spellout of *that*, see Ormazabal (1995), Hawkins (2001), Bošković and Lasnik (2003), Epstein, Pires and Seely (2005) and Nomura (2006). The Categorial Uniformity Principle was devised by

Rizzi (2000, p. 288). The idea in §3.7 that (non-defective) infinitive clauses are introduced by an (overt or null) complementiser dates back to Bresnan (1970). The idea in §3.8 that ECM clauses are *defective* in respect of lacking the CP layer found in full clauses is defended in Chomsky (1999). The *Impenetrability Condition* has its origins in the *Phase Impenetrability Condition* of Chomsky (1998) – but since the notion *phase* is not introduced until chapter 9, for the time being we refer to it simply as the *Impenetrability Condition*: it attempts to capture the intuition that syntactic operations are clause-bound, and so apply one clause at a time; its historical antecedents lie in the Subjacency Condition of Chomsky (1973) (amended by Rizzi 1982) and the Barrierhood Condition of Chomsky (1986b). On finite complementisers being nominative case assigners, see Chomsky (1999, p. 35, fn. 17). The idea that PRO subjects in English carry *null* case derives from work by Chomsky and Lasnik (1993), Chomsky (1995) and Martin (1996, 2001). On the claim that null case is assigned to a PRO subject by C, see Rizzi (1997, p. 304) and Collins (2005a, p. 104). For an alternative proposal that PRO carries 'real' (e.g. nominative, accusative or dative) case, see Cecchetto and Oniga (2004) and Landau (2004, 2006a). The assumption in §3.9 that bare nominals contain a null determiner/quantifier has a long history, dating back to a suggestion made by Chomsky (1965, p. 108) which was taken up and extended in later work by Abney (1987), Bernstein (1993, 2001) and Longobardi (1994, 1996, 2001). On the nature of quantified expressions, see Löbel (1989), Giusti (1991) and Shlonsky (1991). On determiners and Determiner Phrases, see Abney (1987), Bernstein (1993), Giusti (1997), Alexiadou and Wilder (1998), Zamparelli (2000), Grohmann and Haegeman (2002) and Ticio (2003, 2005).

Workbook section

Exercise 3.1

Draw tree diagrams to represent the structure of the following sentences, presenting arguments in support of your analysis and commenting on any null constituents they contain and the reasons for positing them. In addition, say how each of the noun or pronoun expressions in each of the sentences is case-marked.

1	Students enjoy the classes
2	We have fun (**w**)
3	Voters know politicians lie
4	John promised to behave himself (**w**)
5	She sees no need for anyone to apologise
6	They would prefer students to do exams
7	Economists expect salaries to rise (**w**)
8	He might like you to stay (**w**)
9	%I have known you have a tantrum
10	John wanted to help him

In addition, say why *have*-cliticisation is or is not permitted in 11b, 12b, 13b and 14ʙ below:

11 a   They have suffered hardship
  b   They've suffered hardship **(w)**

12 a   The Sioux have suffered hardship
  b   *The Sioux've suffered hardship

13 a   Sioux have suffered hardship
  b   *Sioux've suffered hardship **(w)**

14   SPEAKER A: How are students coping with your *Fantasy Syntax* course?
       SPEAKER B: *Two've given up

Helpful hints

Assume that all clauses other than nonfinite clauses used as the complement of an ECM verb are CPs, and that bare definite nominal arguments are DPs headed by a null definite D, and bare indefinite nominal arguments are QP constituents headed by a null indefinite Q. Assume the conditions on *have*-cliticisation given in (19) in the main text/summary. In relation to 3, consider what case *politicians* has, and how you can use this to determine whether the complement of *know* is a TP or a CP. In 4, use Binding Principle A from exercise 2.2 to help you account for why *himself* is coreferential to *John*. In 5, assume that *no* is a negative quantifier which has a Noun Phrase complement. Take 9 (which is found only in some varieties of English, including my own British one) to be a variant of *I have known you to have a tantrum*. In 10, use Binding Principle B from exercise 2.2 to help you account for why *him* cannot be coreferential to *John*. In relation to the (b, ʙ) examples in 11–14, draw trees to represent the structure of the sentences immediately prior to cliticisation, and then show whether or not the analysis of *have*-cliticisation given here predicts that cliticisation is possible; note that the noun *Sioux* is pronounced |suː|. Show how the ungrammaticality of 13b can be used to evaluate the hypothesis that a bare noun like *Sioux* in 13 is a QP headed by a null qualifier. In addition, say how sentences like 11b can be used to evaluate the plausibility of analyses (such as that proposed by Freidin and Vergnaud 2001) which take pronouns like *they* to be determiners which have a nominal complement whose phonetic features are given a null spellout in the PF component, so that e.g. if *they* refers to *Sioux,* the pronoun *they* would be a DP with the structure shown below:

(i)

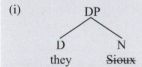

Would it be any more or less plausible to suppose that the (numeral) quantifier *two* in sentences like that produced by speaker ʙ in 14 has a null N complement (interpreted as referring to the noun *students*)?

Model answer for 1

Given the arguments in the main text that all finite clauses contain a TP headed by a T constituent containing an Affix which encodes Tense and (Person and Number) agreement features, the sentence *Students enjoy the classes* will contain a TP headed by a tense affix which carries the features [third-person, plural-number, present-tense], which we can abbreviate to Af_{3PLPR}.

Likewise, given the arguments in the main text that all finite clauses are CPs headed by an (overt or null) complementiser which marks the force of the clause, the overall sentence will be a CP headed by a null finite declarative complementiser [$_C$ ø]. In addition, the indefinite bare noun *students* will be a QP headed by a null quantifier which is generic in interpretation (and so is paraphraseable as 'students in general'). Given these assumptions, sentence 1 will have the structure shown below:

(ii)

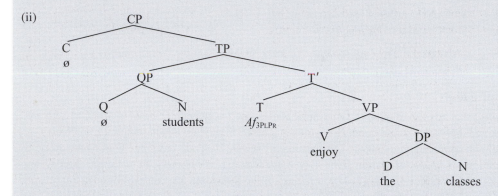

Because there is no auxiliary in T for it to attach to, the tense affix in T is lowered onto the verb *enjoy* by the morphological operation of **Affix Hopping** in the PF component, forming *enjoy*+*Af*$_{3PLPr}$ (which is ultimately spelled out as the third person plural present tense form *enjoy*).

Evidence that the overall clause *Students enjoy the classes* is a CP headed by a null complementiser comes from co-ordination facts in relation to sentences such as:

(iii)   [*Students enjoy the classes*] but [**do they like the lectures**]?

In (iii) the declarative clause *Students enjoy the classes* has been co-ordinated with the interrogative clause *do they like the lectures?* which contains the inverted auxiliary *do*. If (as claimed in the main text) inverted auxiliaries occupy the head C position of CP, it follows that the second of the two co-ordinate clauses in (iii) must be a CP; and if only constituents of the same type can be co-ordinated, it follows that the first clause must also be a CP – as in (ii) above. Evidence in support of positing a null present tense T constituent in (ii) comes from the fact that the T-bar *Af*$_{3PLPr}$ *enjoy the classes* can be co-ordinated with another T-bar like *don't like the lectures*, as we see from (iv) below:

(iv)   Students *enjoy the classes*, but *don't like the lectures*

Evidence that the bare nominal *students* is a QP headed by a null quantifier comes from the fact that it can be co-ordinated with a QP such as *many teachers*, as in:

(v)   *Students* and <u>many teachers</u> enjoy the classes

The DP *the classes* in (i) is assigned accusative case by virtue of being c-commanded by the transitive verb *enjoy*. Accordingly, the DP *the classes* can be substituted by an accusative pronoun, as in:

(vi)   Students enjoy *them*

By contrast, the QP *ø students* is assigned nominative case by virtue of being c-commanded by the finite complementiser *ø*. We therefore correctly predict that this QP can be substituted by a nominative pronoun, as in:

(vii)   *They* enjoy the classes

Additional helpful hints for sentences 2–10

Discuss whether/how your analysis can account for the (un)grammaticality of the sentences below (the relevant grammaticality judgments holding for my own variety of British English).

2a	We have fun and some pain
2b	*We've fun
2c	We have fun and are enjoying syntax
2d	We have fun but will it last?
3a	Voters and most journalists know politicians lie
3b	Voters know politicians and many celebrities lie
3c	Voters know politicians lie and can't be trusted
3d	Voters know politicians lie and don't trust them
3e	Voters know politicians lie and that they do so knowingly
3f	Voters know politicians lie, but do they care?
4a	John promised to behave himself, but will he do so?
4b	John and the vicar promised to behave themselves
4c	John promised to behave himself and has done so
4d	What John promised was to behave himself
4e	John promised to behave himself (How come *himself* refers to *John*?)
5a	She sees no need for him to apologise, but does she think he will?
5b	She sees no need for him to apologise, and would not want him to
6a	They would prefer very much for students to do exams
6b	They would prefer students to do exams and for their papers to remain confidential
6c	What they would very much prefer is for students to do exams
6d	*Students would be preferred to do exams
7a	Salaries are expected to rise
7b	*They expect salaries to rise and for inflation to fall
7c	They expect salaries to rise and inflation to fall
7d	*They expect fully for salaries to rise (cf. They fully expect salaries to rise)
8a	He might like more than anything for you to stay
8b	He might like you to stay and for things to be settled between you
8c	What he might like is for you to stay
8d	*You might be liked to stay
9a	I have known you to have a tantrum (on occasions)
9b	*I've known you've a tantrum (on occasions)
9c	I've never know you have a tantrum or your brother to have one either
9d	You have been known to have a tantrum (cf. *You have been known have a tantrum)
9e	*I've known you have a tantrum and for other people to get upset about it
9f	*I've known occasionally for you to have a tantrum (OK = I've occasionally known you have a tantrum)
10a	What John wanted was to help him

10b   John wanted to help him (Why can't *him* refer to *John*?)

10c   John wanted very much to help him

Exercise 3.2

Account for the (un)grammaticality of the bracketed infinitive complement clause structures in the following sentences in standard varieties of English:

1 a   They were *planning* [to escape]

  b   *They were *planning* [him to escape]

2 a   We *consider* [him to be unsuitable]

  b   *It is *considered* [him to be unsuitable]

3 a   He would *like* [me to leave]

  b   He would *like* [to leave]

4 a   She seems *keen* [for them to participate]

  b   *She seems *keen* [for to participate]

5 a   I received a *request* [to resign]

  b   *I received a *request* [him to resign]

6 a   It was *agreed* [to review the policy]

  b   *It was *agreed* [us to review the policy]

7 a   Congress *decided* [to ratify the treaty]

  b   *Congress *decided* [for him to ratify the treaty]

8 a   She *expected* [to win the nomination]

  b   She *expected* [him/*he to win the nomination]

9 a   He should *let* [you have a break]

  b   *He should *let* [have a break]

10 a   *He *said* [her to like oysters]

  b   *He *said* [to like oysters]

In addition, say how you would analyse structures like 4b in varieties of English (like Belfast English) in which they are grammatical and have a meaning roughly paraphraseable as 'She seems keen for herself to participate.' What if *for-to* can serve as a compound T constituent in such sentences in the relevant varieties (and likewise in sentences such as *I wanted Jimmy for to come with me*; from Henry 1995, p. 85)?

Helpful hints

Note that 1b is intended to have an interpretation paraphraseable as 'They were planning for him to escape,' 9b to have an interpretation paraphraseable as 'He should let himself have a break,' 10a to have an interpretation paraphraseable as 'He said she liked oysters,' and 10b to have an interpretation paraphrasable as 'He said he liked oysters' (where the two occurrences of *he* refer to the same individual). Assume that each of the italicised words in the above examples has its own idiosyncratic selectional properties, and that the selectional properties of any word W are described by saying: 'W selects as its complement an expression headed by . . .' (where in place of the dots you insert the features characterising the relevant head). So, you might say e.g. that a verb like *arrange* can select a complement headed by an infinitival complementiser (either the transitive infinitival complementiser *for* or the null intransitive infinitival complementiser *ø*), whereas an ECM verb like *believe* selects a complement headed by the infinitival T *to*. By contrast, other verbs (it might turn out) don't select a particular kind of infinitive complement – or indeed *any* kind of infinitive complement. Assume that the seemingly subjectless clauses in 1–10 (whether grammatical or not) have a null PRO subject. Pay attention (i) to the selectional properties of the italicised words and (ii) to the case properties of the subjects of the bracketed complement clauses. In the case of the ungrammatical examples, consider whether the ungrammaticality is attributable to a *selectional error* (in that the italicised word is used with a kind of complement which it does not select/allow) or a *case error* (in that the subject of the bracketed complement clause has a case which it cannot be assigned in accordance with the assumptions about case-marking made in the main text) – or both.

Model answer for (1)

Given the CP analysis of finite clauses and control clauses in the text, 1a will have the structure (i) below:

(i)

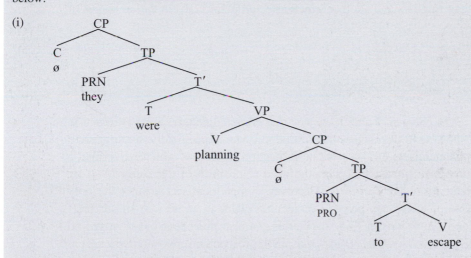

The inherently null complementiser introducing the infinitival control clause assigns null case to the PRO subject which it c-commands. Support for the CP analysis of the bracketed complement clause *to escape* in 1a comes from the fact that (like other CPs, but unlike TPs) it can serve as the focused constituent in pseudo-cleft sentences like:

(ii)   What they were planning was *to escape*

The fact that it is also possible to say:

(iii)   They were planning *for him to escape*

suggests that *plan* can also select a complement headed by the transitive infinitival complementiser *for*. This leads to the greater generalisation that *plan* can select a CP complement headed by an infinitival complementiser (either the accusative-case-assigning complementiser *for* or the null-case-assigning complementiser *ø*). The ungrammaticality of 1b *They were planning him to escape* could be attributable to a spellout error (if the complementiser heading the complement clause is the kind of *for* complementiser which can never be given a null spellout – unlike the *for* introducing an infinitival complement of a verb like *want*).

4 Head movement

4.1 Overview

So far, we have examined a range of syntactic structures which are derived by a series of **merger** operations. We now go on to look at structures whose derivation involves not only merger but also a specific type of movement operation called **head movement**. In this chapter, we focus on two specific types of head movement operation, one which affects auxiliaries in present-day English, and another which affected main verbs in earlier stages of English.

4.2 T-to-C movement

In chapters 2 and 3, we saw that complementisers are positioned in front of subjects in the clauses they introduce. More specifically, we suggested that complementisers head a separate projection in clauses which we termed a **complementiser phrase/CP**, with the head C position of CP being filled by a complementiser like *that/for/if*. However, complementisers are not the only kinds of word which can precede subjects in clauses. As we saw in our brief discussion of questions in §3.6, auxiliaries can also precede subjects in yes-no questions such as *Do you feel like a Coke?* In this respect, inverted auxiliaries seem to resemble complementisers – as the following (love-struck, soap-operesque) dialogue illustrates:

(1) SPEAKER A: Honey-buns, there's something I wanted to ask you
     SPEAKER B: What, sweetie-pie?
     SPEAKER A: **If you will marry me**
     SPEAKER B: (pretending not to hear): What d'you say, darlin'?
     SPEAKER A: **Will you marry me?**

What's the structure of the two bold(-printed) proposals which speaker A makes in (1)? The answer is straightforward enough in the case of *If you will marry me*: it's a clause introduced by the interrogative complementiser/C *if*, and so is a complementiser phrase/CP constituent with the structure (2) below:

(2)

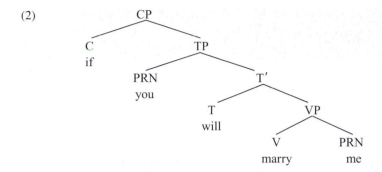

But now consider the structure of the second proposal *Will you marry me?*
What position is occupied by the inverted auxiliary *will?* Since *will* appears to
occupy the same pre-subject position that the complementiser *if* occupies in (2),
a plausible suggestion to make is that the inverted auxiliary actually occupies the
head C position of CP. If this is so, we'd expect *will* and *if* to be mutually exclusive
(on the assumption that we can only insert one word in a given head position
like C, not two words): in other words, if both complementisers and inverted
auxiliaries occupy the head C position of CP, we'd expect to find that a question
can be introduced either by a complementiser or by a preposed auxiliary – but not
by the two together. This is indeed the case, as we see from the ungrammaticality
of speaker B's reply in (3) below:

(3)   SPEAKER A: What d'you want to ask me?
        SPEAKER B: *If will* you marry me

The fact that questions can't contain both a complementiser and an inverted
auxiliary provides us with empirical evidence that inverted auxiliaries occupy the
same structural position as complementisers – i.e. that both occupy the head C
position of CP.

But how can a finite auxiliary (which normally occupies the head T position of
TP) come to be positioned in the head C position of CP? The conventional answer
is that auxiliaries in questions move out of their normal post-subject position into
pre-subject position by a movement operation which in chapter 1 we referred to
as **auxiliary inversion**. Given our assumption that an inverted auxiliary occupies
the head C position of CP, this means that the auxiliary moves from the head T
position in TP into the head C position in CP, as shown by the arrow in (4) below:

(4)

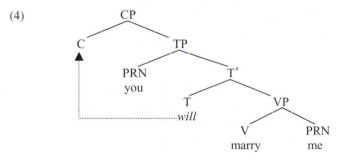

Hence, auxiliary inversion in questions involves **T-to-C movement**.

An important question which is begged by the T-to-C movement analysis in (4) is *why* auxiliaries should move from T to C in main-clause questions. Using a traditional metaphor, let us say that C is a **strong** head in interrogative main clauses in English and that a strong C position has to be filled by an overt word of some kind – either a complementiser directly merged in C, or an auxiliary which moves from T to C. In a complement-clause yes-no question like that bracketed in:

(5)   I wanted to ask [*if* you will marry me]

C is filled by the complementiser *if* – and indeed speaker A's first proposal in (1) might be regarded as an elliptical form of (5) *I wanted to ask you* [*if you will marry me*], with *if* introducing the bracketed complement clause, and constituents other than those of the bracketed clause undergoing ellipsis. However, complementisers like *if* can't be used to introduce main clauses in English, so the strong head C position is instead filled by moving an auxiliary from T to C (i.e. via auxiliary inversion).

In order to understand the mechanics of auxiliary inversion, let's look in rather more detail at the derivation of (1) *Will you marry me?* The verb *marry* merges with the pronoun *me* to form the VP *marry me*. This VP is then merged with the T-auxiliary *will* to form the T-bar *will marry me*, and this T-bar is in turn merged with the pronoun *you* to form the TP *you will marry me*. The resulting TP is then merged with a strong null interrogative complementiser ø to form the CP ø *you will marry me*. Being strong, the null complementiser **attracts** the auxiliary *will* to move from T to C to attach to the null complementiser, so filling the C position.

But what property makes the null complementiser strong enough to attract the auxiliary *will* to move from T to C? One possibility is that the null complementiser in an interrogative main clause is **affixal** in nature, and so must be attached to an overt **host** of an appropriate kind. Since affixes generally only attach to a particular kind of host (e.g. the past tense *-d* affix attaches to verbs but not to nouns, prepositions or adjectives), and since only **tensed** (i.e. present or past tense) auxiliaries move to C, one implementation of this idea is to suppose that the affix carries a tense feature – below denoted as [TNS] – which requires it to attach to a tensed host (i.e. to a present or past tense T constituent). If we suppose that the affix in C in main-clause questions is strong, and that a strong affix can attract a subordinate head to adjoin to it (but cannot itself lower onto a subordinate head), it follows that the only way for a null strong affix in C to find a host is by attracting an auxiliary in T to adjoin to the affix in C, thereby satisfying the requirement for the affix in C to be attached to a tensed host. Thus, at the stage where the null interrogative complementiser is merged with its TP complement, we have the structure (6) below (where ø is a strong affix with a TNS feature requiring it to attach to a tensed host):

(6)

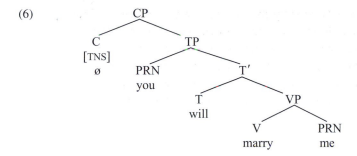

The [TNS] feature on the strong null affix in C attracts the auxiliary *will* to move from T to C (in the manner shown by the arrow below), and the [TNS] feature on C is thereby deleted (this being marked by ~~strikethrough~~) and therafter becomes inactive, so resulting in the following structure:

(7)

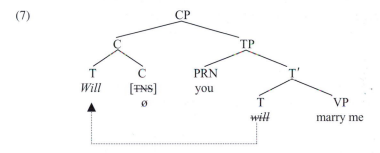

The auxiliary *will* moves from T to C in order to satisfy the requirement of the [TNS] feature on the affix for the affixal null interrogative complementiser to have a present or past tense T constituent affixed to it. This results in the formation of a complex C constituent containing the original null complementiser with the preposed T-auxiliary attached to it. The null complementiser thus behaves like an affixal question particle. Such an interrogative affix analysis is far from implausible from a cross-linguistic point of view, in that (e.g.) yes-no questions in Latin could be formed using the overt question suffix *-ne*, and this could attract a finite verb to attach to it. If we adopt the question-affix analysis, we can say that it is the strong affixal character of an interrogative C (viz. the fact that C in main-clause questions contains a strong null affixal complementiser with a tense feature requiring it to have a T host) which triggers T-to-C movement. Given that English is a largely *suffixal* language (in that it mainly utilises derivational and inflectional suffixes), we can take the null complementiser to be suffixal in nature, so that the attracted auxiliary will end up positioned to the left of it.

4.3   Movement as copying and deletion

An interesting question which arises from the T-to-C movement analysis is what it means for the auxiliary to *move out of T*. If movement of an auxiliary from T to C were to result in the head T position of TP vanishing completely, a sentence such as *Will you marry me?* would have the structure shown in simplified form below:

(8)

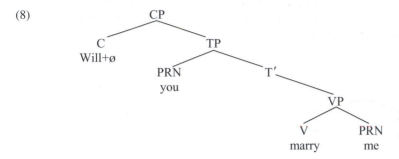

But a structure such as (7) is problematic in that it violates two constituent structure principles which we posited in §2.2, namely:

(9)   **Headedness Principle**
       Every nonterminal node in a syntactic structure is a projection of a head

(10)   **Binarity Principle**
       Every nonterminal node in a syntactic structure is binary-branching

(Note that the *Headedness Principle* has been slightly revised from its original formulation to remove reference to *head word*, in recognition of the point made in §3.4 that not all heads are words.) A tree such as (8) would violate the headedness requirement (9) in that TP and T-bar are nonterminal nodes and yet neither has a head T constituent; (8) would also violate the binarity requirement (10) in that T-bar is a nonterminal node and yet is not binary-branching (since T-bar does not have two daughters) but rather unary-branching (since T-bar has only one daughter).

   It seems clear, then, that movement of an auxiliary from T to C cannot result in the loss of the original T constituent which heads TP: so, T must remain in place in the form of a **null** constituent of some kind. But what kind of item could the relevant null T constituent contain? Our discussion of **gapping** (i.e. head ellipsis) in the previous chapter suggests a possible answer. In §3.4 we suggested that ellipsis of the second (italicised) occurrence of *could* in a sentence such as (11a) below results in a structure such as (11b) containing a null occurrence of *could* (designated as ~~*could*~~):

(11) (a)   He **could** have helped her, or she *could* have helped him
     (b)   He **could** have helped her, or she ~~*could*~~ have helped him

This raises the possibility that T-to-C movement is a composite operation by which a **copy** of an auxiliary in T is first moved into C, and then the original occurrence of the auxiliary in T is **deleted** (by which we mean that its phonetic features are given a **null spellout** and so are unpronounced), leaving a null copy of the auxiliary in T. The assumption that movement is a composite operation involving two suboperations of copying and deletion is the cornerstone of Chomsky's **copy theory of movement**.

To see how the copy theory works, let's look rather more closely at the derivation of *Will you marry me?* Let's suppose that a series of merger operations have applied to derive the structure shown below:

(12)

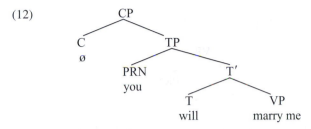

A copy of the T constituent *will* is then **adjoined** (i.e. attached) to the affixal null interrogative complementiser C ø, so forming a complex C constituent which comprises both the original C constituent containing a null complementiser and the T constituent containing *will*. Subsequent deletion of the phonetic features of the original occurrence of *will* in T derives the structure (13) below:

(13)

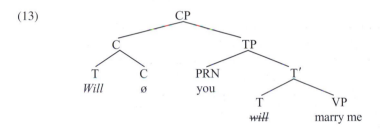

On this view, the T-auxiliary *will* is initially merged with its VP complement *marry me*, forming the T-bar *will marry me*. The resulting T-bar is merged with the pronoun *you* to form the TP *you will marry me*. This TP is then merged with a null interrogative complementiser, forming the CP *ø you will marry me*. The null complementiser (being a strong affix which needs an auxiliary host) attracts a copy of the T-auxiliary *will* to adjoin to it, forming the CP *Will+ø you will marry me*. Subsequent deletion of the phonetic features of the original occurrence of *will* in turn derives *Will+ø you will marry me*. The resulting structure (13) satisfies both the Headedness Principle (9) and the Binarity Principle (10). Considerations of computational efficiency determine that only one copy of a moved constituent is overtly spelled out (since this minimises the amount of material to be pronounced); and considerations of optimal design dictate that the highest copy is the one which is overtly spelled out, since otherwise movement would be undetectable.

An interesting source of evidence in support of the copy theory of movement comes from the study of language acquisition. Young children sometimes produce

auxiliary copying structures like the following (produced by a boy called Sam at age two years and nine months: thanks to Ian Crookston for the data):

(14) (a)   *Can* its wheels *can* spin?
      (b)   *Did* the kitchen light *did* flash?
      (c)   *Is* the steam *is* hot?
      (d)   *Was* that *was* Anna?

What is Sam doing here? The answer seems to be that he has mastered the **copying** component of auxiliary inversion and so is able to adjoin a copy of *will* to the null C constituent: but he has not yet mastered the **deletion** component of auxiliary inversion and so fails to delete the phonetic features of the original occurrence of the auxiliary in T. Accordingly, (14a) above has the simplified structure (15) below for Sam (in which the structure of the DP *its wheels* is not shown because it is irrelevant to the point at hand):

(15)

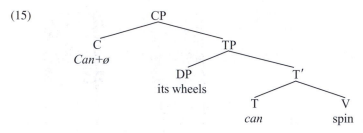

The fact that Sam has adjoined a copy of the T-auxiliary *can* to the null complementiser at the beginning of the overall sentence structure but fails to delete the original occurrence of the auxiliary in T suggests that it is plausible to analyse a movement operation like **auxiliary inversion** as a composite operation involving two separate operations of **copying** and **deletion**.

   In addition to evidence from child grammars we also have evidence from adult grammars in support of the claim that a moved auxiliary leaves behind a null copy of itself. Part of this evidence comes from the phenomenon of *have*-cliticisation which we touched on in §3.3. In this connection, note that *have* cannot cliticise onto the pronoun *I/we/you/they* in inversion structures such as:

(16) (a)   Should **they have**/**they've* called the police?
      (b)   Will **we have**/**we've* finished the rehearsal by 9pm?
      (c)   Would **you have**/**you've* come with me?
      (d)   Could **I have**/**I've* done something to help?

(*'ve* represents the vowel-less clitic form /v/ here.) The sequence *they've* in (16a) does not rhyme with *grave* in careful speech styles, since it is pronounced /ðeɪəv/ not /ðeɪv/. Likewise, the sequence *we've* in (16b) is not homophonous with *weave* in careful speech styles, since *we have* in (16a) can be reduced to /wiəv/ but not /wi:v/. Similarly, *you've* doesn't rhyme with *groove* in (16c), nor *I've* with *hive* in (16d). Why should cliticisation of *have* onto the pronoun be blocked here? We can give a straightforward answer to this question if we posit that when an inverted auxiliary moves from T to C, it leaves behind a null copy of itself in the T position out of which it moves. Given this assumption, a sentence such as (16a) will have the simplified structure shown below (if we assume that nonfinite auxiliaries occupy the head AUX/Auxiliary position of an AUXP/Auxiliary Phrase: see §4.6 for discussion of AUXP):

(17)

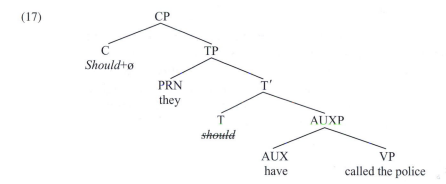

In the previous chapter, we characterised *have*-cliticisation along the following lines:

(18)   *Have* can encliticise onto a word W ending in a vowel or diphthong provided that W c-commands *have* and W is immediately adjacent to *have*

Although in (17) the pronoun *they* ends in a diphthong and c-commands *have*, the two are not immediately adjacent because the null auxiliary ~~should~~ which occupies the head T position of TP intervenes between them and hence blocks *have*-cliticisation thereby accounting for the ungrammaticality of (16a) **Should they've called the police?* Note that a crucial plank in the argumentation here is the assumption that T-to-C movement leaves behind a null copy of the moved auxiliary in the head T position of TP, and this null auxiliary serves to block cliticisation of *have* onto a c-commanding pronoun.

Our discussion of auxiliary inversion here has interesting implications for the derivation of sentences. In this connection, consider how we derive a sentence such as:

(19)   Can you swim?

The first stage is to go to the **lexicon** (= dictionary) and choose a **lexical array** (i.e. a selection of lexical items out of which the sentence is going to be built). In the case of (19), the lexical array will consist of the verb *swim*, the pronoun *you*, the auxiliary *can* and a null affixal interrogative complementiser ø. The next stage is for the auxiliary *can* and the verb *swim* to be taken out of the lexical array and merged, so deriving the T-bar *can swim*. The pronoun *you* is then taken from the lexical array, and merged with the T-bar *can swim* to form the TP *you* *can swim.* The null affixal interrogative complementiser *ø* is then taken from the lexical array and merged with the TP *you can swim* to form the CP *ø you can swim.* Since the null interrogative C is affixal and has a tense feature attracting a tensed head, it triggers movement of a copy of the present tense auxiliary *can* to adjoin to the null affix *ø*, forming *Can+ø you can swim.* Subsequent deletion of the original occurrence of *can* in T derives *Can+ø you ~~can~~ swim.*

4.4   V-to-T movement

Having looked at T-to-C movement in English, we now turn to look at a rather different kind of movement operation, which involves **V-to-T movement** – more specifically, movement of a finite main verb from the head V position of VP into the head T position of TP. We shall see that this kind of verb movement operation was productive in **Elizabethan English** (i.e. the English used during the reign of Queen Elizabeth I, when Shakespeare was writing around 400 years ago), but is no longer productive in present-day English. Since part of the evidence for V-to-T movement involves negative sentences, we begin by looking at the syntax of negation.

In Elizabethan English, clauses containing a finite auxiliary are typically negated by positioning *not* between the (italicised) auxiliary and the (bold-printed) verb: cf.

(20)(a)   She *shall* not **see** me (Falstaff, *Merry Wives of Windsor*, III.iii)
   (b)   I *will* not **think** it (Don Pedro, *Much Ado About Nothing*, III.ii)
   (c)   Thou *hast* not **left** the value of a cord (Gratiano, *Merchant of Venice*, IV.i)

Let's suppose (for the time being, pending a reanalysis of negation in §4.7) that *not* in Elizabethan English is an adverb which functions as the specifier of the verbal expression following it (e.g. *not* is the specifier of *see me* in (20a) above, and hence modifies *see me*). If so, (20a) will have a structure along the lines of (21) below (where *ø* is a null complementiser marking the declarative force of the sentence, and assigning nominative case to the subject *she*):

(21)

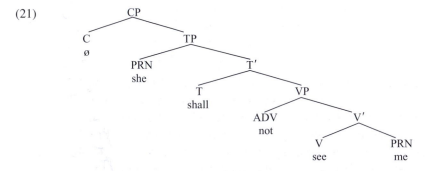

An analysis such as (21) accounts for the position which *not* occupies in front of the verb *see*.

In negative questions, the auxiliary moves from T to C (as in present-day English), leaving *not* in front of the verb: cf.

(22) (a)   **Have** I *not* heard the sea rage like an angry boar? (Petruchio, *Taming of the Shrew*, I.ii)

(b)   **Didst** thou *not* hear somebody? (Borachio, *Much Ado About Nothing*, III.iii)

(c)   **Will** you *not* dance? (King, *Love's Labour's Lost*, V.ii)

If questions involve movement of a finite auxiliary from T to C, then a sentence such as (22a) will involve the T-to-C movement operation shown in (23) below (where we take the string *the sea rage like an angry boar* to be a TP headed by a null counterpart of the infinitival T-constituent *to*, symbolised as *t̵o̵*):

(23)

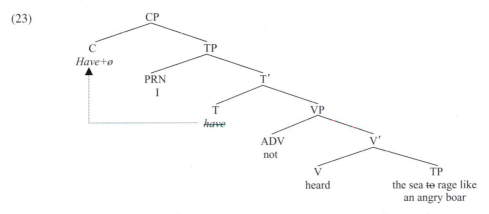

The auxiliary *have* originates in T and then moves to C (i.e. a copy of the auxiliary is adjoined to the strong affixal complementiser in C), leaving behind a copy of *have* in T which is ultimately deleted. The assumption that *not* is a VP-specifier provides a straightforward account of the fact that *not* remains positioned in front of the verb *heard* after *have* moves to C.

However, an interesting aspect of negative sentences in Shakespearean English is that in auxiliariless finite clauses like those in (24) below, the (bold-printed) main verb is positioned in front of *not*: cf.

(24) (a)   I **care** *not* for her (Thurio, *Two Gentlemen of Verona*, V.iv)
(b)   He **heard** *not* that (Julia, *Two Gentlemen of Verona*, IV.ii)
(c)   My master **seeks** *not* me (Speed, *Two Gentlemen of Verona*, I.i)
(d)   I **know** *not* where to hide my head (Trinculo, *The Tempest*, II.ii)

If *not* in Elizabethan English is a VP-specifier which is positioned at the leftmost edge of the Verb Phrase, how can we account for the fact that the verb (which would otherwise be expected to follow the negative particle *not*) ends up positioned in front of *not* in sentences like (24)? The answer is that when a finite T in Elizabethan English contains no auxiliary, the verb moves out of the head V position of VP into the head T position of TP in order to fill T. Accordingly, a sentence like (24a) *I care not for her* will involve the V-to-T movement operation represented by the dotted arrow in (25) below:

(25)

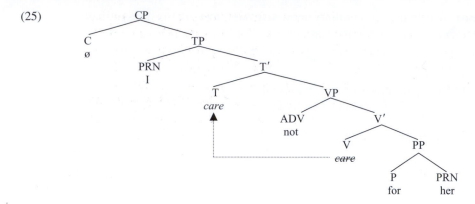

Thus, the verb *care* is first merged in the head V position within VP, and then moves into the head T position in TP, thereby ending up positioned in front of *not* (with the original occurrence of *care* in V being given a null spellout).

An important theoretical question to ask at this juncture is *why* the verb *care* should move from V to T. Using Chomsky's *strength* metaphor, we can suppose that a finite T is **strong** in Elizabethan English and so must be filled: this means that in a sentence in which the T position is not filled by an auxiliary, the verb moves from V to T in order to fill the strong T position. One way of characterising what it means for T to be strong is to suppose that T contains a strong tense affix with a V-feature which requires it to have an (auxiliary or nonauxiliary) verb attached to it as its host. Let's suppose that a strong affix is one which can find a host either by merger, or by attracting some item below it to adjoin to the affix. So, in a structure like (21), the strong (third person singular present) tense affix in T is provided with a host by directly merging the auxiliary *shall* with the tense affix in T, forming *shall+Af* (although the tense affix is not shown in the simplified structure in 21 above); but in a structure like (25), the strong tense affix in T attracts the closest verb which it c-commands (namely the verb *care*) to move to T and attach to the tense affix, so that the affix is provided with a verbal host via movement – as shown in (26) below (where the notation Af_{1SgPr} indicates that the affix has features marking it as first person singular present tense):

(26)

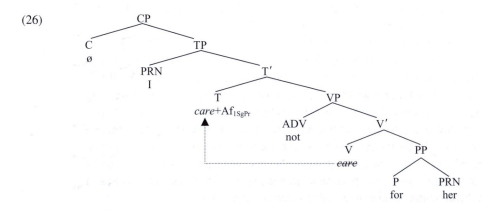

By contrast, T in present-day English contains a **weak** tense affix, and a weak tense affix cannot attract a verb to move from V to T, but rather can only be attached to a verbal host either by merger of an auxiliary like *shall* directly with the null tense affix in T, or by lowering of the tense affix onto the main verb, e.g. in auxiliariless finite clauses such as *He enjoys the classes*. In such auxiliariless clauses, the weak tense affix in T undergoes the morphological operation of **Affix Hopping** in the PF component, lowering the affix onto the main verb in the manner shown by the arrow in (27) below:

(27)

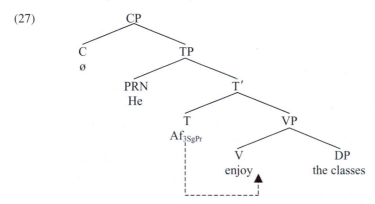

On this view, both strong and weak tense affixes can be directly merged with an auxiliary in T; the two differ in how the affix comes to be attached to a main verb; a strong tense affix (like that found in Elizabethan English) triggers movement of the verb from V to T in structures like (26) above; a weak tense affix (like that found in present-day English) is lowered onto the main verb in the PF component by **Affix Hopping** in structures like (27) above.

   A potential methodological objection which might be made to our use of Shakespearean English data in this section to illustrate V-to-T movement is to question whether it is legitimate to use historical evidence from a 'dead' language variety to illustrate a particular type of syntactic operation permitted by UG. There are three types of response which can be given to this type of objection. One is that if UG involves a set principles innately programmed into the human Language Faculty, it is highly improbable that this genetic endowment will have changed over a mere 400-year time span. Secondly, we have plenty of evidence from (e.g. negative and interrogative sentences in) Shakespeare's plays that main verbs could raise from V to T, and although this evidence comes from written texts (and may represent a more conservative variety than the spoken language at the time), this is equally true of many descriptive grammars of present-day English. And thirdly, there are plenty of present-day languages which show V-to-T movement (e.g. French, Italian, Spanish, German etc.), so it is clear that the phenomenon in question is far from 'dead': we have chosen to illustrate it using data from Elizabethan English rather than (e.g.) French because the central descriptive focus of this book is on *English*, which means that particular phenomena are illustrated using data from some variety of English wherever possible.

4.5   Head movement

There seem to be significant parallels between the kind of movement operation involved in **T-to-C movement** in (23) on the one hand, and **V-to-T movement** in (25) on the other. Both operations involve movement of a word from the head position in one phrase into the head position in a higher phrase. Accordingly, in (23) the auxiliary *have* moves from the head T position of TP into the head C position of CP; and in (25) the verb *care* moves from the head V position of VP into the head T position of TP. This suggests that T-to-C movement and V-to-T movement are two different instances of a more general **head movement** operation by which an item occupying the head position in a lower phrase is moved into the head position in a higher phrase.

As we see from (23) above, questions in Elizabethan English involved the same inversion operation as in present-day English. Given our assumption that inversion involves movement from T to C, an obvious prediction made by the assumption that verbs move from V to T in Elizabethan English is that they can subsequently move from T to C in interrogatives – and this is indeed the case, as we see from the fact that the (italicised) moved verb ends up positioned in front of its (bold-printed) subject in questions like:

(28) (a)   *Saw* **you** my master? (Speed, *Two Gentlemen of Verona*, I.i)
      (b)   *Speakest* **thou** in sober meanings? (Orlando, *As you Like It*, V.ii)
      (c)   *Know* **you** not the cause? (Tranio, *Taming of the Shrew*, IV.ii)

On the account given here, the derivation of a negative question such as (28c) *Know you not the cause?* will involve the two head movement operations shown in simplified form in (29) below:

(29)

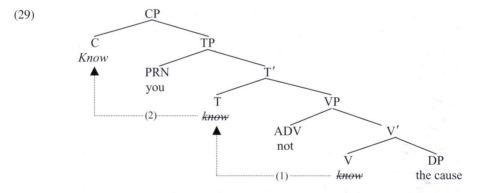

(The structure in (29) is simplified for expository purposes by not showing the verb *know* attaching to a strong tense affix in T, and by not showing movement of the resulting *know+Af* structure to attach to a strong null interrogative affix ø in C, forming the structure *know+Af+ø*.) The verb *know* moves from V to T because a finite T is strong in Elizabethan English, by virtue of containing a strong null tense affix with a V-feature (requiring the affix to attach to a verbal host); and *know* subsequently moves from T to C because an interrogative C is likewise strong by virtue of containing a strong null affix ø with a T-feature (requiring the affix to attach to a T-auxiliary). Consequently, *know* moves through T into C by two successive applications of **head movement** (numbered 1 and 2 above): *know* is first merged in V, then moved to T, and from there moved to C. In structures like (29), head movement is said to apply in a **successive-cyclic** fashion, moving the verb *know* (in successive **cycles** or steps) first from V to T, and then from T to C. Each time the verb moves, it leaves behind a copy of itself which is eventually deleted.

A key assumption made in (29) is that the verb *know* moves to C via the intermediate step of moving to T. This raises the question of why *know* can't move directly from V to C in the manner shown in simplified form in (30) below:

(30)   [$_{CP}$ [$_C$ *Know*] [$_{TP}$ you [$_T$ ø] [$_{VP}$ not [$_V$ *know*] the cause]]]

One reason why the kind of long-distance head-movement operation illustrated in (30) is ruled out is because it violates the following Locality Principle:

(31)   **Head Movement Constraint/HMC**
            Head Movement is only possible between a given head and the head of its complement

If we look at the two movement operations in (29), we see that both obey HMC: operation (1) involves local movement of the verb *know* into T from the head V position of a VP which is the complement of T; and operation (2) involves local movement of *know* into a C position from the head T position of a TP which is the complement of C. Since both head-movement operations are strictly local, there is no violation of HMC. By contrast, direct movement of *know* from V to C in (30) is non-local and violates HMC in that the verb *know* moves from the head V position of VP directly into the head C position of CP, in spite of the fact that VP is not the complement of C. HMC therefore provides a principled account of why (28c) *Know you not the cause?* is ungrammatical in present-day English: the verb *know* cannot move directly to C (because this would violate the HMC requirement for movement to be local), and cannot move through T into C, because verbs can no longer move from V to T in present-day English.

However, such an analysis raises the question of why finite verbs should be able to move from V to T in Elizabethan English, but not in present-day English. Using our earlier *strength* metaphor, we can say that the tense affix carried by a finite T was *strong* in Elizabethan English, but is *weak* in present-day English. Because the affix was strong in finite clauses in Elizabethan English, it could attract a verb to move from V to T; but because the affix is weak in present-day English, T can only be filled by an auxiliary which is directly merged in T, not by a verb moving from V to T. More generally, we can suppose that there is parametric variation with respect to the relative strength of a given type of head, so that (e.g.) a finite T was strong in Elizabethan English but is weak in present-day English.

We can refer to the relevant parameter as the **Head Strength Parameter**. Note that the parameter may have different settings for different types of head in a given language: e.g. a finite T is weak in present-day English, but a finite C is strong in interrogative main clauses.

An interesting possibility raised by our assumption that T was strong in Elizabethan English but is weak in present-day English is that historical change can be characterised in terms of **parameter resetting** – i.e. in terms of the settings of individual parameters changing over time (e.g. a T which was strong at some point in time being reanalysed as weak at a later point in time). One way this can come about is by children analysing the speech input they receive and arriving at a different setting for a given parameter from that adopted by their parents. Another is by transfer of parameter-settings between one language and another brought about by conquests or colonisation. However, since this book is not concerned with historical change, we shall have no more to say about it here.

4.6   Auxiliary Raising

Although we assumed in the previous section that no verbs in present-day English can move from V to T, the picture is complicated by the behaviour of *be* in examples like (32) below:

(32) (a)   She may not *be* suitable
      (b)   She *is* not suitable

In (32a) the copular verb *be* seems to occupy the head V position in VP, and so follows *not*: but in (32b) *is* precedes *not* and so seems to occupy the head T position of TP. This suggests that the copula *be* originates as a main verb (in the head V position of VP) and remains in situ when nonfinite as shown in simplified form in (33a) below, but moves into the head T position of TP when finite as shown in (33b):

(33) (a)   [$_{CP}$ [$_C$ ø] [$_{TP}$ she [$_T$ may] [$_{VP}$ not [$_V$ *be*] suitable]]]

      (b)   [$_{CP}$ [$_C$ ø] [$_{TP}$ she [$_T$ *is*] [$_{VP}$ not [$_V$ ~~*is*~~] suitable]]]

A similar conclusion is suggested by examples such as the following:

(34) (a)   She may not *be* enjoying syntax
      (b)   She *is* not enjoying syntax

In (34a), the head T position of TP is occupied by the modal auxiliary *may*, and the head V position of VP is occupied by the verb *enjoying*: the word *be* therefore seems to occupy some intermediate position between the two. Since *be* (in this use) is an aspectual auxiliary (marking progressive aspect), let's suppose that *be* in (34a) occupies the head AUX/Auxiliary position of an AUXP (i.e. Auxiliary Phrase). However, in (34b) progressive *is* occupies the head T position of TP and hence precedes *not*. One analysis of the relevant data is to suppose that aspectual *be* originates as the head AUX constituent of AUXP and remains in situ when nonfinite as shown in (35a) below, but moves from AUX to T when finite – as shown in (35b) (where *not* is taken to occupy a position to the left of AUXP):

(35) (a)   [CP [C ø] [TP she [T may] not [AUXP [AUX *be*] [VP [V enjoying] syntax]]]]]

(b)   [CP [C ø] [TP she [T *is*] not [AUXP [AUX ~~is~~] [VP [V enjoying] syntax]]]]]

On this view, present-day English would have a *be*-raising operation moving finite forms of *be* from the head V position in VP (or the head AUX position in AUXP) into the head T position in TP. This would mean that present-day English retains a last vestige of raising-to-T.

The different positions occupied by finite and nonfinite forms of *be* are mirrored by the perfect auxiliary *have* – as the examples below illustrate:

(36) (a)   He may not *have* done it
     (b)   He *has* not done it

The head T position of TP in (36a) is occupied by *may* and the head V position of VP by *done*; hence the infinitive form *have* must occupy some position intermediate between the two, e.g. the head AUX position of an AUXP/Auxiliary Phrase, as in (37a) below. However, the fact that the finite form *has* in (36b) is positioned in front of *not* suggests that finite forms of the perfect auxiliary *have* raise from AUX to T in the manner shown informally in (37b) below:

(37) (a)   [CP [C ø] [TP He [T may] not [AUXP [AUX have] [VP [V done] it]]]]]

(b)   [CP [C ø] [TP He [T *has*] not [AUXP [AUX ~~has~~] [VP [V done] it]]]]]

The conclusion which our discussion of (32–37) leads us to is that *have* (in its use as a perfect auxiliary) and *be* (in its use as a progressive auxiliary or copular verb) may originate in a position below *not* and subsequently raise into the head T position of TP.

There is evidence that certain modal auxiliaries also originate in a position below T and subsequently raise into T. In this connection, consider the interpretation of the following negative sentences:

(38) (a)   You must not do that (= 'It is *necessary* for you <u>not</u> to do that')
     (b)   You need not do that (= 'It is <u>not</u> *necessary* for you to do that')

In (38a) the modal *must* has **wide scope** with respect to negation (i.e. *must* has semantic scope over *not*) whereas in (38b) the modal *need* has **narrow scope** with respect to negation (i.e. *need* falls within the semantic scope of *not*). Although wide-scope modals like *must* are directly generated in T (as in (39a) below), there is evidence to suggest that narrow-scope modals like *need* are initially generated in some position below T (e.g. the head AUX position of AUXP), and from there move to T (as in (39b) below):

(39) (a)   [$_{CP}$ [$_C$ ø] [$_{TP}$ you [$_T$ must] not [$_{VP}$ [$_V$ do] that]]]

   (b)   [$_{CP}$ [$_C$ ø] [$_{TP}$ you [$_T$ *need*] not [$_{AUXP}$ [$_{AUX}$ ~~need~~] [$_{VP}$ [$_V$ do] that]]]]

The analysis in (39b) implies that present-day English has an operation by which narrow-scope auxiliaries raise from AUX to T. There are two factors which lend empirical support to the *Auxiliary Raising* analysis in (39b). Firstly, it enables us to provide a principled account of the relevant scope relations in terms of the relation *c-command*: since *must* c-commands *not* in (39a), *must* has scope over *not*; but since *not* c-commands the lower copy of *need* in (39b), *not* can have scope over *need*. The second factor which lends support to the Auxiliary Raising analysis is that it allows us to account for how the polarity item *need* can occur in a structure like (39b), when we saw in §2.6 that a polarity item must be c-commanded by an affective (e.g. negative) constituent, and *not* in (39b) does not c-command *need* in the superficial syntactic structure. We can solve this seeming puzzle if we suppose that *at least one copy* of a polarity item must be c-commanded by an affective constituent (the lower copy of *need* being c-commanded by *not* in 39b). It may be that the two different (T and AUX) positions for auxiliaries can be occupied by different modals in Scots English structures such as:

(40)   He must no can do it (Brown 1991, p. 98)
    'It must be the case that he does not have the capability of doing it'

In (40), *must* is located in T and has scope over *not,* whereas *can* is located in AUX and falls within the scope of *not.*

   If finite forms of BE (in all uses), HAVE (in its use as a perfect auxiliary) and narrow-scope modals like NEED all raise to T, it is clear that the suggestion made in the previous section that T in present-day English is a weak head which does not trigger any form of V-raising is untenable. Rather, the appropriate generalisation would appear to be that in present-day English, only a highly restricted set of verbs (like HAVE, BE and NEED) can raise to T. What do such verbs have in common which differentiates them from other verbs? An answer given by many traditional grammars is that they serve to mark grammatical properties like aspect and modality, and have little or no inherent lexical content (and for this reason they are sometimes called **light verbs**), so in this respect they resemble auxiliaries. Adopting this intuition, we can say that the affix in a finite T in present-day English is only strong enough to trigger movement of an auxiliary like HAVE/BE/NEED to T, not movement of a lexical verb to T. This means that if the head immediately beneath T is an auxiliary (as in (33b, 35b, 37b and 39b) above), the affix attracts it; but if the head beneath T is a main verb (as in (27) above), the affix is instead lowered onto the main verb in the PF component by **Affix Hopping**.

4.7   Another look at negation

In §4.4 and §4.5 we assumed that the negative particle *not* is a VP-specifier which occupies initial position within VP. However, this assumption is problematic in a number of respects. For example, in a sentence such as (35a) *She may not be enjoying syntax*, it is clear that *not* does not occupy a VP-initial position immediately in front of the verb *enjoying*: on the contrary, *not* appears to occupy some position between the modal auxiliary *may* and the aspectual auxiliary *be*. Moreover, we shall argue in chapter 6 that only an **argument** of a verb can occupy the specifier position within VP – and *not* in a negative sentence like *She may not sell it* is not an argument of the verb *sell* (because *not* isn't one of the participants in the act of selling). It is clear, therefore, that we need to rethink our earlier analysis of negation. An alternative analysis which we shall outline in this section (and which has been widely adopted in work since the end of the 1980s) posits that *not* is contained within a separate **NEGP** (= **Negation Phrase**) projection. The specific implementation of this analysis which we will assume here is one which takes the negative particle *not* to be the *specifier* of NEGP (though it should be pointed out that some linguists adopt an alternative analysis under which *not* is taken to be the head NEG constituent of NEGP).

The NEGP analysis is far from implausible from a historical perspective: in earlier varieties of English, sentences containing *not* also contained the negative particle *ne* (with *ne* arguably serving as the head NEG constituent of NEGP and *not* as its specifier). This can be illustrated by the following Middle English example taken from Chaucer's *Wife of Bath's Tale*:

(41)   A lord in his houshold *ne* hath *nat* every vessel al of gold (lines 99–100)
       'A lord in his household does not have all his vessels made entirely of gold'

A plausible analysis of a sentence like (41) is to suppose that *ne* originates as the head NEG constituent of NEGP, with *nat* (= 'not') as its specifier: the verb *hath* originates in the head V position of VP and from there moves to the head NEG position of NEGP, attaching to the negative prefix *ne* to form the complex head *ne+hath* as shown in simplified form in (42) below:

(42)   [NEGP nat [NEG ne+*hath*] [VP [V ~~hath~~] every vessel al of gold]]

The resulting complex head *ne+hath* then attaches to a present tense affix (*Af*) in T, as shown in simplified (and abbreviated) form in (43) below:

(43)   [TP A lord . . . [T ne+hath+*Af*] [NEGP nat [NEG ~~ne+hath~~] [VP [V ~~hath~~] every vessel al of gold]]]

Merger of the TP in (43) with a null declarative complementiser will derive the CP structure associated with (41) *A lord in his houshold ne hath nat every vessel al of gold.*

By Shakespeare's time, *ne* had dropped out of use, leaving the head NEG position of NEGP null (just as in *ne . . . pas* 'not . . . . at.all' negatives in present-day French, *ne* has dropped out of use in colloquial styles). Positing that *not* in Elizabethan English is the specifier of a NEGP headed by a null NEG constituent opens up the possibility that V moves through NEG into T, so that (24a) *I care not for her* has the derivation shown (in simplified form) in (44) below:

(44)

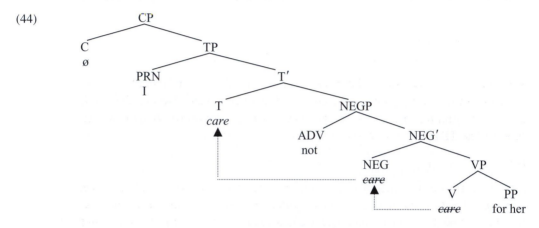

This would mean that head movement applies in a **successive-cyclic** (two-step) fashion. Each of the two head movement operations in (44) – viz. movement of *care* from V to NEG, and then from NEG to T – is local in the sense that it satisfies the **Head Movement Constraint** (31), since in each case movement is from one head position into the next highest head position in the structure. If head movement is driven by affixal properties of heads, and if both T and NEG contain a strong affix with a V-feature which can trigger movement of a main verb, the verb *care* will first move from V to NEG in order to attach to a null negative affix (in much the same way as the verb *hath* in (42) moves from V to Neg to attach to the overt negative affix *ne*), and the resulting complex NEG head (comprising a null negative affix with a verb attached to it) in turn will move from NEG to T in order to attach to a strong tense affix in T.

An important question posed by the analysis in (44) is why sentences like (24a) *I care not for her* are ungrammatical in present-day English. The answer is that neither T nor NEG contains a strong affix with a V-feature in present-day English, and so they are unable to attract a main verb like *care* to move through NEG into T. Still, this assumption in turn raises the question of why we can't simply leave the present tense verb *care* in situ (in the head V position of VP) in present-day English – as in (45) below:

(45)   [CP [C ø] [TP I [T *Af*] [NEGP not [NEG ø] [VP [V care] for her]]]]

One answer is the following. Let's suppose that (just like syntactic operations), morphological and phonological operations in the PF component apply in a **bottom-up** fashion, and process structures in a **cyclic** fashion (i.e. in a step-wise fashion, one projection at a time). What this means is that when the syntax hands over the structure in (45) to the PF component, the lowest maximal projection in the structure (the VP *care for her*) will be processed first, then the next lowest maximal projection (the NEGP *not ∅ care for her*), then the next lowest maximal projection (the TP *I Af not ∅ care for her*) and finally the overall CP (*∅ I Af not ∅ care for her*). Let's also posit that all operations (whether syntactic, morphological or phonological) obey the following UG principle:

(46)   **Earliness Principle**
         Operations must apply as early as possible in a derivation

All of this means that **Affix Hopping** will apply to the tense affix in (45) on the TP cycle – i.e. at the point where we have already processed VP and NEGP, and are now beginning to process TP. The structure which the PF component can 'see' on the TP cycle is (47) below:

(47)   [$_{TP}$ I [$_T$ *Af*] [$_{NEGP}$ not [$_{NEG}$ ∅] [$_{VP}$ [$_V$ care] for her]]]

At this point, we might expect Affix Hopping to apply to lower the tense affix in T onto the verb *care*. There are two possible ways in which we could seek to achieve this. One is by lowering the affix directly from T onto V as in (48a) below, and the other is to lower the affix first onto null NEG head and then onto V in the manner shown in (48b):

(48) (a)   [$_{TP}$ I [$_T$*Af*] [$_{NEGP}$ not [$_{NEG}$ ∅] [$_{VP}$ [$_V$ care] for her]]]

(b)   [$_{TP}$ I [$_T$*Af*] [$_{NEGP}$ not [$_{NEG}$ ∅] [$_{VP}$ [$_V$ care] for her]]]

However, a movement operation like (48a) which lowers the affix directly from T onto V would violate the **Head Movement Constraint** (31), since it involves lowering the head T of TP onto the head V of VP; and yet V is not the next lowest head in the structure (rather, NEG is), and HMC only allows a head to be lowered onto the head immediately beneath it in the structure. Accordingly, we might suppose that Affix Hopping applies in a successive-cyclic fashion, lowering the affix first from T onto NEG, and then from NEG onto V – as in (48b). However, there are two problems posed by any such successive-cyclic lowering operation. The first is that NEG doesn't seem to be the kind of head which is an appropriate host for a tense affix (at least, if we assume that a tense affix attaches to an overt verb, since NEG is neither overt nor a verb): hence, the first step of the two-step movement arrowed in (48b) – namely lowering the affix onto NEG – may be ruled out for this reason. To make matters worse, the second step of lowering the tense affix from NEG onto V in (48b) is also ruled out, because it violates the following UG principle:

(49)   **Strict Cyclicity Principle/SCP**
        At a stage of derivation where a given projection HP is being
        cycled/processed, only operations involving the head H of HP and
        some other constituent c-commanded by H can apply

Lowering the tense affix from T onto NEG in (48b) does not violate **SCP**, since T-to-NEG lowering clearly involves T (by moving the tense affix in T) and also involves a NEG constituent which is c-commanded by T (since this ends up having a tense affix attached to it). But the subsequent operation of lowering the affix from NEG onto V is **anticyclic**, since NEG-to-V lowering does not involve T (in violation of SCP), but rather involves only NEG and V. We therefore correctly predict that sentences like *I not care for her* are ungrammatical in present-day English.

A final point to be made here is that we have excluded from our discussion negative interrogatives like *Shouldn't you be at work?* In such sentences the negative particle *n't* has scope over the modal (so that the sentence has a meaning paraphraseable as 'Is it not the case that you should be at work?') and hence originates in a position above TP. One proposal along these lines would be to suppose that NEGP in such sentences is positioned between CP and TP, and that the auxiliary *should* raises from T through NEG into C, with *n't* cliticising onto the auxiliary. This would allow for the possibility of two types of negation occurring in a sentence such as *Mightn't he not have seen her?* where *not* originates within a NEGP immediately above VP, and *n't* within a NEGP immediately above TP.

4.8   DO-support

In present-day English, the negative counterpart of a sentence like *I care for her* requires DO-support, as we see from (50) below:

(50)   I do not care for her

But how does DO come to appear in such sentences – and why? In order to answer this question, let's look rather more closely at the derivation of sentence (50). Suppose that (as before) the syntactic component of our grammar generates the structure (45) above, repeated as (51) below:

(51)   [CP [C ∅] [TP I [T *Af*] [NEGP not [NEG ∅] [VP [V care] for her]]]]

Since T contains an unattached weak tense affix with a V-feature requiring it to attach to a verbal host, we would expect the affix to be lowered onto an overt verbal stem by Affix Hopping. But if Affix Hopping is a purely *local* operation which lowers an unattached weak tense affix onto the closest head c-commanded by T (hence onto the head word of the expression which is the complement of T), then it follows that all Affix Hopping can do is lower the affix onto the head NEG constituent of NEGP. But, as we have already seen, NEG is not an appropriate host for the affix, since it is neither overt nor verbal. The result is that the affix in T remains stranded (i.e. left without a verbal host to attach to). Let us suppose that when an affix is attached to an (auxiliary or main) verb host, the resulting VERB+AFFIX substructure is spelled out as an appropriately inflected form of the relevant verb (e.g. WAIT+Af$_{3.SG.PRES}$ is spelled out as the regular form *waits*, whereas BE+Af$_{3.SG.PRES}$ is spelled out as the irregular form *is*). However, let us further suppose that when a tense affix is stranded (i.e. unable to find a verbal host to attach to), it is spelled out as an appropriately inflected form of the dummy/expletive auxiliary DO. This being so, the first person singular present tense affix stranded in C in (51) will be spelled out as the first person singular present tense form of DO (namely *do*) – as in (52) below:

(52)   [$_{CP}$ [$_C$ Ø] [$_{TP}$ I [$_T$ do] [$_{NEGP}$ not [$_{NEG}$ Ø] [$_{VP}$ [$_V$ care] for her]]]]]

On this view, there is no DO-insertion operation in the syntax or morphology (somehow inserting the stem DO into a structure which previously did not contain it); rather, a form like *do* in a structure like (52) is simply the spellout of a stranded affix. In other words, a third person singular present tense affix is spelled out as the contracted (affixal) form *-s* in sentences like (53a) below, but as the full form *does* in sentences like (53b) and (53c):

(53) (a)   He like*s* pasta
     (b)   *Does* he like pasta?
     (c)   He *doesn't* like pasta

In much the same way, the third person singular present tense form of the auxilary HAVE/BE is sometimes spelled out as the full form *has/is*, and sometimes as the contracted form *'s*.

    What is implicitly being assumed here is that **Affix Hopping** and **DO-support** are complementary PF operations which provide two different ways of spelling out an affix. We can therefore see them as two facets of an **Affix Attachment** operation, as in (54) below:

(54)   **Affix Attachment**
           When the PF component processes a structure whose head H contains an (undeleted) weak affix which needs a verbal host and which is not already attached to an (auxiliary or main) verb
           (i)   if H has a complement headed by an overt verb, the affix is lowered onto the relevant verb [= **Affix Hopping**]
           (ii)   if not (i.e. if H does not have a complement headed by an overt verb and the affix is stranded), the affix is spelled out as an appropriately inflected form of DO [= **DO-support**]

We can illustrate how (54) works in terms of the italicised structures below:

(55) (a)   *He won the race*
     (b)   He said he would win the race, and *he did*

(c)   He said he would win the race, and *win the race*, *he did*
(d)   *Did he win the race?*
(e)   *Didn't he win the race?*
(f)   Some people don't believe he won the race, but *he* DID *win it*

Consider first (55a), which is derived as follows. The determiner *the* merges with the noun *race* to form the DP *the race*; the verb *win* merges with this DP to form the VP *win the race*. This VP is merged with a T constituent containing a (past tense) affix *Af* to form the T-bar *Af win the race*. This T-bar merges with the pronoun *he* to form the TP *he Af win the race*; and the resulting TP in turn is merged with a null declarative complementiser ∅ to form the CP shown in skeletal form in (56) below:

(56)   [cp [c ∅] [TP He [T *Af*] [VP [V win] the race]]]

The syntactic structure (56) is then sent to the PF component (and the semantic component) to be processed. PF operations apply in a bottom-up, cyclic fashion. On the TP cycle in the PF component, the tense affix in T is lowered onto the verb *win* in accordance with (54i), so that the verb has the form *win+Af*: since the lexical entry for the irregular verb *win* specifies that it is spelled out as *won* when it has a past tense affix attached to it, the overall structure is eventually spelled out as (55a) *He won the race*.

Now consider why DO is used in the elliptical clause *he did* in (55b). This has the syntactic structure shown in (57) below, with the italicised material undergoing ellipsis:

(57)   [cp [c ∅] [TP he [T *Af*] [VP [V ~~win~~] ~~the race~~]]]

The tense affix in T cannot subsequently be lowered onto the verb *win* in the PF component via the **Affix Hopping** operation (54i) because an affix can only attach to an *overt* verb, and the verb ~~win~~ in (57) is not overt (by virtue of having undergone ellipsis); hence the **DO-support** operation in (54ii) has to apply, spelling out the unattached affix as an appropriately inflected form of DO – namely *did*.

Now consider the clause *Win the race, he did* in (55c). Let's suppose that (in the syntax) the VP *win the race* undergoes preposing in order to highlight it, and is thereby moved to the front of the overall clause (to become the specifier of the null complementiser), and that the phonetic features of the original occurrence of the VP *win the race* are given a null spellout, as shown informally in (58) below:

(58)   [cp [VP *win the race*] [c ∅] [TP he [T *Af*] [VP ~~win the race~~]]]

Once again, in the PF component the weak tense affix in T cannot be lowered onto the verb *win* because the complement of T is a VP which contains a null copy of the verb *win* (the overall VP having moved to the front of the sentence, leaving a null copy behind). Accordingly, **DO-support** (54ii) applies once again, and the affix in T is spelled out as *did*.

Let's turn now to look at the derivation of the yes-no question (55d) *Did he win the race?* Suppose that a series of syntactic merger operations have applied to generate the structure (59) below:

(59)   [CP [C ∅] [TP he [T *Af*] [VP [V *win*] *the race*]]]

Suppose also that the interrogative C contains a strong null affix ∅ with a tense feature (requiring it to attach to a T constituent) and hence attracts whatever is contained within T to adjoin to it. Since T in (59) contains only a tense affix, this affix will adjoin to the null affixal complementiser (and the original occurrence of the affix in T will be deleted), so deriving the structure (60) below:

(60)   [CP [C *Af*+∅] [TP he [T ~~*Af*~~] [VP [V *win*] *the race*]]]

The resulting syntactic structure is then sent to the PF component to undergo morphological and phonological processing. Since the tense affix in T gets deleted, it does not undergo Affix Hopping. By contrast, the tense affix (*Af*) in C is not deleted and is unhosted (in the sense that it is not attached to the kind of verbal host that it requires), and hence must undergo **Affix Attachment** (54). However, since the complement of the C constituent which contains the tense affix is not headed by an overt verb (but rather is a TP headed by a null T), Affix Hopping (54i) cannot apply; consequently, DO-support (54ii) applies instead, with the result that the affix is spelled out as the appropriate inflected form of DO, namely *did*.

Now, consider the negative question (55e) *Didn't he win the race?* In keeping with the NEGP analysis of negation outlined in the previous section, let's suppose that after the VP *win the race* has been formed, it is merged with a null NEG head ∅ to form a NEG-bar constituent, and that this in turn is merged with a negative clitic *n't* which serves as its specifier, forming the NEGP *n't ∅ win the race*. This NEGP is then merged with a T containing an abstract tense affix, forming the T-bar *Af n't ∅ win the race*. Suppose that the clitic negative *n't* then attaches to the end of the tense affix, with the original occurrence of *n't* in spec-NEGP ultimately being deleted, so forming the string *Af+n't ~~n't~~ ∅ win the race*. The resulting T-bar is in turn merged with the subject *he*, forming the TP *He Af+n't ~~n't~~ ∅ win the race*. This is then merged with an interrogative C constituent containing a null affix ∅, forming the CP (61) below:

(61)   [CP [C ∅] [TP he [T *Af*+*n't*] [NEGP ~~*n't*~~ [NEG ∅] [VP [V *win*] *the race*]]]]

Since the null affix in C is strong and has a tense feature, it attracts all the material contained in T to adjoin to it, so deriving:

(62)   [CP [C *Af*+*n't*+∅] [TP he [T ~~*Af*+*n't*~~] [NEGP ~~*n't*~~ [NEG ∅] [VP [V *win*] *the race*]]]]

The resulting syntactic structure is then handed over to the PF component. On the CP cycle in the PF component, the tense affix in C will be subject to **Affix Attachment** (54). However, since the complement of C is not a VP headed by an overt verb, Affix Hopping (54i) cannot apply, and DO-support (54ii) applies instead (with the affix being spelled out as an appropriate form of DO), creating the complex head DO+*n't*+∅, which is ultimately spelled out as *didn't*.

An interesting descriptive implication of the analysis presented in (62) is that it is in principle possible that the interrogative form of some auxiliaries may have a different spellout from their non-interrogative counterparts. This is because in their interrogative form they attach to a null affixal interrogative complementiser ø, whereas in their non-interrogative form they do not. A case in point is *be*. When used with a first person singular subject (= *I*), this has the negative interrogative form *aren't* – a form which is not found with an *I* subject (in varieties of English like mine) in non-interrogative uses: cf.

(63) (a)   *Aren't* I entitled to claim Social Security benefits?
      (b)   *I *aren't* entitled to claim Social Security benefits (= *I'm not . . .*)

This can be accounted for by positing that the string $be+Af_{1SgPr}+n't+ø$ found in (63a) can be spelled out as *aren't* – but not the string $be+Af_{1SgPr}+n't$ in (63b) because this is not interrogative (by virtue of having no null interrogative affix attached to it).

   Finally, let's turn to consider the clause *He* DID *win it* in (55f), where capitals mark contrastive stress (and the utterance is used to deny any suggestion that he didn't win the race). One way of handling the relevant phenomenon is to suppose that such sentences contain an invisible positive counterpart of the NEGP constituent which appears in negative sentences. Since positive and negative are two different polarities, we can conflate the two types of (positive and negative) projection into a **POLP** (**Polarity Phrase**) projection. This is not quite as implausible as it may seem, since some American varieties of English (though not my own British one) allow *so* to be used to mark positive polarity in a sentence such as *He did so win it* (meaning 'He really did win it'). We could then say that an emphatic sentence such as *He did (so) win it* has the structure shown below:

(64)   [CP [C ø] [TP he [T *Af*] [PoLP (so) [Pol ø] [VP [V *win*] it]]]]

The affix in T in (64) will have no verbal host immediately beneath it to attach to, because the head immediately beneath T is Pol, and Pol does not contain an overt verbal stem (but rather is a null, non-verbal head). Because the affix in (64) is stranded without a verbal host, it is spelled out as an appropriate form of DO – here, *did*.

4.9   Summary

   In this chapter, we have been concerned with the syntax of **head movement**. We began by looking at **auxiliary inversion** in questions in English in §4.2, arguing that this involves a T-to-C movement operation whereby an auxiliary moves from the head T position of TP into the head C position of CP. We suggested that auxiliaries move to C in main-clause questions because C in such structures is **strong** (perhaps by virtue of containing a strong affix with a tense feature requiring a T constituent to attach to it) and so **attracts** an auxiliary in T to move to C. In §4.3 we argued that movement operations like auxiliary inversion involve two separate **copying** and **deletion** operations: a copy of the auxiliary in

T is adjoined to a null interrogative affix in C, and then the original occurrence of the auxiliary in T is deleted. In §4.4 we saw that finite main verbs in Elizabethan English could move from V to T by an operation of V-to-T movement (as is shown by word order in negative sentences like *I care not for her*), but that this kind of movement is no longer possible in present-day English. We suggested that a null finite T was strong in Elizabethan English (perhaps containing a strong tense affix with a V-feature triggering the raising of verbs to T) but that its counterpart in present-day English is weak (so that a tense affix in T is lowered onto the main verb by the morphological operation of **Affix Hopping**). In §4.5 we argued that T-to-C movement and V-to-T movement are two different reflexes of a more general **head movement** operation, and that head movement is subject to a strict locality condition (imposed by the **Head Movement Constraint**) which requires it to apply in a successive-cyclic (stepwise) fashion, so that head movement is only possible between a given head and the next highest head within the structure containing it. In §4.6 we argued that present-day English has a last vestige of V-to-T raising in finite clauses whereby BE and HAVE and narrow-scope modals like NEED raise from a lower AUX position into the head T position of TP. We suggested that a finite T in present-day English contains a tense affix which is only strong enough to attract an auxiliary-like light verb to move to T, not a lexical verb. In §4.7, we took another look at negation. Revising our earlier analysis of *not* as a VP-specifier, we outlined an alternative analysis under which *not* is the specifier of a NEGP constituent which was headed by *ne* in Chaucerian English, but which is null in present-day English. On this view, Shakespearean negatives like *He heard not that* involve movement of the verb from V through NEG into T. Because NEG and T don't contain a strong enough affix in present-day English, they can no longer trigger movement of a lexical verb. In §4.8 we outlined a morphological account of **Affix Hopping** and DO-**support**. We suggested that once the syntactic component of the grammar has generated a given syntactic structure (e.g. a complete CP), the relevant structure is then sent to the PF component for morphological and phonological processing. If a structure being processed by the PF component contains an unattached weak tense affix, this is lowered onto the head immediately below by **Affix Hopping** if this is an overt verb; if not, the affix is spelled out as an appropriately inflected form of DO.

Key principles and operations which figured in our discussion in this chapter include the following:

(31)　　**Head Movement Constraint/HMC**
　　　　Head Movement is only possible between a given head and the head of its complement

(46)　　**Earliness Principle**
　　　　Operations must apply as early as possible in a derivation

(49)　　**Strict Cyclicity Principle/SCP**
　　　　At a stage of derivation where a given projection HP is being cycled/processed, only operations affecting the head H of HP and some other constituent c-commanded by H can apply

(54)   **Affix Attachment**
         When the PF component processes a structure whose head H contains an
         (undeleted) weak affix which needs a verbal host and which is not already
         attached to an (auxiliary or main) verb

  (i)   if H has a complement headed by an overt verb, the affix is lowered onto the
         relevant verb [= **Affix Hopping**]

  (ii)   if not (i.e. if H does not have a complement headed by an overt verb and the
         affix is stranded), the affix is spelled out as an appropriately inflected form
         of DO [= **DO-support**]

4.10   Bibliographical background

The analysis of auxiliary inversion in §4.2 as involving a strong,
affixal C constituent attracting a subordinate T-auxiliary is adapted from
Chomsky (1993, 1995). On inversion in *so*-sentences like *John can speak French
and so can Mary*, see Toda (2007). The idea in §4.3 that movement involves
copying derives from Chomsky (1995, §3.5); the discussion of which copy of
a moved constituent is overtly spelled out is adapted from Chomsky (2006,
p. 9). Children's *auxiliary copying* structures are discussed in Hiramatsu (2003).
The Head Movement Constraint/HMC outlined in §4.5 has its origins in Travis
(1984); a complication which arises with it is that some languages have a
form of long-distance head movement operation which allows a verb to be
moved out of one clause to the front of another in order to highlight the
verb in some way, and which appears not to obey HMC: for relevant discussion, see Koopman (1984), van Riemsdijk (1989), Lema and Rivero (1990),
Larson and Lefebvre (1991), Manzini (1994), Roberts (1994), Carnie (1995),
Borsley, Rivero and Stephens (1996), Hoge (1998), Holmberg (1999), Toyoshima
(2000), Fanselow (2002) and Landau (2006b). The analysis of *have/be* raising
in §4.6 dates back in spirit to Klima (1964); see Nomura (2006, pp. 303–314)
for discussion of *have/be*-raising in subjunctive clauses. The analysis of narrow-
scope modal auxiliaries as originating in a lower position and subsequently
raising to T is adapted from Roberts (1998) and Nomura (2006). On the defining characteristics of auxiliaries, see Pollock (1989) and Poletto and Benincà
(2004). On the nature of historical change in syntax, see Kroch (2001). The
NEGP analysis of negative clauses in §4.7 has its roots in earlier work by Pollock (1989), Laka (1990), Rizzi (1990), Ouhalla (1990), Iatridou (1990), Belletti
(1990), Zanuttini (1991), Roberts (1993), Haegeman (1995), Chomsky (1995)
and Potsdam (1997, 1998); on negation in earlier varieties of English, see Ingham (2000, 2002, 2007). On sentences like *Shouldn't you be at work?*, see
Cormack and Smith (2000a). The Earliness Principle is taken from Pesetsky
(1995). A range of alternative accounts of the DO-support phenomenon discussed
in §4.8 can be found in Halle and Marantz (1993), Lasnik (1995a, 2000, 2003,
2006), Ochi (1999), Embick and Noyer (2001), Bobaljik (2002) and Freidin
(2004).

Although we have taken head movement to be a syntactic operation here (following Baltin 2002, Roberts 2001b, Donati 2006, Matushansky 2006 and Nomura 2006), it should be noted that Chomsky (1999) takes it to be a morphological operation applying in the PF component, essentially designed to enable affixes to attach to appropriate heads: see Boeckx and Stjepanović (2001), Flagg (2002) and Sauerland and Elbourne (2002) for discussion of this idea. If head movement were indeed a PF operation, we could conflate it with the Affix Attachment operation in (54), by supposing that a tense affix triggers raising of an appropriate host if it is strong enough to do so, but otherwise is lowered onto the relevant host wherever possible, or is spelled out as an appropriate form of DO if stranded. However, the picture is complicated by evidence from Zwart (2001) that head movement has some properties typical of syntactic operations, and others typical of PF operations.

Workbook section

Exercise 4.1

Discuss the derivation of each of the following (declarative or interrogative) sentences, drawing a tree diagram to represent the structure of each sentence and saying why the relevant structure is (or is not) grammatical (in the case of 4, saying why it is ungrammatical as a main clause):

1	He helps her
2	*He d's help her
3	*Helps he her?
4	*If he helps her?
5	Does he help her? **(w)**
6	I wonder if he helps her
7	*I wonder if does he help her
8	*I wonder if helps he her
9	*He helps not her
10	*He not helps her
11	He does not help her **(w)**
12	He doesn't help her
13	Doesn't he help her?
14	He might not help her **(w)**
15	He dare not help her **(w)**

(Note that *d's* in 2 represents unstressed *does*/dəz/.) Say what is unusual about the syntax of sentences like 16 below (the second line of the nursery rhyme *Baa Baa Black Sheep*) – and why such structures appear to be problematic for the assumptions made in §4.6 in the main text:

16   Have you any wool?

Can we overcome the relevant problems if we follow Freidin (2004, p. 115) in supposing that *have* in sentences like 16 is an auxiliary generated in T, and the head V of VP contains a null variant of the verb *got*? (Take *any wool* to be a QP headed by the quantifier *any*.) In addition, say why you think negative imperatives like 17 below (which were grammatical in Elizabethan English) are ungrammatical in present-day English, and why we find 18 instead:

17   *Be not afraid!
18   Don't be afraid!

Next, comment on the syntax of the following negative sentence produced by a boy called Abe at age 2;5.26 (two years, five months, twenty-six days):

19   I not can find it **(w)**

and compare 19 with the corresponding adult structure *I cannot find it*. Then discuss the derivation of each of the following questions produced by a number of different children aged two to four years, and identify the nature of the child's error in each case, comparing the child's structure with its adult counterpart:

20   Is the clock is working?
21   Does it opens?
22   Don't you don't want one?
23   Does it doesn't move? **(w)**

Consider, also, the derivation of the following questions reported (by Akmajian and Heny 1975, p. 17) to have been produced by an unnamed three-year-old girl:

24   Is I can do that?
25   Is you should eat the apple?
26   Is the apple juice won't spill?

Helpful hints

In 13, account for the fact that the sentence is ambiguous between one interpretation paraphraseable as 'Is it the case that he doesn't help her' and another paraphraseable as 'Isn't it the case that he helps her?' In relation to 14, 15 and 19, consider the scope relations between the auxiliary and *not*, and bear in mind the suggestion made in the main text that finite auxiliaries originate in an AUX position below NEG if they fall within the scope of *not*. In relation to 17 and 18, consider the possibility that although a T in finite declarative and interrogative clauses in present-day English is strong enough to attract an auxiliary (but not a lexical verb), T in imperatives is too weak to attract either an auxiliary or a main verb. In 20–23, consider the possibility that children sometimes fail to delete the original occurrence of a moved T constituent. In 22 and 23, consider the possibility that attachment of the clitic *n't* to a tense affix in T may either be treated by the child as a syntactic operation, or as a phonological operation in the PF component which applies *after* the relevant syntactic structure has been formed.

Model answer for 1

Given the assumptions made in the text, 1 will have the simplified syntactic structure (i) below:

(i)

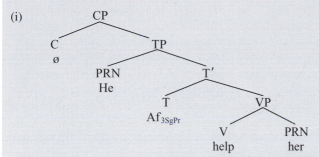

The overall clause is a CP headed by a null declarative complementiser ø which has a TP complement headed by a T constituent which carries a present tense affix which is third person singular by agreement with the subject *he*, and which needs an overt verb stem to attach to. Since tense affixes are not strong enough to trigger raising of main verbs in present-day English, the verb *help* cannot be raised to provide a host for the affix in T. After the syntactic structure in (i) has been formed, it is handed over to the PF component, where it is processed in a bottom-up, cyclic fashion. On the TP-cycle, the tense affix in T is lowered onto the end of the verb *help* by Affix Hopping, which specifies that a weak affix in T is lowered onto the head V of a VP complement of T. Affix Hopping results in the form [*help*+Af$_{3SgPr}$], which is ultimately spelled out as *helps*. The complement pronoun *her* is assigned accusative case in the syntax by the c-commanding transitive verb *help*, and the subject pronoun *he* is assigned nominative case by the c-commanding finite complementiser ø.

Exercise 4.2

Discuss the derivation of the following Shakespearean sentences:

1   Thou marvell'st at my words (Macbeth, *Macbeth*, III.ii)
2   Macbeth doth come (Third Witch, *Macbeth*, I.iii)
3   He loves not you (Lysander, *Midsummer Night's Dream*, III.ii) **(w)**
4   You do not look on me (Jessica, *Merchant of Venice*, II.vi)
5   Wilt thou use thy wit? (Claudio, *Much Ado About Nothing*, V.i)
6   Wrong I mine enemies? (Brutus, *Julius Caesar*, IV.ii)
7   Knows he not thy voice? (First Lord, *All's Well That Ends Well*, IV.i) **(w)**
8   Didst thou not say he comes? (Baptista, *Taming of the Shrew*, III.ii)
9   Canst not rule her? (Leontes, *Winter's Tale*, II.iii)
10   Hath not a Jew eyes? (Shylock, *Merchant of Venice*, III.i)
11   Do not you love me? (Benedick, *Much Ado About Nothing*, V.iv)
12   Buy thou a rope! (Antipholus, *Comedy of Errors*, IV.i)
13   Fear you not him! (Tranio, *Taming of the Shrew*, Iv.iv)
14   Speak not you to him! (Escalus, *Measure for Measure*, V.i)
15   Do not you meddle! (Antonio, *Much Ado About Nothing*, V.i)
16   She not denies it (Leonato, *Much Ado About Nothing*, IV.i) **(w)**

Helpful hints

Assume that 9 has a null finite *pro* subject. Assume also that the sentences in 12–15 are **imperative** in force, and consider the possibility that V raises to C in imperatives in Elizabethan English (see Han 2001), perhaps attaching to a strong imperative affix *Imp*. Consider also the possibility that *not* had a dual status and could either function as an independent word (like present-day English *not*) or could serve as an enclitic particle (like present-day English *n't*) which attached to the end of an immediately adjacent finite T constituent. Finally, say in what way(s) sentence 16 proves problematic in respect of the assumptions made in the main text (and in the model answer below), and see if you can think of possible solutions (e.g. what if the verb raised as far as NEG but not as far as T?). Assume that genitive nominals like *my words*, *mine enemies*, *thy wit*, and *thy voice* are DPs, but do not concern yourself with their internal structure. (We will briefly look at the structure of genitive nominals in the next chapter.)

Model answer for 1 and 2

Relevant aspects of the derivation of 1 (here presented in simplified form) are as follows. The verb *marvel* merges with its PP complement *at my words* to form the VP *marvel at my words*. This in turn is merged with a T constituent containing a strong present tense affix ($= Af$) to form the T-bar *Af marvel at my words*, which is in turn merged with its subject *thou* to form a TP. The tense affix agrees with *thou* and thus carries the features [second-person, singular-number, present-tense], below abbreviated to *2SgPr*. Being strong, the tense affix triggers raising of the verb *marvel* to adjoin to the affix in T. The resulting TP is merged with a null intransitive finite C which marks the declarative force of the sentence and which assigns nominative case to *thou*. 1 thus has the syntactic structure shown in simplified form in (i) below, with the dotted arrow indicating movement of the verb *marvel* from V to T:

(i)

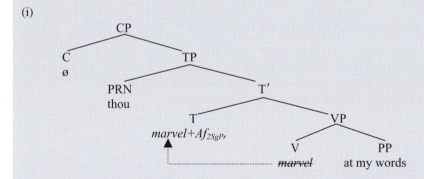

The string *marvel+Af$_{2SgPr}$* is ultimately spelled out as *marvell'st* in the PF component.

Sentence 2 is derived as follows. The verb *come* merges with a tense affix in T, forming the T-bar *Af come*. This will in turn be merged with its subject *Macbeth*, which is a DP headed by a null determiner, in accordance with the **DP hypothesis**. Merging the resulting DP with a null declarative complementiser will derive the syntactic structure shown in (ii) below:

(ii)

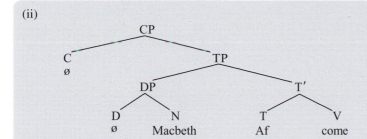

It would seem that the tense affix in T is ultimately spelled out as *doth* (which is a dialectal variant of *does*). What is surprising about this is that the dummy auxiliary DO (in present-day English, at least) is used only to spell out a tense affix which is unable to find a host by any other means. Since finite verbs can raise from V to T in Elizabethan English, what we'd expect to happen in (ii) is for the verb *come* to raise to adjoin to the tense affix in T, so forming the substructure *come+Af*, which would ultimately be spelled out as *cometh* (a dialectal variant of *comes*). However, although this is indeed one possible outcome, this is clearly not what happens in the case of 2 *Macbeth doth come*. Why not?

    Let us suppose that the tense affix in a finite T in a structure like (ii) in Elizabethan English could be either strong or weak, and that Elizabethan English (perhaps because it had V-to-T raising) did not have any T-to-V lowering operation like the Affix Lowering operation found in present-day English. Where T is strong, the tense affix will trigger raising of the main verb from V to T; where it is weak, the verb will remain in situ, and the tense affix will remain unattached, and so will ultimately be spelled out as an appropriately inflected form of DO (here, *doth*). Such an analysis implies that there was considerably more morphosyntactic variation in Shakespearean English than we find in present-day varieties of Standard English – e.g. in respect of a finite tense affix being either strong or weak. Given that Shakespeare's writing contains a mixture of different dialect forms (as we see from the alternation between dialectal variants like *comes/cometh* and *does/doth*), this may not be implausible. However, as noted by Tieken-Boon van Ostade (1988), the origin of *do* is 'one of the great riddles of English linguistic history'.

5 Wh-movement

5.1 Overview

In the previous chapter, we looked at the **head movement** operation by which a head can move into the next highest head position within the structure containing it. In this chapter, we look at a very different kind of movement operation traditionally termed **wh-movement**, by which a wh-expression like *who* or *what languages* moves into the specifier position within CP. In this chapter, we focus on the syntax of wh-questions, though exercise 5.2 at the end of the chapter invites you to think about the syntax of another type of wh-clause, namely relative clauses.

5.2 Wh-questions

So far, we have implicitly assumed that CP comprises a head C constituent (which can be filled by a complementiser or a preposed auxiliary) and a TP complement. However, one question which such an analysis begs is what position is occupied by the bold-printed constituent which precedes the italicised auxiliary in **root interrogatives** (i.e. main-clause questions) such as (1) below:

(1) (a)   **What languages** *can* you speak?
   (b)   **Which one** *would* you like?
   (c)   **Who** *was* she dating?
   (d)   **Where** *are* you going?

Each of the sentences in (1) contains an italicised inverted auxiliary occupying the head C position of CP, preceded by a bold-printed interrogative **wh-expression** – i.e. an expression containing an interrogative word beginning with *wh-* like *what/which/who/where/when/why*. (Note that *how* in questions like *How are you? How well did he behave?* etc. is also treated as a wh-word because it exhibits the same syntactic behaviour as other interrogative words beginning with *wh-*.) Each of the wh-expressions in (1) functions as the complement of the verb at the end of the sentence – as we see from the fact that each of the examples in (1) has a paraphrase like that in (2) below in which the wh-expression occupies complement position after the italicised verb:

(2) (a)   You can *speak* **what languages**?

(b)   You would *like* **which one**?

(c)   She was *dating* **who**?

(d)   You are *going* **where**?

Structures like (2) are termed **wh-in-situ questions**, because the bold-printed wh-expression does not get preposed, but rather remains **in situ** (i.e. 'in place') in the canonical position associated with its grammatical function (e.g. *what languages* in (2a) is the direct object complement of *speak*, and complements are normally positioned after their verbs, so *what languages* is positioned after the verb *speak*). In English, wh-in-situ questions are used primarily as **echo questions**, to echo and question something previously said by someone else (e.g. a sentence like (2c) might be used as an incredulous response to someone who says *She was dating Lord Lancelot Humpalotte*). Echo questions like those in (2) suggest that the wh-expressions in (1) originate as complements of the relevant verbs, and subsequently get moved to the front of the overall clause. But what position do they get moved into, in **non-echoic questions** like (1)?

The answer is obviously that they are moved into some position preceding the inverted auxiliary. Since inverted auxiliaries occupy the head C position of CP, let's suppose that preposed wh-expressions are moved into a position preceding the head C of CP. Given that **specifiers** are positioned before heads, a plausible suggestion to make is that preposed wh-expressions move to become the specifier of C (i.e. move into **spec-C**). If so, a sentence like (2c) *Who was she dating?* will involve the arrowed movement operations shown in (3) below (where *who* has been assigned to the category PRN – though it should be noted that interrogative pronouns like *who* are pronominal quantifiers and hence Q-pronouns, and so *who* could alternatively be assigned to the category Q):

(3)

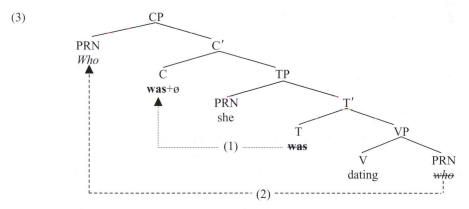

Two different kinds of movement operation (indicated by the numbered arrows) are involved in (3): the movement arrowed in (1) involves the familiar operation of **head movement** by which the bold-printed auxiliary **was** moves from the head T position of TP to the head C position of CP (adjoining to a null affixal interrogative complementiser ∅); by contrast (2) involves movement of an italicised wh-expression from a position below C (here, from the complement position within VP) into the specifier position in CP, and this very different kind of movement operation is known as **wh-movement**. Note that unlike head movement (which, as its name suggests, moves only heads), wh-movement moves maximal projections; for instance, in (1a) *What languages can you speak?* wh-movement moves the quantifier phrase *what languages* which is the maximal projection of the interrogative quantifier *what?* by virtue of being the largest expression headed by the word *what*; and in (1c) *Who was she dating?* it moves the interrogative Q-pronoun *who* (which is a maximal projection by virtue of being the largest expression headed by the word *who*). Let us suppose that every clause/CP must be **typed** (i.e. identified as declarative or interrogative, or exclamative etc. in type) in the syntax, and that a clause is typed as interrogative if it contains an interrogative head or specifier: on this view, movement of the interrogative pronoun *who* to spec-C serves to type the CP in (3) as interrogative.

Evidence in support of the assumption that preposed wh-expressions move into spec-C comes from varieties of English in which a preposed wh-expression can precede a complementiser like *that*. This is true, for example, of interrogative complement clauses in Belfast English like those bracketed below (from Henry 1995, p. 107):

(4) (a)   I wonder [*which dish* **that** they picked]
    (b)   They didn't know [*which model* **that** we had discussed]

Since the complementiser *that* occupies the head C position in the bracketed CP, it seems reasonable to suppose that the wh-expressions *which dish/which model* in front of *that* occupy the specifier position within CP, and this is what Alison Henry argues (these wh-expressions having the status of quantifier phrases headed by the wh-quantifier *which*). In standard varieties of English, sentences like (4) are ungrammatical because they violate the following condition:

(5)   **Complementiser Condition**
       An overt complementiser (like *that/for/if*) cannot have an overt specifier in the superficial structure of a sentence

However, it should be noted that even speakers of Standard English varieties occasionally produce *wh+that* structures in spontaneous speech. However, such structures typically involve a wh-phrase rather than a wh-word preceding *that* – as illustrated by the contrast below:

(6) (a)   %I wonder [*what kind of party* **that** they have in mind]
    (b)   *I wonder [*what* **that** they have in mind]

The italicised expression preceding *that* is a quantifier phrase in (6a), but a pronominal quantifier in (6b).

Although our discussion in this chapter will focus on wh-movement in interrogative clauses, it should be pointed out that there is a wide range of other constructions which have been claimed to involve movement of a (visible or invisible) wh-constituent (albeit without auxilary inversion), including *exclama-tive* clauses like that italicised in (7a) below, relative clauses like that italicised in (7b), comparative clauses like that italicised in (7c) below, *as*-clauses like that italicised in (7d) and so-called *tough*-clauses like that italicised in (7e):

(7) (a)   He hadn't realised *what a fool he was making of himself*
    (b)   She is someone *who you can trust*
    (c)   It is bigger than *I expected it to be*
    (d)   Ames was a spy, *as the FBI eventually discovered*
    (e)   Syntax is tough *to understand*

It is interesting to note that (7c) has a variant form containing the overt wh-word *what* in some (non-standard) varieties of English, where we find *It is bigger than **what** I expected it to be*. We will not attempt to fathom the syntax of constructions like those in (7) here, however – although exercise 5.2 asks you to think about the syntax of relative clauses.

A theoretical point to note in passing is that although the above discussion implicitly assumed that *movement* and *merger* are two entirely distinct types of operation, Chomsky (2001) maintains that *movement* is simply a particular type of *merger* operation. He refers to merger operations which involve taking an item out of the **lexical array** and merging it with some other constituent as **external merge**, and to movement operations by which an item contained within an existing structure is moved to a new position within the same structure as **internal merge**. Accordingly, wh-movement in (3) can be seen as involving an internal merger operation. (By contrast, head movement involves a different type of *adjunction* operation by which one head is adjoined to another – as we saw in the previous chapter.)

5.3   Wh-movement as copying and deletion

A tacit assumption made in our analysis of wh-movement in (3) is that just as a moved head (e.g. an inverted auxiliary) leaves behind a null copy of itself in the position out of which it moves, so too a moved wh-expression leaves behind a copy at its **extraction site** (i.e. in the position out of which it is **extracted**/moved). In earlier work in the 1970s and 1980s, moved constituents were said to leave behind a **trace** in the positions out of which they move (informally denoted as *t*), and traces were treated as being like pronouns in certain respects. A moved constituent and its trace(s) were together said to form a (movement) **chain**, with the highest member of the chain (i.e. the moved constituent) being the **head** of the movement chain, and the lowest member being the **foot** of the chain. Within the framework of Chomsky's more recent **copy theory of movement**, a trace is taken to be a full copy (rather than a pronominal copy) of a moved constituent. Informally, however, we shall sometimes refer to the null copies left behind by movement as **traces** or **trace copies** in later sections and chapters.

The assumption that moved wh-expressions leave a copy behind can be defended not only on theoretical grounds (in terms of our desire to develop a unified theory of movement in which both minimal and maximal projections leave behind copies when they move), but also on empirical grounds. One such empirical argument comes from the familiar phenomenon of *have*-cliticisation in sentences like:

(8)   I have/I've been to Rome more often than I have/*I've to Paris

Although *have* can cliticise onto *I* in the string *I've been to Rome* in (8), cliticisation is not possible in the string *I've to Paris*. Why should this be? Let us make the reasonable assumption that *I've to Paris* in (8) is an elliptical variant of *I've been to Paris*, so that (8) has the fuller structure shown informally in (9) below, with strikethrough indicating that the ellipsed V receives a null spellout in the PF component:

(9)   I have been to Rome more often than I have ~~been~~ to Paris

The relevant type of cliticisation operation is subject to a constraint which can be characterised informally in the following terms:

(10)   Cliticisation is barred when a clitic is followed by a null constituent

(where 'is followed by' can be given an order-free formulation in terms of the relation c-command, in ways that I leave the technophiles among you to fathom for yourselves). This accounts for the ungrammaticality of the string *I've to Paris* in (8), since *have* is immediately followed by a null copy of the verb *been* and so the constraint (10) blocks *have* from cliticising onto *I*.

In the light of the constraint in (10), consider why cliticisation is permitted (in my own British English variety) in (11) below:

(11) (a)   They have very little money in their bank account
     (b)   They've very little money in their bank account

but not in (12):

(12) (a)   I wonder [how much money they have in their bank account]
     (b)   *I wonder [how much money they've in their bank account]

The bracketed clauses in (12) are interrogative complement clauses which show wh-movement of an interrogative expression to the front of the clause (the moved wh-expression being *how much money*, comprising a quantifier *much* with the complement *money* and the specifier *how*). If (as we claim here) wh-movement involves a copying operation, (12b) will have the fuller structure shown in (13) below:

(13)   I wonder [how much money they have ~~how much money~~ in their bank account]

That is, the wh-QP *how much money* will originate as the complement of the verb *have*, and a copy of this constituent will then be placed at the front of the bracketed interrogative complement clause, with the original occurrence of the QP receiving a null spellout (marked by ~~strikethrough~~). But the null QP following the clitic *have* will then block *have* from contracting onto *they* in accordance with the cliticisation constraint in (10). Thus, the ungrammaticality of sentences like (12b) is consistent with the claim that wh-movement involves copying.

A different kind of evidence in support of the claim that preposed wh-expressions leave behind a null copy when they move comes from a phenomenon which we can call **preposition copying**. In this connection, consider the following Shakespearean wh-structures:

(14) (a) *In what enormity* is Marcius poor **in**? (Menenius, *Coriolanus*, II.i)

    (b) *To what form but that he is* should wit larded with malice and malice forced with wit turn him **to**? (Thersites, *Troilus and Cressida*, V.i)

    (c) . . . that fair [*for which* love groan'd **for**] (Prologue to Act II, *Romeo and Juliet*)

(14a, b) are interrogative clauses, and the bracketed structure in (14c) is a **relative clause** – so called because it contains a relative wh-pronoun *which* relating (more specifically, referring back) to the preceding noun expression *that fair*. In these examples, an italicised prepositional wh-phrase (i.e. a Prepositional Phrase containing a wh-word like *what/which*) has been moved to the front of the relevant clause by wh-movement. But a (bold-printed) copy of the preposition also appears at the end of the clause. In case you think that this is a Shakespearean quirk (or – Heaven forbid – a slip of the quill on the part of Will), the examples in (15) below show much the same thing happening in (bracketed) **relative clauses** in present-day English:

(15) (a) But if this ever-changing world [*in which* we live **in**] makes you give in and cry, say 'Live and Let Die' (Sir Paul McCartney, theme song from the James Bond movie *Live and Let Die*)

    (b) IKEA only actually has ten stores [*from which* to sell **from**] (Economics reporter, BBC Radio 5)

    (c) Israeli soldiers fired an anti-tank missile and hit a police post [*in which* the Palestinian policeman who was killed had been **in**] (News reporter, BBC Radio 5)

    (d) Tiger Woods (*about whom* this Masters seems to be all **about**) is due to tee off shortly (Sports reporter, BBC Radio 5)

    (e) The hearing mechanism is a peripheral, passive system *over which* we have no control **over** (undergraduate exam paper)

How can we account for preposition copying in structures like (14) and (15)?

The **copy theory of movement** enables us to provide a principled answer to this question. Let's suppose that wh-movement is a composite operation involving two suboperations of **copying** and **deletion**: the first stage is for a copy of the moved wh-expression to be moved into spec-C; the second stage is for the original occurrence of the wh-expression to be deleted. From this perspective, preposition copying arises when the preposition at the original extraction site undergoes copying but not deletion. To see what this means in more concrete terms, consider the syntax of (14a) *In what enormity is Marcius poor in?* This is derived as follows. The wh-quantifier *what* merges with the noun *enormity* to derive the quantifier phrase/QP *what enormity*. This in turn is merged with the preposition *in* to form the Prepositional Phrase/PP *in what enormity*. This PP is then merged with the adjective *poor* to form the Adjectival Phrase/AP *poor in what enormity*. This AP is merged with the copular verb *is* to form the Verb Phrase/VP *is poor in what enormity*. This VP is merged with a finite T constituent which triggers raising of the verb *is* from V to T; the resulting T-bar constituent is merged with its subject *Marcius* (which is a DP headed by a null determiner) to form the tense phrase/TP *ø Marcius is i̶s̶ poor in what enormity*. Merging this with a strong C into which *is* moves forms the C-bar *Is ø Marcius i̶s̶ i̶s̶ poor in what enormity?* Moving a copy of the PP *in what enormity* into spec-C in turn derives the structure shown in simplified form in (16) below (with copies of moved constituents shown in italics):

(16)

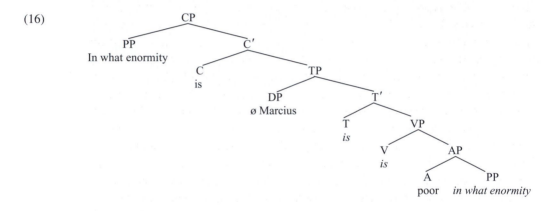

The two italicised copies of the moved copular verb *is* are deleted by operation of **copy deletion**. But consider how copy deletion affects the copy left behind by movement of the PP *in what enormity* to spec-C. If we suppose that copy deletion in (14a) deletes the smallest phrase containing the wh-word *what*, it will delete the quantifier phrase *what enormity* rather than the Prepositional Phrase *in what enormity*, so deriving (14a) *In what enormity is Marcius poor in?* Thus, preposition copying structures like (14) and (15) provide evidence that wh-movement is a composite operation involving wh-copying and wh-deletion.

A related piece of evidence that wh-movement leaves behind a copy comes from speech errors involving **wh-copying**, e.g. in relative clauses such as that bracketed below:

(17)   It's a world record [**which** many of us thought *which* wasn't on the books at all] (Athletics commentator, BBC2 TV)

What's the nature of the speech error made by the tongue-tied (or brain-drained) BBC reporter in (17)? The answer is that when moving the relative pronoun *which* from its initial italicised position to its subsequent bold-printed position, our intrepid reporter successfully merges a copy of *which* in the bold-printed position, but fails to delete the original occurrence of *which* in the italicised position. Such speech errors provide us with further evidence that wh-movement is a composite operation involving both copying and deletion.

An additional piece of evidence in support of wh-movement involving a copying operation comes from sentences such as those below:

(18) (a)   *What hope* **of finding any survivors** could there be**?**
      (b)   *What hope* could there be **of finding any survivors?**

(19) (a)   *What proof* **that he was implicated** have you found?
      (b)   *What proof* have you found **that he was implicated**?

In order to try and understand what's going on here, let's take a closer look at the derivation of (18). The expression *what hope of finding any survivors* in (18a) is a QP comprising the quantifier *what* and an NP complement which in turn comprises the noun *hope* and its PP complement *of finding any survivors* (with the polarity item *any* being able to occur because it is c-commanded by the interrogative quantifier *what*: see §2.6). The overall QP *what hope of finding any survivors* is initially merged as the complement of the verb *be*, but ultimately moves to the front of the overall sentence in (18a): this is unproblematic, since it involves wh-movement of the whole QP. But in (18b), it would seem as if only part of this QP (= the string *what hope*) undergoes wh-movement, leaving behind the remnant PP *of finding any survivors*. The problem with this is that the string *what hope* is not a constituent, only a subpart of the overall QP *what hope of finding any survivors*. Given the standard assumption that only complete constituents can undergo movement, we clearly cannot maintain that the nonconstituent string *what hope* gets moved on its own. So how can we account for sentences like (18b)? Copy theory provides us with an answer, if we suppose that wh-movement places a copy of the complete QP *what hope of finding survivors* at the front of the overall sentence, so deriving the structure shown in skeletal form in (20) below:

(20)   **What hope of finding any survivors** could there be *what hope of finding any survivors*

If we further suppose that the PP *of finding any survivors* is spelled out in its original position (i.e. in the italicised position it occupied before wh-movement applied) but the remaining constituents of the QP (the quantifier *what* and the noun *hope*) are spelled out in the superficial (bold-printed) position in which they end up after wh-movement, (18b) will be spelled out in the manner shown in simplified form below after copy-deletion has applied (with ~~strikethrough~~ indicating constituents which receive a null spellout):

(21)   **What hope ~~of finding any survivors~~** could there be *~~what hope~~ of finding*
          any survivors

As should be obvious, such an analysis relies crucially on the assumption that moved constituents leave behind full copies of themselves. It also assumes the possibility of **split spellout** or **discontinuous spellout**, in the sense that (in sentences like (18) and (19) above) a PP or CP which is the complement of a particular type of moved constituent can be spelled out in one position (in the position where it originated), and the remainder of the constituent spelled out in another (in the position where it ends up). More generally, it suggests that (in certain structures) there is a choice regarding which part of a movement chain gets deleted. A further possibility which this opens up is that wh-in-situ structures in languages like Chinese may involve wh-movement, but with the moved wh-expression being spelled out in its initial position (at the foot of the movement chain) rather than in its final position (at the head of the movement chain).

A different type of argument in support of the copy theory of movement can be formulated in connection with the interpretation of reflexive anaphors like *himself* in sentences such as:

(22)   Joe wonders which picture of himself Jim bought

In (22), the reflexive anaphor *himself* can refer either to *Joe* or to *Jim*. An obvious problem posed by the latter interpretation is that a reflexive has to be c-commanded by a local antecedent (one contained within the same TP, as we saw in §2.7), and yet *Jim* does not c-command *himself* in (22). How can we account for the dual interpretation of *himself*? The copy theory of movement provides a principled answer to this question. The QP *which picture of himself* is initially merged as the complement of the verb *bought* but is subsequently moved to front of the *bought* clause, leaving behind a copy in its original position, so deriving the structure shown in skeletal form in (23) below:

(23)   [CP [TP Joe wonders [CP **which picture of himself** [TP Jim bought
                                        which picture of himself]]]]

Given the two-copy structure in (23), the possibility of *himself* referring to *Jim* can be attributed to the fact that the italicised copy of *himself* is c-commanded by (and contained within the same TP as) *Jim*. On the other hand, the possibility of *himself* referring to *Joe* can be attributed to the fact that the bold-printed copy of **himself** is c-commanded by (and occurs within the same TP as) *Joe*.

In this section, we have seen that there is a range of empirical evidence which supports the claim that a constituent which undergoes wh-movement leaves behind a copy at its extraction site. This copy is normally given a null spellout in the PF component, though we have seen that copies may sometimes have an overt spellout, or indeed part of a moved phrase may be spelled out in one position, and part in another. We have also seen that copies of moved wh-constituents are visible in the semantic component, and play an important role in relation to the interpretation of anaphors.

5.4   Driving wh-movement and auxiliary inversion

An important question raised by the analysis outlined above is what triggers wh-movement. In recent work, Chomsky has suggested that an **edge feature** is the mechanism which drives movement of wh-expressions to spec-C. More specifically, he maintains that just as T in finite clauses carries an EPP feature requiring it to be extended into a TP projection containing a specifier on the edge of TP, so too C in questions carries an edge feature [EF] requiring it to be extended into a CP projection containing a specifier on the edge of CP. These two types of feature differ in that the EPP feature on T works in conjunction with agreement (so that T requires as its subject a constituent which it agrees with in person/number), whereas the edge feature on C operates independently of agreement, allowing C (in principle) to attract any type of constituent to move to the specifier position within CP. However, questions in languages like English are subject to the following condition:

(24)   **Interrogative Condition**
A clause is interpreted as a non-echoic question if (and only if) it is a CP with an interrogative specifier (i.e. a specifier containing an interrogative word)

If wh-words like *who/what/where* etc. originate within TP, it follows that the edge feature on an interrogative C will need to attract an interrogative expression to move to spec-C in order for the relevant clause to be interpreted as interrogative in accordance with (24).

We can illustrate how the edge feature analysis of wh-movement works by looking at the derivation of the bracketed interrogative complement clause below:

(25)   He wants to know [where you are going]

The bracketed wh-question clause in (25) is derived as follows. The verb *going* is merged with its complement *where* to form the VP *going where*. The present tense T-auxiliary *are* is then merged with the resulting VP to form the T-bar *are going where*. The pronoun *you* is in turn merged with this T-bar to form the TP *you are going where*. A null interrogative complementiser [$_C$ ∅] is subsequently merged with the resulting TP. Since English (unlike Chinese) is the kind of language which requires wh-movement in non-echoic wh-questions, C also has an edge feature [EF] requiring it to have a specifier (with the specifier having to be interrogative in order for the resulting structure to be interpreted as a question in accordance with 24). Thus, merging C with its TP complement will form the C-bar in (26) below (with the edge feature on C being bracketed, following the convention that features are enclosed in square brackets):

(26)

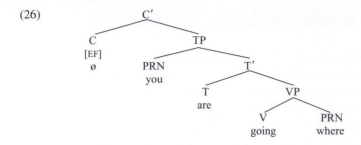

(The locative adverbial pronoun *where* is categorised here as a PRN/pronoun, though – like other adverbial wh-pronouns such as *how* and *when* – it could equally be categorised as an ADV/adverb.) The edge feature on C enables it to **attract** the wh-pronoun *where* to move from its VP-complement position in (26) to CP-specifier position. If 'EF is always deleted when satisfied' in English (Chomsky 2006, p. 8), the edge feature carried by C will be deleted (and thereby inactivated) once its requirements are satisfied (deletion being indicated by ~~strikethrough~~), so that (arrowed) wh-movement derives the structure (27) below:

(27)

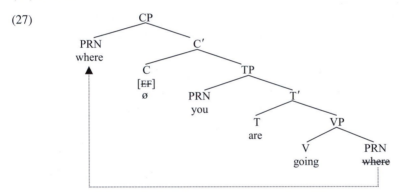

There is no auxiliary inversion (hence no movement of the auxiliary *are* from T to C) because (27) is a complement clause, and an interrogative C does not carry a tense feature triggering auxiliary inversion in complement clauses.

By contrast, main-clause wh-questions involve auxiliary inversion as well as wh-movement, as we see from sentences like (28) below:

(28)   Who were you phoning?

The derivation of (28) proceeds as follows. The wh-pronoun *who* merges with the verb *phoning* to form the VP *phoning who*. The resulting VP is subsequently merged with the past tense auxiliary *were* to form the T-bar *were phoning who*, which is itself merged with the pronoun *you* to form the TP *you were phoning who*. This TP is then merged with a null interrogative C which carries an edge feature. Since (28) is also a main-clause question, C will additionally carry a tense feature [TNS]. Given these assumptions, merging C with the TP *you were phoning who* will derive the following structure:

(29)

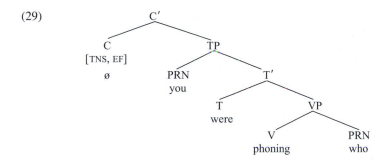

The tense feature on C attracts the past tense auxiliary *were* to move to C (attaching to a null affixal interrogative complementiser). The edge feature on the interrogative C triggers movement of the interrogative pronoun *who* to spec-C, so deriving the structure shown below (with the tense and edge features on C being deleted once their requirements are met, and arrows indicating movements which take place in the course of the derivation):

(30)

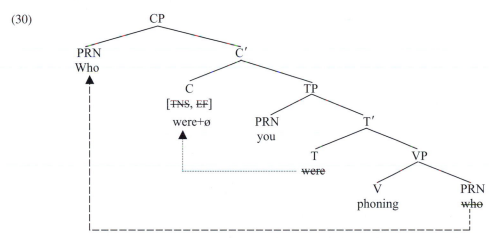

And (30) is the superficial syntactic structure of (28) *Who were you phoning?*

A key assumption embodied in the analysis presented here is that questions in English obey the Interrogative Condition (24) above, which specifies that 'A clause is interpreted as a non-echoic question if (and only if) it is a CP with an interrogative specifier (i.e. a specifier containing an interrogative word).' This assumption has interesting implications for the syntax of yes-no questions such as:

(31)   Is it raining?

It implies that not only (non-echoic) wh-questions but also (non-echoic) yes-no questions are CPs with an interrogative specifier. This in turn suggests that yes-no questions contain a **null yes-no question particle** which is directly generated in spec-C (i.e. which is positioned in spec-C by simple merger rather than movement). From a historical perspective, such an analysis is by no means implausible, since Elizabethan English had main-clause yes-no questions introduced by the overt question word *whether*, as illustrated below:

(32) (a)   Whether had you rather lead mine eyes or eye your master's heels?
             (Mrs Page, *Merry Wives of Windsor*, III.ii)

     (b)   Whether dost thou profess thyself a knave or a fool? (Lafeu, *All's Well That Ends Well*, IV.v)

This raises the possibility that yes-no questions have essentially the same syntax in present-day English as in Elizabethan English, save that they could be introduced by the overt interrogative adverb *whether* in Elizabethan English, but are introduced by a null counterpart of *whether* (which we can denote as ~~whether~~) in present-day English.

A second piece of evidence in support of the null yes-no question particle analysis comes from the fact that yes-no questions can be introduced by *whether* when they are transposed into reported speech (and so occur in a complement clause), as we see from the examples below:

(33) (a)   'Are you feeling better?,' he asked
     (b)   He asked *whether* I was feeling better

A third piece of evidence is that yes-no questions with auxiliary inversion resemble *whether* questions in that in both cases *yes/no* are appropriate answers: cf.

(34) (a)   When he asked 'Did you vote for Larry Loudmouth?,' I said 'Yes' and you said 'No'
     (b)   When he asked whether we voted for Larry Loudmouth, I said 'Yes' and you said 'No'

A fourth argument is that main-clause yes-no questions can be tagged by *or not* in precisely the same way as complement-clause *whether* questions: cf.

(35) (a)   Has he finished *or not*?
     (b)   I can't say whether he has finished *or not*

If yes-no questions are CPs containing a null counterpart of *whether* in spec-C, we can arrive at a unitary characterisation of (non-echoic) questions as *CPs with an interrogative specifier*.

What all of this means is that (31) *Is it raining?* will be derived as follows. The present tense auxiliary *is* merges with the verb *raining* to form the T-bar *is raining*. The resulting T-bar merges with the subject *it* to form the TP *it is raining*. This TP in turn merges with a null C which has a tense feature and an edge feature. The tense feature of C attracts (a copy of) the T constituent *is* to merge with C; the requirement imposed by the edge feature of the interrogative C for CP to have an interrogative specifier is met by merging a null yes-no question particle in spec-C (which, for concreteness, we will take to be a null counterpart of the adverb *whether*, below symbolised as ~~whether~~), ultimately deriving the structure shown below (after deletion of the features of C and of the original occurrence of *is*):

(36)

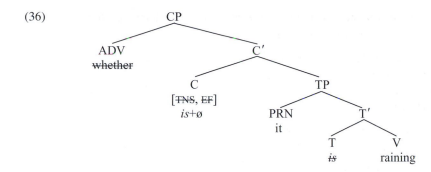

If the yes-no question particle is a null counterpart of *whether*, the lexical entry for *whether* will need to specify that it receives a null spellout in main clauses but is spelled out as |weðə(r)| elsewhere.

5.5   Pied-piping of material in the domain of a wh-word

The wh-questions we have analysed so far have all involved movement of a wh-word to spec-C. However, sometimes it's more than just a wh-word which gets preposed under wh-movement. For example, if we look at the wh-movement counterpart of a wh-in-situ question like (37a) below, we find that when the wh-quantifier *which* is moved to the front of the sentence, the noun *assignment* has to be moved together with it:

(37) (a)   You have done *which* **assignment**?
     (b)   *Which have you done **assignment**?
     (c)   *Which* **assignment** have you done?

To use the relevant technical term, when a wh-quantifier is moved to spec-C, subordinate material in its c-command **domain** (i.e. material c-commanded by the wh-quantifier) has to be **pied-piped** (i.e. dragged) along with it: consequently, when the wh-quantifier *which* moves in (37), it pied-pipes the noun *assignment* with it, so that the whole quantifier phrase *which assignment* moves to spec-C – as in (37c). (The colourful **pied-piping** metaphor was coined by Ross 1967, based on a traditional fairy story in which the pied-piper in the village of Hamelin enticed a group of children to follow him out of a rat-infested village by playing his pipe.) Why should this be? In order to try and answer this question, let's consider how (37c) is derived.

The quantifier *which* merges with the noun *assignment* to form the QP *which assignment*. This in turn is merged with the verb *done* to form the VP *done which assignment*. The resulting VP is subsequently merged with the present tense auxiliary *have* to form the T-bar *have done which assignment*, which is itself merged with the pronoun *you* to form the TP *you have done which assignment*. TP is then merged with a null interrogative C. Since (37c) is a main-clause question, C will carry tense and edge features. Consequently, merging C with the TP *you have done which assignment* will derive the following structure:

(38)

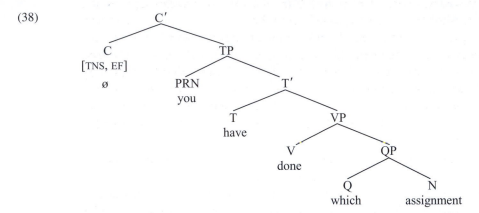

The tense feature of C attracts the present tense auxiliary *have* to move to C, attaching to a null affix in C. The edge feature of C attracts an interrogative expression to move to the specifier position on the edge of CP.

However, a question which arises at this point is why C can't simply attract the wh-word *which* on its own to move to spec-C, so deriving the structure (39) below (with arrows marking wh-movement and auxiliary inversion):

(39)

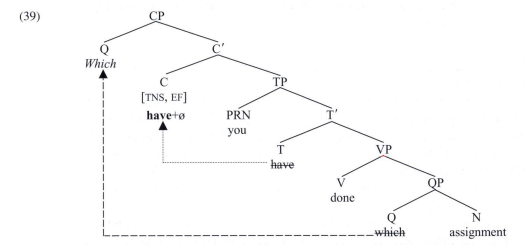

The resulting derivation crashes, as we see from the ungrammaticality of (37b) *Which have you done assignment?* Why should this be?

The answer is that movement of *which* on its own violates the following UG condition on movement chains:

(40)   **Chain Uniformity Condition**
'A chain is uniform with regard to phrase structure status' (Chomsky 1995, p. 253)

(40) requires every copy in a movement chain to be uniform. This condition rules out the possibility of *which* moving on its own in (39) for the following reason. In (39), the moved wh-word *which* in spec-C has the status of a maximal projection by virtue of being the largest expression headed by the word *which*; by contrast, the null copy ~~which~~ left behind by wh-movement has the status of a minimal projection by virtue of being the head Q constituent of the QP ~~which~~ *assignment*. The resulting wh-chain thus violates the Chain Uniformity Condition (40) by having a maximal projection at its head and a minimal projection at its foot. In simpler terms, the Chain Uniformity Condition means that since the original occurrence of the quantifier *which* heads a QP, all other copies of *which* in the movement chain must also head a QP – and this will only be the case if QP rather than Q moves. (As should be apparent, the Chain Uniformity Condition will also bar movement of an intermediate projection to spec-C.)

However, while we have now accounted for why the quantifier *which* cannot move on its own in (37b), we have not accounted for how the whole quantifier phrase *which assignment* comes to move in (37c) *Which assignment have you done?* Why should this be? The answer lies in a further condition which can be formulated as follows:

(41)   **Attract Smallest Condition/ASC**
       A head which attracts a particular type of item attracts the smallest
       constituent containing such an item which will not lead to violation of any
       UG principle

What this implies in relation to a movement operation like wh-movement is that we move the wh-word on its own wherever possible, but that if movement of the wh-word on its own is prevented by some UG principle, we then move the next smallest possible constituent containing the wh-word (as long as this doesn't involve violation of any UG principle): because the Chain Uniformity Condition prevents intermediate projections from undergoing movement, this means that (if a wh-word cannot move on its own) we move the smallest possible maximal projection containing the wh-word . . . and so on. Let's see how this works for a structure such as (38).

The edge feature on the interrogative C in (38) means that the interrogative C attracts an interrogative constituent. The Attract Smallest Condition/ASC (41) means that C attracts the *smallest possible* interrogative constituent to move to spec-C. The smallest syntactic constituent is a head, so ASC tells us that what we should do first is try and move the head interrogative Q *which* of the QP *which assignment* to spec-C. However (as we have just seen), movement of the wh-word *which* on its own is blocked by the Chain Uniformity Condition (40). Hence, in conformity with ASC, we try moving the next smallest constituent containing the interrogative word *which*, and this is the QP *which assignment*. Moving QP to spec-C derives the structure shown below:

(42)

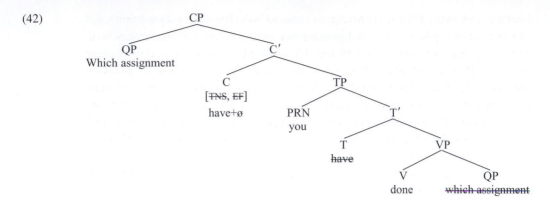

The resulting structure is convergent/well-formed (as we see from the grammaticality of (37c) *Which assignment have you done?*) and is interpreted as a non-echoic question (in accordance with (24) above) by virtue of being a CP with an interrogative specifier.

Our discussion here shows that when movement of a wh-word on its own is not possible, a maximal projection containing the wh-word is moved instead. Note, however, that we can't just move *any* maximal projection containing a wh-word. For example, although the Verb Phrase *done which assignment* in (38) is a maximal projection (more specifically, the maximal projection of the verb *done*) and contains the wh-word *which*, it cannot undergo wh-movement – as we see from the ungrammaticality of

(43)   **Done which assignment have you?*

Why should this be? The answer is that in consequence of the Attract Smallest Condition (41), C can only attract the *smallest* maximal projection which doesn't violate any UG principle: since the smaller maximal projection *which assignment* can move on its own without violating any constraint, there is no reason whatever to move the larger maximal projection *done which assignment*.

Although we have attributed the requirement for moving the *smallest possible* constituent to the Attract Smallest Condition/ASC (41), it should be noted that ASC can arguably be subsumed under a more general condition which Chomsky sketches in the following terms:

(44)   **Economy Condition**
'Derivations and representations . . . are required to be minimal, with no superfluous steps in derivations and no superfluous symbols in representations' (Chomsky 1989, p. 69)

(44) amounts to requiring that structures (i.e. 'representations') be as simple (i.e. 'minimal') as possible, and that the syntactic operations involved in derivations should likewise be as simple as possible.

The conclusion which emerges from our discussion in this section is the following. An interrogative C carries an edge feature enabling C to attract an interrogative word. Where the relevant wh-word is the head of a larger phrase, the Chain Uniformity Condition will prevent movement of the wh-word on its own, and the Economy Condition/Attract Smallest Condition will require movement of the smallest constituent containing the wh-word. If we further suppose that (in consequence of the Chain Uniformity Condition) only a maximal projection can move to spec-C, this condition (taken together with the Interrogative Condition (24)) leads to the generalisation that an interrogative C with an edge feature attracts the smallest possible maximal projection containing an interrogative wh-word to become its specifier.

A further type of sentence in which material in the (c-command) domain of a wh-word is pied-piped along with a preposed wh-word is found in possessive structures such as the following:

(45) (a)   You have borrowed *whose car?*

   (b)   *Whose* have you borrowed *car?*

   (c)   *Whose car* have you borrowed?

In the echo-question (45a), the interrogative phrase *whose car* remains in situ in complement position within the Verb Phrase. In the corresponding non-echo questions in (45b,c) the genitive pronoun *whose* undergoes wh-movement on its own in (45b) but leads to an ungrammatical outcome, whereas the larger expression *whose car* undergoes wh-movement in (45c) and results in a grammatical sentence. So, it would seem that movement of *whose* to the front of the overall sentence requires the noun *car* to be pied-piped along with *whose*. Why should this be?

In order to answer this question, we need to understand the structure of the wh-expression *whose car*. At first sight, it might seem as if *whose* is the head of the phrase *whose car*. However, closer reflection suggests that this cannot be so because *whose* carries genitive case and yet *whose car* is the complement of the transitive verb *borrow* in (45) and so must be accusative. Moreover, *whose* in (45) can be substituted by a phrasal genitive (as in 'Which of the men's car did you borrow?'); and since phrases can occupy the specifier (but not the head) position within a projection, it seems more likely that genitives are the specifiers of the expressions containing them. Furthermore, *whose car* is definite in interpretation (in the sense that it has a meaning paraphraseable as '*the car belonging to who?*'), suggesting that it must be a DP headed by a definite determiner (and indeed there are a number of languages which have a type of possessive structure paraphraseable in English as *whose the car* – e.g. Hungarian). Since there is no overt determiner in a structure like *whose car*, it is plausible to suppose that its head must be a null counterpart of the definite D constituent *the*.

Given these assumptions, (45c) *Whose car have you borrowed?* will be derived as follows. The noun *car* is merged with a null definite determiner marking possession, and this forms the D-bar *ø car*. This D-bar is in turn merged with its pronoun specifier *whose* forming the DP *whose ø car*. The resulting DP is merged with the verb *borrowed*, forming the VP *borrowed whose ø car*. The relevant VP is merged with the present tense T-auxiliary *have*, forming the T-bar *have borrowed whose ø car*, which in turn is merged with its subject *you* forming the TP *you have borrowed whose ø car*. This TP is then merged with an interrogative C carrying tense and edge features, so forming the C-bar below:

(46)

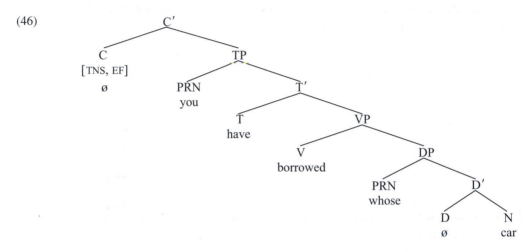

The tense feature of C triggers movement of the present tense auxiliary *have* from T to C, and the edge feature of C attracts the smallest possible maximal projection containing an interrogative word to move to spec-C. Now, the smallest maximal projection containing an interrogative word in (46) is the genitive pronoun *whose* itself, which is a maximal projection by virtue of being the largest expression headed by *whose*. Hence, we might expect *whose* to move to spec-C on its own, so deriving the structure associated with (45b) **Whose have you borrowed car?* But the resulting sentence is ungrammatical. Why?

   The answer lies in a constraint identified by Ross (1967) which we can paraphrase as follows:

(47)   **Left Branch Condition/LBC**
         In languages like English, the leftmost constituent of a nominal expression
         cannot be extracted out of the expression containing it

(*Nominal expressions* can be taken to include DP and QP. In an order-free model of syntax like that assumed in Minimalism, where syntactic structures are not linearly ordered, and word order is added by linearisation conditions in the PF component, the LBC will have to be formulated in structural terms, e.g. as barring extraction of any constituent from the *edge* of the relevant kinds of expression.) If we look at (46), we see that the genitive pronoun *whose* is the leftmost constituent of the DP *whose ø car*. Consequently, the Left Branch Condition (47) prevents *whose* from being extracted out of the DP containing it, so accounting for the ungrammaticality of (45b) **Whose have you borrowed car?* In accordance with the Economy Condition (44), we therefore try preposing the next smallest maximal projection containing *whose*, namely the DP *whose ø car*. Moving this DP to spec-C has the effect of pied-piping the noun *car* along with the interrogative word *whose*, and derives the structure shown in (48) below (simplified by showing only overt constituents and not showing the internal structure of TP or DP):

(48)

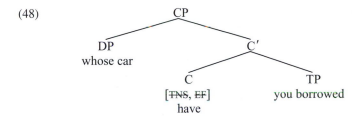

This leads to convergence, as we see from the grammaticality of (45c) *Whose car have you borrowed?*

5.6   Pied-piping of a superordinate preposition

An interesting question raised by the *economy* analysis sketched above is how we account for what happens in clauses like those bracketed in (49) below:

(49)   They asked [**to** *whom* he was referring]

In formal styles of English, the superordinate preposition *to* is **pied-piped** along with the interrogative pronoun *whom*, so that the whole PP *to whom* moves to spec-C position within the bracketed clause. Why should a superordinate preposition be pied-piped along with the subordinate wh-pronoun in such cases? In order to try and answer this question, let's look at the derivation of (49).

Given the assumptions made here, the bracketed interrogative complement clause in (49) will be derived as follows. The preposition *to* merges with the pronoun *whom* to form the PP *to whom*. This PP in turn is merged with the verb *referring* to form the VP *referring to whom*. This VP is then merged with the past tense auxiliary *was*, forming the T-bar *was referring to whom*, and this in turn is merged with the subject pronoun *he* to form the TP *he was referring to whom*.

Merging the resulting TP with a null interrogative complementiser carrying an edge feature [EF] will derive the structure below:

(50)

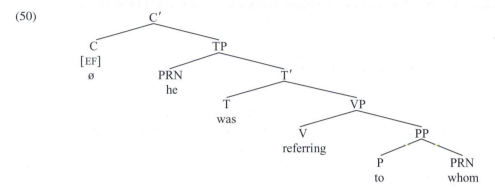

We'd then expect the edge feature of C to trigger movement of the smallest maximal projection containing an interrogative word to the specifier position within CP. Since the pronoun *whom* is a maximal projection containing an interrogative word (by virtue of being the largest expression headed by the interrogative word *whom*), economy considerations would lead us to expect that *whom* will be moved on its own. And yet, this is not the case: instead, the whole PP *to whom* undergoes movement to the spec-C at the front of the embedded clause. Why should this be?

The answer suggested by Chomsky (1995, p. 264) is that extracting *whom* out of the Prepositional Phrase containing it violates a constraint which 'bars preposition stranding'. Although Chomsky does not elaborate on the nature of the relevant constraint, for concreteness let us suppose that it can be subsumed under the Impenetrability Condition which we outlined in §3.8, as will be the case if we revise the latter by the addition of the material italicised below:

(51)   **Impenetrability Condition**
A constituent in the domain of a complementiser *or preposition* is impenetrable to (and so cannot be attracted by) a higher head c-commanding the relevant complementiser/*preposition*

(Recall that *domain* means 'c-command domain', so that a constituent is within the domain of a preposition if it is c-commanded by the preposition – i.e. if it is the complement of the preposition, or is contained within the complement of the preposition.) If the head C of CP in (50) attracts the wh-pronoun *whom* to move directly to spec-C, the Impenetrability Condition (51) will be violated, because *whom* is c-commanded by the preposition *to* and is attracted by a C constituent which c-commands the preposition *to*. Because the Impenetrability Condition bars C from attracting *whom* on its own, C instead attracts the next smallest maximal projection containing *whom* – namely the PP *to whom*.

However, while the analysis presented above accounts for why prepositions are pied-piped along with their complements in formal styles of English (and indeed in many other languages – e.g. French, Italian, Spanish, Greek, Japanese and so forth), what it fails to account for is why prepositions can be **stranded** (i.e. left behind) under wh-movement in informal styles of English, e.g. in sentences such as:

(52)   They asked [*who* he was referring **to**]

After all, under the account offered above, a sentence like (52) ought to violate the Impenetrability Condition (51), and hence would be expected to be ungrammatical. It would therefore seem that colloquial English manages to bypass the Impenetrability Condition somehow. But how?

In this connection, consider the following examples:

(53) (a)   They went *how far inside the tunnel*? (ECHO QUESTION)
     (b)   *How far* did they go *inside the tunnel*? (NON-ECHOIC QUESTION)

If we suppose that *the tunnel* is the complement of the preposition *inside* and *how far* is its specifier, the wh-PP *how far inside the tunnel* in (53a) will have the structure shown in simplified form in (54) below:

(54)   [$_{PP}$ how far [$_{P'}$ [$_P$ inside] the tunnel]]

That is to say, the preposition *inside* merges with its complement *the tunnel* to form the P-bar *inside the tunnel*, and this P-bar is in turn merged with the wh-specifier *how far* to form the PP *how far inside the tunnel*. As the grammaticality of (53b) shows, the specifier *how far* can be extracted out of the PP containing it without violating the Impenetrability Condition (51). This is because the Impenetrability Condition only bars extraction of a constituent in the domain of (i.e. c-commanded by) the preposition, and the specifier *how far* is not c-commanded by the preposition *inside*. More generally, the Impenetrability Condition allows material to be extracted from the *edge* of a Prepositional Phrase, but not from its (c-command) *domain*.

Assuming that movement is permitted from the edge of a Prepositional Phrase, let's now consider how *who* comes to be moved out of its containing preposition phrase in colloquial English sentences like (52) *They asked who he was referring to*. Let us suppose that it is a property of prepositions in colloquial English that they can have an edge feature which allows a wh-expression in the domain of the preposition to move to the edge of PP. This will allow *who* to move from complement to specifier position within the PP (thereby deleting the edge feature on P) in a structure such as (55) below:

(55)

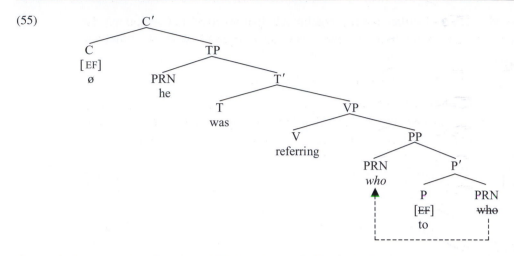

Once *who* has moved to the edge of PP, it no longer falls within the (c-command) domain of the preposition, and so can freely be attracted by the edge feature on the complementiser to move into the spec-C position at the front of the interrogative clause (so deriving the structure associated with *who he was referring to*). On this view, the key difference between preposition pied-piping and preposition stranding lies in whether or not P has an edge feature which can trigger wh-movement to the edge of PP. In informal (but not formal) styles of English, P can have an an edge feature which allows a wh-expression within its domain to move to the edge of PP, and thereafter be extracted from its containing PP.

Added plausibility is given to the edge feature analysis by the fact that in informal (but not formal) styles of English, we find WH+PREPOSITION sentence fragments such as that produced by speaker B below:

(56)   SPEAKER A: He has been talking to someone
          SPEAKER B: *Who to?/*Whom to?*

It would seem that in sentence fragments like those italicised in (56), it is possible for the wh-word to move in front of the preposition in informal (but not formal) styles of English. Since *whom* is used in formal (but not informal) styles of English, it follows that only *who* and not *whom* can occur in the kind of informal structure found in (56B). Such structures are consistent with the suggestion made here that a preposition can have an edge feature attracting a wh-expression to become its specifier in informal (but not formal) styles of English.

5.7   Long-distance wh-movement

The account of (non-echoic) wh-questions which we have presented so far amounts to claiming that the smallest possible maximal projection containing an interrogative word moves to the specifier position in the CP containing it. But this assumption raises interesting questions about what happens in questions like (57) below where an interrogative word originates in a lower clause (as the complement of the verb *hiding*) and moves to the spec-C position in a higher clause:

(57)   *What* might he think that she is hiding ~~what~~?

Such structures (in which a wh-expression originating in a lower clause moves to spec-C in a higher clause) are said to involve **long-distance wh-movement** (and hence are referred to as **long-distance questions**). In this section, we look at how long-distance wh-movement works.

At first sight, the answer might seem to be obvious. Thus, we might imagine that wh-movement in a sentence like (57) has the effect of moving the interrogative pronoun *what* directly from the position in which it originates (as the object of the verb *hiding*) into the position where it ends up (as the specifier of the inverted auxiliary *might*), in the manner shown by the arrow below;

(58)   [$_{CP}$ *What* [$_C$ might] he think [$_{CP}$ [$_C$ that] she is hiding ~~what~~]]

However, any such direct movement of *what* into the main-clause spec-C position would violate the Impenetrability Condition, presented in its original form in (59) below:

(59)   **Impenetrability Condition**
              A constituent in the domain of (i.e. c-commanded by) a complementiser is
              impenetrable to (and so cannot be attracted by) a higher head
              c-commanding the complementiser

The problem posed by one-step wh-movement in (58) is that it violates the Impenetrability Condition (59). This is because *what* originates within the domain of the embedded clause complementiser *that* (i.e. it originates in a position where it is c-commanded by *that*) and is subsequently attracted by the main-clause complementiser to move to the spec-C position in the main clause: since the main-clause complementiser c-commands the embedded-clause complementiser *that*, this leads to violation of the constraint (59). Thus, an analysis such as (58) would wrongly predict that sentences like (57) are ungrammatical.

However, we can avoid violation of the Impenetrability Condition if we suppose that wh-movement in sentences like (57) applies in two separate steps, moving the wh-pronoun *what* first to the spec-C position in the complement clause (in front of the complementiser *that*), and then into the spec-C position at the front of the main clause – as shown by the two arrows below;

(60)   [$_{CP}$ *What* [$_C$ might] he think [$_{CP}$ ~~what~~ [$_C$ that] she is hiding ~~what~~]]

Once *what* has moved to become the specifier of the complementiser *that*, it is no longer in the domain of *that* and hence is free to be attracted by the main-clause complementiser to move into spec-C in the main clause. On this view, wh-movement is a *local* (clause-bound) operation which applies in a *successive-cyclic* fashion, moving a wh-expression first to the front of the clause in which it originates, then to the front of the next highest clause . . . and so on until the wh-expression reaches its ultimate landing site at the front of the interrogative clause. (Note that movement of *what* to become the specifier of *that* in (60) does not violate the Complementiser Condition (5), as long as *what* subsequently moves elsewhere.)

The implication of the discussion above is that a UG principle (= the Impenetrability Condition) requires wh-movement to be a local operation moving wh-expressions one clause at a time. However, there is also a second UG principle (devised by Rizzi 1990, p. 7) which similarly requires long-distance movement to take place one clause at a time. Adapting this constraint from the earlier framework used by Luigi Rizzi to that utilised here, we can formulate it as follows:

(61)   **Relativised Minimality Condition/RMC**
A constituent X can only be affected by (e.g. agree with or be attracted by) the minimal (i.e. closest) constituent of the relevant type above it (i.e. c-commanding X)

It follows from (61) that a constituent undergoing wh-movement can only be attracted to become the specifier of the minimal/closest C constituent above it. It also follows that a constituent undergoing head movement can only be attracted to adjoin to the minimal/closest head above it (so that the Relativised Minimality Condition can be said to subsume – and thereby obviate the need for – the Head Movement Constraint outlined in §4.5). As should be clear, long-distance (single-step) wh-movement in the manner of (58) above would violate RMC because *what* moves directly to become the specifier of the main clause C constituent containing *might*, and yet this is not the closest C constituent above the original copy of *what*. Since the closest C constituent above the position in which *what* originates is the embedded clause complementiser *that*, RMC requires *what* to become the specifier of the embedded C constituent containing *that* before subsequently becoming the specifier of the next highest C constituent in the structure, namely the main clause C containing *might*: consequently, RMC requires wh-movement to apply one clause at a time, as in (60) above.

If (as assumed here) wh-movement is driven by an edge feature on C, and if wh-movement applies in a successive-cyclic (one-clause-at-a-time) fashion, it follows that the head C in each of the clauses through which a wh-expression moves must have an edge feature of its own, enabling it to attract a wh-expression to move to its specifier position. Given this assumption, (57) will be derived as follows. The verb *hiding* merges with the interrogative pronoun *what* to form the VP *hiding what*. This VP is merged with the T-auxiliary *is* to form the T-bar *is hiding what*, which is then merged with the pronoun *she* to form the TP *she is hiding what*. The resulting TP is merged with the complementiser *that* to form the C-bar *that she is hiding what*. The complementiser *that* has an edge feature which attracts *what* to move to its specifier position, thereby deriving the following structure (with the edge feature on C being deleted once its requirements have been satisfied, and the original copy of *what* also being deleted):

(62)

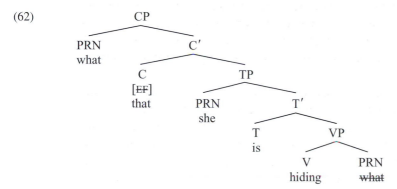

(Note that a structure like (62) does not violate the Complementiser Condition (5) which bars an overt complementiser from having an overt specifier, since (62) is an intermediate stage of derivation, and the Complementiser Condition holds only of final/superficial syntactic structures.) The CP in (62) is then merged as the complement of the verb *think*, forming the VP *think what that she is hiding what*. The resulting VP is merged as the complement of the past tense modal T-auxiliary *might*, forming the T-bar *might think what that she is hiding what*. This T-bar is itself merged with the subject pronoun *he*, forming the TP *he might think what that she is hiding what*. The TP thereby formed is merged with a null C constituent *ø* which (in main-clause questions) carries both a tense feature and an edge feature, so forming the C-bar *ø he might think what that she is hiding what*. The tense feature of the null affixal complementiser attracts the T-auxiliary *might* to move from T to adjoin to C, and the edge feature of the complementiser attracts a copy of the interrogative pronoun *what* to move to become the specifier of C, so deriving the structure shown in simplified form in (63) below (with arrows indicating movements which take place in the course of the derivation):

(63)

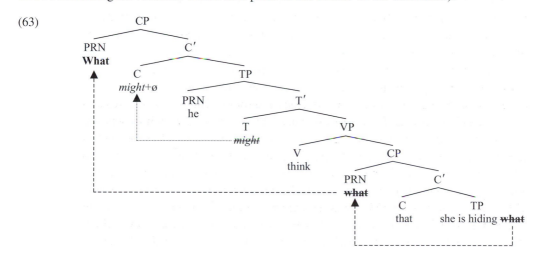

On this view, long-distance wh-movement proceeds in a successive-cyclic fashion (i.e. in a succession of short steps, one clause at a time), with each individual step involving a *local* operation in which a wh-expression is attracted to become the specifier of the closest C constituent above it (thereby satisfying the Relativised Minimality Condition (61)).

The key assumption being made here is that UG principles such as Chomsky's Impenetrability Condition and Rizzi's Relativised Minimality Condition require long-distance wh-movement to take place in a series of short-distance steps. There is a considerable amount of empirical evidence (both from English and from other languages) that wh-movement is indeed a local operation which moves a wh-expression one clause at a time. Since our concern here is with English, in the remainder of this section, we examine evidence from a number of varieties of English.

An interesting piece of evidence that wh-expressions move one clause at a time is offered by McCloskey (2000, 2002), based on observations about **quantifier stranding/floating** in West Ulster English. In this variety, a wh-word can be modified by the universal quantifier *all*, giving rise to questions such as:

(64)   *What all* did you get for Christmas?
        ='What are all the things which you got for Christmas?'

McCloskey argues that in such sentences, the quantifier and the wh-word originate as a single constituent. He further maintains that under wh-movement, the wh-word *what* can either pied-pipe the quantifier *all* along with it as in (64) above, or can move on its own leaving the quantifier *all* stranded. In this connection, consider the sentences below:

(65) (a)   *What all* do you think that he'll say that we should buy?
     (b)   *What* do you think *all* that he'll say that we should buy?
     (c)   *What* do you think that he'll say *all* that we should buy?
     (d)   *What* do you think that he'll say that we should buy *all*?

McCloskey claims (2000, p. 63) that '*All* in wh-quantifier float constructions appears in positions for which there is considerable independent evidence that they are either positions in which wh-movement originates or positions through which wh-movement passes. We have in these observations a new kind of argument for the successive-cyclic character of long wh-movement.'

McCloskey argues that the derivation of (65a–d) proceeds along the following lines (simplified in a number of ways). The quantifier *all* merges with its complement *what* to form the structure [*all what*]. The wh-word *what* then raises to become the specifier of *all*, forming the overt QP [*what all*]. (To simplify exposition, we only show the overt constituents of QP here, hence not the null copy of *what* following *all*.) The resulting QP [*what all*] is merged as the object of *buy*, forming [*buy what all*]. If *what* undergoes wh-movement on its own in subsequent stages of derivation, we derive (65d) '*What* do you think that he'll say that we should buy *all*?' But suppose that the quantifier *all* is pied-piped along with *what* under wh-movement until we reach the stage shown in skeletal form below:

(66)   [CP *what all* [C that] we should buy]

If wh-movement then extracts *what* on its own, the quantifier *all* will be stranded in the most deeply embedded spec-C position, so deriving (65c) '*What* do you think that he'll say *all* that we should buy?' By contrast, if *all* is pied-piped along with *what* until the end of the intermediate C-cycle, we derive:

(67)   [CP *what all* [C that] he'll say that we should buy]

If wh-movement then extracts *what* on its own, the quantifier *all* will be stranded in the intermediate spec-C position and we will ultimately derive (65b) '*What* do you think *all* that he'll say that we should buy?' But if *all* continues to be pied-piped along with *what* throughout the remaining stages of derivation, we ultimately derive (65a) '*What all* do you think that he'll say that we should buy?'

A further piece of evidence that wh-expressions move one clause at a time comes from auxiliary inversion in Belfast English. In her (1995) book *Belfast English*, Alison Henry notes that in long-distance wh-questions in Belfast English, not only the main clause C but also intermediate C constituents show T-to-C movement (i.e. auxiliary inversion), as illustrated below:

(68)   What *did* Mary claim [*did* they steal]? (Henry 1995, p. 108)

We can account for auxiliary inversion in structures like (68) in a straightforward fashion if we suppose that (in this kind of variety) the head C of any clause which has an interrogative specifier can trigger auxiliary inversion. If so, the fact that the complement clause shows auxiliary inversion provides evidence that the preposed wh-word *what* moves through the spec-C position in the bracketed complement clause in (68) before subsequently moving into the main-clause spec-C position.

A further piece of evidence leading to the same conclusion comes from the interpretation of reflexive anaphors like *himself* in standard varieties of English. As we saw in exercise 2.2, these are subject to Principle A of Binding Theory which requires an anaphor to be locally bound and hence to have an antecedent within the TP most immediately containing it. This requirement can be illustrated by the contrast below:

(69) (a)   *Jim was surprised that [TP Peter wasn't sure [CP that [**TP** Mary liked
                                                                this picture of himself best]]]

      (b)   Jim was surprised that [TP Peter wasn't sure [CP which picture of himself
                                                                [**TP** Mary liked best]]]

In (69a), the TP most immediately containing the reflexive anaphor *himself* is the bold-printed TP whose subject is *Mary*, and since there is no suitable (third person masculine singular) antecedent for *himself* within this TP, the resulting sentence violates Binding Principle A and so is ill-formed. However, in (69b) the wh-phrase *which picture of himself* has been moved to the specifier position within the bracketed CP, and the TP most immediately containing the reflexive anaphor is the italicised TP whose subject is *Peter*. Since this italicised TP does indeed contain a c-commanding antecedent for *himself* (namely its subject *Peter*), there is no violation of Principle A if *himself* is construed as bound by *Peter* – though Principle A prevents *Jim* from being the antecedent of *himself*.

In the light of this restriction, consider the following sentence:

(70)   Which picture of himself wasn't he sure that Mary liked best?

In (70), the antecedent of *himself* is *he* – and yet *himself* is clearly not c-commanded by *he*, as we see from (71) below (simplified in numerous ways, including by showing only overt constituents):

(71)

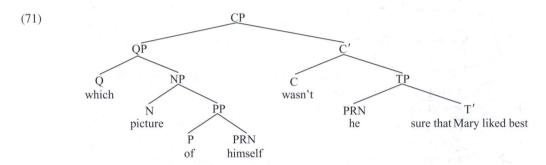

In fact, the only elements c-commanded by the pronoun *he* in (71) are T-bar and its constituents. But if *he* does not c-command *himself* in (71), how come *he* is interpreted as the antecedent of *himself* when we would have expected such a structure to violate Principle A of Binding Theory and hence to be ill-formed?

We can provide a principled answer to this question if we suppose that wh-movement operates in a successive-cyclic fashion, and involves an intermediate stage of derivation represented in (72) below (simplified by showing overt constituents only):

(72)   [$_{TP}$ He wasn't sure [$_{CP}$ which picture of himself that [$_{TP}$ Mary liked best]]]

In (72), the anaphor *himself* has a c-commanding antecedent within the italicised TP most immediately containing it – namely the pronoun *he*. If the requirements of Principle A can be satisfied at any stage of derivation, it follows that the assumption that a sentence like (70) involves an intermediate stage of derivation like (72) enables us to account for why *himself* is construed as bound by *he*. More generally, sentences like (72) provide us with evidence that long-distance wh-movement involves successive-cyclic movement through intermediate spec-C positions – and hence that wh-movement is an inherently local operation. At a subsequent stage of derivation, the wh-QP *which picture of himself* moves into spec-C in the main clause, so deriving the structure (71) associated with (70) *Which picture of himself wasn't he sure that Mary liked best?*

A final piece of evidence that wh-expressions move one clause at a time comes from the phenomenon of **wh-copying** in Child English. Ros Thornton (1995) reports children producing long-distance wh-copy questions such as the following (p. 147):

(73)(a)   **What** do you think [*what* Cookie Monster eats]?

(b)   **How** do you think [*how* Superman fixed the car]?

In such cases, it would appear that the wh-word moves to the italicised spec-C position within the bracketed complement clause before moving into its final landing-site in the bold-printed spec-C position in the main clause. While the children concerned 'know' that the original occurrence of the wh-word receives a null spellout, they wrongly assume that any wh-copy in any spec-C position can be overtly spelled out (whereas only the highest such copy is overtly spelled out in adult English). Children's wh-copying structures thus provide evidence that wh-expressions move one clause at a time.

Overall, then, we see that there is a considerable body of empirical evidence which supports the hypothesis that (in consequence of UG principles like the Impenetrability Condition and the Relativised Minimality Condition) long-distance wh-movement is successive-cyclic in nature and involves wh-expressions moving one clause at a time through intermediate spec-C positions (attracted by an edge feature on each of the relevant C constituents).

A final question to be answered in relation to our discussion of long-distance wh-movement in this section is why long-distance wh-movement is not possible in structures such as (74b) below:

(74)(a)   [$_{CP}$ [$_C$ ø] she might ask [$_{CP}$ *where* [$_C$ ø$_{Int}$] he has been ~~where~~]]

(b)   *[$_{CP}$ *Where* [$_C$ might] she ask [$_{CP}$ ~~where~~ [$_C$ ø$_{Int}$] he has been ~~where~~]]

The wh-adverb *where* originates as the complement of *been* in (74) and in the (a) example is attracted by an edge feature on the null interrogative complementiser introducing the embedded clause to become its specifier, so deriving *She might ask where he has been*. However, given our assumption that any C constituent can carry an edge feature, the obvious question which arises at this juncture is what prevents the head C constituent of the main clause CP from carrying an edge feature which attracts *where* to move further to the front of the overall sentence in the (b) example. A plausible answer is that further movement is prevented by the following constraint:

(75)   **Freezing Constraint**

         An element moved to a position dedicated to some scope-discourse interpretive property . . . is frozen in place (Rizzi and Shlonsky 2005, p. 1)

If we assume that the specifier position of an interrogative C is the *scope position* for a moved interrogative expression (marking the fact that it has scope over all the constituents that it c-commands, hence over all the other constituents of the clause), then (in the case of interrogatives) (75) amounts to claiming that once an interrogative wh-expression moves into the specifier position of an interrogative complementiser, it immediately becomes *frozen* in place and is unable to move further. Part of the reason for this may be that a verb like *ask* requires an interrogative complement, and we saw that the Interrogative Condition outlined in (24) above means that a clause is only interpreted as interrogative if it is a CP with an interrogative specifier. An alternative way of thinking about the same problem is to suppose that an interrogative wh-expression which falls within the scope of (i.e. originates in a position c-commanded by) an interrogative complementiser cannot move out of the CP headed by the relevant complementiser. Either assumption will prevent *where* from moving out of the embedded CP in (74).

5.8   Multiple wh-questions

So far, all the questions which we have looked at have contained only a single interrogative wh-expression. However, alongside such questions, we also find **multiple wh-questions** – i.e. questions containing more than one interrogative wh-expression. A salient syntactic property of such questions in English is that only *one* of the wh-expressions can be preposed – as we can illustrate in relation to the following set of examples:

(76) (a)   He might think *who* has done **what**?
      (b)   *Who* might he think has done **what**?
      (c)   ****What** might he think *who* has done?
      (d)   **Who **what** might he think has done?
      (e)   ****What** *who* might he think has done?

(76a) is an echo question in which the highlighted wh-words *who* and *what* remain in situ; (76b–e) are non-echoic questions in which either or both of the two wh-words are preposed. If we try and prepose the highlighted wh-words in (76), we find that only one of the two can be preposed (not both of them), and moreover the preposed item has to be *who* and not *what*. Why should this be? In order to get a clearer idea of what's going on here, let's take a closer look at the derivation of (76a). The verb *done* merges with the interrogative pronoun *what* to form the VP *done what*. The present tense T-auxiliary *has* merges with this VP to form the T-bar *has done what*, and this in turn merges with the interrogative pronoun *who* to form the TP *who has done what*. The resulting TP is merged with a null declarative complementiser (a null counterpart of *that*, below shown as ∅) with an edge feature, to form the C-bar shown below:

(77)

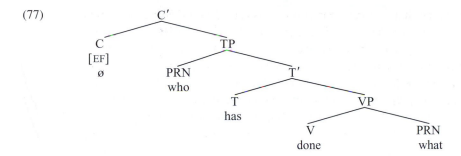

The edge feature on C enables it to attract a wh-expression which it c-commands to move to become the specifier of C. But an obvious problem which arises in the case of a structure like (77) is that there are two different wh-expressions c-commanded by the null complementiser, namely *who* and *what*. Since C can only attract a single wh-expression to move to spec-C, it is clear that only one of the two wh-words can move to spec-C – but which? Since we know from (76) that it is *who* rather than *what* which must be preposed in (77) and since *who* is higher up in the structure than *what*, such sentences provide evidence for the existence of a **superiority effect** – i.e. a requirement for C to attract the *highest* wh-word in the structure. Why should this be? A plausible suggestion to make is that this is because C has to attract the *closest* interrogative word which it c-commands. This requirement is a consequence of a principle of Universal Grammar (proposed by Richards 1997) which we can outline informally as follows:

(78)   **Attract Closest Condition**
         A head which attracts a given kind of constituent attracts the *closest* constituent of the relevant kind

The **Attract Closest Condition** is related to the Locality Principle which we posited in §1.5, and can be seen as the obverse of the Relativised Minimality Condition – and indeed all three conditions can arguably be subsumed within the Economy Condition (44), given that economy considerations require us to *move the smallest constituent possible the shortest distance possible*. And since the Chain Uniformity Condition tells us that only a maximal projection can be attracted to move into a specifier position, the various conditions which UG imposes on movement mean that wh-movement will in effect be subject to the condition in (79) below:

(79)   **Wh-Attraction Condition**
         The edge feature on C attracts the smallest possible maximal projection containing the closest wh-word to move to spec-C

What this means is that we first identify the closest wh-word to C, and then move the smallest possible maximal projection containing it to spec-C; if that's barred for some reason, we move the next smallest maximal projection containing the wh-word . . . and so on.

After this brief excursus, let's now return to the derivation of (76b) *Who might he think has done what?* Suppose that we have reached the stage of derivation in (77) above. In accordance with the Attract Closest Condition (78), C identifies *who* as the closest wh-word, and in compliance with the Chain Uniformity Condition (40) and the Economy Condition (44) attracts the smallest possible maximal projection containing *who* to move to spec-C. However, since *who* is itself a maximal projection (by virtue of being the largest expression headed by the word *who*), this means that *who* is attracted to move to spec-C, thereby deriving the structure shown below:

(80)

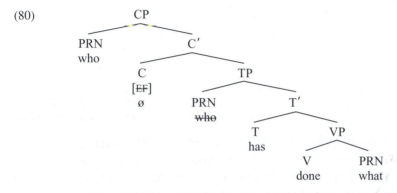

As shown in (80), wh-movement leads to deletion of the edge feature on C, and to the original occurrence of *who* ultimately being given a null spellout.

The derivation continues by merging the CP in (80) as the complement of the verb *think*, forming the VP *think who ø who has done what*. This VP is then merged with the T-auxiliary *might* to form the T-bar *might think who ø who has done what*, and this in turn merges with the pronoun *he* to form the TP *he might think who ø who has done what*. The resulting TP is then merged with a C constituent which (as in all main-clause questions) carries a tense feature and an edge feature, so forming the following structure:

(81)

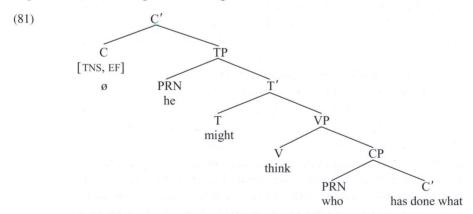

In accordance with the Attract Closest Condition (78), the tense feature on C in (81) attracts the closest T-auxiliary (= *might*) to move to C. In conformity with the same principle, the edge feature on C attracts the closest interrogative word (= *who*) to move to become the specifier of C, so deriving the structure shown below (simplified in the same ways as for 81):

(82)

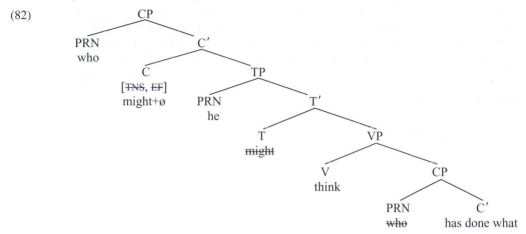

In short, the assumption that movement operations like wh-movement are subject to the **Attract Closest Condition** (78) provides a principled account of why it is *who* rather than *what* which undergoes wh-movement in (76). Moreover, given the assumption that (in a language like English) the edge feature on C is immediately deleted (and thereby inactivated) once C has attracted the closest wh-expression, it follows that no more than one wh-expression can be moved to the front of any given clause.

5.9   Summary

We began this chapter in §5.2 by arguing that main-clause wh-questions are CPs headed by a C constituent which attracts a tensed auxiliary to move to C via **head movement**, and a wh-expression to move into spec-C via **wh-movement**. In §5.3 we argued that wh-movement involves a copying operation whereby a moved wh-expression leaves behind a null copy of itself at its extraction site (i.e. in the position out of which it is extracted/moved); and we noted that in earlier work, copies were analysed as **traces**. In §5.4 we outlined an analysis of wh-questions under which an interrogative C carries an edge feature which attracts an interrogative wh-word to move to spec-C, and also (in main-clause questions) a tense feature which attracts a tensed auxiliary to adjoin to C and so triggers auxiliary inversion. We saw that wh-movement provides a way of satisfying the Interrogative Condition which specifies that a CP is only interpreted as a non-echoic question if it has an interrogative specifier. We saw that the same condition also requires us to assume that yes-no questions are CPs containing a null yes-no question particle (which can be thought of as a null counterpart of *whether*). In §5.5 we noted that an interrogative word like *which* heading a larger phrase like *which assignment* cannot be preposed on its own (since this would violate the Chain Uniformity Condition), but rather has to pied-pipe the noun *assignment* along with it (e.g. in a sentence like *Which assignment have you done?*). We saw that pied-piping of the noun *assignment* along with the wh-word *which* is the consequence of an **Attract Smallest Condition** which requires C to attract the smallest possible constituent containing the wh-word (and we noted that this condition can be subsumed under a more general **Economy Condition**). We also noted that (since the Chain Uniformity Condition requires the specifier position within CP to be filled by a maximal projection), C attracts the smallest possible maximal projection containing an interrogative word to move to spec-C. We saw how Ross's **Left Branch Condition** prevents genitive possessors like *whose* from being extracted out of the DP containing them, with the result that the whole DP containing *whose* has to be preposed in sentences such as *Whose car have you borrowed?* In §5.6, we observed that in formal styles of English, a wh-expression which is the complement of a preposition pied-pipes the preposition along with it when it undergoes wh-movement, so that the whole Prepositional Phrase moves to spec-C in sentences like *To whom was he referring?* We argued that this is a consequence of the **Impenetrability Condition** which prevents a constituent in the domain of a preposition (or complementiser) from being attracted by a higher head, so forcing the preposition to be pied-piped along with the wh-expression under wh-movement. We went on to suggest that in informal styles of English, prepositions can carry an edge feature which enables a wh-expression in the domain of the preposition to move to the edge of PP and thereafter to be extracted out of PP, so leaving the preposition stranded. In §5.7, we presented evidence that wh-movement in long-distance questions like *What might he think that she is hiding?* applies in a successive-cyclic fashion (one clause at a time), with *what* first moving into the spec-C position at the front of the *that*-clause before subsequently going on to move into the spec-C position in the main clause. We noted that successive-cyclic application of wh-movement is forced by locality principles such as Chomsky's **Impenetrability Condition** (which bars a constituent within the domain of C from being attracted by a higher head), and Rizzi's **Relativised Minimality Condition** (which requires a wh-expression to be attracted by the closest C constituent above it). In §5.8, we looked at the syntax of multiple wh-questions, noting that in consequence of the **Attract Closest Condition**, C in multiple wh-questions attracts the *closest* wh-word which it c-commands. We noted that this condition (in conjunction with the Chain Uniformity and Economy conditions) means that the edge feature on C attracts *the smallest possible maximal projection containing the closest wh-word* to move to spec-C.

Overall, the main goal of this chapter has been to look at the syntax of preposed interrogative wh-expressions. Preposed wh-expressions end up (via movement) in an **A-bar position** – i.e. a specifier position which can be occupied by either an argument or an adjunct. Because it moves wh-expressions into spec-C and spec-C is an A-bar position, wh-movement can be regarded as a particular instance of a more general **A-bar movement** operation.

Key conditions on movement operations (or on the structures they produce) introduced in this chapter include the following:

(5)   **Complementiser Condition**
An overt complementiser (like *that/for/if*) cannot have an overt specifier in the superficial structure of a sentence

(24)   **Interrogative Condition**
A clause is interpreted as a non-echoic question if (and only if) it is a CP with an interrogative specifier (i.e. a specifier containing an interrogative word)

(40)   **Chain Uniformity Condition**
'A chain is uniform with regard to phrase structure status' (Chomsky 1995, p. 253)

(41)   **Attract Smallest Condition/ASC**
A head which attracts a particular type of item attracts the smallest constituent containing such an item which will not lead to violation of any UG principle

(44)   **Economy Condition**
'Derivations and representations . . . are required to be minimal, with no superfluous steps in derivations and no superfluous symbols in representations' (Chomsky 1989, p. 69)

(47)   **Left Branch Condition/LBC**
In languages like English, the leftmost constituent of a nominal expression cannot be extracted out of the expression containing it

(51)   **Impenetrability Condition**
A constituent in the domain of a complementiser or preposition is impenetrable to (and so cannot be attracted by) a higher head c-commanding the relevant complementiser/preposition (Recall that a constituent is in the domain of a head H if it is c-commanded by H.)

(61)   **Relativised Minimality Condition/RMC**
A constituent X can only be affected by (e.g. agree with or be attracted by) the minimal (i.e. closest) constituent of the relevant type above it (i.e. c-commanding X)

(75)   **Freezing Constraint**
An element moved to a position dedicated to some scope-discourse interpretive property . . . is frozen in place (Rizzi and Shlonsky 2005, p. 1)

(78)   **Attract Closest Condition**
A head which attracts a given kind of constituent attracts the *closest* constituent of the relevant kind

(79)   **Wh-Attraction Condition**
The edge feature on C attracts the smallest possible maximal projection containing the closest wh-word to move to spec-C

5.10   Bibliographical background

On the idea of clause-typing in §5.2, see Cheng (1997). The *Complementiser Condition* outlined in §5.2 derives from the Multiply Filled COMP Filter of Chomsky and Lasnik (1977): for further discussion, see Seppänen and Trotta (2000) and Zwicky (2002). See Kennedy and Merchant (2000), Lechner (2001), Kennedy (2002), Bhatt and Pancheva (2004) and Grosu and Horvath (2006) for discussion of comparative structures like (7c) in the main text, Potts (2002) for discussion of *as*-structures like (7d), and Chomsky (1977) for discussion of *tough* structures like (7e). Chomsky's claim that there are two types of Merger operation (internal and external) is extended in Citko (2005), who argues for a third type of Merger operation which she calls *Parallel Merge*, and claims that this is found in co-ordinate structures like *I wonder what Gretel recommended and Hansel read.* On wh-movement in rhetorical questions, see Sprouse (2007). The idea in §5.3 that there is parametric variation with respect to which copies in a movement chain are overtly spelled out and which are deleted is developed in Bobaljik (1995), Brody (1995), Groat and O'Neil (1996), Pesetsky (1997, 1998), Richards (1997), Roberts (1997), Franks (1999), Runner (1998), Cormack and Smith (1999), Nunes (1999, 2001, 2004), Bošković (2001), Fanselow and Ćavar (2002), Bobaljik (2002), Landau (2006b) and Polinsky and Potsdam (2006). The idea that wh-in-situ structures may involve a form of wh-movement in which the initial copy at the foot of the movement chain is overtly spelled out is developed in Pesetsky (2000) and Reintges, LeSourd and Chung (2002): see Watanabe (2001) for a more general discussion of wh-in-situ structures. The idea in §5.4 that wh-movement is driven by an edge feature derives from Chomsky (2005b). The claim that a clause is interpreted as interrogative if it has an interrogative specifier is taken from Radford *et al.* (1999). The idea that yes-no questions contain an abstract yes-no question particle derives from earlier work by Katz and Postal (1964), Grimshaw (1993) and Roberts (1993); the idea that this particle is a null counterpart of *whether* is suggested by Bresnan (1970). In relation to the claim in §5.5 that structures like **Which/Whose was he driving car?* involve violation of a Chain Uniformity or Left Branch condition, it should be noted that numerous languages permit either or both such structures: for discussion, see Uriagereka (1988), Borsley and Jaworska (1998), Corver (1990), Franks and Progovac (1994), Zlatić (1997), Merchant (2001), Fanselow and Ćavar (2002), Davies and Dubinsky (2004) and Bošković (2004, 2005). On the Attract Smallest Condition, see Akiyama (2004). The analysis of possessive structures presented in the text is loosely based on Abney (1987): see Chomsky (1995, p. 263) for a variant of this. For alternative accounts of the preposition pied-piping phenomenon discussed in §5.6, see Abels (2003), Heck (2004), Radford (2004a, pp. 211–15), Watanabe (2006) and Boeckx (2007). On the Relativised Minimality Condition, see Rizzi (1990, 2001a); on preposition stranding, see Abels (2003) and Almeida and Yoshida (2007). For more detailed discussion of sentences like

Which picture of himself wasn't he sure that Mary liked best? see Belletti and Rizzi (1988), Uriagereka (1988), Lebeaux (1991), Fox (2000) and Barss (2001). Additional evidence that wh-movement applies in a local (one-clause-at-a-time) fashion comes from a variety of other phenomena, including spellout of multiple copies of a moved wh-expression in Frisian (Hiemstra 1986), Romani (McDaniel 1989), German (Felser 2004), Afrikaans (Hong 2005) and Punjabi (Yang 2006); stranding of material on the edge of intermediate CPs, including prepositions in Afrikaans (du Plessis 1977) and *else* in Child English sentences like *What do you want else to eat?* (Boecks 2007); partial wh-movement in German and a variety of languages (see e.g. Cole 1982, McDaniel 1986, Saddy 1991, Cole and Hermon 2000 and Bruening 2006); postverbal subjects in French (Kayne and Pollock 1978), Spanish (Torrego 1984) and Basque (Ortiz de Urbina 1989); wh-marking of complementisers in Irish (McCloskey 2001, 2002) and of subject pronouns in Ewe (Collins 1993); and exceptional accusative case-marking by a higher transitive verb of the wh-subject of a lower finite clause (reported for English by Kayne (1984, p. 5) and for Hungarian by Bejar and Massam (1999, p. 66)). On the Freezing Constraint, see Rizzi and Shlonsky (2005) and Rizzi (2006). On the semantic properties of multiple wh-questions like those discussed in §5.8, see Dayal (2002). The Attract Closest Condition has its historical antecedents in the Superiority Condition of Chomsky (1973) and the Minimal Link Condition of Chomsky (1995) and is related to the Defective Intervention Constraint of Chomsky (1998): for an alternative account of superiority effects, see Hornstein (1995); for an experimental study of superiority effects, see Clifton, Fanselow and Frazier (2006). Although in languages like English only one wh-expression can be fronted in a wh-question, it should be pointed out that there are languages like Bulgarian which allow multiple wh-fronting question structures which can be paraphrased in English as 'Who what to whom said?': see Rudin (1988) and Bošković (2002a). Although we do not discuss other types of wh-construction (e.g. relative clauses) in the text, for alternative accounts of their syntax see Fabb (1990), Borsley (1992, 1997), Sag (1997), Wiltschko (1998), del Gobbo (2003), Authier and Reed (2005), Adger and Ramchand (2005) and de Vries (2002, 2006), as well as the collection of papers in Alexiadou, Law, Meinunger and Wilder (2000).

Workbook section

Exercise 5.1

Discuss the derivation of the wh-clauses below, drawing tree diagrams to show their superficial structure and saying why they are grammatical or ungrammatical in standard varieties of English.

1 a   Which film have you seen?
  b   *Which have you seen film?

2 a   Dare anyone say anything? **(w)**

  b   Do you speak French?

3 a   To whom/?To who have they spoken? **(w)**

  b   *To who've they spoken? **(w)**

  c   Who have they spoken to? **(w)**

  d   Who've they spoken to? **(w)**

4 a   Which picture of who have you chosen? **(w)**

  b   *Which picture of who've you chosen? **(w)**

  c   *Who've you chosen which picture of?

  d   Which picture have you chosen of who?

5 a   What excuse has he given?

  b   *What has he given excuse?

  c   *What excuse he has given?

  d   *What he has given excuse?

6 a   In how many places has he hidden?

  b   How many places has he hidden in?

  c   *In how many has he hidden places?

  d   *How has he hidden in many places?

7 a   To whom/?To who do you think that they were talking?

  b   Who/?Whom do you think that they were talking to?

8 a   Whose car will he think has crashed into what?

  b   *What will he think whose car has crashed into?

9 a   He is wondering who has done what **(w)**

  b   *He is wondering what who has done **(w)**

  c   *Who is he wondering has done what? **(w)**

  d   *What is he wondering who has done? **(w)**

10 a   Which of the two dresses do you think (that) she will prefer?

  b   Which do you think of the two dresses (%that) she will prefer?

In addition, discuss the syntax of child wh-questions like that in (11) below:

11   Who will he think who the cat was chasing? (= 'Who will he think the cat was chasing?') **(w)**

And comment on relevant aspects of the syntax of the *which/how* clauses in (12) below:

12 a   To which of these groups do you consider that you belong to?

  b   May we ask you to indicate which of these ethnic groups that you belong to?

  c   It's difficult to see how that we can keep these players

(12a and 12b are from an official form issued by the Tax Office in the town I live in, and 12c was produced by an England soccer star on TV.) Say what is interesting about the *which/how* clauses in (12), what their counterparts would be in 'standard' varieties of English, and how the two varieties differ.

    Finally, comment on relevant aspects of the syntax of the Shakespearean questions in (13) below, the African American English questions in (14) (from Green 1998, pp. 98–99) and the bracketed interrogative complement clauses in Belfast English (adapted from Henry 1995) in (15–16):

13 a	What sayst thou? (Olivia, *Twelfth Night*, III.iv)
b	What dost thou say? (Othello, *Othello*, III.iii)
c	What didst not like? (Othello, *Othello*, III.iii)
14 a	What I'm gon' do? (= 'What am I going to do?')
b	How she's doing? (= 'How is she doing?')
15 a	They wondered [which one that he chose]
b	They wondered [which one did he choose]
c	*They wondered [which one that did he choose]
16 a	They wondered [if/whether (*that) we had gone]
b	*They wondered [if/whether had we gone]
c	They wondered [had we gone]

Helpful hints

In 2a, assume that *dare*, *anyone* and *anything* are **polarity items** (see §2.6), and so must be c-commanded by an interrogative constituent; assume also that *dare* originates in T. In 3 and 7, a prefixed question mark ? indicates that the use of *who(m)* in the relevant sentence (for speakers like me) leads to stylistic incongruity (in that the accusative form *whom* and preposition pied-piping occur in more formal styles, and the accusative form *who* and preposition stranding in less formal styles). In 3 and 4, assume (for the purposes of this exercise) that *have* can cliticise onto a preceding word W if W ends in a vowel or diphthong, if W c-commands *have* and if there is no (overt or null) constituent intervening between W and *have*. In 4, take *which picture of who* to be a QP formed by merging the quantifier *which* with the NP *picture of who*; in relation to 4d, bear in mind the discussion of *split spellout* in §5.3. In 6, take *how many places* to be a QP formed by merging the Q *many* with the N *places* to form the Q-bar *many places* and assume that this Q-bar is then merged with the wh-adverb *how* to form the QP *how many places* (so that the degree adverb *how* is the specifier of this QP): note that, irrelevantly, 6c is grammatical on a different interpretation on which *how* is a manner adverb with a meaning paraphraseable as 'In what way?' In 10, assume that *which of the two dresses* is a QP which has the internal constituent structure [QP [Q which] [PP [P of] [DP [D the] [NumP [Num two] [N dresses]]]]], in which *two* is a numeral quantifier (= Num), and *of* is a preposition which (in this type of use) is sometimes said to have the function of marking genitive case; in relation to 10b, note that the percentage sign in front of *that* means that this type of structure is only acceptable in some varieties of English if *that* is omitted, and bear in mind the discussion of *split spellout* in the main text. In 11, bear in mind that the same child also produced *How much do you think how much the bad guy stole?* In 12b and 12c, concern yourself only with the structure of the *which/how*-clauses, not with the structure of the main clause; and take *these ethnic groups* to be a DP but don't concern yourself with its structure. In 16, consider the possibility that both *if* and *whether* are complementisers in Belfast English (though only *if* is a complementiser in Standard English).

Model answer for 1

(1a) is derived as follows. The interrogative quantifier *which* is merged with the noun *film* to form the QP *which film*. This is merged with the (perfect participle) verb *seen* to form the VP *seen which film*. This VP is in turn merged with the (present) tense auxiliary *have* to form the T-bar *have seen which film*. The resulting T-bar is merged with the pronoun *you* to form the TP *you have seen which film*. This TP is merged with a null C constituent carrying a tense feature and an edge feature, so forming the C-bar in (i) below:

(i)

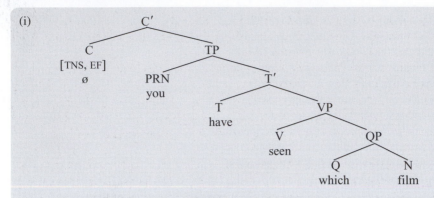

The tense feature of C attracts the present tense auxiliary *have* to move from T to C. In consequence of the Wh-Attraction Condition, the edge feature of C attracts the smallest possible maximal projection containing the closest interrogative word to move to spec-C. Since the closest interrogative word to C (and indeed the only interrogative word in the structure) is *which*, and the smallest maximal projection containing *which* is the QP *which film*, and since preposing this QP on its own does not violate any syntactic constraints, the QP *which film* moves to spec-C. Assuming that the features of C are deleted once their requirements are satisfied, the structure which results after head-movement and wh-movement have applied is that shown in simplified form below:

(ii)

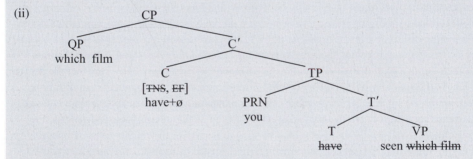

The discussion in the main text was mainly limited to wh-movement interrogative clauses. However, wh-movement can also be argued to take place in **relative clauses** like those bracketed below:

(i) (a) It's hard to find *someone* [**who** you can relate to]
     (b) Can you think of *things* [**which** she might need]?

The bracketed structures are termed **relative clauses** because they contain a (bold-printed) **relative pronoun** (*who/whose/which*) that 'relates to' (i.e. refers back to) an italicised **antecedent** in a higher clause (generally one which immediately precedes the bold-printed relative wh-expression). Make the following set of assumptions about the syntax of relative clauses:

I   Relative clauses are CPs headed by a complementiser like *that/for/ø* which has an edge feature triggering movement of a relative pronoun (like *who/which/where/when/why*) to spec-C

II   A relative pronoun occupying spec-C position in a relative clause is given a null spellout in the PF component – optionally in a finite clause, obligatorily in an infinitive clause (= *Relative Pronoun Spellout Condition*)

III   An overt complementiser (like *that/for/if*) cannot have an overt specifier in the superficial structure of a sentence (*Complementiser Condition*)

(Recall that in the main text, we noted that in some varieties, the Complementiser Condition only holds where spec-C is occupied by a pronoun rather than by a noun expression. Note that the term *overt specifier* is intended to denote a constituent in spec-C which contains one or more overt items.)

In the light of the assumptions made in I–III above, discuss the derivation of the bracketed relative clauses in the sentences below, drawing tree diagrams to show their superficial structure and saying why they are grammatical or ungrammatical in standard varieties of English:

1 a   There is no-one else [who you can blame]
  b   There is no-one else [you can blame]
  c   *There is no-one else [who that you can blame]
  d   There is no-one else [that you can blame]
2 a   There is no-one else [for you to blame] (**w**)
  b   There is no-one else [to blame] (**w**)
  c   *There is no-one else [who for you to blame] (**w**)
  d   *There is no-one else [who to blame] (**w**)
3 a   *There is no-one [who that you can talk to]
  b   There is no-one [that you can talk to]
  c   There is no-one [who you can talk to]
  d   There is no-one [to whom you can talk] (**w**)
  e   *There is no-one [to whom that you can talk]
  f   *There is no-one [to you can talk] (**w**)
4 a   *This is the way [how he behaved]
  b   This is the way [he behaved]
  c   *This is the way [how that he behaved]
  d   This is the way [that he behaved]
5 a   *I need someone [who to love me]
  b   I need someone [to love me]
  c   *I need someone [who to love]
  d   I need someone [to love]
6 a   I need a place [in which to stay]
  b   *I need a place [in to stay]
  c   *I need a place [which to stay in]
  d   I need a place [to stay in]
  e   *I need a place [where to stay]
  f   I need a place [to stay]
7 a   *I need a place [in which for her to stay]
  b   *I need a place [in for her to stay]
  c   *I need a place [which for her to stay in]
  d   I need a place [for her to stay in]
  e   *I need a place [where for her to stay]
  f   I need a place [for her to stay]

8 a   *This is no way [how to behave]
   b   This is no way [to behave]
   c   *This is no way [how for you to behave]
   d   This is no way [for you to behave]

In addition, comment on the syntax of the bracketed relative clause in the sentence in (9) below
(produced by a sports commentator on Sky TV):

9   As Liverpool chase the game, there may be more room [in which for Manchester United
        to manoeuvre]

and say what its 'Standard English' counterpart would be and why. Finally, consider the following:

10 a   The world [in which we are living] is changing
   b   The world [which we are living in] is changing
   c   %The world [in which we are living in] is changing

Contrary to what is said in the main text, assume that preposition pied-piping is obligatory in
English (and universally), but that languages (and language varieties) may differ with regard to
which link/s of the wh-chain the preposition is spelled out on.

Helpful hints

In relation to 4 and 8, assume that *how* is a pronominal manner adverb (which you can categorise
as ADV) which originates as the complement of the verb *behave*: try and identify the way in
which *how* differs from other relative pronouns like *who/which/where/why*.

Model answer for 1a,b

The bracketed relative clause in 1a is derived as follows. The verb *blame* is merged with the
relative pronoun *who* to form the VP *blame who*. The resulting VP is merged with the present
tense auxiliary *can* to form the T-bar *can blame who*, and this is then merged with the subject *you*
to form the TP *you can blame who*. This TP is subsequently merged with a null complementiser
(perhaps a null counterpart of *that*) which carries an edge feature, so deriving the structure shown
in (ii) below:

(ii)

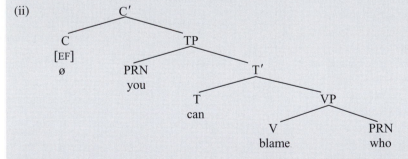

In accordance with the Wh-Attraction Condition, the edge feature on the relative clause C
constituent attracts the smallest possible maximal projection containing a relative pronoun to
move to spec-C. The smallest such maximal projection is the pronoun *who*, which is a maximal
projection containing a relative pronoun by virtue of being the largest expression headed by the
relative pronoun *who*. Hence, *who* moves to spec-C, and thereby erases the edge feature of C, so

deriving the structure shown in simplified form below, which is the superficial structure of the bracketed relative clause in 1a:

(iii)

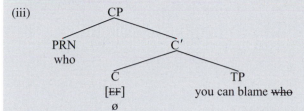

Given that a relative pronoun occupying the specifier position in a relative clause can be given a null spellout in the PF component, an alternative possibility is for the relative pronoun *who* in spec-C to be given a null spellout at PF, so deriving (iv) below, which is the superficial structure associated with the bracketed relative clause in 1b:

(iv)

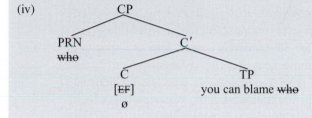

6 A-movement

6.1 Overview

In this chapter, we look at the syntax of **subjects**. So far, we have assumed that subjects originate in the specifier position within TP and remain there (unless the subject is a wh-expression which undergoes wh-movement and moves to spec-C, e.g. in sentences like *Who did he say was coming?*). However, in this chapter we shall argue that subjects originate internally within the Verb Phrase as arguments of verbs, and are subsequently raised into the specifier position within TP, with the relevant movement operation being triggered by an EPP feature carried by T. Since spec-T is an **A-position** (i.e. a position which can generally only be occupied by argument expressions), the operation by which subjects move into spec-T is traditionally known as **A-movement**.

6.2 Subjects in Belfast English

Let's begin our discussion of the syntax of subjects by looking at some interesting data from Belfast English (kindly supplied to me by Alison Henry). Alongside Standard English constructions like (1a,b) below:

(1) (a)   *Some students* should get distinctions
    (b)   *Lots of students* have missed the classes

Belfast English also has structures like (2a,b):

(2)(a)   There should *some students* get distinctions
    (b)   There have *lots of students* missed the classes

Sentences like (2a,b) are called *expletive* structures because they contain the **expletive** pronoun *there*. (The fact that *there* is not a **locative** pronoun in this kind of use is shown by the impossibility of replacing it by locative *here* or questioning it by the interrogative locative *where?* or focusing it by assigning it contrastive stress.) For the time being, we concentrate on the derivation of Belfast English sentences like (2a,b) before turning to consider the derivation of Standard English sentences like (1a,b).

One question to ask about the sentences in (2a,b) is where the expletive pronoun *there* is positioned. Since *there* immediately precedes the tensed auxiliary *should/have*, a reasonable conjecture is that *there* is the subject/specifier of *should/have* and hence occupies the spec-T position. If this is so, we'd expect to find that the auxiliary can move in front of the expletive subject (via T-to-C movement) in questions – and this is indeed the case in Belfast English, as the sentences in (3) below illustrate:

(3) (a)   **Should** *there* <u>some students</u> get distinctions?
    (b)   **Have** *there* <u>lots of students</u> missed the classes?

But what position is occupied by the underlined quantified expressions *some students/lots of students* in (3)? Since they immediately precede the verbs *get/missed* and since subjects precede verbs, it seems reasonable to conclude that the expressions *some students/lots of students* function as the subjects of the verbs *get/missed* and (since subjects are typically specifiers) occupy **spec-V** (i.e. specifier position within VP). If these assumptions are correct, (2a) will have the structure (4) below (simplified by not showing the internal structure of the expressions *some students/distinctions*: we can take both of these to be QP/Quantifier Phrase expressions, headed by the overt quantifier *some* in one case and by a null quantifier [$_Q$ ø] in the other):

(4)

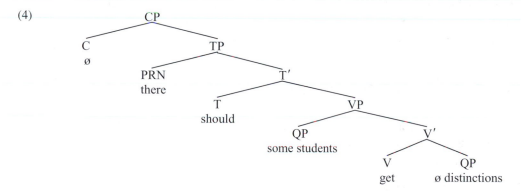

The analysis in (4) claims that the sentence contains two subjects/specifiers: *there* is the specifier (and subject) of *should*, and *some students* is the specifier (and subject) of *get*. The two subjects serve two different functions: the expression *some students* has the semantic function of denoting the recipients of the distinctions, and so could be said to be the *semantic* subject of the sentence; by contrast, the pronoun *there* satisfies the syntactic requirement of the EPP feature on T (requiring T to have a specifier which is a noun or pronoun expression), and so could be said to be the *syntactic* subject of the sentence.

Given the assumptions in (4), sentence (2a) will be derived as follows. The noun *distinctions* merges with a null quantifier [$_Q$ ø] to form the QP *ø distinctions*. By virtue of being the complement of the verb *get*, this QP is merged with the V *get* to form the **V-bar** (incomplete verb expression) *get ø distinctions*. The resulting V-bar is then merged with the subject of *get*, namely the QP *some students* (itself formed by merging the quantifier *some* with the noun *students*),

so deriving the VP *some students get ø distinctions*. This VP is in turn merged
with the past tense T-auxiliary *should*, forming the T-bar *should some students get
ø distinctions*. Let's suppose that every T constituent has an EPP feature requiring
it to have a noun or pronoun expression as its specifier. In sentences like (2a,b) in
Belfast English, the requirement for T to have such a specifier can be satisfied by
merging expletive *there* with the T-bar *should some students get ø distinctions*, so
forming the TP *There should some students get ø distinctions*. The resulting TP
is then merged with a null declarative complementiser, forming the CP shown in
(4) above.

But what about the derivation of the corresponding Standard English sentence
(1a) *Some students should get distinctions*? Let's suppose that the derivation of
(1a) runs parallel to the derivation of (2a) until the point where the auxiliary
should merges with the VP *some students get ø distinctions* to form the T-bar
should some students get ø distinctions. As before, let's assume that [T *should*]
has an EPP feature requiring it to project a structural subject/specifier. But let's
also suppose that the requirement for [T *should*] to have a specifier of its own
cannot be satisfied by merging expletive *there* in spec-T because in standard
varieties of English *there* can generally only occur in structures containing an
intransitive verb like *be, become, exist, occur, arise, remain* etc. Instead, the EPP
requirement for T to have a subject with person/number properties is satisfied by
moving the subject *some students* from its original position in spec-V into a new
position in spec-T, in the manner shown by the arrow below:

(5)

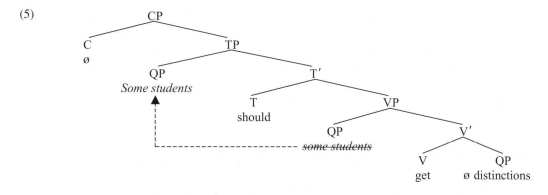

Since spec-T is an A-position which can only be occupied by an argument
expression (i.e. an expression which originates as the subject or complement of a
verb or other predicate), the kind of movement operation illustrated by the dotted
arrow in (5) is called **A-movement**.

Given the arguments presented in chapters 4 and 5 that Head Movement and
Wh-Movement are composite operations involving copying and deletion, we
would expect the same to be true of A-movement. One piece of evidence in
support of a copying analysis of A-movement comes from **scope** properties in
relation to sentences such as (6a) below, which will have the syntactic structure
shown in simplified form in (6b) if *everyone* originates as the subject of the verb

finished and is then raised up (by A-movement) to become the subject of the present tense auxiliary *have*:

(6) (a)   Everyone hasn't finished the assignment yet
    (b)   [CP [C ø] [TP *Everyone* [T has] [NEGP not [Neg ø] [VP ~~everyone~~ [V finished]
                                              the assignment yet]]]]

For many speakers, sentences like (6a) are ambiguous between (i) a reading on which the quantifier expression *everyone* has **scope** over *not* so that the sentence means much the same as 'Everyone is in the position of not having finished the assignment yet,' and (ii) another reading on which *everyone* falls within the scope of *not* (so that the sentence means much the same as 'Not everyone is yet in the position of having finished the assignment'). We can account for this scope ambiguity in a principled fashion if we suppose that A-movement involves copying, that scope is defined in terms of c-command (so that a scope-bearing constituent has scope over constituents which it c-commands), and that the scope of a universally quantified expression like *everyone* in negative structures like (6b) can be determined either in relation to the initial position of *everyone* or in relation to its final position. In (6b) *everyone* is initially merged in a position (marked by ~~strikethrough~~) in which it is c-commanded by (and so falls within the scope of) *not*; but via A-movement it ends up in an (italicised) position in which it c-commands (and so has scope over) *not*. The scope ambiguity in (6a) therefore reflects the two different positions occupied by *everyone* in the course of the derivation.

The claim that (non-expletive) subjects like *some students/lots of students* in sentences like (1) originate internally within the VP containing the relevant verb (and from there move into spec-T in sentences like (1) above) is known in the relevant literature as the **VP-Internal Subject Hypothesis (= VPISH)**, and this has been almost universally adopted in research since the mid 1980s. Below, we look at some of the evidence in support of VPISH.

6.3   Idioms

An interesting piece of evidence in support of the VP-Internal Subject Hypothesis comes from the syntax of **idioms**. We can define idioms as expressions (like those italicised below) which have an idiosyncratic meaning which is not a purely compositional function of the meaning of their individual parts:

(7) (a)   Let's have a couple of drinks to *break the ice*
    (b)   Be careful not to *upset the applecart*
    (c)   The president must *bite the bullet*

There seems to be a constraint that only a string of words which forms a unitary constituent can be an idiom. So, while we find idioms like those in (7) which are of the form *verb+complement* (but where the subject isn't part of the idiom), we don't find idioms of the form *subject+verb* where the verb has a complement which isn't part of the idiom: this is because in *subject+verb+complement* structures, the verb and its complement form a unitary constituent (a V-bar), whereas the subject and the verb do not – and only unitary constituents can be idioms.

In the light of the constraint that an idiom is a unitary constituent with an idiosyncratic interpretation, consider idioms such as the following:

(8) (a)   All hell broke loose
    (b)   The shit hit the fan
    (c)   The cat got his tongue

In (8), not only is the choice of verb and complement fixed, but so too is the choice of subject. In such idioms, we can't replace the subject, verb or complement by near synonyms – as we see from the fact that sentences like (9) below are ungrammatical (on the intended idiomatic interpretation):

(9) (a)   *The whole inferno escaped
    (b)   *Camel dung was sucked into the air conditioning
    (c)   *A furry feline bit his lingual articulator

However, what is puzzling about idioms like (8) is that one or more auxiliaries can freely be positioned between the subject and verb: cf.

(10) (a)   All hell *will* break loose
     (b)   All hell *has* broken loose
     (c)   All hell *could have* broken loose

(11) (a)   The shit *might* hit the fan
     (b)   The shit *has* hit the fan
     (c)   The shit *must have* hit the fan

How can we reconcile our earlier claim that only a string of words which form a unitary constituent can constitute an idiom with the fact that *all hell . . . break loose* is a discontinuous string in (10), since the subject *all hell* and the predicate *break loose* are separated by the intervening auxiliaries *will/has/could have*? To put the question another way: how can we account for the fact that although the choice of subject, verb and complement is fixed, the choice of auxiliary is not?

The VP-Internal Subject Hypothesis provides a straightforward answer, if we suppose that subjects originate internally within VP, and that clausal idioms like those in (8) are *VP idioms* which require a fixed choice of head, complement and specifier in the VP containing them. For instance, in the case of (8a), the relevant VP idiom requires the specific word *break* as its head verb, the specific adjective *loose* as its complement and the specific quantifier phrase *all hell* as its subject/specifier. We can then account for the fact that *all hell* surfaces in front of the auxiliary *will* in (8a) by positing that the QP *all hell* originates in spec-V as the subject of *break loose*, and is then raised (via A-movement) into spec-T to become the subject of *will break loose*. Given these assumptions, (8a) will be derived as follows. The verb *break* merges with the adjective *loose* to form the idiomatic V-bar *break loose*. This is then merged with its QP subject *all hell* to form the idiomatic VP *all hell break loose*. The resulting VP is merged with the tense auxiliary *will* to form the T-bar *will all hell break loose*. Since finite auxiliaries carry an EPP feature requiring them to have a subject specifier with person/number features, the subject *all hell* moves from being the subject of *break* to becoming the subject of *will* – as shown in simplified form below:

(12)

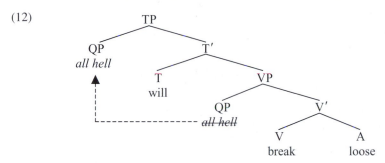

We can then say that (in the relevant idiom) *all hell* must be the sister of *break loose*, and that this condition will be met only if *all hell* originates in spec-V as the subject (and sister) of the V-bar *break loose*. We can account for how the subject *all hell* comes to be separated from its predicate *break loose* by positing that subjects originate internally within VP and from there raise to spec-T (via **A-movement**) across an intervening T constituent like *will*, so that the subject and predicate thereby come to be separated from each other – movement of the subject to spec-T being driven by an EPP feature carried by [$_T$ *will*] requiring *will* to have a subject with person/number features. Subsequently, the TP in (12) is merged with a null declarative complementiser, so deriving the structure associated with (10a) *All hell will break loose*.

6.4   Argument structure and theta-roles

The assumption that subjects originate internally within VP ties up in interesting ways with a traditional idea from predicate logic maintaining that **propositions** (which can be thought of as representing the substantive semantic content of clauses) comprise a **predicate** and a set of **arguments**. Simplifying somewhat, we can say that a predicate is an expression denoting an activity or event, and an argument is an expression denoting a participant in the relevant activity or event. For example, in sentences such as those below, the italicised verbs are predicates and the bracketed expressions represent their arguments:

(13) (a)   [The guests] have *arrived*
     (b)   [The police] have *arrested* [the suspect]

In other words, the arguments of a verb are typically its subject and complement(s). A verb like *arrive*, when used with a single [bracketed] argument in a structure like (13a), is said to be a **one-place predicate**; and a verb like *arrest* when used with two [bracketed] arguments in a structure like (13b) is said to be a **two-place predicate**.

However, there is an important sense in which it is not enough simply to say that in a sentence such as (13b) *The police have arrested the suspect* the verb *arrest* is a predicate which has two arguments – the internal argument *the suspect* and the external argument *the police*. After all, such a description fails to account for the fact that these two arguments play very different semantic roles in relation to the act of *arrest* – i.e. it fails to account for the fact that *the police* are the individuals who perform the act (and hence get to verbally and physically abuse the suspect), and that *the suspect* is the person who suffers the consequences of the act (e.g. being manhandled, handcuffed, thrown into the back of a windowless vehicle and beaten up). Hence, any adequate account of argument structure should provide a description of the semantic role which each argument plays.

In research spanning more than half a century, linguists have attempted to devise a universal typology of the semantic roles played by arguments in relation to their predicates. In the table in (14) below are listed a number of terms used to describe some of these roles (the convention being that terms denoting semantic roles are CAPITALISED), and for each role an informal gloss is given, together with an illustrative example (in which the italicised expression has the semantic role specified):

(14)   **List of roles played by arguments with respect to predicates**

Role	Gloss	Example
THEME	Entity undergoing the effect of some action	*Mary* fell over
AGENT	Entity instigating some action	*Debbie* killed Harry
EXPERIENCER	Entity experiencing some psychological state	*I* like syntax
LOCATIVE	Place in which something is situated or takes place	He hid it *under the bed*
GOAL	Entity representing the destination of some other entity	John went *home*
SOURCE	Entity from which something moves	He returned *from Paris*
INSTRUMENT	Means used to perform some action	He hit it *with a hammer*

We can illustrate how the terminology in (14) can be used to describe the semantic roles played by arguments in terms of the following examples:

(15) (a)   [The FBI] arrested   [Larry Luckless]
            [AGENT]   [THEME]
     (b)   [The suspect] received   [a caution]
            [GOAL]   [THEME]
     (c)   [The audience] enjoyed   [the play]
            [EXPERIENCER]   [THEME]
     (d)   [The president] went   [to Boston]
            [THEME]   [GOAL]

(e)	[They] stayed	[in a hotel]
	[THEME]	[LOCATIVE]
(f)	[The noise] came	[from the house]
	[THEME]	[SOURCE]

Given that – as we see from these examples – the THEME role is a central one, it has become customary over the past two decades to refer to the relevant semantic roles as **thematic roles**; and since the Greek letter θ ($=$ *theta*) corresponds to *th* in English and the word *thematic* begins with *th*, it has become standard practice to also use the synonymous expression **theta-role** or **θ-role** (pronounced *theeta-role* by some and *thayta-role* by others). Using this terminology, we can say (e.g.) that in (15a) *the FBI* is the AGENT argument of the predicate *arrested*, and that *Larry Luckless* is the THEME argument of *arrested*.

Thematic relations (like AGENT and THEME) have been argued to play a central role in the description of a range of linguistic phenomena. For example, it has been claimed that the distribution of certain types of adverb is thematically determined. Thus, Gruber (1976) maintains that adverbs like *deliberately* can only be associated with AGENT arguments: cf.

(16) (a)   *John* ($=$ AGENT) **deliberately** rolled the ball down the hill
     (b)   **The ball* ($=$ THEME) **deliberately** rolled down the hill

Likewise, Fillmore (1972, p. 10) argues that the adverb *personally* can only be associated with EXPERIENCER arguments: cf.

(17) (a)   **Personally**, your proposal doesn't interest *me* ($=$ EXPERIENCER)
     (b)   ****Personally**, you hit *me* ($=$ THEME)

And indeed thematic structure has been argued to play an important role in a wide range of other phenomena (e.g. the syntax of passives and reflexives) – but space limitations prevent us from reviewing the relevant evidence here.

If we look closely at the examples in (15), we see a fairly obvious pattern emerging. Each of the bracketed argument expressions in (15) carries one and only one θ-role, and no two arguments of any predicate carry the same θ-role. Chomsky (1981) suggested that these thematic properties of arguments are the consequence of a principle of Universal Grammar traditionally referred to as the **θ-criterion**, and outlined in (18) below:

(18)   **Theta-criterion/θ-criterion**
            Each argument bears one and only one θ-role, and each θ-role is assigned to one and only one argument (Chomsky 1981, p. 36)

A principle along the lines of (18) has been assumed (in some form or other) in much subsequent work.

However, an important question raised by (18) is precisely how arguments come to be assigned theta-roles. To put this question in a more concrete form, consider how the object *the suspect* comes to be assigned its theta-role of THEME complement of the predicate *arrested* in (13b) *The police have arrested the suspect.* Since *the suspect* is the complement of the verb *arrested* and since verbs merge with their complements, a principled answer would be to suppose that theta-roles are assigned to arguments in accordance with the hypothesis (19) below:

(19)   **Predicate-Internal Theta-Marking Hypothesis**
         An argument is theta-marked (i.e. assigned a theta-role) via merger with a predicate

The hypothesis in (19) will also account for the theta-marking of subjects, if we assume that subjects originate as arguments of verbs. To see how, let's look at the derivation of (13b) *The police have arrested the suspect.*

The verb *arrested* merges with its direct object complement *the suspect* (a DP formed by merging the determiner *the* with the noun *suspect*). In accordance with the Predicate-Internal Theta-Marking Hypothesis (19), the object *the suspect* will be theta-marked via merger with the verbal predicate *arrested*. If the lexical entry for the verb *arrest* specifies that its complement plays the thematic role of THEME argument of *arrest*, merging the verb *arrested* with its complement *the suspect* will result in *the suspect* being assigned the theta-role of THEME argument of *arrested*. The V-bar thereby formed is then merged with the subject DP *the police* (itself formed by merging the determiner *the* with the noun *police*) to form the VP shown in (20) below (simplified by not showing the internal structure of the two DPs):

(20)

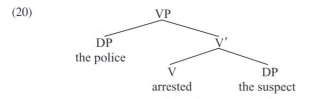

If the lexical entry for the verb *arrest* specifies that its subject has the thematic role of AGENT argument of *arrest*, merging *the police* with the V-bar *arrested the suspect* will result in *the police* being assigned the theta-role of AGENT argument of the predicate *arrested*. Introducing some new terminology at this point, we can say that in a structure such as (20), the complement *the suspect* is the **internal argument** of the verb *arrested* (in the sense that it is the argument contained within the immediate V-bar projection of the verb, and hence is a sister of the verb), whereas the subject *the police* is the **external argument** of the verb *arrested* (in that it occupies a position external to the V-bar constituent which is the immediate projection of the verb *arrested*). We can equivalently say that the verb *arrested* is **first-merged** with its complement *the suspect* and **second-merged** with its subject *the police*.

The VP in (20) is then merged with the present tense auxiliary [$_T$ *have*], forming the T-bar *have the police arrested the suspect.* Since a finite T has an [EPP] feature requiring it to have a subject of its own, the DP *the police* moves from being the subject of *arrested* to becoming the subject of [$_T$ *have*], forming

The police have ~~the police~~ *arrested the suspect.* Merging the resulting TP with a null complementiser marking the declarative force of the sentence in turn derives the (simplified) structure in (21) below:

(21)

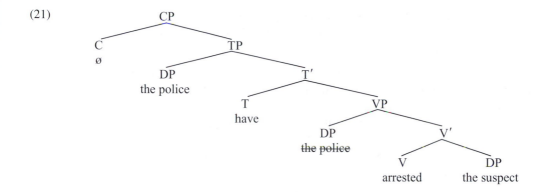

The analysis in (21) is consistent with the **θ-criterion** (18) in that each argument is assigned a single theta-role which is different from that assigned to any other argument of the same predicate (*the suspect* being the THEME argument of *arrested* and *the police* being its AGENT argument). (21) is also consistent with the **Predicate-Internal Theta-Marking Hypothesis** (19), since *the suspect* is assigned the thematic role of THEME argument of *arrested* by being first-merged with *arrested*, and *the police* is assigned the thematic role of AGENT argument of *arrested* by being second-merged with *arrested*. Since only predicative heads can assign theta-roles, and since neither T nor C is a predicative head, neither T nor C assigns any theta-role to any constituent in (21).

Our discussion here suggests that thematic considerations lend further support to the VP-Internal Subject Hypothesis. By positing that all arguments of a verb (including its subject) originate internally within VP, we can arrive at a unitary and principled account of θ-marking in terms of the Predicate-Internal Theta-Marking Hypothesis (19), since we can say that a verb only theta-marks an argument with which it is merged (via a first- or second-merge operation).

6.5   Unaccusative predicates

The overall conclusion to be drawn from our discussion so far is that subjects originate internally within VP, as theta-marked arguments of the verb. In all the structures we have looked at until now, the Verb Phrase has contained both a complement and a specifier (the specifier being the subject of the verb). However, in this and subsequent sections we look at VPs which contain a verb and a complement *but no specifier*, and where it is the complement of the verb which subsequently moves to spec-T.

One such type of VP are those headed by a special subclass of intransitive verbs which have the property that they can be used both in expletive structures such as (22a–24a) below, and in non-expletive structures like those in (22b–24b):

(22) (a)   There <u>have</u> **arisen** *several complications*
     (b)   *Several complications* have **arisen**

(23) (a)   There <u>could</u> have **occurred** *a diplomatic incident*
     (b)   *A diplomatic incident* could have **occurred**

(24) (a)   There <u>does</u> still **remain** *some hope of finding survivors*
     (b)   *Some hope of finding survivors* does still **remain**

We shall argue here that the italicised arguments originate as the complements of the bold-printed verbs in both types of structure: they remain in situ as the complement of the verb in the expletive (a) structures, but raise to become the subject of the underlined T-auxiliary *have/could/does* in the non-expletive (b) structures. However, the bold-printed verbs in (22–24) differ from transitive verbs taking a noun expression as their complement in that they don't assign accusative case to their complement, but rather nominative case. Although the nominative–accusative case contrast is invisible in noun expressions in English, it is visible in languages like Icelandic with a richer case system. And in Icelandic, the (italicised) complement of an unaccusative verb receives *nominative* (= NOM) case even in expletive structures where it remains in situ and follows the verb – as the following example (which Matthew Whelpton kindly persuaded Johannes Gisli Jónsson to provide for me) illustrates:

(25)   Það hafa **komið** *nokkrir*NOM *gestir*NOM
        There have come some guests

Because they don't assign accusative case to their complements, verbs like those bold-printed in (22–24) are known as **unaccusative predicates**.

Given that the complements of unaccusative predicates are not assigned accusative case, it would be only natural to question whether they actually are complements (rather than e.g. subjects which end up positioned after the unaccusative verb rather than in front of it). In fact, there is strong syntactic evidence in support of analysing them as complements. Part of the evidence comes from their behaviour in relation to a constraint on movement operations discovered by Huang (1982), which can be characterised in the following terms:

(26)   **Constraint on Extraction Domains/CED**
        Only complements allow material to be extracted out of them, not specifiers or adjuncts

We can illustrate Huang's CED constraint in terms of the following contrasts:

(27) (a)   He was taking [pictures of *who*]?
     (b)   *Who* was he taking [pictures of ~~who~~]?

(28) (a)   [Part of *what*] has broken?
     (b)   **What* has [part of ~~what~~] broken?

(29) (a)   He was angry [when she broke *what*]?
     (b)   **What was he angry [when she *broke* ~~what~~]?

(27a, 28a, 29a) are echo questions in which the wh-pronoun *who/what* remains in situ, while (27b, 28b, 29b) are their wh-movement counterparts. In (27b), *who* is extracted out of a bracketed nominal expression which is the complement of the verb *taking*, and yields a grammatical outcome because there is no violation of CED (extraction out of complement expressions being permitted by CED). By contrast, in (28b) *what* is extracted out of a bracketed expression which is the subject (and hence specifier) of the auxiliary *has*, and since CED blocks extraction out of specifiers, the resulting sentence is ungrammatical. Likewise in (29b) *what* is extracted out of a bracketed adjunct clause, and since CED blocks extraction out of adjuncts, the sentence is ungrammatical.

In the light of Huang's CED constraint, consider a sentence such as:

(30)   *How many survivors* does there remain [some hope of finding
                                                 ~~how many survivors~~]

Here, the wh-phrase *how many survivors* has been extracted (via **wh-movement**) out of the bracketed expression *some hope of finding how many survivors*. Given that the Condition on Extraction Domains tells us that only complements allow material to be extracted out of them, it follows that the bracketed expression in (30) must be the complement of the verb *remain*. By extension, we can assume that the italicised expressions in (22–24) are likewise the complements of the bold-printed verbs.

Not all intransitive verbs allow their arguments to be positioned after them, however – as we see from the ungrammaticality of sentences such as (31) below:

(31) (a)   **When the Snail Rail train arrived five hours late, there complained *many passengers*
     (b)   **In the dentist's surgery, there groaned *a toothless patient*
     (c)   **Every time General Wynott Nukem goes past, there salutes *a guard at the gate*

Intransitive verbs like *complain/groan/salute* are known as **unergative verbs**: they differ from unaccusatives in that the subject of an unergative verb has the thematic role of an AGENT argument, whereas the subject of an unaccusative verb has the thematic property of being a THEME argument.

In addition to those already noted, there are a number of other important syntactic differences between unaccusative verbs and other types of verb (e.g. unergative verbs or transitive verbs). For example, Alison Henry (1995) observes that in one dialect of Belfast English (which she calls dialect A) unaccusative verbs can have (italicised) postverbal subjects in imperative structures like:

(32) (a)   Leave *you* now!
   (b)   Arrive *you* before 6 o'clock!
   (c)   Be going *you* out of the door when he arrives!

By contrast, other (e.g. unergative or transitive) verbs don't allow postverbal imperative subjects, so that imperatives such as (33) below are ungrammatical in the relevant dialect:

(33) (a)   *Read *you* that book!
   (b)   *Eat *you* up!
   (c)   *Always *laugh* you at his jokes!

Additional evidence for positing that unaccusative verbs are syntactically distinct from other verbs comes from **auxiliary selection** facts in relation to earlier stages of English when there were two perfect aspect auxiliaries (*have* and *be*), each taking a complement headed by a specific kind of verb. Unaccusative verbs differed from transitive or unergative verbs in being used with the perfect auxiliary *be*, as the sentences in (34) below (taken from various plays by Shakespeare) illustrate:

(34) (a)   Mistress Page *is* **come** with me (Mrs Ford, *Merry Wives of Windsor*, V.v)
   (b)   *Is* the duke **gone**? Then *is* your cause **gone** too (Duke, *Measure for Measure*, V.i)
   (c)   How chance thou *art* **returned** so soon? (Antipholus, *Comedy of Errors*, I.ii)
   (d)   She *is* **fallen** into a pit of ink (Leonato, *Much Ado About Nothing*, IV.i)

A last vestige of structures like (34) survives in present-day English sentences such as *All hope of finding survivors is now gone*.

Verbs which (when used intransitively) are unaccusative predicates include MOTION predicates such as *arrive/come/fall/go/leave/return/rise* etc. and EXISTENTIAL predicates (i.e. verbs indicating the existence or coming into being of a state of affairs, or a change of state, or the cessation of a state) like *appear/arise/be/become/begin/change/die/exist/happen/occur/remain/start/stay/stop/turn*. An unaccusative verb like *fall* typically allows inanimate as well as animate subjects (cf. *My wife fell off a stool/The temperature fell sharply*), whereas an unergative predicate like *complain* typically allows only an animate subject (cf. *My wife complained/!The temperature complained*).

As we have seen, there is a considerable body of empirical evidence that unaccusative subjects behave differently from subjects of other (e.g. unergative or transitive) verbs. Why should this be? The answer given by the VP-Internal Subject Hypothesis is that the subjects of unaccusative verbs do not originate as the subjects of their associated verbs at all, but rather as their *complements*, and that unaccusative structures with postverbal arguments involve leaving the relevant argument in situ in VP-complement position – e.g. in unaccusative expletive structures such as (22–24) above, and in Belfast English unaccusative imperatives such as (32). This being so, a sentence such as (22a) *There have*

arisen several complications will be derived as follows. The quantifier *several*
merges with the noun *complications* to form the QP *several complications*. This
is merged as the complement of the unaccusative verb *arisen*, forming the VP
arisen several complications. The resulting VP is merged with the auxiliary *have*
to form the T-bar shown in simplified form below:

(35)

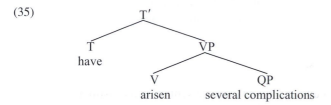

The EPP feature carried by the finite T constituent *have* requires it to have a nominal (i.e. noun or pronoun) expression as its specifier. This requirement is satisfied
by merging expletive *there* in spec-T. The resulting TP *there have arisen several
complications* is then merged with a null declarative-force complementiser to
form the CP (36) below:

(36)

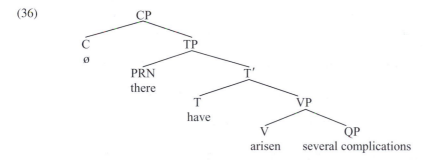

And (36) is the structure of (22a) *There have arisen several complications*.

However, an alternative way for the T constituent in (35) to satisfy the EPP
requirement to have a nominal specifier is for T to attract a nominal to move
to spec-T. In accordance with the **Attract Closest Condition**, T will attract the
closest nominal within the structure containing it. Since the only nominal in (35)
is the QP *several complications*, T therefore attracts this QP to move to spec-T
in the manner shown in simplified form in (37) below:

(37)

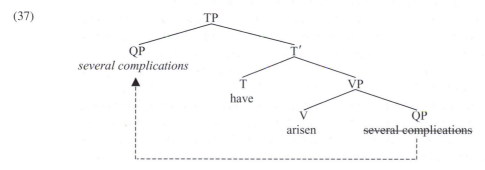

The type of movement involved is the familiar **A-movement** operation which moves an argument from a position lower down in a sentence to become the structural subject (and specifier) of TP. The resulting TP in (37) is subsequently merged with a null complementiser marking the declarative force of the sentence, so generating the structure associated with *Several complications have arisen*.

The A-movement analysis of unaccusative subjects in (37) above allows us to provide an interesting account of sentences pairs like that in (38) below:

(38) (a)   All hope of finding survivors has gone
      (b)   All hope has gone of finding survivors

Since GO is an unaccusative verb, the QP *all hope of finding survivors* will originate as the complement of *gone*. Merging *gone* with this QP will derive the VP *gone all hope of finding survivors*. The resulting VP is merged with the T constituent *has* to form the T-bar *has gone all hope of finding survivors*. Since T has an EPP feature requiring it to project a specifier, the QP *all hope of finding survivors* is raised to spec-T, leaving an italicised copy behind in the position in which it originated. Merging the resulting TP with a null complementiser marking the declarative force of the sentence derives the structure shown in simplified form in (39) below:

(39)   [$_{CP}$ [$_C$ ∅] [$_{TP}$ [$_{QP}$ **All hope of finding survivors**] [$_T$ has] [$_{VP}$ [$_V$ gone]
                                    [$_{QP}$ *all hope of finding survivors*]]]]

In the case of (38a), the whole of the QP *all hope of finding survivors* is spelled out in the bold-printed spec-T position which it moves to, and the italicised copy of the moved QP in VP-complement position is deleted in its entirety – as shown in simplified form in (40) below:

(40)   [$_{CP}$ [$_C$ ∅] [$_{TP}$ [$_{QP}$ **All hope of finding survivors**] [$_T$ has] [$_{VP}$ [$_V$ gone]
                                    [$_{QP}$ ~~*all hope of finding survivors*~~]]]]

In the case of (38b), the quantifier *all* and the noun *hope* are spelled out in the bold-printed position they move to in (39), and the PP *of finding survivors* is spelled out in the VP-complement position in which it originates – as shown in (41) below:

(41)   [$_{CP}$ [$_C$ ∅] [$_{TP}$ [$_{QP}$ **All hope ~~of finding survivors~~**] [$_T$ has] [$_{VP}$ [$_V$ gone]
                                    [$_{QP}$ ~~*all hope*~~ *of finding survivors*]]]]

(41) thus presents us with another example of the **discontinuous/split spellout** phenomenon highlighted in §5.3. It also provides evidence in support of taking A-movement (like other movement operations) to be a composite operation involving copying and deletion.

6.6 Passive predicates

A class of predicates which are similar in some respects to unaccusative predicates are **passive predicates**. Traditional grammarians maintain that the bold-printed verbs in sentences such as the (a) examples in (42–44) below are in the **active voice**, whereas the italicised verbs in the corresponding (b) sentences are in the **passive voice** (and have the status of **passive participles**):

(42) (a) Hundreds of passers-by **saw** the attack
(b) The attack was *seen* by hundreds of passers-by

(43) (a) Lex Luthor **stole** the kryptonite
(b) The kryptonite was *stolen* by Lex Luthor

(44)(a) They **took** everything
(b) Everything was *taken*

There are four main properties which differentiate passive sentences from their active counterparts. One is that passive (though not active) sentences generally require the auxiliary BE. Another is that the main verb in passive sentences is in the passive participle form (cf. *seen/stolen/taken*), which is generally homophonous with the perfect participle form. A third is that passive sentences may (though need not) contain a *by*-phrase in which the complement of *by* plays the same thematic role as the subject in the corresponding active sentence: for example, *hundreds of passers-by* in the active structure (42a) serves as the subject of *saw the attack*, whereas in the passive structure (42b) it serves as the complement of the preposition *by* (though in both cases it has the thematic role of EXPERIENCER argument of *see*). The fourth difference is that the expression which serves as the complement of an active verb surfaces as the subject in the corresponding passive construction: for example, *the attack* is the complement of *saw* in the active structure (42a), but is the subject of *was* in the passive structure (42b). Since this chapter is concerned with A-movement (and hence the syntax of subjects), we focus on the syntax of the superficial subjects of passive sentences, setting aside the derivation of *by*-phrases.

Passive predicates resemble unaccusatives in that alongside structures like those in (45a–47a) below containing preverbal subjects they also allow expletive structures like (45b–47b) in which the italicised argument can be postverbal (providing it is an indefinite expression):

(45) (a) *No evidence of any corruption* was found
(b) There was found *no evidence of any corruption*

(46) (a) *Several cases of syntactophobia* have been reported
(b) There have been reported *several cases of syntactophobia*

(47) (a)   *A significant change of policy* has been announced
     (b)   There has been announced *a significant change of policy*

How can we account for the dual position of the italicised expressions in such structures?

The answer given within the framework outlined here is that a passive subject is initially merged as the thematic complement of the main verb (i.e. it originates as the complement of the main verb as in (45b–47b) and so receives the θ-role which the relevant verb assigns to its complement), and subsequently moves from V-complement position into T-specifier position in passive sentences such as (45a–47a).

On this view, the derivation of sentences like (45) will proceed as follows. The noun *corruption* merges with the quantifier *any* to form the QP *any corruption*. The resulting QP then merges with the preposition *of* to form the PP *of any corruption*. This PP in turn merges with the noun *evidence* to form the NP *evidence of any corruption*. The resulting NP is merged with the negative quantifier *no* to form the QP *no evidence of any corruption*. This QP is merged as the complement of the passive verb *found* (and thereby assigned the thematic role of THEME argument of *found*) to form the VP *found no evidence of any corruption*. The VP thus formed is merged with the auxiliary *was* forming the T-bar *was found no evidence of any corruption*. The auxiliary [$_T$ *was*] carries an EPP feature requiring it to have a specifier. This requirement can be satisfied by merging the expletive pronoun *there* in spec-T, deriving the TP *There was found no evidence of any corruption*. Merging this TP with a null complementiser marking the declarative force of the sentence will derive the structure shown in simplified form in (48) below:

(48)

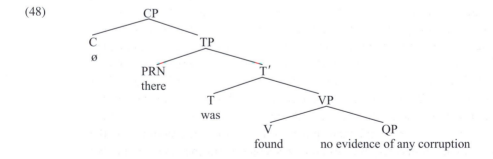

However, an alternative way of satisfying the EPP feature of T is not to merge *there* in spec-T, but rather to **passivise** the QP *no evidence of any corruption* – i.e. to move it from being the thematic object of *found* to becoming the structural subject of *was*. Merging the resulting TP with a null complementiser which marks the sentence as declarative in force derives the CP shown in simplified form in (49) below (with the arrow showing the movement which took place on the T-cycle):

(49)

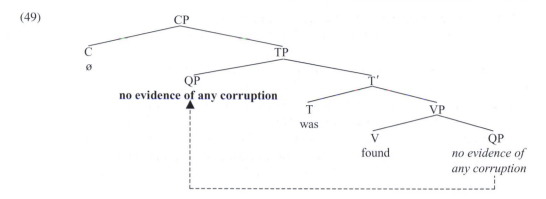

The arrowed movement operation (traditionally called **passivisation**) by which QP moves from thematic complement position into structural subject position turns out to be a particular instance of the more general **A-movement** operation which serves to create structural subjects (i.e. to move arguments into spec-T in order to satisfy the EPP feature of T). Note that an assumption implicit in the analyses in (48) and (49) is that verb phrases headed by intransitive passive participles remain subjectless throughout the derivation, because the T constituent *was* is the head which requires a structural subject by virtue of its EPP feature, not the verb *found* (suggesting that it is functional heads like T and C which trigger movement, not lexical heads like V).

In the case of (45a) *No evidence of any corruption was found*, the whole of the QP *no evidence of any corruption* is spelled out in the bold-printed spec-T position in (49) at the **head** of the movement chain, and all the material in the italicised V-complement position at the **foot** of the movement chain is deleted. However, in §5.3 we saw that some structures in which a moved noun has a prepositional complement may allow **discontinuous spellout**, with the noun and any preceding expressions modifying it being spelled out at the head (i.e. on the highest link) of the movement chain, and its prepositional or clausal complement being spelled out at the foot (i.e. on the lowest link) of the movement chain. Discontinuous spellout is also permitted in (49), allowing for the possibility of the quantifier *no* and the noun *evidence* being spelled out in the bold-printed position at the head (i.e. top) of the movement chain, and the PP *of any corruption* being spelled out in the italicised VP-complement position at the foot (i.e. bottom) of the movement chain, so deriving the structure associated with the sentence in (50) below:

(50)   **No evidence** was found *of any corruption*

Sentences such as (50) thus provide evidence that passive subjects originate as complements, if *of any corruption* is a remnant of the preposed complement *no evidence of any corruption*.

Further evidence that passive subjects originate as complements comes from the distribution of idiomatic nominals like those italicised below:

(51) (a)   They **paid** *little heed* to what he said
     (b)   *Little heed* was **paid** to what he said

(52) (a)   They **paid** *due homage* to General Ghouly
     (b)   *Due homage* was **paid** to General Ghouly

(53) (a)   The FBI **kept** *close tabs* on the CIA
     (b)   *Close tabs* were **kept** on the CIA by the FBI

In expressions such as *pay heed/homage to* and *keep tabs on*, the verb *pay/keep* and the noun expression containing *heed/tabs/homage* together form an idiom. Given the arguments in §6.3 that idioms are unitary constituents, it is apparent that the bold-printed verb and the italicised noun expression must form a unitary constituent when they are first introduced into the derivation. This will clearly be the case if we suppose that the noun expression originates as the complement of the associated verb (as in 51a–53a), and becomes the subject of the passive auxiliary *was/were* in (51b–53b) via passivisation/A-movement.

A claim which is implicit in the hypothesis that passive subjects originate as thematic objects is that the subjects of active verbs and the complements of passive verbs have the same thematic function. Evidence that this is indeed the case comes from the traditional observation that the two are subject to the same pragmatic restrictions on the choice of expression which can occupy the relevant position, as we see from sentences such as the following (where ?, ?! and ! mark increasing degrees of anomaly):

(54) (a)   *The students/?The camels/?!The flowers/!The ideas* were arrested
     (b)   They arrested *the students/?the camels/?!the flowers/!the ideas*

We can account for this if we suppose that pragmatic restrictions on the choice of admissible arguments for a given predicate depend jointly on the semantic properties of the predicate and the thematic role of the argument: it will then follow that two expressions which fulfil the same thematic role in respect of a given predicate will be subject to the same pragmatic restrictions on argument choice. Since passive subjects like those italicised in (54a) originate as complements, they will have the same θ-role (and so be subject to the same pragmatic restrictions on argument choice) as active complements like those italicised in (54b).

We can arrive at the same conclusion (that passive subjects originate as thematic complements) on theoretical grounds. It seems reasonable to suppose that thematic structure is mapped into syntactic structure in a uniform fashion, and that this is regulated by a UG principle such as the following:

(55)   **Uniform Theta Assignment Hypothesis/UTAH**
        Constituents which fulfil the same thematic role with respect to a given
        predicate occupy the same initial position in the syntax

It follows from UTAH that if passive subjects have the same theta-role as active objects, it is plausible to suppose that passive subjects originate in the same V-complement position as active objects.

6.7 Long-distance passivisation

Thus far, the instances of passivization which we have looked at have been clause-internal in the sense that they have involved movement from complement to subject position within the same clause. However, passivisation is also able to apply across certain types of clause boundary – as can be illustrated in relation to structures such as (56) and (57) below:

(56) (a) There are alleged to have been **stolen** *a number of portraits of the queen*

(b) *A number of portraits of the queen* are alleged to have been **stolen**

(57) (a) There are believed to have **occurred** *several riots*

(b) *Several riots* are believed to have **occurred**

It seems clear that the italicised expression in each case is the thematic complement of the bold-printed verb in the infinitive clause, so that *a number of portraits of the queen* is the thematic complement of the passive verb *stolen* in (56), and *several riots* is the thematic complement of the unaccusative verb *occurred* in (57). In (56a, 57a) the italicised argument remains in situ as the complement of the bold-printed verb; but in (56b, 57b) the italicised argument moves to become the structural subject of the auxiliary *are*. Let's look rather more closely at the derivation of sentences like (57a) and (57b).

(57a) is derived as follows. The quantifier *several* merges with the noun *riots* to form the QP *several riots*. This QP merges with (and is assigned the θ-role of THEME argument of) the unaccusative verb *occurred* to form the VP *occurred several riots*. The resulting VP merges with the perfect auxiliary *have* to form the AUXP *have occurred several riots*. This in turn merges with the infinitival tense particle *to*, so forming the T-bar *to have occurred several riots*. As we saw in §3.2, infinitival *to* (like all T-constituents) has an EPP feature which requires it to have a noun or pronoun expression as its subject/specifier. One way of satisfying this requirement is for expletive *there* to be merged in spec-T, forming the TP *there to have occurred several riots*. The resulting TP merges with the passive verb *believed* to form the VP *believed there to have occurred several riots*. This VP then merges with the present tense T-auxiliary *are* to form the T-bar *are believed there to have occurred several riots*. A T-constituent like *are* has an EPP feature requiring it to have a suitable subject of its own, and one way of satisfying this requirement is for T to attract a (pro)noun expression which it c-commands to become its subject. Given the Attract Closest Condition (recapituated below from §5.8):

(58)   **Attract Closest Condition/ACC**
A head which attracts a given kind of constituent attracts the *closest*
constituent of the relevant kind

it follows that T will attract the *closest* noun or pronoun expression within its
(c-command) domain. Accordingly, the T-auxiliary *are* attracts the expletive
pronoun *there* to become its subject (via passivisation), so forming the TP *there
are believed* ~~there~~ *to have occurred several riots*. This TP is then merged with
a null C marking the sentence as declarative in force, so deriving the following
structure:

(59)

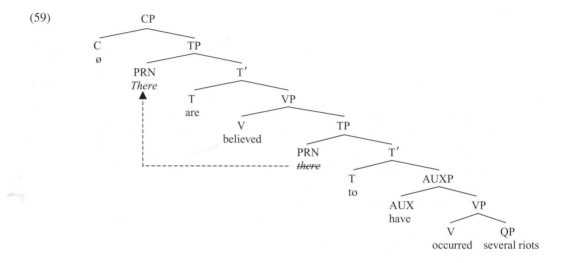

And (59) is the structure of (57a) *There are believed to have occurred several
riots*.

Now consider the derivation of (57b) *Several riots are believed to have
occurred*. Assume that the derivation proceeds as for (57a) until we reach the
stage where we have formed the T-bar *to have occurred several riots*. But this
time, suppose that the EPP requirement that the infinitival T-constituent *to* should
have a subject of its own is satisfied by moving the QP *several riots* to spec-T
to become the subject of *to*, so forming the TP *several riots to have occurred
~~several riots~~*. The resulting TP merges with the passive verb *believed* to form
the VP *believed several riots to have occurred ~~several riots~~*. This then merges
with the present tense T-auxiliary *are* to form the T-bar *are believed several riots
to have occurred ~~several riots~~*. Since the T-constituent *are* has an EPP feature, it
will attract the closest noun or pronoun expression (= the QP *several riots*) to
become its subject/specifier, so forming the TP *several riots are believed ~~several
riots~~ to have occurred ~~several riots~~*. The resulting TP is then merged with a null
C constituent marking the sentence as declarative in force, so forming the CP
shown below:

(60)

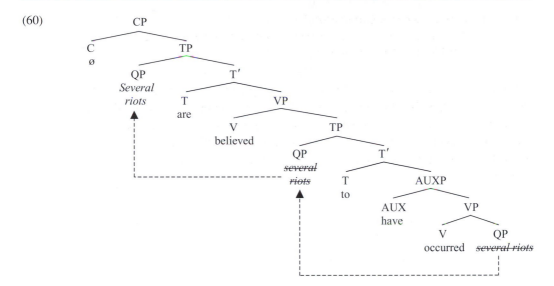

Our discussion illustrates that (in consequence of the EPP feature on T) long-distance passivisation takes place in a series of short steps (i.e. in a *successive-cyclic* fashion), moving the relevant expression one TP at a time. Since operations which move a noun or pronoun expression into spec-T are instances of A-movement, long-distance passivisation involves a series of applications of the familiar **A-movement** operation: thus, each of the two arrowed movements in (60) is a particular instance of A-movement.

In the previous chapter, we noted that movement operations obey the **Relativised Minimality Condition** (61) below:

(61)   **Relativised Minimality Condition/RMC**
        A constituent X can only be affected by (e.g. agree with or be attracted by)
        the minimal (i.e. closest) constituent of the relevant type above it (i.e.
        c-commanding X)

As we saw in §5.6, this means that a constituent undergoing wh-movement is attracted by the closest C constituent above it. However, it also means that a constituent undergoing A-movement is likewise attracted by the closest T constituent above it. As should be clear, A-movement in (60) conforms to RMC, in that the QP *several riots* is first attracted to become the specifier of the closest T constituent above it (= the embedded clause T constituent containing infinitival *to*), and then attracted to become the specifier of the next closest T constituent above it (= the main-clause T constituent containing *are*). As should be apparent, there is considerable overlap between the Attract Closest Condition/ACC in (58) and the Relativised Minimality Condition/RMC (61) – one is in effect the converse of the other. Thus, ACC says that a head H can only attract the closest expression X of the relevant type which it c-commands, whereas RMC says that an expression X can only be attracted by the closest head H of the relevant type which c-commands it. Accordingly, ACP and RMC represent two different approaches to capturing the *locality* property of syntactic operations.

A key assumption made in (59) and (60) is that the *to*-infinitive complement of the verb *believed* is a TP and not a CP. This is in line with our assumption in §3.8 that *believe* is an ECM verb when used with an infinitival complement (i.e. an Exceptional Case-Marking verb able to assign accusative case to the subject of its complement), and that its complement is a defective clause (lacking the CP layer found in complete clauses) and hence a TP. Recall that we have independent evidence from contrasts such as:

(62) (a)   Nobody intended [*you* to get hurt]
     (b)   *You* weren't intended [to get hurt]

(63) (a)   Nobody intended [for *you* to get hurt]
     (b)   *You* weren't intended [for to get hurt]

that an italicised expression contained within a TP complement like that bracketed in (62) can passivise, but not one contained within a CP complement like that bracketed in (63).

It is traditionally said that passivisation is an operation by which the complement of a VP becomes the subject/specifier of a higher TP. However, while this is true of the kind of passive structures which we have looked at so far, it is not true of those like (64) below:

(64) (a)   *All hell* was said to have **broken loose**
     (b)   *The shit* is expected to **hit the fan**

In (64a,b) the italicised passivised nominal is an idiomatic expression which originates as the *subject* of the bold-printed expression – demonstrating that passivisation can target subjects as well as complements. The derivation of (64b) proceeds as follows. The verb *hit* merges with the DP *the fan* to form the V-bar *hit the fan*. This V-bar in turn merges with the DP *the shit* to form the (idiomatic) VP *the shit hit the fan*. This VP is merged with the infinitival T-constituent *to*, forming the T-bar *to the shit hit the fan*. In conformity with the Attract Closest Condition (58), the EPP feature on [$_T$ *to*] enables it to attract the closest noun expression (= *the shit*) to become its subject, so forming the TP *the shit to ~~the shit~~ hit the fan*. The resulting TP is merged as the complement of the passive verb *expected*, forming the VP *expected the shit to ~~the shit~~ hit the fan*. This VP is then merged as the complement of the present tense T-auxiliary *is*, forming the T-bar *is expected the shit to ~~the shit~~ hit the fan*. In conformity with the Attract Closest Condition (58), the EPP feature on the T-auxiliary *is* enables it to attract the closest nominal (= *the shit*) to become its subject, so forming the TP *The shit is expected ~~the shit~~ to ~~the shit~~ hit the fan*. Merging this TP with a null complementiser marking the sentence as declarative in force derives the structure below:

(65)

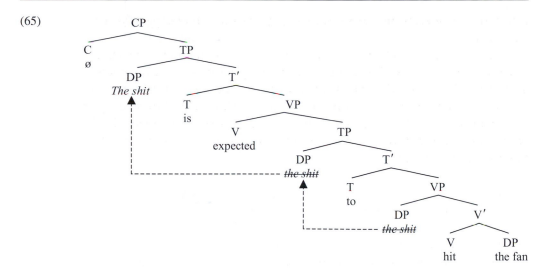

Although structures like (65) are traditionally said to involve **long-distance passivisation**, in actual fact they involve two separate local A-movement operations
by which the idiomatic nominal *the shit* moves first to become the specifier of
the lower TP (thereby becoming the subject of infinitival *to*) and then to become
the specifier of the higher TP (thereby becoming the subject of *is*). In each case
(in conformity with the Attract Closest Condition) T attracts the closest nominal
expression which it c-commands to move to spec-T, and the relevant movement
operation also satisfies the Relativised Minimality Condition (61), which requires
a constituent undergoing A-movement to become the specifier of the closest T
constituent above it.

6.8   Raising

A further type of structure which involves movement of an argument
expression out of one clause to become the subject of another clause is illustrated
by the (b) examples in (66–69) below:

(66) (a)   There does **seem** [to remain *some hope of peace*]
      (b)   *Some hope of peace* does **seem** [to remain]

(67) (a)   There does **appear** [to have been made *remarkably little progress on
                                                                disarmament*]
      (b)   *Remarkably little progress on disarmament* does **appear** [to have
                                                                been made]

(68) (a)   It would **seem** [that *Senator Slyme* has been lying to Congress]
      (b)   *Senator Slyme* would **seem** [to have been lying to Congress]

(69) (a)   It would **appear** [that *they* have underestimated her]
      (b)   *They* would appear [to have underestimated her]

In (66), the italicised expression *some hope of peace* is the thematic complement of the unaccusative predicate *remain*; it remains in situ in the expletive structure (66a), but raises to become the subject of the *seem*-clause in (66b). In (67), the italicised expression *remarkably little progress on disarmament* is the thematic complement of the passive verb *made*; it remains in situ in the expletive structure (67a) but raises to become the subject of the *appear*-clause in (67b). In (68), the italicised expression *Senator Slyme* is the thematic subject of the verb *lying*: if the complement clause is a finite clause as in (68a), it surfaces as the subject of the complement clause; but if the complement clause is infinitival as in (68b), it surfaces as the subject of the *seem*-clause. Likewise, in (69) the italicised pronoun *they* is the thematic subject of the verb *underestimate*: if the complement clause is finite as in (69a), it surfaces as the subject of the complement clause; if the complement clause is infinitival as in (69b), it surfaces as the subject of the *appear* clause.

Examples like (66–69) suggest that verbs like *seem* and *appear* resemble passive verbs in that they allow an expression which is a theta-marked argument of a predicate in a lower clause to raise to become the subject of the *seem/appear*-clause. Given this assumption, a sentence such as (66b) will have the following simplified derivation. At the point where the QP *some hope of ø peace* has been formed (the noun *peace* having been merged with a null quantifier), it will be merged with (and θ-marked by) the verb *remain* to form the VP *remain some hope of ø peace*. This VP is then merged with the infinitival tense particle *to*, forming the T-bar *to remain some hope of ø peace*. Infinitival *to* (like all T constituents) has an EPP feature requiring it to have a noun or pronoun expression as its subject. One way of satisfying this requirement is by merging the expletive pronoun *there* in spec-T, so deriving the TP *there to remain some hope of ø peace*. The resulting infinitival TP is subsequently merged with the verb *seem* to form the VP *seem there to remain some hope of ø peace*. This in turn is merged with the present tense auxiliary *does* to form the T-bar *does seem there to remain some hope of ø peace*. Like all T constituents, [$_T$ *does*] has an EPP feature which enables it to attract the closest noun or pronoun expression (= the expletive pronoun *there*) to become its subject, so forming the TP *There does seem* ~~there~~ *to remain some hope of ø peace*. This TP is then merged with a null complementiser marking the sentence as declarative in force, so forming the structure shown in simplified form below (with movement indicated by an arrow):

(70)   [$_{CP}$ [$_C$ ø] [$_{TP}$ *there* [$_T$ does] [$_{VP}$ [$_V$ seem] [$_{TP}$ ~~*there*~~ [$_T$ to] [$_{VP}$ [$_V$ remain] some hope of ø peace]]]]]

And (70) is the structure of (66a) *There does seem to remain some hope of peace*.

Now consider the derivation of (66b) *Some hope of peace does seem to remain*. Assume that this proceeds as for (66a) until we have formed the T-bar *to remain some hope of ø peace*. Since infinitival *to* (like all T constituents in English) has an EPP feature, it can (in conformity with the Attract Closest Condition (58)) attract the closest nominal (= *some hope of ø peace*) to become its subject, so forming the TP *some hope of ø peace to remain* ~~some hope of ø peace~~. The resulting TP is then merged with the verb *seem* to form the VP *seem some hope of ø peace to remain* ~~some hope of ø peace~~. This VP is in turn merged with the present tense T constituent *does* to form the T-bar *does seem some hope of ø peace to remain* ~~some hope of ø peace~~. Like all T constituents, the T-auxiliary *does* has an EPP feature which allows it to attract the closest nominal (= *some hope of ø peace*) to become its subject, so forming the TP *some hope of ø peace does seem* ~~some hope of ø peace~~ to remain ~~some hope of ø peace~~. Merging this TP with a null declarative complementiser forms the following structure (with arrows indicating A-movement operations which take place in the course of the derivation):

(71)

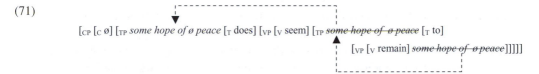

The movement operation by which the noun or pronoun expression moves from being the specifier of a lower TP to becoming the specifier of a higher TP in (70) and (71) is traditionally known as (**subject**) **raising** (because it *raises* a noun or pronoun expression from being the subject of a lower clause to becoming the subject of a higher clause) but in reality it turns out to be yet another instance of the more general **A-movement** operation by which T attracts the closest nominal which it c-commands to become its specifier (and thereby move to spec-T). Words like *seem/appear* (when used with an infinitival complement) have the property that the subject of the *seem/appear*-clause is created by being raised out of a complement clause, and so (for this reason) are known as **raising predicates**. The parallels between raising in structures like (71) and long-distance passivisation in structures like (60) should be obvious.

Note in addition that the assumption that the nominal *some hope of peace* moves from its underlying position as the complement of the verb *remain* into its superficial position as the subject of *does* in two successive steps (moving one TP at a time) means that A-movement in (71) obeys the Relativised Minimality Condition (which requires a constituent undergoing A-movement to become the specifier of the closest T constituent above it, each time it moves).

6.9   Comparing raising and control predicates

It might at first sight seem tempting to conclude from our discussion of long-distance passivisation structures like (65) and raising structures like (71) that all clauses containing a structure of the form *verb+to+infinitive* have a derivation in which some expression is raised out of the infinitive complement to become the subject of the main clause. However, any such conclusion would be undermined by our claim in §3.2 and §3.7 that some verbs which take *to+infinitive* complements are **control predicates** (i.e. predicates which can take an infinitive complement with a PRO subject which is controlled by/refers book to the subject of the main clause). In this connection, consider the difference between the two types of infinitive structure illustrated below:

(72) (a)   He does seem [to scare them]
      (b)   He does want [to scare them]

As used in (72), the verb *seem* is a **raising predicate**, but the verb *want* is a **control predicate**. We will see that this reflects the fact that the verbs *seem* and *want* differ in respect of their argument structure. We can illustrate this by sketching the derivation of the two sentences.

In the raising structure (72a), the verb *scare* merges with (and assigns the EXPERIENCER θ-role to) its internal argument/thematic complement *them*. The resulting V-bar *scare them* then merges with (and assigns the AGENT θ-role to) its external argument/thematic subject *he*. The resulting VP *he scare them* is subsequently merged with the infinitival tense particle *to*, so forming the T-bar *to he scare them*. Like all T constituents, *to* has an EPP feature which enables it to attract the closest noun or pronoun expression to become its subject, so forming the TP *he to ~~he~~ scare them*. This in turn merges with the raising verb *seem* to form the VP *seem he to ~~he~~ scare them*. The resulting VP is then merged with the (emphatic) T-auxiliary *does*. The EPP feature carried by [$_T$ *does*] enables it to attract *he* to become its subject, so forming the TP *he does seem ~~he~~ to ~~he~~ scare them*. This TP is merged with a null C which marks the clause as declarative in force, so forming the structure shown in simplified form below (with each of the arrows marking a separate application of A-movement):

(73)

$$[_{CP} [_C \text{ø}] [_{TP} \textit{he} [_T \text{does}] [_{VP} [_V \text{seem}] [_{TP} \textit{he} [_T \text{to}] [_{VP} \textit{he} [_V \text{scare}] \text{them}]]]]]$$

The successive-cyclic (one-TP-at-a-time) application of A-movement in (73) satisfies the Relativised Minimality Condition (61), which requires an A-moved constituent to become the specifier of the closest T constituent above it: accordingly, *he* becomes the specifier of the embedded clause T constituent *to* before moving on to become the specifier of the main clause T constituent containing *does*.

A key assumption made in the raising analysis in (73) is that the verb *seem* (as used there) is a one-place predicate whose only argument is its infinitival TP complement, to which it assigns an appropriate θ-role – that of THEME argument of *seem*. This means that the VP headed by *seem* has no thematic subject: note, in particular, that the verb *seem* does not θ-mark the pronoun *he*, since *he* is θ-marked by *scare*, and the **θ-criterion** (18) rules out the possibility of any argument being θ-marked by more than one predicate. Nor does the VP headed by *seem* have a structural subject at any stage of derivation, since *he* raises to become first the subject of the lower TP headed by infinitival *to*, and then to become the subject of the higher TP headed by the present tense T-auxiliary *does*. This underlines the point that syntactic movement operations typically move a constituent to the edge (i.e. head or specifier position) of a *functional projection* like TP or CP.

The property of having a THEME complement but no thematic subject means that raising predicates like *seem* have essentially the same thematic properties as unaccusative verbs like *come* discussed in §6.5. Not surprisingly, therefore, many intransitive verbs like those below allow a dual use as (i) an unaccusative verb with an italicised nominal complement as in the relevant (a) example below, and (ii) a raising verb with an underlined infinitival TP complement as in the corresponding (b) example:

(74) (a) There appeared *a grotesque face* at the window
    (b) His attitude appears <u>to have changed</u>

(75) (a) There has never before happened *anything quite so momentous*
    (b) It happened <u>to be raining at the time</u>

(76) (a) There remain *doubts about his competence*
    (b) That remains <u>to be seen</u>

(77) (a) There began *a long period of negotiation*
    (b) The situation began <u>to get worse</u>

In such sentences, a raising verb is a one-place predicate with a TP as its complement, whereas an unaccusative verb is a one-place predicate with a noun or pronoun expression as its complement.

Having looked at the raising infinitive structure (72a), let's now turn to consider the derivation of the control infinitive structure (72b) *He does want to scare them*. As before, the verb *scare* merges with (and assigns the EXPERIENCER θ-role to) its internal argument (i.e. thematic complement) *them*. The resulting V-bar *scare them* then merges with (and assigns the AGENT θ-role to) its external argument. Given the assumption we made in §3.2 that control infinitives have a particular kind of null pronominal subject known as 'big *PRO*', the thematic subject of *scare them* will be *PRO*, and this will be merged in spec-V (in accordance with the VP-Internal Subject Hypothesis), and thereby be assigned the θ-role of AGENT argument of *scare*. The resulting VP *PRO scare them* then merges with infinitival *to*, forming the T-bar *to PRO scare them*. The EPP feature of infinitival *to* enables it to attract *PRO* to become its subject, so forming the TP *PRO to ~~PRO~~ scare them*. Given the conclusion we drew in §3.7 that control infinitives are CPs, this TP will in turn merge with a null infinitival complementiser to form the CP *ø PRO to ~~PRO~~ scare them*. The CP thereby formed serves as the internal argument (and thematic complement) of the verb *want*, so is merged with *want* and thereby assigned the θ-role of THEME argument of *want*. The resulting V-bar *want ø PRO to ~~PRO~~ scare them* then merges with its external argument (and thematic subject) *he*, assigning *he* the thematic role of EXPERIENCER argument of *want*. The resulting VP *he want ø PRO to ~~PRO~~ scare them* is then merged with the T-auxiliary *does*, forming the T-bar *does he want ø PRO to ~~PRO~~ scare them*. The EPP feature carried by [$_T$ *does*] enables it to attract the closest noun or pronoun expression which it c-commands (= *he*) to become its subject, so forming the TP *he does ~~he~~ want ø PRO to ~~PRO~~ scare them*. Merging the resulting TP with a null declarative complementiser forms the structure shown in simplified form below (with arrows indicating the two different A-movement operations taking place in the course of the derivation):

(78)   [$_{CP}$ [$_C$ ø] [$_{TP}$ *He* [$_T$ does] [$_{VP}$ ~~he~~ [$_V$ want] [$_{CP}$ [$_C$ ø] [$_{TP}$ PRO [$_T$ to] [$_{VP}$ ~~PRO~~ [$_V$ scare] them]]]]]]

The resulting structure satisfies the θ-**criterion** (18) (which requires each argument to be assigned a single θ-role, and each θ-role to be assigned to a single argument), in that *he* is the EXPERIENCER argument of *want*, the bracketed CP is the THEME complement of *want*, PRO is the AGENT argument of *scare*, and *them* is the EXPERIENCER argument of *scare*.

The analysis of control predicates presented here differs from that presented in chapter 3 in that it assumes that the PRO subject of a control infinitive like that bracketed in (72b) *He does want to scare them* is merged in spec-V, and not (as assumed in chapter 3) in spec-T. The requirement for PRO to be generated in spec-V follows from the **VP-Internal Subject Hypothesis** and the **Predicate-Internal Theta-Marking Hypothesis**, which posit that arguments are generated and theta-marked internally to a projection of their predicate, so that PRO (by virtue of being the AGENT argument of *scare*) is generated as the specifier of the VP headed by *scare*. However, given that all T constituents in English have an EPP feature, the EPP feature on infinitival *to* will attract PRO to move out of the VP in which it originates into the specifier position within the TP headed by infinitival *to*. Since movement of an empty category like PRO out of the VP into spec-T is by nature invisible, an obvious question which arises is whether there is any empirical evidence that PRO moves to spec-T rather than remaining in situ within VP. The answer, as we shall see, is 'Yes'.

One piece of evidence suggesting that PRO *does* indeed move to spec-T in control infinitives comes from the syntax of constituents like those italicised in (79) below which have the property that they are construed as modifying a bold-printed antecedent which is not immediately adjacent to them:

(79) (a)   **They** were *both* priding themselves on their achievements
   (b)   **I** don't *myself* think that Capuccino was the best choice for manager of the England team
   (c)   **He** was *personally* held responsible

Both in (79a) is a **floating quantifier** (and *each/all* can be used in a similar fashion); *myself* in (79b) is a **floating emphatic reflexive**; and *personally* in (79c) is an **argument-oriented adverb** (construed as modifying an argument, in this case *he*). In each sentence in (79), the italicised expression is construed as modifying the bold-printed subject of the clause. Contrasts such as those in (80) and (81) below:

(80) (a)   **Two republican senators** were *themselves* thought to have been implicated

    (b)   *There were *themselves* thought to have been implicated **two republican senators**

(81) (a)   **Two republican senators** are *both* thought to have been implicated

    (b)   *There are *both* thought to have been implicated **two republican senators**

suggest that a floating modifier must be c-commanded by its bold-printed antecedent.

In the light of the requirement for a floating modifier to be c-commanded by its antecedent, consider the syntax of the bracketed clauses in the following sentences:

(82) (a)   [To *both* be betrayed by their friends] would be disastrous for Romeo and Juliet

    (b)   [To *themselves* be indicted] would be unfair on the company directors

    (c)   It was upsetting [to *personally* have been accused of corruption]

In each of these examples, the bracketed clause is a control clause containing a PRO argument. In each case, PRO is the thematic complement of a passive participle (viz. *betrayed/indicted/accused*). Hence, if control *to* had no EPP feature and PRO remained in situ, the TP in the bracketed infinitive complement in (82b) would have the skeletal structure (83a) below, but if (as suggested here) control *to* has an EPP feature, this will trigger movement of PRO to become the structural subject of *to* – as in (83b):

(83) (a)   [CP [C ø] [TP [T to] [AUXP *themselves* [AUX be] [VP [V indicted] **PRO**]]]]

    (b)   [CP [C ø] [TP **PRO** [T to] [AUXP *themselves* [AUX be] [VP [V indicted] ~~PRO~~]]]]

Given the requirement for a floating emphatic reflexive to be c-commanded by its antecedent, and given that PRO is the intended antecedent of *themselves* in (83), it is clear that (83a) cannot be the right structure, since PRO does not c-command *themselves* in (83a). By contrast, movement of PRO to spec-T in (83b) means that PRO will indeed c-command *themselves*, so correctly predicting that (82b) is grammatical. Thus, sentences such as (82) provide us with empirical evidence that PRO moves to spec-T in control clauses, and thereby becomes the subject of infinitival *to*. This in turn is consistent with our more general claim that all T constituents in English have an EPP feature requiring them to have a subject.

Having compared the syntax of control predicates with that of raising predicates, we end this chapter by looking briefly at the question of how we can determine whether a given predicate which selects an infinitival *to* complement is a control predicate or a raising predicate. In this connection, it should be noted that there are a number of syntactic differences between raising and control predicates which are a direct reflection of the different thematic properties of these two types of predicate. For example, raising predicates like *seem* can have expletive *it/there* subjects, whereas control predicates like *want* cannot: cf.

(84) (a)   *It* **seems/*wants** to be assumed that he lied to Congress
     (b)   *There* **seem/*want** to remain several unsolved mysteries

(The expletive nature of *it* in (84a) is shown by the fact that it cannot be substituted by a referential pronoun like *this/that*, or questioned by *what?* Likewise, the expletive nature of *there* in (84b) is shown by the fact that it cannot be substituted by a referential locative pronoun like *here*, or questioned by *where?*) This is because control predicates like *want* are two-place predicates which project a thematic subject (an EXPERIENCER in the case of *want*, so that the subject of *want* must be an expression denoting a sentient entity capable of experiencing desires), and non-referential expressions like expletive *it/there* clearly do not denote sentient entities and so cannot serve as the thematic subject of a verb like *want*. By contrast, raising predicates like *seem* have no thematic subject, and hence impose no restrictions on the choice of structural subject in their clause, so allowing a (non-thematic) expletive subject.

   Similarly, raising predicates like *seem* (but not control predicates like *want*) allow idiomatic subjects such as those italicised below:

(85)   Whenever they meet . . .
     (a)   *all hell* **seems/*wants** to break loose
     (b)   *the fur* **seems/*wants** to fly
     (c)   *the cat* **seems/*wants** to get his tongue

The ungrammaticality of sentences like **All hell wants to break loose* can be attributed to the fact that *want* is a control predicate, and hence (in order to derive such a structure) it would be necessary to assume that *all hell* originates as the subject of *want*, and that *break loose* has a separate PRO subject of its own: but this would violate the requirement that (in its idiomatic use) *all hell* can only occur as the subject of *break loose*, and conversely *break loose* (in its idiomatic use) only allows *all hell* as its subject. By contrast, *All hell seems to break loose* is grammatical because *seem* is a raising predicate, and so *all hell* can originate as the subject of *break loose* and then be raised up to become the subject of the tense affix in T in the *seem* clause.

   A further property which differentiates the two types of predicate is that raising predicates like *seem* preserve synonymy under long-distance passivisation, so that (86a) below is synonymous with (86b):

(86) (a)   John seems to have helped Mary
     (b)   =Mary seems to have been helped by John

By contrast, control predicates like *want* do not preserve synonymy in long-distance passives, as we see from the fact that (87a) below is not synonymous with (87b):

(87)(a)   John wants to help Mary
   (b)   ≠Mary wants to be helped by John

Moreover, there are pragmatic restrictions on the choice of subject which control predicates like *want* allow (in that the subject generally has to be a rational animate being, not an inanimate entity) – as we see from (88) below (where ! marks pragmatic anomaly):

(88)   *My cat/!My gesture* wants to be appreciated

By contrast, raising predicates freely allow animate or inanimate subjects: cf.

(89)   *My cat/My gesture* seems to have been appreciated

The different properties of the two types of predicate stem from the fact that control predicates like *want* θ-mark their subjects, whereas raising predicates like *seem* do not: so, since *want* selects an EXPERIENCER subject as its external argument (and prototypical EXPERIENCERS are animate beings), *want* allows an animate subject like *my cat*, but not an inanimate subject like *my gesture*. By contrast, since raising predicates like *seem* do not θ-mark their subjects, they allow a free choice of subject.

   An important point to note is that although our discussion of *raising* and *control* predicates has revolved around verbs, a parallel distinction is found in adjectives. For example, in sentences such as:

(90) (a)   *John* is **likely** to win the race
   (b)   *John* is **keen** to win the race

the adjective *likely* is a raising predicate and *keen* a control predicate. We can see this from the fact that *likely* allows expletive and idiomatic subjects, but *keen* does not: cf.

(91) (a)   *There* is **likely**/*****keen** to be a strike
   (b)   *All hell* is **likely**/*****keen** to break loose

This is one reason why throughout this chapter we have talked about different types of *predicate* (e.g. drawing a distinction between raising and control predicates) rather than different types of *verb*.

6.10   Summary

This chapter has primarily been concerned with the syntax of subjects. In §6.2 we argued that Belfast English structures such as *There should some students get distinctions* provide us with evidence that subjects originate internally within VP, and we noted that this claim is known as the **VP-Internal Subject Hypothesis/VPISH**. We also maintained that sentences such as *Some students should get distinctions* involve movement of *some students* from the specifier position within VP to the specifier position within TP, and we saw that the relevant movement operation is known as **A-movement**. In §6.3 we suggested that idiomatic structures like *All hell will break loose* provide empirical support for the VPISH. In §6.4 we argued that the VP-Internal Subject Hypothesis allows us to posit a uniform mapping (i.e. relationship) between thematic argument structure and (initial) syntactic structure, if we suppose that all arguments of a predicate originate (and are theta-marked) internally within a projection of the predicate. In §6.5, we looked at the syntax of **unaccusative predicates** like *arise/remain/occur* etc. and hypothesised that the argument of an unaccusative verb originates as its complement but differs from the complement of a transitive verb in that it receives nominative rather than accusative case. We highlighted a number of further differences between unaccusative predicates and other types of predicate (e.g. in relation to the position of subjects in Belfast English imperatives, and auxiliary selection in earlier varieties of English). In §6.6, we looked at the structure of simple passive clauses, arguing that a passive subject originates as the thematic complement of a subjectless passive participle, and is raised into spec-T (via A-movement) in order to satisfy the EPP feature of T. In §6.7 we saw that passivisation can be a **long-distance** operation involving movement of an argument contained within an infinitival TP which is the complement of a passive participle. We saw that (in consequence of every T carrying an EPP feature requiring it to have a subject) the passivised nominal moves in a successive-cyclic fashion, first into the closest spec-T position above it, then into the next closest one (and so on) – in conformity with the Relativised Minimality Condition. In §6.8 we argued that predicates like *seem/appear* function as **raising predicates** in the sense that their subjects originate internally within their infinitive complement, and from there are raised to the spec-T position within the *seem/appear*-clause: hence, in a sentence such as *All hell would appear to have broken loose*, the idiomatic expression *all hell* originates as the subject of *broken loose* and from there is raised up (one TP at a time) first to become the specifier of the lower TP headed by infinitival *to*, and then to become the specifier of the higher TP headed by *would*. In §6.9, we contrasted raising predicates with control predicates, noting that they differ in that control predicates theta-mark their subjects (and hence generally require an animate subject) and have a CP complement, whereas raising predicates do not theta-mark their subjects (and hence freely allow inanimate, expletive and idiomatic subjects) and have a TP complement. We also noted that (unlike control predicates), raising predicates preserve synonymy under long-distance passivisation.

Key constructs which our discussion in this chapter made use of include the following:

(18)   **Theta Criterion/θ-criterion**
Each argument bears one and only one θ-role, and each θ-role is assigned to one and only one argument

(19)   **Predicate-Internal Theta-Marking Hypothesis**
An argument is theta-marked (i.e. assigned a theta-role) via merger with a predicate

(26)   **Constraint on Extraction Domains/CED**
Only complements allow material to be extracted out of them, not specifiers or adjuncts

(55)   **Uniform Theta Assignment Hypothesis/UTAH**
Constituents which fulfil the same thematic role with respect to a given predicate occupy the same initial position in the syntax

(58)   **Attract Closest Condition/ACC**
A head which attracts a given kind of constituent attracts the *closest* constituent of the relevant kind

(61)   **Relativised Minimality Condition/RMC**
A constituent X can only be affected by (e.g. agree with or be attracted by) the minimal (i.e. closest) constituent of the relevant type above it (i.e. c-commanding X)

6.11   Bibliographical background

Evidence adduced in support of the VP-internal Subject Hypothesis outlined in §6.2 can be found in a variety of works dating back to the mid 1980s, including Kitagawa (1986), Speas (1986), Contreras (1987), Zagona (1987), Kuroda (1988), Sportiche (1988), Rosen (1990), Ernst (1991), Koopman and Sportiche (1991), Woolford (1991), Burton and Grimshaw (1992), McNally (1992), Guilfoyle, Hung and Travis (1992), Huang (1993) and McCloskey (1997). For further discussion of quantifier scope in A-movement structures, see Lebeaux (1995), Hornstein (1995), Romero (1997), Sauerland (1998), Lasnik (1998, 1999), Fox (2000), Boeckx (2000, 2001) and Fox and Nissenbaum (2004). It should be noted that some linguists have attempted to eliminate EPP as a factor in driving movement of a subject out of VP into spec-T (e.g. Epstein, Pires and Seely 2005). The ideas on theta-roles discussed in §6.4 date back to pioneering work by Gruber (1965), Fillmore (1968, 1972) and Jackendoff (1972): the Theta Criterion is taken from Chomsky (1981). The idea in §6.5 that subjects of unaccusative verbs originate as their complements dates back to work by Burzio (1986) on Italian and Contreras (1986) on Spanish. For attempts to develop a Minimalist counterpart of the Constraint on Extraction Domains, see Nunes and Uriagereka

(2000), Sabel (2002), Rackowski and Richards (2005) and Chomsky (2005b). The use of (the counterpart of) BE rather than HAVE as a perfect auxiliary with unaccusative verbs is found in a number of languages – e.g. Italian and French (cf. Burzio 1986), Sardinian (cf. Jones 1994), German and Dutch (cf. Haegeman 1994) and Danish (cf. Spencer 1991): see Sorace (2000) for further discussion of auxilary selection. On unaccusative structures like *The stockmarket dropped 250 points today*, see Nakajima (2006). On the syntax of *by*-phrases in passive structures like those discussed in §6.6, see Jaeggli (1986), Roberts (1987), Baker, Johnson and Roberts (1989), Afarli (1989), Mahajan (1994), Goodall (1997) and Collins (2005a). The Uniform Theta Assignment Hypothesis was devised by Baker (1988, p. 46, 1997, p. 74): it is rejected (inter alia) by proponents of the *Movement Theory of Control* (see below). For evidence that long-distance A-movement applies in a successive-cyclic fashion, see Bošković (2002b), Lasnik (2006) and Boeckx (2007). For more detail on the properties of raising predicates discussed in §6.8 and on the differences between control and raising predicates discussed in §6.9, see Davies and Dubinsky (2004). Note that some verbs (e.g. *begin*, *continue*, *fail* and *start*) are ambiguous between being raising or control verbs (in the sense that they can be used as either): see Perlmutter (1970) and (on the learnability problem which this poses for children) Becker (2006). Finally, it should be noted that this chapter presents the classical theory of control assumed by Chomsky in his own work. An alternative *Movement Theory of Control/MTC* has been developed by Bowers (1973), O'Neil (1995), Hornstein (1999, 2001, 2003), Boeckx (2000, 2007), Manzini and Roussou (2000), Boeckx and Hornstein (2003, 2004, 2006a,b) and Grohmann (2003): the key assumption of the movement analysis is that in a sentence such as *Jim will try to open it*, the nominal *Jim* originates as the subject of the embedded clause verb *open* and then raises up to become the subject of (and acquire an additional theta-role from) the main clause verb *try*. For a critique of the *movement* analysis, see Landau (2006a). For a very different account of control which posits that PRO does not exist and that control clauses are subjectless, see Jackendoff and Culicover (2003) and Culicover and Jackendoff (2001, 2005, 2006).

Workbook section

Exercise 6.1

Say whether the italicized verbs as used in the type of construction illustrated in the examples below function as raising or control predicates, and what evidence there is to support your analysis. Provide a detailed outline of the derivation of any *one* of the control sentences and any *one* of the raising sentences, giving arguments in support of your answer.

1   Employers *tend* to exploit employees
2   He has *decided* to admit it **(w)**
3   We *came* to appreciate the classes

4   You *have* to help me
5   They *failed* to hit the target
6   He *tried* to rectify the situation
7   He *refused* to sign the petition
8   He's *beginning* to irritate me
9   They *attempted* to pervert the course of justice
10   I *happened* to be passing your house
11   He is *going* to help me (**w**)
12   He is *bound* to win
13   John *looks* to be a good student
14   He *needs* to have a shave
15   They *managed* to open the door
16   We *intend* to close the store
17   The weather is *threatening* to ruin the weekend
18   We are *hoping* to get a visa
19   She has *chosen* to ignore him
20   They are *planning* to visit London

In addition, comment on what is interesting about the following sentence (produced by a former captain of the England soccer team in a TV interview):

21   Racism has been trying to be cut out of the game for a number of years now

Helpful hints

You might like to consider how sentences such as the following can help you determine whether a particular predicate is a raising or control predicate. The (a) sentence in each case shows whether the verb concerned allows an inanimate subject, the (b) sentence whether it allows an expletive subject, the (c) sentence whether it allows an idiomatic subject, and the (d) sentence whether it allows long-distance passivisation with preservation of synonymy.

1a   Syntax tends to baffle people
1b   There tends to be a lot of confusion about syntax
1c   All hell tends to break loose
1d   Employees tend to be exploited by employers
2a   *Your attitude has decided to upset him
2b   *There has decided to be a strike
2c   *The cat has decided to be out of the bag
2d   *Syntax has decided to be abandoned by John
3a   Her behaviour came to annoy him
3b   There came to be an understanding between them
3c   The shit eventually came to hit the fan
3d   The classes came to be appreciated by the students
4a   The situation has to improve
4b   There has to be some form of compromise
4c   The chickens have to come home to roost before long
4d   The matter has to be settled
5a   My car failed to start
5b   There failed to be any improvement in the situation

5c   The shit won't fail to hit the fan

5d   Their disagreements failed to be resolved amicably

6a   *The game tried to end in a draw

6b   *There tried to be renewed efforts to achieve peace

6c   *The shit tried to hit the fan

6d   *The conflict tried to be resolved peacefully

7a   *The situation has refused to improve

7b   *There refused to be any form of compromise

7c   *The cat refused to get his tongue

7d   *The offer refused to be accepted

8a   The situation is beginning to deteriorate

8b   It's beginning to snow

8c   The fur is beginning to fly

8d   Taxes are beginning to be lowered

9a   *The decision attempted to upset her

9b   *There attempted to be a compromise

9c   *The cat attempted to be out of the bag

9d   *The decision attempted to be rescinded

10a   An ambulance happened to be passing

10b   It happened to have been raining at the time

10c   All hell suddenly happened to break loose

10d   The incident happens to have been caught on camera

11a   The situation is going to get worse

11b   There is going to be a storm later

11c   The chickens are going to come home to roost

11d   Taxes are going to be cut

12a   The car is bound to break down

12b   There is bound to be an inquest

12c   The shit is bound to hit the fan

12d   Election promises are bound to be broken

13a   The situation looks to have improved

13b   There looks to be no chance of getting a ticket

13c   The cat looks to have got his tongue

13d   All the tickets look to have been sold

14a   The quality of teaching needs to improve

14b   There needs to be goodwill on all sides

14c   All hell needs to break loose

14d   The government needs to be overthrown

15a   *The situation managed to upset her

15b   *There managed to be a compromise

15c   *All hell managed to break loose

15d   *Taxes managed to be cut

16a   *Your arguments intended to convince me

16b   *There had intended to be a meeting in the morning

16c   *The shit intended to hit the fan

16d   *Taxes intended to be lowered

17a	The strike is threatening to undermine profitability
17b	There is threatening to be a hostile takeover
17c	All hell is threatening to break loose
17d	Punitive measures are threatening to be taken
18a	*Your attitude is hoping to exacerbate the situation
18b	*There is hoping to be an increase in profits
18c	*The cat is hoping to get his tongue
18d	*Taxes are hoping to be reduced
19a	*The situation has chosen to upset her
19b	*It has chosen to rain
19c	*All hell has chosen to break loose
19d	*The decision has chosen to be revoked
20a	*The decision planned to upset her
20b	*There hadn't planned to be a strike
20c	*The cat had planned to get his tongue
20d	*London plans to be visited next week

Non-native speakers of English might find it useful to note the meaning of the following idioms:

All hell broke loose = 'A chaotic situation arose'

The cat is out of the bag = 'The secret has been discovered'

The cat has got his tongue = 'He is speechless'

The shit hit the fan = 'The relevant action had dire consequences'

The chickens came home to roost = 'The consequences of the action in question became apparent'

Model answer for 1

There are a number of reasons for suggesting that *tend* functions as a raising predicate when it takes an infinitive complement. For one thing (as we would expect if *tend* is a one-place raising predicate which does not theta-mark its subject), *tend* imposes no restrictions on its choice of subject, and so freely allows either an expression like *Professor Brainstorm* (denoting an animate being) or an expression like *Syntax* (denoting an inanimate entity) as the subject of its containing clause – as illustrated in (i) below:

(i)   *Professor Brainstorm/Syntax* tends to baffle people

Moreover, *tend* allows a non-thematic subject like expletive *there/it* – as in the examples below:

(ii)   *There* tends to be a lot of confusion about syntax
(iii)   *It* tends to be assumed that syntax is hard

(We can tell that *there* is an expletive pronoun in (ii) from the fact that it cannot be substituted by *here* or questioned by *where?* Likewise, *it* must be expletive in (iii) because it cannot be substituted by *this/that* or questioned by *what?*) Moreover, *tend* can have an idiomatic subject, as in (iv) below:

(iv)   *All hell* tends to break loose

Given that *all hell* can serve only as the subject of *break loose* in the relevant idiom in (iv), it is clear that we could not analyse *tend* as a control predicate in (iv) and claim that *all hell* originates as the subject of *tend* and *PRO* as the subject of *break loose*, since this would violate the requirement that *all hell* can occur only as the subject of *break loose* and conversely that *break loose* can only have the subject *all hell* (in the relevant idiom). By contrast, if *tend* is a raising predicate, we can claim that *all hell* originates as the subject of *break loose* and then raises up to become the subject of the (null T constituent in the) *tend* clause. Furthermore, *tend* preserves synonymy under long-distance passivisation, as we can see from the fact that (v) and (vi) are synonymous:

(v)   Employers tend to exploit employees
(vi)   =Employees tend to be exploited by employers

If (as argued here) *tend* is a raising predicate, sentence 1 will be derived as follows. The noun *employees* merges with a null quantifier (which has a generic interpretation paraphraseable as 'employees in general') to form the QP *ø employees*. The resulting QP merges with (and is assigned the θ-role of THEME argument of) the verb *exploit* to form the V-bar *exploit ø employees*. The QP *ø employers* (itself formed by merging a null generic quantifier with the noun *employers*) is then merged with (and assigned the θ-role of AGENT argument of) this V-bar, forming the VP *ø employers exploit ø employees*. This VP is merged as the complement of the infinitival tense particle *to*, forming the T-bar *to ø employers exploit ø employees*. Infinitival *to* (like all T constituents) has an EPP feature which enables it to attract the closest nominal (= the QP *ø employers*) to become its subject, so forming the TP *ø employers to ~~ø employers~~ exploit ø employees*. The relevant TP is in turn merged with the verb *tend*, forming the VP *tend ø employers to ~~ø employers~~ exploit ø employees* (with the TP complement of *tend* having the semantic function of being a THEME argument of *tend*). The resulting VP is merged with a T-constituent containing a present tense affix (= Af) forming the T-bar *Af tend ø employers to ~~ø employers~~ exploit ø employees*. The EPP feature on T enables it to attract the closest nominal which it c-commands (= the QP *ø employers*) to become its subject, so forming the TP *ø employers Af tend ~~ø employers~~ to ~~ø employers~~ exploit ø employees*. The resulting TP is merged with a null declarative C to form the CP shown in simplified form below (with arrows showing the two A-movement operations which take place in the course of the derivation):

(vii)   [$_{CP}$ [$_C$ ø] [$_{TP}$ ø *employers* [$_T$ Af] [$_{VP}$ [$_V$ tend] [$_{TP}$ *ø employers* [$_T$ to] [$_{VP}$ *ø employers* [$_V$ exploit]

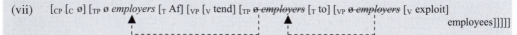

employees]]]]]

The derivation satisfies the **θ-criterion** by virtue of the fact that each argument carries one and only one θ-role: i.e. *ø employees* is the THEME argument of *exploit*, *ø employers* is the AGENT argument of *exploit* and the TP complement of *tend* is its THEME argument. It also satisfies the Relativised Minimality Condition (which requires a constituent undergoing A-movement to become the specifier of the closest T constituent above it) in that the QP *ø employers* moves into the spec-T position in the complement clause before moving into the spec-T position in the main clause.

Exercise 6.2

Discuss the derivation of the following sentences:

1 a   There are certain to remain some problems
  b   There were reported to remain some problems **(w)**
  c   There were thought likely to remain some problems

2 a   A change of policy was envisaged (**w**)
  b   A change is thought to be envisaged (**w**)
  c   A change seems likely to be envisaged

3 a   Differences of opinion are emerging (**w**)
  b   Differences of opinion are starting to emerge (**w**)
  c   Differences of opinion appear to be starting to emerge

4 a   He is leaving the country
  b   He is planning to leave the country (**w**)
  c   He is thought to be planning to leave the country

5 a   No details are going to be revealed
  b   No details of any threats are expected to emerge (**w**)
  c   No details are expected to emerge of any threats (**w**)

6 a   Nothing has happened
  b   Nothing is expected to happen (**w**)
  c   Nothing is thought likely to happen

Helpful hints

Assume that the infinitive form *be* is an auxiliary occupying the head AUX position of AUXP in 2b, 2c, 3c, 4c and 5a. Assume that T always has an EPP feature, whether finite or infinitival. In addition, assume that the verbs *leave/plan* in 4 have an AGENT external argument, but that all other arguments in 1–6 are THEME internal arguments of their associated predicates. In relation to 5b and 5c assume that *any* is a partitive quantifier which has the property of being a polarity item and so must be c-commanded by a negative or interrogative constituent; in relation to 5c, bear in mind the discussion of discontinuous spellout in the text.

Model answer for 1a

The quantifier *some* merges with the noun *problems* to form the QP *some problems*. This QP is merged with (and assigned the θ-role of THEME complement of) the unaccusative predicate *remain* to form the VP *remain some problems*. This in turn is merged with the infinitival tense particle *to*, forming the TP *to remain some problems*. Like all T constituents, infinitival *to* has an EPP feature requiring it to have a noun or pronoun expression as its subject, and this requirement can be met by merging the expletive pronoun *there* with the T-bar already formed, so generating the TP *there to remain some problems*. This TP is then merged with the raising adjective *certain* to form the AP *certain there to remain some problems*. The resulting TP in turn is merged with the copular verb *are* to form the VP *are certain there to remain some problems*. This VP is subsequently merged with a null finite T which attracts the copula *are* to move from V to T in the manner showed by the dotted arrow in (i), so forming the following structure (simplified by not showing the internal structure of the QP *some problems*):

(i)

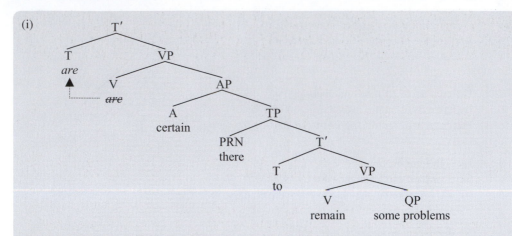

Like all T constituents, the T-auxiliary *are* has an EPP feature (not shown above) which allows it to attract the closest noun or pronoun expression (= *there*) to move to spec-T to become its subject in the manner shown in simplified form in (ii) below:

(ii)

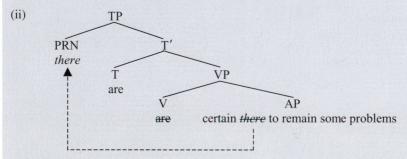

The TP in (ii) is subsequently merged with a null complementiser which serves to mark the sentence as declarative in force. The arrowed A-movement operation satisfies the Relativised Minimality Condition (which requires a constituent undergoing A-movement to become the specifier of the closest T constituent above it), since the arrowed movement operation in (ii) moves *there* from being the specifier of the T constituent in the embedded clause to becoming the specifier of the T constituent in the main clause – as shown in simplified schematic form below:

(iii)   [CP [C ø] [TP *there* [T are] ~~are~~ certain [TP ~~there~~ [T to] remain some problems]]]

The analysis presented here assumes that *certain* is a raising adjective. Evidence that this is so comes from the fact that clauses containing *certain* allow expletive and idiomatic subjects, as in:

(iv)(a) *It* is certain to be raining in Manchester
   (b) *The fur* is certain to fly

The expletive nature of *it* in (iva) is shown by the fact that it cannot be substituted by referential pronouns like *this/that* or questioned by *what?*

7 Agreement, case and A-movement

7.1 Overview

In this chapter, we take a look at the syntax of agreement. We begin by outlining the claim made by Chomsky in recent work that agreement involves a relation between a **probe** and a **goal** (though it should be noted that the term *goal* in this chapter is used in an entirely different way from the term GOAL – written in capital letters – which was used to denote the thematic role played by a particular kind of argument in relation to its predicate in §6.4). We look at the nature of agreement (exploring its relation with case-marking on the one hand, and with movement on the other) and examine the consequences of this for control infinitives on the one hand and raising infinitives on the other.

7.2 Agreement

In traditional grammars, finite auxiliaries are said to agree with their subjects. Since (within the framework used here) finite auxiliaries occupy the head T position of TP and their subjects are in spec-T, in earlier work agreement was said to involve a specifier–head relationship (between T and its specifier). However, there are both theoretical and empirical reasons for doubting that agreement involves a spec–head relation. From a theoretical perspective, Minimalist considerations lead us to the conclusion that we should restrict the range of syntactic relations used in linguistic description, perhaps limiting them to the relation **c-command**. From a descriptive perspective, a spec–head account of agreement is problematic in that it fails to account for agreement between the auxiliary *were* and the nominal *several prizes* in passive structures such as:

(1)   There **were** awarded *several prizes*

Since the auxiliary *were* occupies the head T position of TP in (1) and the expletive pronoun *there* is in spec-T, a spec–head account of agreement would lead us to expect that *were* should agree with *there*. But instead, *were* agrees with the in situ complement *several prizes* of the passive participle *awarded*. What is going on here? In order to try and understand this, let's take a closer look at the derivation of (1).

The quantifier *several* merges with the noun *prizes* to form the QP *several prizes*. This QP is merged with the passive verb *awarded* to form the VP *awarded several prizes*. The resulting VP is in turn merged with the passive auxiliary BE, forming the T-bar shown in simplified form in (2) below (where the notation BE indicates that the morphological form of the relevant item hasn't yet been determined):

(2)

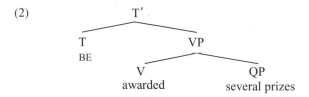

The tense auxiliary [T BE] needs to agree with an appropriate nominal within the structure containing it. Let us suppose that the 'timing' of operations such as agreement, case-marking and movement is determined by the following principle:

(3)   **Earliness Principle**
             Operations must apply as early as possible in a derivation

Given (3), T-agreement must apply as early as possible in the derivation, and hence will apply as soon as BE is introduced into the structure. On the assumption that c-command is central to syntactic operations, T will agree with a nominal (i.e. a noun or pronoun expression) which it c-commands. Accordingly, as soon as the structure in (2) is formed, [T BE] searches for a nominal which it c-commands to agree with.

To use the relevant technical terminology, by virtue of being the highest head in the overall structure at this point in the derivation, BE serves as a **probe** which searches for a c-commanded nominal **goal** to agree with. The only nominal goal c-commanded by [T BE] within the structure in (2) is the QP *several prizes*: [T BE] therefore agrees in person and number with *several prizes*, and so is ultimately spelled out as the third person plural form *were* in the PF component. Chomsky refers to person and number features together as **φ-features** (where φ is the Greek letter *phi*, pronounced in the same way as *fie* in English): using this terminology, we can say that the probe [T BE] agrees in φ-features with the goal *several prizes*. Let us suppose that expletive *there* is directly merged in spec-T in order to satisfy the EPP requirement for T to project a nominal specifier, and that the resulting TP is in turn merged with a null declarative complementiser to form the CP shown in simplified form below:

(4)

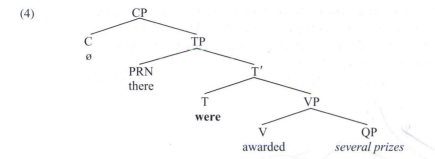

(4) is then the structure of (1) *There were awarded several prizes*.

However, there are a number of details which we have omitted in (4); one relates to the **case** assigned to the complement (*several prizes*) of the passive participle *awarded*. Although case is not overtly marked on the relevant noun expressions in English, evidence from languages like Icelandic with a richer case system suggests that the complement of a passive participle in finite expletive clauses is assigned nominative case via agreement with T – as the following contrast (from Sigurðsson 1996, p. 12) illustrates:

(5) (a)   Það voru   lesnar *fjórar   bækur*
          There were read four_{NOM.PL} books_{NOM.PL}

   (b)   Það var   skilað *fjórum bókum*
          There was returned four_{DAT.PL} books_{DAT.PL}

In (5a), the auxiliary *voru* is a third person plural form which agrees with the NOM.PL/nominative plural complement *fjórar bækur* 'four books'. In (5b), the auxiliary is in the agreementless form *var* 'was', and the complement of the passive participle is DAT.PL/dative plural. (*Var* is a third person singular form, but can be treated as an agreementless form if we characterise agreement by saying that 'An auxiliary is first/second person if it agrees with a first/second person subject, but third person otherwise; it is plural if it agrees with a plural subject, but singular otherwise.' This means that a third person singular auxiliary can arise either by agreement with a third person singular expression or – as here – can be a **default** form used as a fall-back when the auxiliary doesn't agree with anything.) Sigurðsson argues that it is an inherent lexical property of the participle *skilað* 'returned' that (like around a quarter of transitive verbs in Icelandic) it assigns so-called **inherent** dative case to its complement (inherent case being assigned by a verb to one of its arguments which has a specific thematic role, and hence being thematically based). Consequently, (because it can't agree with a non-nominative complement) the auxiliary surfaces in the agreementless form *var* in (5b); by contrast, the participle *lesnar* 'read' in (5a) does not assign inherent case to its complement, and instead the complement is assigned (so-called) **structural** nominative case via agreement with the past tense auxiliary *voru* 'were'.

Icelandic data like (5) suggest that there is a systematic relationship between nominative case assignment and T-agreement: they are two different reflexes of an **agreement** relationship between a finite T probe and a nominal goal. In consequence of the agreement relationship between the two, the T probe agrees with a nominal goal which it c-commands, and the nominal goal is assigned nominative case. Accordingly, *several prizes* in (4) receives nominative case via agreement with [$_T$ *are*].

The approach to case assignment outlined here (in which subjects are assigned nominative case via agreement with a finite T) might at first sight seem to be competely at odds with our earlier claim in §3.6 and §3.7 that subjects are case-marked by a c-commanding C constituent. But in one sense, our revised hypothesis that finite subjects are case-marked by T is a natural refinement of our earlier analysis. In chapter 3, we argued that a noun or pronoun expression is case-marked by the closest case assigner which c-commands it: since we also assumed in chapter 3 that subjects originate in spec-T, it was natural to assume that they are case-marked by the closest functional head above them, namely C. But once we move to an analysis like that in chapter 6, in which subjects originate internally within VP, our assumption that they are case-marked by the closest functional head above them leads to the conclusion that nominative subjects are case-marked by T rather than by C (because T is the closest functional head above a VP-internal subject). The apparent discrepancy between these two approaches can be resolved if (as suggested in recent work) agreement features originate on C but are 'handed over' to T in the course of the derivation (for theoretical reasons which we look at in chapter 9).

7.3   Feature Valuation

Let's think through rather more carefully what it means to say that case is systematically related to agreement, and what the mechanism is by which case and agreement operate. To illustrate our discussion, consider the derivation of a simple passive such as that produced by speaker B below:

(6)   SPEAKER A: What happened to the protestors?
         SPEAKER B: *They were arrested*

Here, discourse factors determine that a third person plural pronoun is required in order to refer back to the third person plural expression *the protestors*, and that a past tense auxiliary is required because the event described took place in the past. So (as it were) the person/number features of *they* and the past tense feature of *were* are determined in advance, before the items enter the derivation. By contrast the case feature assigned to *they* and the person/number features assigned to *were* are determined via an agreement operation in the course of the derivation: e.g. if the subject had been the third person singular pronoun *one*, the auxiliary would have been third person singular via agreement with *one* (as in *One was arrested*); and if THEY had been used as the object of a transitive verb (as in *The police arrested them*), it would have surfaced in the accusative form *them* rather than the nominative form *they*.

Generalising at this point, let's suppose that noun and pronoun expressions like THEY enter the syntax with their (person and number) φ-features already **valued**, but their case feature as yet **unvalued**. (The notation THEY is used here to provide a case-independent characterisation of the word which is variously spelled out as *they/them/their* depending on the case assigned to it in the syntax.) Using a transparent feature notation, let's say that THEY enters the derivation carrying the features [3-Pers, Pl-Num, u-Case], where *Pers* = person, *Pl* = plural, *Num* = number and *u* = unvalued. Similarly, let's suppose that finite T constituents (like the tense auxiliary BE) enter the derivation with their tense feature already valued, but their person and number φ-features as yet unvalued (because they will be valued via agreement with an appropriate goal). This means BE enters the derivation with the features [Past-Tns, u-Pers, u-Num]. In the light of these assumptions, let's see how the derivation of (6B) proceeds.

The pronoun THEY is the thematic complement of the passive verb *arrested* and so merges with it to form the VP *arrested* THEY. This is in turn merged with the tense auxiliary BE, forming the structure (7) below (where already valued features are shown in **bold**, and unvalued features in *italics*):

(7)

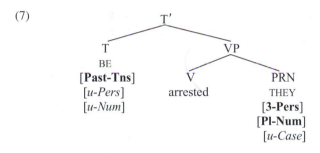

The T-auxiliary BE will probe at this point and search for a suitable goal, locating THEY as the only potential goal in its c-command domain. The unvalued φ-features on the probe are then valued by the goal, and (conversely) the unvalued case feature on the goal is valued by the probe. (In Chomsky's use of these terms, it is the unvalued person/number features which serve as probes rather than the item BE itself, but this is a distinction which we shall overlook throughout, in order to simplify exposition.) For concreteness, let us suppose that agreement can be characterised as involving the two Feature Valuation suboperations sketched below:

(8)   **Agreement**
        When a probe (like T) agrees with a goal in its local domain
(i)   the unvalued (person/number) φ-features on the probe will be valued (i.e. assigned a value which is a copy of that on the goal)
(ii)   the unvalued case feature on the goal will be valued (i.e. assigned a value dependent on the nature of the probe – e.g. nominative if the probe is a finite T)

In the light of our characterisation of agreement in (8), let's return to consider what happens when we reach the stage of derivation in (7) above where agreement applies. In consequence of φ-feature-valuation suboperation in (8i), the values of the person/number features of THEY are copied onto BE, so that the unvalued person and number features [*u-Pers, u-Num*] on BE in (7) are assigned the values [*3-Pers, Pl-Num*] carried by THEY. At the same time, via the case valuation suboperation (8ii), the unvalued case feature [*u-Case*] carried by the goal THEY is valued as nominative by the finite T-probe BE. Thus, application of Agreement to the structure in (7) results in the structure shown in (9) below (where the underlined features are the ones which have been valued via Agreement):

(9)

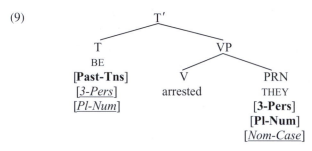

Since all the features carried by BE are now valued, BE can ultimately be spelled out in the phonology as the third person plural past tense form *were*. Likewise, since all the features carried by THEY are also valued at this point, THEY can ultimately be spelled out as the third person plural nominative form *they*. However, the derivation in (9) is not yet terminated: the EPP feature of T (not shown above) will subsequently trigger A-movement of *they* to become the structural subject of *were*, and the resulting TP *they were arrested* ~~they~~ will then be merged with a null declarative complementiser to form the structure shown in skeletal form below:

(10)   [CP [C Ø] [TP They [T were] [VP [V arrested] ~~they~~]]]

But since our immediate concern is with case and agreement, we skip over these details here.

7.4   Uninterpretable features and Feature Deletion

Our discussion of how case and agreement work in a sentence such as (6B) has wider implications. One of these is that items may enter the derivation with some of their features already **valued** and others as yet **unvalued**: e.g. BE enters the derivation in (7) with its tense feature valued, but its (person and number) φ-features unvalued; and THEY enters with its φ-features valued but its case feature unvalued. This raises the question of which features are initially valued when they first enter the derivation, which are initially unvalued – and why. Chomsky (1998) argues that the difference between valued and unvalued grammatical features correlates with a related distinction between those grammatical features which are **interpretable** (in the sense that they play a role in semantic interpretation) and those which are **uninterpretable** (and hence play no role in semantic interpretation). For example, it seems clear that the case feature of a pronoun like THEY is uninterpretable, since a subject pronoun surfaces as nominative, accusative or genitive depending on the type of [bracketed] clause it is in, without any effect on meaning – as the examples in (11) below illustrate:

(11) (a)   It seems [*they* were arrested]
  (b)   He expected [*them* to be arrested]
  (c)   He was shocked at [*their* being arrested]

By contrast, the (person/number/gender) φ-features of pronouns are interpretable, since e.g. a first person singular pronoun like *I* clearly differs in meaning from a third person plural pronoun like *they*, and a masculine pronoun like *he* differs in meaning from a feminine pronoun like *she*. We can illustrate the interpretable and uninterpretable features carried by auxiliaries (or, more abstractly, finite T constituents) in terms of the sentences below:

(12) (a)   She *is* working/She *was* working
  (b)   He *is* writing the assignment/He *has* written the assignment
  (c)   He insists that she *is* respected/He insists that she *be* respected
  (d)   They *are* working/*They *am* working

The choice of tense feature on the auxiliary *is/was* determines whether the sentence is interpreted as describing a present or past state of affairs, and so **tense** is clearly an interpretable feature. Likewise, the choice between the progressive auxiliary *is* and the perfect auxiliary *has* in (12b) determines whether the sentence is interpreted as describing an action which is in progress or one which is completed, and so **aspect** is also an interpretable feature of the auxiliary. In much the same way, the choice between the indicative auxiliary *is* and its subjunctive counterpart *be* in (12c) determines whether the sentence is interpreted as describing a *realis* (i.e. existing) state of affairs or an *irrealis* one (i.e. one which does not exist at present but which may exist in the future), and so **mood** must also be an interpretable feature of auxiliaries. By contrast, the (person/number) φ-features of auxiliaries are uninterpretable, in that they serve purely to mark agreement with a particular nominal: consequently, if we replace the third person plural T-auxiliary *are* by the first person singular form *am* in a sentence like (12d) with a third person plural subject, we do not change the meaning of the sentence but rather simply make it ungrammatical. We can summarise the picture which we get from sentences like (11) and (12) above in terms of the table in (13) below:

(13)   **Table of interpretable and uninterpretable features**

Type of constituent	interpretable features include	uninterpretable features include
T-constituent	tense, aspect and mood	person and number
noun expression or pronoun	person, number and gender	case

However, there are a number of potential complications which cloud the picture painted in (13). For example, the person and number (and gender, if such they have) features on expletive pronouns appear to be uninterpretable, as do the gender features on nouns in languages with arbitrary grammatical gender (such as the feminine gender of the French noun *table* 'table'). Similarly, where tense is determined by *sequence of tense* requirements, it may be an uninterpretable feature. However, we set aside such complications here.

As we saw in the simplified model of grammar which we presented in §1.3, each structure generated by the syntactic component of the grammar is subsequently sent to the **PF component** of the grammar to be **spelled out** (i.e. assigned a **PF representation** which provides a representation of its **Phonetic Form**). If we assume that unvalued features are **illegible** to (and hence cannot be processed by) the **PF component**, it follows that every unvalued feature in a derivation must be valued in the course of the derivation, or else the derivation will **crash** (i.e. fail) because the PF component is unable to **spell out** unvalued features: in the words of Chomsky (2006, p. 13) 'If transferred to the interface unvalued, uninterpretable features will cause the derivation to crash.' In more concrete terms, this amounts to saying that unless the syntax specifies whether we require e.g. a first person singular or third person plural present tense form of BE, the derivation will crash because the PF component cannot determine whether to spell out BE as *am* or *are*.

In addition to being sent to the PF component, each structure generated by the syntactic component of the grammar is simultaneously sent to the **semantic component**, where it is converted into an appropriate **semantic representation**. Clearly, interpretable features play an important role in computing semantic representations. Equally clearly, however, uninterpretable features play no role whatever in this process: indeed, since they are illegible to the semantic component, we need to devise some way of ensuring that uninterpretable features do not input into the semantic component. How can we do this?

The answer suggested in work by Chomsky over the past decade is that uninterpretable features are *deleted* in the course of the derivation, and thereby become invisible to the syntactic and semantic components (while remaining visible to the PF component). But how? As a first approximation (to be slightly revised in terms of the *Completeness Condition* below), let us suppose that Feature Deletion works along the lines sketched informally below:

(14)   **Feature Deletion**
        An uninterpretable feature is deleted immediately any operation it is
        involved in applies, and is thereafter invisible in the syntactic and semantic
        components (but visible in the PF component)

By saying that a feature becomes *invisible* in the syntax once it is deleted, we mean that it becomes inactive: for example, an EPP feature can no longer trigger movement once deleted, and a pronoun which has been assigned case cannot subsequently be assigned another case. Chomsky supposes that a constituent is only **active** for an operation like agreement, case-marking or movement if it carries an

undeleted uninterpretable feature of some kind, and that once the relevant uninterpretable feature has been deleted, the constituent carrying it becomes inactive
for further operations of the relevant kind.

To illustrate how this works, consider the case-marking of the italicised subject
of the bracketed complement clause in the sentences below:

(15) (a)   They believe [*John* to be lying]
     (b)   They believe [*John* is lying]

In (15a), the complement-clause subject *John* is not assigned case by any constituent internally within its own bracketed clause, and so can receive exceptional
accusative case from the transitive verb *believe* in the higher clause – as we see
from *They believe him to be lying*. But in (15b), *John* is assigned nominative case
by the finite T constituent *is* within its own clause, and consequently (given (14)
above) is inactivated for further case/agreement operations at that point, and so
cannot subsequently be assigned accusative case by the verb *believe* – as we see
from the ungrammaticality of **They believe him is lying*.

In the light of our characterisation of Feature Deletion in (14) above, let's
reconsider how agreement applies in a structure like (7) above, repeated as (16)
below (though with the addition of the uninterpretable EPP feature on T):

(16)

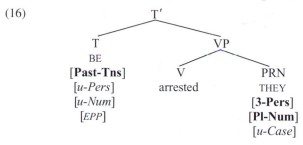

The agreement features of the probe BE are valued as third person plural via the
φ-feature-valuation suboperation (8i); the case feature of the goal THEY is valued
as nominative via the case valuation suboperation (8ii); and the EPP feature on
T triggers movement of the goal THEY to spec-T. But at the same time as these
operations apply, the Feature Deletion operation in (14) also applies, concomitantly deleting the uninterpretable (italicised) person, number and EPP features on
the probe, and the uninterpretable (italicised) case feature on the goal. The result
of all these various operations applying is to derive the structure in (17) below:

(17)

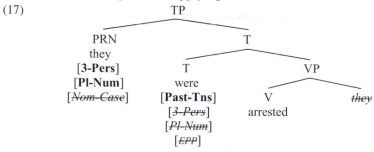

(Items are shown in their spellout forms, and the structure is simplified by showing the original occurrence of THEY as *they*.) In accordance with (14), the deleted
uninterpretable features will be invisible in the semantic and syntactic components – hence *they* and *were* will be inactive for further operations which involve
case or agreement features (e.g. agreement, case assignment and A-movement).
However, the deleted features will remain visible in the PF component: accordingly, the PF component can 'see' the deleted [nominative-case] feature on the
pronoun THEY and so spells out the pronoun in the nominative form *they*; likewise,
the PF component can 'see' the deleted [third-person, plural-number] features on
the T-constituent BE, and so spells it out as the third person plural form *were*.

An interesting complication which arises from our assumption in (14) that
uninterpretable features are deleted once they have 'done their work' is the
following. If case-marking were to apply before agreement or movement in (16)
above, the uninterpretable case feature on the pronoun *they* would be inactivated,
and the pronoun would then no longer be active for agreement or movement. One
way of getting round this problem is to suppose that agreement, case-marking,
A-movement and Feature Deletion all apply simultaneously on the T-cycle in
(16), and to assume that this is the consequence of a more general condition such
as (18) below:

(18)   **Simultaneity Condition**
            All syntactic operations involving a given probe P apply simultaneously

And indeed we shall assume (18) for the time being (though we will revisit this
issue in chapter 9). In a fairly obvious sense, (18) follows from the Earliness
Principle (3), in the sense that e.g. if all (case and agreement) Feature Valuation,
Feature Deletion and agreement operations which apply on the T-cycle apply as
early as possible, they will apply simultaneously.

7.5   Expletive *it* subjects

So far, all the constructions we have looked at have involved a finite
T agreeing with a noun or pronoun expression which carries interpretable per-
son/number φ-features. However, English has two **expletive pronouns** which
(by virtue of being non-referential) carry no interpretable φ-features. One of
these is *expletive it* in sentences such as:

(19) (a)   *It* is said that he has taken bribes
     (b)   *It* can be difficult to cope with long-term illness
     (c)   *It*'s a pity that she can't come

The pronoun *it* in sentences like these appears to be an **expletive**, since it cannot
be replaced by a referential pronoun like *this* or *that*, and cannot be questioned
by *what*. Let's examine the syntax of expletive *it* by looking at the derivation of
a sentence like (19a).

If (as we did in our earlier discussion of (4) above) we assume that expletive pronouns are directly merged in spec-T, the main clause in sentence (19a) will be derived as follows. The (passive participle) verb *said* is merged with its CP complement *that he has taken bribes* to form the VP *said that he has taken bribes*. Merging this VP with the tense auxiliary BE forms the structure shown in simplified form below:

(20)

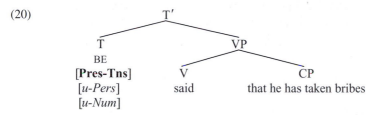

In accordance with the Earliness Principle (3), we might expect T-agreement to apply at this point.

Accordingly, the probe BE (which is active by virtue of its uninterpretable person/number φ-features) searches for an active goal to value its unvalued φ-features. It might at first sight seem as if the CP headed by *that* is an appropriate goal, and is a third person singular expression which can value the person/number features of BE. However, it seems unlikely that such clauses have person/number features. One reason for thinking this is that even if the *that*-clause in (20) is co-ordinated with another *that*-clause as in (21) below, the verb BE remains in the singular form *is*:

(21)   It is said [*that he has taken bribes* and *that he has embezzled company*

                                                                                                    funds]

If each of the italicised clauses in (21) were singular in number, we would expect the bracketed co-ordinate clause to be plural (in the same way as the co-ordinate structure *John and Mary* is a plural expression in a sentence like *John and Mary are very happy together*): but the fact that the passive auxiliary *is* remains singular in (21) suggests that the CP has no number properties of its own. Nor indeed does the *that*-clause in (21) have an unvalued case feature which could make it into an active goal, since a *that*-clause cannot be used in a position like that italicised in (22) below where it would be assigned accusative case by a transitive preposition such as *of*, suggesting that *that*-clauses are caseless:

(22)   There have been reports of bribery/**of that he has taken bribes*

If the CP in (20) has no uninterpretable case feature, it is inactive and so cannot value the φ-features of BE.

However, a question we might ask about (20) is whether BE could instead agree with the subject of the *that*-clause, namely *he*: after all, *he* enters the derivation with an uninterpretable case feature (making it active), and is a third person singular expression and so could seemingly value the unvalued person and number features of BE. Yet it is clear that BE does not in fact agree with *he*, since if we replace *he* by the first person plural subject *we*, BE still surfaces in the third person singular form *is* – as in (23) below:

(23)   It *is* said [_{CP} that [_{TP} **we** have taken bribes]]

Something, then, must prevent BE from agreeing with *we* in (23) – but what? The answer is that by the time we have reached the stage of derivation in (23), the case feature on *we* has already been valued as nominative and deleted, and so is invisible to other probes (and hence inactive) at this point – see (14) above. Consequently, BE cannot agree with *we* in (23) – and by the same token, BE cannot agree with *he* in (20). (For reasons which I leave you to work out for yourself, the Impenetrability Condition outlined in §3.8 would also prevent *is* from agreeing with *we* in (23), because the T constituent *is* c-commands the complementiser *that* which in turn c-commands the pronoun *we*.)

So far, what we have established in relation to the structure in (20) is that BE cannot agree with the CP headed by the complementiser *that* because *that* is inactive and has no φ-features or case feature; nor can BE agree with *he*, because the case feature on *he* has been valued and deleted and so is inactive at this point (and in any case, the Impenetrability Condition would prevent this). It is precisely because BE cannot agree with CP or with any of its constituents that expletive *it* has to be used, in order to value the φ-features of T and to satisfy the EPP feature on T requiring it to have a subject of its own. In keeping with the Minimalist spirit of positing only the minimal apparatus which is conceptually necessary, let's further suppose that expletive *it* has 'a full complement of φ-features' (Chomsky 1998, p. 44) but that (as Martin Atkinson suggested in conversation) these are the only features it carries. Now, while *it* clearly carries an interpretable (neuter/inanimate) gender feature when used as a referential pronoun (e.g. in a sentence like *This book has lots of exercises in it*, where *it* refers back to *this book*), it has no semantic interpretation in its use as an expletive pronoun, and so can be assumed to carry no interpretable gender feature in such a use. The reason for positing that expletive *it* is a caseless pronoun is that it is already active by virtue of its uninterpretable φ-features, and hence does not 'need' a case feature to make it active for agreement (unlike subjects with interpretable φ-features). Some suggestive evidence that expletive *it* may be a caseless pronoun comes from the fact that it has no genitive form *its* – at least for speakers like me who don't say **He was annoyed at its being claimed that he lied*.

If the reasoning in the previous paragraph is along the right lines, expletive *it* enters the derivation carrying the features [third-person, singular-number]. Since expletive *it* is a 'meaningless' expletive pronoun, these features will be *uninterpretable*. Given this assumption, merging *it* as the specifier of the T-bar in (20) above will derive the structure (24) below (with interpretable features shown in bold, and uninterpretable features in italics):

(24)

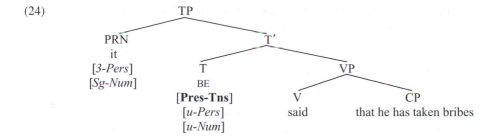

Chomsky (1999) suggests that expletive *it* can serve as a probe (active by virtue of its uninterpretable person/number features) which locates the T-auxiliary BE as a suitable goal (active by virtue of its uninterpretable and unvalued person/number features). If this is so, agreement between the two will lead to valuation of the unvalued person/number features on BE, and deletion of the uninterpretable person/number features on both BE and *it*.

However, such an account of expletive structures is problematic from a theoretical perspective. For one thing, a probe is typically the head of a phrase (and hence a minimal projection), whereas *it* in (24) is a specifier (and hence a maximal projection). Moreover, agreement (e.g. in a structure like (16) above) typically involves a goal valuing unvalued person/number features on a probe, whereas under the account offered above, agreement in (24) involves the converse situation of a probe valuing person/number features on a goal. The conclusion we reach is thus that an expletive 'can't be a probe' (Noam Chomsky, p.c., 5 June 2005) and that having an expletive as a probe is 'an option barred under narrower . . . conceptions of the role of the probe in controlling operations' (Chomsky 2006, p. 6). Consequently, BE must be the probe in (24) and expletive *it* the goal. However, given the assumption that a probe can only agree with a goal which it c-commands, it follows that the expletive goal *it* cannot be directly merged in spec-T, because if so it would not be c-commanded by the probe BE, and agreement would not be able to apply – with the result that the derivation would crash (because unvalued features would not be valued, and uninterpretable features would not be deleted), and sentence (23) would wrongly be predicted to be ungrammatical. Since a goal must occupy a lower position than its probe, the conclusion we reach is thus that expletive *it* must originate in a position below the T-auxiliary BE. But where?

Bearing in mind that the core assumption of the VP-Internal Subject Hypothesis outlined in §6.2 is that subjects originate within VP and subsequently raise from their original position within VP into the specifier position within TP, a plausible suggestion is that expletive pronouns likewise originate internally within VP, and subsequently raise to the subject/specifier position within TP. In this connection, compare the following pair of sentences:

(25) (a)   They had said that he has taken bribes
     (b)   I won't have *it* said that he has taken bribes

In (25a), *said* is an active perfect participle, and the specifier position within the VP headed by *said* is occupied by the external argument of the verb *said* (namely its subject *they*). However, *said* in (25b) is a passive participle form of the verb, and it is a property of passive verbs that they project no external argument, with the result that the specifier position is free to be occupied by an expletive. In (25b), expletive *it* appears immediately in front of (and hence can plausibly be taken to originate as the specifier of) the passive participle *said*.

Let us therefore suppose that in sentence (19a) *It is said that he has taken bribes*, the expletive pronoun *it* originates in spec-V. This means that the main clause in (19a) will be derived as follows. The passive participle *said* merges with its CP complement *that he has taken bribes* to form the V-bar *said that he has taken bribes*. This V-bar is then merged with the expletive pronoun *it*, deriving the VP *it said that he has taken bribes*. The resulting VP merges with a present tense T constituent containing the passive auxiliary BE, so deriving the structure shown in simplified form below:

(26)

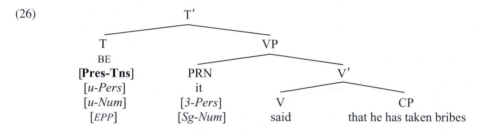

At this point, BE can serve as an active probe which locates the c-commanded expletive pronoun *it* as an active goal (both BE and *it* being active by virtue of their uninterpretable person/number features). Via agreement (8), the goal *it* values the unvalued person/number features on the probe BE. At the same time as agreement applies, the EPP feature on the T-auxiliary BE attracts the goal *it* to move to spec-T. Feature Deletion (14) results in deletion of the uninterpretable person/number features on both probe and goal, and of the EPP feature on the probe. Simultaneous application of agreement, case-marking, movement and deletion thus derives the structure in (27) below (where outline font marks a copy which receives a null spellout in the PF component):

(27)

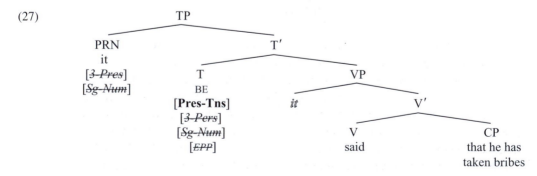

The resulting structure (27) is subsequently merged with a null C constituent carrying an interpretable declarative-force feature. Since the initially unvalued person/number features on BE have been valued, and all uninterpretable features on both BE and *it* have been deleted, the relevant derivation converges. Given that deleted features remain visible in the PF component, the T-auxiliary BE will be spelled out as the third person singular present tense form *is*.

7.6   Expletive *there* subjects

Having looked at the syntax of expletive *it* in the previous section, we now turn to look at expletive *there*. As a starting point for our discussion, we'll go back to the very first sentence we looked at in this chapter, namely (1) *There were awarded several prizes*. However, given the conclusion we reached in the previous section that expletives originate internally within VP, our earlier analysis in (4) above (which assumed that expletive *there* originates in spec-T) will now have to be revised along the following lines. The (passive participle) verb *awarded* merges with the QP complement *several prizes* to form the V-bar *awarded several prizes*. This V-bar is then merged with the expletive pronoun *there* to form the VP *there awarded several prizes*. Let's assume that (like expletive *it*) expletive *there* carries no case feature (and hence has no genitive form, as we see from the ungrammaticality of **She was upset by there's being nobody to help her*). Let's also suppose that the only feature carried by expletive *there* is an uninterpretable person feature, and let's further suppose that *there* is intrinsically third person (consistent with the fact that a number of other words beginning with *th-* are third person – e.g. *this*, *that*, *these*, *those* and *the*). Given these (and earlier) assumptions, the VP headed by the passive participle *awarded* will have the following structure:

(28)

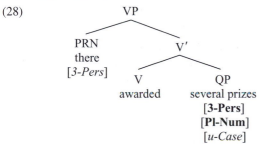

A question which arises at this juncture is whether the uninterpretable person feature on *there* can be deleted via agreement with the QP *several prizes*. The answer is 'No', because there is no probe–goal agreement relation between *there* and *several prizes*. There are two reasons why *there* cannot agree with *several prizes*. For one thing, *there* is not the head of a phrase (and so is not a minimal projection), and hence cannot serve as a probe: rather, *there* is a specifier (and maximal projection) and hence can only serve as a goal, not as a probe. Secondly, agreement typically involves a relation between a *valued* feature on one member of a probe–goal pair and a matching *unvalued* feature on the other (with the unvalued feature being valued via agreement); but since *there* and *several prizes* both enter the derivation valued as [third-person], there cannot in principle be any agreement relation between them. Consequently, agreement cannot apply at the stage of derivation in (28).

The derivation therefore continues by merging the VP already formed in (28) with a past tense T constituent containing the passive auxiliary BE, so deriving the structure shown in simplified form below:

(29)

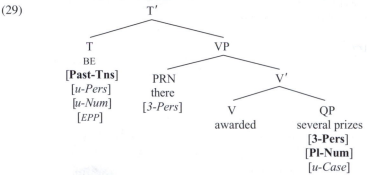

Given the Earliness Principle (3), agreement and case assignment will apply at this point in the derivation. Because BE is the head of the overall structure (and is active by virtue of its uninterpretable person and number features) it serves as a probe which searches for goals which can value its unvalued features. Let us further suppose that a probe first locates the closest appropriate goal, and then (if that is unable to value and delete all its features) locates the next closest goal ... and so on, until the point where all features of the probe have been valued and deleted (at which point the probe stops searching for further goals). Accordingly, when T-BE probes, it locates *there* as the closest possible goal. However, since *there* (being numberless) cannot value its unvalued number feature, T-BE continues to probe and locates the QP *several prizes* as a second goal. Thus, T-BE locates two suitable goals: one is *there* (which is active by virtue of its uninterpretable person feature); the other is the QP *several prizes* (which is active by virtue of its uninterpretable case feature). Let's suppose that when a probe locates more than one active goal, it undergoes simultaneous **multiple agreement** with all active goals accessible to it. Accordingly, via the φ-feature-valuation suboperation (8i), the T-probe BE agrees in person with both goals (the third person expressions *there* and *several prizes*) and the unvalued person feature on BE is thereby valued as third person. However, BE also agrees in number with the plural expression *several prizes*, and so the unvalued number feature on BE is valued as plural. At the same time, the unvalued case feature on the goal *several prizes* is valued as nominative by the finite T-probe, in accordance with the case valuation suboperation (8ii) above. The EPP feature on T attracts the closest goal, and so triggers movement of *there* to spec-T. In accordance with Feature Deletion (14), the uninterpretable person and number features on BE, the uninterpretable case feature on *several prizes* and the uninterpretable EPP feature on BE are deleted. Simultaneous application of agreement, case-marking, movement and deletion thus derives the structure shown below (where ᴏᴜᴛʟɪɴᴇ font marks a copy which receives a null spellout in the PF component):

(30)

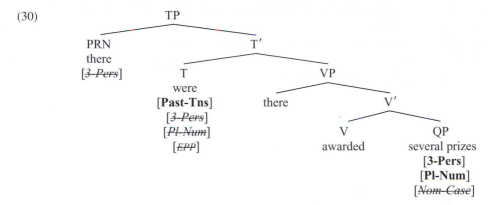

The resulting TP is then merged with a null C carrying an interpretable declarative force feature. Since all features are valued, the derivation converges at the PF interface; since all uninterpretable features have been deleted, it also converges at the semantics interface.

Our assumption that T in (29) undergoes multiple agreement with both the expletive goal *there* and the non-expletive goal *several prizes* and that *there* is intrinsically third person carries with it the tacit implication that the non-expletive goal must likewise be a third person expression, if we make the plausible assumption that a probe cannot agree in person with multiple goals which have different person properties (because this will lead to a feature mismatch). Such an assumption accounts for contrasts like:

(31) (a)   Only I am going to the party
(b)   *There am/is only I going to the party

In (31a), the only goal for the T-probe BE is the first person singular expression *only I*, and consequently BE can agree with this (single) goal and thereby be marked as first person singular. But in (31b), BE has two goals which it must agree with – namely the first person singular expression *only I* and the third person expletive *there*. If BE agrees in person and number with *only I*, it will be marked as first person singular and ultimately be spelled out as *am*: but this will mean that *am* does not agree in person with *there*. On the other hand, if BE agrees in person with *there* and in number with *only I*, it will be marked as third person singular and ultimately be spelled out as *is*: but this will mean that *is* does not agree in person with *only I*. Because of the resulting feature mismatch, (31b) is ungrammatical. An interesting way of obviating this mismatch is found in colloquial structures like *There's only me going to the party*, where the pronoun *me* has accusative case (perhaps assigned by BE in the same way as in structures like *It's me*): if only a nominative expression can be the goal for T-agreement, we can account for the absence of agreement between *is* and *me* in such structures, and for why the verb *is* gets spelled out in the default third person singular form.

An important question to ask in the context of our discussion of expletive *it* in the previous section and expletive *there* in this section is what conditions govern the use of expletives. What I shall suggest here is that the relevant conditions can be characterised as follows:

(32)   **Expletive Conditions**
  (i)   External Argument Condition:
          An expletive can only be merged as the highest argument of a verb with no external argument
  (ii)   Indefiniteness Condition:
          Expletive *there* can only be merged with a verb which has an indefinite nominal or pronominal internal argument
  (iii)   Inactivity Condition:
          Expletive *it* can only be merged with a constituent which does not contain a nominal or pronominal expression with active case- or φ-features

The conditions in (32) provide us with a basis to account for contrasts such as the following, where the bold-printed pronouns are expletives:

(33) (a)   **There** was awarded *only one prize*
    (b)   *__It__ was awarded *only one prize*

(34) (a)   **It** is said *that he has taken bribes*
    (b)   *__There__ is said *that he has taken bribes*

(35) (a)   *__There__ was impeached *the president*
    (b)   *__It__ was impeached *the president*

Sentences (33a) and (33b) both satisfy the External Argument Condition (32i) because the verb *arrested* is a passive participle with no external argument: (32a) also satisfies the Indefiniteness Condition (32ii) because the italicised associate of *there* is an indefinite expression; by contrast, (33b) violates the Inactivity Condition (32iii) because the italicised associate of *it* is the QP *only one prize* and this is active by virtue of its uninterpretable case feature. Sentences (34a) and (34b) both satisfy the External Argument Condition (32i) because the verb *said* is a passive participle with no external argument: (34a) also satisfies the Inactivity Condition (32iii) because the italicised associate of *it* is a clause whose head C *that* carries no active person/number/case feature (nor are any of the constituents of the *that*-clause active, their uninterpretable features having been valued and deleted at an earlier stage of derivation); but (34b) violates the Indefiniteness Condition (32ii) because the italicised associate of *there* is not an indefinite noun or pronoun expression. Sentences (35a) and (35b) both satisfy the External Argument Condition (32i) because the verb *impeached* is a passive participle with no external argument: (35a) violates the Indefiniteness Condition because the italicised associate of *there* is not an indefinite expression but rather the definite

DP *the president*; and (35b) violates the Inactivity Condition because the italicised associate of *it* is the DP *the president* and this is active by virtue of its
uninterpretable case feature. The only grammatical outcome for a structure in
which a passive participle has a definite DP complement in English is not to use
an expletive but rather to passivise the complement – as in *The president was
impeached*. So, we see that the conditions in (32) provide a descriptively adequate
account of the syntax of expletives. Incidentally, note that an interesting consequence of the Inactivity Condition (32iii) is that a weather verb like *rain* which
has no thematic argument will require use of expletive *it*: and given the *highest
argument* condition in (32i), *it* will originate as the highest (and only) argument
of the verb *rain*, in the same VP-complement position as an unaccusative subject
(with *it* subsequently raising to spec-T and yielding a structure like *It is raining
it̶*, with strikethrough marking the initial position of *it*).

However, the conditions in (32) are essentially descriptive stipulations which
lack explanatory force. The question we need to ask therefore is *why* such conditions should obtain. Consider first the External Argument Condition (32i). If we
suppose that a Verb Phrase can only have a single specifier and that the italicised
external argument of the verb in a transitive structure like (36a) below originates
as the specifier for the verb, then it follows that the verb cannot also have an
expletive specifier like that bold-printed as in (36b):

(36) (a)   *A spokesman for the president* has denied allegations of impropriety
     (b)   ***There** has *a spokesman for the president* denied allegations of impropriety

An alternative possibility is to follow Felser and Rupp (2001, p. 312) in analysing
an expletive as 'a thematic or quasi-thematic subject', so that 'the expletive is
characterised as an argument expression'. More specifically, they maintain that
expletive *there* 'is thematic without referring to an actual participant or event
depicted – rather, in the spirit of Kratzer (1995), we may take it to be associated
with an abstract location' (p. 312). If an expletive is 'the last argument to be
added' in a derivation (p. 314), it follows that (in a sentence like *There occurred
several unfortunate incidents*), the expletive will be merged in spec-V: thus, the
QP *several unfortunate incidents* will be the first argument to be merged with
the verb *occur* (as its complement), and the expletive *there* the second argument
(as the specifier of *occur*). We should also note in passing that expletive *it* (in
some uses, at least) has argument-like properties, e.g. in being able to serve as
the antecedent of PRO in sentences like *It can be difficult to achieve one's goals
without PRO being impossible*.

The question of why the Inactivity Condition in (32iii) should hold also seems
to have a relatively straightforward answer: given that VP is merged as the
complement of T, and a finite T carries agreement features which require it to
agree with an active constituent within VP, we can see the function of using
expletive *it* in a structure which would otherwise lack a goal active for agreement
as being to provide an active goal which can value unvalued person/number
features on a T-probe – as was implicit in our earlier discussion of sentences like

(19a) *It is said that he has taken bribes*. Moreover, given the assumption that (in consequence of the Economy Condition) an active head probes only as far as it needs to in order to satisfy its requirements, we can see why expletive *it* cannot be used in a structure like (33b) **It was awarded only one prize*: this is because if *it* is merged as the specifier of the verb *awarded*, the T constituent BE will agree in person and number with the closest φ-complete goal *it*, so leaving the case feature on *only one prize* unvalued and undeleted, and thereby causing the derivation to crash.

What remains to be accounted for is the Indefiniteness Condition (31ii). This condition raises two questions: firstly, why an expletive should be used at all, and secondly, why (if one is used) it has to be *there* and not *it*. Let's look at each of these questions in turn. Use of an expletive in association with an indefinite internal argument may well be motivated by semantic considerations. Thus, indefinites which move to spec-T are ambiguous between a specific and a non-specific reading, whereas indefinites which remain in situ within VP in expletive structures allow only a non-specific reading – as illustrated by the contrast below:

(37) (a)   *A man* is in the room
     (b)   There is *a man* in the room

So, while *a man* in (37a) can have either a specific or a non-specific interpretation, in (37b) it can only have a non-specific interpretation. This suggests that the use of an expletive pronoun in sentences like (37b) is a device for ensuring that the associated indefinite expression does not receive a specific interpretation.

However, this still leaves us with the question of why *there* rather than *it* should be the expletive pronoun used in conjunction with an indefinite internal argument. The answer we shall suggest here is that the choice of pronoun in an expletive structure is determined by the Economy Condition, in the sense that economy considerations dictate that (in expletive structures) we use an expletive carrying as few uninterpretable features as possible. Since *there* carries only one uninterpretable feature (its third person feature) and *it* carries two (its third person and singular number features), what this means in practical terms is that *there* will be used wherever possible, with *it* only being used when use of *there* results in ungrammaticality.

We can illustrate how the economy account works by considering why *there* is used rather than *it* in sentences with an indefinite associate like (33a) *There was awarded only one prize*. Given the assumptions made here, (33a) will be derived as follows. The passive verb *awarded* merges with its indefinite complement *only one prize* to form the V-bar *awarded only one prize*. This is then merged with expletive *there* to form the VP *there awarded only one prize*. The resulting VP is then merged with a past tense T constituent containing the passive auxiliary BE, so deriving the structure shown below:

(38)

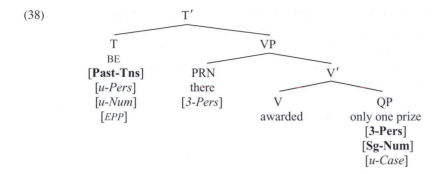

The active T-probe BE locates two active goals within its search space – namely the expletive pronoun *there* (active by virtue of its uninterpretable person feature) and the QP *only one prize* (active by virtue of its uninterpretable case feature). Four things then happen at the same time: (i) BE agrees in person with *there*, and in person and number with *only one prize*; (ii) the unvalued case feature on *only one prize* is valued as nominative; (iii) the EPP feature on T triggers movement of the closest goal (= expletive *there*) to spec-T; and (iv) all uninterpretable features on the probe and goals are deleted. The result of these four operations is to derive the structure in (39) below:

(39)

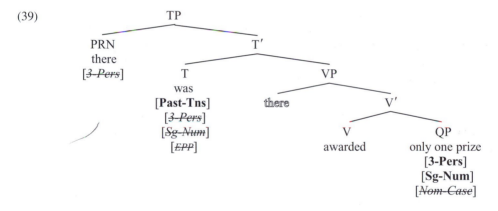

The resulting TP is subsequently merged with a null C containing an inter-pretable declarative force feature. The resulting derivation converges both at the PF interface (because all features have been valued) and at the semantics interface (because all uninterpretable features have been deleted). Since use of expletive *there* in (39) leads to convergence, economy considerations rule out the use of expletive *it* in structures with an indefinite associate (because *it* is more 'costly' to use by virtue of having two uninterpretable features which need to be deleted).

But now consider why expletive *it* (but not expletive *there*) is used in a sentence like (19a) above, repeated as (40a) below:

(40) (a)   *It* is said that he has taken bribes
     (b)   **There* is said that he has taken bribes

The main clause in each of the sentences in (40) will be derived by merging the verb *said* with its *that*-clause complement to form the V-bar *said that he has taken bribes*, and then merging this V-bar with the expletive pronoun *it* or *there*. The resulting VP is then merged with a present tense T constituent containing the progressive auxiliary BE, so forming the T-bar in (41) below:

(41)

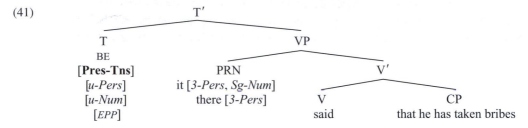

If the expletive used is *there*, the unvalued and uninterpretable person feature on BE can be valued via agreement with *there*, but not the unvalued and uninterpretable number feature on BE. The result is that the derivation crashes, and the corresponding sentence (40b) is ungrammatical. Because use of the more economical expletive *there* would cause the derivation to crash, expletive *it* is used instead: agreement between the probe BE and the expletive goal *it* in (41) will both value and delete the unvalued person/number features on BE, and delete the uninterpretable person/number features on *it*. The resulting sentence (40a) is therefore correctly predicted to be grammatical.

7.7   Agreement and A-movement

So far, we have seen that agreement plays an important role not only in valuing the φ-features of T but also in valuing the case features of nominals. However, as we will see in this section, there is also evidence that agreement also plays an important role in A-movement. To see why, let's return to consider the derivation of our earlier sentence (6B) *They were arrested*. Assume that the derivation proceeds as sketched earlier until we reach the stage of derivation in (16) above, repeated as (42) below:

(42)

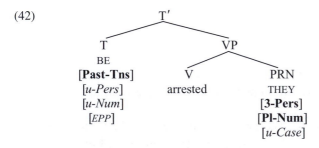

In (42), [T BE] is an active probe (by virtue of its uninterpretable person and number features) and has an uninterpretable EPP feature. It therefore searches for an active goal which can value and delete its person/number features, locating the pronoun THEY (which is active by virtue of its uninterpretable case feature and which has person and number features that can match those of BE). Since the matching goal THEY is a definite pronoun, the EPP feature of [T BE] cannot be deleted by merging an expletive in spec-T, but rather can only be deleted by movement of the goal to spec-T: accordingly, THEY moves to become the specifier of BE. Assuming that agreement, case marking and Feature Deletion work as before, the structure which is formed at the end of the T-cycle will be that shown below:

(43)

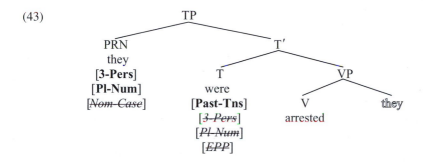

(To avoid excessive visual clutter, the trace copy of *they* left behind in VP-complement position is shown here simply as t͟h͟e͟y͟, but is in fact an identical copy of *they*, containing the same features as *they*. The same typographical convention will be used throughout the rest of this chapter.) The TP in (43) is subsequently merged with a null declarative-force C, so terminating the syntactic derivation. Since all uninterpretable features have been deleted, the derivation **converges** – i.e. results in a syntactic structure which can subsequently be mapped into well-formed phonetic and semantic representations.

A key assumption underlying the analysis sketched here is that T triggers movement of a goal with which it agrees in person/number. In a passive sentence like (5B) *They were arrested*, the goal which agrees with T and which moves to spec-T is the thematic complement of the verb *arrested*. But in an active sentence like:

(44)   He has arrested them

it is the subject *he* which agrees with T and moves to spec-T, and not the complement *them*. Why should this be? In order to answer this question, let's look at how (44) is derived.

The verb *arrested* merges with its THEME complement *them* to form the V-bar *arrested them*. This V-bar is in turn merged with its AGENT argument *he* to form the VP *he arrested them*. The resulting VP is then merged with a present tense T constituent to form the T-bar shown in simplified form below:

(45)

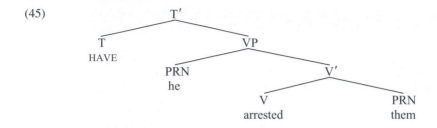

T serves as a probe at this point and looks for a goal to value (and delete) its unvalued person/number features. However, if (as we assumed in our discussion of the passive structure in (43) above) T can agree with the complement of a verb, an important question to ask is why T can't agree with the complement *them* in an active structure like (45), and why in fact HAVE must agree with the subject *he* and hence is ultimately spelled out as the third person singular present tense form *has*.

One reason is that (by the time we reach the stage of derivation in (45) above) the pronoun *them* will already have had its case feature valued (as accusative) and deleted, and so will no longer be active for case/agreement operations. If all structural case assignment involves agreement (as tacitly assumed in (8) above), it follows that accusative case assignment will involve the kind of operation outlined informally below:

(46)   **Accusative Case Assignment**
An unvalued case feature on a goal is valued as accusative via agreement with a transitive probe

Agreement between a transitive verb and its object is invisible in English (in the sense that it has no overt phonetic manifestation), but is visible in languages like Swahili with overt object-agreement morphology. Given the Earliness Principle (3), the pronoun *them* in (45) will have had its case feature valued as accusative (and deleted) via agreement with the transitive verb *arrested* on the V-cycle, and so be inactive for subsequent case/agreement operations by the time we reach the T-cycle in (45) above. Consequently, when the T-probe HAVE searches for a goal in (45), the only active goal (with an unvalued case feature) which it locates is the pronoun *he*. Accordingly, HAVE agrees with, assigns nominative case to, and attracts *he* to move to spec-T, so forming a TP whose overt constituents are *He has arrested them*. Merging the resulting TP with a null declarative complementiser derives the structure associated with (44) *He has arrested them*.

A second reason why the T-probe HAVE can't agree with the object *them* in (45) is the following. We suggested earlier that a head probes only as far as it needs to in order to ensure that all its unvalued features are valued. When T-HAVE probes in (45), the closest goal which it locates is the subject *he*. Since *he* can value all the unvalued (person/number) agreement features on T, there is no need for T to probe any further and therefore (in consequence of the Economy Condition) no possibility of T probing further and agreeing with the object *them*.

7.8   EPP and agreement in control infinitives

The analysis presented in the previous section assumes that a finite T carries an EPP feature which (in conjunction with agreement) drives A-movement. But what about the kind of infinitival [$_T$ *to*] constituent found in **control** clauses? In the previous chapter, we argued that infinitival *to* in a control clause like that bracketed in (47a) below has an EPP feature which attracts PRO to move out of the VP in which it originates into spec-T in the manner indicated by the arrow in (47b):

(47)   (a)   They don't want [to see you]

(b)   They don't want [$_{CP}$ [$_C$ ${}^{\emptyset}$] [$_{TP}$ PRO [$_T$ to] [$_{VP}$ P̶R̶O̶ [$_V$ see] you]]]

Let's likewise suppose that PRO is assigned null case by agreement with a c-commanding T with null (non-finite) tense in much the same way as subjects in tensed clauses are assigned nominative case by agreement with a c-commanding T which has finite (present or past) tense. More specifically, let's assume that *to* in control infinitives contains not only an abstract non-finite tense feature, but also abstract φ-features; and let's further suppose that null case assignment can be characterised informally as follows:

(48)   **Null Case Assignment**
An unvalued case feature on a pronoun goal is valued as null via agreement with a T-probe carrying null (non-finite) tense

In the light of these assumptions, consider the derivation of the bracketed control clause in:

(49)   They have decided [PRO to help you]

Decide is a control predicate (as we see from the fact that (49) is paraphraseable as *They have decided that they will help you*, and from the fact that *decide* does not allow an expletive subject in a sentence like *There has decided to be an enquiry*). Given the VP-Internal Subject Hypothesis, the PRO subject of the bracketed infinitive clause will originate in spec-V, as the specifier of *help you*. More specifically, the derivation proceeds as follows. The verb *help* merges with its complement *you*, and the resulting V-bar *help you* in turn merges with its PRO subject to form the VP PRO *help you*. Merging control *to* with this VP forms the T-bar *to* PRO *help you*. Let's suppose that since PRO refers back to *they* in (49), PRO (as used here) carries the interpretable features [**3-Pers, Pl-Num**]; let's also suppose that PRO enters the derivation with an unvalued case feature [*u-Case*]. In addition, let's assume that control *to* carries an interpretable nonfinite tense feature [**Nf-Tns**] (denoting an irrealis event which has not yet happened but may happen in the future), and also has uninterpretable (and unvalued) person/number features. Finally (for the reasons given in §6.9), let's assume that *to* carries an EPP feature in control clauses. Given all these assumptions, merging *to* with

[VP PRO *help you*] will form the T-bar (50) below (simplified by showing only features on constituents of immediate concern to us):

(50)

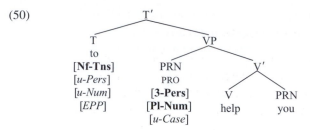

Since *to* is the highest head in the structure and is active (by virtue of its uninterpretable φ-features), it serves as a probe which searches for a goal to value and delete its φ-features. Since *to* c-commands PRO and PRO is active by virtue of its uninterpretable case feature, PRO can serve as a goal for the probe *to*. The unvalued φ-features on the probe are assigned the same third person plural values as those on the goal by agreement (8) and are deleted by Feature Deletion (14). The unvalued case feature on PRO is assigned the value [*Null-Case*] by Null Case Assignment (48) and deleted by Feature Deletion (14). The EPP feature of *to* is deleted by movement of PRO to spec-T. The result of applying these various operations is to derive the TP shown in simplified form in (51) below:

(51)

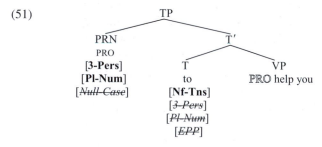

The resulting TP is subsequently merged with the null nonfinite complementiser which introduces control clauses. As required, the structure which will serve as input to the semantic component contains only (bold-printed) interpretable features – all uninterpretable features having been deleted.

7.9   EPP and person agreement in defective clauses

In §7.7 we suggested that a finite T has an EPP feature which triggers movement of the closest active matching goal to spec-T, in conformity with the Attract Closest Condition. In §7.8, we suggested that control *to* likewise carries an EPP feature triggering movement of the closest active goal to spec-T. If (as we did in the previous chapter) we make the unitary assumption that all T constituents in English have an EPP feature, it follows that raising *to* will likewise carry an EPP feature. A piece of empirical evidence which lends support to this claim comes from the syntax of the italicised floating quantifiers in sentences such as the following (a floating quantifier being one separated from its antecedent, underlined below):

(52)   The boys would seem to me *both/all* to have been treated fairly

One way of accounting for such structures is to suppose that the QP *both/all the boys* originates as the complement of the passive participle *treated*, and then moves to become the specifier of infinitival *to*. Subsequently, the DP *the boys* moves on its own to become the specifier of the T-auxiliary *would*, leaving the quantifier *all/both* 'floating' or 'stranded' as the specifier of infinitival *to*. From this perspective, the floating/stranded quantifier provides evidence of A-movement through the specifier of a defective infinitival clause.

A further piece of evidence leading to the same conclusion is offered by Chomsky (2001, fn. 56) on the basis of (somewhat contrived) sentences like (53) below:

(53)   John seems to Fred [to appear to himself [to like Mary]]

Here, *himself* refers to *John*, not to *Fred*. This is puzzling if we assume that the antecedent of a reflexive must be an argument locally c-commanding the reflexive (and hence contained within the same TP as the reflexive), since if raising *to* has no EPP feature and *John* moves directly from being the subject of the *like*-clause to becoming the subject of the *seem*-clause, the lefthand bracketed TP containing the reflexive will contain no antecedent for *himself*, and hence we will wrongly predict that structures like (53) are ill-formed. By contrast, argues Chomsky, if we posit that raising *to* does indeed have an EPP feature, *John* will move from being subject of *like Mary* to becoming subject of *to like Mary*, then later becoming subject of *to appear to himself to like Mary*, before finally moving to become the subject of the null T constituent in the *seem*-clause. This will mean that a null copy of *John* is left behind as the subject of each of the two infinitive clauses, as shown in skeletal form in (54) below:

(54)   *John* seems to Fred [~~*John*~~ to appear to himself [~~*John*~~ to like Mary]]

Since the reflexive *himself* is locally c-commanded by the bold-printed copy ***John*** in (54) within the lefthand bracketed TP containing the reflexive, (54) correctly predicts that *himself* will be interpreted as referring to *John*. (Recall that lower copies of moved constituents are deleted in the phonological component but remain visible in the syntactic and semantic components.)

Structures like (53) suggest that raising *to* must have an EPP feature triggering movement of an argument to spec-T. But it's important to bear in mind that the EPP feature on T works in conjunction with the person/number φ-features of T: more specifically, the EPP feature on T triggers movement to spec-T of an active goal which T agrees with in respect of one or more φ-features (i.e. in person or number or both). It therefore follows that T in raising clauses must carry one or more φ-features if it is to trigger movement of a goal carrying φ-features of its own. Now it clearly cannot be the case that raising *to* carries both person and number, since if it did we would wrongly predict that raising clauses require a null PRO subject, given that infinitival *to* assigns null case to its subject by (48) when carrying both person and number. The conclusion we reach, therefore, is that raising *to* must carry only *one* φ-feature. But which φ-feature – person or number?

The answer is provided by raising sentences such as the following:

(55)   There do seem to remain several problems

On the assumption that raising *to* carries an EPP feature requiring it to attract a subject, the expletive pronoun *there* will raise (in successive-cyclic fashion) from its original position as the specifier of the unaccusative verb *remain* to become the specifier of infinitival *to*, and thereafter raise still further to become the specifier of the present tense T-auxiliary *do*, in the manner shown by the arrows in the skeletal structure in (56) below:

(56)   [CP [C ø] [TP *There* [T do] [VP [V seem] [TP *there* [T to] [VP *there* [V remain] several problems]]]]]

If the EPP feature on a T-constituent attracts a goal which the probe agrees with in respect of one or more φ-features, movement of *there* to become the specifier of raising *to* on the subordinate clause T-cycle means that the φ-feature carried by *to* in (56) must match that carried by expletive *there*. Since we argued in §7.6 that expletive *there* carries person (but not number), it follows that *to* in (56) must carry a person feature. This being so, the EPP feature of raising *to* will require it to project a specifier carrying a person feature, and expletive *there* clearly satisfies this requirement.

Our conclusion can be generalised from raising sentences like (55) to long-distance expletive passives like (57a) below, involving the movement operation arrowed in (57b):

(57)
(a)   There are thought to remain several problems

(b)   [CP [C ø] [TP *There* [T are] [VP [V thought] [TP *there* [T to] [VP *there* [V remain] several problems]]]]]

Passive *to* (i.e. the kind of *to* found in long-distance passives) cannot carry both person and number features, since otherwise it would wrongly be predicted to require a subject with null case. Since *there* is attracted to become the specifier of *to* in (57b) and *there* has a person feature, it seems reasonable to conclude that passive *to* (like raising *to*) carries person but not number.

We can generalise our finding still further to infinitival TPs like those bracketed below:

(58) (a)   They were expecting [TP *the visitors* to be met at the airport]
     (b)   They were expecting [TP *there* to be someone to meet the visitors at the airport]

(59) (a)   I will arrange [CP for [TP *the visitors* to be met at the airport]]
   (b)   I will arrange [CP for [TP *there* to be someone to meet the visitors at the airport]]

The bracketed TPs in (58) are ECM clauses (with the properties noted in §3.9). Since *the visitors* originates as the thematic complement of the passive verb *met* in (58a) but ends up as the subject of [T to], it is clear that the head T of the bracketed complement-clause TP must contain an EPP feature and at least one φ-feature. Since the infinitive subject can be expletive *there* in (58b), and since *there* carries only person, it follows that the head T of an ECM clause must carry a person feature as well as an EPP feature. But if we suppose that a nonfinite T which carries a full set of person and number features (like the head T of a control clause) assigns null case to its subject, then it is apparent from the fact that the subject of an ECM clause is an overt constituent and hence does not have null case that the head T of an ECM clause must also be defective, and so carry an EPP feature and a person feature, but no number feature. Our conclusion can be generalised in a straightforward fashion to *for*-infinitive structures like those bracketed in (59): if we define ECM structures as structures in which a constituent within TP is assigned case by an external head lying outside the relevant TP, it follows that *for*-infinitives are also ECM structures.

Our argumentation here leads us to the following more general conclusions about the feature composition of T in English:

(60)   **Feature Composition of T in English**
   (i)   T always carries an EPP feature and a person feature in all types of (finite and nonfinite, main and complement) clauses
   (ii)   T also carries a number feature in complete clauses which are CPs (i.e. in finite clauses and control clauses), though not in defective clauses which are only TPs (hence not in raising clauses, or long-distance passives or ECM clauses)

In the light of these assumptions, consider the derivation of the following sentence:

(61)   Several prizes are thought likely [to be awarded]

Since the bracketed infinitive complement in (61) is the TP complement of the raising adjective *likely*, it is a defective clause and so [T to] will carry uninterpretable EPP and person features (but no number feature) in accordance with (60i, ii). This means that at the point where *to* is merged with its complement we have the structure shown in skeletal form below:

(62)   [T to] be awarded [several prizes]
            [*u-Pers*]   [**3-Pers**]
            [*EPP*]   [**Pl-Num**]
                             [*u-Case*]

Since [$_T$ *to*] is the highest head in the structure at this point and is active by virtue of its uninterpretable person feature, [$_T$ *to*] serves as a probe which searches for an active goal and locates *several prizes*, which is active by virtue of its unvalued case feature. The unvalued person feature on the probe *to* is valued as third person (and deleted) via agreement in person with the goal *several prizes*. But what of the unvalued case feature on the goal *several prizes*? This cannot be valued by infinitival *to* in (62) because *to* is not a case assigner (and, more generally, it would seem that only non-defective probes can be structural case assigners); consequently, the case feature of *several prizes* cannot be deleted either, on the assumption that an unvalued feature can only be deleted as part of an operation which values it. The EPP feature of *to* is deleted by movement of *several prizes* to spec-T, thereby deriving the structure (63) below (simplified in various ways, including by showing the deleted copy of *several prizes* without its features):

(63)   [several prizes]   [$_T$ to]   be awarded several prizes
         [3-Pers]   [*3-Pers*]
         [Pl-Num]   [*EPP*]
         [*u-Case*]

Note that *several prizes* remains active at this point, because its uninterpretable case feature has not yet been valued or deleted. Merging the structure (63) with the raising adjective *likely*, merging the resulting AP with the passive verb *thought* and then merging the resulting VP with a finite present tense T constituent containing BE will derive:

(64)   [$_T$ BE]   thought likely [several prizes] [$_T$ to]   be awarded several prizes
         [Pres-Tns]   **[3-Pers]**   [*3-Pers*]
         [*u-Pers*]   **[Pl-Num]**   [*EPP*]
         [*u-Num*]   [*u-Case*]
         [*EPP*]

Because it is the head of the overall TP structure and is active by virtue of its uninterpretable φ-features, BE serves as a probe which searches for an active goal and locates *several prizes* (which is active by virtue of the fact that its uninterpretable case feature has not been valued or deleted at this point); consequently, the goal *several prizes* values and deletes the uninterpretable person/number features of the probe BE. By virtue of being finite and non-defective, BE values the unvalued case feature of the agreeing nominal *several prizes* as nominative, and deletes it. The EPP feature of BE is deleted by moving *several prizes* to spec-T, so deriving:

(65)   [several prizes]   [$_T$ BE]   thought likely *t*   [$_T$ to]   be awarded *t*
         [3-Pers]   **[Pres-Tns]**   [*3-Pers*]
         [Pl-Num]   [*3-Pers*]   [*EPP*]
         [*Nom-Case*]   [*Pl-Num*]
                               [*EPP*]

                                   (*t* denoting a null trace copy of *several prizes*)

The resulting TP is subsequently merged with a null declarative complementiser, and BE is ultimately spelled out as *are*. Since all unvalued features have been valued and all uninterpretable features have been deleted, the derivation **converges** (i.e. results in a well-formed structure which can be assigned an appropriate phonetic representation and an appropriate semantic representation).

7.10 Defective clauses with expletive subjects

In the previous section, we looked at the syntax of defective clauses which have thematic subjects; in this section, we turn to look at defective clauses with expletive subjects. Let's begin by comparing the derivation of (61) above with the derivation of the corresponding expletive sentence:

(66)   There are thought likely to be awarded several prizes

The derivation of (66) proceeds as follows. The passive verb *awarded* merges with its complement *several prizes* to form the V-bar *awarded several prizes*. Since the internal argument *several prizes* is indefinite, the resulting V-bar can be merged with the expletive pronoun *there* (in accordance with the Indefiniteness Condition (32ii) above) to form the VP *there awarded several prizes*. This VP is then merged with the passive auxiliary *be* to form the AUXP *be there awarded several prizes*. The resulting AUXP is subsequently merged with infinitival *to* (which – by virtue of heading the complement of the raising adjective *likely* – is a defective T constituent carrying person and EPP features only) to form the structure shown in skeletal form below:

(67)

[$_T$ to]	be	there	awarded	[several prizes]
[*u-Pers*]		[*3-Pers*]		[**3-Pers**]
[*EPP*]				[**Pl-Num**]
				[*u-Case*]

Given what we have said so far, we might suppose that what happens at this point is the following. Infinitival *to* (by virtue of being the head of the overall structure and being active) serves as a probe and identifies *there* as the closest active goal which can value its unvalued person feature. Agreement in person between *to* and the third person expletive pronoun *there* results in the unvalued person feature on *to* being valued as third person via (8), and in the uninterpretable person features on both *to* and *there* being deleted. The EPP feature on *to* attracts *there* to become the subject/specifier of *to*.

However, closer reflection suggests that there is something wrong with the story told in the previous paragraph. The problem is that if the person feature on *there* is deleted via agreement with infinitival *to*, *there* will be inactivated at the end of the T-cycle, once it has moved to become the specifier of infinitival *to*, and this will wrongly predict that sentences such as the following should be grammatical:

(68)   *It is thought likely there to be awarded several prizes

However, the fact that this sentence is ungrammatical (while that in (66) above is grammatical) suggests that *there* does not have its person feature deleted or inactivated at this point. Why should this be? The answer lies in a condition on deletion of case/agreement features which we can outline in the following terms (where α is a probe and β a goal, or conversely β is a probe and α a goal):

(69)   **Completeness Condition**
         An uninterpretable case/agreement feature on a constituent α is deleted
         when α agrees (in respect of one or more φ-features) with a φ-complete
         constituent β (i.e. with a non-defective β which carries a complete set of
         φ-features – *both* person *and* number)

In consequence of the Completeness Condition (69), the uninterpretable person feature on the expletive goal *there* cannot be deleted by the T-probe *to* in (67) because *to* is a defective probe (by virtue of carrying person but not number), and only agreement with a φ-complete probe (i.e. one with both person and number) can delete case/agreement features on a goal. The EPP feature on *to* triggers movement of the closest active goal (= *there*) to spec-T and (if movement of any goal – whether φ-complete or not – to spec-T deletes the EPP feature on T) is thereby deleted, deriving:

(70)   there   [T to]   be ~~there~~ awarded   [several prizes]
         [*3-Pers*]   [~~*3-Pers*~~]   [**3-Pers**]
                    [~~*EPP*~~]   [**Pl-Num**]
                                                         [*u-Case*]

Merging the TP in (70) with the raising adjective *likely*, merging the resulting AP with the passive verb *thought* and merging the resulting VP with a present tense T containing BE will derive:

(71)   [T BE]   thought likely [there]   [T to]   be ~~there~~ awarded [several prizes]
         [**Pres-Tns**]   [*3-Pers*]   [~~*3-Pers*~~]   [**3-Pers**]
         [*u-Pers*]   [~~*EPP*~~]   [**Pl-Num**]
         [*u-Num*]   [*u-Case*]
         [*EPP*]

At this point, [T BE] is the highest head in the overall structure and so serves as a probe. Its uninterpretable person and number features make it active, and mean that [T BE] looks for one or more active goals which can value its person/number features. When T-BE probes, the closest active goal which it locates is the expletive pronoun *there* (active by virtue of its undeleted uninterpretable third person feature). However, because expletive *there* is a defective pronoun carrying only person (and not number), *there* can value (but cannot delete) only the person feature on T-BE, and (lacking number) *there* can neither value nor delete the number feature on T-BE. Let us suppose that economy requirements impose the following condition on probes, as indeed we tacitly assumed earlier:

(72)   **Probe Condition**
          A head probes only as far as is needed in order to find a goal which can value any unvalued features on the probe, and delete any uninterpretable features on the probe

This will mean that T-BE in (71) must probe beyond *there* in order to find a goal which can both value and delete all its features. T-BE therefore probes further, and locates the next closest active goal, which is the quantifier phrase *several prizes* (active by virtue of its undeleted uninterpretable case feature, and carrying both person and number features). Accordingly, the probe BE simultaneously agrees with both *there* and *several prizes*. The unvalued person feature of BE will be valued as third person via agreement with the third person goals *there* and *several prizes*, and the unvalued number feature of BE will be valued as plural via agreement with the plural goal *several prizes*. The uninterpretable person/number features on the probe BE are deleted in accordance with the Completeness Condition (69) because BE agrees with the φ-complete goal *several prizes*. The unvalued case feature on the goal *several prizes* will be valued as nominative via (8ii) and deleted via agreement with the φ-complete probe BE in conformity with the Completeness Condition (69). The EPP feature of BE attracts the closest active goal (namely *there*) to move to become the specifier of BE (movement resulting in deletion of the EPP feature on BE), so deriving:

(73)   there   [T BE]   thought likely *t*   [T to]   be *t*   [several prizes]
                                                                awarded

          [~~3-Pers~~]   [**Pres-Tns**]   [~~3-Pers~~]   [**3-Pers**]
                     [~~3-Pers~~]   [~~EPP~~]   [**Pl-Num**]
                     [~~Pl-Num~~]   [~~Nom-Case~~]
                     [~~EPP~~]
          (*t* denoting a null trace copy of *there*)

The resulting structure will then be merged with a null declarative complementiser, and BE will ultimately be spelled out as the third person plural present tense form *are*. As required, all uninterpretable features have been deleted from (73), so only the bold interpretable features are seen by the semantic component.

Note that an important assumption which is incorporated into the analysis presented here is that all the agreement, case assignment, movement and deletion operations which apply on the T-cycle apply simultaneously, in conformity with the Simultaneity Condition (18). A further key assumption we have made is that T can agree with multiple goals, so that (e.g.) [T BE] agrees with both *there* and *several prizes* in (71). At first sight, it might seem that allowing a probe to agree with multiple goals creates unwelcome asymmetries between *movement* and *agreement*. This is because (in consequence of the Attract Closest Condition) the EPP feature of T only triggers movement of a single goal (viz. the *closest* one) to spec-T, whereas agreement can target more than one goal. However, this potential difference between movement and agreement can be reconciled if we suppose that an agreeing head probes only as far as the closest (φ-complete) goal which can value and delete *all* its agreement features – so allowing BE to probe as far as *several prizes* in (71). It would then follow that agreement and EPP features alike can only probe as far as the closest constituent which will satisfy all their requirements – and this condition in turn is arguably reducible to the Economy Condition of Chomsky (1989, p. 69) requiring that there should be 'no superfluous steps in derivations' (so that once a probe has satisfied its requirements, it ceases to probe any further). Since the EPP feature on BE in (71) searches for a goal with person, it ceases to probe once it locates the closest person-specified goal, namely *there*. But since the agreement features on BE require a φ-complete goal with both person and number, they probe as far as the QP *several prizes*.

Finally, let's turn to consider the derivation of an ECM structure such as:

(74)   John is expecting there to be several problems

This is derived as follows. The verb *be* merges with its QP complement *several problems* to form the V-bar *be several problems*. This V-bar is then merged with the expletive pronoun *there* to form the VP *there be several problems*. The resulting VP is in turn merged with infinitival *to* (which, being defective in ECM clauses, carries only EPP and person features), so forming the structure shown in simplified form below:

(75)   [T to]   there   be   [several problems]
         [*u-Pers*]   [*3-Pers*]   **[3-Pers]**
         [*EPP*]   **[Pl-Num]**
                                       [*u-Case*]

The unvalued, uninterpretable person feature on the probe *to* is valued as third person via multiple agreement with the two third person goals *there* and *several problems*; it is also deleted via person agreement with the φ-complete goal *several problems*. The unvalued, uninterpretable case feature on the goal *several problems* cannot be valued or deleted by the probe *to* (and likewise, the uninterpretable third person feature on the expletive goal *there* cannot be deleted by the probe *to*), because *to* is a defective probe which does not have a complete set of φ-features (in that *to* has person but not number). The EPP feature on *to* triggers raising of the closest person-specified goal (= *there*) to spec-T and is thereafter deleted, so deriving the structure shown below:

(76)   there   [T to]   ~~there~~ be   [several problems]
         [*3-Pers*]   [~~3-Pers~~]   **[3-Pers]**
                    [~~EPP~~]   **[Pl-Num]**
                                               [*u-Case*]

The ECM verb *expecting* then merges with the TP in (76) (and with its subject *John*) to form the VP shown in (77) below:

(77)   John   expecting   there   [T to]   ~~there~~ be   [several problems]
            [u-Pers]   [3-Pers]   [~~3-Pers~~]   **[3-Pers]**
            [u-Num]   [~~EPP~~]   **[Pl-Num]**
                                                                            [u-Case]

If (as we have assumed), structural case-marking involves agreement between probe and goal, it follows that the transitive verb *expecting* in (77) will enter the derivation with unvalued, uninterpretable person and number features which make it an active probe. The verb *expecting* thus probes until all its agreement features have been valued. It locates expletive *there* as a goal (active by virtue of its uninterpretable person feature), but since *there* can only value the person (and not the number) feature on the verb *expecting*, it continues to probe until it locates a goal like the QP *several problems* which is active (by virtue of its unvalued and uninterpretable case feature) and which carries both person *and number* features. Accordingly, the (abstract) person and number features on the verb *expecting* are valued as third person via agreement with both *there* and *several problems*, and as plural via agreement with *several problems*: the person and number features on the probe *expecting* are also deleted via agreement with the φ-complete goal *several problems*. The case feature on the goal *several problems* is valued as accusative in accordance with (46) above (and concomitantly deleted) via agreement with the φ-complete probe *expecting* (the transitivity of the verb *expecting* being reflected in the fact that it has an external argument – namely *John*). The uninterpretable third person feature on the expletive goal *there* is deleted via person agreement with the φ-complete probe *expecting*. After all these various operations have taken place simultaneously, we derive the structure in (78) below at the end of the V-cycle:

(78)   John   expecting   there   [T to]   ~~there~~ be   [several problems]
            [~~3-Pers~~]   [~~3-Pers~~]   [~~3-Pers~~]   **[3-Pers]**
            [~~Pl-Num~~]   [~~EPP~~]   **[Pl-Num]**
                                                                            [~~Acc-Case~~]

Merging the resulting VP with a T constituent containing the progressive auxiliary BE, and then merging the resulting TP with a null declarative complementiser ultimately derives the structure associated with (74) *John is expecting there to be several problems.*

An interesting descriptive observation which we note in passing is that the verb BE seems to function as an unaccusative predicate (like REMAIN) in structures such as (79) below:

(79)   **There** has remained/been *some dissatisfaction*

However, BE differs from other unaccusative predicates in seemingly requiring the use of expletive *there* with an indefinite associate – as we see from (80) below:

(80)   *Some dissatisfaction* has remained/*been

This might perhaps suggest that (when used as an existential predicate – i.e. a predicate describing the existence of some entity) BE is listed in the lexicon as obligatorily requiring expletive *there* as its specifier (with *there* perhaps serving as a locative argument).

7.11   Summary

In this chapter, we have taken a look at Chomsky's recent work on case, agreement and movement. In §7.2, we saw that agreement plays an integral role in case assignment, in that nominative case is assigned to a nominal (i.e. noun or pronoun expression) which agrees in person and number with a finite T. In §7.3, we argued that some features enter the derivation already valued (e.g. the tense feature of T and the person/number φ-features of non-expletive nominals), whereas others (e.g. the φ-features of T and the case feature of nominals) are initially unvalued and are assigned values in the course of the derivation via a case/agreement Feature-Valuation operation. In §7.4, we argued that agreement and case-marking involve a relation between an active probe and an active goal, and that probe and goal are only active if they carry one or more uninterpretable features (e.g. uninterpretable φ-features or case features). We also saw that uninterpretable features have to be deleted in the course of the derivation by a Feature Deletion operation, in order to ensure that they do not feed into the semantic component and thereby cause the derivation to crash (because they are illegible in the semantic component), and we posited that a feature becomes inactive in the syntax and invisible to the semantic component once deleted (while remaining visible to the PF component). In §7.5, we suggested that expletive *it* enters the derivation with uninterpretable third person and singular number features, and that these value, delete and in turn are deleted by those of the auxiliary *is* in sentences such as *It is said that he has taken bribes*; we argued that an expletive originates within an intransitive VP which has no external argument. In §7.6, we argued that expletive *there* carries only an uninterpretable third person feature. We looked at the distribution of expletive pronouns and concluded that expletive *there* is used in structures where a verb has an indefinite (pro)nominal internal argument, and expletive *it* in structures where there is no other active agreeing (pro)nominal goal. In §7.7, we outlined Chomsky's agreement-based account of A-movement under which A-movement involves an agreement relation between an active probe with an EPP feature and an active goal, and we noted that the EPP feature of T is satisfied (and deleted) by movement of the closest active goal to spec-T. In §7.8, we looked at the syntax of infinitive clauses. We saw that the PRO subject of a control infinitive originates within VP and that it is attracted to move to spec-T by an infinitival *to* which carries nonfinite tense and an EPP feature, and which agrees in person and number with and assigns null case to PRO. In §7.9, we went on to argue that T in other types of infinitive clause (e.g. the infinitival complements of raising, passive and ECM predicates) is defective in that although it carries uninterpretable EPP and person features (the latter serving to make T *active*), it lacks the number feature carried by T in finite/control clauses. And in §7.10, we extended this analysis to defective clauses with expletive subjects.

Key assumptions which we have made in this chapter are summarised below (in some cases, slightly revised in terms of assumptions made later in the text):

(81) **Earliness Principle** (= 3)
      Operations apply as early as possible in a derivation

(82) **Feature Composition of T in English** (= 60)
  (i)   T always carries an EPP feature and a person feature in all types of (finite and nonfinite, main and complement) clauses
  (ii) T also carries a number feature in complete clauses which are CPs (i.e. in finite clauses and control clauses), though not in defective clauses which are only TPs (hence not in raising clauses, or long-distance passives or ECM clauses)

(83) **Feature Valuation**: **Agreement and Case Assignment** (= 8)
      When an active probe (like T) agrees with one or more active goals in its local domain
  (i)   the unvalued (person/number) φ-features on the probe will be valued (i.e. assigned a value which is a copy of that on the goal/s)
  (ii) the unvalued case feature/s on the goal/s will be valued (i.e. assigned a value dependent on the nature of the probe – e.g. nominative if the probe is a finite T, null case if the probe is a null T with nonfinite tense, accusative if the probe is transitive)

(84) **Feature Deletion** (= 14)
  (i)   An uninterpretable case/agreement feature on a constituent α is deleted when α agrees (in respect of one or more φ-features) with a φ-complete constituent β which carries a complete set of person and number φ-features (= **Completeness Condition**)
  (ii) An uninterpretable EPP feature on a probe is deleted by movement of the closest active goal of the relevant type to become the specifier of the probe (= **EPP Condition**)
  (iii) Once deleted, a feature becomes invisible in the syntactic and semantic components (and hence inactive in the syntax) while remaining visible in the PF component (**Invisibility Condition**)

(85) **Simultaneity Condition** (= 18)
      All syntactic operations which involve a given probe apply simultaneously

(86) **Expletive Conditions** (= 32)
  (i)   External Argument Condition:
        An expletive can only be merged as the highest argument of a verb with no external argument
  (ii) Indefiniteness Condition:
        Expletive *there* can only be merged with a verb which has an indefinite nominal or pronominal internal argument

(iii)   Inactivity Condition:
          Expletive *it* can only be merged with a constituent which does not contain a
          nominal or pronominal expression with active case- or φ-features

(87)   **Probe Condition** (= 72)
          A head probes only as far as is needed in order to find a goal which can
          value any unvalued features on the probe, and delete any uninterpretable
          features on the probe

7.12   Bibliographical background

The probe–goal account of agreement and case assignment sketched
in §7.2 is based on Chomsky (1998, 1999, 2001). See Sigurðsson (2006) for
an alternative account of case assignment. The Earliness Principle derives from
work by Pesetsky (1995) and Rezac (2003). The spec-T account of expletives
derives from Chomsky (1999). On dative complements in Icelandic, see Svenonius (2002a, b). On so-called 'semantic agreement' in British English structures
like *The government are ruining the country*, see den Dikken (2001) and Sauerland and Elbourne (2002). On the idea that agreement features originate on C
and are 'handed down' to T, see Chomsky (2005b, 2006) and Miyagawa (2005,
2006); we will return to this in chapter 9. For an alternative view of agreement
as involving feature sharing, see Pesetsky and Torrego (2007). On the claim
made in §7.6 that CPs headed by the complementiser *that* are caseless, see
Safir (1986). The claim made in §7.7 that the only feature carried by expletive
there is an uninterpretable person feature derives from Chomsky (1998, 1999,
2001): for alternative analyses of expletive *there* structures, see Jenkins (1975),
Lasnik (1992, 1995b), Groat (1995), Moro (1997), Sobin (1997), Schütze (1999),
Felser and Rupp (2001), Bowers (2002), Lasnik (2003), Han (2004), Hazout
(2004a,b), Sobin (2004), Williams (2006) and Hornstein (2007). On structures
such as *There were three fish caught in the lake*, see Chomsky (1999), Bowers (2002), Caponigro and Schütze (2003) and Rezac (2006). On agreement in
structures like *There's lots of people in the room*, see Sobin (1997), Schütze
(1999) and den Dikken (2001). On multiple agreement, see Chomsky (2001,
2005b), Hiraira (2001, 2005) and Henderson (2006). On the semantic properties
of indefinites, see Milsark (1974, 1977), Jenkins (1975), Diesing (1992), Groat
(1995) and Felser and Rupp (2001). The claim in §7.8 that A-movement involves
agreement is made in Chomsky (1998, 1999, 2001). In relation to control clauses
discussed in §7.9, see Stowell (1982) and Martin (2001) on the tense properties
of control *to*, and Martin (2001) on the agreement properties of control *to*; see
Bowers (2002) and Landau (2006a) for alternative analyses of the case-marking
of PRO subjects. The claim that infinitival *to* in defective clauses carries EPP and
person features follows Chomsky (1999); the *Completeness Condition* is derived
from the same source. The analysis of floating quantifiers presented in the text
is adapted from Sportiche (1988). A potential problem for the claim in §7.10

that defective clauses carry an incomplete set of agreement features is posed by languages which use subjunctive clauses in contexts where English uses infinitives (e.g. in *seem*-type raising structures): in such clauses, T carries a complete set of agreement features, but is defective in respect of its tense properties (in being untensed, and hence showing no tense contrasts): see Uchibori (2000), Landau (2006a) and Polinsky and Potsdam (2006). This suggests that a broader cross-linguistic characterisation of the notion of *defective clause* is required.

Workbook section

Exercise 7.1

Discuss the derivation of the following sentences, paying particular attention to the syntax of case, agreement and EPP features:

1   Many miners may die
2   Many miners are thought to have died (**w**)
3   No prize was awarded
4   No prize is likely to be awarded
5   They are hoping to be promoted (**w**)
6   They appear to be hoping to be promoted
7   She is expecting him to be promoted
8   She seems to be expecting him to be promoted
9   He is believed to want to be promoted
10   He appears to be believed to want to be promoted

Helpful hints

When *have* or *be* occurs immediately after infinitival *to*, take it to be the head AUX constituent of an AUXP projection; and in 4, assume that *is* functions as a copula and raises from V to T in the manner described in §4.6. Bear in mind the key assumptions summarised in (81–87) in the main text.

Model answer for 1

The verb *die* is an unaccusative predicate – as we see from the postverbal position of the italicised subject in a (somewhat contrived) expletive sentence like

(i)   Never before had there died *so many miners* in a single accident

and from the fact its Italian counterpart *morire* is used in conjunction with the perfect auxiliary *essere* 'be', as we see in:

(ii)   Sono morti parecchi minatori
        Are   died several   miners
        'Several miners have died'

Accordingly, sentence 1 is derived as follows. The unaccusative verb *die* is merged with the QP *many miners* to form the VP *die many miners*. This is then merged with a present tense T constituent containing the modal auxiliary *may* to form the structure shown below:

(iii)

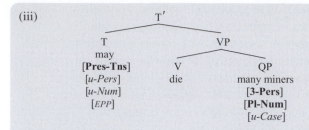

The T-auxiliary *may* is a probe by virtue of being the head of the overall structure and carries (abstract) uninterpretable person and number features in accordance with (82), and these make it active. It searches for an active goal and locates the QP *several miners* (which is active by virtue of its uninterpretable case feature). Via agreement with the φ-complete goal *several miners*, the φ-features on the probe *may* are valued as third person plural in accordance with (83i), and deleted in accordance with (84i). Via agreement with the finite φ-complete probe *may*, the case feature on the goal *several miners* is valued as nominative in accordance with (83ii), and deleted in accordance with (84i). The EPP feature on T is deleted by movement of the closest goal *several miners* to spec-T, in conformity with (84ii). These various (agreement, case-marking, movement and deletion) operations apply simultaneously on the T-cycle in accordance with (85), so deriving the TP shown in (iv) below:

(iv)

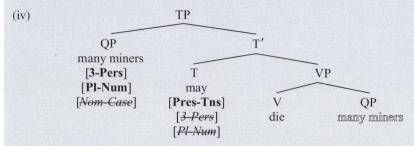

The resulting TP is then merged with a null complementiser containing an interpretable declarative force feature. In accordance with (84iii), deleted features are invisible in the semantic component, but visible in the PF component (though there is no overt spellout of the abstract person/number agreement features on the modal auxiliary *may*). Since all unvalued features have been valued (and all uninterpretable features deleted), the derivation converges both at the interface with the PF component and at the interface with the semantic component.

Exercise 7.2

Discuss the syntax of the following expletive sentences, paying particular attention to case-marking and agreement, and to the choice of expletive pronoun:

1   There remains every hope of finding survivors
2   There does appear to remain some discontent
3   *There does appear some discontent to remain
4   It is said that there have been some demonstrations **(w)**
5   *It is said there to have been some demonstrations
6   There are said to have been some demonstrations

7   It is thought to be recognised that there do appear to remain problems

8   I believe it to be essential for there to be some safeguards

9   It would seem that it is snowing

10   The jury found there to be no evidence of corruption

In addition, say what problems seem to be posed for the analysis of expletives given in the main text by sentences such as 11:

11   It's a pity that expletives cause problems

Helpful hints

Take a nonfinite form of BE/HAVE to be an AUX (heading an AUXP) in *to have . . .* in 5 and 6 and in *to be . . .* in 7. Take any nonfinite form of BE to be a copular V heading a VP when followed by a QP (like *some demonstrations* in 4, 5 and 6, *some safeguards* in 8 or *no evidence of corruption* in 10. In 9, assume that *snow* is an unaccusative verb, and that its subject originates in the same position as other unacusative subjects. Bear in mind the key assumptions summarised in (81–87) in the main text. Assume that the complementiser *for* in example 8 has the same case/agreement properties as a transitive ECM verb. Consider the effect of taking *a pity* to be a predicate rather than an argument in 11.

Model answer for 1

Given the assumptions made in the text, sentence 1 will be derived as follows. The noun *hope* is merged with its PP complement *of finding survivors* (whose structure need not concern us here) to form the NP *hope of finding survivors*. This NP is merged with the quantifier *every* to form the QP *every hope of finding survivors*. The resulting QP is merged as the complement of the unaccusative verb *remain* to form the V-bar *remain every hope of finding survivors*. This V-bar is then merged with expletive *there* to form the VP *there remain every hope of finding survivors*, with *there* being merged as the highest argument of a verb (*remain*) which has an indefinite internal argument *every hope of finding survivors* but no external argument, so that Expletive Conditions (86i, ii) are satisfied. The resulting VP in turn is merged with an affixal finite T constituent (denoted as *Af*) to form the structure shown in simplified form in (i) below:

(i)

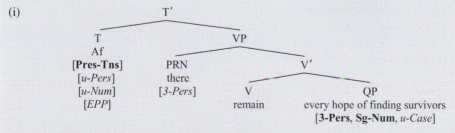

(Note that expletive *it* could not be used in place of *there* here, because the Inactivity Condition would prevent *it* from being merged with a V-bar like that in (i) which contains a constituent with an active case feature, such as the QP *every hope of finding survivors*.) The affixal T constituent serves as a probe because it is the highest head in the structure, and because its uninterpretable person/number features make it active. Consequently, T searches for active goals, locating the expletive pronoun *there*, which is active by virtue of its uninterpretable person feature. However, since *there* carries no number feature and so cannot value the number feature on T, the T head probes further until it locates the (person-and-number-specified) QP *every hope of finding*

survivors (active by virtue of having an uninterpretable case feature). The person/number features on T are valued as third person singular (in accordance with (83i)) via multiple agreement with *there* and *every hope of finding survivors*, and deleted (in accordance with (84i)) via agreement with the φ-complete goal *every hope of finding survivors*. The uninterpretable person feature on expletive *there* is deleted via agreement with the φ-complete (affixal) T-probe, in accordance with (84i). Via agreement with the φ-complete affix in T, the unvalued case feature on *every hope of finding survivors* is valued as nominative in conformity with (83ii) and deleted in accordance with (84i). The uninterpretable EPP feature on the T-probe (which requires T to have a specifier with person) is deleted by movement of the closest person-specified goal (= *there*) to spec-T, in conformity with (84ii). These various agreement, case assignment, movement and deletion operations take place simultaneously on the T-cycle, in conformity with (85), so deriving the TP shown below:

(ii)

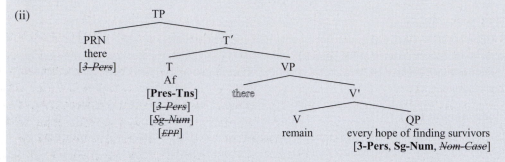

The resulting TP is then merged with a null complementiser containing an interpretable declarative force feature. The entire structure in (ii) (including both interpretable and uninterpretable features) is then handed over to the PF component, where the affix in T is lowered onto the verb *remain*, which is consequently spelled out as the third person singular present tense form *remains*. The structure in (ii) is simultaneously handed over to the semantic component, where only undeleted features (i.e. the bold-printed interpretable features) are visible in accordance with (84iii). Since all unvalued features have been valued (and all uninterpretable features deleted), the derivation converges both at the interface with the PF component and at the interface with the semantic component.

8 Split projections

8.1 Overview

Hitherto, we have assumed a simple model of clause structure in which complete clauses are CP+TP+VP structures. However, in this chapter, we review work suggesting that CP, TP and VP should be *split* into more than one type of projection – hence the title of this chapter. We begin by looking at arguments that the CP layer of clause structure should be split into a number of separate (**Force Phrase**, **Topic Phrase** and **Focus Phrase**) projections. We then go on to explore the possibility of splitting TP into separate **Tense Phrase**, **Aspect Phrase** and **Mood Phrase** projections. In the remainder of the chapter, we look at evidence that verb phrases should be split into two separate projections – one headed by a **lexical verb** and the other by an abstract **light verb**.

8.2 Split CP: Force, Topic and Focus projections

Our discussion of wh-movement in chapter 5 was concerned with movement of wh-expressions to the periphery of clauses (i.e. to a position above TP). However, as examples like (1) below illustrate, it is not simply wh-constituents which undergo movement to the clause periphery:

(1)   *No other colleague* would he turn to

In (1), *no other colleague* (which is the complement of the preposition *to*) has been **focused/focalised** – i.e. moved to the front of the sentence in order to **focus** it (and thereby give it special emphasis). At first sight, it would appear that the focused negative expression moves into spec-C and that the pre-subject auxiliary *would* moves from T to C in the manner shown in (2) below (simplified inter alia by not showing *he* originating in spec-V):

(2)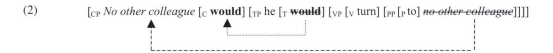

[CP *No other colleague* [C **would**] [TP he [T **would**] [VP [V turn] [PP [P to] *no other colleague*]]]]

However, one problem posed by the CP analysis of focusing/focalisation sketched in (2) is that a structure containing a preposed focused constituent can occur after a complementiser like *that*, as in (3) below:

(3)   I am absolutely convinced [**that** *no other colleague* would he turn to]

This suggests that there must be more than one type of CP projection 'above' TP in clauses: more specifically, there must be one type of projection which hosts preposed focused constituents, and another type of projection which hosts complementisers. Reasoning along these lines, Luigi Rizzi (1997, 2001b, 2004) suggests that CP should be *split* into a number of different projections – an analysis widely referred to as the **split CP hypothesis**. More specifically, he suggests that complementisers (by virtue of their role in specifying whether a given clause is declarative, interrogative, imperative or exclamative in **force**) should be analysed as **Force** markers heading a **ForceP** (= Force Phrase) projection, and that focused constituents should be analysed as contained within a separate **FocP** (= Focus Phrase) headed by a **Foc** constituent (= Focus marker). If we suppose that the preposed negative expression italicised in (3) is focused and that the complementiser *that* serves to mark the complement clause as declarative in force, the bracketed complement clause in (3) will have the structure shown in simplified form below:

(4)

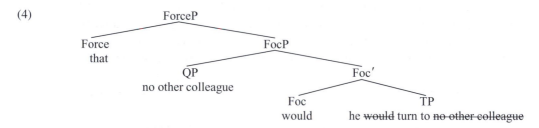

The focused QP/quantifier phrase *no other colleague* originates as the complement of the preposition *to* and (by virtue of being focused) moves from complement position within PP into specifier position within FocP. The auxiliary *would* originates in T and from there moves into the head Foc position of FocP. One way of describing the relevant data is to suppose that the head Foc constituent of FocP carries an edge feature [EF] which allows it to attract a negative expression to move into spec-FocP (in which position the preposed negative expression is interpreted as being focused), and that Foc is a strong (affixal) head carrying a tense feature which attracts the auxiliary *would* to move from T into Foc.

From a discourse perspective, a focused constituent typically represents *new* information (i.e. information not previously mentioned in the discourse and unfamiliar to the hearer). In this connection, consider the following dialogue:

(5)   SPEAKER A: Would you ever cheat in really tough exams?
           SPEAKER B: *Under no circumstances* would I cheat in exams

Here, the new information given by speaker B is that there are *no circumstances* under which he would cheat in exams: accordingly, the italicised preposed negative phrase is said to be *focused* in 5B.

In respect of their information content, focused constituents differ from another class of preposed expressions which serve as the **topic** of the clause immediately containing them. Topics typically represent *old* information (i.e. information which has already been mentioned in the discourse and hence is known to the hearer). In this connection, consider the sentence produced by speaker B below:

(6)   SPEAKER A: The demonstrators have been looting shops and setting fire to cars

    SPEAKER B: *That kind of behaviour*, we cannot tolerate in a civilised society

Here, the italicised phrase *that kind of behaviour* refers back to the activity of looting shops and setting fire to cars mentioned earlier by speaker A, and so is the **topic** of the discourse. Since the topic *that kind of behaviour* is the complement of the verb *tolerate* it would be expected to occupy the canonical complement position following *tolerate*. Instead, it ends up at the front of the overall sentence, and so would seem to have undergone a movement operation of some kind. Since the relevant movement operation serves to mark the preposed constituent as the topic of the sentence, it is widely known as **topicalisation**. However, since it moves a maximal projection to a specifier position on the periphery of the clause, topicalisation can (like focusing and wh-movement) be regarded as a particular instance of the more general **A-bar movement** operation we looked at in chapter 5, whereby a moved constituent is attracted into an A-bar specifier position (i.e. the kind of specifier position which can be occupied by arguments and adjuncts alike).

Rizzi argues that just as focused constituents occupy the specifier position within a Focus Phrase, so too topicalised constituents occupy the specifier position within a **Topic Phrase**. This in turn raises the question of where Topic Phrases are positioned relative to other constituents within the clause. In this connection, consider the italicised clause in (7) below:

(7)   He had seen something truly evil – prisoners being ritually raped, tortured and mutilated. He prayed *that atrocities like those, never again would he witness*

In the italicised clause in (7), *that* marks the declarative force of the clause; *atrocities like those* is the object of the verb *witness* and has been preposed in order to mark it as the topic of the sentence (since it refers back to the acts of rape, torture and mutilation mentioned in the previous sentence); the preposed negative adverbial phrase *never again* is a focused constituent, and hence requires auxiliary inversion. Thus, the italicised *that*-clause in (7) has the simplified structure

shown below:

(8)

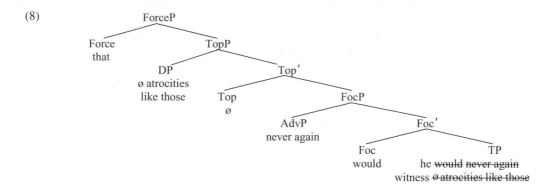

We can assume that the head Top constituent of the Topic Phrase carries an edge feature which allows it to attract a maximal projection to move into the specifier position within the Topic Phrase – in which position the preposed maximal projection is interpreted as the topic of the relevant sentence. If we further assume that Top is a weak head (and so does not carry a tense feature attracting a tensed auxiliary), we can account for the fact that the auxiliary *would* remains in the strong Foc position and does not raise to the weak Top position.

Rizzi's **split CP** analysis raises interesting questions about the syntax of the kind of wh-movement operation which we find (inter alia) in interrogatives, relatives and exclamatives. Within the unitary (unsplit) CP analysis outlined in chapter 5, it was clear that wh-phrases moved into spec-C; but if CP can be split into a number of distinct projections (including a Force Phrase, a Topic Phrase and a Focus Phrase), the question arises as to which of these projections serves as the landing-site for wh-movement. Rizzi (1997, p. 289) suggests that 'relative operators occupy the highest specifier position, the spec of Force'. In this connection, consider the syntax of the bracketed relative clauses in (9) below:

(9) (a)   A university is the kind of place [in which, that kind of behaviour, we cannot tolerate]

(b)   Syntax is the kind of subject [which only very rarely will students enjoy]

In (9a), the preposed wh-expression *in which* precedes the preposed topic *that kind of behaviour*; in (9b) the preposed relative pronoun *which* precedes the preposed focused expression *only very rarely*. If Rizzi is right in suggesting that preposed relative operator expressions occupy specifier position within the Force Phrase, the bracketed relative clauses in (9a,b) above will have the simplified structures shown below:

(10) (a)   [ForceP *in which* [Force ∅] [TopP **that kind of behaviour** [Top ∅] [TP we cannot tolerate **t** *t*]]]

(b)   [ForceP *which* [Force ∅] [FocP **only very rarely** [Foc w̲i̲l̲l̲] [TP students t̲ enjoy *t* **t**]]]

(To save space, trace copies of moved constituents are shown as *t* and printed in the same typeface as their antecedent.)

In much the same way, Rizzi argues that an interrogative wh-expression occupies spec-Force in complement-clause questions. Evidence in support of this claim comes from sentences such as the following (from Culicover 1991):

(11) (a)   Lee wonders [whether under no circumstances at all would Robin volunteer]
    (b)   Lee wonders [why under no circumstances at all would Robin volunteer]

Here, the wh-expressions *whether/why* occur to the left of the focused negative phrase *under no circumstances*, suggesting that *whether/why* do not occupy specifier position within FocP but rather some higher position – and since ForceP is the highest projection within the clause, it is plausible to suppose that *whether/why* occupy the specifier position within ForceP in structures like (11). Further evidence in support of the same conclusion comes from contrasts such as the following:

(12) (a)   I cannot see [*how*, **this kind of behaviour**, we can tolerate
                                    in a civilised society]
    (b)   *I cannot see [*this kind of behaviour*, **how** we can tolerate
                                    in a civilised society]

The observation that an (italicised) interrogative wh-expression can be followed – but not preceded – by a (bold-printed) topic in complement-clause questions like those bracketed in (12) is consistent with the view that a preposed wh-expression in a complement-clause question occupies spec-ForceP, and hence is positioned above a topic phrase. Further evidence in support of this conclusion comes from the fact that in colloquial English we often find structures like those below (from Radford (1988, p. 500), recorded from radio and TV broadcasts), in which an (italicised) preposed interrogative expression precedes the (underlined) complementiser introducing a [bracketed] embedded clause:

(13) (a)   I'm not sure [*what kind of ban* that FIFA has in mind]
    (b)   We'll see [*what sort of pace* that Daley Thompson's running at]
    (c)   It'll probably be evident from the field [*which of the players* that are feeling the heat most]

If the (underlined) complementiser is a Force head, it is plausible to supposed that the (italicised) interrogative expression preceding it occupies the specifier position within ForceP.

A question raised by Rizzi's analysis of relative and interrogative wh-clauses is where preposed wh-expressions move in exclamative clauses. In this connection, consider (14) below:

(14) (a)   *How many of their policies* **only rarely** do politicians get around to implementing!
    (b)   *In how many countries*, that kind of behaviour, autocratic leaders would simply not tolerate!

(c)   *In how many countries of the world*, <u>such behaviour</u>, **under no circumstances** would autocratic leaders tolerate!

In (14a), the italicised exclamative wh-expression *how many of their policies* precedes the bold-printed focused constituent **only rarely**. In (14b) the exclamative wh-phrase *in how many countries* precedes the underlined topic *that kind of behaviour*. And in (14c), an italicised exclamative expression precedes both an underlined topicalised expression and a bold-printed focused expression. Although the resulting sentences are clearly somewhat contrived, they suggest that exclamative wh-expressions (like wh-pronouns in relative clauses and interrogative wh-expressions in complement-clause questions) move into the specifier position within ForceP.

From what we have said so far, it might seem plausible to conclude that relative, interrogative and exclamative wh-expressions always move to the specifier position within ForceP. However, Rizzi (1997, p. 299) maintains that a preposed interrogative wh-expression 'ends up in Spec of Foc in main questions'. Furthermore, he maintains (p. 295) that 'There can be . . . only one structural Focus position per clause.' The twin assumptions that interrogative wh-expressions in main-clause questions move to the specifier position in a Focus Phrase and that no clause may contain more than one Focus Phrase projection together provide a straightforward account of the ungrammaticality of main clause questions such as (15) below:

(15) (a)   *What never again will you do?
     (b)   *What will never again you do?

If both *what* and *never again* (when preposed) move into the specifier position within FocP, if Foc allows only one focused constituent as its specifier, and if no clause may contain more than one FocP constituent, it follows that (15a) will be ruled out by virtue of Foc having two specifiers (*what* and *never again*) and that (15b) will be ruled out by virtue of requiring two Focus Phrase constituents (one hosting *what* and another hosting *never again*). Likewise, multiple wh-movement questions (i.e. questions in which more than one wh-expression is preposed) such as (16) below will be ruled out in a similar fashion:

(16) (a)   *Who where did he send?
     (b)   *Who did where he send?

Thus, the conclusion which Rizzi's observation leads us to is that wh-expressions move to the edge of a Focus Phrase projection in main-clause wh-questions, but move to spec-ForceP in other types of clause.

Further evidence in support of the claim that interrogative wh-expressions move to spec-FocP (and not to spec-ForceP) in main-clause questions comes from contrasts such as:

(17) (a)   **That kind of behaviour**, *how* can we tolerate in a civilised society?
     (b)   **How can **that kind of behaviour** we tolerate in a civilised society?

If *how* were in spec-ForceP, we would be unable to account for the observation that it follows the bold-printed topic phrase in (17a), given Rizzi's assumption that ForceP is always the highest projection in a split CP. By contrast, if *how* is in spec-FocP, the order of projections in (17a) is precisely as in (8), with FocP being positioned under TopP, and TopP being positioned under a ForceP projection with a null head.

What remains to be accounted for is why the italicised focused wh-word cannot precede the bold-printed topic in (17b). The answer relates to the syntax of the auxiliary *can* which occupies the head Foc position of FocP in (17b). *Can* originates in the head T position of TP and in order to get into Foc must either move directly from T to Foc, or move (in successive-cyclic fashion) through Top into Foc – these two possibilities being shown by the arrowed movements in the (abbreviated) structure below:

(18)   [ForceP [Force Ø] [FocP how [Foc *can*] [TopP that kind of behaviour [Top ø] [TP we [T *can*] tolerate...]]]]

However, direct movement from T to Foc (represented by the dotted arrow) is ruled out because it would violate the Head Movement Constraint (which allows a head to move only into the next highest head position in the structure containing it); and successive-cyclic movement from V through Top into Foc (represented by the two solid arrows) is ruled out because Top is a weak head, and so cannot attract T to move to Top. Consequently, the topic must be positioned above the focused wh-expression in main-clause questions like (17) in English.

A further question raised by Rizzi's analysis is why interrogative wh-expressions should occupy two different types of position, moving to spec-FocP in a main-clause question structure like (19a) below, but to spec-ForceP in a complement-clause question structure like that bracketed in (19b):

(19) (a)   [ForceP [Force Ø] [FocP *what dress* [Foc were] [TP you [T ~~were~~] wearing]]]?
     (b)   He asked [ForceP *what dress* [Force Ø] [TP you [T were] wearing]]

Part of the answer may lie in the semantic properties of interrogative wh-words, which not only make them suitable candidates for focusing (because a focused expression carries new information, and interrogative wh-words ask for new information), but also mark interrogative force. By virtue of having properties making them suitable to be focused, they can occupy the specifier position in a Focus Phrase as in (19a); but by virtue of being interrogative in force, they can alternatively occupy specifier position within a Force Phrase as in (19b). More generally, it would appear that constituents which are able to move to the specifier position in FocP share in common the semantic property that they are *operator expressions* (i.e. expressions containing an operator). Negative and interrogative expressions contain an operator which licenses (i.e. allows the occurrence of) a subordinate polarity item such as partitive *any*, whereas exclamative and relative wh-expressions do not – as we see from the contrast below:

(20) (a)   <u>What sympathy</u> did *any* of the protestors get?
   (b)   <u>Not a grain of sympathy</u> did *any* of the protestors get
   (c)   *<u>What a lot of sympathy</u> *any* of the protestors got!
   (d)   *He was surprised at the sympathy <u>which</u> *any* of the protestors got

Consequently, operator expressions like the underlined interrogative expression in (20a) and the underlined negative expression in (20b) can move to spec-FocP, but not non-operator expressions like the underlined exclamative expression in (20c) or the underlined relative pronoun in (20d). Instead, exclamative and relative wh-expressions move to the specifier position within a Force Phrase (which might more appropriately be called a *Type Phrase*, given that a relative pronoun marks a clause as relative in *type* rather than in *force*).

However, all of this still leaves the question of why interrogative expressions move to spec-ForceP (and not to spec-FocP) in embedded questions like (19b). It may well be that the answer lies in *selection*. In the use illustrated in (19b), the verb *ask* selects an interrogative complement. If we suppose that a question-asking predicate like *ask* requires a complement with an interrogative edge (i.e. with an interrogative expression on the edge of the relevant projection which serves to mark the relevant clause as interrogative in type), then it follows that movement of an interrogative wh-expression in an interrogative complement clause must be to the specifier position of the highest head in the selected structure – hence to spec-ForceP. By contrast, a main clause is unselected, and so a focused interrogative wh-expression moves only as far as spec-FocP (perhaps for economy reasons, there being no necessity for further movement to spec-ForceP in a main clause: however, we shall offer an alternative answer at the end of §9.4). If Foc is a strong head and Force a weak head, we can account for why auxiliary inversion occurs in main-clause questions like (19a), but not in complement-clause questions like (19b).

On the other hand, because preposed negative expressions are operator expressions but do not mark force (as we see from the fact that there are no predicates which select a negative complement), they move to spec-FocP in both main and complement clauses alike. And because Foc is always a strong head, we can account for why we find auxiliary inversion in complement clauses like that bracketed in (3) above *I am absolutely convinced* [*that no other colleague would he turn to*]. The bracketed complement clause in (3) would have the structure shown in simplified form in (21) below:

(21)   [$_{\text{ForceP}}$ [$_{\text{Force}}$ that] [$_{\text{FocP}}$ no other colleague [$_{\text{Foc}}$ *would*] [$_{\text{TP}}$ he [$_{\text{T}}$ ~~*would*~~] turn
to ~~no other colleague~~]]]

Its main-clause counterpart *No other colleague would he turn to* would have an analogous structure, save for the head Force constituent of ForceP being null.

A final descriptive detail which needs to be added relates to the spellout of the Force head in structures such as the following:

(22) (a)   He admitted [ForceP [Force that/ø] [TP he [T is] really enjoying syntax]]

   (b)   He admitted [ForceP [Force that/*ø] [TopP syntax [Top ø] [TP he [T is] really enjoying ~~syntax~~]]]

   (c)   He admitted [ForceP [Force that/*ø] [FocP nothing else [Foc would]

                     [TP he [T ~~would~~] rather do ~~nothing else~~]]]

As these examples illustrate, the Force head in a finite declarative clause can be spelled out as *that* irrespective of whether its complement is a TP as in (22a), or a TopP as in (22b), or a FocP as in (22c). By contrast, a declarative Force head can only have a null spellout in structures like (22a) where it has a TP complement. One way of handling the relevant contast is in terms of *selection* if we suppose that a null declarative complementiser can only select a TP complement, whereas the overt complementiser *that* can select a much wider range of complements (e.g. TP or TopP, or FocP) – a solution which obviously presupposes that we treat *that* and ø as distinct complementisers.

Although in this section we have outlined Rizzi's *split CP* analysis of the left periphery of clauses, it should be noted that (because we have little further to say about topicalisation and focalisation), we shall for the most part revert to using the traditional unsplit CP analysis of the clause periphery in the rest of the book, and thus follow Chomsky (2005b, p. 9) in adopting the convention that 'C is shorthand for the region that Rizzi (1997) calls the *left periphery*.'

8.3   Split TP: Aspect and Mood projections

Parallel to Rizzi's pioneering work on splitting the peripheral C head into a number of separate types of head (such as Force, Topic and Finiteness), there have been attempts over the past two decades to split the inflectional head termed INFL in Chomsky (1981) into separate inflectional heads including not only Tense, but also Aspect, Mood and Agreement. However, Chomsky (1995) argued against the postulation of Agr[eement] heads on the twin grounds that (i) agreement is a relation rather than a category, and (ii) agreement features are uninterpretable, and hence a head which carried only agreement features could not be assigned any interpretation at the semantics interface, and would cause the derivation to crash: accordingly, Chomsky (1995, p. 355) proposed 'eliminating Agr [heads] from UG entirely' on conceptual grounds. However, Tense, Aspect and Mood are interpretable features, and so there are no such conceptual objections to positing that these are each realised on different functional heads. Since we have argued throughout our book that all clauses contain a T constituent carrying an interpretable tense feature, in this section we concentrate on the question of whether there is evidence for positing the existence of Aspect and Mood heads in English.

Felser (1999a) argues that in verb–particle structures such as *take the rubbish out*, the verb *take* originates immediately adjacent to the particle *out* (as in *take out the rubbish*), but subsequently moves into the head Aspect position of an Aspect Phrase projection which is positioned above VP but below TP, so becoming separated from the particle, and resulting in structures such as:

(23) (a)   [CP [C ∅] [TP he [T was] [AspP [Asp taking] [VP the rubbish [V ~~taking~~] out]]]]
  (b)   [CP [C ∅] [TP he [T had] [AspP [Asp taken] [VP the rubbish [V ~~taken~~] out]]]]
  (c)   [CP [C ∅] [TP he [T ∅] [AspP [Asp took] [VP the rubbish [V ~~took~~] out]]]]

The assumption that the verb TAKE moves into a position above the V position in which it originates accounts for how the verb *take* comes to be separated from the particle *out*, while the assumption that movement is to a head below T accounts for why the verb cannot subsequently undergo T-to-C movement, e.g. in sentences such as:

(24)   *Took he out the rubbish?

Felser argues that perception verb complements such as that bracketed in (25a) below have the status of Aspect Phrases, so that the bracketed complement clause in (25a) has the structure shown in highly simplified form in (25b):

(25) (a)   We saw [him taking the rubbish out]
  (b)   We saw [AsP him [Asp taking] the rubbish out]

She argues that the verb *take* raises from the head V position of VP into the head Asp position of AspP, while its subject *him* raises to the specifier position within AspP and is assigned exceptional accusative case by the transitive verb *saw*.

However, while evidence of the kind outlined above in support of positing an independent Aspect head in English is suggestive, it should be pointed out that it is far from conclusive. For example (as we will see in §8.5), it turns out that a split projection analysis of Verb Phrases can handle the syntax of the kind of verb–particle structures discussed by Felser, without the need for positing an independent Aspect head. The analyses we present throughout the rest of this book, therefore, will ignore the possibility that English may have an Aspect head (except in structures like *She may (not) be telling the truth/She may (not) have told the truth/She may (not) have been telling the truth*, which contain one or more overt aspectual auxiliaries *be/have* positioned below the T-auxiliary *may* and – in negative clauses – below the negative particle *not*: in such cases, each occurrence of the aspectual auxiliary could be argued to head a separate AspP projection – though we will continue to label such projections AUXP, as in earlier chapters).

Having very briefly surveyed evidence for positing an Aspect head, we now turn to look at evidence put forward by Schütze (2004) that English finite clauses contain a further kind of inflectional head which marks the property of (indicative, subjunctive or imperative) **Mood** (abbreviated to **M**). Schütze claims that there is empirical evidence in support of positing a Mood Phrase/MP projection between TP and CP, so that canonical negative clauses are of the form CP+MP+TP+NEGP+VP. (A complication which we will overlook here is

Schütze's assumption that non-negative clauses contain a positive counterpart of NEGP: see the discussion of POLP in §4.8.) He maintains that M is the locus of modals and mood morphemes: more specifically, he posits that M can contain either a modal auxiliary stem (e.g. *can/will/must*), or an abstract (indicative or subjunctive) mood morpheme, below denoted as $\emptyset_{IND}$ and $\emptyset_{SUB}$ respectively. Schütze further assumes that an indicative mood morpheme is spelled out as an inflected form of DO when not attached to any other verbal stem (so that DO-support is found in indicative but not subjunctive clauses). By contrast, T is the locus of tense affixes, in the sense that 'The only elements generated under T are tense affixes' (Schütze 2004, p. 507). T can contain either a strong affix which acquires a host by triggering movement of a lexical verb from V to T, or a weak affix which acquires a host by raising to attach to an auxiliary in M. Neg is the locus of the negative particles *not/n't*, and Schütze posits that these are generated in the head Neg position of of NEGP (and not in the specifier position of NEGP as we assumed in §4.7): he also assumes that Neg is not a strong head and so blocks a lexical verb raising from V to T (because direct movement of the verb from V to T is barred by the Head Movement Constraint, and successive-cyclic movement of the verb from V through Neg into T is barred by virtue of Neg not being strong and so being unable to attract V to move to Neg); however, a clitic negative like *n't* can itself cliticise to an M head above it. Subject–auxiliary inversion is treated as M-to-C movement, so only a constituent in M (not one in T) can undergo inversion and raise to C: subjects are also assumed to raise to spec-M rather than to spec-T. Schütze argues that his account obviates the need for positing the traditional Affix Lowering operation (by which an affix in T is lowered onto a verb in V), and that Head Movement is driven by the requirement for an affix to be attached to an appropriate kind of head (a strong affix remaining in situ and triggering raising of a head below it, and a weak affix raising to attach to a head above it).

How Schütze's system works can be illustrated (in a simplified fashion) as follows. Consider first a simple indicative clause structure like (26) below containing a modal such as *will* and a present tense affix Af_{PRES} (with the subject *he* originating as the specifier of the verb *help* and raising to become the specifier of the modal *will* – as shown by the arrow):

(26)

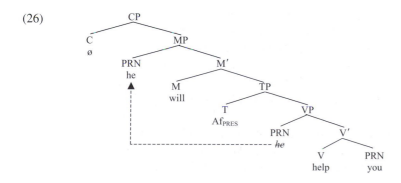

If the affix in T is weak (and so finds a host by attaching to the head immediately above it), it will raise to attach to the modal stem *will* in M, so forming:

(27)   [CP [C ∅] [MP he [M will+*Af*PRES] [TP [T ~~*Af*PRES~~] [VP ~~he~~ [V help] you]]]]

The modal is spelled out as *will* if (as here) the affix is present tense, and as *would* if it is past tense. The M constituent containing *will+affix* can then undergo subsequent movement to adjoin to a null interrogative C in a main-clause question structure such as:

(28)   [CP ~~whether~~ [C *will*+*Af*PRES+∅] [MP he [M ~~will+*Af*PRES~~]
                                [TP [T ~~*Af*PRES~~] [VP ~~he~~ [V help] you]]]]

so ultimately deriving *Will he help you?* By contrast, if the T-affix in (26) were strong, it would attract the verb *help* to adjoin to it, so leaving the modal *will* without a tense affix (and thereby causing the derivation to crash, because the PF component has no spellout for a tenseless form of a modal like *will*).

Now consider what happens in an auxiliariless indicative clause structure such as the following:

(29)   [CP [C ∅] [MP they [M ∅IND] [TP [T *Af*PRES] [VP ~~they~~ [V like] you]]]]

If the affix in T is strong in (29), it will trigger movement of the verb *like* from V to T, so forming the structure:

(30)   [CP [C ∅] [MP they [M ∅IND] [TP [T *like*+*Af*PRES] [VP ~~they~~ [V ~~like~~] you]]]]

Since the requirement for *like* to have a tense affix and for the tense affix to be attached to an overt verb stem is satisfied by raising the verb from V to T, no further movement is possible in this kind of structure (the null indicative mood morpheme in M not being a strong affix), and the sentence will be spelled out as *They like you*. By contrast, if the T-affix is weak in (30), it will raise to attach to the null mood morpheme in M, so forming the structure:

(31)   [CP [C ∅] [MP they [M ∅IND+*Af*PRES] [TP [T ~~*Af*PRES~~] [VP ~~they~~ [V like] you]]]]

Since the resulting indicative M constituent contains no verbal stem, it is spelled out as an appropriately inflected form of supportive DO, so deriving *They do like you*. In order to account for the fact that sentences like *They do like you* are ungrammatical in standard varieties of English unless DO is emphatic, Schütze invokes an economy condition which amounts to 'Use as few words as possible' – a principle which is claimed to rule out *They do like you* on the grounds that it has the more economical counterpart *They like you*.

Now consider a negative indicative clause such as that below:

(32)   [CP [C ∅] [MP he [M ∅IND] [TP [T *Af*PRES] [NEGP [Neg not]
                                [VP ~~he~~ [V appreciate] you]]]]]

If the affix in T is strong here, the verb *appreciate* cannot raise from V to attach to the affix in T because single-step movement is blocked by the Head Movement

Constraint, and multiple-step movement is blocked by the fact that Neg is not a strong head and so cannot attract a lexical verb to attach to it: in either eventuality, the derivation will crash. But if the affix in T is weak, it will raise to attach to the indicative mood head, so forming the structure:

(33)   [$_{CP}$ [$_C$ ø] [$_{MP}$ he [$_M$ ø$_{IND}$+Af$_{PRES}$] [$_{TP}$ [$_T$ ~~Af$_{PRES}$~~] [$_{NEGP}$ [$_{Neg}$ not]

[$_{VP}$ ~~he~~ [$_V$ appreciate] you]]]]]

If (as here) M contains no verbal stem, the INDICATIVE MOOD+PRESENT TENSE morphemes in M will be spelled out as an appropriately inflected form of DO, so deriving *He does not appreciate you*.

Schütze claims that a significant advantage of his split TP analysis is that it dispenses with the need for positing the traditional Affix Lowering operation by which an affix in T is lowered onto a verb in V. However, it is not clear that Schütze entirely succeeds in attaining this goal. In this connection, consider a structure like that below in which T contains a strong affix which triggers raising of the verb from V to T:

(34)   [$_{CP}$ [$_C$ ø] [$_{MP}$ he [$_M$ ø$_{IND}$] [$_{TP}$ [$_T$ *like*+Af$_{PRES}$] [$_{VP}$ ~~he~~ [$_V$ ~~like$_{PRES}$~~] you]]]]

An apparent problem which arises here is that in order to determine whether to spell out the verb as *likes* or *like*, the PF component needs to 'know' whether the verb is indicative, subjunctive or imperative in mood, since *-s* is an indicative mood inflection. However, the mood feature is marked on M rather than on T. Consequently, some way needs to be found of marking the verb in T for mood. We clearly cannot raise the verb from T to M, since this would wrongly predict that the verb would be eligible to undergo M-to-C movement in interrogatives (i.e. auxiliary inversion). The only possibility would seem to be to lower the null indicative mood morpheme from M onto C via Affix Lowering, so deriving the structure (35) below:

(35)   [$_{CP}$ [$_C$ ø] [$_{MP}$ he [$_M$ ø$_{IND}$] [$_{TP}$ [$_T$ like+Af+ø$_{IND}$] [$_{VP}$ ~~he~~ [$_V$ ~~like~~] you]]]]

The verb could then be spelled out as the third person singular present indicative form *likes*. However, such an analysis would undermine Schütze's argument that his analysis dispenses with the need for Affix Lowering. Moreover, the problem is compounded if M is the locus of the (third person singular) agreement features in the clause, as will be the case if movement of the subject out of VP into spec-MP is contingent on agreement between M and the subject: then not only mood features but also agreement features will have to be lowered from M onto the verb in T by Affix Lowering.

Overall, Schütze's postulation of an M head independent of T faces two main problems. One is that derivations will crash if the 'wrong' choice of items is made. For example, as noted earlier, a structure like (26) will crash if T contains a strong (rather than a weak) affix, because modal *will* is left without a tense affix to attach to it, and the PF component has no spellout for tenseless modals. This poses a problem if we follow Chomsky (2006, p. 2) in positing that grammars should meet a condition of 'efficient computation'. Moreover, Schütze's analysis would seem to still require the Affix Lowering operation which it was designed to dispense with. Thus, while the idea that Mood should head a separate projection from Tense is far from implausible, the particular implementation of this idea in Schütze's analysis of English seems problematic, and hence we will not pursue this possibility any further in the remainder of the book. Instead, in the rest of this chapter we will look at work which has become widely accepted arguing that Verb Phrases should be split into at least two distinct projections.

8.4   Split VP: Transitive ergative structures

Having looked at evidence that CP and TP can be split into a number of different projections, we now turn to look at evidence arguing that VPs should be split into two distinct projections – an outer *shell* and an inner *core*. This has become known as the **VP-shell** (or **split VP**) analysis.

The sentences which we have analysed so far have generally contained simple Verb Phrases headed by a verb with a single complement. Such single-complement structures can easily be accommodated within the binary-branching framework adopted here, since all we need say is that a verb merges with its complement to form a (binary-branching) V-bar constituent, and that the resulting V-bar merges with its subject to form a binary-branching VP constituent. However, a particular problem for the binary-branching framework is posed by three-place predicates like those italicised in (36) below which have a (bold-printed) subject and two (bracketed) complements:

(36) (a)   **He** *rolled* [the ball] [down the hill]
   (b)   **He** *filled* [the bath] [with water]
   (c)   **He** *broke* [the vase] [into pieces]
   (d)   **They** *withdrew* [the troops] [from Ruritania]

If we assume that complements are sisters to heads, it might seem as if the V-bar constituent headed by *rolled* in (36a) has the structure (37) below:

(37)

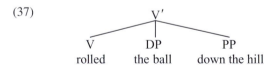

However, a structure such as (37) is problematic within the framework adopted here. After all, it is a ternary-branching structure (V-bar branches into the three separate constituents, namely the V *rolled*, the DP *the ball* and the PP *down the hill*), and this poses an obvious problem within a framework which assumes that the merger operation which forms phrases is an inherently **binary** operation which can only combine constituents in a *pairwise* fashion. Moreover, a ternary-branching structure such as (37) would wrongly predict that the string *the ball*

down the hill does not form a constituent, and so cannot be coordinated with another similar string (given the traditional assumption that only identical constituents can be conjoined) – yet this prediction is falsified by sentences such as:

(38)   He rolled *the ball down the hill* and *the acorn up the mountain*

How can we overcome these problems?

One answer is to suppose that transitive structures like *He rolled the ball down the hill* have a complex internal structure which is parallel in some respects to causative structures like *He made the ball roll down the hill* (where MAKE has roughly the same meaning as CAUSE). On this view *the ball roll down the hill* would serve as a VP complement of a null causative verb (which can be thought of as an invisible counterpart of MAKE). We can further suppose that the null causative verb is affixal in nature, and so triggers raising of the verb *roll* to adjoin to the causative verb, deriving a structure loosely paraphraseable as *He made+roll [the ball ~~roll~~ down the hill]*, where ~~roll~~ is a null copy of the moved verb *roll*. We could then say that the string *the ball down the hill* in (38) is a VP remnant headed by a null copy of the moved verb *roll*. Since this string is a VP constituent, we correctly predict that it can be co-ordinated with another VP remnant like *the acorn up the mountain* – as is indeed the case in (38).

Analysing structures like *roll the ball down the hill* as transitive counterparts of intransitive structures is by no means implausible, since many three-place transitive predicates like *roll* can also be used as two-place intransitive predicates in which the (italicised) DP which immediately follows the (bold-printed) verb in the three-place structure functions as the subject in the two-place structure – as we see from sentence pairs such as the following:

(39) (a)   They will **roll** *the ball* down the hill
     (b)   *The ball* will **roll** down the hill

(40) (a)   He **filled** *the bath* with water
     (b)   *The bath* **filled** with water

(41) (a)   He **broke** *the vase* into pieces
     (b)   *The vase* **broke** into pieces

(42) (a)   They **withdrew** *the troops* from Ruritania
     (b)   *The troops* **withdrew** from Ruritania

(43) (a)   They **closed** *the store* down
     (b)   *The store* **closed** down

(44) (a)   They **moved** *the headquarters* to Brooklyn
     (b)   *The headquarters* **moved** to Brooklyn

(Verbs which allow this dual use as either three-place transitive predicates or two-place intransitive predicates are sometimes referred to as **ergative predicates**.) Moreover, the italicised DP seems to play the same thematic role with respect to the bold-printed verb in each pair of examples: for example, *the ball* is the

THEME argument of *roll* (i.e. the entity which undergoes a rolling motion) both in (39a) *They will roll the ball down the hill* and in (39b) *The ball will roll down the hill*. Evidence that *the ball* plays the same semantic role in both sentences comes from the fact that the italicised argument is subject to the same pragmatic restrictions on the choice of expression which can fulfil the relevant argument function in each type of sentence: cf.

(45) (a)   *The ball/The rock/!The theory/!Sincerity* will **roll** gently down the hill
   (b)   They will **roll** *the ball/the rock/!the theory/!sincerity* gently down the hill

If principles of UG correlate thematic structure with syntactic structure in a uniform fashion (in accordance with the **Uniform Theta Assignment Hypothesis/UTAH** discussed in §6.6), then it follows that two arguments which fulfil the same thematic function with respect to a given predicate must be merged in the same position in the syntax.

An analysis within the spirit of UTAH would be to assume that both a transitive structure like (39a) *They will roll the ball down the hill* and its intransitive counterpart (39b) *The ball will roll down the hill* contain the same 'core' VP structure [vp *the ball* [v *roll*] *down the hill*]. However, the question which then arises is how the verb *roll* comes to precede the DP *the ball* in the transitive Verb Phrase *roll the ball down the hill*. A plausible answer to this question is to suppose that the verb *roll* moves from its initial position below *the ball* into a higher verb position above *the ball*. Such an analysis requires us to split transitive Verb Phrases into two separate projections, and to analyse them as comprising an outer shell and an inner core.

More concretely, let's make the following assumptions about how the transitive structure (39a) is derived. The lexical verb (= V) *roll* is merged with its PP complement *down the hill* to form the V-bar *roll down the hill*, and this is then merged with the DP *the ball* to form the VP structure (46) below:

(46)

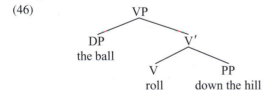

The VP in (46) is then merged as the complement of an abstract causative **light verb (v)** – i.e. a null verb with much the same causative interpretation as the verb MAKE (so that *They will roll the ball down the hill* has a similar interpretation to *They will make the ball roll down the hill*). Let's also suppose that this causative light verb is a strong affix, and attracts the verb *roll* to adjoin to it, forming a structure which can be paraphrased literally as 'make+roll the ball down the hill' – a structure which has an overt counterpart in French structures like *faire rouler la balle en bas de la colline*, literally 'make roll the ball into bottom of the hill'). The resulting v-bar structure is then merged with the subject *they* (which is assigned the θ-role of AGENT argument of the causative light verb), to form the complex vP (47) below (lower-case letters being used to denote the light verb, and the dotted arrow showing movement of the verb *roll* to adjoin to the null light verb ø):

(47)

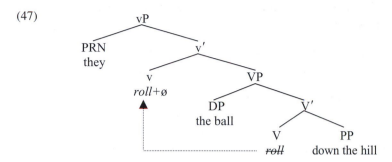

(The affixal light verb is treated as a suffix here, since English is a language which largely uses derivational suffixes, e.g. adding the suffix *-en* to an adjective like *sharp* to form the verb *sharpen* 'make sharp'.)

Subsequently, the vP in (47) merges with the T constituent *will*, the subject *we* raises into spec-T and the resulting TP is merged with a null declarative complementiser, forming the structure (48) below (where the arrows show movements which have taken place in the course of the derivation):

(48)

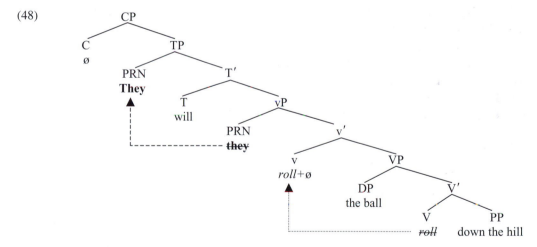

The analysis in (48) correctly specifies the word order in (39a) *They will roll the ball down the hill*.

The VP-shell/split VP analysis in (48) provides an interesting account of an otherwise puzzling aspect of the syntax of sentences like (39a) – namely the fact that adverbs like *gently* can be positioned either before *roll* or after *the ball*, as we see from:

(49) (a)   They will *gently* **roll** the ball down the hill
     (b)   They will **roll** the ball *gently* down the hill

Let's suppose that adverbs like *gently* are **adjuncts**, and that **adjunction** is a different kind of operation from **merger**. Merger extends a constituent into a larger type of projection, so that (e.g.) merging T with an appropriate complement extends T into T-bar, and merging T-bar with an appropriate specifier extends T-bar into TP. By contrast, adjunction extends a constituent into a larger projection of the same type (e.g. adjoining a moved V to a T head forms a larger T head, and adjoining an adverb to an intermediate projection like T-bar extends T-bar into another T-bar constituent). Let's further suppose that *gently* is the kind of adverb which can adjoin to an intermediate verbal projection. Given this assumption and the light-verb analysis in (48), we can then propose the following derivations for (49a–b).

In (49a), the verb *roll* merges with the PP *down the hill* to form the V-bar *roll down the hill*, and this V-bar in turn merges with the DP *the ball* to form the VP *the ball roll down the hill*, with the structure shown in (46) above. This VP then merges with a null causative light-verb ø to which the verb *roll* adjoins, forming the v-bar *roll+ø the ball* ~~roll~~ *down the hill*. The adverb *gently* adjoins to the resulting v-bar to form the larger v-bar *gently roll+ø the ball* ~~roll~~ *down the hill*; and this larger v-bar in turn merges with the subject *they* to form the vP *they gently roll+ø the ball* ~~roll~~ *down the hill*. The vP thereby formed merges with the T constituent *will*, forming the T-bar *will they gently roll+ø the ball* ~~roll~~ *down the hill*. The subject *they* raises to spec-T forming the TP *they will* ~~they~~ *gently roll+ø the ball* ~~roll~~ *down the hill*. This TP is then merged with a null declarative complementiser to derive the structure shown in simplified form in (50) below (with arrows showing movements which have taken place):

(50)

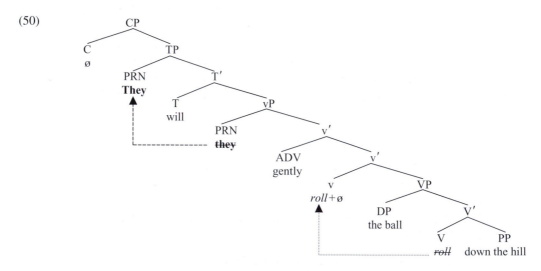

The structure (50) correctly specifies the word order in (49a) *They will gently roll the ball down the hill*.

Now consider how (49b) *They will roll the ball gently down the hill* is derived. As before, the verb *roll* merges with the PP *down the hill*, forming the V-bar *roll*

down the hill. The adverb *gently* is then adjoined to this V-bar to form the larger
V-bar *gently roll down the hill*. This V-bar in turn merges with the DP *the ball*
to form the VP *the ball gently roll down the hill*. The resulting VP is merged
with a causative light verb [$_v$ ø] to which the verb *roll* adjoins, so forming the
v-bar *roll+ø the ball gently ~~roll~~ down the hill*. This v-bar is then merged with
the subject *we* to form the vP *they roll+ø the ball gently ~~roll~~ down the hill*. The
vP thereby formed merges with [$_T$ *will*], forming the T-bar *will they roll+ø the
ball gently ~~roll~~ down the hill*. The subject they raises to spec-T, and TP is merged
with a null declarative C to form the CP (51) below:

(51)

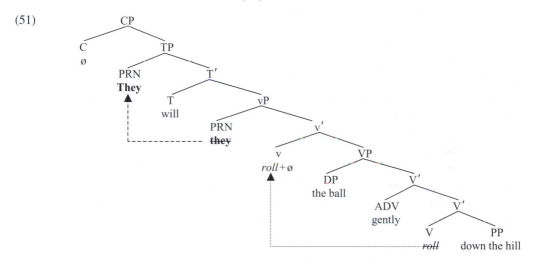

The different positions occupied by the adverb *gently* in (50) and (51) reflect a
subtle meaning difference between (49a) and (49b): (49a) means that the action
which initiated the rolling motion was gentle, whereas (49b) means that the
rolling motion itself was gentle. If we assume that adjuncts can be spelled out
either to the left or to the right of the constituent they adjoin to, we can account
for sentences such as (52) below in which the adverb appears at the end of the
sentence:

(52)   They will roll the ball down the hill gently

In such a sentence, the adverb *gently* could be adjoined to (and spelled out to the
right of) either V-bar or v-bar, so correctly predicting that the sentence is subtly
ambiguous.

   A light-verb analysis also offers us an interesting account of adverb position
in sentences like:

(53) (a)   He had *deliberately* rolled the ball **gently** down the hill
     (b)   *He had **gently** rolled the ball *deliberately* down the hill

Let's suppose that *deliberately* (by virtue of its meaning) can only be an adjunct to
a projection of an agentive verb (i.e. a verb whose subject has the thematic role of
AGENT). Given our earlier assumption that the light-verb [$_v$ ø] is a causative verb

with an AGENT subject, the contrast in (53) can be accounted for straightforwardly: in (53a) *deliberately* is contained within a vP headed by a null agentive causative light verb; but in (53b) it is contained with a VP headed by the nonagentive verb *roll*. (The verb *roll* is a nonagentive predicate because its subject has the θ-role THEME, not AGENT.) We can then say that adverbs like *deliberately* can adjoin to a v-bar headed by an agentive light verb, but not to V-bar.

This in turn might lead us to expect to find a corresponding class of adverbs which can adjoin to V-bar but not v-bar. In this connection, consider the following contrast (adapted from Bowers 1993, p. 609):

(54) (a)   Mary jumped the horse *perfectly* over the last fence
     (b)   *Mary *perfectly* jumped the horse over the last fence

Given the assumptions made here, the derivation of (54a) would be parallel to that of (51) in relevant respects, while the derivation of (54b) would be parallel to that of (50). If we assume that the adverb *perfectly* (in the relevant use) can function only as an adjunct to a V-projection, the contrast between (54a) and (54b) can be accounted for straightforwardly: in (54a), *perfectly* is adjoined to V-bar, whereas in (54b) it is adjoined to v-bar – in violation of the requirement that it can only adjoin to a V-projection.

An interesting question raised by the VP-shell/split VP analysis of transitive structures outlined in this section is how the DP *the ball* in a structure like (51) comes to be assigned accusative case (as we see from the fact that it can be substituted by an accusative pronoun like *them* in a sentence such as *They will roll them gently down the hill*). In §7.7, we suggested that a transitive probe assigns accusative case to a goal with an unvalued case feature which it c-commands and agrees with in person and number. This raises the question of what is the transitive probe in (51) which assigns accusative case to the DP *the ball*. It cannot be the head V of VP, since this does not c-command the DP *the ball* at any stage of derivation. Instead, it must be the light verb, because this does indeed c-command the DP *the ball* on the edge of VP. If structural case assignment involves agreement, it follows that (in the relevant kind of structures) a transitive light verb (i.e. one with a thematic external argument) carries a set of (invisible) person and number agreement features and assigns accusative case to a c-commanded (pro)nominal goal with an unvalued case feature. What this means in more concrete terms is that the light verb in (51) agrees (invisibly) with and assigns (invisible) accusative case to DP *the ball* (accusative case only being directly visible in pronouns like *me/us/him/them*).

8.5   Split VP: Other transitive structures

As we saw in the previous section, the VP-shell analysis provides an interesting solution to the problems posed by ergative verbs when they are used as transitive verbs with two complements. (In their intransitive use, they have the same syntax as the *unaccusative* structures to be discussed in §8.7.) However, the problems posed by transitive verbs which take two complements arise not only with transitive ergative structures (like those in (39–44) above) which have intransitive counterparts, but also with two-complement transitive verbs like those bold-printed below (their complements being bracketed):

(55) (a)   They will **load** [the truck] [with hay]
     (b)   He **gave** [no explanation] [to his friends]
     (c)   They **took** [everything] [from her]
     (d)   Nobody can **blame** [you] [for the accident]

Verbs like those in (55) cannot be used intransitively, as we see from the ungrammaticality of:

(56) (a)   *The truck will load with hay
     (b)   *No explanation gave to his friends
     (c)   *Everything took from her
     (d)   *You can blame for the accident

However, it is interesting to note that in structures like (55) too we find that adverbs belonging to the same class as *gently* can be positioned either before the verb or between its two complements: cf.

(57) (a)   They will *carefully* load the truck with hay
     (b)   They will load the truck *carefully* with hay

This suggests that (in spite of the fact that the relevant verbs have no intransitive counterpart) a split projection analysis is appropriate for structures like (55) also. If so, a sentence such as (55a) will have the structure shown in simplified form in (58) below (with arrows showing movements which take place):

(58)

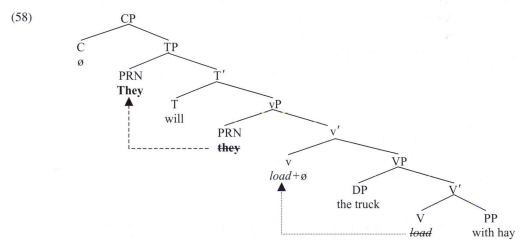

We can then say that the adverb *carefully* adjoins to v-bar in (57a), and to V-bar in (57b). If we suppose that verbs like *load* are essentially affixal in nature (in the sense that they must adjoin to a null causative light verb with an AGENT external argument), we can account for the ungrammaticality of intransitive structures such as (56a) *The truck will load with hay*. In (58), the light verb agrees (invisibly) with and assigns (invisible) accusative case to the DP *the truck*.

The split vP analysis can be extended to deal with VERB+PARTICLE structures like *He was taking the rubbish out* which involve a VP containing both a (pro)nominal direct object complement and a prepositional particle without the need for positing an Aspect Phrase projection. More concretely, structures like those in (23) above can be replaced by a split vP analysis along the lines shown below:

(59) (a)   [CP [C ø] [TP he [T was] [vP [v taking] [VP the rubbish [V ~~taking~~] out]]]]
    (b)   [CP [C ø] [TP he [T had] [vP [v taken] [VP the rubbish [V ~~taken~~] out]]]]
    (c)   [CP [C ø] [TP he [T ø] [vP [v took] [VP the rubbish [V ~~took~~] out]]]]

On this view, the verb TAKE originates in the head V position of VP and subsequently raises into the head v position of vP – not into the head Asp position of AspP, as claimed in Felser (1999a). The light verb heading vP agrees (invisibly) with and assigns (invisible) accusative case to the DP *the rubbish*.

The VP-shell analysis outlined above can also be extended to so-called **resultative predicates** which have both nominal and adjectival complements – i.e. to structures such as those below:

(60) (a)   The acid will turn the litmus-paper red
    (b)   They may paint the house pink

In (60a), the verb *turn* originates in the head V position of VP, with the DP *the litmus-paper* as its subject and the adjective *red* as its complement (precisely as in *The litmus-paper will turn red*): *turn* then raises to adjoin to a causative light-verb ø heading vP; the subject of this light verb (the DP *the acid*) in turn raises from spec-v to spec-T, and the resulting TP merges with a null declarative complementiser – as shown informally in (61) below:

(61)   [CP [C ø][TP **the acid** [T will] [vP **the acid** [v *turn*+ø] [VP the litmus-paper [V *turn*] red]]]]

The light verb heading vP agrees (invisibly) with and assigns (invisible) accusative case to the DP *the litmus-paper*.

A further set of structures which are amenable to a split vP analysis are sentences such as the following:

(62) (a)   Duncan must **persuade** <u>Dougal</u> *that he should be less frugal*
    (b)   Duncan must **persuade** <u>Dougal</u> *to be less frugal*

In these examples, the bold-printed verb *persuade* has two complements – an underlined direct object DP complement (*Dougal*) and an italicised CP complement. The CP complement is a finite clause headed by *that* in the first example, and an infinitival clause with a null complementiser and a null PRO subject in the second. (Because the PRO subject in sentences like (62b) is controlled by the matrix direct object *Dougal,* the relevant type of sentence is called an **Object Control** structure.) Under a traditional unsplit VP analysis, we would have to say that the Verb Phrases in the embedded clauses in sentences like those in (62a,b) have the respective initial structures shown in skeletal form in (63a,b) below (if we suppose that *Duncan* and *Dougal* are both DPs headed by a null definite determiner):

(63)

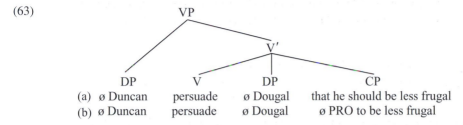

	DP	V	DP	CP
(a)	ø Duncan	persuade	ø Dougal	that he should be less frugal
(b)	ø Duncan	persuade	ø Dougal	ø PRO to be less frugal

However, structures such as these would be incompatible with the Binarity Principle which we posited in §2.2 because they contain a ternary-branching V-bar constituent. By contrast, we can develop a binary-branching split vP analysis of this type of Verb Phrase in the following terms. In (62a), the verb *persuade* merges with its CP complement to form the V-bar *persuade that he should be less frugal*, and the resulting V-bar is then merged with the DP *ø Dougal* to form the VP *ø Dougal persuade that he should be less frugal* (with a meaning loosely paraphraseable as 'Dougal realise that he should be less frugal'). This VP is then merged with a null causative light verb to form the v-bar [ᵥ *ø*] *ø Dougal persuade that he should be less frugal*, and the v-bar thereby formed is in turn merged with its external argument *ø Duncan* to form the vP *ø Duncan* [ᵥ *ø*] *ø Dougal persuade that he should be less frugal*. The lexical verb *persuade* adjoins to the light verb (as shown by the arrow below), so forming the following structure (with a meaning roughly paraphraseable as 'Duncan make Dougal realise that he should be less frugal'):

(64)

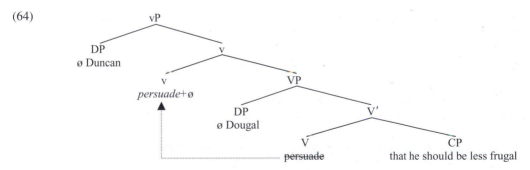

Subsequently, the vP in (64) is merged with the T-auxiliary *must*, the DP *ø Duncan* raises up to become the subject of *must*, and the resulting TP is merged with a null declarative complementiser, so forming the structure associated with (62a). (62b) has an essentially parallel derivation, except that the CP complement of *persuade* is headed by a null complementiser and has a null PRO subject. From a theoretical perspective, the crucial point to note is that the split vP analysis enables us to maintain that sentences like those in (62) have a binary-branching structure.

If we look back at structures like (64), (61), (59), (58) (51), (50) and (48), an interesting generalisation which emerges about internal arguments is that when a transitive V has both a (pro)nominal (e.g. QP, DP or PRN) complement and another kind of complement (whether prepositional, adjectival or clausal), the (pro)nominal complement is merged in a *higher* position than (and so precedes) the other complement. Conversely, when a verb has both a clausal complement and another kind of complement, the clausal complement is merged in a *lower* position than (and so follows) the other complement. This suggests the following condition on the relative order in which different types of internal argument are merged:

(65)   **Merger Condition**
        Where V has a clausal internal argument and some other type/s of internal argument, the clausal argument is the first to be merged with V; where V has a (pro)nominal internal argument and some other type/s of internal argument, the (pro)nominal argument is the last one merged with V

We can illustrate how (65) works in terms of the following sentence:

(66)   She bet several dollars with him that she would beat him

In (66), the first internal argument to be merged with the verb *bet* is its CP complement *that she would beat him*, forming the intermediate V-projection *bet that she would beat him*; the second internal argument to be merged with the verb *bet* is the PP *with him*, forming the even larger intermediate V-projection *with him bet that she would beat him*; the third and last internal argument to be merged with the verb *bet* is the QP *several dollars*, forming the complete VP projection *several dollars with him bet that she would beat him*. Subsequently merging this VP with a light verb which triggers raising of the verb *bet* from V to v will generate the surface order *bet several dollars with him that she would beat him*. The important point to note here is that (in conformity with the Merger Condition (65)), the first argument to be merged with the verb *bet* is its CP complement, and the last is the nominal (QP) complement *several dollars*.

An important question to ask is *why* internal arguments should be merged in the order specified in the Merger Condition (65). The reason why a (pro)nominal argument is merged higher within VP than any other arguments may be that (in order to be assigned case) it must be merged as close to its case assigner as possible – and indeed a light verb cannot assign accusative case to a nominal if there is an overt constituent intervening between the two (so that an intervening adverbial adjunct blocks accusative case marking, e.g. in structures such as **He closed immediately the door*). The reason why clausal arguments are merged lower than other arguments may be to avoid the parsing problems which Chomsky (1965) claims are posed by centre-embedded clauses (i.e. by structures like 'John

admitted *that he had been arrested for shoplifting* to her' in which the italicised *that*-clause is embedded in a position between the bold-printed verb and its underlined Prepositional Phrase complement).

So far, our discussion has largely been concerned with how to deal with transitive structures containing a three-place predicate with two internal arguments. This raises the question of how to deal with the complements of simple (two-place) transitive predicates (which have subject and object arguments) like *read* in (67) below:

(67)   He will read the book

Chomsky (1995) proposes a light-verb analysis of two-place transitive predicates under which (67) would (at the end of the vP cycle) have a structure along the lines of (68) below (with the arrow showing movement of the verb *read* from V to adjoin to a null light verb in v):

(68)

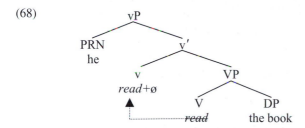

That is, *read* would originate as the head V of VP, and would then be raised to adjoin to a null agentive light-verb *ø* (and the structure in (68) can be paraphrased as 'He performed the action of reading the book').

If all agentive Verb Phrases have a split vP structure containing both a light verb and a lexical verb, this has important implications for the syntax of **unergative** Verb Phrases (i.e. Verb Phrases with an AGENT subject but no direct object) such as those italicised below:

(69) (a)   He might *resign from the club*
     (b)   He might *protest*

If an AGENT argument is merged as the specifier of a light verb which has a complement headed by a lexical verb, the italicised Verb Phrases in (69a,b) will have the respective derivations shown in (70a,b) below:

(70)   (a)   (b)

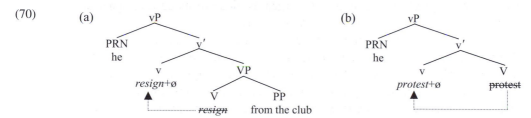

The v-bar constituents in (70a,b) would have an interpretation loosely para-phraseable as 'perform the action of resigning from the club/protesting'. An analysis such as (70a) would account for the possibility of positioning an adverb like *discreetly* either immediately before the PP *from the club* (as in *resign discreetly from the club*) or immediately before the verb *resign* (as in *discreetly resign from the club*), depending on whether the adverb is adjoined to a projection of the lexical verb or to a projection of the light verb. The assumption that both transitive and ergative Verb Phrases have a split projection structure would take us one step nearer to the position of being able to maintain that *all* verb phrases have a split vP structure. However, this raises the question of whether a split vP analysis position can be defended for other types of verb phrase – a question which we explore in the next two sections.

8.6   Split VP: Unaccusative structures

Thus far, we have argued that clauses with AGENT or EXPERIENCER subjects have a shell structure comprising an inner VP headed by a lexical verb and an outer vP headed by a light verb. However, we will now go on to present evidence that a split projection analysis is also appropriate for intransitive clauses. In this section, we look at clauses containing an **unaccusative** verb.

In §6.5, we suggested that the arguments of unaccusative predicates like *come/go* originate as their complements. However, there are reasons for thinking that the syntax of unaccusative Verb Phrases is rather more complex than we suggested there. In this connection, consider unaccusative imperative structures such as the following in (dialect A of) Belfast English (See Henry 1995: note that *youse* is the plural form of *you* – corresponding to American English *y'all*):

(71)(a)   Go you to school!
   (b)   Run youse to the telephone!
   (c)   Walk you into the garden!

If postverbal arguments of unaccusative predicates are **in situ** complements, this means that each of the verbs in (71) must have two complements. If we make the traditional assumption that complements are sisters of a head, this means that if both *you* and *to school* are complements of the verb *go* in (71a), they must be sisters of *go*, and hence the VP headed by *go* must have the (simplified) structure (72) below:

(72)

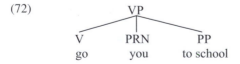

VP
V — PRN — PP
go   you   to school

However, a ternary-branching structure such as (72) is incompatible with a frame-work such as that used here which assumes that the merger operation by which phrases are formed is inherently binary.

Since analysing unaccusative subjects in such structures as underlying comple-ments proves problematic, let's consider whether they might instead be analysed as specifiers. On this view, we can suppose that the inner VP core of a Belfast English unaccusative imperative structure such as (71a) *Go you to school!* is not (72) above, but rather (73) below:

(73)

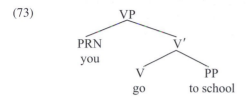

Thus, in conformity with the Merger Condition (65), the verb *go* first merges with its PP complement *to school* to form the V-bar *go to school* and then merges with the pronoun *you* to form the VP *you go to school*. Assuming such an analysis, we can say that it is a property of unaccusative predicates that all their arguments originate within VP. But the problem posed by a structure like (73) is that it provides us with no way of accounting for the fact that unaccusative subjects like *you* in (71a) *Go you to school!* surface postverbally. How can we overcome this problem? One answer is the following. Let us suppose that VPs like (73) which are headed by an unaccusative verb are embedded as the complement of a null light verb, and that the unaccusative verb raises to adjoin to the light verb in the manner indicated by the arrow in (74) below:

(74)

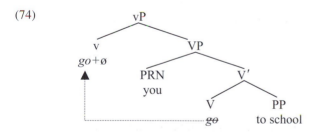

If (as Alison Henry argues) subjects remain in situ in imperatives in dialect A of Belfast English, the postverbal position of unaccusative subjects in sentences such as (71) can be accounted for straightforwardly. And the split VP analysis in (74) is consistent with the assumption that the merger operation by which phrases are formed is intrinsically binary.

Moreover, the split VP analysis enables us to provide an interesting account of the position of adverbs like *quickly* in unaccusative imperatives (in dialect A of Belfast English) such as:

(75)   Go you quickly to school!

If we suppose that adverbs like *quickly* are adjuncts which can merge with an intermediate verbal projection (e.g. a single-bar projection comprising a verb and its complement), we can say that *quickly* in (75) is adjoined to the V-bar *go to school* in (74). What remains to be accounted for (in relation to the syntax of imperative subjects in dialect A of Belfast English) is the fact that subjects of transitive and unergative verbs occur in preverbal (not postverbal) position: cf.

(76) (a)   *You* read that book!
   (b)   *Read *you* that book!

(77) (a)   *Youse* tell the truth!
   (b)   *Tell *youse* the truth

(78) (a)   *You* protest!
   (b)   *Protest *you*!

Why should this be? If we assume (as in our discussion of (68) above) that transitive verbs originate as the head V of a VP complement of a null agentive light verb, an imperative such as (76a) will contain a vP with the simplified structure shown in (79) below (where the dotted arrow indicates movement of the verb *read* to adjoin to the null light verb heading vP):

(79)

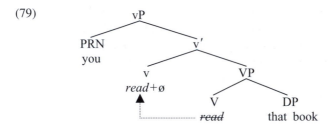

The AGENT subject *you* will originate in spec-v, as the subject of the agentive light-verb *ø*. Even after the verb *read* adjoins to the null light verb, the subject *you* will still be positioned in front of the resulting verbal complex *read+ø*. As should be obvious, we can extend the light-verb analysis from transitive verbs like *read* to unergative verbs like *protest* if we assume (as in (70) above) that unergative subjects (like transitive subjects) originate as specifiers of an agentive light verb.

Given these assumptions, we could then say that the difference between unaccusative subjects and transitive/unergative subjects is that unaccusative subjects originate within VP (as the argument of a lexical verb), whereas transitive/unergative subjects originate in spec-v (as the external argument of a light verb). If we hypothesise that Verb Phrases always contain an outer vP shell headed by a strong (affixal) light verb and an inner VP core headed by a lexical verb, and that lexical verbs always raise from V to v, the postverbal position of unaccusative subjects can be accounted for by positing that the subject remains in situ in such structures. Such a hypothesis can be extended to account for the intransitive use of ergative predicates in sentences like (39b–44b) above, so that intransitive ergatives can be analysed in a parallel fashion to unaccusatives.

The light-verb analysis of unaccusatives sketched here also offers us a way of accounting for the observation that in Early Modern English, the perfect auxiliary used with unaccusative verbs was BE (as we saw in §6.5), whereas that used with transitive and unergative verbs was HAVE. We can account for this by positing that the perfect auxiliary HAVE selected a vP complement with an external argument, whereas the perfect auxiliary BE selected a complement headed by an intransitive light verb with no external argument. The distinction has been lost in present-day English, with perfect HAVE being used with both types of vP structure.

Further evidence in support of the claim that unaccusative clauses have a split VP structure comes from the fact that it enables us to account for the observation that unaccusative verbs can occur in the three types of structure illustrated below:

(80) (a)   A loud scream came from inside the house
     (b)   From inside the house came a loud scream
     (c)   There came a loud scream from inside the house

If unaccusative clauses have a split VP structure, we can account for this as follows. In (80a), the unaccusative verb *come* is first-merged with its PP argument (forming the V-bar *come from inside the house*), and second-merged with its indefinite QP argument (forming the VP *a loud scream come from inside the house*) – the order of merger of the two arguments being in conformity with the Merger Condition (65). The resulting VP is then merged with a null light-verb ∅, forming the vP ∅ *a loud scream come from inside the house*. The strong/affixal light verb triggers raising of the verb *come* from V to v – in the manner shown by the arrow below:

(81)

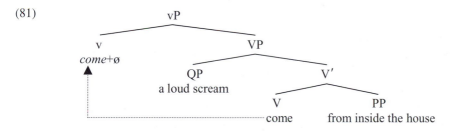

The vP in (81) is then merged with a finite T constituent containing an abstract affix carrying an interpretable past tense feature, together with uninterpretable (unvalued) person and number features, and an uninterpretable EPP feature. The T-affix agrees in person and number with, assigns nominative case to and triggers movement to spec-T of the QP *a loud scream*, so forming a TP which is merged with a null declarative complementiser to form the structure shown in simplified form below:

(82)   [CP [C ∅] [TP a loud scream [T Af]
             [vP [v come+∅] [vP a loud scream [v come] from inside the house]]]]]

The past tense affix in T lowers onto the head v of vP in the PF component, with the result that the verb COME is spelled out as the past tense form *came* in (80a) *A loud scream came from inside the house*.

The type of structure found in (80b) *From inside the house came a loud scream* is traditionally said to involve **locative inversion**, in the sense that the locative PP complement *from inside the house* ends up positioned in front of the verb *came*. One way of handling such a structure is to suppose that the EPP feature on T can be satisfied by raising the locative PP *from inside the house* (rather than the QP *a loud scream*) to spec-T, so generating the structure in (83) below:

(83)   [$_{CP}$ [$_C$ ø] [$_{TP}$ from inside the house [$_T$ Af] [$_{vP}$ [$_v$ come+ø]
                    [$_{VP}$ a loud scream [$_V$ ~~come~~] ~~from inside the house~~]]]]

Evidence in support of the analysis in (83) comes from sentences such as:

(84)   He trembled when he heard **that** *from inside the house* had come a loud
         scream

The fact that the italicised locative PP follows the bold-printed complementiser in (84) suggests that the inverted locative PP is in spec-T rather than spec-C.

Now consider the derivation of the unaccusative expletive sentence (80c) *There came a loud scream from inside the house*. In §7.6, we proposed a number of conditions on the syntax of expletive pronouns in English, including the following:

(85)   **External Argument Condition**
         An expletive can only be merged as the highest argument of a verb which
         has no external argument

We rationalised (85) by supposing that expletives occupy the same structural position as external arguments, with the result that the two are mutually exclusive. Given the claim made in this chapter that external arguments occupy spec-v, a plausible extension of the same reasoning would be to suppose that expletives likewise originate in spec-v. This being so, (80c) will be derived as follows.

The verb *come* is first-merged with its PP argument (forming the V-bar *come from inside the house*), and second-merged with its indefinite QP argument (forming the VP *a loud scream come from inside the house*). The resulting VP is then merged with a null light-verb ø, forming the v-bar ø *a loud scream come from inside the house*, and the resulting v-bar is in turn merged with expletive *there* to form the vP *there* ø *a loud scream come from inside the house*. The strong/affixal light verb triggers raising of the verb *come* from V to v – in the manner shown by the arrow in (86) below:

(86)

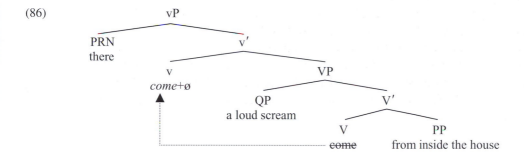

The vP in (86) is then merged with a finite T constituent containing an abstract affix (*Af*) carrying an interpretable past tense feature, together with uninterpretable (unvalued) person and number features, and an uninterpretable EPP feature. The T-affix agrees in person with (and triggers movement to spec-T of) expletive *there*, and agrees in person and number with (and assigns nominative case to) the QP *a loud scream*, so forming a TP which is merged with a null declarative complementiser to form the structure shown in simplified form below:

(87)   [CP [C ø] [TP there [T Af] [vP there [v come+ø] [VP a loud scream
                                                 [V come] from inside the house]]]]]

The past tense affix in T lowers onto the head v of vP in the PF component, with the result that the verb COME is spelled out as the past tense form *came* in (80c) *There came a loud scream from inside the house*. The overall conclusion which our discussion in this section leads us to is thus that the split VP analysis allows us to provide a principled account of (inverted and uninverted, expletive and unexpletive) unaccusative structures.

    A minor descriptive detail to note, however, is that the assumption that expletives originate within vP requires us to modify the conditions on the use of expletives which we posited in the previous chapter along the following lines:

(88)   **Expletive Conditions** (revised)
    (i)   External Argument Condition:
              An expletive can only be merged as the last/highest argument of a light verb
              with no external argument (i.e. in spec-v)
    (ii)   Indefiniteness Condition:
              Expletive *there* can only be merged as the specifier of a light verb whose VP
              complement has an indefinite nominal or pronominal internal argument
    (iii)   Inactivity Condition:
              Expletive *it* can only be merged as the specifier of a light verb which does
              not c-command any accessible nominal or pronominal expression with
              some active case- or φ-feature(s)

8.7   Split VP: Passive and raising structures

A further class of intransitive clauses that can be argued to contain a split vP are passives like:

(89)   The horse was jumped perfectly over the fence

The passive subject *the horse* originates as an internal argument of the verb *jumped* here. Since passive verb forms are intransitive, the passive participle *jumped* cannot assign accusative case to the DP *the horse* here; rather, the DP *the horse* is assigned nominative case by the T-auxiliary *was*. Accordingly, the derivation of (89) proceeds as follows.

The verb *jump* first merges with its PP argument *over the fence* to form the intermediate V-projection *jump over the fence*. The adverb *perfectly* adjoins to this structure, forming the even larger V-projection *perfectly jump over the fence*. The resulting structure is then merged with the DP argument *the horse*, to form the VP *the horse perfectly jump over the fence* (the order of merger of the PP and DP internal arguments being in conformity with the Merger Condition (65)). The VP thereby formed is then merged with an intransitive light verb (with no external argument), and this attracts the verb *jump* to attach to it, so forming the vP in (90) below (with an arrow showing movement of the verb *jump* from V to v):

(90)

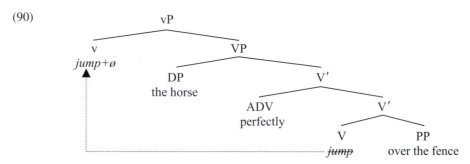

Since the vP in (90) is a passive structure, the light verb is spelled out as the passive participle suffix *-ed*, with the result that the verb JUMP is ultimately spelled out in the PF component as the passive participle form *jumped*. (Indeed, Chomsky 1999 labels the light verb found in passive structures as PRT.)

The vP in (90) is subsequently merged with a past tense T constituent containing the passive auxiliary BE. This serves as a probe and locates the DP *the horse* as a goal which is active by virtue of its unvalued case feature. T agrees with, assigns nominative case to and attracts the DP *the horse* to move to spec-T. The resulting TP is merged with a null declarative complementiser, deriving the CP shown in simplified form below (with only overt constituents of vP being shown):

(91)   [CP [C ø] [TP the horse [T was] [vP [v jumped] perfectly over the fence]]]

Thus, the assumption that passive Verb Phrases have a split VP structure accounts for how the passive verb *jumped* comes to be positioned in front of the adverb *perfectly* even though the adverb *perfectly* modifies the expression *jump over the fence*.

Yet another class of intransitive predicates for which a split VP analysis can be argued to be appropriate are **raising** predicates like *seem*. In this connection, consider the syntax of a raising sentence such as:

(92)   The president does seem to me to have upset several people

Given the assumptions made in this chapter, (92) will be derived as follows. The verb *upset* merges with its QP complement *several people* to form the VP *upset several people*. This in turn merges with a null causative light verb, which (by virtue of being affixal in nature) triggers raising of the verb *upset* to adjoin to the light verb (as shown by the dotted arrow below); the resulting v-bar merges with its external AGENT argument *the president* to form the vP in (93) below (paraphraseable informally as 'The president caused-to-get-upset several people'):

(93)

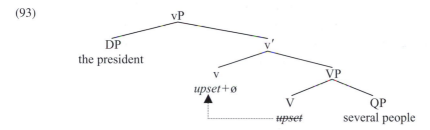

This vP in is then merged with the aspectual auxiliary *have* to form an AUXP (which could equally be termed an AspP), and this AUXP is in turn merged with [$_T$ *to*]. If (as we argued in §7.9) T in raising infinitives has an EPP feature and an unvalued person feature, the subject *the president* will be attracted to move to spec-T, so deriving the structure shown in simplified form in (94) below (with the arrow marking A-movement):

(94)

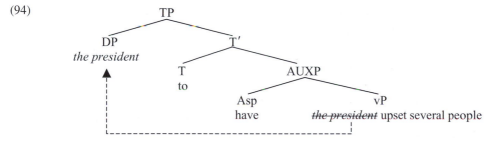

The TP in (94) is then merged as the complement of *seem*, forming the V-bar *seem the president to have upset several people* (omitting trace copies and other empty categories, to make exposition less abstract). Let's suppose that *to me* is the EXPERIENCER argument of *seem* and is merged as the specifier of the resulting

V-bar, forming the VP shown in (95) below (simplified by not showing null copies of moved constituents and other empty categories):

(95)

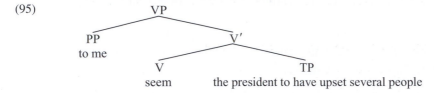

On the assumption that all Verb Phrases contain an outer vP shell, the VP in (95) will then merge with a null (affixal) light verb, triggering raising of the verb *seem* to adjoin to the light verb. Merging the resulting vP with a finite T constituent containing (emphatic) DO will derive the structure shown in simplified form below (with the arrow showing the verb movement that took place on the vP cycle):

(96)

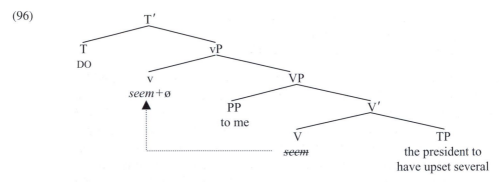

[T DO] serves as a probe looking for an active nominal goal. If a (non-expletive) nominal can only be an active goal if it has an unvalued case feature, then neither the pronoun *me* (assigned accusative case by the transitive preposition *to*) nor the QP *several people* (assigned accusative case by the transitive verb *upset*) will be accessible goals. Consequently, the DP *the president* (which is active by virtue of having an unvalued case feature) is the only nominal which can serve as the goal of [T DO] in (96). Accordingly, DO assigns nominative case to *the president* (and conversely agrees with *the president*, with DO ultimately being spelled out at PF as *does*), and the EPP and uninterpretable person/number features of DO ensure that *the president* moves into spec-T, so deriving the structure shown in simplified form below:

(97)

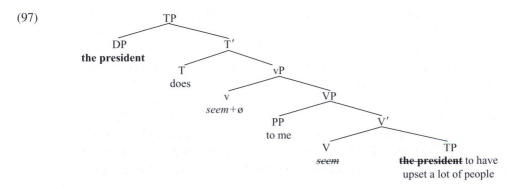

The resulting TP will then be merged with a null declarative complementiser, forming the CP structure associated with (92) *The president does seem to me to have upset several people*. We can assume that the related sentence (98) below:

(98)   The president does seem to have upset several people

has an essentially parallel derivation, except that the verb *seem* in (98) projects no EXPERIENCER argument, so that the structure formed when *seem* is merged with its TP complement will not be (95) above, but rather [$_{VP}$ [$_V$ *seem*] [$_{TP}$ *the president* [$_T$ *to*] *have upset several people*]].

An interesting corollary of the light-verb analysis of raising verbs like *seem* is that the Italian counterpart of *seem* is used with the perfect auxiliary *essere* 'be' rather than *avere* 'have' – as we can illustrate in relation to:

(99)   Maria mi è sempre sembrata essere simpatica
              Maria me is always seemed be nice
              'Maria has always seemed to me to be nice'

(The position of the EXPERIENCER argument *mi* 'to me' in (99) is accounted for by the fact that it is a clitic pronoun, and clitics attach to the left of a finite auxiliary or nonauxiliary verb in Italian – in this case attaching to the left of *è* 'is'.) Earlier, we suggested that in languages with the HAVE/BE contrast, HAVE typically selects a vP complement with a thematic external argument, whereas BE selects a vP complement with no thematic external argument. In this context, it is interesting to note (e.g. in relation to structures like (96) above) that the light verb found in clauses containing a raising predicate like SEEM projects no external argument, and hence would be expected to occur with (the relevant counterpart of) the perfect auxiliary BE in a language with the HAVE/BE contrast. Data such as (99) are thus consistent with the light-verb analysis of raising predicates like SEEM outlined here.

8.8   Summary

We began this chapter in §8.2 by outlining the claim made by Rizzi that in clauses which contain preposed focus/topic expressions, CP *splits* into a number of separate projections, viz. a Force Phrase/**ForceP**, a Topic Phrase/**TopP** and a Focus Phrase/**FocP** (with the Focus head being strong and so triggering movement of an auxiliary from T to Foc, but the Topic and Force heads being weak). We posited that preposed topics move to the specifier position in TopP, preposed negative expressions move to the specifier position in the Focus Phrase (as do preposed wh-expressions in main-clause questions) and wh-expressions in other types of structure move to the specifier of the Force Phrase. In §8.3, we looked at suggestions for splitting TP into distinct Tense, Aspect and Mood projections. We began by looking at claims by Felser that in verb–particle structures such as *He took the rubbish out* the verb *took* raises to an Aspect position above

V but below T, but concluded that the case for positing an Aspect head in such structures was not entirely convincing. We also looked at proposals in Schütze (2004) in support of positing a separate M/Mood head, with M being the locus of modals and mood morphemes, and T being the locus of tense affixes: we noted (but questioned) Schütze's argument that this would eliminate Affix Lowering. In §8.4, we presented a number of arguments suggesting that VPs should be split into two distinct projections – an inner VP core headed by a lexical verb and an outer vP **shell** headed by an affixal **light verb**. In particular, we looked at the syntax of **ergative** verbs like *roll* which are used both intransitively in structures like *The ball rolled down the hill* and transitively in structures like *They rolled the ball down the hill*. We argued that the Verb Phrase in transitive ergative structures comprises an inner VP core headed by a lexical verb/V contained within an outer vP shell headed by a causative light verb/v with an AGENT subject, and that the affixal light verb attracts the verb *roll* to raise from V to v. We also showed how the shell analysis can help us account for the distribution of adverbs in such structures. We argued that the direct object (*the ball*) is assigned accusative case under c-command via agreement with the light verb. In §8.5, we extended the shell analysis to a variety of other double-complement transitive structures including prepositional structures such as *load the cart with hay*, resultatives like *turn the litmus-paper red*, verb–particle structures like *take the rubbish out* and Object Control structures like *persuade Dougal to be less frugal*. We also showed how the vP shell analysis could be extended to simple transitive structures like *John read the book*, and to unergative structures like *He may resign (from the job)*. In §8.6, we argued in favour of a shell analysis for intransitive clauses containing an unaccusative verb. We began by showing how a split VP analysis of unaccusative clauses would account for the word order found in Belfast English imperatives such as *Go you to school!* and went on to show how it would handle standard English unaccusative structures such as *A loud scream came from inside the house*, locative inversion structures like *From inside the house came a loud scream* and expletive structures such as *There came a loud scream from inside the house*. In §8.7, we then went on to extend the shell analysis to passives like *The horse was jumped perfectly over the fence*, and to raising structures such as *They seem to me to be fine*. We concluded that all transitive and intransitive Verb Phrases alike have a shell structure in which the verb raises from V to v, with AGENT and EXPERIENCER external arguments (and expletive subjects) originating in spec-v, and all other arguments originating within VP.

Key assumptions made in this chapter include the following:

(100)   Under the version of the split CP analysis outlined in this chapter:
   (i)   A preposed wh-expression moves to spec-FocP in a main clause wh-question, but to spec-ForceP in other types of wh-clause
   (ii)   A preposed negative expression moves to spec-FocP
   (iii)   A preposed topic moves to spec-TopP
   (iv)   Foc is a strong head attracting an auxiliary in T to move to Foc, but Top and Force are weak heads

(v)   A null declarative complementiser (viz. the null counterpart of *that*) can only have a TP complement

(101)   Under Schütze's version of the *split TP* analysis outlined in this chapter:
(i)   Clauses are of the form CP+MP+TP(+NEGP)+VP
(ii)   M contains either a modal stem or an abstract (indicative/subjunctive) mood morpheme
(iii)   An indicative mood morpheme is spelled out as a DO-form when not attached to a verbal stem
(iv)   T contains either a strong affix which triggers raising of V to T, or a weak affix which raises to M
(v)   Neg is non-affixal and cannot attract V to raise to Neg; however, clitic *n't* raises to attach to M
(vi)   Auxiliary inversion is movement from M to C

(102)   Under the version of the *split VP* analysis outlined in this chapter:
(i)   All Verb Phrases contain a light verb projection (vP) and a subordinate lexical verb projection (VP), with the lexical verb originating in V and adjoining to a null affixal light verb in v.
(ii)   The specifier position within vP can be filled by an AGENT or EXPERIENCER external argument or a non-thematic expletive, but otherwise is empty; other arguments are internal arguments and are merged with V.
(iii)   In transitive clauses, v agrees with and assigns accusative case to a (pro)nominal goal with an unvalued case feature which is c-commanded by v.

Two key sets of *conditions* which we posited earlier in our discussion of split VPs in the chapter are the following:

(65)   **Merger Condition**
Where V has a clausal internal argument and some other type/s of internal argument, the clausal argument is the first to be merged with V; where V has a (pro)nominal internal argument and some other type/s of internal argument, the (pro)nominal argument is the last one merged with V

(88)   **Expletive Conditions** (revised)
(i)   External Argument Condition:
An expletive can only be merged as the last/highest argument of a light verb with no external argument (i.e. in spec-v)
(ii)   Indefiniteness Condition:
Expletive *there* can only be merged as the specifier of a light verb whose VP complement has an indefinite nominal or pronominal internal argument
(iii)   Inactivity Condition:
Expletive *it* can only be merged as the specifier of a light verb which does not c-command any accessible nominal or pronominal expression with some active case- or φ-feature(s)

8.9   Bibliographical background

The split CP analysis of the clause periphery in §8.2 derives from work by Rizzi (1997, 2001b, 2004) and Haegeman (2000): for a critique, see Newmeyer (2005). On differences between focusing and topicalisation, see Rizzi (1997), Cormack and Smith (2000b), Smith and Cormack (2002), Alexopoulou and Kolliakou (2002), Drubig (2003) and Green (2007). For evidence that what appear to be clausal subjects like the clause underlined in *That the defendant is guilty has been proved beyond all reasonable doubt* are actually topics, see Emonds (1976), Koster (1978), Williams (1980), Stowell (1981), Safir (1986), Bresnan (1994), Postal (1998) and Alrenga (2005). On the difference between clause *type* and *force*, see Huddleston (1994). For alternative analyses of negative preposing, see Sobin (2003), Branigan (2005) and Maekawa (2007). For arguments against a feature-based account of focus, see Neeleman and Szendrői (2004). In relation to the claim in §8.3 that TP can be split into a number of separate projections including an Aspect Phrase/AspP projection, it should be noted that a number of studies have postulated the existence of an Aspect head (independent of Tense) in a wide range of languages, including Russian (Tenny 1987), Greek (Alexiadou 1997), Spanish and Basque (Laka 1990), Breton and Welsh (Hendrick 1991), Scots Gaelic (Ramchand 1996), Irish (Guilfoyle 1994), Chinese (Borer 1993), Nweh (Nkemnji 1995), Egyptian Arabic (Diesing and Jelinek 1995), English (Felser 1999a, Adger 2003, van Gelderen 2004 and Thompson 2006) and Lithuanian (Franks and Lavine 2006). On the possibility that *small clauses* like that bracketed in *I consider* [*Mary (as) unsuitable for the post*] may contain an Aspect Projection, see Jiménez (2000a,b). For further discussion of the syntax and semantics of Aspect, see the collection of papers in Verkuyl, de Swart and van Hout (2005). On the idea that resultative participles (like *opened* in *the carefully opened package*) incorporate an Aspect head, see Embick (2004). On the claim that clauses may contain a Mood Projection/MP, see Cinque (1999, 2002, 2004), Schütze (2004) and Haegeman (2006): in relation to Schütze's claim that positing a Mood Phrase projection eliminates the need for lowering operations like Affix Lowering, see the defence of lowering operations in Richards (2004). The claim that structures like *She's like you* (where *'s* is a contracted form of *does*) are ruled out by an Economy Condition derives from Emonds (1994, p. 168) and Freidin (2004, p. 119). Note that we have only discussed some of the wide range of split TP analyses proposed in the relevant research literature – excluding, for example, the claim made by Pollock (1989) and Belletti (1990) that clauses contain a Subject Agreement projection (AgrSP), or the related claim by Rizzi and Shlonsky (2005) that they contain a Subject Projection (SubjP): for evidence against an AgrSP projection, see Iatridou (1990) and Chomsky (1995). The split vP analysis outlined in §§8.4–8.7 dates back in spirit to work by Larson (1988, 1990), Hale and Keyser (1991, 1993a, 1994), Chomsky (1995) and Kratzer (1993, 1996). On the idea that causative verbs like Italian *fare* 'make' may be the spellout of a causative light verb, see Folli and Harley (2007). For technical accounts of differences between Adjunction and Merger, see Stepanov (2001) and Chomsky (2001). For arguments that *do* is a light verb in elliptical structures such as *John will roll a ball down the hill and Paul will do so as well*, see See Stroik (2001) and Haddican (2007). For alternative analyses of resultative structures, see Keyser and Roeper (1992), Carrier and Randall (1992) and Oya (2002). For an analysis of unergative verbs involving object incorporation, see Baker (1988) and Hale and Keyser (1993a). For further discussion of Object Control structures, see Bowers (1993); for an analysis of the control verb *promise*, see Larson (1991). On the use of the perfect auxiliary BE in unaccusative structures, see Sorace (2000). For a range of alternative accounts of locative inversion, see Bresnan (1994), Levin and Rappaport Hovav (1995), Collins (1997), Culicover and Levine (2001), Nakajima (2001), Bowers (2002) and Hornstein (2007). In relation to the disussion of raising in §8.7, see Collins (2005b) for a split projection analysis of structures like *John seems to Mary to be nice*. The discussion of passives in §8.8 excludes expletive passives such as *There were several prizes awarded*: see Chomsky (1999) and Bowers (2002) for two different analyses of this type of structure. Although we have assumed only two 'layers' of structure within the Verb Phrase here, it should be noted that a number of linguists have proposed additional 'layers' of structure within the Verb Phrase, such as an Object (Agreement) Phrase (Koizumi 1993, 1995; Radford 1997a, §§10.4–10.6), an Acc(usative) Phrase (Beck and Johnson 2004), a Transitivity Phrase (Bowers 2002), a Voice Phrase (Collins 1997, 2005a), a Participial Phrase (Collins 2005a) and an Applicative Phrase (McGinnis 2004). Space limitations mean that we have excluded from discussion here the possibility that Noun Phrases may have a split projection structure parallel to that found in Verb Phrases, on which see Carstens (2000, 2001), Adger (2003) and Radford (2004a, §9.9). Likewise, it has been proposed that Prepositional Phrases (in languages which allow preposition stranding) may have a split projection structure: see Boeckx (2007).

Workbook section

Exercise 8.1

Discuss how the structure of the bracketed clauses in the sentences below would be analysed within
the framework of the *split CP* analysis outlined in §8.2 of the main text.

1   He admitted [that they will only rarely enjoy this course]
2   *He admitted [only rarely will they enjoy this course]
3   *He admitted [that only rarely they will enjoy this course]
4   *He admitted [this course, they will only rarely enjoy]
5   *He admitted [that this course will they only rarely enjoy]
6   He admitted [that this course, only rarely will they enjoy] **(w)**

7   *He admitted [that this course will only rarely they enjoy] **(w)**

8   *He admitted [that only rarely will this course, they enjoy] **(w)**

9   *He admitted [only rarely, this course, they will enjoy] **(w)**

10   This is a course [which only rarely will they enjoy] **(w)**

Then comment on how the wh-clauses in the following sentences might be analysed within the split CP framework (14 and 15 being from the Leonard corpus on the CHILDES database, MacWhinney 1995):

11   What a mine of useless information that I am! (Irish TV celebrity, BBC1 TV) **(w)**

12   I wonder which dress that they picked (Belfast English, from Henry 1995, p. 107)

13   He protested that how could he have known she would be killed? (= semi-indirect speech)

14   What Kent's gonna play with? (produced by a child with Specific Language Impairment) **(w)**

15   What's he gon(na) kill? (produced by the same child as 14) **(w)**

In addition, say whether contrasts such as those below can be handled within the framework of assumptions presented in the main text, and if not try and develop an alternative analysis.

16   What under no circumstances would John do for Mary? (Maekawa 2007, p. 158)

17   *Under no circumstances what would John do for Mary? (Maekawa 2007, p. 159)

18   Not long after the robbery, the police arrested a suspect

19   *Not long after the robbery did the police arrest a suspect

20   None of the girls would John admit that he had lied to

21   *None of the girls would John admit that had he lied to

Finally, say how you think the following sentences could be derived under the *split TP* analysis outlined in §8.3 of the main text, highlighting any problems which arise.

22   He should receive a pardon

23   Should he not receive a pardon? **(w)**

24   Did he receive a pardon? **(w)**

25   Didn't she demand that he receive a pardon?

26   She demanded that he not receive a pardon

Helpful hints

To simplify your discussion of sentences 1–10, concern yourself only with the structure of the left periphery of the bracketed clauses in these examples (i.e. the Force/Topic/Focus Phrase projections above the TP layer). Assume that the TP has the skeletal structure [$_{TP}$ *they* [$_T$ *will*] *only rarely enjoy this course*] but don't concern yourself with its precise internal structure. Assume that the complementiser *that* occupies the head Force position of a ForceP projection (marking the relevant clause as declarative in force); that *only rarely* is an ADVP constituent (whose internal structure need not concern you) which moves to the edge of a FocP projection when preposed; and that the DP *this course* moves to the edge of a TopP projection when preposed. Assume that a clause only contains a FocP projection if it contains a focused constituent preceding the subject, and only contains a TopP constituent if it contains a topic constituent preceding the subject.

   In sentences 11–15, likewise concern yourself only with the structure of the left periphery of the wh-clauses. Bear in mind the claim made in the main text that focused wh-interrogative expressions can either move to become the specifier of a strong Focus head (in main-clause questions) or of a weak Force head (in embedded questions), but that exclamative wh-expressions move to the specifier position within the Force Phrase in main-clause questions and embedded questions alike. In 14–15, bear in mind the possibility that some language learners may initially assume that an interrogative wh-word can have more than one landing-site (in virtue of being focused on the one hand, and interrogative in force on the other). In relation to 16–17, consider whether preposed negative and interrogative expressions might have different landing-sites (e.g. in the specifier of a Negative Phrase/NEGP or Interrogative Phrase/IntP respectively). In 18–19, consider whether some preposed negative expressions may be topicalised rather than focused; take *not long after the robbery* to be a prepositional phrase/PP, but do not concern yourself with its internal structure. In 20–21, consider the possibility that preposed negative expressions can move to spec-ForceP in an embedded clause out of which they are extracted. In relation to sentences 22–26, make the set of assumptions summarised in (101) above; you can simplify your discussion of 22–26 by not assuming the split VP analysis of Verb Phrases, if you wish.

Model answer for 1

Rizzi posits that CP splits into multiple projections in clauses which contain a preposed topic or focus constituent. However, neither the main *admitted* clause nor the complement *enjoy* clause contains a preposed topic or focus constituent in 1; hence, neither contains a FocP or TopP projection. Accordingly, both clauses in 1 will be simple ForceP projections whose head serves to mark declarative force, the main clause headed by a null Force head, and the complement clause headed by *that*. However, since our concern here is with the structure of the bracketed *that*-clause which serves as the complement of the verb *admitted*, we concentrate on how this is derived.

Assume (as in the *helpful hints*) that we have reached a stage of derivation where we have formed the TP *they will only rarely enjoy this course*. This is merged with a Force head containing the complementiser *that*, so forming the structure shown in highly simplified form in (i) below:

(i)   [ForceP [Force that] [TP they [T will] only rarely enjoy this course]]

Given the assumption made in the main text that English allows a declarative Force head to have a null spellout when it has a TP complement, we correctly predict that alongside sentence 1 we can also have a sentence like (ii) below, in which the bracketed complement clause contains a null complementiser:

(ii)   He admitted [they will only rarely enjoy syntax]

Model answer for 22

Given the assumptions made in the *helpful hints* (adapted from Schütze 2004), sentence 22 will have the structure shown below (simplified inter alia by not showing the subject *he* originating within VP, and by not splitting VP into two separate vP/VP projections):

(i)   [CP [C ø] [MP he [M shall] [TP [T AfPAST] [VP [V receive] [a pardon]]]]]

By hypothesis, the past tense affix in T can be either weak or strong. If it is weak, it will raise to attach to the modal stem *shall* in M, so deriving the structure:

(ii)   [CP [C ø] [MP he [M shall+AfPAST] [TP [T AfPAST] [VP [V receive] a pardon]]]]

The PF component will then spell out the string *shall+AfPAST* as the past tense form *should*. However, if (as Schütze assumes) T can also contain a strong affix, the strong affix in T will trigger raising of the verb *receive* from V to T, so deriving:

(iii)   [CP [C ø] [MP he [M shall] [TP [T *receive*+AfPAST] [VP [V receive] a pardon]]]]

However, this will leave the modal stem *shall* in M without a tense affix, and since the PF component has no means of spelling out untensed modals, the resulting derivation will crash. What this illustrates is that the split TP analysis developed by Schütze over generates in certain respects, and hence could be argued not to meet Chomsky's (2006, p. 2) criterion of 'efficient computation'. In this instance, one way of circumventing the over generation problem would be to suppose that it is a lexical property of modals that they select a TP complement headed by a weak T constituent (though we can't use the mechanism of *selection* to resolve all the over generation problems posed by Schütze's analysis).

Exercise 8.2

Discuss how the syntax of sentences 1–16 below could be analysed within the split VP framework, giving arguments in support of your analysis. Comment in particular on the syntax of the italicised constituents, saying what position each one occupies, what case (if any) it receives and how.

1   They will increase *the price* gradually to 90 dollars
2   He will explain *the procedures* (**w**)
3   He should apologise profusely to her (**w**)
4   This could make *him* angry
5   Tourists may smuggle *drugs* illegally into the country
6   He should ask *her* confidentially if she is taking drugs
7   They will tell *you* politely to leave (**w**)
8   There may suddenly appear *a ghost* at the window
9   From inside the mineshaft emerged *the miners*
10   *It* was put hastily in the bag (**w**)
11   *You* are expected to go immediately to the police (**w**)
12   *The police* were reported by the press to have arrested a suspect (**w**)
13   *It* must be proved to the jury beyond all doubt that the defendant is guilty
14   *Several politicians* are widely thought to be suspected of corruption
15   There does seem to me to remain *some unrest* in Utopia (**w**)
16   *Some evidence* would certainly appear to have emerged recently of corruption

In addition, comment on the syntax of the following sentences reported by Bowerman (1982) to have been produced by young children (their names and ages in *years; months* being indicated in parentheses):

17   I disappeared (i.e. 'hid') a bear in the back of the car (Scott 5;0)
18   She came (i.e. 'brought') it over here (Christy 3;4)
19   Somebody fell (i.e. 'knocked') it off (Eva 3;8)
20   I'm staying (i.e. 'keeping') it in the water (Eva 3;2)

Helpful hints

Treat the *if*-clause in 6, the *to*-clause in 7 and the *that*-clause in 13 as CPs, and the *to*-clauses in 11, 12, 14, 15 and 16 as TPs, but do not concern yourself with their internal structure. Treat the *by*-phrase in the passive sentence in 12 as an internal argument of the verb *reported*. Take the PP *beyond all doubt* in 13 to be an adjunct. In relation to 16, bear in mind the treatment of discontinuous constituents in earlier chapters. More generally, assume that (in these sentences) an (adverbial or prepositional) adjunct which follows a verb adjoins to a projection of V, whereas an adjunct which precedes a verb adjoins to a projection of *v* (the relevant projection to which the adverb adjoins in each case being one containing V/v and its complement).

Model answer for 1

The verb *increase* can be used not only as an transitive verb in sentences such as 1 above, but also as an intransitive verb in sentences such as:

(i)   The price will increase gradually to 90 dollars

Accordingly, we can take *increase* to be an ergative predicate which (in intransitive uses) has the same syntax as an unaccusative verb. This means that 1 is derived as follows. The verb *increase* merges with its GOAL PP argument *to 90 dollars* to form the V-bar *increase to 90 dollars*. The adverb *gradually* is then adjoined to this V-bar to form the even larger V-bar *gradually increase to 90 dollars*. The THEME DP argument *the price* is then merged with the resulting V-bar to form the VP shown below:

(ii)

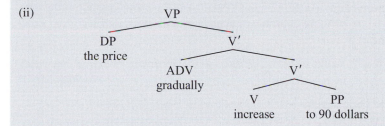

The order in which the internal arguments are merged with the verb *increase* in (ii) is in accordance with the Merger Condition (65), in that the DP argument *the price* is the last internal argument to be merged with the verb (and is thus the highest internal argument in the structure). The VP in (ii) then merges with a causative light-verb *ø* to generate a v-bar which in turn merges with its external AGENT argument (= *they*), so forming the structure (iii) below:

(iii)

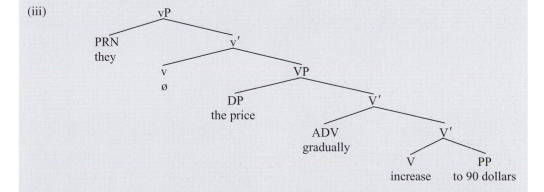

The transitive light-verb [v ø] agrees (invisibly) with and assigns (invisible) accusative case to the DP *the price*. Being a strong, affixal head, the light verb also attracts the verb *increase* to move from V to adjoin to v, as shown by the arrow below:

(iv)

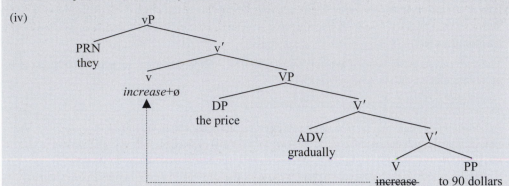

The vP in (iv) is subsequently merged with a T constituent containing *will*, and T-*will* agrees (invisibly) with and assigns nominative case to the subject *they*. T also has an EPP feature which triggers raising of the subject *they* to spec-T. Merging TP with a null declarative C forms the CP shown in simplified form below (with the constituents marked by ~~strikethrough~~ being given a null spellout in the PF component):

(v)   [$_{CP}$ [$_C$ ø] [$_{TP}$ they [$_T$ will] [$_{vP}$ ~~they~~ [$_v$ increase+ø] [$_{VP}$ the price gradually [$_V$ ~~increase~~]
                                                                                                 to 90 dollars]]]]

If the adverb *gradually* had been adjoined to v-bar rather than to V-bar, the resulting structure would instead have been:

(vi)   [$_{CP}$ [$_C$ ø] [$_{TP}$ they [$_T$ will] [$_{vP}$ ~~they~~ gradually [$_v$ increase+ø] [$_{VP}$ the price [$_V$ ~~increase~~]
                                                                                                 to 90 dollars]]]]

and (vi) would be spelled out as the sentence *They will gradually increase the price to 90 dollars*.

9 Phases

9.1 Overview

In this chapter, we look at recent work by Chomsky suggesting that syntactic structure is built up in **phases** (with phases including CP and transitive vP). At the end of each phase, part of the syntactic structure already formed undergoes **transfer** to the phonological and semantic components, with the result that the relevant part of the structure is inaccessible to further syntactic operations from that point on. (An incidental point of detail to note is that we shall simplify exposition – and follow Chomsky – by adopting a split projection analysis of Verb Phrases, but not of TP or CP constituents.)

9.2 Phases

In chapter 7, we noted Chomsky's claim that syntactic operations involve a relation between a **probe** P and a **local goal** G which is sufficiently 'close' to the probe (or, in the case of **multiple agreement**, a relation between a probe and more than one local goal). However, an important question to ask is why probe–goal relations must be local. In this connection, Chomsky (2001, p. 13) remarks that 'the P, G relation must be local' in order 'to minimise search' (i.e. in order to ensure that a minimal amount of searching will enable a probe to find an appropriate goal). His claim that locality is forced by the need 'to minimise search' suggests a processing explanation (albeit Chomsky has always maintained that the overall goal of linguisic theory is to develop a theory of *competence* rather than of *performance*). The implication is that the Language Faculty can only process limited amounts of structure at one time, and can only hold a limited amount of structure in its 'active memory' (Chomsky 1999, p. 9). In order to ensure a 'reduction of computational burden' (1999, p. 9) Chomsky proposes that 'the derivation of EXP[ressions] proceeds by *phase*' (p. 9), so that syntactic structures are built up one *phase* at a time. He maintains (2001, p. 14) that 'phases should be as small as possible, to minimise memory', suggesting (1999, p. 9) that they are 'propositional' in nature, and include CP and transitive vP (i.e. a vP with an AGENT or EXPERIENCER external argument, which he denotes as v*P). His rationale for taking CP and v*P as phases is that

CP represents a complete clausal complex (including a specification of *force*), and v*P represents a complete thematic (argument structure) complex (including an external argument).

Once all the operations which apply within a given phase have been completed, the **domain** of the phase (i.e. the complement of its head) becomes **impenetrable** to further syntactic operations. Chomsky refers to this condition as the **Phase Impenetrability Condition/PIC** – and we can formulate it as follows:

(1)   **Phase Impenetrability Condition/PIC**
       The c-command domain of a phase head is impenetrable to an external
       probe (i.e. a goal which is c-commanded by the head of a phase is
       impenetrable to any probe c-commanding the phase)

(As should be self-evident, this condition is a modification of the **Impenetrability Condition** that we posited in earlier chapters.) The reason why the domain of the phase head is impenetrable to an external probe (according to Chomsky 2001, p. 5) is that once a complete phase has been formed, the domain of the phase undergoes a **transfer** operation by which the relevant (domain) structure is simultaneously sent to the phonological component to be assigned an appropriate phonetic representation, and to the semantic component to be assigned an appropriate semantic representation – and from that point on, the relevant domain is no longer accessible to the syntax. So, for example, once a complete CP phase has been formed, the TP which is the domain (i.e. complement) of the phase head C will be sent to the phonological and semantic components for processing. As a result, TP is no longer visible in the syntax, and hence neither TP itself nor any constituent of TP can subsequently serve as a goal for a higher probe of any kind: i.e. no probe c-commanding CP can enter into a relation with TP or any constituent of TP.

In order to make our discussion more concrete, consider the derivation of the following sentence:

(2)   Will Ruritania withdraw troops from Utopia?

Given the split projection (vP+VP) analysis of Verb Phrases outlined in the previous chapter, (2) will be derived as follows. The V *withdraw* first merges with the PP *from ∅ Utopia* (with *Utopia* being a DP headed by a null determiner, given the DP hypothesis) to form the V-bar *withdraw from Utopia*, and then merges with the QP *troops* (comprising a null partitive quantifier ∅ and the noun *troops*) to form the VP *withdraw ∅ troops from Utopia*. The resulting VP is merged with a causative light verb whose external AGENT argument is ∅ *Ruritania* (another definite DP headed by a null determiner). The light verb agrees (invisibly) with and assigns (invisible) accusative case to the QP ∅ *troops*; moreover, being affixal in nature, the light verb triggers movement of the verb *withdraw* from its original (italicised) position in V to v, so resulting in the structure shown below (with the arrow marking movement):

(3)

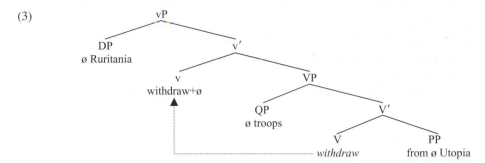

Since a transitive vP (i.e. a vP with a thematic external argument) is a phase, and since the vP in (3) is transitive and has the external argument *ø Ruritania*, the VP constituent (by virtue of being the domain/complement of the light verb which is the head of the phase) will undergo **transfer** to the phonological and semantic components at this point, and thereafter cease to be accessible to further syntactic operations. Let's suppose that transfer results in lower copies of moved constituents receiving a null spellout in the PF component, and that uninterpretable features which have been deleted are removed from the structure handed over to the semantic component, but not from the structure handed over to the phonological component. Consequently, the phonological component will not spell out the original (italicised) copy of the verb *withdraw* in (3), and only the items *troops* and *from Utopia* will be given an overt phonetic spellout.

The **syntactic computation** then proceeds once more, with [T *will*] being merged with the vP in (3) to form the T-bar shown below (simplified by showing only those items within VP which received an overt spellout in the PF component after the VP underwent transfer at the end of the vP phase, and using outline font to indicate that the items in question have already undergone transfer):

(4)

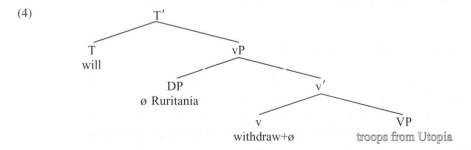

Since [T *will*] has uninterpretable (and unvalued) person/number features, it is an active probe which searches for a local goal to value and delete its unvalued features. Neither the QP *ø troops* nor the DP *ø Utopia* are accessible to the probe *will* (since both are contained within a VP which has already been transferred to the phonological and semantic components); however, the DP *ø Ruritania* is accessible to *will* and is syntactically active by virtue of its uninterpretable case feature. Hence, *will* agrees (invisibly) with and assigns (invisible) nominative case to the DP ø *Ruritania*. The auxiliary [T *will*] also has an EPP feature requiring movement of the closest goal which it agrees with to spec-T; accordingly, the DP ø *Ruritania* is moved from its original (italicised) position in spec-v to become the specifier of *will*, as shown by the arrow below:

(5)

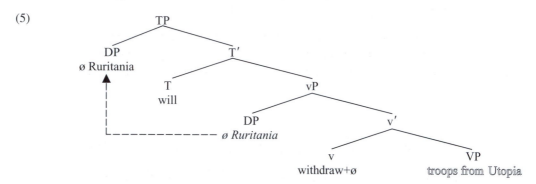

The resulting TP is merged with a null interrogative C. Let's suppose that (as suggested in §5.4) yes-no questions contain a null yes-no question particle merged in spec-C (perhaps a null counterpart of the adverb *whether*), and that C has a tense feature which attracts *will* to move from its original (italicised) position in T to adjoin to the null C heading CP in the manner shown by the arrow below:

(6)

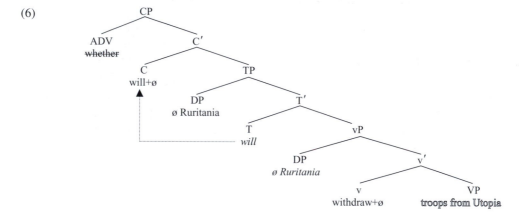

Since CP is a phase and the domain of the head of a phase is spelled out at the end of a phase, TP undergoes **transfer** to the phonological and semantic components at this point. The transfer operation results in the italicised copies of the auxiliary *will* and the DP ø *Ruritania* receiving a null spellout in the phonological component.

However, we are now left with something of a problem. We have come to the end of the derivation, but so far neither C nor the null yes-no question particle which serves as its specifier have been 'handed over' to the phonological and semantic components for further processing. One way of ensuring that this happens is to make the additional assumption in (7ii) below about transfer:

(7) **Transfer**
 (i)   At the end of each phase, the domain (i.e. complement of the phase head) undergoes *transfer*
 (ii) At the end of the overall derivation, all remaining constituents undergo transfer

In the case of (6), the two remaining constituents which have not yet undergone **transfer** are the C constituent containing *will* and the null yes-no question operator in spec-C. Accordingly, these undergo transfer to the phonological/semantic components at the end of the overall derivation.

9.3   Intransitive and defective clauses

Our illustrative account of **phases** in the previous section involved a structure containing a transitive vP phase and a CP phase. However, since neither intransitive clauses (i.e. those containing a vP with no external argument) nor defective clauses (i.e. clauses which are TPs lacking a CP projection) are phases, things work differently in such structures – as we can illustrate in relation to the derivation of:

(8)   There are thought by many to remain some problems in Utopia

The unaccusative verb *remain* merges with its LOCATIVE complement *in ø Utopia* (*Utopia* being a DP headed by a null determiner) to form the V-bar *remain in ø Utopia*, and this V-bar is in turn merged with its THEME argument (the quantifier phrase *some problems*) to form the VP *some problems remain in ø Utopia*. This VP in turn is merged with a null light verb which, being affixal, triggers movement of the verb *remain* from its italicised position in V to adjoin to the light verb. If (as argued in the previous chapter) expletives originate in spec-v, at the end of the v-cycle we will have the following structure:

(9)

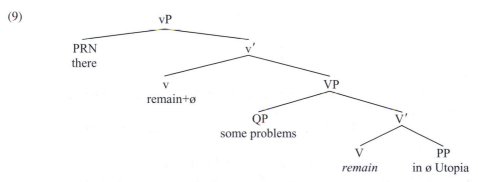

Although a transitive vP is a phase (and so requires its domain to be spelled out at the end of the v-cycle), the vP in (9) is not a phase because it is *intransitive* by

virtue of having no thematic external argument (i.e. no AGENT or EXPERIENCER subject) – as can be seen from the fact that the spec-v position in (9) is occupied by the non-thematic expletive pronoun *there*. Accordingly, the VP complement does not undergo transfer at this point, and the syntactic derivation proceeds by merging the resulting vP with infinitival *to*. If (as argued in §7.9) infinitival *to* has an EPP feature and a person feature in defective clauses, *to* will attract expletive *there* (which is a third person pronoun) to move to spec-T, so deriving:

(10)

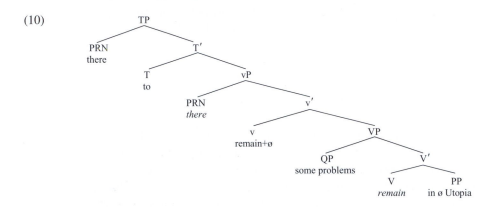

The (passive participle) verb *thought* is then introduced into the derivation, and merges with the TP in (10) to form a V-bar which in turn merges with the PP *by many* to form the VP shown below (though an incidental detail to note in passing is that some linguists take passive *by*-phrases to be adjuncts):

(11)

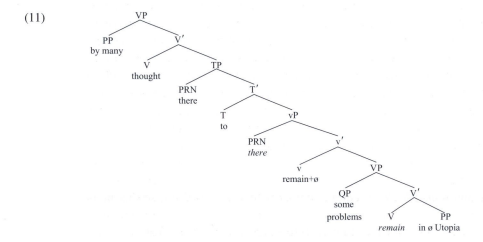

The resulting VP is then merged as the complement of a light verb which (being affixal) attracts the verb THINK to adjoin to it. If we suppose that the light verb is participial in nature (which is why Chomsky (1999) uses the label PRT to denote it), we can account for why the verb *think* is ultimately spelled out as the passive participle *thought*. Merging the resulting vP with the passive auxiliary BE will derive the following T-bar constituent (where the verb THINK is shown in its passive participle spellout form *thought*):

(12)

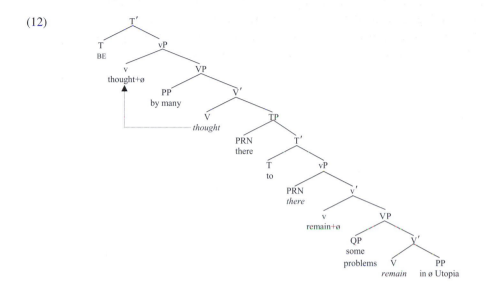

At this point, BE is an active probe by virtue of its uninterpretable (and unvalued) φ-features, and so it searches for an active local goal to value its person/number features. In chapter 7, we suggested that a head carrying unvalued person and number features keeps on probing until it locates the closest active φ-complete goal which can value (and delete) its person and number features. Accordingly, BE will not stop probing when it locates the expletive pronoun *there* (active by virtue of its uninterpretable person feature, but φ-incomplete by virtue of lacking number) and will continue to probe deeper into the structure until it locates the φ-complete third person plural goal *some problems* (active by virtue of its uninterpretable and unvalued case feature and φ-complete by virtue of carrying both person and number). Both *there* and *some problems* are accessible goals for BE since neither is contained within a structure which has undergone transfer. (We can assume that the pronoun *many* is not active at this point, because it falls within the domain of a closer probe *by* which will already have valued its case feature as accusative and deleted it.) Accordingly, BE simultaneously agrees in person with *there* and *some problems*, and in number with *some problems*, so that BE is assigned the feature values [third-person, plural-number]. Since *some problems* is φ-complete, it can delete the uninterpretable person and number features of BE. Conversely, BE (by virtue of being finite) can value the unvalued case feature of *some problems* as nominative, and (because BE is also φ-complete) can delete the relevant case feature (and also the person feature of *there*). The EPP feature of T is deleted by moving the closest active goal (i.e. *there*) from its original position as the specifier of *to* into its derived position as the specifier of BE (movement being indicated by an arrow below). Merging the resulting TP with a null declarative complementiser derives the CP structure shown in simplified form below:

(13)

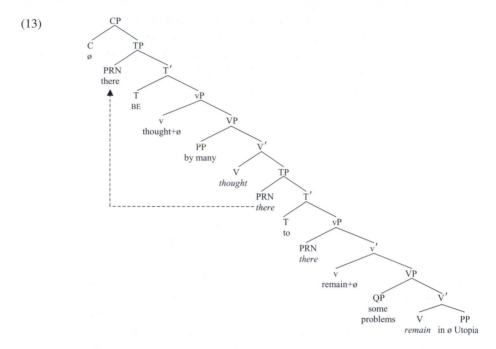

Since CP is a phase, the TP headed by [T BE] which constitutes its domain will undergo transfer at this point, in accordance with (7i). The italicised copies of moved constituents will be given a null spellout, and the auxiliary BE in T will be spelled out as *are* in the phonological component (since it has been valued as third person plural in the course of the derivation). The null C heading CP subsequently undergoes transfer by (7ii), and is assigned a null spellout in the phonological component, and interpreted in the semantic component as marking the relevant sentence as declarative in force.

   In the context of our discussion of phases here, the key point which emerges is that neither an intransitive vP nor a defective TP clause constitutes a phase – e.g. in the case of (13), not the intransitive vP containing *remain*, nor the vP containing the passive participle *thought*, nor the defective TP complement of *thought*. In consequence, the relevant vP and TP constituents are still accessible in the syntax when BE is introduced into the derivation, so allowing BE to agree with *some problems*.

9.4   Phases and A-bar movement

   The phase-based theory of syntax outlined in the previous section has far-reaching consequences for the operation of A-bar movement operations like wh-movement – as we can illustrate in relation to the following sentence:

(14)   Where is it thought that he will go?

The derivation of (15) proceeds as follows. The unaccusative verb *go* is merged with its GOAL argument (the locative adverbial pronoun *where*) to form the V-bar *go where*, which in turn is merged with its THEME argument *he* to form the VP *he go where*. This VP is then merged with a null affixal light verb which triggers raising of the verb *go* to v from its original position in V, as shown by the arrow below:

(15)

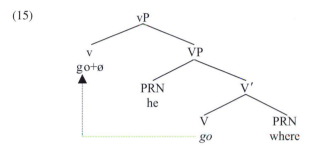

Since vP is intransitive (by virtue of the fact that the light verb has no external argument), vP is not a phase, and transfer cannot apply at this point. The syntactic computation therefore continues, with [T *will*] merging with the vP in (15). *Will* agrees with (and assigns nominative case to) *he*, and the EPP feature of *will* triggers raising of *he* from its original position in spec-V to spec-T (as shown by the arrow below). Merging the complementiser *that* with the resulting TP forms the CP shown in (16) below:

(16)

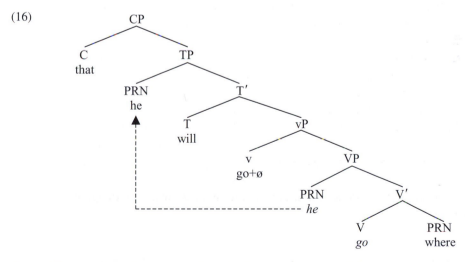

Since CP is a phase, its domain (i.e. its TP complement) will undergo transfer at this point. This means that neither TP nor any of the constituents of TP will subsequently be accessible to further syntactic operations – i.e. in effect, TP and its constituents of TP are *frozen* in place once TP undergoes transfer.

However, this causes an obvious problem, since if all constituents of TP are frozen in place at this point, the wh-word *where* will be unable to move from the (sentence-final) V-complement position it occupies in (16) to the (sentence-initial) main clause C-specifier position which it occupies in (14) *Where is it thought that he will go?* As we saw in §5.6, we can overcome this problem if we posit that wh-movement applies in a **successive-cyclic** fashion (one clause at a time), and that the complementiser *that* in structures like (16) has an **edge feature** which triggers movement of the closest wh-expression (= *where*) to become the specifier of the complement-clause CP headed by *that* before *where* subsequently moves on to become the specifier of the main clause C constituent containing the inverted auxiliary *is*. Assuming this to be so, *where* will move from the clause-final position which it occupies in (16) above as the complement of *go* into the clause-initial position which it occupies in (17) below as the specifier of *that* (movement being indicated by an arrow):

(17)

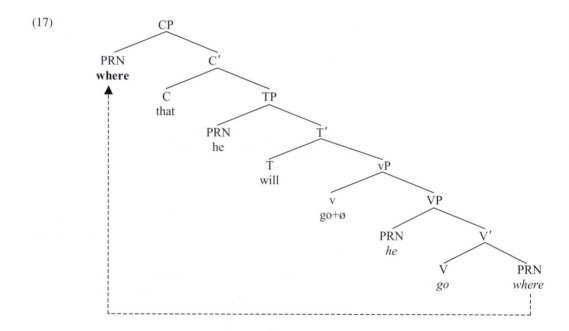

At this point (once all the operations which apply on the C-cycle have applied) the domain of C (i.e. its TP complement) will undergo transfer in accordance with (7i), because CP is a phase: one consequence of this is that the italicised lower copies of moved constituents will be marked as receiving a null spellout in the phonological component.

After transfer of TP is completed, the syntactic computation continues. The CP in (17) is merged as the complement of the verb THINK, and the resulting VP is in turn merged as the complement of a participial light verb (ensuring that THINK is eventually spelled out as the passive participle *thought*), with the verb THINK (below shown as *thought*) raising to adjoin to the light verb. The expletive pronoun *it* is merged as the specifier of the vP. A present tense T constituent containing the passive auxiliary BE is then merged with the vP already formed, and [T BE] agrees with the third person singular expletive pronoun *it* (so that BE is eventually spelled out as *is*), and the EPP feature on [T BE] attracts *it* to raise to spec-T. Merging the resulting TP with a null affixal interrogative C will trigger raising of BE from its original (italicised) position in T to C; since the interrogative C also has an edge feature, it will attract interrogative *where* to move from the italicised spec-C position in the complement clause into spec-C position in the main clause, so deriving the CP shown in simplified form below (with movements triggered by the main-clause C constituent being arrowed):

(18)

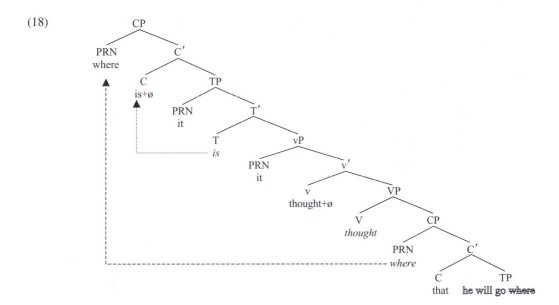

Since CP is a phase, its domain (= the main clause TP) will undergo transfer by (7i) at this point, so that the italicised copies of *is*, *thought* and *where* will receive a null spellout in the phonological component. If we assume an additional transfer condition (7ii) to the effect that 'at the end of the overall derivation, all remaining constituents undergo transfer', the remaining constituents *where* and *is* + ø on the edge of the root CP undergo transfer by (7ii).

What our overall discussion in this section tells us is that just as A-movement applies in a successive-cyclic fashion (so that each time a new T constituent is introduced into the derivation, it can attract the closest nominal goal to become its specifier), so too (within a phase-based theory of syntax) A-bar movement operations like wh-movement must apply in a successive-cyclic fashion (one phase at a time): this means that each time a new phase head like C is introduced into a wh-structure, it will serve as a probe which attracts the closest wh-goal to move into its specifier position.

9.5   A-bar movement in transitive clauses

In the previous section, we looked at how wh-movement applies in *intransitive* clauses within Chomsky's phase-based theory of syntax. However, the picture is more complicated in the case of A-bar movement out of a transitive vP. Since transitive vPs are phases, it follows that in structures containing one or more *transitive* vPs, wh-movement will have to pass through intermediate spec-v positions as well. We can illustrate how this works by looking at the derivation of the transitive sentence

(19)   What have they done?

This will be derived as follows. The verb DO (shown below in its spellout form *done*) merges with its thematic complement *what* to form the VP *done what*, and the resulting VP is merged with a transitive light verb whose external argument is *they*. The light verb agrees with and assigns accusative case to *what*, and (by virtue of being affixal) triggers raising of *done* from V to v. Let's suppose that just as C can have an edge feature attracting movement of a wh-expression, so too a transitive light verb (by virtue of being a phase head, like C) can have a wh-attracting edge feature. This being so, *what* will be moved to become a second (outer) specifier for vP, forming the structure below:

(20)

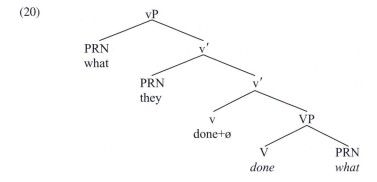

An assumption implicit in this analysis is that a head can have **multiple specifiers** – in the case of (20), an inner specifier *they* representing the external argument of the light verb, and an outer specifier *what* which is attracted by the edge feature of the light verb. Since a transitive vP is a phase, the VP domain *done what* in (20) will undergo transfer at the end of the vP phase in accordance with (7:), and the two italicised copies of moved constituents will thereby be given a null spellout.

The derivation then proceeds by merging [$_T$ *have*] with the vP in (20), forming the T-bar below:

(21)

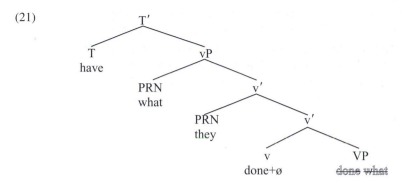

The T-probe *have* is active by virtue of its unvalued uninterpretable person/ number agreement features, and searches for a nominal goal to value and delete its agreement features and become its subject. Since the closest nominal goal c-commanded by T-*have* is the pronoun *what*, let's ask why *have* can't agree with and attract *what* to become its subject. One way of ruling out the possibility of T agreeing with and attracting *what* would be in terms of a condition such as the following:

(22)   **Inactivation Condition**
        A goal with a case feature becomes inactive for agreement with (or attraction by) an **A-head** like T once its case feature has been valued and deleted

(An A-head is a probe like T or transitive v which enters the derivation carrying one or more unvalued agreement features, and which acts as a case assigner if it has a complete set of agreement features.) Another condition which would prevent *what* from moving to spec-T in (20) is a constraint proposed in Chomsky (2005b) which we can characterise as follows:

(23)   **Mixed Chains Constraint**
        Movement cannot give rise to a mixed chain containing one copy of a constituent which has moved to the edge of a phase, and another which has moved to the edge of a non-phasal projection

Since *what* has moved to the edge of the vP phase in (21), the *Mixed Chains Constraint* (23) bars movement of *what* to the edge of TP, because this would result in a chain in which *what* moves to the edge of a phasal projection (= vP), and then from there moves to the edge of a non-phasal projection (= TP).

To summarise: the Inactivation Condition (22) means *what* is inactive and so cannot agree with *have*, and the Mixed Chains Constraint (23) further prevents *what* from moving to spec-T. By contrast, the pronoun *they* is active at this point because its case feature has not yet been valued. If we follow Boeckx (2007, p. 83) in supposing that a pronoun like *what* with an already valued case feature is 'transparent' for T, then T can see 'through' *what* and locate the pronoun *they* as the closest active goal. Accordingly, *have* agrees with, assigns nominative case to and attracts the pronoun *they* to move to spec-T, so deriving:

(24)

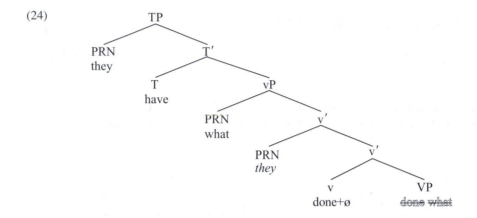

This TP is then merged with a null complementiser with a tense feature which triggers movement of *have* from T to C, and an edge feature which triggers movement of *what* to spec-C, so deriving:

(25)

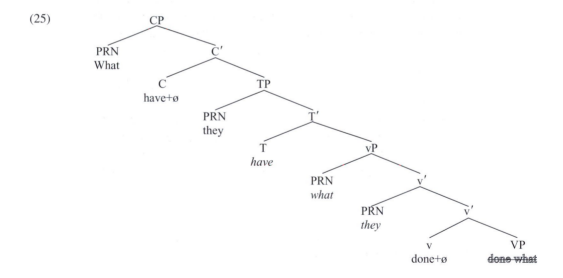

At the end of the CP phase, TP undergoes transfer in accordance with (7i) and the italicised copies of moved constituents receive a null spellout in the phonological component. Subsequently, the constituents at the edge of CP (i.e. its specifier *what* and its head *have* + *ø*) undergo transfer in accordance with (7ii).

   Our discussion of the derivation of (20) *What have they done?* shows us that A-bar movement in transitive clauses will involve movement through spec-v into spec-C. An obvious implication of this is that wh-questions like (26a) below which contain two transitive clauses will correspondingly involve successive-cyclic wh-movement through two spec-v positions (and likewise through two spec-C positions) – as shown in skeletal form in (26b):

(26) (a)   What might she think that they will do?

(b)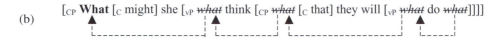

More generally, a sentence containing *n* transitive verbs and *m* CPs inter-vening between the original position of a wh-expression and its ultimate landing-site will involve movement through *n* spec-v positions and *m* spec-C positions.

As our discussion in this section illustrates, theoretical considerations lead us to conclude that, if CPs and transitive vPs are phases, wh-movement must involve movement through intermediate spec-C positions, and also through inter-mediate spec-v positions in transitive clauses. In §5.7, we presented empirical evidence that long-distance wh-movement involves movement through interme-diate spec-C positions. An obvious question to ask at this juncture, therefore, is what empirical evidence there is that a wh-expression extracted out of a transitive vP first moves to the edge of vP before subsequently moving to the edge of CP. Since (as we see in the case of A-movement) a probe which attracts a goal to become its specifier may agree with the attracted goal in respect of one or more features, what we might expect to find is that a transitive v agrees (in respect of one or more features) with a goal which it attracts to become its specifier. However, since English has impoverished agreement morphology, we will have to look at other languages for evidence of such agreement.

In this connection, it is interesting to note that there is evidence that wh-movement out of a transitive Verb Phrase triggers agreement marking on the verb in some languages. We can illustrate this phenomenon in terms of the following Chamorro example (adapted from Reintges, LeSourd and Chung 2006, p. 169):

(27)   Hafa si*n*anganenña si Joaquin nu hagu bi*n*indenña
          What told the Joaquin to you sold
          'What did Joaquin tell you that he sold?'

The crucial aspect of the example in (27) is that the direct object *hafa* 'what' has been moved out of its original position as the object of the embedded clause to the front of the main clause, and that this movement triggers agreement on both the verb in the embedded clause and the verb in the main clause, each of which therefore end up carrying the italicised (object-agreement) infix *in*. This suggests that a transitive light verb carrying an edge feature attracts a wh-marked goal and undergoes overtly marked agreement with the goal.

A different pattern of agreement (in respect of number–gender concord features) between a transitive light verb and an attracted wh-expression is illustrated by participle agreement in French in clauses such as (28b) below:

(28) (a)   Il a *commis* quelle bêtise?
             He has committed what blunder
             'What blunder did he make?'

     (b)   Quelle bêtise il a *commise*?
             What blunder he has committed
             'What blunder did he make?'

The participle *commis* 'committed' is in the default (masculine singular) form in (28a), and does not agree with the feminine singular in situ wh-object *quelle bêtise* 'what blunder' (the final *-e* in these words can be taken to be an orthographic marker of a feminine singular form). However, the participle *commise* in (28b) contains the feminine singular marker *-e* and agrees with its preposed feminine singular object *quelle bêtise* 'what blunder' and consequently rhymes with *bêtise*. What's going on here?

Let's look first at the derivation of (28a). The QP *quelle bêtise* 'what blunder' in (28a) is merged as the complement of the verb *commis* 'committed' forming the VP *commis quelle bêtise* 'committed what blunder'. The resulting VP is then merged with a null transitive light verb, and the resulting v-bar is in turn merged with its external AGENT argument *il* 'he'. Since the light verb has an external argument, it assigns accusative case to the QP object *quelle bêtise* 'what blunder'. Being affixal, the light verb attracts the verb *commis* 'committed' to adjoin to it, in the manner shown by the arrow below:

(29)

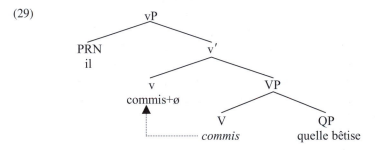

By hypothesis, the light verb has no edge feature in wh-in-situ questions, so there is no movement of the wh-phrase *quelle bêtise* 'what blunder' to spec-v. Subsequently the vP (29) is merged as the complement of the auxiliary *a* 'has' which agrees in person/number φ-features with (and triggers movement to spec-T of) the subject *il* 'he'. Merging the resulting TP with a null complementiser which likewise has no edge feature derives the structure associated with (28a) *Il a commis quelle bêtise?* (literally 'He has committed what blunder?').

Now consider the derivation of (28b). This is similar to that of (28a), until we reach the stage of derivation shown in (29) above. However, in a non-echoic question, the light verb will have an edge feature which attracts the wh-marked object *quelle bêtise* 'what blunder' to move to become an additional (outer) specifier for the vP, in the manner shown by the arrow below:

(30)

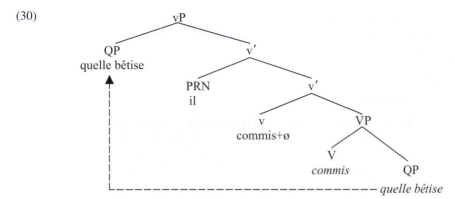

The resulting vP (30) is then merged as the complement of the auxiliary *a* 'has' which agrees in φ-features with (and triggers movement to spec-T of) the subject *il* 'he'. Merging the resulting TP with a null interrogative complementiser which has a wh-attracting edge feature triggers movement of the wh-phrase to spec-C, so deriving the structure associated with (28b) *Quelle bêtise il a commise?* (literally 'What blunder he has committed?').

In the light of the assumptions made above, consider why the participle surfaces in the agreeing (feminine singular) form *commise* 'committed' in the wh-movement structure (28b), but not in the non-agreeing (default) form *commis* in the wh-in-situ structure (28a). In this connection, it is interesting to note that in Irish, a complementiser only overtly agrees with a wh-expression which it attracts to move to spec-C (not with an in situ wh-expression). What this suggests is that French participles only overtly inflect for number/gender agreement with their object if they have an edge feature which forces movement of a nominal through spec-v. However, any such assumption requires us to suppose that wh-movement proceeds through spec-v in transitive clauses, and hence lends further support to Chomsky's claim that transitive vPs are phases.

Further evidence in support of successive-cyclic wh-movement through spec-v in transitive clauses comes from observations about mutation in Welsh made in Tallerman (1993). Tallerman claims that wh-traces trigger so-called **soft mutation** of the initial consonant of a following word. In this connection, consider the sentence in (31) below (where PROG denotes a progressive aspect marker):

(31)   Beth wyt ti 'n *feddwl* oedd gin I?
          What are you PROG think was with me
          'What do you think I had?'

What is particularly interesting here is that the italicised verb has undergone soft mutation, so that in place of the radical form *meddwl* 'think', we find the mutated form *feddwl*. Given independent evidence that Tallerman produces in support of claiming that wh-traces induce mutation, an obvious way of accounting for the use of the mutated verb form *feddwl* 'think' in (31) is to suppose that the wh-pronoun *beth* 'what' moves through spec-v on its way to the front of the overall sentence. We can then suppose that a wh-copy on the edge of vP triggers soft mutation on the lexical verb adjoined to the light-verb heading the vP.

9.6   Uninterpretable features and feature inheritance

Throughout the book so far, we have assumed that a non-phasal head like T (in finite clauses) enters the derivation carrying not only an interpretable tense feature, but also uninterpretable agreement features which are valued via agreement with (and work in conjunction with EPP to trigger movement of) an active noun or pronoun expression which is assigned nominative case via agreement with T. However, in recent work, Chomsky (2005b, 2006) has argued that non-phasal heads enter the derivation carrying only interpretable features, and that they **inherit** their uninterpretable features from the phase head immediately above them. This means (for example) that the phase head C is not only the locus (i.e. source) of certain interpretable features (e.g. C marks declarative, interrogative or imperative force) but is also the locus of the uninterpretable agreement features carried by T. Indeed, this idea had already been anticipated in earlier work: cf. Chomsky's suggestion (1999, p. 35, fn. 17) that 'The locus of nominative case and subject–verb agreement is C, not T.' Chomsky's reasoning is along the following lines. T only carries a complete set of (person and number) agreement features in a clause where T is selected by C, not in a defective (CP-less) clause. In this connection, consider the contrast between the two complement clauses bracketed below:

(32) (a)   It would seem [$_{CP}$ [$_C$ that] [$_{TP}$ he [$_T$ has] left]]
   (b)   He would seem [$_{TP}$ [$_T$ to] have left]

Given the assumptions we made in chapter 7, the bracketed TP in (32a) is selected by the C constituent *that*, and the head T of TP is the auxiliary *has* which carries a complete set of person/number agreement features. By contrast, the TP in the raising structure in (32b) is not selected by C, and its head T constituent *to* is defective in that it does not carry a complete set of agreement features. Reasoning thus, Chomsky concludes that the person/number agreement features of T must originate on C, and subsequently 'be inherited by' or 'be handed over to' or 'percolate down onto' (three different metaphors expressing the same idea) the T constituent immediately beneath C.

An interesting piece of evidence in support of the claim that C is the locus of agreement features comes from the phenomenon of *complementiser–subject agreement* found in a number of languages. For example, Haegeman (1992, p. 47) notes that in West Flemish 'the complementiser of the finite clause agrees in person and number with the grammatical subject of the sentence it introduces', and provides a list of illustrative examples (p. 49) which include the following:

(33) (a)   Kpeinzen *dank* **ik** morgen goan
             I.think that$_{1.Sg}$ I tomorrow go
             'I think that I'll go tomorrow'

   (b)   Kpeinzen *daj* **gie** morgen goat
             I.think that$_{2.Sg}$ (you) tomorrow go
             'I think that you will go tomorrow'

   (c)   Kpeinzen *dan* **Valère en Pol** morgen goan
             I.think that$_{3.Pl}$ Valère and Pol tomorrow go
             'I think that Valere and Paul will go tomorrow'

In these examples, the (italicised) complementiser overtly inflects for agreement in person and number with the (bold-printed) subject of its clause. However, since the finite verb in the clause also inflects for agreement with the subject, it would seem that agreement features are copied from C onto T (so that both C and T end up bearing a copy of the relevant agreement features).

A parallel phenomenon of *complementiser agreement* is found in a non-standard variety of English spoken by people who come from the Boston area of Massachusetts, in which C agrees with a preposed (italicised) wh-expression that it attracts to move to spec-C, e.g. in stuctures such as the following (from Kimball and Aissen 1971, p. 246):

(34)   Where are the boys [*who* Tom **think** [Dick **believe**
                                        [Harry **expect** to be late]]]

Here, the head C constituent of each of the bracketed CPs attracts the italicised relative pronoun *who* (which is plural by virtue of having the plural noun *boys* as its antecedent) to move to spec-C. C ultimately 'hands over' these agreement features to the bold-printed verbs in the head v position of vP (perhaps via a downward feature-percolation operation in the PF component, of which Affix Lowering may be a particular instance). Note that sentences such as (34) also provide independent evidence for successive-cyclic wh-movement through intermediate spec-C positions, since each of the bold-printed verbs in each of the three bracketed CPs is a plural form agreeing with the plural wh-pronoun *who*. Interestingly, Radford (1992, p. 55) reports that two-year-old children sometimes produce parallel structures such as those below (the names of the children producing each utterance being shown in parentheses, together with their ages in years; months):

(35) (a)   *What'***s** the wheels doing? (Holly 2;0)
   (b)   *What'***s** those? (Alistair 2;6)
   (c)   *What'***s** you doing? (Ellen 2;9)
   (d)   *What'***s** they called now? (James 2;10)

So, for example, the child producing (35a) allows the auxiliary *(i)s* occupying the head C position of CP to agree with the wh-pronoun *what* which it attracts to move to spec-C. In structures such as (34–35), it would appear that C retains its agreement features, rather than handing them over to T.

Further evidence for agreement originating on C comes from infinitival CPs such as those bracketed below:

(36) (a)   I would like very much [$_{CP}$ [$_C$ for] [$_{TP}$ him [$_T$ to] win the race]]

   (b)   I would like very much [$_{CP}$ [$_C$ ø] [$_{TP}$ PRO [$_T$ to] win the race]]

The locus of case assignment in (36) seems to be the complementiser introducing the clause, in that the prepositional complementiser *for* requires the *him* subject of its TP complement to be assigned accusative case, whereas the null complementiser ø requires the PRO subject of its TP complement to be assigned null case. If structural case assignment works hand in hand with agreement (as we saw in the previous chapter), this means that the complementisers must also carry a complete set of (person and number) agreement features. However, if the case and agreement features were to remain on the complementiser, we would expect the complementiser to agree with and case-mark the infinitive subject, and attract it to raise to the edge of CP. However, this would wrongly predict that *for*-infinitive structures like that in (37) below should be grammatical:

(37)   *I would like very much [$_{CP}$ him [$_C$ for] [$_{TP}$ [$_T$ to] win the race]]

Instead, it is the infinitival T constituent *to* which attracts the complement clause subject to raise from its initial position as specifier of the vP *win the race* to become the specifier of infinitival *to*. How can this be?

An answer consistent with Chomsky's *inheritance* analysis is the following. Let us suppose that a series of merger operations on the complement clause CP phase in (36a) give rise to the structure shown in simplified form below (with the material in outline font having already undergone transfer):

(38)   [$_{CP}$ [$_C$ for] [$_{TP}$ [$_T$ to] [$_{vP}$ him [$_v$ win] the race]]]

Let us further suppose that the complementiser is the initial locus of subject case assignment and subject agreement properties within the clause, but that the complementiser 'hands over' its uninterpretable case and agreement features to the head T constituent of its TP complement. In consequence, the infinitival T probe *to* agrees with and assigns accusative case to the subject *him* of the vP *him win the race*, and attracts it to raise to spec-T, as shown by the arrow below:

(39)   [$_{CP}$ [$_C$ for] [$_{TP}$ him [$_T$ to] [$_{vP}$ him [$_v$ win] the race]]]

Likewise, in a control infinitive clause such as that bracketed in (36b) above, infinitival *to* inherits the uninterpretable case assignment and agreement features of the null complementiser introducing the clause, and so agrees with and assigns null case to the infinitive subject, and attracts it to raise to spec-T. (An implicit assumption in our discussion here is that complementisers – and other case assigners – carry an uninterpretable case-assignment feature which determines the value which they assign to an unvalued case feature on an accessible goal.)

Chomsky argues that in the same way as a C phase head 'hands over' its subject case assignment and subject agreement feature to the head immediately beneath it (i.e. to T), so too a transitive light verb which serves as a phase head 'hands over' its object case assignment and object agreement features to the head immediately beneath it (i.e. to V). One type of structure in which this happens are ECM structures such as the following:

(40)(a)   The DA will **prove** *the witness* <u>conclusively</u> to have lied (adapted from Bowers 1993, p. 632)

(b)   I **suspect** *him* <u>strongly</u> to be a liar (Authier 1991, p. 729)

(c)   I've **believed** *Gary* <u>for a long time now</u> to be a fool (Kayne 1984, p. 114)

(d)   I have **found** *Bob* <u>recently</u> to be morose (Postal 1974, p. 146)

If (as we have assumed hitherto) the (*italicised*) infinitive subject were superficially positioned in the specifier position of an infinitival TP complement clause, and if accusative case in transitive Verb Phrases is assigned by a superordinate light verb, the light verb in the main clause would agree with and assign accusative case to the infinitive subject. However, the problem is that this doesn't account for why – in sentences like (40) above – the (italicised) subject of the ECM clause is followed by an (underlined) adverbial or prepositional expression which modifies the (bold-printed) main-clause verb. If the italicised adverbial/prepositional expression is contained within the main-clause VP (by virtue of modifying a projection of the main-clause verb), it follows that the bold-printed accusative subject of the infinitive complement must also be inside the main clause VP. How can this be? The answer is that the subject of the ECM clause raises up to become the object of the main-clause verb by an operation traditionally termed **(subject-to-) object-raising**. To illustrate how this analysis works, let's take a closer look at the derivation of (40a).

Let's suppose we have reached a stage of derivation at which we have formed the infinitival TP *the witness to have lied*. This TP is merged with the verb *prove* to form the V-projection *prove the witness to have lied*. The adverb *conclusively* is then adjoined to this V-projection to form the even larger V-projection *conclusively prove the witness to have lied* (which we will label as VP because it is the largest structure headed by the V *prove*). The resulting structure is in turn merged with a null light verb, forming the v-projection *ø conclusively prove the witness to have lied*, and this in turn is merged with the DP *the DA* to form a vP. Let us suppose that a transitive light verb can carry a set of agreement and (accusative) case-assignment features, and that it hands these over to the head immediately beneath it (i.e. to the head V of VP). Let us further suppose that V (like T) can carry an EPP feature when it inherits agreement features from the phase head above it. Given these assumptions, the lexical V *prove* will (invisibly) agree with and assign (invisible) accusative case to the DP *the witness*, and (by virtue of its EPP feature) will also attract it to move to spec-V. The verb *prove* is in turn attracted by the affixal light verb to move from V to v, so deriving the structure shown below (with arrows indicating movement):

(41)

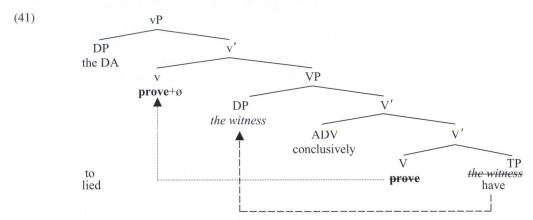

Given that the (italicised) moved DP thereby becomes the object of the verb *prove*, it is clear that the relevant movement operation is another instance of A-movement. The vP in (41) is subsequently merged with the T-auxiliary *will*, which attracts the DP *the DA* to move to spec-T, so forming a TP which is merged with a null declarative complementiser to form the CP shown in skeletal form below (in which only overt constituents of vP are shown):

(42)   [$_{CP}$ [$_C$ ø] [$_{TP}$ the DA [$_T$ will]
                    [$_{vP}$ [$_v$ prove] the witness conclusively to have lied]]]

The analysis in (42) accounts for how the accusative subject of the infinitive complement clause comes to be positioned in front of an adverb modifying a projection of the verb in the main clause, and how the accusative DP *the witness* comes to be adjacent to the transitive verb *prove*.

Now consider the corresponding ECM expletive structure in (43) below, where the subject of the ECM clause is expletive *there*:

(43)   The DA will prove *there* conclusively to have been a conspiracy

Given that we analysed expletive *there* in §7.6 as carrying only a third person feature, the V *prove* will inherit case assignment and agreement features from *v*, and will agree in person with *there* and in person and number with *a conspiracy*, and will assign accusative case to the indefinite nominal *a conspiracy*. (It will not assign case to expletive *there*, because this is a caseless pronoun.) It will also attract the closest (pro)nominal expression it agrees with (namely expletive *there*) to move to the outer edge of VP. Consequently, expletive *there* will end up in a position above (and hence be spelled out to the left of) the adverb *conclusively*.

A key assumption made in the preceding paragraph is that V inherits its agreement features and its ability to assign accusative case from the light verb which heads the vP phase. One reason for thinking that the relevant case and agreement features originate on the light verb can be illustrated in relation to the following contrast:

(44) (a) The DA has proved the defendant conclusively to have committed the murder

(b) The defendant has been proved conclusively to have committed the murder

The matrix vPs in these two sentences have the respective structures shown below, prior to agreement, case-marking and movement of the (italicised) infinitive subject *the defendant*:

(45) (a) [$_{vP}$ the DA [$_v$ ø] [$_{VP}$ conclusively [$_V$ prove] [$_{TP}$ *the defendant* [$_T$ to] have committed the murder]]]

(b) [$_{vP}$ [$_v$ ø] [$_{VP}$ conclusively [$_V$ prove] [$_{TP}$ *the defendant* [$_T$ to] have committed the murder]]]

Why should it be that the V *prove* subsequently agrees with, case-marks and attracts the italicised infinitive subject in the active structure (45a), but not in the passive structure (45b) (where the matrix T constituent – not shown in 45b above – agrees with, assigns nominative case to and attracts the infinitive subject)? Whether or not V agrees with, case-marks and attracts the italicised infinitive subject cannot be determined by the internal structure of VP, since this contains the same two constituents in the two sentences (namely the verb *prove* and the TP complement *the defendant to have committed the murder*). Rather, what determines that accusative case is assigned to the infinitive subject in the transitive sentence (45a) but not in the intransitive passive sentence (45b) is the fact that the vP has a thematic external argument (namely *the DA*, which occupies the specifier position within vP) in the transitive structure (45a), but has no external argument (and hence no specifier) in the intransitive structure (45b). A plausible way of accounting for this is to suppose that a light verb only carries agreement features (and only has the ability to assign accusative case) if it has a thematic external argument. However, since it is V rather than v which agrees with, assigns accusative case to and attracts the infinitive subject in ECM structures, it is clear that v must 'hand over' its agreement features to V once the vP phase is formed.

However, while v hands over its case and agreement features to V in ECM structures like (46a) below, it seems clear that this does not happen in structures like (46b):

(46) (a) [$_{vP}$ the DA [$_v$ ø] [$_{VP}$ [$_V$ prove] [$_{TP}$ *the witness* to have lied]]]

(b) [$_{vP}$ they [$_v$ ø] [$_{VP}$ *the ball* [$_V$ roll] down the hill]]

The reason is that while V-*prove* c-commands (and so can agree with and assign accusative case to) the DP *the witness* in (46a), V-*roll* does not c-command (and so cannot agree with and case-mark) the DP *the ball* in (46b). On the contrary, only v (and not V) c-commands *the ball* in (46b), so it seems clear that the light verb must retain its case/agreement features in such structures, and not hand them over to V. This raises the question of why a transitive light verb should hand over its case/agreement features to V in ECM structures like (46a), but not in simple transitive structures like (46b). One possible answer could be that UG prevents a light verb *v* from case-marking any constituent in the c-command domain of a lexical verb V (perhaps because V is itself a potential case assigner, and one case assigner cannot case-mark a constituent within the domain of another case assigner): this would mean that v can only case-mark a goal within its own **immediate domain** (i.e. a goal which is c-commanded by v but not by V). If so, then *v* will be able to directly case-mark the DP *the ball* in (46b) because this DP is within the domain of (and so follows) the light verb, but is not within the domain of (and so does not follow) V; but by contrast, v will not be able to case-mark the DP *the witness* in (46a) because this DP falls within the domain of (and so follows) the V *prove*. We could then suppose that v only hands over its case and agreement features to V when v finds no accessible goal to case mark within its own immediate domain: this would mean that *v* must hand its case/agreement features over to V in ECM structures like (46a), but not in simple transitives like (46b). (An alternative solution which might be envisaged is that v always hands over its case/agreement properties to V, and that V-*roll* can only case-mark the DP *the ball* in a structure like 46b after it has raised to adjoin to v: this kind of solution poses other problems, and so will not be pursued here.)

To summarise our discussion in this section: in recent work, Chomsky argues that phase heads enter the derivation carrying both interpretable and uninterpretable features, but that other heads enter the derivation carrying only interpretable features. After a series of Merger operations have applied to build up a particular phase structure (and before case/agreement/movement operations apply), the phase head can 'hand over' its uninterpretable features to the head beneath it, so that e.g. T can inherit agreement features from C in a finite clause, and V can inherit agreement features from v in a transitive clause. This means that in a finite ECM structure like (44a) *The DA has proved the defendant conclusively to have committed the murder*, T will agree with, assign nominative case to and attract the DP *the DA* to move to spec-T, while V will agree with, assign accusative case to and attract the DP *the defendant* to move to spec-V.

9.7   Independent probes

Hitherto, we have adopted the classic bottom-up *cyclic* account of derivations under which e.g. (within a given clause) T-operations (i.e. movement and agreement operations involving a T-probe and one or more goals) apply before C-operations (i.e. operations involving a C-probe and one or more goals): and indeed, this sequential ordering of operations was assumed to be a consequence of the Earliness Principle, in that T is introduced into the derivation before C, so T-operations apply immediately T is introduced into the derivation, and hence before C-operations. However, the revised conception of derivations outlined in the previous section means that this view is no longer tenable. After all, if T inherits its uninterpretable agreement features from C (as Chomsky claims), then it follows that the percolation operation by which uninterpretable features percolate down from C to T must take place before T can serve as a probe for agreement, case-marking and movement, since it is only once T has acquired uninterpretable agreement features from C that it can become an active probe for agreement, case and movement operations. Consequently, in recent work, Chomsky maintains that it is only after Merger operations have built up a complete phase structure that movement and agreement operations can apply. Furthermore, he also posits that each separate head within a phase can probe independently of any other probe within the same phase, in a random fashion (with some possibilities yielding a convergent outcome, and others causing a crash). In this section, we look at evidence that different heads within a phase can probe independently and in any order (e.g. C can probe before T, or T can probe before C, or C and T can probe simultaneously). However, before doing this (and by way of background information), let's first examine two constraints on movement which will play an important part in our subsequent exposition.

In this connection, consider the following contrast:

(47) (a)   They believe [John to be innocent]
   (b)   John is believed [to be innocent]
   (c)   They believe [John is innocent]
   (d)   *John is believed [is innocent]

As we see from (47a,b), the subject of a defective TP (e.g. an infinitive clause which is the complement of a ECM predicate like *believe*) can passivise, but not the subject of a non-defective (e.g. finite) TP. This suggests that the specifier of a non-defective TP is barred from undergoing further A-movement operations. However, contrasts such as that below:

(48) (a)   Of which party do you believe [the leader to have committed suicide]?
   (b)   *Of which party do you believe [the leader has committed suicide]?

suggest that A-bar movement is likewise possible out of the subject of a defective TP as in (48a), but not out of the subject of a complete (non-defective) TP as in (48b). The observation that both A-movement and A-bar movement are barred out of the subject/specifier of a complete TP leads Chomsky (2005b) to suggest that the subject/specifier of a complete TP is *invisible* to further operations (and hence to higher probes). We can characterise this constraint as follows:

(49)   **Invisibility Condition**
         The specifier of a complete (non-defective) TP is invisible to any higher probe

The constraint in (49) provides a straightforward account of why the subject of the bracketed complete TP cannot be passivised in (47d), and why the PP *of which party* cannot be extracted out of the DP *the leader of which party*, which is the subject of the bracketed complete TP in (48b).

A second constraint which will also play a part in our discussion below can be illustrated in terms of the ungrammaticality of:

(50)   *Of which car is it unclear which driver they arrested?

On the main-clause CP phase, wh-movement will involve the movement operation indicated by the arrow in the structure shown below (simplified in numerous ways, including by showing only CPs, and only wh-copies on the edge of CP):

(51)   [$_{CP}$ **Of which car** is it unclear [$_{CP}$ *which driver **of which car*** they arrested]]

What prevents the PP *of which car* from being extracted out of the DP *which driver of which car*? Chomsky (2005b) suggests the following constraint:

(52)   **Specifier Condition**
           No subextraction is possible out of a constituent which is a specifier of a
           phase head

Since the DP *which driver of which car* occupies spec-C in (51) and hence is the specifier of the phase head C, the Specifier Condition (52) prevents the PP *of which car* from being subextracted out of it.

Having outlined two background assumptions about conditions on movement, let's now turn to the main point of our discussion in this section – namely to argue that different heads (like C and T) probe independently of each other on a given phase. Chomsky (2005b) observes that traditional bottom-up cyclic accounts of syntax fail to account for contrasts such as the following (the relevant grammaticality judgments being Chomsky's, and being somewhat less sharp for some other speakers):

(53)(a)   *Of which car has the driver caused a scandal?
    (b)   Of which car was the driver arrested?

More specifically, he maintains that the existing bottom-up account would wrongly predict that (53b) is ungrammatical. To see why both sentences would be predicted to be ungrammatical under a bottom-up account, let's take a look at the derivation of each of the two sentences in (53), beginning with (53a). This is derived as follows.

The verb *cause* merges with the QP *a scandal* to form the VP *cause a scandal*. This VP in turn merges with a transitive light verb to form a v-bar which in turn merges with the DP *the driver of which car* to form the vP shown in simplified form below (with the verb *cause* raising to attach to the light verb, and the QP *a scandal* being assigned accusative case by V, which inherits case/agreement features from v):

(54)

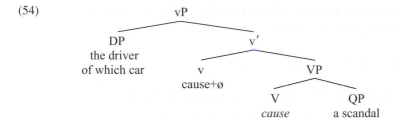

The vP in (54) is then merged with the past tense T-auxiliary HAVE, which agrees with, case-marks, and triggers movement of the DP *the driver of which car* to spec-T (as well as determining that the verb *cause* is spelled out in the perfect participle form *caused*). Merging the resulting TP with a null interrogative C forms the structure shown below (simplified in a number of ways, including by only showing overt constituents of vP):

(55)

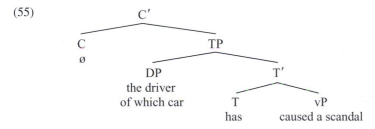

The interrogative C carries a tense feature triggering movement of *has* from T to C, and an edge feature triggering movement of a maximal projection containing a wh-word to spec-C. We might therefore expect C to be able to trigger movement of the wh-PP *of which car* to spec-C, as in (56) below:

(56)

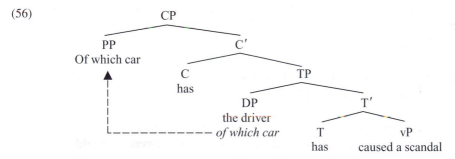

However, the resulting sentence (53a) *Of which car has the driver caused a scandal?* is ungrammatical. The reason is that the arrowed movement in (56) violates the Invisibility Condition (49) which renders the specifier of a non-defective TP invisible to a higher probe: since the DP *the driver of which car* in (55) is the specifier of a finite (non-defective) TP headed by the finite T-auxiliary *has*, the whole DP is invisible to the higher probe C, and hence C cannot attract the PP *of which car* to move to spec-C, with the result that the movement arrowed in (56) is barred.

Now consider how we would derive (53b) *Of which car was the driver arrested?* In terms of our existing assumptions, this would be derived as follows. The verb *arrest* merges with its complement *the driver of which car* to form the VP *arrest the driver of which car*. This VP is in turn merged with an intransitive light verb (with no external argument) which triggers raising of the verb *arrest* from V to v, forming the vP shown in simplified form below:

(57)

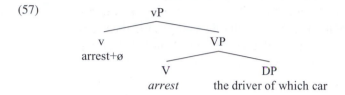

The participial nature of the light verb means that the verb ARREST is ultimately spelled out in the passive participle form *arrested*. The vP in (57) is then merged with the past tense T-auxiliary BE, which agrees with, case-marks and triggers movement of the DP *the driver of which car* to spec-T. Merging the resulting TP with a null interrogative C forms the structure shown in skeletal form below (simplified in a number of ways, including by not showing null constituents of vP):

(58)

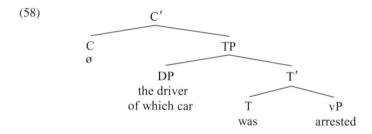

As in all finite main-clause non-echoic questions, C carries a tense feature triggering movement of *was* from T to C, and an edge feature triggering movement of a wh-expression (more precisely, a maximal projection containing a wh-word) to spec-C. We might therefore expect C to be able to attract the PP *of which car* to move to spec-C in the manner shown by the arrow below:

(59)

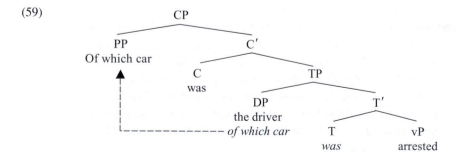

However, subextraction of the PP *of which car* out of the DP *the driver of which car* is blocked by the Invisibility Condition (49), which renders the specifier of a non-defective TP invisible to any higher probe. Accordingly, the C-probe in (58) cannot 'see' the PP *of which car*, because this PP is part of a larger DP *the driver of which car*, which is itself invisible to a higher probe like C. Consequently, on our existing assumptions, sentence (53b) *Of which car was the driver arrested?* is wrongly predicted to be ungrammatical. What has gone wrong here?

Chomsky (2005b, p. 13) suggests that the answer lies in the traditional (bottom-up) assumption that operations involving lower (= subordinate) probes must necessarily apply before operations involving higher (= superordinate) probes. He argues instead for the alternative position that (within a given phase) different heads can probe in a random fashion – either one before the other, or *simultaneously* ('in parallel', to use the terminology of Chomsky (2005b, p. 13)). Let's see how the *parallel probes* assumption helps us account for the contrast between (53a) and (53b).

Consider first the derivation of (53b) *Of which car was the driver arrested?* and suppose that we have arrived at a stage of derivation at which we have formed the vP shown in (57) above. Let's further suppose that this vP merges with a past tense T constituent containing BE to form a TP which in turn merges with a null interrogative C constituent, deriving the CP shown below:

(60)

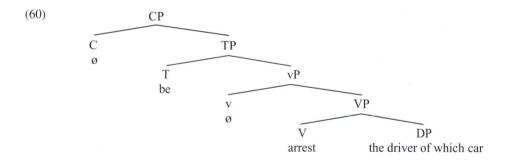

In other words, assume that the v, T and C heads within the CP phase are all introduced into the derivation before any of them can probe. In order to simplify our discussion, let's set aside the head movement operations by which the verb *arrest* adjoins to the participial light verb *v*, and the T constituent containing BE adjoins to C, and instead concentrate on the movement to the edge of TP and CP. Consider first what happens if C and T probe simultaneously. This means that at the same time as the T-auxiliary BE agrees with the (bold-printed) DP *the driver of which car* and attracts a copy of it to move to spec-T, the null interrogative C constituent simultaneously attracts a copy of the (italicised) PP *of which car* to move to spec-C. These operations lead to the formation of the structure (61) below (with the inner arrow showing A-movement to spec-T, and the outer arrow showing A-bar movement to spec-C):

(61)

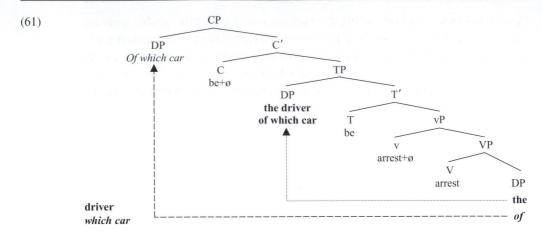

There is no violation of the Invisibility Condition (49) because the PP *of which car* is being extracted out of a DP (*the driver of which car*) at the foot of the tree which is the complement of the verb *arrest*, and not out of a DP which is the subject of a non-defective T. Dual movement results in a structure containing three copies of the PP *of which car* – namely the original one within VP, a second one which ends up in spec-T as part of the moved DP *the driver of which car*, and a third one which moves on its own from complement position in VP into specifier position within CP. Given that only the highest copy of a moved constituent is overtly spelled out, it follows that only the highest of the three copies of the PP *of which car* will be overtly spelled out (namely that in spec-C): likewise, only the highest copy of the string *the driver* is overtly spelled out (namely that in spec-T). Assuming that BE is ultimately spelled out as *was* and ARREST as the passive participle *arrested*, the structure in (61) will be spelled out in the PF component as (53b) *Of which car was the driver arrested?*

Now let's return to consider the derivation of the ungrammatical sentence (53a) **Of which car has the driver caused a scandal?* Let's suppose that we have reached a stage of derivation at which we have formed the vP phase in (54) above, and that we then merge this vP with the T-auxiliary HAVE to form a TP which is in turn merged with an interrogative C constituent to form the CP shown below:

(62)

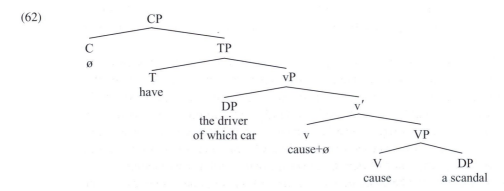

Given Chomsky's assumption that C and T can probe simultaneously, what we might expect to be possible here is for T to agree with and case-mark the DP *the driver of which car* and attract a copy of it to move to spec-T, and for C to simultaneously attract a copy of the PP *of which car* to move to spec-C (as well as attracting a copy of the auxiliary HAVE to move to C), as shown by the arrows in the structure below (simplified in familiar ways):

(63)

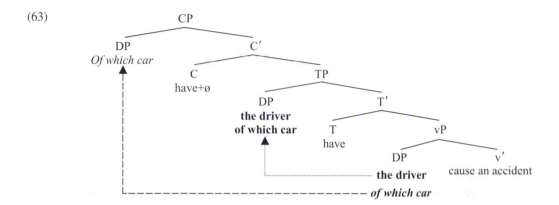

Since HAVE/CAUSE are spelled out as *has/caused* in the PF component and only the highest copy of each constituent is overtly spelled out, the resulting structure will ultimately be spelled out as (53b) **Of which car has the driver caused a scandal?* But the resulting sentence is ungrammatical. Why should this be? The answer is that subextraction of the PP *of which car* out of the DP *the driver of which car* violates the Specifier Condition (52) which bars subextraction out of a constituent which is a specifier of a phase. Since vP in (63) is a phase (by virtue of the light verb having a thematic external argument), and since the DP *the driver of which car* is the specifier of this vP phase, the wh-movement operation indicated by the slashed arrow in (63) leads to violation of the Specifier Condition, and to consequent ungrammaticality. Note, incidentally, that it would not be possible to attempt to avoid violating the Specifier Condition by moving the PP *of which car* to spec-v at the stage of derivation in (54) above (and subsequently to spec-C) because (as Chomsky 2005b, p. 14 notes) the PP *of which car* in (54) is not in the search domain of (i.e. is not c-commanded by) the null light verb.

So far in this section, we have outlined Chomsky's account of why subextraction is possible out of the subject of a passive clause, but not out of the subject of a transitive clause. Note that a crucial theoretical assumption underlying Chomsky's analysis is that C and T can probe independently and *simultaneously*. However, there is evidence from simple transitive sentences like (19) *What have they done?* that C and T do not always probe simultaneously. In this connection, suppose that we have reached the stage of derivation shown below (with *what* having moved to the edge of the vP phase on the v-cycle, and VP having undergone transfer at the end of the vP phase):

(64)

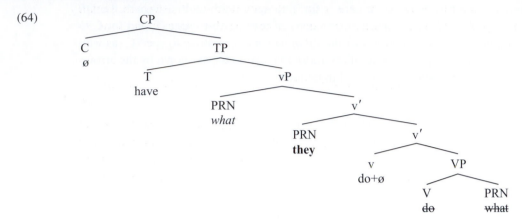

At this point, T needs to be able to attract the bold-printed subject *they* to move to spec-T, and C needs to be able to attract the italicised wh-object *what* to move to spec-C. Let us suppose that only the highest copy (or link) in a movement chain is *visible* to a superordinate probe in the syntax – a constraint which we can characterise as follows:

(65)   **Visibility Condition**
          Only the highest copy in a movement chain is visible in the syntax (other
          copies being inert)

Moreover, suppose that we capture Chomsky's (2005b, p. 8) insight that a 'probe agrees with goals in its domain as far as a goal with no unvalued features, which blocks further search' in terms of a condition along the following lines:

(66)   **Intervention Condition**
          Probe P cannot target goal G if there is some other visible goal of the same
          kind as G intervening between the two and if the intervening goal is inactive
          for P

Independent motivation for such a condition (according to Chomsky 1998, p. 45, fn. 94) comes from the ungrammaticality of double-*there* sentences such as:

(67)   *There <u>are</u> likely *there* to be <u>problems</u>

where the intervening italicised occurrence of *there* blocks agreement between *are* and *problems*.

In the light of the Intervention Condition in (66), let's now consider what happens next in (64). Suppose that T probes first and C afterwards, or that T and C probe simultaneously. In either eventuality, the Intervention Condition (66) will prevent the T-auxiliary *have* from targeting the subject *they* because the (italicised) highest occurrence of the pronoun *what* intervenes between the two, and because *what* is inactive for A-operations (i.e. operations involving a probe like T which is an A-head) because its case feature was deleted on the vP phase.

But now let's make the alternative assumption that C probes before T in (64). If so, C will attract *what* to move to spec-C, thereby deriving the structure shown in simplified form below (with DO ultimately being spelled out as *done* in the PF component):

(68)   [CP *what* [C ø] [TP [T have] [vP what <u>they</u> [v done] [VP [v done] what]]]]

Subsequently, the T-auxiliary *have* can probe separately and attract the subject *they* to move to spec-T, because although the copy of *what* which intervenes between *have* and *they* is inactive, it is not the highest copy of *what* (the highest copy of *what* being the italicised one at the front of the overall sentence). Movement of the subject *they* to spec-T derives the structure:

(69)   [CP *what* [C ø] [TP <u>they</u> [T have] [vP what they [v done] [VP [v done] what]]]]

Subsequent auxiliary inversion together with deletion of all but the highest copies will then derive the superficial structure associated with *What have they done?* Thus, only if C probes before T in an object-question structure like (64) will the derivation yield a successful outcome.

Since C and T sometimes probe simultaneously and sometimes sequentially, Chomsky (2005b, p. 17) concludes that 'All options are open' so that C and T can probe 'in either order, or simultaneously, with only certain choices converging' (i.e. resulting in a well-formed sentence). In other words, sometimes C probes before T, sometimes T probes before C, and sometimes the two probe at the same time.

9.8   Subject questions

The assumption that T and C function as independent probes has interesting implications for the syntax of *subject questions* (i.e. clauses whose subject is interrogative) like those below:

(70) (a)   Who died?
     (b)   Who killed the president?

(70a) is derived as follows. DIE is an unaccusative predicate which merges with the pronoun *who* to form the VP *die who*. This VP is then merged with a null light verb, thereby forming the vP *ø die who*. The resulting vP is then merged with a T constituent containing a past tense affix (below denoted as *Af*) so forming a TP which is in turn merged with an interrogative C to form the CP

shown below:

(71)

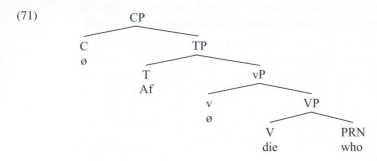

C, T and v then probe independently of each other. The light verb attracts the verb *die* to adjoin to it. Since C and T both locate the same goal *who*, they probe simultaneously. (If C were to probe before T, T would be unable to agree with, case-mark or attract *who*; if T were to probe before C and attract *who* to spec-T, the Invisibility Condition would prevent C from subsequently attracting *who* to move from spec-T to spec-C – as indeed would a constraint against *mixed chains*.) The T-affix picks out *who* as a goal which is active by virtue of its unvalued case feature, and agrees with and assigns nominative case to *who*, and also attracts a copy of *who* to move to spec-T. C probes simultaneously and identifies *who* as the closest (and only) interrogative goal in its search domain, and attracts a separate copy of *who* to move to spec-C, in the manner shown by the arrows below:

(72)

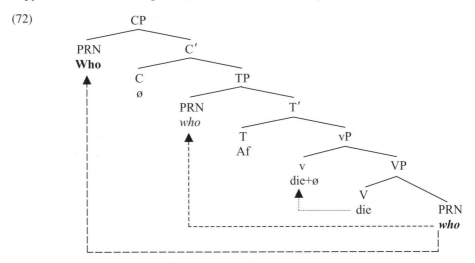

As (72) shows, one copy of *who* is created in spec-T via A-movement, and a second (separate) copy of *who* is created in spec-C via A-bar movement. In the PF component, the highest copy of *who* (= the one in spec-C) is given an overt spellout. There is no T-to-C movement (and hence no DO-support) in subject questions, because C does not attract T when C attracts a wh-constituent which is itself attracted by T (and *who* is attracted by both T and C in 72). Consequently, the past tense affix remains in T in the syntax, and is lowered from T onto V in the PF component, with the result that the verb DIE is ultimately spelled out as *died*.

The derivation of (70b) *Who killed the president?* is similar in key respects. The verb *kill* merges with the DP *the president* to form the VP *kill the president*. This VP is then merged with a null light verb (which attracts the verb *kill*) to form a v-bar which is itself merged with the pronoun *who* to form a vP. This vP is then merged with a T constituent containing a past tense affix (= *Af*), so forming a TP. The resulting TP is merged with an interrogative C, forming a CP. The agreement features on T probe and pick out *who* as their goal, agreement between the two resulting in T being marked as third person singular, and in *who* being marked as tensed. The movement features on the two heads (viz. the edge and tense features on C, and the EPP feature on T) then probe simultaneously (i.e. in parallel), each attracting a copy of *who* to move into its own specifier position – as shown by the arrows below:

(73)

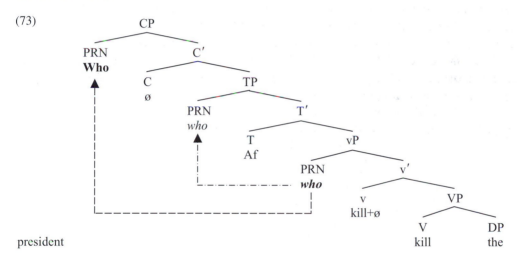

president

As before, only the highest copy of *who* (= the one in spec-C) is overtly spelled out in the PF component. Since the copy of *who* attracted by C is in a thematic argument position (in spec-v), there is no T-to-C movement and the past tense affix in T lowers onto v via Affix Hopping, with the result that the verb KILL is ultimately spelled out as the past tense form *killed*, so deriving (70b) *Who killed the president?*

A key assumption made in the analysis of subject questions in (72) and (73) above is that it results in a structure in which there is one copy of *who* in spec-T and a separate copy of *who* in spec-C. The assumption that there is a copy of *who* in spec-T gains empirical support from sentences like:

(74) (a)   Who might appear to himself to have been victimised?
     (b)   Who is considered by himself to be the best candidate?

We noted in §2.7 that a reflexive anaphor like *himself* can only be bound by (i.e. refer to) a c-commanding expression within the minimal TP containing the reflexive. If the only movement which *who* undergoes in (74) is A-bar movement from complement position in VP into specifier position within TP (as shown by the arrow below), (74a) will have the following skeletal structure:

(75)   [cp Who [c ø] **[TP** [T might] appear to himself [TP [T to] have been victimised *who*]]]

But since *himself* has no antecedent c-commanding it within the closest (bold-printed, enlarged and bracketed) TP immediately containing it, such a derivation wrongly predicts that (74a) is ungrammatical. By contrast, if *who* undergoes successive-cyclic A-movement to both spec-T positions and undergoes separate A-bar movement to spec-C, we derive the structure shown in skeletal form below (with the higher arrows showing A-movement, and the lower arrow showing A-bar movement):

(76)

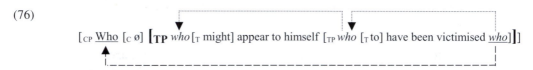

[cp Who [c ø] **[TP** *who* [T might] appear to himself [TP *who* [T to] have been victimised *who*]]]

Given the analysis in (76), the copy of *who* which occupies the specifier position within the bold-printed (enlarged) TP can serve as the antecedent of *himself*, thereby accounting for the well-formedness of (74a). Accordingly, sentences like those in (74) provide us with evidence that a copy of the subject moves to spec-T in subject questions.

But what evidence is there that a separate copy of the subject moves to spec-C? Relevant evidence comes from the observation made by Pesetsky and Torrego (2001) that *who* in subject questions can be substituted by *who on earth* or *who the hell*: cf.

(77) (a)   *Who on earth* killed the president?
     (b)   *Who the hell* killed the president?

As Pesetsky (1987) notes (and as the examples in (78) below illustrate), wh-expressions like *who on earth* and *who the hell* have the property that they cannot remain in situ, but rather must move to spec-C:

(78) (a)   *Who on earth/Who the hell* is she going out with?
     (b)   *She is going out with *who on earth/who the hell*?

If wh-expressions like those italicised in (78) always move to spec-C, it follows that the italicised subjects in (77) must likewise have moved to spec-C – and hence it is plausible to suppose that the same is true of the subject *who* in (70b) *Who killed the president?* Thus, we have empirical evidence that in subject questions, one copy of the interrogative subject moves to spec-T and a separate copy moves to spec-C.

9.9 More on subextraction

Given that (as we earlier saw in relation to the ungrammaticality of (53a) *Of which car has the driver caused a scandal?*) subextraction out of the nominative subject of a transitive clause is not permitted, it is interesting to note that *raising* sentences such as (79) below are grammatical:

(79)   Of which car would the driver appear to have caused a scandal?

In order to try and understand what's going on here, let's take a closer look at the derivation of (79). The DP *the driver of which car* originates as the specifier of the vP which is eventually spelled out as *caused a scandal*, and (via successive-cyclic A-movement) becomes first the specifier of infinitival *to* and then the specifier of *would*, so creating three copies of the DP in question. At some stage of derivation, the PP *of which car* must be extracted out of one of the three (italicised) copies of the DP, and be moved to the (bold-printed) spec-C position in the schematic structure (80) below:

(80)   [CP **Of which car** [C would] [TP *the driver of which car*₃ [T would] appear
          [TP *the driver of which car*₂ [T to] have [vP *the driver of which car*₁
                                    [v caused] a scandal]]]]

The grammaticality of sentence (79) leads to the conclusion that it must be possible to subextract the PP *of which car* out of one or more of the three italicised copies of the DP *the driver of which car* in (80). But which one(s)?

It seems clear that the relevant PP cannot be subextracted out of the lowest copy of the italicised DP (carrying the subscript number 1) in (80), because this would violate the *Specifier Condition* (52) which bars subextraction out of the specifier of a phase head. Nor can the PP in question be subextracted out of the highest copy of the italicised DP (carrying the subscript number 3), because this would violate the *Invisibility Condition* (49) which renders the specifier of a non-defective (e.g. finite) TP invisible to a higher probe. The conclusion we reach is thus that the PP must be subextracted from the intermediate copy of the italicised DP (carrying the subscript number 2), in the manner shown by the arrow below:

(81)   [CP **Of which car** [C would] [TP *the driver of which car*₃ [T would] appear

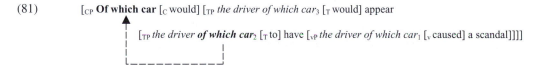

          [TP *the driver **of which car**₂ [T to] have [vP *the driver of which car*₁ [v caused] a scandal]]]]

The arrowed movement in (81) does not violate the Invisibility Condition (49), because subextraction is out of the subject of a *defective* clause (i.e. a TP which is not the immediate complement of a C head). Nor does the arrowed movement violate the *Specifier Condition* (52), because the PP is not extracted out of the specifier of a phase head.

A closer look at the derivation in (81) is also revealing in respect of what it tells us about how T and C probe. First, the (non-phasal/defective) T constituent containing infinitival *to* attracts the DP *the driver of which car* to become its specifier. Then the higher (non-defective) T constituent containing *would* and the interrogative C constituent probe in parallel, T attracting a copy of *the driver of which car* to move to spec-T, and C simultaneously attracting the interrogative PP *of which car* to move to spec-C (the possibility of moving the whole DP to become the specifier of T-*would* and from there moving the wh-PP to spec-C being ruled out by the Invisibility Condition). As noted earlier, Chomsky (2005b, p. 1) concludes from this kind of structure that C and T can probe either sequentially ('in either order' – i.e. with C probing before T, or T probing before C) or simultaneously, 'with only certain choices converging' (i.e. resulting in grammaticality).

Our discussion here leads us to the wider conclusion that subextraction is possible from the subject of a defective clause (i.e. one which is a TP but not a CP), but not from the subject of a complete clause (i.e. one which is a CP). If this is so, we should expect to find that subextraction is also possible from the subject of a defective ECM clause with an accusative subject. In this connection, consider the following contrast:

(82) (a)   Of which car hadn't they expected [the driver to enter the race]?
 (b)   *Of which car hadn't it been expected [for the driver to enter the race]?

In the case of (82a), the DP *the driver of which car* originates in spec-v and is subsequently raised to spec-T via A-movement, as shown by the arrow in the simplified structure below:

(83) [$_{TP}$ *the driver of which car* [$_T$ to] [$_{vP}$ *the driver of which car* [$_v$ enter] the race]]

The TP in (83) is then merged as the complement of the ECM verb *expect*, forming the VP below:

(84) [$_{VP}$ [$_V$ expect] [$_{TP}$ *the driver of which car* [$_T$ to] [$_{vP}$ *the driver of which car*
               [$_v$ enter] the race]]]

This VP is in turn merged as the complement of a null light verb with an AGENT subject, forming the vP phase shown below:

(85) [$_{vP}$ they [$_v$ ø] [$_{VP}$ [$_V$ expect] [$_{TP}$ *the driver of which car* [$_T$ to] [$_{vP}$ *the driver*
               of which car [$_v$ enter] the race]]]]

Chomsky (2005b) posits that just as a CP phase contains a higher probe (= C) which can trigger A-bar movement and a lower probe (= T) which can trigger A-movement (to spec-T) of a DP which it agrees with and case-marks, so too a vP phase has a parallel structure. Consequently a vP phase contains both a higher

probe (the light verb *v*) which can trigger A-bar movement, and a lower probe
(= the lexical verb *V*) which can trigger A-movement (to spec-V) of a DP that
it agrees with and case-marks. If we further suppose that the twin heads of a
phase (C and T in the case of a CP phase; v and V in the case of a vP phase)
can probe in parallel, what this allows for is the following possibility. In (85), the
transitive V *expect* agrees (invisibly) with, assigns accusative case to and triggers
A-movement to spec-V of a copy of the DP *the driver of which car* (as shown
by the lower arrow below); simultaneously, the null light-verb *ø* triggers A-bar
movement to spec-v of a copy of the wh-PP *of which car* (as shown by the upper
arrow):

(86)

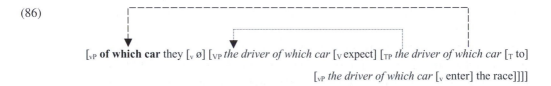

[$_{vP}$ **of which car** they [$_v$ ø] [$_{VP}$ *the driver of which car* [$_V$ expect] [$_{TP}$ *the driver of which car* [$_T$ to]

[$_{vP}$ *the driver of which car* [$_v$ enter] the race]]]]

On the subsequent CP phase, the pronoun *they* will move to spec-T and the wh-PP
of which car to spec-C, thereby deriving the structure associated with (82a) *Of
which car hadn't they expected the driver to enter the race?*

Our discussion of (82a) above illustrates that subextraction is possible from
the accusative subject of a defective clause (i.e. a clause which is a TP but not a
CP). But why, then, should subextraction be barred out of the accusative subject
in (82b) **Of which car hadn't it been expected [for the driver to enter the race]*?
The answer is that the bracketed clause containing the accusative subject in this
case is a complete clause (i.e. one which is both a CP and a TP), and hence a
phase. Given that CPs are phases, the only way in which the wh-PP *of which car*
can move into spec-C in the main clause is by first moving into spec-C in the
complement clause. On the assumptions made here, the complement clause will
have the structure shown in simplified form below:

(87)   [$_{CP}$ **of which car** [$_C$ for] [$_{TP}$ *the driver of which car$_2$* [$_T$ to] [$_{vP}$ *the driver of
which car$_1$* [$_v$ enter] the race]]]

However, the problem posed by this structure is that subextraction of the bold-
printed wh-PP from copy 1 of the italicised DP *the driver of which car* violates the
Specifier Condition (52) which bars subextraction out of the specifier of a phase
head (the phase head in this case being a light verb with an italicised external
argument); moreover, subextraction of the wh-PP out of copy 2 is blocked by
the Invisibility Condition (49) which renders invisible the specifier of a non-
defective TP (i.e. a TP which is the complement of a phasal C head). Since there
is no way for the wh-PP *of which car* to move to spec-C, the associated sentence
(82b) **Of which car hadn't it been expected for the driver to enter the race?* is
ungrammatical.

Our discussion of subextraction from accusative subjects in this section leads us to the more general conclusion that subextraction is possible from the subject of a defective clause (= TP), but not from the subject of a complete clause (= CP).

9.10   Summary

In this chapter, we have taken a look at Chomsky's phase-based theory of syntax. In §9.2, we noted Chomsky's claim that the computational component of the Language Faculty can only hold limited amounts of syntactic structure in its working memory at any one time, and that clause structure is built up in **phases** (with phases including CP and transitive vP). At the end of each phase, the **domain** (i.e. complement of the phase head) undergoes transfer to the phonological and semantic components, with the result that neither the domain nor any constituent it contains are accessible to further syntactic operations from that point on. In §9.3, we saw that intransitive vPs and defective clauses (i.e. clauses which are TPs but not CPs) are not phases, and hence allow A-movement out of their complement, as in structures such as *Several problems are thought to remain in Utopia*. In §9.4, we saw that a phase-based theory of syntax requires us to assume that long-distance A-bar movement (e.g. of wh-expressions) involves movement through intermediate spec-C positions, since CP is a phase and only constituents on the **edge** of a phase can undergo subsequent syntactic operations. In §9.5, we saw that a phase-based theory likewise requires us to posit that A-bar movement in transitive clauses involves movement through intermediate spec-v positions – and we noted that there is empirical evidence in support of this assumption from morphological marking of verbs in Chamorro, past participle agreement in French, and mutation in Welsh. In §9.6, we saw that in recent work, Chomsky has suggested that phase heads (like C and a transitive v with a thematic external argument) enter the derivation carrying both interpretable and uninterpretable features, and can hand over their uninterpretable features to a subordinate head (so that e.g. C hands over its uninterpretable agreement features to T in a finite clause). We suggested that a light verb with an external argument retains its uninterpretable case/agreement features if it can locate a suitable goal within its immediate domain, but otherwise hands them down to the V head immediately beneath it. In §9.7, we outlined the proposal in Chomsky (2005b) that different heads (like C and T) within the same phase probe independently (either simultaneously or sequentially) once a phasal structure like CP has been formed. We saw that this allows us to account for why subextraction is barred in an active sentence such as **Of which car has the driver caused a scandal?* but not in a passive such as *Of which car was the driver arrested?* In §9.8, we went on to show that this analysis implies that subject questions like *Who was arrested?* involve A-movement of one copy of *who* from V-complement position into spec-T, and simultaneous A-bar movement of a separate copy of *who* from V-complement position into spec-C. In §9.9, we saw that subextraction is possible from the specifier position in a defective clause – hence from the subject of an infinitival TP which is the complement of a raising, passive or ECM predicate.

Some of the key assumptions made in this chapter are repeated below:

(7)   **Transfer**
   (i)   At the end of each phase, the domain (i.e. complement of the phase head) undergoes *transfer*
   (ii) At the end of the overall derivation, all remaining constituents undergo transfer

(22)   **Inactivation Condition**
         A goal with a case feature becomes inactive for agreement with (or attraction by) an A-head like T once its case feature has been valued and deleted

(23)   **Mixed Chains Constraint**
         Movement cannot give rise to a mixed chain containing one copy of a constituent which has moved to the edge of a phase, and another which has moved to the edge of a non-phasal projection

(49)   **Invisibility Condition**
         The specifier of a complete (non-defective) TP is invisible to any higher probe

(52)   **Specifier Condition**
         No subextraction is possible out of a constituent which is a specifier of a phase head

(65)   **Visibility Condition**
         Only the highest copy in a movement chain is visible in the syntax (other copies being inert)

(66)   **Intervention Condition**
         Probe P cannot target goal G if there is some other visible goal of the same kind as G intervening between the two and if the intervening goal is inactive for P

9.11 Bibliographical background

The account of phases in §§9.2–9.5 is based on work by Chomsky (1998, 1999, 2001, 2002, 2005a). The version of the Phase Impenetrability Condition presented in §9.2 is adapted from Chomsky (2001, p. 5, ex. 6). The assumption in §9.5 that heads can have multiple specifiers echoes a claim made in Chomsky (1998, p. 16). The *Mixed Chains Constraint* proposed in Chomsky (2005b) has its historical antecedents in the *Improper Movement Constraint* discussed in Chomsky (1981), Ura (1993), Müller and Sternefeld (1993) and Ura

(2001). For further evidence of morphological marking of intermediate verbs in long-distance wh-movement structures, see Georgopoulos (1985, 1991) on Palauan, Chung (1994, 1998, 2004) on Chamorro, den Dikken (2001) on Kilega, Branigan and MacKenzie (2002) on Innu-aimûn, Bruening (2001, 2004) on Passamaquoddy, and Rackowski and Richards (2005) on Tagalog. On French past participle agreement, see Kayne (1989), Branigan (1992), Ura (1993, 2001), Bošković (1997), Richards (1997), Sportiche (1998) and Radford and Vincent (2007). On wh-marking of complementisers in Irish, see McCloskey (2001). The account of Welsh mutation given in the main text is based on Tallerman (1993); see Willis (2000) for a rather different analysis. For an alternative analysis of long-distance wh-movement, see Ishii (2006a,b). The account of feature inheritance in §9.6 is adapted from work by Chomsky (2005b, 2006), Miyagawa (2005, 2006) and Richards (2007). Although the analysis of ECM structures presented in the text posits that the embedded subject raises up to become the matrix object, it should be noted that there was considerable controversy about this in the 1970s: see e.g. Chomsky (1973), Postal (1974), Lightfoot (1976), Bresnan (1976) and Bach (1977); see also Runner (2006). On Complementiser Agreement, see Rizzi (1990), Haegeman (1992), Boeckx (2003), Carstens (2003), Kornfilt (2004) and Miyagawa (2005); for discussion of a related phenomenon in the Boston variety of English, see Kimball and Aissen (1971) and Kayne (2005). On the idea that case assigners carry an uninterpretable feature specifying what case they assign, see Chomsky (1981) and Adger (2003). The discussion in §§9.7–9.9 draws heavily on Chomsky (2005b, 2006). On why there is no auxiliary inversion in subject questions, see Radford (2007). On subextraction from subjects, see Broekhuis (2006). For discussion of a wide range of issues relating to phases, see the collection of papers in McGinnis and Richards (2005).

Workbook section

Exercise 9.1

Discuss the role played by phases in the derivation of the following sentences:

1   Where did he arrange for her to go?
2   Where does she think they've gone?
3   Who knows what she will say?
4   What does it appear that he thinks was said to her?
5   What is he thought to want her to do?
6   How many prizes seem to have been awarded?
7   How many prizes do there seem to have been awarded?
8   What kind of prize do you want to award?
9   What did the DA make the defendant out to have done?

10   How much money can you show him to have stolen? (**w**)
11   How much discontent do you believe there sincerely to remain in the office?
12   Who do you expect it to emerge explicitly from the report that bribes were paid
      to?

Helpful hints

In 6 and 7 take *how many prizes* to be a QP, with *many* as its head, *prizes* as its complement and *how* as its specifier; likewise, in 10 and 11 take *how much money/discontent* to be a QP, with *much* as its head, *money/discontent* as its complement and *how* as its specifier. Recall the discussion of pied-piping in §§5.5–5.6, expletive pronouns at the end of §8.6 and ECM structures in §9.6.

Model answer for 1

The unaccusative verb *go* merges with its (locative adverbial pronoun) complement *where* to form the V-bar *go where*. This V-bar is then merged with the pronoun (which is ultimately spelled out as) *her* to form the VP *her go where*. The resulting VP is in turn merged with a null intransitive light verb, forming the vP *ø her go where*. Since the light verb has no external argument, it is not a phase head and so has no edge feature and cannot trigger wh-movement. The resulting vP merges with infinitival *to*, forming a TP which is in turn merged with the complementiser *for* to form the CP shown below:

(i)

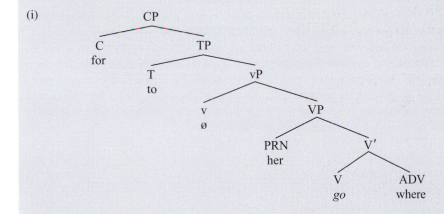

If all structural case assignment involves agreement between a probe and a goal, and if uninterpretable features originate on phase heads, then the complementiser *for* will enter the derivation carrying a set of unvalued (and uninterpretable) person and number agreement features, and a feature which enables it to assign accusative case to a goal with an unvalued case feature. Since there is no accessible goal within its immediate domain, the uninterpretable case and agreement features on the complementiser *for* percolate down onto (and so are inherited by) T. At this point, C, T and v probe independently. The light verb v attracts V-*go* to adjoin to it. Since T has inherited a set of case and agreement features from C, T will agree with and case-mark the pronoun *her*, and (by virtue of its EPP feature) will attract *her* to move to spec-T. Since CP is a phase, C will carry an edge feature triggering movement of *where* to spec-C, so deriving the structure shown below:

(ii)

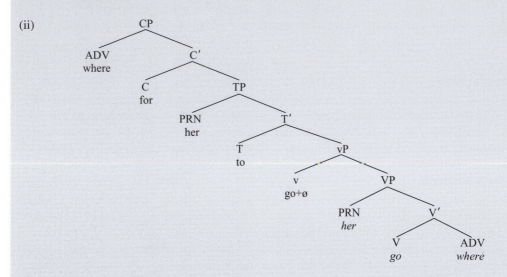

At the end of the C-cycle, the domain of C (i.e. its TP complement) will undergo transfer (to the phonological and semantic components) and thereafter be inaccessible to further syntactic operations; italicised trace copies of moved constituents will be deleted.

The resulting CP is then merged with the verb *arrange*, forming the VP *arrange where for her to go*. This is in turn merged with a light verb, forming the v-bar *ø arrange where for her to go*. The resulting v-bar is merged with its AGENT external argument *he*. Since the light verb is transitive by virtue of having an external argument, vP is a phase, and so the light verb probes at this point. By virtue of being strong/affixal, the light verb attracts the verb *arrange* to adjoin to it. By virtue of being a phase head, the light verb also has an edge feature triggering movement of *where* to spec-v, so deriving the structure shown below (simplified by not showing the structure of the embedded CP or the null constituents which it contains):

(iii)

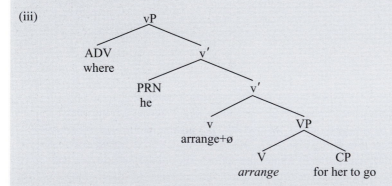

At the end of the vP phase, the VP domain will undergo transfer, and the italicised trace copy of the verb *arrange* will have a null spellout in the PF component.

The vP in (iii) is then merged as the complement of a finite T constituent containing a past tense affix, and the resulting TP is then merged with an interrogative C to form the CP phase in

(iv) below (simplified by showing only overt constituents of vP):

(iv)

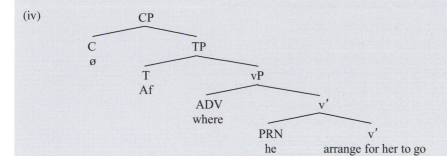

The phase head C carries a set of (unvalued and uninterpretable person/number) agreement features, and a feature enabling it to assign nominative case. Since there is no potential goal within the immediate domain of C, these case/agreement features percolate down onto (and so are inherited by) T. C and T then probe independently. By virtue of being a phase head, C has an edge feature which triggers movement of the interrogative goal *where* to spec-C. C also has a tense feature which triggers movement of the affix *Af* from T to C. The past tense affix in T agrees with and case-marks the pronoun *he*, attracting it to move to spec-T. If *where* counts as a potential intervener blocking T from targeting *where* in (iv) (which will arguably not be so if *where* is an adverb which does not carry a case feature), movement of *where* to spec-C will have to take place before movement of *he* to spec-T. At any rate, the result of these three different movement operations is to derive the structure shown below (simplified by showing only overt constituents of vP):

(v)

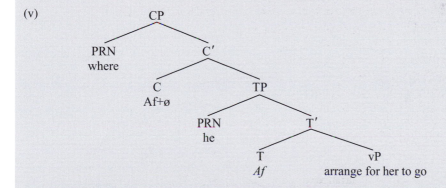

The TP domain undergoes transfer in accordance with (7i) in the main text (with the italicised copy of the affix in T receiving a null spellout). The copy of the affix stranded in C undergoes DO-support in the PF component, with DO ultimately being spelled out as *did* because it is attached to a past tense affix. The constituents on the edge of CP undergo transfer in accordance with (7ii) in the main text.

Discuss the syntax of subextraction in the sentences below:

1   Of which drugs did they find traces?
2   Of which drugs were traces found?
3   Of which drugs were there found traces?
4   Of which drugs did traces remain in the blood? **(w)**
5   Of which drugs did there remain traces in the blood?
6   *Of which drugs did traces contaminate the blood? **(w)**
7   Of which drugs do you think they found traces?
8   *Of which drugs do you wonder what traces they found?
9   Of which drugs are traces believed to have contaminated the blood?
10   Of which drugs do they believe traces to have contaminated the blood?
11   *Of which drugs do they believe traces contaminated the blood?
12   Of which drugs do they believe traces were found in the blood?
13   *Of which drugs would it be unlikely for traces to contaminate the blood?
14   Of which drugs would it be unlikely for traces to be found in the blood?

Model answer for 1

The verb *find* merges with the QP *ø traces of which drugs* (with ø being a null partitive quantifier) to form the VP *find ø traces of which drugs*. The resulting VP then merges with a light verb to form a v-bar which in turn merges with its AGENT external argument *they* to form an even larger v-projection, with the verb *find* raising from V to v. By virtue of having an external argument, the light verb will carry agreement features which percolate from v to V, allowing V to agree with and assign accusative case to its QP complement *ø traces of which drugs*. Since a light verb with an external argument is also a phase head and so has an edge feature, the light verb attracts the wh-PP *of which drugs* to move to spec-v in the manner shown by the arrow below:

(i)

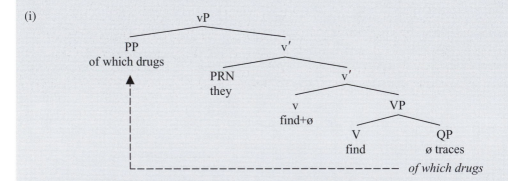

There is no violation of any extraction constraint because the QP is subextracted out of a complement, not out of an adjunct or specifier. The VP complement of the phase head undergoes spellout at this point, in accordance with (7i) in the main text.

 The vP (i) then merges with a T constituent containing a past tense affix, forming a TP which in turn merges with an interrogative C to form the CP below (simplified by showing only overt constituents of vP):

(ii)

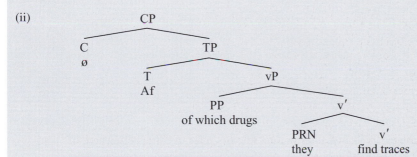

C enters the derivation carrying uninterpretable case and agreement features, and hands these over to T. C and T then probe independently. T agrees with and assigns nominative case to the pronoun *they* and attracts it to move to spec-T (there being no intervention effect because the intervening PP *of which drugs* is not the kind of constituent which serves as a potential goal for agreement with T, since such a goal can only be a constituent whose head carries an initially unvalued case feature, and the head P of PP is not such a constituent). The edge feature on C attracts the interrogative PP *of which drugs* to move to spec-C, and the tense feature on C attracts the affix in T to move to C, so deriving the structure shown below (again simplified by showing only overt constituents of vP):

(iii)

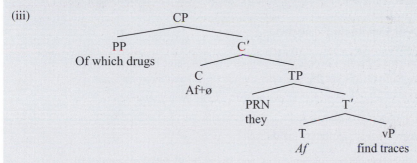

The TP domain undergoes transfer in accordance with (7i) in the main text (with the italicised copy of the affix in T receiving a null spellout). The copy of the affix in C undergoes DO-support in the PF component, with DO being ultimately spelled out as *did* because it is attached to a past tense affix. The constituents on the edge of CP undergo transfer in accordance with (7ii) in the main text.

Glossary and list of abbreviations

Bold print is used to indicate technical terms, and to cross-refer to entries elsewhere in the glossary. Abbreviations used here are: ch. = chapter; § = chapter/section number; ex. = exercise.

A: See **Adjective**, **A-head**, **A-position**, **binding**.

A-bar: An **A-bar position** is a position which can be occupied by arguments or adjuncts alike. For example, the specifier position within CP is said to be an A-bar position because it can contain not only an argument like the italicised wh-phrase in '*Which car* did he fix?' but also an adjunct like the italicised adverb in '*How* did he fix the car?' **A-bar movement** is a movement operation (like **wh-movement**) which moves an argument or adjunct expression to an A-bar position. On **A-bar head**, see **A-head**.

ACC: Attract Closest Condition: see **attract**.

acc(usative): See **case**.

acquisition: The process by which people acquire their first language (= L1 acquisition) or a second language which is not their mother tongue (= L2 acquisition).

active: A contrast is traditionally drawn between sentence pairs such as (i) and (ii) below:

(i)   The thieves stole the jewels
(ii)   The jewels were stolen by the thieves

(i) is said to be an **active** clause (or sentence), and (ii) to be its **passive** counterpart; similarly, the verb *stole* is said to be an active verb (or a verb in the active **voice**) in (i), whereas the verb *stolen* is said to be a passive verb (or a verb in the passive voice – more specifically, a passive **participle**) in (ii); likewise, the auxiliary *were* in (ii) is said to be a passive **auxiliary**. In a different use, a **probe** or **goal** is said to be active for movement/agreement if it carries an undeleted uninterpretable feature, and to be **inactive** once the relevant feature has been deleted: see §7.4.

adequacy, criteria of: These are the criteria which an adequate grammar or linguistic theory must meet. See §1.3.

adjacency condition: A condition requiring that two expressions must be immediately adjacent (i.e. there must be no constituent intervening between the two) in order for some operation to apply. For example, *have* must be immediately adjacent to *they* in order to **cliticise** onto it in structures such as *They've gone* home.

adjective: This is a category of word (abbreviated to A) which often denotes states (e.g. *happy*, *sad*), which typically has an adverb counterpart in *-ly* (cf. *sad/sadly*), which typically has comparative/ superlative forms in *-er/-est* (cf. *sadder/saddest*), which can often take the prefix *un-* (cf. *unhappy*), which can often form a noun by the addition of the suffix *-ness* (cf. *sadness*) etc.

adjoin: See **adjunction**.

adjunct: One way in which this term is used is to denote an optional constituent typically used to specify e.g. the time, place or manner in which an event takes place. Another way in which it is used is to denote a constituent which has been attached to another to form a larger constituent of the same type. (See **adjunction**).

adjunction: This is a process by which one constituent is adjoined (= attached) to another to form a larger constituent of the same type. For example, we could say that in a sentence like 'He should not go,' the negative particle *not* (in the guise of its contracted form *n't*) can be adjoined to the auxiliary *should* to form the negative auxiliary *shouldn't*. In a sentence such as *He gently rolled the ball down the hill*, the adverb *gently* can be taken to be an adverb which adjoins to a verbal projection, extending it into a larger projection of the same kind: see §8.4.

adposition: A cover term subsuming **preposition** and **postposition**. For example, the English word *in* is a preposition since it is positioned before its complement (cf. *in Tokyo*), whereas its Japanese counterpart is a postposition because it is positioned after its complement *Tokyo*. Both words are **adpositions**.

ADV/adverb: This is a category of word which typically indicates manner (e.g. 'wait *patiently*') or degree (e.g. '*exceedingly* patient'). In English, most (but not all) adverbs end in *-ly* (cf. *quickly* – but also *almost*).

Af: See **affix**.

affective: An affective constituent is an (e.g. negative, interrogative or conditional) expression which can have a **polarity expression** like (partitive) *any* in its scope. So, for example, interrogative *if* is an affective constituent as we see from the fact that an interrogative *if*-clause can contain partitive *any* in a sentence such as 'I wonder *if* he has *any* news about Jim.' See §2.6.

affix/affixal: The term **affix** (abbreviated to *Af*) is typically used to describe a grammatical morpheme which cannot stand on its own as an independent word, but which must be attached to a host word of an appropriate kind. An affix which attaches to the beginning of a word (e.g. *un-* in *unhappy*) is called a **prefix:** an affix which attaches to the end of a word (e.g. *-s* in *chases*) is called a **suffix**. An **affixal** head is one which behaves like an affix in needing to attach to a particular kind of host word. See also **Clitic**. **Affix Hopping** (or **Affix Lowering**) is an operation by which an unattached affix in T is lowered onto a verb: see §3.4. **Affix Attachment** is an operation whereby an unattached tense affix lowers onto a verb where possible, but is otherwise supported by use of the dummy auxiliary *do:* see §4.8.

AGENT: This is a term used to describe the semantic (= thematic) role which a particular type of argument plays in a given sentence. It typically denotes a person who deliberately causes some state of affairs to come about: hence e.g. *John* plays the thematic role of AGENT in a sentence such as '*John* smashed the bottle.' See §6.4.

agreement: An operation by which (e.g. in a sentence like *They are lying*) the person/number features of the auxiliary *are* get assigned the same values as those of its subject *they*, so that *are* is third person plural because it agrees in **person** and **number** with its third person plural subject *they*. See ch.7.

A-head: An A-head is the kind of head (like T) which allows as its specifier an argument expression but not an adjunct expression. An **A-bar head** is the kind of head (like C) which allows as its specifier either an argument or an adjunct expression.

A-movement: Movement from one **A-position** to another (typically, from a subject or complement position into another subject position). See ch.6.

A-position: A position which can be occupied by an **argument**, but not by a nonargument expression (e.g. not by an adjunct). In practice, the term denotes a subject position, or a lexical complement position (i.e. a position occupied by a constituent which is the complement of a **lexical/substantive** head).

anaphor: This is an expression (like *himself*) which cannot have independent reference, but which must take its reference from an appropriate **antecedent** (i.e. expression which it refers to) within the same phrase or sentence. Hence, while we can say 'John is deluding himself' (where *himself* refers back to *John*), we cannot say *'Himself is waiting,' since the anaphor *himself* here has no antecedent. A traditional distinction is drawn between **reflexive anaphors** (i.e. *self* forms like *myself/ourselves/yourself/your-selves/himself/herself/itself/themselves*) and the **reciprocal anaphors** *each other/one another* (cf. 'They help each other/one another'). See §2.7 and ex.2.2.

animate: The term animate is used to denote (the gender of) an expression which denotes a living being (e.g. a human being or animal), while the term **inanimate** is used in relation to an expression which denotes lifeless entities. For example, the **relative pronoun** *who* could be said to be animate in gender and the relative pronoun *which* inanimate – hence we say *someone who upsets people* and *something which upsets people*.

antecedent: An expression which is referred to by a pronoun or anaphor of some kind. For example, in 'John cut himself shaving,' *John* is the antecedent of the anaphor *himself*, since *himself* refers back to *John*. In a sentence such as 'He is someone who we respect,' the antecedent of the **relative pronoun** *who* is *someone*.

anticyclic: See **cycle**.

AP: Adjectival Phrase – i.e. a phrase headed by an adjective, such as *fond of chocolate*, *keen on sport*, *good at syntax* etc.

A-position: A position which can only be occupied by an argument, hence a position in which an argument originates (e.g. as the subject or complement of a verb), or one in which it moves to become the specifier of an A-head (and so comes to occupy a position like spec-TP).

arbitrary: When we say that an expression has 'arbitrary reference', we mean that it can denote an unspecified set of individuals, and hence have much the same meaning as English *one/people* or French *on*. In a sentence such as 'It is difficult [PRO to learn Japanese],' the bracketed clause is said to have an abstract pronoun subject PRO which can have arbitrary reference, in which case the sentence is paraphraseable as 'It's difficult for *people* to learn Japanese.' See §3.2.

argument: This is a term borrowed by linguists from philosophy (more specifically, from predicate calculus) to describe the role played by particular types of expression in the semantic structure of sentences. In a sentence such as 'John hit Fred,' the overall sentence is said to be a **proposition** (a term used to describe the semantic content of a clause), and to consist of the predicate *hit* and its two arguments *John* and *Fred*. The two arguments represent the two participants in the act of hitting, and the predicate is the expression (in this case the verb *hit*) which describes the activity in which they are engaged. By extension, in a sentence such as 'John says he hates syntax' the predicate in the main clause is the verb *says*, and its two arguments are *John* and the clause *he hates syntax*; the argument *he hates syntax* is in turn a proposition whose predicate is *hates*, and whose two arguments are *he* and *syntax*. Since the complement of a verb is positioned internally within V-bar whereas the subject of a verb is positioned outside V-bar, complements are also referred to as **internal arguments**, and subjects as **external arguments**. Expressions which do not function as arguments are **nonarguments**. The **argument structure** of a predicate provides a description of the set of **arguments** associated with the **predicate**, and the **theta-role** which each fulfils in relation to the predicate. A **one-/two-/three-place predicate** is a predicate which has one/two/three arguments. See 6.4.

array: The **lexical array** for a given expression denotes the set of lexical items out of which the expression is formed.

article: A term used in traditional grammar to describe a particular subclass of determiner/quantifier: the word *the* is traditionally called the **definite article**, and the word *a* is termed the **indefinite article**.

aspect/AspP: Aspect is a term typically used to denote the duration of the activity described by a verb (e.g. whether the activity is ongoing or completed). In sentences such as:

(i)   He has taken the medicine
(ii)   He is taking the medicine

the auxiliary *has* is said to be an auxiliary which marks **perfect aspect** (and hence to be a **perfect auxiliary**), in that it marks the perfection (in the sense of 'completion' or 'termination') of the activity of taking the medicine; for analogous reasons, *taken* is said to be a **perfect participle** verb form in (i) (though is referred to in traditional grammars as a 'past participle'). Similarly, *is* functions as an auxiliary which marks **progressive aspect** in (ii), because it relates to an activity which is ongoing or in progress (for this reason, *is* in (ii) is also referred to as a **progressive auxiliary**); in the same way, the verb *taking* in (ii) is said to be the **progressive participle** form of the verb (though is sometimes known in traditional grammars as a 'present participle'). An auxiliary which marks aspect (like *have* and *be* in the above examples) is referred to as an **aspectual auxiliary**. An **Aspect Phrase/AspP** is a phrase headed by an item which marks (e.g. perfect or progressive) aspect.

associate: An expression which represents the thematic argument in an expletive *there* construction, and which is associated with the expletive subject *there*: e.g. *several prizes* in *There were awarded several prizes*.

asymmetric c-command: See **c-command**.

attract/attraction: To say that a head H **attracts** a constituent C is to say that H triggers movement of C to some position on the **edge** of HP (so that C may move to adjoin to H, or to become the specifier of H). The **Attract Closest Condition** requires that a head which **attracts** a particular type of constituent X attracts the **closest** X which it c-commands. The **Attract Smallest Condition** requires that a head which **attracts** a particular type of item attracts the smallest constituent containing such an item which will not lead to violation of any UG principle. The **Wh-Attraction Condition** specifies that a head H which attracts a wh-word attracts the smallest possible maximal projection containing the closest wh-word to become the specifier of H.

attribute: See **value**.

AUX/auxiliary: A term used to **categorise** items such as *will/would/can/could/shall/ should/may/might/must/ought* and some uses of *have/be/do/need/dare*. Such items have a number of idiosyncratic properties, including the fact that they can undergo **inversion** (e.g. in questions like '*Can* you speak French?'). By contrast, **main verbs** (i.e. verbs which are not auxiliaries) cannot undergo inversion – as we see from the ungrammaticality of **'Speak* you French?'

auxiliary copying: A phenomenon whereby a moved auxiliary leaves behind an overt copy of itself when it moves – as with *can* in a Child English question like *What can I can have for dinner?*

auxiliary inversion: See **inversion**.

auxiliary selection: This term relates to the type of verb which a given auxiliary selects as its complement: e.g. in many languages (the counterpart of) BE when used as a perfect auxiliary selects only a complement headed by a verb with no *external argument* (see **argument**), whereas (the counterpart of) HAVE selects a complement headed by a verb with an external argument.

AUXP: Auxiliary projection/Auxiliary phrase – i.e. a phrase headed by an auxiliary which does not occupy the head T position of TP. See §4.6.

B: On **Principle B** of Binding Theory, see ex. 2.2.

bar: When used as a suffix attached to a category label such as N, V, P etc. (as in N-bar, V-bar, P-bar, T-bar etc.), it denotes an **intermediate projection** which is larger than a word but smaller than a phrase. Hence, in a phrase such as *university policy on drugs*, we might say that the string *policy on drugs* is an N-bar, since it is a projection of the head noun *policy*, but is an intermediate projection in that it has a larger projection into the NP *university policy on drugs*. The term **bar notation** used in the theory known as **X-bar syntax** refers to a system of representing projection levels which posits that (first-) merge of a head H with its complement forms an H-bar constituent, and (second-) merge of a head with a specifier forms an H-double-bar constituent (with the **maximal projection** of H being labelled HP). On **A-bar position**, see **A-bar**.

bare: A **bare form** (of a word) is one which is uninflected. A **bare infinitive** structure is one which contains a verb in the infinitive form, but does not contain the infinitive particle *to* (e.g. the italicised clause in 'He won't let *you help him*'). A **bare noun** is a noun used without any quantifier or determiner to modify it (e.g. *fish* in '*Fish* is expensive'). A **bare clause** is one not introduced by an overt complementiser (e.g. *he was tired* in 'John said *he was tired*.' A theory of **bare phrase structure** is one in which there are no category labels or projection levels associated with constituents: see §2.8.

base form: The base form of a verb is the simplest, uninflected form of the verb (the form under which the relevant verb would be listed in an English dictionary) – hence forms like *go/be/have/see/want/love* are the base forms of the relevant verbs. The base form can typically function either as an **infinitive** (cf. 'Try to *stay*'), an **imperative** (cf. '*Stay* with me tonight!'), a present tense **indicative** form ('They sometimes *stay* with me') or a **subjunctive** form (cf. 'I demand that he *stay* with me').

Binarity Principle: A principle of Universal Grammar specifying that all nonterminal nodes in syntactic structures (i.e. tree-diagrams) are **binary-branching**. See §2.2.

binary: A term relating to a two-way contrast. For example, **number** is a binary property in English, in that we have a two-way contrast between **singular** forms like *cat* and **plural** forms like *cats*. It is widely assumed that **parameters** have binary settings, that features have binary values, and that all branching in syntactic structure is binary.

binary-branching: A tree diagram in which every nonterminal node has two daughters is binary-branching; a category/node which has two daughters is also binary-branching. See §2.2.

bind/binder/binding: To say that one constituent X binds (or serves as the binder for) another constituent Y (and conversely that Y is bound by X) is to say that X determines properties (usually referential properties) of Y. For example, in a sentence such as 'John blamed himself,' the reflexive anaphor *himself* is bound by *John* in the sense that the referential properties of *himself* are determined by *John* (so that the two refer to the same individual). The **c-command condition on binding** says that a bound form must be c-commanded by its antecedent. On principles A, B and C of **Binding Theory**, see ex.2.2.

bottom-up: To say that a syntactic structure is derived in a **bottom-up** fashion is to say that the structure is built up from bottom to top, with lower parts of the structure being formed before higher parts.

bound: In a traditional use of this term, a bound form is one which cannot stand alone and be used as an independent word, but rather must be attached to some other morpheme (e.g. negative *n't*, which has to attach to some auxiliary such as *could*). In a completely different use of the term, a bound constituent is one which has a binder (i.e. antecedent) within the structure containing it. See **bind**.

bracketing: A technique for representing the categorial status of an expression, whereby the expression is enclosed within a pair of square brackets, and the lefthand bracket is **labelled** with an appropriate category symbol – e.g. [D the].

branch: A term used to represent a solid line linking a pair of nodes in a tree diagram, marking a mother/daughter (i.e. containment) relation between them.

C: See **complementiser**.

canonical: A term used to mean 'usual', 'typical' or 'normal', as in 'The canonical word order in English is specifier+head+complement.'

case: The different case forms of a pronoun are the different forms which the pronoun has in different sentence positions. It is traditionally said that English has three cases – **nominative** (abbreviated to **Nom**), **accusative** (= **Acc**, sometimes also referred to as **objective**) and **genitive** (= **Gen**). Personal pronouns typically inflect overtly for all three cases, whereas noun expressions inflect only for genitive case. The different case forms of typical pronouns and noun expressions are given below:

nominative	I	we	you	he	she	it	they	who	the king
accusative	me	us	you	him	her	it	them	who(m)	the king
genitive	my	our	your	his	her	its	their	whose	the
	mine	ours	yours		hers		theirs	whose	king's

As is apparent, some pronouns have two distinct genitive forms: a **weak** (shorter) form used when they are immediately followed by a noun (as in 'This is *my car*'), and a **strong** (longer) form used when they are not immediately followed by a noun (as in 'This car is *mine*'). In Chomsky and Lasnik (1993), it is suggested that the null subject PRO found in **control** constructions carries null case. In languages like English where certain types of expression are assigned case by virtue of the structural position they occupy in a given clause (e.g. accusative if c-commanded by a transitive head, nominative if c-commanded by finite intransitive head), the relevant expressions are said to receive **structural case**. Where a constituent is assigned case by virtue of its semantic function (e.g. a GOAL complement of certain types of verb is assigned dative case in German), it is said to receive **inherent case**. In languages like Icelandic where subjects can be assigned a variety of cases (e.g. some are accusative and others dative, depending on the choice of verb and its semantic properties), subjects are said to have **quirky case**. In the Italian counterpart of a structure like 'She gave him them,' the **direct object** corresponding to English 'them' is assigned accusative case, and the indirect object corresponding to English 'him' is assigned a distinct case, traditionally called **dative case**. (On direct and indirect objects, see **object**.) On **nominative case assignment**, see §3.6 and §7.3; on **accusative case assignment**, see §3.9, §7.7 and § 8.4; on **null case assignment**, see §3.7 and §7.8; and on the syntax of **genitives**, see §5.5.

case particle: Some linguists take *of* in structures like *destruction of the city* or *fond of pasta* to be a particle marking **genitive** case and belonging to the category K of 'case particle'. On this analysis, the *of*-phrase (*of the city*) is taken to have genitive case, and *of* is said to be the morpheme which marks genitive case.

categorial: Categorial information is information about the grammatical category that an item belongs to. A categorial property is one associated with members of a particular grammatical category. **The Categorial Uniformity Principle** is a principle suggested by Luigi Rizzi (2000, p. 288) to the effect that all expressions of the same type belong to the same category (e.g. all declarative clauses are CPs, both main clauses and complement clauses).

categorise/categorisation: Assign(ing) an expression to a (grammatical) **category**.

category: A term used to denote a set of expressions which share a common set of linguistic properties. In syntax, the term is used for expressions which share a common set of grammatical properties. For example, *boy* and *girl* belong to the (grammatical) category **noun** because they both inflect for plural number (cf. *boys/girls*), and can both be used to end a sentence such as 'The police haven't yet found the missing – .' In traditional grammar, the term **parts of speech** was used in place of **categories**.

causative verb: A verb which has much the same sense as 'cause'. For example, the verb *have* in sentences such as 'He had them expelled' or 'He had them review the case' might be said to be causative in sense (hence to be a causative verb).

c-command: A structural relation between two constituents. To say that one constituent X c-commands another constituent Y is (informally) to say that X is no lower than Y in the structure (i.e. either X is higher up in the structure than Y, or the two are at the same height). More formally, a constituent X c-commands its sister constituent Y and any constituent Z that is contained within Y. If we think of a tree diagram as a network of train stations, we can say that one constituent X c-commands another constituent Y if you can get from X to Y by taking a northbound train, getting off at the first station, changing trains there and then travelling one or more stops south on a different line. A constituent X **asymmetrically c-commands** another constituent Y if X c-commands Y but Y does not c-command X. See §2.6.

c-command condition on binding: A condition to the effect that a bound constituent (e.g. a **reflexive anaphor** like *himself* or the trace of a moved constituent) must be **c-commanded** by its **antecedent** (i.e. by the expression which binds it). See §2.7 and exercise 2.2.

CED: See **Condition on Extraction Domains**.

chain: A set of constituents comprising an expression and any trace copies associated with it. Where a constituent does not undergo movement, it forms a single-membered chain.

Chain Uniformity Condition: A condition which specifies that all the links in a movement chain must have the same structural status (e.g. all the links must be maximal projections).

clause: A clause is defined in traditional grammar as an expression which contains (at least) a **subject** and a **predicate**, and which may contain other types of expression as well (e.g. one or more **complements** and/or **adjuncts**). In most cases, the predicate in a clause is a lexical (= main) verb, so that there will be as many different clauses in a sentence as there are different lexical verbs. For example, in a sentence such as 'She may think that you are cheating on her,' there are two lexical verbs (*think* and *cheating*), and hence two clauses. The *cheating* clause is *that you are cheating on her*, and the *think* clause is *She may think that you are cheating on her*, so that the *cheating* clause is one of the constituents of the *think* clause. More specifically, the *cheating* clause is the **complement** of the *think* clause, and so is said to function as a **complement clause** in this type of sentence. Clauses whose predicate is not a verb (i.e. verbless clauses) are known as **small clauses**: hence, in 'John considers [Mary intelligent],' the bracketed expression is sometimes referred to as a **small clause**.

cleft sentence: A structure such as 'It was *syntax* that he hated most,' where *syntax* is said to occupy **focus position** within the cleft sentence.

clitic(isation): The term **clitic** denotes an item which is (generally) a reduced form of another word, and which has the property that (in its reduced form) it must cliticise (i.e. attach itself to) an appropriate kind of **host** (i.e. to another word or phrase). For example, we could say that the contracted negative particle *n't* is a clitic form of the negative particle *not* which attaches itself to a finite auxiliary verb, so giving rise to forms like *isn't, shouldn't, mightn't* etc. Likewise, we could say that *'ve* is a clitic form of *have* which attaches itself to a pronoun ending in a vowel, so giving rise to forms like *we've, you've, they've* etc. When a clitic attaches to the end of another word, it is said to be an **enclitic** (and hence to **encliticise** onto the relevant word). Clitics differ from **affixes** in a number of ways. For example, a clitic is generally a reduced form of a full word, and has a corresponding full form (so that *'ll* is the clitic form of *will*, for example), whereas an affix (like noun plural *-s* in *cats*) has no full-word counterpart. Moreover, clitics can attach to phrases (e.g. *'s* can attach to *the president* in *The president's lying*), whereas an affix typically attaches to a word stem (e.g. the past tense *-ed* affix attaches to the verb stem *snow* in *snowed*).

closest: In structures in which a head X attracts a particular kind of constituent Y to move to the **edge** of XP, X is said to attract the **closest** constituent of type Y, in accordance with the **Attract Closest Condition**. See also **local**.

cognition/cognitive: (Relating to) the study of human knowledge.

common noun: See **noun**.

COMP: See **complementiser**.

comparative: The comparative form of an adjective or adverb is the form (typically ending in *-er*) used when comparing two individuals or properties: cf. 'John is *taller* than Mary,' where *taller* is the comparative form of the adjective *tall*.

competence: A term used to represent native speakers' knowledge of the grammar of their native language(s).

complement: This is a term used to denote a specific grammatical function (in the same way that the term **subject** denotes a specific grammatical function). A complement is an expression which is directly **merged** with (and hence is the **sister** of) a head word, thereby projecting the head into a larger structure of essentially the same kind. In 'close the door', *the door* is the complement of the verb *close*; in 'after dinner', *dinner* is the complement of the preposition *after*; in 'good at physics', *at physics* is the complement of the adjective *good*; in 'loss of face', *of face* is the complement of the noun *loss*. As these examples illustrate, complements typically follow their heads in English. The choice of complement (and the morphological form of the complement) is determined by properties of the head: for example, an auxiliary such as *will* requires as its complement an expression headed by a verb in the infinitive form (cf. 'He will *go/*going/*gone*'). Moreover, complements bear a close semantic relation to their heads (e.g. in 'Kill him,' *him* is the complement of the verb *kill* and plays the semantic role of THEME argument of the verb *kill*). Thus, a complement has a close morphological, syntactic and semantic relation to its head. A **complement clause** is a clause which is used as the complement of some other word (typically as the complement of a verb, adjective or noun). Thus, in a sentence such as 'He never expected that she would come,' the clause *that she would come* serves as the complement of the verb *expected*, and so is a complement clause. On **complement selection**, see **selection**.

complementiser: This term is used in two ways. On the one hand, it denotes a particular category of clause-introducing word such as *that/if/for*, as used in sentences such as 'I think *that* you should apologize,' 'I doubt *if* she realises,' 'They're keen *for* you to show up.' On the other hand, it is used to denote the pre-subject position in clauses ('the complementiser position') which is typically occupied by a complementiser like *that/if/for*, but which can also be occupied by an inverted auxiliary in sentences such as 'Can you help?,' where *can* is said to occupy the complementiser position in the clause. A **complementiser phrase** (**CP**) is a phrase/clause/expression headed by a complementiser (or by an auxiliary or verb occupying the complementiser position). The **Complementiser Condition** specifies that no overt complementiser (like *if/that/for*) can have an overt specifier in the superficial structure of a sentence. The term **complementiser** is abbreviated to COMP in earlier work and to **C** in later work.

Completeness Condition: A principle of grammar specifying that uninterpretable case/agreement features on a constituent α can only be deleted via agreement with a constituent β which carries a complete set of person and number features.

complex sentence: One which contains more than one **clause**.

component: A grammar is said to have three main components: a **syntactic/computational component** which generates syntactic structures, a **semantic component** which assigns each such syntactic structure an appropriate **semantic interpretation** and a **PF component** which assigns each syntactic structure generated by the computational component an appropriate **phonetic form**. See §1.3.

computational component: See **component**.

concord: A traditional term to describe an operation whereby a noun and any adjectives or determiners modifying it are assigned the same values for features such as number, gender and case.

condition: A grammatical principle. The **Condition on Extraction Domains** is a principle specifying that only complements allow constituents to be extracted out of them, not specifiers or adjuncts. See §6.5.

conditional: A term used to represent a type of clause (typically introduced by *if* or *unless*) which lays down conditions – e.g. 'If you don't behave, I'll bar you,' or 'Unless you behave, I'll bar you.' In these examples, the clauses *If you don't behave* and *Unless you behave* are **conditional clauses**.

CONJ: See **conjunction**.

conjoin: To join together two or more expressions by a **coordinating conjunction** such as *and/or/but*. For example, in 'Naughty but nice', *naughty* has been conjoined with *nice* (and conversely *nice* has been conjoined with *naughty*).

conjunct: One of a set of expressions which have been **conjoined**. For example, in 'Rather tired but otherwise alright', the two conjuncts (i.e. expressions which have been conjoined) are *rather tired* and *otherwise alright*.

conjunction/CONJ: A word which is used to join two or more expressions together. For example, in a sentence such as 'John was tired but happy,' the word *but* serves the function of being a **coordinating conjunction** because it coordinates (i.e. joins together) the adjectives *tired* and *happy*. In 'John felt angry and Mary felt bitter,' the conjunction *and* is used to coordinate the two clauses *John felt angry* and *Mary felt bitter*. In traditional grammar, **complementisers** like *that/for/if* are categorised as (one particular type of) subordinating conjunction.

constituent: A term denoting a structural unit – i.e. an expression which is one of the components out of which a phrase or sentence is built up. For example, the two constituents of a **Prepositional Phrase** (= PP) such as 'into touch' (e.g. as a reply to 'Where did the ball go?') are the preposition *into* and the noun *touch*. To say that X is an **immediate constituent** of Y is to say that Y **immediately contains** X (see **contain**), or equivalently that Y is the mother of X: see §2.7.

constituent structure: The constituent structure (or **phrase structure**, or **syntactic structure**) of an expression is (a representation of) the set of constituents which the expression contains. Syntactic structure is usually represented in terms of a **labelled bracketing** or a **tree diagram**.

constrained: see **restrictive**.

constraint: A structural restriction which blocks the application of some process to a particular type of structure. The term tends to be used with the rather more specific meaning of 'A grammatical principle which prevents certain types of grammatical operation from applying to certain types of structure.' The terms **condition** and **principle** are used in much the same way.

contain/containment: To say that one constituent X **contains** another constituent Y is to say that Y is one of the constituents out of which X is formed by a merger operation of some kind. In terms of tree diagrams, we can say that X contains Y if X occurs higher up in the tree than Y, and X is connected to Y by a continuous (unbroken) set of downward branches (the branches being represented by the solid lines connecting pairs of nodes in a tree diagram). If we think of a tree diagram as a network of train stations, we can say that X **contains** Y if it is possible to get from X to Y by travelling one or more stations south. To say that one constituent X **immediately contains** another constituent Y is to say that Y occurs immediately below X in a tree and is connected to X via a branch (or that X contains Y and there is no intervening constituent Z which contains Y and which is contained by X). To say that a tree diagram represents **containment** relations is to say that it shows which constituents are contained within which other constituents. See §2.6.

content: This term is generally used to refer to the semantic content (i.e. meaning) of an expression (typically, of a word). However, it can also be used is a more general way to refer to the linguistic properties of an expression: e.g. the expression **phonetic content** is sometimes used to refer to the phonetic form of (e.g.) a word: hence, we might say that PRO is a pronoun which has no phonetic content (meaning that it is a 'silent' pronoun with no audible form).

contentives/content words: Words which have intrinsic descriptive content (as opposed to **functors**, i.e. words which serve essentially to mark particular grammatical functions). Nouns, verbs, adjectives and (most) prepositions are traditionally classified as contentives, while pronouns, auxiliaries, determiners, complementisers and particles of various kinds (e.g. infinitival *to*, genitive *of*) are classified as functors.

contraction: A process by which two different words are combined into a single word, with either or both words being reduced in form. For example, by contraction, *want to* can be reduced to *wanna*, *going to* to *gonna*, *he is* to *he's*, *they have* to *they've*, *did not* to *didn't* etc. See also **cliticisation**.

contrastive: In a sentence like '*Syntax*, I hate but *phonology* I enjoy,' the expressions *syntax* and *phonology* are contrasted, and each is said to be **contrastive** in use.

control(ler)/control predicate: In non-finite clauses with a PRO subject which has an antecedent, the antecedent is said to be the **controller** of PRO (or to **control** PRO), and conversely PRO is said to be controlled by its antecedent; and the relevant kind of structure is called a **control structure**. So, in a structure like 'John tried PRO to quit,' *John* is the controller of PRO, and conversely PRO is controlled by *John*. The relevant phenomenon is referred to as **Subject Control** where the (italicised) controller is the subject of the higher verb (as in '*John* tried PRO to quit'), and as **Object Control** where it is the object to the higher verb (as in 'John persuaded *Mary* PRO to quit'). The term **control predicate** denotes a word like *try* or *persuade* which takes an infinitive complement with a (controlled) PRO subject. See §3.2.

converge(nce): A **derivation** converges (and hence results in a well-formed sentence) if the resulting **PF representation** contains only phonetic features, and the associated **semantic representation** contains only (semantically) interpretable features.

coordinate/coordination: A **coordinate structure** is a structure containing two or more expressions joined together by a coordinating **conjunction** such as *and/but/or/nor* (e.g. 'John and Mary' is a coordinate structure). **Coordination** is an operation by which two or more expressions are joined together by a coordinating conjunction.

copula/copular verb: A 'linking verb', used to link a subject with a nonverbal predicate. The main copular verb in English is *be* (though verbs like *become*, *remain*, *stay* etc. have much the same linking function). In sentences such as 'They are lazy,' 'They are fools' and 'They are outside,' the verb *are* is said to be a **copula** in that it links the subject *they* to the adjectival predicate *lazy*, or the nominal predicate *fools*, or the prepositional predicate *outside*.

copy/copying: The **copy theory of movement** is a theory developed by Chomsky which maintains that a moved constituent leaves behind a (**trace**) copy of itself when it moves, with the copy generally having its phonetic features deleted and so being **null:** see §4.3, §5.3 and §6.2. **Feature Copying** is an operation by which the value of a feature on one constituent is copied onto another (e.g. the values of the person/number features of a subject are copied onto an auxiliary): see §7.3.

coreferential: Two expressions are coreferential if they refer to the same entity. For example, in 'John cut himself while shaving,' *himself* and *John* are cofererential in the sense that they refer to the same individual.

count/countability: A **count(able) noun** is a noun which can be counted. Hence, a noun such as *chair* is a count noun since we can say 'One chair, two chairs, three chairs etc.'; but a noun such as *furniture* is a **noncount/uncountable/mass noun** since we cannot say '*one furniture, *two furnitures etc.'. The **countability** properties of a noun determine whether the relevant item is a **count noun** or not.

CP: complementiser phrase (See **complementiser**).

crash: A derivation is said to **crash** if one or more features carried by one or more constituents is **illegible** at either or both of the **interface levels** (the phonetics interface and the semantics interface). For example, if the person or number features of HAVE remain unvalued in a sentence such as 'He HAVE left,' the resulting sentence will crash at the phonetics interface, since the PF component will be unable to determine whether HAVE should be spelled out as *have* or *has*.

cyclic: An operation (like argreement or movement) is said to apply in a **cyclic** fashion if it first applies to the lowest constituent of the relevant kind in the structure, then to the next lowest, and then to the next lowest but one (and so on). An operation is **anticyclic** if it does not apply in a cyclic fashion.

D: See **determiner**.

Dat: An abbreviation for **dative case**. See **case**.

daughter: A node X is the daughter of another node Y if Y is the next highest node up in the tree from X, and the two are connected by a **branch** (solid line).

declarative: A term used as a classification of the **force** (i.e. semantic type) of a clause which is used to make a statement (as opposed to an **interrogative**, **exclamative** or **imperative** clause).

default: A default value or property is one which obtains if all else fails (i.e. if other conditions are not satisfied). For example, if we say that -ϕ is the default verbal inflection for regular verbs in English, we mean that regular verbs carry the inflection -*s* if third person singular present tense forms, -*d* if past, perfect or passive forms, -*ing* if progressive or gerund forms, and -ϕ otherwise (by default).

defective: A defective item is one which lacks certain properties. For example, if we suppose that T constituents generally carry person and number features, then infinitival *to* in all infinitive structures except **control** infinitives is a defective T constituent in that (under Chomsky's analysis) it carries person but not number. Any clause containing a defective T constituent is a **defective clause**.

definite: Expressions containing determiners like *the*, *this*, *that* etc. are said to have **definite reference** in that they refer to an entity which is assumed to be known to the addressee(s): e.g. in a sentence such as 'I hated the course,' the DP *the course* refers to a specific (e.g. Minimalist Syntax) course whose identity is assumed to be known to the hearer/reader. In much the same way, personal pronouns like *he/she/it/they* etc. are said to have definite reference. By contrast, expressions containing the article *a* are **indefinite**, in that (e.g.) if you say 'I'm taking a course,' you don't assume that the hearer/reader knows which course you are taking.

definite article: See **article**.

DEG: A degree word like *so/too/how*.

deletion: An operation by which affected features on a constituent are made invisible to the semantic component and/or are not given an audible exponent in the PF component (and so are silent).

demonstrative: This is a term used to refer to words like *this/that*, *these/those* and *here/there* which indicate a location relatively nearer to or further from the speaker (e.g. *this book* means 'the book relatively close to me', and *that book* means 'the book somewhat further away from me').

derivation: The derivation of a phrase or clause is the set of syntactic (e.g. merger, movement, agreement and case-marking) operations used to form the relevant structure. The derivation of a word is the set of morphological operations used to form the word.

derive: To **derive** a structure it to say how it is formed (i.e. specify the operations by which it is formed).

derived structure: A structure which is produced by the application of one or more syntactic (merger, movement or agreement) operations.

descriptive adequacy: A grammar of a particular language attains descriptive adequacy if it correctly specifies which strings of words do (and don't) form grammatical phrases and sentences in the language, and correctly describes the structure and interpretation of the relevant phrases and sentences. See §1.3.

DET/determiner: A word like *the/this/that* which is typically used to modify a noun, but which has no descriptive content of its own. Most determiners can be used either prenominally (i.e. in front of a noun that they modify) or pronominally (i.e. used on their own without a following noun) – cf. 'I don't like *that idea*/I don't like *that*).'

Determiner Phrase: A phrase like *the king (of Utopia)* which comprises a determiner *the*, and a noun complement like *king* or a Noun Phrase complement like *king of Utopia*. In work before the mid 1980s, a structure like *the king of Utopia* would have been analysed as a noun phrase (= NP), comprising the head noun *king*, its complement *of Utopia* and its specifier *the*. Since Abney (1987), such expressions have been taken to have the status of **DP**/Determiner Phrase.

direct object: See **object**.

discontinuous spellout: This phenomenon (also termed *split spellout*) arises when part of a moved phrase is spelled out in the position in which it originates, and the remainder in the position in which it ends up – as in 'How much do you believe *of what he tells you?*,' where the wh-phrase *how much of what he tells you* moves to the front of the sentence, with *how much* being spelled out in the position it moves to, and *of what he tells you* being spelled out in the position in which it originates. See §5.3.

discourse: Discourse factors are factors relating to the extrasentential setting in which an expression occurs (where extrasentential means 'outside the immediate sentence containing the relevant expression'). For example, to say that the reference of PRO is discourse-determined in a sentence such as 'It would be wise PRO to prepare yourself for the worst' means that PRO has no antecedent within the sentence immediately containing it, but rather refers to some individual(s) outside the sentence (in this case, the person being spoken to).

ditransitive: A ditransitive structure is a double-object structure like *She gave me them*, where the transitive verb *gave* has two objects (*me* and *them*). See **object**.

domain: The **domain** (or, more fully, **c-command domain**) of a head H is the set of constituents c-commanded by H – namely its sister and all the constituents contained within its sister. For example, the domain of C includes its TP complement and all constituents of the relevant TP.

DO-support: This refers to the use of the 'dummy' (i.e. meaningless) auxiliary *do* to form questions, negatives or tags in sentences which would otherwise contain no auxiliary. Hence, because a nonauxiliary verb like *want* requires *do*-support in questions/negatives/tags, we have sentences such as '*Does* he want some?,' 'He *doesn't* want any' and 'He wants some, *does* he?' See §4.8.

double-object construction: See **object**.

DP: See **Determiner Phrase**.

DP Hypothesis: The hypothesis that all definite expressions have the status of DPs – not just nominals like *the president* which contain an overt determiner, but also proper names like *John*.

D-pronoun: A pronoun like *that* in 'I don't like *that*' which seems to be a pronominal determiner.

dummy: A word with no intrinsic lexical semantic content (e.g. the expletive pronoun *there* and the auxiliary *do*).

Earliness Principle: A principle which says that linguistic operations must apply as early in a derivation as possible.

Early Modern English/EME: The type of English found in the early seventeenth century (i.e. at around the time Shakespeare wrote most of his plays, between 1590 and 1620).

echo question: A type of sentence used to question something which someone else has just said (often in an air of incredulity), repeating all or most of what they have just said. For example, if I say 'I've just met Nim Chimpsky' and you don't believe me (or don't know who I'm talking about), you could reply with an echo question such as 'You've just met who?'

ECM: See **Exceptional Case Marking**.

Economy Condition: A condition which requires that (all other things being equal) syntactic representations should contain as few constituents and syntactic derivations involve as few grammatical operations as possible.

edge: The edge of a given projection HP is that part of HP which excludes the complement of H (hence, that part of the structure which includes the head H and any specifier/s or adjunct/s which it has).

Elizabethan English: The type of English found in the early seventeenth century, during the reign of Queen Elizabeth I (i.e. at around the time Shakespeare wrote most of his plays, between 1590 and 1620).

ellipsis/elliptical: Ellipsis is an operation by which an expression is omitted (in the sense that its phonetic features are deleted and so unpronounced), e.g. in order to avoid repetition. For example, in a sentence such as 'I will do it if you will do it,' we can ellipse (i.e. omit) the second occurrence of *do it* to avoid repetition, and hence say 'I will do it if you will.' An **elliptical** structure is one containing an 'understood' constituent which has undergone **ellipsis** (i.e. been omitted).

embedded clause: A clause which is positioned internally within another constituent. For example, in a sentence such as 'He may suspect that I hid them,' the *hid*-clause (= *that I hid them*) is embedded within (and is the complement of) the Verb Phrase headed by the verb *suspect*. Likewise, in 'The fact that he didn't apologise is significant,' the *that*-clause (*that he didn't apologise*) is an embedded clause in the sense that it is embedded within a Noun Phrase headed by the noun *fact*. A clause which is not embedded within any other expression is a **root clause** (see **root**) or **main clause**.

EME: See **Early Modern English**.

empirical evidence: Evidence based on observed linguistic phenomena. In syntax, the term 'empirical evidence' usually means 'evidence based on grammaticality judgments by native speakers'. For example, the fact that sentences like *'Himself likes you' are judged ungrammatical by native speakers of Standard English provides us with empirical evidence that anaphors like *himself* can't be used without an appropriate antecedent (i.e. an expression which they refer back to).

empty: A constituent is empty/null if it is 'silent' and hence has no overt phonetic form. Empty categories include null subject pronouns like PRO and *pro*, null relative pronouns (like the null counterpart of *who* in *someone I know well*), null determiners (like that in 'ø *John* is tired') and null trace copies of moved constituents. See ch.3.

enclitic/encliticise: See **clitic**.

entry: A **lexical entry** is an entry for a particular word in a dictionary (and hence by extension refers to the set of information about the word given in the relevant dictionary entry).

EPP: This was originally an abbreviation for the **Extended Projection Principle**, which posited that every T constituent must be extended into a TP projection which has a **specifier**. In more recent work, the requirement for a T constituent like *will* to have a specifier is said to be a consequence of T carrying an [EPP] feature requiring it to project a specifier. The **EPP Condition** specifies that an uninterpretable EPP feature on a probe is deleted by movement of the closest active goal of the relevant type to become the specifier of the probe.

ergative: This term originally applied to languages like Basque in which the complement of a transitive verb and the subject of an intransitive verb are assigned the same morphological case. However, by extension, it has come to be used to denote verbs like *break* which occur both in structures like 'Someone broke the window' and in structures like 'The window broke,' where *the window* seems to play the same semantic/thematic role in both types of sentences, in spite of being the complement of *broke* in one sentence and the subject of *broke* in the other. See §8.4.

Exceptional Case Marking/ECM: Accusative subjects of infinitive clauses (e.g. *him* in 'I believe *him to be innocent*') are said to carry exceptional accusative case (in that the case of the accusative subject is assigned by the main-clause verb *believe*, and it is exceptional for the case of the subject of one clause to be assigned by the verb in a higher clause). Verbs (like *believe*) which take an infinitive complement with an accusative subject are said to be **ECM verbs**. See §3.8 and §9.6.

exclamative: A type of structure used to exclaim surprise, delight, annoyance etc. In English syntax, the term is restricted largely to clauses beginning with wh-exclamative words like *What*! or *How*! – e.g. 'What a fool I was!' or 'How blind I was!' See §8.2.

existential: An existential sentence is one which is about the existence of some entity. For example, a sentence such as 'Is there any coffee left?' questions the existence of coffee. Consequently, the word *any* here is sometimes said to be an **existential quantifier** (as is *some* in a sentence like 'There is some coffee in the pot').

experience: Children's experience is the speech input which they receive (or, more generally, the speech activity which they observe) in the course of acquiring their native language.

EXPERIENCER: A term used in the analysis of semantic/thematic roles to denote the entity which experiences some emotional or cognitive state – e.g. *John* in 'John felt unhappy' or 'John thought about his predicament'. See §6.4.

explanatory adequacy: A linguistic theory meets the criterion of explanatory adequacy if it explains why grammars have the properties that they do, and how children come to acquire grammars in such a short period of time. See §1.3.

expletive: A 'dummy' constituent with no inherent semantic content, such as the pronoun *there* in existential sentences like 'There is no truth in the rumour,' or the pronoun *it* in sentences such as *It is unclear why he resigned.* See §7.5, §7.6 and §8.6.

expression: This word is used in the text as an informal term meaning a string (i.e. continuous sequence) of one or more words which form a **constituent.**

Extended Projection Principle: See **EPP**.

external argument. See **argument**. The **External Argument Condition** on the use of expletives specifies that an expletive can only be merged as the highest argument of a (light) verb with no external argument.

extract/extraction: Extract(ion) is another term for **move(ment)**, and so denotes an operation by which one constituent is moved out of another. E.g. in a structure such as 'Who do you think [he saw –]' the pronoun *who* has been extracted (or **subextracted**) out of the bracketed clause (i.e. it is been moved out of the position marked –), and moved to the front of the overall sentence. The **extraction site** for a moved constituent is the position which it occupied before undergoing movement.

F: This symbol is used as a convenient notational device to denote an abstract functional head (or an abstract feature) of some kind.

Faculty of Language: see **Language Faculty**.

feature: A device used to describe a particular grammatical property. For example, the distinction between count and noncount nouns might be described in terms of a feature such as [±COUNT]. On **Feature Copying**, see **copying**. **Feature Deletion** is an operation by which uninterpretable features are deleted: see §7.4.

feminine: This term is used in discussion of grammatical **gender** to denote pronouns like *she/her/hers* which refer to female entities.

FHC: See **Functional Head Constraint**.

filled: To say that a given position in a structure must be filled is to say that it cannot remain empty but rather must be occupied (usually by an overt constituent of an appropriate kind).

finite: The term **finite verb/finite clause** denotes (a clause containing) an auxiliary or nonauxiliary verb which can have a nominative subject like *I/we/he/she/they*. For example, compare the two bracketed clauses in:

(i)   What if [people annoy her]?
(ii)   Don't let [people annoy her]

The bracketed clause and the verb *annoy* in (i) are finite because in place of the subject *people* we can have a nominative pronoun like *they*; by contrast, the bracketed clause and the verb *annoy* are **nonfinite** in (ii) because *people* cannot be replaced by a nominative pronoun like *they* (only by an accusative pronoun like *them*): cf.

(iii)   What if [*they* annoy her]?
(iv)   Don't let [*them/*they* annoy her]

By contrast, a verb or clause which has a subject with accusative or null case in English is nonfinite; hence the bracketed clauses and italicised verbs are nonfinite in the examples below:

(v)   Don't let [them *annoy* her]
(vi)   You should try [PRO to *help*]

Nonfinite forms include **infinitive** forms like *be*, and **participle** forms like *being/been*.

first-merge: See **merge**.

first person: See **person**.

FL: Faculty of Language: See **Language Faculty**.

floating quantifier: A quantifier which is separated from the expression which it quantifies. For example, in a sentence such as 'The students have *all* passed their exams,' *all* quantifies (but is not positioned next to) *the students*, so that *all* is a floating quantifier here.

Foc/Focalised/Focus/Focusing/FocP: **Focus** position in a sentence is a position occupied by a constituent which is emphasised in some way (usually in order to mark it as containing 'new' or 'unfamiliar' information). For example, in a **cleft sentence** such as 'It's *syntax* that they hate most' or a **pseudo-cleft** sentence such as 'What they hate most is *syntax*,' the expression *syntax* is said to occupy **focus position** within the relevant sentence, and to be **focused/focalised**. **Focusing** denotes a movement operation by which a constituent is moved into a focus position at the beginning of a clause in order to highlight it (e.g. to mark it as introducing new information). Thus, in a sentence like '*Nothing* could they do to save her,' the expression *nothing* has been focused by being moved to the front of the overall sentence from its underlying position as the complement of the verb *do*. In work on split CP projections by Luigi Rizzi (discussed in §8.2), preposed focused expressions are said to occupy the specifier position within a **FocP** ('Focus Phrase') projection which is headed by an abstract **Foc** ('Focus') head.

foot: The foot of a (movement) chain is the constituent which occupies the lowest position in the chain.

Force/ForceP: The complementisers *that/if* in a sentence such as *I didn't know* [*that/if he was lying*] are said to indicate that the bracketed clauses are declarative/interrogative in force (in the sense that they have the force of a question/a statement). In work on split CP projections by Luigi Rizzi (discussed in §8.2), complementisers are said to constitute a **Force** head which can project into a **Force Phrase/Force P**.

formal: In an expression such as **formal speech style**, the word *formal* denotes a very careful and stylised form of speech (as opposed to the kind of informal colloquial speech style used in a casual conversation in a bar): in an expression such as **formal features**, the word formal means 'grammatical' (i.e. features which play a role in morphology/syntax).

fragment: An utterance which is not a complete sentence (in the sense that it does not constitute a clause). So, a phrase such as 'A new dress' used in reply to a question such as 'What did you buy?' would be a **sentence fragment**. (By contrast, a sentence such as 'I bought a new dress' would not be a sentence fragment, since it contains a complete clause.)

Freezing Constraint: A principle of grammar specifying that any constituent occupying a position which reflects its scope/discourse properties is frozen in place.

front/fronting: Fronting is an informal term to denote a movement operation by which a given expression is **fronted** – i.e. moved to the front of some phrase or sentence.

function: Expressions such as **subject**, **specifier**, **complement**, **object**, **head** and **adjunct** are said to denote the grammatical function which a particular expression fulfils in a particular structure (which in turn relates to the position which it occupies and certain of its grammatical properties – e.g. case and agreement properties).

functional category/Functional Head Constraint/function word/functor: A word which has no **descriptive content** and which serves an essentially grammatical function is said to be a **function word** or **functor** (by contrast, a word which has descriptive content is a **content word** or **contentive**). A **functional category** is a category whose members are function words: hence, categories such as complementiser, auxiliary, infinitive particle, case particle or determiner are all functional categories – as well as the expressions they head (e.g. C-bar/CP, T-bar/TP, D-bar/DP etc.). The **Functional Head Constraint** is a grammatical principle which specifies that the complement of a certain type of functional head (including C and D) cannot be preposed on its own without also moving the functional head: see §2.5.

gapping: A form of **ellipsis** in which the head word is omitted from one (or more) of the conjuncts in a coordinate structure in order to avoid repetition. For example, the italicised second occurrence of *bought* can be gapped (i.e. omitted) in a sentence such as 'John bought an apple and Mary *bought* a pear,' giving 'John bought an apple, and Mary a pear.'

Gen: In one use, an abbreviation for **genitive case**; in another, an abbreviation for **gender**.

gender: A grammatical property whereby words are divided into different grammatical classes which play a role in **agreement/concord** relationships. In French, for example, nouns are intrinsically masculine or feminine in gender (e.g. *pommier* 'apple tree' is masculine, but *pomme* 'apple' is feminine), and articles inflect for gender, so that *un* 'a' is the masculine form of the indefinite article, and *une* is its feminine form. Articles in French have to agree in gender with the nouns they modify; hence we say *un pommier* 'an apple tree', but *une pomme* 'an apple'. In English, nouns no longer have inherent gender properties, and their modifiers don't inflect for gender either. Only certain pronouns like *he/she/it* carry gender properties in modern English, and these are traditionally said to carry **masculine/feminine/neuter** gender respectively (though the term **inanimate** is sometimes used in place of **neuter**).

generate/generative: The syntactic component of a grammar is said to **generate** (i.e. specify how to form) a set of syntactic structures. A grammar which does so is said to be a **generative grammar**.

generic: To say that an expression like *eggs* in a sentence such as 'Eggs are fattening' has a generic interpretation is to say that it is interpreted as meaning 'eggs in general'.

genitive: See **case**.

gerund: When used in conjunction with the progressive aspect auxiliary *be*, verb forms ending in *-ing* are **progressive participles**; in other uses they generally function as **gerunds**. In particular, *-ing* verb forms are gerunds when they can be used as subjects, or as complements of verbs or prepositions, and when (in literary styles) they can have a genitive subject like *my*. Thus *writing* is a gerund (verb form) in a sentence such as 'She was annoyed at [my *writing* to her mother],' since the bracketed gerund structure is used as the complement of the preposition *at*, and has a genitive subject *my*.

GOAL/goal: The term GOAL is used in the analysis of semantic/thematic roles to denote the entity towards which something moves – e.g. *Mary* in 'John sent *Mary* a letter': see §6.4. In a different sense, the term **goal** represents a constituent which agrees with or is attracted by a higher head which serves as a **probe**: see §7.2.

grammar: In traditional terms, the word grammar relates to the study of morphology and syntax. In a broader Chomskyan sense, grammar includes the study of phonology and semantics: i.e. a grammar of a language is a computational system which derives the Phonetic Form and Semantic Representation of expressions.

grammatical: An expression is **grammatical** if it contains no morphological or syntactic error, and **ungrammatical** if it contains one or more morphological or syntactic errors. **Grammatical features** are (e.g. person, number, gender, case etc.) features which play a role in grammatical operations (e.g. in determining case or agreement properties).

have-**cliticisation:** An operation by which *have* (in the guise of its contracted clitic variant /v/) attaches to an immediately preceding word ending in a vowel or diphthong, resulting in forms such as *I've, we've, they've* etc.

head: This term has two main uses. The head (constituent) of a phrase is the key word which determines the properties of the phrase. So, in a phrase such as *fond of fast food*, the head of the phrase is the adjective *fond*, and consequently the phrase is an Adjectival Phrase (and hence can occupy typical positions associated with adjectival expressions – e.g. as the complement of *is* in 'He is *fond of fast food*'). In many cases, the term *head* is more or less equivalent to the term *word* (e.g. in sentences such as 'An accusative pronoun can be used as the complement of a transitive head'). In a different use of the same word, the head of a movement chain is the highest constituent in the chain.

headed/Headedness Principle: An expression is **headed** if it has a **head**. The **Headedness Principle** specifies that every constituent must be headed (i.e. must have a head). So, for example, an expression like *fond of fast food* is headed by the adjective *fond* and so is an Adjectival Phrase. See **head**.

head-first/-last: A head-first structure is one in which the head of an expression is positioned before its complement(s); a head-last structure is one in which the head of an expression is positioned after its complement(s). See §1.6.

head movement: Movement of a word from one head position to another (e.g. movement of an auxiliary from T to C, or of a verb from V to T, or of a noun from N to D). See ch.4.

Head Movement Constraint/HMC: A principle of Universal grammar which specifies that movement between one head position and another is only possible between the head of a given structure and the head of its complement. See §4.5.

Head Position Parameter: The parameter which determines whether a language positions heads before or after their complements. See §1.6.

Head Strength Parameter: A parameter whose setting determines whether a given kind of head is **strong** and can trigger movement of a lower head to attach to it, or **weak** and so cannot attract a lower head to move to attach to it. See §4.5.

HMC: See **Head Movement Constraint**.

homophonous: Two different expressions are homophonous if they have the same phonetic form (e.g. *we've* and *weave*).

host: An expression to which a **clitic** or **affix** attaches. For example, if *n't* cliticises onto *could* in expressions like *couldn't*, we can say that *could* is the host onto which *n't* cliticises.

I: See **INFL**.

idiom: A string of words which has an idiosyncratic meaning (e.g. *hit the roof* in the sense of 'get angry').

I-language: I-language is a linguistic system internalised (i.e. internally represented) within the brain. See §1.3.

illegible: See **legible**.

immediate constituent: See **constituent**.

immediately contain: See **contain**.

Imp: A symbol used to designate an (affixal) imperative morpheme which occupies the head C position of CP in imperatives: see ex. 4.2.

impenetrable/Impenetrability Condition. The **Impenetrability Condition** says that a constituent within the domain of a complementiser is impenetrable/inaccessible to (and hence cannot be affected by) a head c-commanding the relevant complementiser. See also **Phase Impenetrability Condition**.

imperative: A term employed to classify a type of sentence used to issue an order (e.g. 'Be quiet!,' 'Don't say anything!'), and also to classify the type of verb-form used in an imperative sentence (e.g. *be* is a verb in the **imperative mood** in 'Be quiet!').

inactive: See **active**. The **Inactivity Condition** on expletive *it* specifies that it can only be merged with a constituent which does not contain a nominal or pronominal expression with active case- or φ-features. The **Inactivation Condition** specifies that a goal with a case feature becomes inactive for agreement with (or attraction by) an A-head like T once its case feature has been valued and deleted.

inanimate: See **animate**.

Inclusiveness Condition: A grammatical principle proposed by Chomsky (1999, p. 2) which 'bars introduction of new elements (features) in the course of a derivation'.

indefinite: See **definite**. The **Indefiniteness Condition** on expletive *there* specifies that it can only be merged with a verb which has an indefinite nominal or pronominal internal argument. If we adopt a split projection analysis of Verb Phrases, this can be recast as saying that expletive *there* can only be merged as the specifier of a light verb whose VP complement has an indefinite nominal or pronominal internal argument.

indefinite article: See **article**.

indicative: Indicative (auxiliary and main) verb forms are finite forms which are used (inter alia) in declarative and interrogative clauses (i.e. statements and questions). Thus, the italicised items are said to be indicative in **mood** in the following sentences: 'He *is* teasing you,' '*Can* he speak French?,' 'He *had* been smoking,' 'He *loves* chocolate,' 'He *hated* syntax.' An **indicative clause** is a clause which contains an indicative (auxiliary or nonauxiliary) verb. See **mood**.

indirect object: See **object**.

infinitive/infinitival: The infinitive (or infinitival) form of a verb is the (uninflected) form which is used (inter alia) when the verb is the complement of a modal auxiliary like *can*, or of the infinitive particle *to*. Accordingly, the italicised verbs are infinitive/infinitival forms in sentences like 'He can *speak* French' and 'He's trying to *learn* French.' An **infinitive/infinitival clause** is a clause which contains a verb in the infinitive form. Hence, the bracketed clauses are infinitive clauses in: 'He is trying [to help her]' and 'Why not let [him help her]?' (In both examples, *help* is an infinitive verb form, and *to* when used with an infinitive complement is said to be an **infinitive particle**.) Since clauses are analysed as phrases within the framework used here, the term **infinitive phrase** can be used interchangeably with **infinitive clause**, to denote a TP projection headed by the infinitive particle *to* (or by a null counterpart of the infinitive particle *to*).

INFL: A category devised by Chomsky (1981) whose members include finite auxiliaries (which are INFLected for tense/agreement), and the INFinitivaL particle *to*. INFL was abbreviated to **I** in Chomsky (1986) and replaced by T (-tense marker) in later work.

inflection/inflectional: An inflection is an **affix** which marks grammatical properties such as number, person, tense, case. For example, a plural noun such as *dogs* in English comprises the stem form *dog* and the plural number inflection *-s*. **Inflectional morphology** is the grammar of **inflections**.

inherent case: See **case**.

inherit/inheritance: An operation by which cerain uninterpretable features (e.g. agreement features) on a phrase head are handed down to (and thereby inherited by) the non-phasal head immediately beneath the phase head: see §9.6.

initial grammar: The earliest grammar of their native language developed by infants.

innateness hypothesis: The hypothesis that children have a biologically endowed innate language faculty. See §1.4.

in situ: A constituent is said to remain *in situ* (i.e. 'in place') if it doesn't undergo a given kind of movement operation.

interface levels: Levels at which the grammar interfaces (i.e. connects) with speech and thought systems which lie outside the domain of grammar. **Phonetic Form** is the level at which the grammar interfaces with articulatory–perceptual (speech) systems, and **semantic representation** is the level at which it interfaces with conceptual–intentional (thought) systems.

intermediate projection: See **project(ion)**.

internal argument: See **argument**.

internalised grammar: A grammar which is internally represented within the mind/brain.

interpretable: A feature is (semantically) interpretable if it has semantic content: so, for example, a feature such as [Plural-Number] on a pronoun like *they* is interpretable, but a phonological feature like [+nasal] is **uninterpretable**, and so too are many grammatical/formal features (e.g. case features). See §7.4.

interpretation: To say that an expression has a particular (semantic) interpretation is to say that it expresses a particular meaning. So, for example, we might say that a sentence such as 'He loves you more than Sam' has two different interpretations – one on which *Sam* has a subject interpretation and is implicitly understood as the subject of *loves you*, and a second on which *Sam* has an object interpretation and is implicitly understood as the object of *he loves*. The first interpretation can be paraphrased as 'He loves you more than Sam loves you,' and the second as 'He loves you more than he loves Sam.'

interrogative: An interrogative clause or sentence is one which asks a question. The **Interrogative Condition** specifies that a clause is interpreted as a **non-echoic question** if (and only if) it is a CP with an interrogative specifier (i.e. a specifier containing an interrogative word). See **question**.

Intervention Condition: A principle of grammar specifying that probe P cannot target goal G if there is some other visible goal of the same kind as G intervening between the two and if the intervening goal is inactive for P.

intransitive: See **transitive**.

intuitions: Judgments given by native speakers about the grammaticality, interpretation and structure of expressions in their language.

inversion/inverted: A term used to denote a movement process by which the relative order of two expressions is reversed. It is most frequently used in relation to the more specific operation by which an auxiliary (and, in earlier stages of English, nonauxiliary) verb comes to be positioned before its subject, e.g. in questions such as 'Can you speak Swahili?,' where *can* is positioned in front of its subject *you*. See ch.4. An **inverted auxiliary/verb** is one which is positioned in front of its subject (e.g. *will* in 'Will I pass the syntax exam?').

Invisibility Condition: A principle of grammar specifying that the specifier of a complete (non-defective) TP is invisible to any higher probe.

irrealis: An infinitive complement like that italicised in 'They would prefer (*for*) *you to abstain*' is said to denote an *irrealis* (a Latin word meaning 'unreal') event in the sense that the act of abstention is a hypothetical event which has not yet happened and may never happen.

island: A structure out of which no subpart can be extracted. For example, co-ordinate structures like *William and Harry* are **islands** in this sense. Hence, in a sentence like 'I admire William and Harry,' we can topicalise the whole co-ordinate structure *William and Harry* by moving it to the front of the overall sentence (as in 'William and Harry, I admire'), but we cannot topicalise *Harry* alone (as we see from the ungrammaticality of *'Harry* I admire William and').

K: See **case particle**.

label: A notational device used to represent linguistic (particularly categorial) properties of constituents. For example, if we say that the word *man* belongs to the category N of noun, we are using N as a label to indicate the categorial properties of the word *man* (i.e. to tell us what grammatical category *man* belongs to).

labelled bracketing: See **bracketing**.

landing-site: The landing-site for a moved constituent is the position it ends up in after it has been moved (e.g. the specifier position within CP is the landing-site for a moved wh-expression).

Language Faculty: Chomsky argues that humans beings have an innate Language Faculty (or **Faculty of Language**, **FL**) which provides them with an algorithm (i.e. set of procedures or program) for acquiring a grammar of their native language(s). See §1.4.

LBC: See **Left Branch Condition**.

learnability: A criterion of adequacy for linguistic theory. An adequate theory must explain how children come to learn the grammar of their native languages in such a short period of time, and hence must provide for grammars of languages which are easily learnable by children. See §1.3.

Left Branch Condition: A **constraint** which specifies that in languages like English, the leftmost constituent of a nominal expression cannot be moved out of the expression containing it.

legible: To say that syntactic structures must be **legible** at the semantics and phonetics interfaces is to say that the structures inputted to the **semantic component** of the grammar must contain only features which contribute to semantic interpretation, and that the structures inputted to the **PF component** must contain only features which contribute to determining the phonetic form of an expression. Any structure which is not legible at a given interface is said to be **illegible** to the relevant interface.

level: In the sense in which this term is used in this book, constituents like T, T-bar and TP represent different **projection levels** – i.e. successively larger types of category

(T being a **minimal projection**, T-bar an **intermediate projection** and TP a **maximal projection**). See **projection**.

lexical/lexicon: The word **lexical** is used in a number of different ways. Since a **lexicon** is a dictionary (i.e. a list of all the words in a language and their idiosyncratic linguistic properties), the expression **lexical item** in effect means 'word', the expression **lexical entry** means 'the entry in the dictionary for a particular word', the term **lexical property** means 'property of some individual word', the term **lexical learning** means 'learning words and their idiosyncratic properties' and the term **lexical array** means 'the set of words out of which a given expression is formed'. However, the word lexical is also used in a second sense, in which it is contrasted with **functional** (and hence means 'non-functional'). In this second sense, a **lexical category** is a category whose members are **contentives** (i.e. items with idiosyncratic descriptive content): hence, categories such as noun, verb, adjective or preposition are lexical categories in this sense. So, for example, the term **lexical verb** means 'main verb' (i.e. a nonauxiliary verb like *go, find, hate, want* etc.).

light verb: This term is traditionally used to denote verbs (e.g. like *take/make* in expressions like *make fun of* and *take heed of*) with relatively little semantic content. However, in recent work on **VP shells** discussed in §8.4–§8.7, this term is extended to denote an abstract affixal verb (often with a causative sense like that of *make*) to which a noun, adjective or verb adjoins. For example, it might be claimed that the suffix *-en* in a verb like *sadden* is an affixal light verb which combines with adjectives like *black, white* and *sad* to form the causative verb *sadden* (which has a meaning loosely paraphraseable as 'make sad', or 'cause to become sad'). This type of analysis can be extended to verbs like *roll* as they are used in sentences like 'He *rolled* the ball down the hill,' if we assume that *roll* here is used causatively (and so has a meaning paraphraseable as 'make roll', or 'cause to roll'), and hence involves adjunction of the verb *roll* to an abstract light verb (which can be thought of as a null verbal counterpart of *-en*). A light verb is denoted as **V**.

link: A constituent (or position) which is part of a movement **chain**.

local/locality: One constituent X can agree with another constituent Y only if Y is in the **local c-command domain** of X – i.e. only if Y is c-commanded by X and if Y is sufficiently close to X. The closeness requirement is a consequence of a universal **Locality Principle**. In recent work, Chomsky has defined closeness (for syntactic operations like agreement) in terms of the **Phase Impenetrability Condition**.

locative: This is a term which denotes the semantic/thematic function of a constituent. A locative expression is one which denotes place. So, for example, *there/where* are locative pronouns in sentences such as 'Are you going *there*?' or '*Where* are you going?' **Locative inversion** is an operation by which a locative expression is positioned in front of its associated verb, e.g. as in *Down the hill rolled the ball*. See §8.6.

locus: To say that T is the **locus** of tense is to say that the tense property of a tensed clause or tensed auxiliary or main verb originates as a tense feature (or tense affix) carried by the head T constituent of TP.

long-distance movement: A long-distance movement operation is one which moves a constituent out of one clause (TP/CP) into another.

M: mood.

main clause: See **root clause**.

main verb: A non-auxiliary verb. See **auxiliary**.

masc(uline): This term is used in discussions of grammatical **gender** to denote pronouns like *he/him/his* which refer to male entities.

mass noun: See **count noun**.

matrix: In a sentence such as 'I think *he lied*,' the (italicised) *lied* clause is an **embedded/complement clause** (by virtue of being embedded as the complement of the verb *think*), and the *think* clause is the **matrix clause**, in the sense that it is the clause immediately containing the *lied* clause.

maximal projection: See **projection**.

Merge(r): An operation by which two constituents are combined together to form a single larger constituent: see ch.2. The **Merger Condition** is a principle of grammar specifying that when a lexical verb V is merged with more than one **internal argument** of the relevant kind, a clausal internal argument is the first to be merged with V (and so is positioned lower within VP than any other internal argument), and a (pro)nominal internal argument the last to be merged with V (and so is positioned higher within VP than any other internal argument). The first argument merged with a head H (i.e. its complement) is said to be **first-merged** with H, and the second argument merged with H (i.e. its specifier) is said to be second-merged with H.

Minimalism/Minimalist Program: A theory of grammar developed by Chomsky whose core assumption is that grammars are minimally complex, perfect systems of optimal design. See §1.3.

minimal projection: See **projection**.

Mixed Chains Constraint: A principle of grammar specifying that movement cannot give rise to a mixed chain containing one copy of a constituent which has moved to the edge of a phase, and another which has moved to the edge of a non-phasal projection.

modal/modality: A modal auxiliary is an auxiliary which expresses **modality** (i.e. notions such as possibility, futurity or necessity). The set of modal auxiliaries found in English is usually assumed to include *will/would/can/could/shall/should/may/might/must/ought*, and *need/dare* when followed by a 'bare' (*to*-less) infinitive complement.

modifier/modify: In an expression such as *tall men*, it is traditionally said that the adjective *tall* **modifies** (i.e. attributes some property to) or is a **modifier** of the noun *men*. Likewise, in a sentence such as 'Eat slowly!,' the adverb *slowly* is said to **modify** the verb *eat* (in the sense that it describes the manner in which the speaker is being told to eat).

module: An individual component of a larger system. For example, a grammar might be said to contain a **case module** – i.e. a component which accounts for the case properties of relevant constituents.

mood: This is a term describing inflectional properties of finite verbs. (Auxiliary and nonauxiliary) verbs in English can be in the **indicative mood**, **subjunctive mood** or **imperative mood**. Examples of each type of mood are given by the italicised verb forms in the following: 'He *hates* [= indicative] spaghetti'; 'The court ordered that he *be* [= subjunctive] detained indefinitely'; '*Keep* [= imperative] quiet!' The mood of the verb determines aspects of the interpretation of the relevant clause, so that e.g. subjunctive verbs occur in **irrealis** clauses. A **Mood Phase/MP** is a phrase headed by an item which marks (e.g. indicative or subjunctive) mood.

morpheme: The smallest unit of grammatical structure. Thus, a plural noun such as *cats* comprises two morphemes, namely the stem *cat* and the plural suffix -*s*.

morphology/morphological: Morphology studies how **morphemes** are combined together to form words. **Morphological** properties are properties relating to the form of words (i.e. relating to the inflections or affixes they carry). For example, it is a morphological property of regular count nouns that they have a plural form ending in -*s*.

morphosyntactic: A morphosyntactic property is a 'grammatical' property, i.e. a property which affects (or is affected by) relevant aspects of morphology and syntax. For instance, **case** is a morphosyntactic property in that (e.g.) pronouns have different morphological forms and occupy different syntactic positions according to their case: e.g. the nominative form of the first person plural pronoun is *we* and its accusative form is *us*; the two occupy different syntactic positions in that the nominative form occurs as the subject of a finite verb, whereas the accusative form occurs as the complement of a transitive verb or preposition: cf. '*We* disagree,' 'Join *us*.'

mother: A constituent X is the mother of another constituent Y if X is the next highest node up in the tree from Y, and the two are connected by a branch (solid line). See §2.6.

move/movement: An operation by which (a copy of) a constituent is displaced from one position in a given structure and comes to occupy another position in the structure.

MP: Mood Phrase (see **Mood**).

multiple agreement: Agreement between a **probe** and more than one **goal**. See §7.6.

multiple specifiers: In his (1995) book and subsequent work, Chomsky suggests that certain types of head may allow more than one specifier (e.g. a light verb with an external argument/subject as its inner specifier may attract a wh-expression to become its outer specifier: see §9.5).

multiple wh-questions: Questions containing more than one wh-word. See §5.8.

N: See **noun**.

natural language: A language acquired in a natural setting by human beings (hence, excluding e.g. computer languages, animal communication systems etc.).

NEG: The head constituent of a **NEGP** (i.e. of a Negation Phrase constituent which contains *not* as its specifier). See §4.7.

negation: A process or construction in which some proposition is said to be false. Negation involves the use of some negative item such as *not*, *n't*, *nobody*, *nothing*, *never* etc. – though most discussions of negation in English tend to be about the negative adverbs *not/n't*. See §4.7.

negative evidence: In the context of discussions about the nature of the evidence which children make use of in acquiring their native language(s), this term relates to evidence based on the nonoccurrence of certain structures in the child's speech input, or on correction of children by others (e.g. adults). See §1.7.

negative particle: This term typically denotes the negative adverbs *not/n't*.

NEGP: See **NEG**.

neuter: See **gender**.

node: A term used to denote each point in a tree diagram which carries a category label. Each node represents a separate constituent in the relevant structure.

Nom: An abbreviation for **nominative**. See **case**.

nominal: This is the adjective associated with the word *noun*, so that in principle a **nominal (expression)** is an expression containing or comprising a noun. However, the term is sometimes extended to mean 'expression containing or comprising a noun *or pronoun*'.

nominative: See **case**.

nonargument: See **argument**.

nonauxiliary verb: A 'lexical verb' or 'main verb' (like *want, try, hate, smell, buy* etc.) which requires DO-**support** to form questions, negatives and tags.

nonconstituent: A nonconstituent string is a sequence of words which do not together form a constituent.

noncount noun: See **count noun**.

non-echoic question: A question which can be used in any context, not just to echo something previously said.

No-Negative-Evidence Hypothesis: The hypothesis that children acquire their native language(s) on the basis of positive evidence alone, and do not make use of negative evidence. See §1.7.

nonfinite: See **finite**.

non-terminal: See **terminal**.

noun/N: A category of word (whose members include items such as *boy/friend/thought/sadness/computer*) which typically denotes an entity of some kind. In traditional grammar, a distinction is drawn between **common nouns** and **proper nouns**. Proper nouns are names of individual people (e.g. *Chomsky*), places (e.g. *Colchester, Essex, England*), dates (e.g. *Tuesday, February, Easter*), magazines (e.g. *Cosmopolitan*) etc., whereas common nouns (e.g. *boy, table, syntax* etc.) are nouns denoting general (non-individual) entities. Proper nouns have the semantic property of having unique reference, and the syntactic property that (unless themselves modified) they generally can't be modified by a determiner (cf. *the London).

Noun Phrase/NP: A phrase whose head is a noun. In work prior to the mid 1980s, a structure such as *the king of Utopia* was taken to be a noun phrase/NP comprising the head noun *king*, its complement *of Utopia* and its specifier *the*. In more recent work, such expressions are taken to be **Determiner Phrases/DPs** comprising the head determiner *the* and a Noun Phrase/NP complement *king of Utopia*, with the NP in turn comprising the head noun *king* and its complement *of Utopia*. See §2.3 and §3.11.

NP: See **Noun Phrase**.

N-pronoun: A pronoun like *one* in 'Mary bought a green one' which has the morphological and syntactic properties of a (count) noun.

null: A null constituent is one which is **'silent'** or 'unpronounced' and so has no overt phonetic form. See ch.3.

null case: The case carried by PRO (see **case**).

null subject: A subject which has grammatical and semantic properties but no overt phonetic form. There are a variety of different types of null subject, including the null *pro* subject which can be used in any finite clause in a language like Italian, the null counterpart of *you* found in English imperative clauses like 'Shut the door!,' the null PRO subject found in non-finite control clauses like that bracketed in 'The prisoners tried [PRO to escape]' and the null truncated subject found in sentences like 'Can't find my pen. Must be on my desk at home.' See §3.2.

null subject language: This term is used to denote a language which allows any finite clause of any kind to have a null *pro* subject. For example, Italian is a null subject language and so allows us to say 'Sei simpatica' (literally 'Are nice,' meaning 'You are nice'); by contrast, English is a **non-null subject language** in the sense that it doesn't allow the subject to be omitted in this type of structure (hence *'Are nice' is ungrammatical in English).

Null Subject Parameter: A parameter whose setting determines whether a language is a **null subject language** or not. See §1.6.

Num/number: A term used to denote the contrast between singular and plural forms. In English, we find number contrasts in nouns (cf. 'one *dog*', 'two *dogs*'), in some determiners (cf. '*this* book', '*these* books'), in pronouns (cf. *it/they*) and in finite (auxiliary or main) verbs (cf. 'It *smells*,' 'They *smell*').

object: The complement of a transitive item (e.g. in 'Help *me*,' *me* is the object of the transitive verb *help*; and in 'for *me*', *me* is the object of the transitive preposition *for*). The term **object** is generally restricted to complements which carry accusative case – i.e. to nominal or pronominal complements: hence, *nothing* would be the object (and complement) of *said* in 'He said *nothing*,' but the *that*-clause would be the **complement** (but not the object) of *said* in 'He said [that he was tired]' – though some traditional grammars extend the term object to cover clausal complements as well as (pro)nominal complements. In sentences such as 'She gave him them,' the verb *give* is traditionally said to be **ditransitive** by virtue of having two objects, namely *him* and *them:* the first object (representing the recipient) is termed the **indirect object**, and the second object (representing the gift) is termed the **direct object**; the relevant construction is known as the **double object construction**. Where a verb has a single object (e.g. *nothing* in 'He said nothing'), this is the direct object of the relevant verb.

objective: Another term for **accusative**. See **case**.

one-place predicate: A predicate which has only one argument. See **argument**.

operator: This term is used in syntax to denote (e.g.) interrogative and negative expressions which have the syntactic properties that they trigger auxiliary inversion (cf. 'What *have you* done?,' 'Nothing *have I* done') and allow a polarity item like partitive/existential *any* to occur in their scope (cf. 'What can *anyone* do?,' 'Nothing can *anyone* do').

overt: An expression is overt if it has a non-null phonetic form, but **null** if it has no phonetic content. Thus, *him* is an overt pronoun, but **PRO** is a null pronoun. The term **overt structure** is used in this book (though not more generally) as an informal expository term to refer to a simplified representation of the structure of a given expression which shows only the overt constituents which it contains (and hence excludes trace copies and other null constituents).

P: See **preposition**.

Parameters/Parametric: A parameter is a dimension of grammatical variation between different languages or different language varieties (e.g. the **Null Subject Parameter**, **Head Position Parameter**, **Wh-Parameter**). **Parametric variation** relates to differences between languages which reflect differences in the setting of one or more parameters. See §1.6.

Parameter-setting: The process by which children determine which setting of a parameter is appropriate for the native language they are acquiring. See §1.7.

paraphrase: A paraphrase is an expression which has roughly the same meaning as the expression which it is being used to paraphrase, but which brings out the relevant meaning more clearly. For example, we can bring out the ambiguity of a sentence like *He loves you more than me* by saying that it has two different **interpretations**, one of which can be paraphrased as 'He loves you more than he loves me,' and the other of which can be paraphrased as 'He loves you more than I love you.'

partial: A **labelled bracketing** is **partial** if it shows only part of the structure of a given sentence or expression (other parts being omitted to simplify exposition).

participle: A non-finite verb form which encodes **aspect** or **voice**. In European languages, participles have no person properties but (in languages like Latin or Icelandic which have a richer morphology than English) have number/gender/case properties. English has three types of participle: **progressive participles** (ending in *-ing*) used in conjunction with the progressive aspect auxiliary *be* in sentences like 'It is *raining*'; **perfect participles** (generally ending in *-d* or *-n*) used in conjunction with the perfect aspect auxiliary *have* in sentences like 'He has *gone* home'; and **passive participles** (also generally ending in *-d* or *-n*) used in conjunction with the passive voice auxiliary *be* in sentences like 'He was *arrested* by Percy Plodd.'

particle: This is an informal term used to describe a range of (typically monosyllabic) items which are invariable in form, and which don't fit easily into traditional systems of grammatical categories. For example, infinitival *to* (cf. 'Try *to* be nice') is said to be an **infinitive particle**; *of* as used in expressions like 'loss *of* face' is sometimes said to be a **genitive case particle**; *not* and *n't* are said to be **negative particles**. The term is sometimes extended to include prepositions used without a complement (e.g. *down* in 'He fell *down*').

partitive: A partitive quantifier is a word like *some/any* which quantifies over part of the members of a given set (as in '*Some* students enjoy syntax').

part of speech: See **category**.

passive: See **active**, **passivisation**.

passive participle: See **active**, **participle**.

passivisation: A movement operation whereby an expression which is the **thematic** complement of a verb becomes the subject of the same clause (as in '*The jewels* were stolen') or the subject of another clause (as in '*The minister* was said to have lied to Parliament'). See §6.6–§6.7.

past tense: See **tense**.

PATIENT: A particular type of **theta-role**, denoting an entity which suffers the consequences of some action. For example, in a sentence such as 'John killed *Harry*,' *Harry* is the patient argument of the verb *kill*. The more recent term THEME is often used in place of the traditional term PATIENT. See §6.4.

perfect: In one sense of the word, in a sentence like 'He has gone home,' *has* is an auxiliary marking **perfect aspect**, and *gone* is a **perfect participle**: see **aspect**, **participle**. In a different sense, by claiming that language is a perfect system, Chomsky means that grammars produce structures which are 'perfect' in the sense that they are precisely of the form required to interface with speech and thought systems.

performance: A term which denotes observed language behaviour – e.g. the kind of things people actually say when they speak a language, and what meanings they assign to sentences produced by themselves or other people. Performance can be impaired by factors such as tiredness or drunkenness, giving rise to **performance errors**. Performance is contrasted with **competence** (which denotes fluent native speakers' knowledge of the grammar of their native language). See §1.3.

periphery: The periphery of a clause is that part of the clause structure which is positioned above TP – in other words the **edge** of CP (or its counterpart in a **split CP** system like that discussed in §8.2).

Pers: An abbreviation of **person/press**.

person/pers: In traditional grammar, English is said to have three grammatical persons. A **first person** expression (e.g. *I/we*) is one whose reference includes the speaker(s); a **second person** expression (e.g. *you*) is one which excludes the speaker(s) but includes the addressee(s) (i.e. the person or people being spoken to); a **third person** expression (e.g. *he/she/it/they*) is one whose reference excludes both the speaker(s) and the addressee(s) – i.e. an expression which refers to someone or something other than the speaker(s) or addressee(s).

personal pronouns: These are pronouns which carry inherent **person** properties – i.e. first person pronouns such as *I/we*, second person pronouns such as *you* and third person pronouns such as *he/she/it/they*. See **person**.

PF(representation): (A representation of the) **Phonetic Form** (of an expression). See **representation**. The **PF component** of a grammar is the component which converts the syntactic structures generated by the computational component of the grammar into PF-representations, via a series of morphological and phonological operations. A **PF-clitic** is a clitic which attaches to another item in the PF component (not in the syntax), so that the two form a single phonetic word, but are not a single word in the syntax.

phase: In work outlined in chapter 9, Chomsky argues that syntactic structures are build up in phases (phases including complementiser phrases and transitive Verb Phrases), and that once a phase has been produced, the domain/complement of the head of the phase undergoes **transfer** to the PF component and the semantic component, and thereby becomes impenetrable to further operations in the syntax.

Phase Impenetrability Condition/PIC: A **constraint** on grammatical operations which specifies that the domain/complement of a phase head is impenetrable/inaccessible to an external probe (i.e. to a c-commanding probe which lies outside relevant **phase**). See §9.2.

phi-features/φ-features: Person and number features (and, in languages which have grammatical gender, gender features as well).

Phonetic Form: See **interface levels**.

phonetic representation: See **representation**.

phonological features: Features used to describe sound properties. For example, the difference between nasal and oral sounds might be described in terms of the feature [±NASAL].

phrase: The term **phrase** is used to denote an expression larger than a word which is a **maximal projection**: see **projection**. In traditional grammar, the term refers strictly to non-clausal expressions (hence, 'reading a book' is a phrase, but 'He is reading a book' is a clause, not a phrase). However, in more recent work, **clauses** are analysed as types of phrases: e.g. 'He will resign' is a tense phrase (TP), and 'That he will resign' is a complementiser phrase (CP). See §2.3 and §2.4.

phrase-marker/P-marker: A tree diagram used to represent the syntactic structure of a phrase or sentence. See §2.6.

phrase structure: See **constituent structure**.

PIC: See **Phase Impenetrability Condition**.

pied-piping: A process by which a moved constituent drags one or more other constituents along with it when it moves. For example, if we compare a sentence like 'Who were you talking to?' with 'To whom were you talking?,' we can say that in both cases the pronoun *who* is moved to the front of the sentence, but that in the second sentence the preposition *to* is **pied-piped** along with the pronoun *who*. See §5.5 and §5.6.

PITMH: See **Predicate-Internal Theta-Marking Hypothesis**. See §6.4.

Pl: See **plural**.

plural/pl: A plural expression is one which denotes more than one entity (e.g. *these cars* is a plural expression, whereas *this car* is a **singular** expression).

P-marker: See **phrase-marker**.

polarity/PolP: a **polarity item/expression** is a word/phrase (e.g. a word like *ever* or a phrase like *at all* or *care a damn*) which has an inherent **affective** polarity, and hence is restricted to occurring within the scope of an affective (e.g. negative, interrogative or conditional) constituent (see **affective**). A **Polarity Phrase/PolP** constituent is a phrase which marks whether a sentence is positive or negative (See §4.8).

positive evidence: In discussions of child language acquisition, this expression denotes evidence based on the actual occurrence of certain types of structure in the child's speech input. For example, hearing an adult say *Open it* gives a child **positive evidence** that verbs are canonically positioned before their complements in English. See §1.7.

possessive: A possessive structure is one which indicates possession: the term is most commonly used in relation to expressions like '*John's* book' or '*his* book' (where the italicised expressions denote the person who possesses the book). The italicised possessor in each structure is said to be **genitive** in **case**.

postposition: A type of word which is the counterpart of a **preposition** in languages which position prepositions after their complements. See **adposition**.

postulate: A postulate is a theoretical assumption or hypothesis; to postulate is to hypothesise.

PP: See **Prepositional Phrase**.

PPT: See **Principles-and-Parameters Theory**.

Pr: An abbreviation for the feature [present-tense]. See **tense**.

pragmatics: The study of how nonlinguistic knowledge is integrated with linguistic knowledge in our use of language.

precede(nce): To say that one constituent **precedes** another is to say that it is positioned to its left (on the printed page) and that neither constituent contains the other. **Precedence** is left-to-right linear ordering.

predicate: See **argument**, **clause**, **predicative**.

Predicate-Internal Theta-Marking Hypothesis/PITMH: The hypothesis that an argument is assigned a **theta-role** via merger with a **predicate**. See §6.4.

predication: The process by which a **predicate** is combined with a **subject** in order to form a **proposition**. For example, in a sentence such as 'Boris likes vodka,' the property of liking vodka is said to be predicated of *Boris*.

predicative: In structures such as 'John is *in Paris/very silly/a liar*,' the italicised expressions are said to be predicative in that they predicate the property of being in Paris/being very silly/being a liar of John (i.e. they attribute the relevant property to John). A nominal like *a liar* when used predicatively is also referred to as a **predicate nominal**.

prefix: See **affix**.

prenominal: A prenominal expression is one which is positioned in front of a noun expression. For example, both *a* and *red* are prenominal in an expression such as *a red car*.

preposing: An informal term to indicate a movement operation by which a constituent is moved further to the left within a phrase or sentence.

preposition/P: A preposition is a word generally used to express location, manner etc. – e.g. *at/in/on/under/by/with/from/against/down* etc. In English, it is a characteristic property of prepositions that they are invariable, and that they can generally be modified by *straight/right*. Where a preposition has a nominal or pronominal complement, it is said to be **transitive**; where it has no complement, it is said to be **intransitive**. Hence *down* is a transitive preposition in 'He fell *down* the stairs,' but an intransitive preposition in 'He fell *down.'*

Prepositional Phrase/PP: A phrase whose head is a preposition – e.g. *in town*, *on Sunday*, *to the market*, *for someone else* etc.

preposition stranding: See **stranding**.

Pres/present tense: See **tense**.

principles: **Principles of Universal Grammar/UG principles** describe potentially universal properties of natural language grammars: the terms **condition** and **constraint** are also used with much the same meaning as the term **principle**. Potential principles of Universal Grammar include the **Headedness Principle, Binarity Principle, Attract Closest Condition** and **Phase Impenetrability Condition**.

Principles-and-Parameters Theory/PPT: This theory, developed in Chomsky (1981) and much subsequent work, claims that natural language grammars incorporate not only a set of innate universal **principles** which account for those aspects of grammar which are common to all languages, but also a set of **parameters** which account for those aspects of grammar which vary from one language to another. See **principles** and **parameter**.

PRN: An abbreviation for **pronoun**.

PRO: A null-case pronoun (known informally as 'big PRO', because it is written in capital letters) which represents the understood subject of an infinitive complement of a control predicate, e.g. in a structure such as 'John decided PRO to leave.' See §3.2

pro: A null nominative-case pronoun (known informally as 'little pro', because it is written in lower-case letters) which represents the understood null subject of a finite clause in a **null subject language**. A Shakespearean sentence such as 'Wilt come?' (= 'Will you come?,' Stephano, *The Tempest*, III.ii) could be argued to have a null *pro* subject, and hence to have the structure 'Wilt *pro* come?,' with *pro* having essentially the same interpretation as the second person singular pronoun *thou*. See §3.2.

probe: When a **head** is merged with its complement, it serves as a **probe** which searches for a matching goal within its complement (i.e. an expression which it can agree with): see §7.2. The **Probe Condition** is a principle of grammar specifying that a head probes only as far as is needed in order to find a goal which can value any unvalued features (and delete any uninterpretable features) on the probe.

proform: A proform is an expression (typically a word) which has no specific content of its own, but which derives its content from an **antecedent**. For example, in a sentence such as 'Mary may have been tired, but she didn't seem *so*,' the antecedent of the word *so* is the adjective *tired*: hence *so* (in the use illustrated here) can be said to be an adjectival proform.

PROG: Progressive aspect marker. See **aspect**.

progressive: See **aspect**.

project(ion): A **projection** is a constituent containing a head word. For example, a Noun Phrase such as *students of Linguistics* is a **projection** of its head noun *students* (equivalently, we can say that the noun *students* here **projects** into the Noun Phrase *students of linguistics*). A **minimal projection** is a constituent which is not a projection of some other constituent: hence, heads (i.e. words) are minimal projections. An **intermediate projection** is a constituent which is larger than a word, but smaller than a phrase (e.g. *is working* in 'He is working'). A **maximal projection** is a constituent which is not contained within any larger constituent with the same head. So, for example, in a sentence like 'I've heard several *accounts of what happened*,' the italicised noun phrase expression *accounts of what happened* is a maximal projection, since it is a projection of the noun *accounts* but is not contained within any larger projection of the noun *accounts* (if we assume that *several accounts of what happened* is a quantifier phrase headed by the quantifier *several*). By contrast, in a sentence such as 'I've heard several *accounts*,' the italicised noun *accounts* is both a minimal projection (by virtue of the fact that it is not a projection of some other head) and a maximal projection (by virtue of the fact that it is not contained within any larger structure which has the same head noun). The **Projection Principle** is a UG principle suggested in earlier work by Chomsky (1981, p. 29) which requires that the properties of lexical items should remain constant throughout the derivation: a related principle is the **Inclusiveness Condition**.

pronominal: A pronominal (expression) is a non-anaphoric pronoun like *him* which obeys **Principle B** of **Binding Theory** (and hence must not refer to any higher expression within the closest TP most immediately containing it). See Ex.2.2.

pronoun/PRN: The word *pronoun* is composed of the two morphemes – namely *pro* (meaning 'on behalf of') and *noun:* hence, a pronoun is traditionally said to be a word used in place of a noun expression. Pronouns differ from nouns in that they have no intrinsic descriptive content, and so are functors. There are a range of different types of pronoun found in English, including the pronominal noun *one(s)* used in sentences like 'I'll take the red *one(s)*,' pronominal quantifiers like *any* in 'I couldn't find *any*' and pronominal determiners like *this* in 'This is hard.' The term *pronoun* is most frequently used to indicate a class of items (like *he/him/his*) traditionally referred to as **personal pronouns** (though analysed in much recent work as pronominal determiners).

proper noun: See **noun**.

proposition: This is a term used to describe the semantic content (i.e. meaning) of a sentence. For example, we might say that the sentence 'Does John smoke?' questions the truth of the proposition that 'John smokes.'

pseudo-cleft sentence: A sentence such as 'What he hated most was *syntax*,' where *syntax* is said to occupy **focus position** within the overall sentence.

Q: In one use, an abbreviation for **quantifier**; in another use, an abbreviation for **question particle**.

QP/Quantifier Phrase: A phrase whose head is a quantifier – e.g. an expression such as *many people*, or *few of the students*.

Q-pronoun: A pronoun like *many* in 'I don't eat *many*' which seems to be a pronominal quantifier.

quantifier/Q: A quantifier is a special type of word used to denote quantity. Typical quantifiers include the universal quantifiers *all/both*, the distributive quantifiers *each/every*, the existential/partitive quantifiers *some/any* etc.

quantifier floating: See **floating quantifier**.

question: This refers to a type of sentence which is used to ask whether something is true, or to ask about the identity of some entity. See **Yes-no question** and **Wh-question**.

question particle/Q: The analysis of yes-no questions presented in §5.4 suggests that they contain a null question particle (i.e. a null counterpart of *whether*).

quirky case: See **case**.

raising (**predicate**): The term **raising** is used in two senses. In its most general sense, it denotes any movement operation which involves moving some constituent from a 'lower' to a 'higher' position in a structure. However, it also has a more specific sense, indicating a particular kind of **A-movement** operation by which an expression is moved from being the subject of one clause to becoming the subject of another. The term **raising predicate** denotes a word like *seem* whose subject is raised out of subject position in a complement clause to become subject of the (TP constituent in the) *seem* clause. See §6.8 and §6.9.

realis: A realis verb form is one which can be used to describe a real state of affairs, and is typically **indicative** in **mood** – e.g. the italicised verbs in 'He **cheats/cheated** at cards.'

reciprocal: See **anaphor**.

reduced: A reduced form is a form of a word which has lost one or more of its segments (i.e. vowel/consonants), and/or which contains a vowel which loses its defining characteristics and is realised as a neutral vowel like schwa /ə/. For example, the auxiliary *have* has the full (**unreduced**) form /hæv/ when stressed, but has the various reduced forms /həv/, /əv/ and /v/ when unstressed.

reference/referential/referring: The reference of an expression is the entity (e.g. object, concept, state of affairs) in the external world to which it refers. A **referential/referring expression** is one which refers to such an entity; conversely, a **nonreferential expression** is one which does not refer to any such entity. For example the second *there* in a sentence such as '*There* was nobody *there*' is referential (it can be paraphrased as 'in that place'), whereas the first *there* is nonreferential and so cannot have its reference questioned by *where?* (cf. *'*Where* was nobody there?').

reflexive: See **anaphor**.

relative pronoun/relative clause: In a sentence such as 'He's someone [*who* you can trust],' the bracketed clause is said to be a *relative clause* because it 'relates to' (i.e. modifies, or restricts the reference of) the pronoun *someone*. The pronoun *who* which introduces the clause is said to be a **relative pronoun**, since it 'relates to' the expression *someone* (in the sense that *someone* is the **antecedent** of *who*).

Relativised Minimality Condition: A principle of grammar which specifies that a constituent X can only be affected (e.g. attracted) by the minimal (i.e. closest) constituent of the relevant type above it (i.e. c-commanding X).

representation: A **syntactic representation** (or **structural representation**) is a notation/device (typically, a tree diagram or labelled bracketing) used to represent the **syntactic structure** of an expression (i.e. the way in which it is structured out of words and phrases): a **semantic representation** is a representation of linguistic aspects of the meaning of an expression; a **PF-representation** or **phonetic representation** is a representation of the phonetic form of an expression.

restrictive: A restrictive theory is one which is constrained by virtue of imposing strong **constraints** on the types of structures and operations found in natural language grammars. See §1.3.

resultative: A verb such as *paint* in a sentence such as 'John *painted* his house pink' is said to be a resultative verb in that the result of the action of painting is that the house becomes pink. See §8.4.

R-expression: A referring expression comprising or containing a noun, like *John* or *the man next door*. See ex.2.2.

root: The root of a tree diagram is the topmost node in the tree. Hence, a **root clause** is a free-standing clause, i.e. a clause which is not contained within any other expression. In traditional grammar, a root clause is termed a *principal clause, independent clause* or **main clause**. By contrast, an **embedded clause** is a clause which is contained within some larger expression; and a **complement clause** is an (embedded) clause which is used as the complement of some item. So, in a sentence such as 'I think he loves you,' the *think* clause (i.e. the expression *I think he loves you*) is a root clause, whereas the *loves* clause (i.e. the expression *he loves you*) is an embedded clause. Moreover, the *loves* clause is also a complement clause, since it serves as the complement of the verb *think*.

S/S′/S-bar: Category labels used in work in the 1960s and 1970s to designate a **sentence** or **clause**. See §2.3 and §2.4.

scope: The scope of an expression is the set of constituents which it modifies or which fall within (what we might informally call) its 'sphere of influence'. For example, a sentence like *He cannot be telling the truth* has a meaning paraphraseable as 'It is not possible that he is telling the truth,' and in such a sentence the negative *not* is said to have scope over the modal auxiliary *can* (and conversely *can* is said to fall within the scope of *not,* or to have **narrow scope** with respect to *not*). By contrast, a sentence such as *You mustn't tell lies* has a meaning paraphraseable as 'It is necessary that you not tell lies,' and in such a sentence, the auxiliary *must* is said to have scope over (or to have **wide scope** with respect to) the negative particle *n't*.

SCP: See **Strict Cyclicity Principle**.

second-merge: See **merge**.

second person: See **person**.

select(ion)/selectional: When a word has a particular type of complement, it is said to **select** (i.e. 'take' or 'allow') the relevant type of complement (and the relevant phenomenon is referred to as **complement selection**). For example, we can say that the word *expect* has the **selectional property** that it can select an infinitive complement (e.g. in structures like 'They expect *to* win').

semantics/semantic component: Semantics is the study of linguistic aspects of meaning. The **semantic component** of a grammar is the component which maps syntactic structures into semantic representations. See **representation**.

sentence: This term is usually used to denote a **root clause** – i.e. a free-standing clause which is not contained within some larger expression. See **root**.

sentence fragment: See **fragment**.

Sg: An abbreviation for **singular**.

Shakespeare: Shakespeare's plays were written between (around) 1590 and 1620, and are examples of **Early Modern English/Elizabethan English** (though some have suggested that Shakespeare's English is rather conservative, and hence is more representative of a slightly earlier stage of English).

shell: This term is used in connection with the idea (discussed in §8.4–§8.7) that Verb Phrases comprise two different projections, an outer vP shell headed by a **light verb**, and an inner VP core headed by a **lexical verb**.

silent: See **null**.

simple sentence: One which contains a single **clause**.

Simultaneity Condition: A principle of grammar specifying that all syntactic operations which involve a given probe apply simultaneously.

singular: A singular expression is one which denotes a single entity (e.g. *this car* is a **singular/Sg** expression, whereas *these cars* is a **plural/Pl** expression).

sister: Two nodes are sisters if they have the same mother (i.e. if they are directly merged with each other at some stage of derivation). See §2.6.

small clause: See **clause**.

SOURCE: A term used in the analysis of semantic/thematic roles to denote the entity from which something moves – e.g. the italicised expression in 'John returned *from Paris*.' See §6.4.

Spec: See **specifier**. Terms like **spec-C/spec-T/spec-V** (etc.) denote the specifier position within CP/TP/VP (etc.).

specification: The specification of an item is the set of features which it carries.

specifier/spec: The grammatical function fulfilled by certain types of constituent which precede the head of their containing phrase. For example, in a sentence such as 'John is working,' *John* is superficially the specifier (and subject) of *is working*. In a sentence such as 'What did John do?' *what* is superficially the specifier of the CP headed by a C constituent containing the inverted auxiliary *did*. In a phrase such as 'straight through the window', *straight* is the specifier of the PP headed by the preposition *through*. A **specifier-first** structure is one which has its specifier positioned in front of its head. The **Specifier Condition** in ch. 9 bars subextraction out of a constituent which is a specifier of a phase head.

spellout: The 'pronunciation' of an expression: e.g. to say that an item has a **null spellout** is to say that it is 'silent' and so has a null phonetic form.

split CP/split projection/split TP/split VP: Work discussed in ch. 8 suggests that CP, TP and VP can be split into a number of separate projections/phrases.

split spellout: See **discontinuous spellout**.

star: An asterisk (*) used in front of an expression to indicate that the expression is ungrammatical.

stem: The stem of a word is the form to which inflectional affixes are added. So, a verb form like *going* comprises the stem *go* and the inflectional suffix *-ing*.

strand/stranded/stranding: A stranded preposition is one which has been separated from its complement (by movement of the complement). For example, in an echo question like 'You're waiting for who?,' the preposition *for* has not been stranded, since it is immediately followed by its complement *who*. But in '*Who* are you waiting *for*?,' the preposition *for* has been **stranded**, in that it has been separated from its complement *who*: the relevant phenomenon is termed **preposition stranding**.

Strict Cyclicity Principle/SCP: A UG principle which specifies that a **cyclic** operation can only affect the overall head H of a structure and some other constituent c-commanded by H. See §4.7.

string: A continuous sequence of words contained within the same phrase or sentence. For example, in the sentence 'They hate syntax,' the sequences *They hate*, *hate syntax* and *They hate syntax* are all strings – but *They syntax* is not. Note that a string need not be a **constituent**.

strong: A strong head is one which can attract (i.e. trigger movement of) another head; a **weak** head is one which cannot trigger movement. For example, C in an interrogative main clause is strong in present-day English, and so attracts an auxiliary to move from T to C – e.g. in sentences like *Can you speak French?* On an entirely different use of these terms in the expressions **weak/strong genitive pronoun**, see **case**.

structural: See **case, representation**.

structure: See **constituent structure**.

stylistic variation: Variation correlated with stylistic factors. For example, *whom* is used in formal styles and *who* in other styles in sentences like 'He is someone *whom/who* I admire greatly.'

subextraction: See **extraction**.

subject: The (superficial structural) subject of a clause is a noun or pronoun expression which is normally positioned between a complementiser and an (auxiliary or nonauxiliary) verb. Syntactic characteristics of subjects include the fact that they can trigger agreement with auxiliaries (as in 'The president is lying,' where the auxiliary *is* agrees with the subject *the president*), and they can be inverted with auxiliaries in main clause questions (as in 'Is the president lying?,' where the auxiliary *is* has been inverted with the subject *the president*).

subjunctive: In a (formal style) sentence such as 'The judge ordered that he *be* detained indefinitely,' the passive auxiliary verb *be* is traditionally said to be in the **subjunctive mood**, since although it has exactly the same form as the infinitive form *be* (e.g. in infinitive structures such as 'To *be* or not to *be* – that is the question'), it has a nominative subject *he*, and hence is a **finite** verb form. In present-day spoken English, constructions containing subjunctive verbs are generally avoided, as they are felt to be archaic or excessively formal in style by many speakers. See **mood**.

substantive: A **substantive category** is a category (like noun, verb, adjective, adverb, preposition) whose members are **contentives** (i.e. items with idiosyncratic descriptive content).

substitution: A technique used to determine the category which a given expression belongs to. An expression belongs to a given type of category if it can be substituted (i.e. replaced) in phrases or sentences like that in which it occurs by another expression which clearly belongs to the category in question. For example, we might say that *clearer* is an adverb in 'John speaks *clearer* than you' because it can be replaced by the adverbial expression *more clearly*.

successive-cyclic movement: Movement in a succession of short steps.

suffix: See **affix**.

superiority effect: A phenomenon which arises when a head has to target the highest/closest constituent of a given type in a structure.

superlative: The superlative is a form of an adjective/adverb (typically carrying the suffix *-est*) used to mark the highest value for a particular property in comparison with others. For example, *hardest* is the superlative form of *hard* in 'John is the *hardest* worker because he works *hardest*.'

syntactic representation/structure: See **representation**.

syntax: The component of a grammar which determines how words are combined together to form phrases and sentences.

T: A tense-marking constituent containing either a tensed auxiliary, or an abstract tense affix *Tns*, or a non-finite tense particle like infinitival *to*. **T-to-C movement** is movement of an auxiliary or nonauxiliary verb from the head T position of TP into the head C position of CP – as with the italicised inverted auxiliary in '*Is* it raining?'

taxonomy: A system for classifying entities into types

tense: Finite auxiliary and main verbs in English show a binary (two-way) tense contrast, traditionally said to be between **present (Pres/Pr) tense** forms and **past tense** forms.

Thus, in 'John *hates* syntax,' *hates* is a present tense verb form, whereas in 'John *hated* syntax,' *hated* is a past tense verb form (an alternative classification which many linguists prefer is into [±PAST] verb forms, so that *hated* is [+PAST], and *hates* [−PAST]). This present/past tense distinction correlates (to some extent) with time-reference, so that (e.g.) past tense verbs typically describe an event taking place in the past, whereas present-tense verbs typically describe an event taking place in the present (or future). However, the correlation is an imperfect one, since e.g. in a sentence such as 'I *might* go there tomorrow,' the auxiliary *might* carries the past tense inflection -*t* (found on past tense main verbs like *left*) but does not denote past time.

tensed: A tensed (auxiliary or nonauxiliary) verb-form is one which carries (present/past) **tense** – e.g. *is, will, could, hates, went* etc. By extension, a tensed clause is one containing a tensed auxiliary or main verb. See **tense**.

terminal node: A terminal node in a tree diagram is one at the bottom of the tree; a non-terminal node is one which is not at the bottom of the tree.

ternary: Three-way. For example, person properties might be described in terms of a ternary (three-valued) feature such as [1/2/3-Pers], with first person pronouns like *we* being [1-Pers], second person pronouns like *you* being [2-Pers] and third person pronouns like they being [3-Pers]. A ternary-branching constituent is one which has three daughters.

thematic role: See **theta-role**.

THEME: The name of a specific theta-role (sometimes also termed PATIENT) representing the entity undergoing the effect of some action (e.g. *Harry* in 'William teased *Harry*').

theory of grammar: A theory which specifies the types of categories, relations, operations and principles found in natural language grammars. See §1.3.

theta criterion/θ-criterion: A principle of Universal Grammar which specifies that each argument should bear one and only one theta-role, and that each theta-role associated with a given predicate should be assigned to one and only one argument. See §6.4.

theta-mark/θ-mark: To say that a predicate **theta-marks** its arguments is to say that it determines the theta-role played by its arguments. See §6.4.

Theta-role/θ-role/thematic role: The semantic role played by an argument in relation to its predicate (e.g. AGENT, THEME, GOAL etc.). For example, in a sentence like *William teased Harry*, the verb *tease* assigns the θ-role AGENT to its subject *William* and the theta-role THEME to its complement *Harry*. See §6.4.

third person: See **person**.

three-place predicate: A predicate (typically a verb) which takes three arguments – e.g. the verb *give* in 'John gave Mary something' (where the three arguments of *give* are *John, Mary* and *something*). See **argument**.

Top/Topic/Topicalisation/TopP: In a dialogue such as the following:

> SPEAKER A: I've been having problems with the Fantasy Syntax seminar
> SPEAKER B: *That kind of course*, very few students seem to be able to get their heads round

the italicised expression *that kind of course* can be said to be the **topic** of the sentence produced by speaker B, in the sense that it refers back to *the Fantasy Syntax seminar* mentioned by the previous speaker. An expression which represents 'old' or 'familiar' information in this way is said to be a **topic**. The movement operation by which the italicised expression moves from being the complement of the preposition *round* to the front of the overall sentence is traditionally termed **topicalisation**. In work by Luigi Rizzi on split CP projections discussed in §8.2, topic expressions which occur at the beginning of clauses are said to be contained within a **TopP 'Topic Phrase'** projection, headed by an abstract **Top** (= 'Topic') constituent.

TP: Tense projection/Tense phrase – i.e. phrase headed by a tense-marked auxiliary or an abstract tense affix *Af*. See §§2.2–2.3.

trace (theory): A **trace** of a moved constituent is a null copy left behind (as a result of movement) in each position out of which a constituent moves. **Trace theory** is a theory which posits that moved constituents leave behind a trace **copy** in each position out of which they move. See §4.3, §5.3 and §6.2.

transfer: See **phase**.

transitive: A word is traditionally said to be transitive (in a given use) if it assigns **accusative** case to a noun or pronoun expression which it **c-commands**. So, *likes* in 'John *likes* him' is a transitive verb, since it assigns accusative case to its complement *him*. Likewise, infinitival *for* is a transitive complementiser, since it assigns accusative case to the subject of its infinitive complement (cf. 'I'm keen [for *him* to participate more actively]'). A verb or complementiser is **intransitive** (in a particular structure) if it does not assign accusative case to any constituent in the relevant structure.

tree (diagram): A form of graph used to represent the syntactic structure of a phrase or sentence.

truncate/truncation: Truncation is an operation by which a sentence is shortened by omitting one or more unstressed words at the beginning. For example, we can truncate a question like *Are you going anywhere nice on holiday?* by omitting *are* to form *You going anywhere nice on holiday?* and can further truncate the sentence by omitting *you* to give *Going anywhere nice on holiday?*

T-to-C movement: See **T**.

two-place predicate: A predicate which has two arguments – e.g. *tease* in 'William *teased* Harry' where the two arguments of the predicate *tease* are *William* and *Harry*. See **argument**.

UG: See **Universal Grammar**.

unaccusative: An unaccusative predicate is a word like *come* whose apparent 'subject' originates as its complement. See §6.5.

unary-branching: A unary-branching node is one which has a single daughter.

unbound: A constituent is unbound if it has no appropriate antecedent in an appropriate position within a given structure. For example, *himself* is unbound in a sentence such as *'She helped *himself*,' since *she* is not an appropriate antecedent for *himself*, and there is no other appropriate antecedent for *himself* anywhere within the sentence.

uncountable: See **count**.

unergative: An unergative predicate is a verb like *groan* in a sentence such as 'He was *groaning*' which has an AGENT subject but no overt object (though may have an incorporated object: see §8.5).

ungrammatical: See **grammatical**.

Uniform Theta Assignment Hypothesis/UTAH: A hypothesis (developed by Baker 1988) which maintains that each theta-role assigned by a particular kind of predicate is canonically associated with a specific syntactic position: e.g. spec-v is the canonical position associated with an AGENT argument. See §6.6.

uninterpretable: See **interpretable**.

Universal Grammar/UG: Those aspects of grammar which are universal, and which are assumed by Chomsky to be part of the innate knowledge which a child is born with.

universality: A criterion of adequacy for a theory of grammar, requiring that the theory be applicable to all natural languages. See §1.3.

unreduced: See **reduced**.

unspecified: To say that a constituent is **unspecified** for a given feature is to say that it lacks (a value for) the relevant feature.

unvalued: See **value**.

UTAH: See **Uniform Theta Assignment Hypothesis**.

V: See **verb**.

v: See **light verb**.

value: In relation to a feature such as [Singular-Number], **number** is said to be an **attribute** (and represents the property being described) and **singular** its **value**. To **value** a feature is to assign it a value. For example, a finite auxiliary enters the derivation with its person and number features **unvalued** (i.e. not assigned any value), and these are then valued via agreement with the subject in the course of the derivation. See §7.3.

variety: A particular (e.g. geographical or social) form of a language.

verb/V: A category of word which has the morphological property that it can carry a specific range of inflections (e.g. the verb *show* can carry past tense *-d*, third person singular present tense *-s*, perfect *-n* and progressive *-ing*, giving rise to *shows/showed/shown/showing*), and the syntactic property that it can head the complement of infinitival *to* (cf. 'Do you want to *show* me?'). On **verb movement**, see **V-to-T movement**.

Verb Phrase/VP: A phrase which is headed by a verb – e.g. the italicised phrase in 'They will *help you*.' See ch. 2.

Visibility Condition: A principle of grammar specifying that only the highest copy in a movement chain is visible in the syntax (other copies being inert).

voice: See **active**.

VP/VPISH: On VP, see **Verb Phrase**. A **VP-adverb** is an adverb (like *perfectly*) which adjoins to a projection of a lexical verb (V). The **VP-Internal Subject Hypothesis/ VPISH** is the hypothesis that subjects originate internally within the Verb Phrase: see ch. 6. The **VP-shell** analysis maintains that verb phrases can be split into (at least) two separate projections, a lower one headed by a lexical verb, and a higher one headed by a **light verb**: see ch. 8.

vP: A phrase (maximal projection) headed by a light verb. A **vP-adverb** is an adverb which adjoins to a projection of a **light verb** (v).

V-to-T movement: Movement of a verb out of the head V position in VP into the head T position in TP (also known as **verb movement**). See §4.4.

weak: See **strong**.

wh: This is widely used as a feature carried by constituents which undergo wh-movement: hence e.g. the relative pronoun *who* in *someone who I think is lying* can be described as a wh-pronoun, as can the interrogative pronoun *who* in *Who are you waiting for?* and the exclamative quantifier *what* in *What fun we had!*

Wh-Attraction Condition: See **attract**.

wh-copying: A phenomenon whereby a moved wh-expression leaves behind an overt copy of itself when it moves – as with movement of *who* in a Child English question such as *Who do you think who chased the cat?*

wh-expression: An expression containing a **wh-word**.

wh-movement: A type of movement operation whereby a **wh-expression** is moved to the front of a particular type of structure (e.g. to the front of the overall sentence in '*Where* has he gone?'). See ch. 5.

Wh-Parameter: A parameter whose setting determines whether wh-expressions are (or are not) moved to the front of an appropriate type of clause (e.g. in wh-questions). See §1.6.

wh-phrase: A phrase containing a **wh-word**.

wh-question: A question which contains a **wh-word**, e.g. 'What are you doing?'

wh-word: A word which begins with wh (e.g. *who/what/which/where/when/why*), or which has a similar syntax to *wh*-words (e.g. *how*).

word order: The linear sequencing (left-to-right ordering) of words within a phrase or sentence.

X-bar syntax: A theory of synactic structure which makes use of the **bar notation:** see **bar**.

yes-no question: A question to which 'Yes' or 'No' would be an appropriate answer – e.g. 'Is it raining?'

References

Abeillé, A. & Borsley, R. D. (2006) 'Comparative correlatives and parameters', ms., University of Essex.

Abels, K. (2003) 'Successive-cyclicity, anti-locality and adposition stranding', PhD diss., University of Connecticut.

Abney, S. P. (1987) 'The English Noun Phrase in its sentential aspect', PhD diss., MIT.

Acquaviva, P. (2002) 'The morphological dimension of polarity licensing', *Linguistics* 40: 925–959.

Adger, D. (2003) *Core Syntax: A Minimalist Approach*, Oxford University Press, Oxford.

Adger, D. & Ramchand, G. (2005) 'Merge and Move: Wh-dependencies revisited', *Linguistic Inquiry* 36: 161–193.

Afarli, T. A. (1989) 'Passive in Norwegian and in English', *Linguistic Inquiry* 20: 101–108.

Akiyama, M. (2004) 'Multiple nominative constructions in Japanese and Economy', *Linguistic Inquiry* 35: 671–683.

Akmajian, A. & Heny, F. (1975) *An Introduction to the Principles of Transformational Syntax*, MIT Press, Cambridge Mass.

Alexiadou, A. (1997) *Adverb Placement: A Case Study in Antisymmetric Syntax*, Benjamins, Amsterdam.

Alexiadou, A. E. & Anagnostopoulou, E. (1998) 'Parameterizing AGR: Word Order, V-Movement and EPP checking', *Natural Language and Linguistic Theory* 16: 491–539.

Alexiadou, A., Law, P., Meinunger, A. and Wilder, C. (eds) (2000) *The Syntax of Relative Clauses*, John Benjamins, Amsterdam.

Alexiadou, A. & Wilder, C. (eds) (1998) *Possessors, Predicates and Movement in the Determiner Phrase*, John Benjamins, Amsterdam.

Alexopoulou, T. & Kolliakou, D. (2002) 'On Linkhood, Topicalisation and Clitic Left Dislocation', *Journal of Linguistics* 38: 193–245.

Almeida, D. A. de A. & Yoshida, M. (2007) 'A problem for the preposition stranding generalization', *Linguistic Inquiry* 38: 349–362.

Alrenga, P. (2005) 'A sentential subject asymmetry in English and its implications for complement selection', *Syntax* 8: 175–207.

Anderson, S. R. & Lightfoot, D. W. (2002) *The Language Organ: Linguistics as Cognitive Physiology*, Cambridge University Press, Cambridge.

Antony, L. M. & Hornstein, N. (2003) *Chomsky and His Critics*, Blackwell, Oxford.

Authier, J.-M. (1989) 'Arbitrary null objects and unselective binding', in Jaeggli & Safir (eds), pp. 45–67.

(1991) 'V-governed expletives, case theory and the projection principle', *Linguistic Inquiry* 22: 721–40.

Authier, J. M. & Reed, L. (2005) 'The diverse nature of non-interrogative Wh', *Linguistic Inquiry* 36: 635–647.

Bach, E. (1977) 'Review of Paul M. Postal *On Raising*', *Language* 53: 621–654.

Baker, M. (1988) *Incorporation*, University of Chicago Press, Chicago.

Baker, M. (1997) 'Thematic roles and syntactic structure', in L. Haegeman (ed.) *Elements of Grammar*, Kluwer, Dordrecht, pp. 73–137.

Baker, M., Johnson, K. & Roberts, I. (1989) 'Passive arguments raised', *Linguistic Inquiry* 20: 219–251.

Baltin, M. (2002) 'Movement to the higher V is remnant movement', *Linguistic Inquiry* 33: 653–659.

Baltin, M. & Collins, C. (eds) (2001) *The Handbook of Contemporary Syntactic Theory*, Blackwell, Oxford.

Barbosa, P. (1995) 'Null subjects', PhD diss., MIT.
    (2000) 'Clitics: a Window into the Null Subject Property', in J. Costa (ed.), *Portuguese Syntax: Comparative Studies*, Oxford University Press, New York, pp. 31–93.
    (2007) 'Two kinds of subject *pro*', ms., Universidade do Minho.

Barbosa, P., Duarte M. E. L. & Kato, M. A. (2005) 'Null subjects in European and Brasilian Portuguese', *Journal of Portuguese Linguistics* 4: 11–52.

Barss, A. (2001) 'Syntactic reconstruction effects', in Baltin & Collins (eds), pp. 670–696.

Basilico, D. (2003) 'The topic of small clauses', *Linguistic Inquiry* 34: 1–35.

Beck, S. & Johnson, K. (2004) 'Double objects again', *Linguistic Inquiry* 35: 97–124.

Becker, M. (2006) 'There began to be a learnability puzzle', *Linguistic Inquiry* 37: 441–456.

Bejar, S. & Massam, D. (1999) 'Multiple case checking', *Syntax* 2: 65–79.

Belletti, A. (1990) *Generalized Verb Movement: Aspects of Verb Syntax*, Rosenberg and Sellier, Turin.

Belletti, A. & Rizzi, L. (1988) 'Psych-verbs and θ-theory', *Natural Language and Linguistic Theory* 6: 291–352.

Benmamoun, E. (2006) 'Licensing configurations: The puzzle of head negative polarity items', *Linguistic Inquiry* 37: 141–149.

Bernstein, J. B. (1993) 'Topics in the syntax of nominal structures across Romance', PhD diss., City University of New York.
    (2001) 'The DP hypothesis: Identifying clausal properties in the nominal domain', in Baltin and Collins (eds), pp. 536–561.

Bhatt, R. & Pancheva, R. (2004) 'Late merger of degree clauses', *Linguistic Inquiry* 35: 1–45.

Bloomfield, L. (1935) *Language*, George Allen and Unwin, London.

Bobaljik, J. (1995) 'Morphosyntax: The syntax of verbal inflection', PhD diss., MIT.
    (2002) 'A-chains at the PF-interface: Copies and "covert" movement', *Natural Language and Linguistic Theory*, 20: 197–267.

Boeckx, C. (2000) 'A note on Contraction', *Linguistic Inquiry* 31: 357–366.
    (2001) 'Scope reconstruction and A-movement', *Natural Language and Linguistic Theory* 19: 503–548.
    (2003) *Islands and Chains: Resumption as Stranding*, Benjamins, Amsterdam.
    (2007) *Understanding Minimalist Syntax*, Blackwell, Oxford.

Boeckx, C. & Hornstein, N. (2003) 'Reply to Control is not movement', *Linguistic Inquiry* 34: 269–280.

(2004) 'Movement under control', *Linguistic Inquiry* 35: 431–452.

(2006a) 'The virtues of control as movement', *Syntax* 9: 118–130.

(2006b) 'Control in Icelandic and theories of Control', *Linguistic Inquiry* 37: 591–606.

Boeckx, C. & Stjepanović, S. (2001) 'Head-ing towards PF', *Linguistic Inquiry* 32: 345–355.

Borer, H. (1993) 'The projection of arguments', in E. Benedicto & J. Runner (eds), *Functional Projections UMass Occasional Papers* 17, GLSA publications, Amherst Mass.

Borroff, M. L. (2006) 'Degree phrase inversion in the scope of negation', *Linguistic Inquiry* 37: 514–521.

Borsley, R. D. (1992) 'More on the difference between English restrictive and non-restrictive relative clauses', *Journal of Linguistics* 28: 139–148.

(1997) 'Relative clauses and the theory of phrase structure', *Linguistic Inquiry* 28: 629–647.

Borsley, R. & Jaworska, E. (1998) 'A note on prepositions and case-marking in Polish', *Linguistic Inquiry* 19: 685–691.

Borsley, R., Rivero, M. L. & Stephens, J. (1996) 'Long head movement in Breton', in R. Borsley & I. Roberts (eds), *The Syntax of the Celtic Languages: A Comparative Perspective*, Cambridge University Press, Cambridge, pp. 53–74.

Bošković, Z. (1997) 'On certain violations of the superiority condition, AgrO and economy of derivation', *Journal of Linguistics* 33: 227–254.

(2001) *On the Nature of the Syntax–Phonology Interface: Cliticization and Related Phenomena*, Elsevier, Amsterdam.

(2002a) 'On multiple *wh*-fronting', *Linguistic Inquiry* 33: 351–383.

(2002b) 'A-Movement and the EPP', *Syntax* 5: 167–218.

(2004) 'Topicalization, Focalization, Lexical Insertion and Scrambling', *Linguistic Inquiry* 35: 613–638.

(2005) 'On the locality of left branch extraction and the structure of NP', *Studia Linguistica* 59: 1–45.

Bošković, Z. & Lasnik, H. (2003) 'On the distribution of null complementisers', *Linguistic Inquiry* 34: 527–46.

Bowerman, M. (1982) 'Evaluating competing linguistic models with language acquisition data: Implications of developmental errors with causative verbs', *Quaderni di Semantica* 3: 5–66.

(1988) 'The "no negative evidence" problem: How do children avoid an overly general grammar?', in J. Hawkins (ed.), *Explaining Language Universals*, Blackwell, Oxford, pp. 73–101.

Bowers, J. (1973) 'Grammatical relations', PhD diss., MIT.

(1993) 'The syntax of predication', *Linguistic Inquiry* 24: 591–656.

(2002) 'Transitivity', *Linguistic Inquiry* 33: 183–224.

Braine, M. D. S. (1971) 'Three suggestions regarding grammatical analyses of children's language', in C. A. Ferguson & D. I. Slobin (eds), *Studies of Child Language Development*, Holt Rinehart and Winston, New York, pp. 421–429.

Branigan, P. (1992) 'Subjects and complementisers', PhD diss., MIT.

(2005) 'The phase theoretic basis for subject–aux inversion', unpublished paper, Memorial University (www.ucs.mun.ca/~branigan/papers).

Branigan, P. & MacKenzie, M. (2002) 'Altruism, Ā-movement and object agreement in Innu-aimûn', *Linguistic Inquiry* 33: 385–407.

Bresnan, J. (1970) 'On complementizers: Toward a syntactic theory of complement types', *Foundations of Language* 6: 297–321.

(1972) 'Theory of complementation in English syntax', PhD diss., MIT (published as Bresnan 1979).

(1976) 'Nonarguments for Raising', *Linguistic Inquiry* 7: 265–299.

(1979) *Theory of Complementation in English Syntax*, Garland, New York (published version of Bresnan 1972).

(1994) 'Locative inversion and the architecture of Universal Grammar', *Language* 70: 72–131.

Brody, M. (1995) *A Radically Minimalist Theory*, MIT Press, Cambridge Mass.

Broekhuis, H. (2006) 'Extraction from subjects: Some remarks on Chomsky's "On Phases"', in H. Broekhuis, N. Corver & R. Huybreghts (eds), *Organising Grammar*, Mouton de Gruyter, Berlin, pp. 59–68.

Brown, K. (1991) 'Double modals in Hawick Scots', in P. Trudgill & J. K. Chambers (eds), *Dialects of English*, Longman, London, pp. 74–103.

Brown, R., Cazden, C. & Bellugi, U. (1968) 'The child's grammar from I to III', in J. P. Hill (ed.), *Minnesota Symposium on Child Development*, vol. 2, pp. 28–73.

Brown, R. & Hanlon, C. (1970) 'Derivational complexity and order of acquisition in child speech', in J. R. Hayes (ed.), *Cognition and the Development of Language*, Wiley, New York, pp. 11–53.

Bruening, B. (2001) 'Syntax at the edge: Cross-clausal phenomena and the syntax of Passamaquoddy', PhD diss., MIT.

(2004) 'Two types of wh-scope-marking in Passamaquoddy', *Natural Language and Linguistic Theory* 22: 229–305.

(2006) 'Differences between the wh-scope-marking and wh-copy constructions in Passamaquoddy', *Linguistic Inquiry* 37: 25–49.

(2007) 'Wh-in-situ does not correlate with *wh*-indefinites or question particles', *Linguistic Inquiry* 38: 139–166.

Büring, D. (2005) *Binding Theory*, Cambridge University Press, Cambridge.

Burton, S. & Grimshaw, J. (1992) 'Coordination and VP-internal subjects', *Linguistic Inquiry* 23: 305–13.

Burzio, L. (1986) *Italian Syntax*, Reidel, Dordrecht.

Caponigro, I. & Schütze, C. T. (2003) 'Parameterizing passive participle movement', *Linguistic Inquiry* 34: 293–308.

Cardinaletti, A. & Starke, M. (1999) 'The typology of structural deficiency: A case study of the three classes of pronouns', in H. van Riemsdijk (ed.), *Clitics in the Languages of Europe*, Mouton de Gruyter, Berlin, pp. 145–233.

Carlson, K., Dickey, M. W. & Kennedy, C. (2005) 'Structural economy in the processing and representation of gapping sentences', *Syntax* 8: 208–228.

Carnie, A. (1995) 'Nonverbal predication and Head Movement', PhD diss., MIT.

Carrier, J. & Randall, J. H. (1992) 'The argument structure and syntactic structure of resultatives', *Linguistic Inquiry* 23: 173–234.

Carstens, V. (2000) 'Concord in Minimalist Theory', *Linguistic Inquiry* 31: 319–355.

(2001) 'Multiple agreement and case deletion: Against φ-(in)completeness', *Syntax* 4: 147–163.

(2003) 'Rethinking complementiser agreement: agree with a case-checked goal', *Linguistic Inquiry* 34: 393–412.

Cecchetto, C. & Oniga, R. (2004) 'A challenge to null case theory', *Linguistic Inquiry* 35: 141–149.

Cheng, L. (1997) *On the Typology of Wh-Questions*, Garland, New York.

Cheng, L. & Corver, N. (eds) (2006) *Wh-Movement: Moving On*, MIT Press, Cambridge Mass.

Cheng, L. & Rooryck, J. (2000) 'Licensing *Wh*-in-situ', *Syntax* 3: 1–19.

Chierchia, G. (2006) 'Broaden your views: Implicatures of domain widening and the "logicality" of language', *Linguistic Inquiry* 37: 535–590.

Chomsky, N. (1955) 'The logical structure of linguistic theory', mimeo, MIT (subsequently published as Chomsky 1975).

(1957) *Syntactic Structures*, Mouton, The Hague.

(1965) *Aspects of the Theory of Syntax*, MIT Press, Cambridge Mass.

(1968) Interview with S. Hampshire in *The Listener*, May 1968.

(1970) 'Remarks on nominalization', in R. A. Jacobs and P. S. Rosenbaum (eds) *Readings in English Transformational Grammar*, Ginn, Waltham, Mass., pp. 184–221.

(1972) *Language and Mind* (enlarged edition), Harcourt Brace Jovanovich, New York.

(1973) 'Conditions on transformations', in S. R. Anderson & P. Kiparsky (eds), *A Festschrift for Morris Halle*, Holt, Rinehart and Winston, New York, pp. 232–286.

(1975) *The Logical Structure of Linguistic Theory*, Plenum Press, New York (published version of Chomsky 1955).

(1977) 'On Wh-movement', in Culicover *et al.* (eds), pp. 71–132.

(1980) 'On binding', *Linguistic Inquiry* 11: 1–46.

(1981) *Lectures on Government and Binding*, Foris, Dordrecht.

(1982) *Some Concepts and Consequences of the Theory of Government and Binding*, MIT Press, Cambridge Mass.

(1986a) *Knowledge of Language: Its Nature, Origin and Use*, Praeger, New York.

(1986b) *Barriers*, MIT Press, Cambridge Mass.

(1989) 'Some notes on economy of derivation and representation', *MIT Working Papers in Linguistics* 10: 43–74 (reprinted as chapter 2 of Chomsky 1995).

(1993) 'A Minimalist Program for linguistic theory', in Hale and Keyser (eds), pp. 1–52 (reprinted as chapter 3 of Chomsky 1995).

(1995) *The Minimalist Program*, MIT Press, Cambridge Mass.

(1998) *Minimalist Inquiries: The Framework*, MIT Occasional Papers in Linguistics, no. 15 (also published in R. Martin, D. Michaels and J. Uriagereka (eds), *Step by Step: Essays on Minimalism in Honor of Howard Lasnik*, MIT Press, Cambridge Mass., pp. 89–155).

(1999) *Derivation by Phase*, MIT Occasional Papers in Linguistics, no. 18 (also published in M. Kenstowicz (ed.) (2001) *Ken Hale: A Life in Language*, MIT Press, Cambridge Mass., pp.1–52).

(2001) 'Beyond explanatory adequacy', unpublished manuscript, MIT. (A published version appeared in A. Belletti (ed.) (2004) *Structures and Beyond: The Cartography of Syntactic Structures*, vol. 3, Oxford University Press, pp. 104–131.)

(2002) *On Nature and Language*, Cambridge University Press, Cambridge.

(2005a) 'Three factors in language design', *Linguistic Inquiry* 36: 1–22.

(2005b) 'On Phases', unpublished paper, MIT (to appear in R. Freidin, C. P. Otero & M.-L. Zubizaretta (eds), *Foundational Issues in Linguistic Theory*, MIT Press, Cambridge Mass.).

(2006) 'Approaching UG from below', unpublished paper, MIT.

Chomsky, N. & Lasnik, H. (1977) 'Filters and Control', *Linguistic Inquiry* 8: 425–504.

(1993) 'The theory of principles and parameters', in J. Jacobs, A. von Stechow, W. Sternefeld & T. Venneman (eds), *Syntax: An International Handbook of Contemporary Research*, Mouton de Gruyter, Berlin, pp. 506–569 (reprinted in Chomsky 1995, pp. 13–127).

Chung, S. (1994) '*Wh*-agreement and "Referentiality" in Chamorro', *Linguistic Inquiry* 25: 1–45.

(1998) *The Design of Agreement: Evidence from Chamorro*, University of Chicago Press, Chicago.

(2004) 'Restructuring and verb-initial order in Chamorro', *Syntax*: 7: 199–233.

Cinque, G. (1999) *Adverbs and Functional Heads*, Oxford University Press, Oxford.

(2002) *Functional Structure in DP and IP: The Cartography of Syntactic Structures*, vol. 1, Oxford University Press, Oxford.

(2004) '"Restructuring" and functional structure', in A. Belletti (ed.), *The Cartography of Syntactic Structures*, vol. 3, *Structures and Beyond*, Oxford University Press, Oxford, pp. 132–191.

Cinque, G. & Kayne, R. S. (eds) (2005) *Handbook of Comparative Syntax*, Oxford University Press, Oxford.

Citko, B. (2005) 'On the nature of Merge: External Merge, Internal Merge and Parallel Merge', *Linguistic Inquiry* 36: 475–496.

Clahsen, H. (2008) 'Chomskyan syntactic theory and language disorders', in M. J. Ball, M. Perkins, N. Mueller & S. Howard (eds), *The Handbook of Clinical Linguistics*, Blackwell, Oxford, pp. 165–183.

Clifton, C., Fanselow, G. & Frazier, L. (2006) 'Amnestying superiority violations: Processing multiple questions', *Linguistic Inquiry* 37: 51–68.

Cole, P. (1982) *Imbabura Quechua*, North-Holland, The Hague.

Cole, P. & Hermon, G. (1998) 'The typology of wh-movement: *Wh*-questions in Malay', *Syntax* 1: 221–258.

(2000) 'Partial wh-movement: Evidence from Malay', in Lutz *et al.* (eds), pp. 101–130.

Collins, C. (1993) 'Topics in Ewe syntax', PhD diss., MIT.

(1997) *Local Economy*, MIT Press, Cambridge Mass.

(2005a) 'A smuggling approach to the passive in English', *Syntax* 8: 81–120.

(2005b) 'A smuggling approach to raising in English', *Linguistic Inquiry* 36: 289–298.

Collins, C. & Thráinsson, H. (1993) 'Object shift in double object constructions and the theory of Case', *MIT Working Papers in Linguistics* 19: 131–174.

Contreras, H. (1986) 'Spanish bare NPs and the ECP', in I. Bordelois, H. Contreras & K. Zagona (eds), *Generative Studies in Spanish Syntax*, Foris, Dordrecht, pp. 25–49.

Contreras, J. (1987) 'Small clauses in Spanish and English', *Natural Language and Linguistic Theory*, 5: 225–244.

Coppock, L. (2002) 'Gapping: In defense of deletion', *Chicago Linguistics Society* 37: 133–148.

Cormack, A. & Smith, N. (1999) 'Where is a sign merged?', *Glot International* 4,6: 21.
   (2000a) 'Head Movement and negation in English', *Transactions of the Philological Society* 98: 49–85.
   (2000b) 'Fronting: The Syntax and Pragmatics of "Focus" and "Topic"', *UCL Working Papers in Linguistics* 20: 387–417.
Corver, N. (1990) 'The syntax of left branch extractions', PhD diss., Tilburg University.
Crain, S. & Pietroski, P. (2002) 'Why language acquisition is a snap', *The Linguistic Review* 19: 163–183.
Culicover, P. W. (1991) 'Topicalization, inversion and complementiser in English', in D. Delfitto, M. Everaert, A. Evers & F. Stuurman (eds), *OTS Working Papers: Going Romance and Beyond*, University of Utrecht, pp. 1–45.
Culicover, P. W. & Jackendoff, R. (2001) 'Control is not movement', *Linguistic Inquiry* 30: 483–512.
   (2005) *Simpler Syntax*, Oxford University Press, Oxford.
   (2006) 'Turn over control to the semantics', *Syntax* 9: 131–152.
Culicover, P. W. & Levine, R. D. (2001) 'Stylistic inversion in English: A reconsideration', *Natural Language and Linguistic Theory* 19: 283–310.
Culicover, P. W. & Nowak, A. (2003) *Dynamical Grammar: Minimalism, Acquisition and Change*, Oxford University Press, Oxford.
Culicover, P. W., Wasow, T. & Akmajian, A. (eds) (1977) *Formal Syntax*, Academic Press, New York.
Cummins, S. & Roberge, Y. (2004) 'Null objects in French and English', in J. Auger, C. Clements & B. Vance (eds), *Contemporary Approaches to Romance Linguistics*, John Benjamins, Amsterdam, pp.121–138.
   (2005) 'A modular account of null objects in French', *Syntax* 8: 44–64.
Curtiss, S. (1977) *Genie: A Psycholinguistic Study of a Modern Day "Wild Child"*, Academic Press, London.
Davies, W. D. & Dubinsky, S. (2004) *The Grammar of Raising and Control: A Course in Syntactic Argumentation*, Blackwell, Oxford.
Dayal, V. (2002) 'Single-pair versus multiple-pair answers: Wh-in-situ and scope', *Linguistic Inquiry* 33: 512–520.
Déchaine, R.-M. & Wiltschko, M. (2002) 'Decomposing pronouns', *Linguistic Inquiry* 33: 409–442.
del Gobbo, F. (2003) 'Appositives at the interface', PhD diss., University of California, Irvine.
den Dikken, M. (2001) 'Pluringulars, pronouns and quirky agreement', *The Linguistic Review* 18: 19–41.
Denham, K. (2000) 'Optional *wh*-movement in Babine-Witsuwit'en', *Natural Language and Linguistic Theory* 18: 199–251.
Déprez, V. (2000) 'Parallel (a)symmetyries and the internal structure of negative expressions', *Natural Language and Linguistic Theory* 18: 253–342.
de Vries, M. (2002) *The Syntax of Relativization*, LOT, Utrecht.
   (2006) 'The syntax of appositive relativization: On specifying co-ordination, false free relatives and promotion', *Linguistic Inquiry* 37: 229–270.
Diesing, M. (1992) *Indefinites*, MIT Press, Cambridge Mass.
Diesing, M. & Jelinek, E. (1995) 'Distributing arguments', *Natural Language Semantics* 3: 123–76.

Donati, C. (2006) 'On *wh*-head movement', in Cheng & Corver (eds), pp. 21–46.

Drubig, H. N. (2003) 'Toward a typology of focus and focus constructions', *Linguistics* 41: 1–50.

du Plessis, H. (1977) 'Wh-movement in Afrikaans', *Linguistic Inquiry* 8: 211–222.

Embick, D. (2004) 'On the structure of resultative participles in English', *Linguistic Inquiry* 35: 355–392.

Embick, D. & Noyer, R. (2001) 'Movement operations after Syntax', *Linguistic Inquiry* 32: 555–595.

Emonds, J. E. (1976) *A Transformational Approach to English Syntax*, Academic Press, New York.

(1994) 'Two principles of economy', in G. Cinque, J. Koster, J.-Y. Pollock, L. Rizzi & R. Zanuttini (eds), *Paths towards Universal Grammar: Studies in Honor of Richard Kayne*, Georgetown University Press, Washington DC, pp. 155–172.

Epstein, S. D., Pires A. & Seely, T. D. (2005) 'EPP in T: More controversial subjects', *Syntax*, 8: 65–80.

Ernst, T. (1991) 'On the scope principle', *Linguistic Inquiry* 22: 750–6.

Escribano, J. L. G. (2004) 'NPs as just NPs', unpublished paper, University of Oviedo.

Everett, D. (2005) 'Biology and language: A consideration of alternatives', *Journal of Linguistics* 41: 157–175.

(2006) 'Biology and language: Response to Anderson & Lightfoot', *Journal of Linguistics* 42: 385–393.

Fabb, N. (1990) 'The difference between English restrictive and non-restrictive clauses', *Journal of Linguistics* 26: 57–78.

Fanselow, G. (2002) 'Against remnant VP-movement', in A. Alexiadou, E. Anagnostopoulou, S. Barbiers & H.-M. Gaertner (eds), *Dimensions of Movement: From Features to Remnants*, John Benjamins, Amsterdam, pp. 91–125.

Fanselow, G. & Ćavar, D. (2002) 'Distributed deletion', in A. Alexiadou (ed.), *Theoretical Approaches to Universals*, John Benjamins, Amsterdam, pp. 65–107.

Farrell, P. (1990) 'Null objects in Brazilian Portuguese', *Natural Language and Linguistic Theory* 8: 325–346.

Fauconnier, G. (1975) 'Polarity and the scale principle', *Chicago Linguistics Society* 11: 188–199.

(1978) 'Implication reversal in a natural language', in F. Guenthner & S. J. Schmidt (eds), *Formal Semantics and Pragmatics for Natural Languages*, Reidel, Dordrecht, pp. 289–302.

Felser, C. (1999a) *Verbal Complement Clauses: A Minimalist Study of Direct Perception Constructions*, Benjamins, Amsterdam.

(1999b) 'Perception and control: A Minimalist analysis of English direct perception complements', *Journal of Linguistics* 34: 351–385.

(2004) 'Wh-copying, phases and successive cyclicity', *Lingua* 114: 543–574.

Felser, C. & Rupp, L. (2001) 'Expletives as arguments: Germanic existential sentences revisited', *Linguistische Berichte*, 187: 289–324.

Fillmore, C. J. (1968) 'The case for case', in E. Bach & R. T. Harms (eds), *Universals in Linguistic Theory*, Holt, Rinehart & Winston, New York, pp. 1–88.

(1972) 'Subjects, speakers and roles' in D. Davidson & G. Harman (eds), *Semantics of Natural Language*, Reidel, Dordrecht.

Fitch, W. T., Hauser, M. D. & Chomsky, N. (2005) 'The evolution of the language faculty: Clarification and implications', *Cognition* 97: 179–210.

Flagg, E. (2002) 'Interface issues in the English imperative', PhD diss., Cambridge Mass.

Fodor, J. D. (2001) 'Setting syntactic parameters', in Baltin & Collins (eds), pp. 730–767.

Fodor, J. D. & Crowther, C. (2002) 'Understanding stimulus poverty arguments', *The Linguistic Review* 19: 105–145.

Fodor, J. D. & Sakas, W. G. (2005) 'The subset principle in syntax: Costs of compliance', *Journal of Linguistics* 41: 513–569.

Folli, R. & Harley, H. (2007) 'Causation, obligation and Argument Structure: On the nature of little v', *Linguistic Inquiry* 38: 197–238.

Fox, D. (2000) *Economy and Semantic Interpretation*, MIT Press, Cambridge Mass.

Fox, D. & Nissenbaum, J. (2004) 'Condition A and scope reconstruction', *Linguistic Inquiry* 35: 475–485.

Frank, R. & Vijay-Shanker, K. (2001) 'Primitive c-command', *Syntax* 4: 164–204.

Franks, S. (1999) 'Optimality theory and clitics at PF', *Formal Approaches to Slavic Linguistics* 7: 101–116.

Franks, S. & Lavine, J. E. (2006) 'Case and word order in Lithuanian', *Journal of Linguistics* 42: 239–288.

Franks, S. & Progovac L. (1994) 'On the placement of Serbo-Croatian clitics', *Indiana Linguistic Studies* 7: 69–78.

Frazier, L. & Clifton, C. (2005) 'The syntax–discourse divide: Processing ellipsis', *Syntax* 8: 121–174.

Freidin, R. (2004) '*Syntactic Structures* redux', *Syntax* 7: 101–127.

Freidin, R. & Vergnaud, J. R. (2001) 'Exquisite connections: some remarks on the evolution of linguistic theory', *Lingua* 111: 639–666.

Georgopoulos, C. (1985) 'Variable in Palauan syntax', *Natural Language and Linguistic Theory* 3: 59–94.

   (1991) *Syntactic Variables: Resumptive Pronouns and A'-binding in Palauan*, Kluwer, Dordrecht.

Giannikidou, A. (1997) 'The landscape of polarity items', PhD diss., University of Groningen.

   (1998) *Polarity Sensitivity as (Non)veridical Dependency*, John Benjamins, Amsterdam.

   (1999) 'Affective dependencies', *Linguistics and Philosophy* 22: 367–421.

Giorgi, A. (2007) 'On the nature of long-distance anaphors', *Linguistic Inquiry* 38: 321–342.

Giusti, G. (1991) 'The categorial status of quantifier nominals', *Linguistische Berichte* 136: 438–452.

   (1997) 'The categorial status of determiners', in L. Haegeman (ed.), *The New Comparative Syntax*, Cambridge University Press, Cambridge, pp. 94–113.

Givón, T. (2002) *Biolinguistics: The Santa Barbara Lectures*, John Benjamins, Amsterdam.

Goodall, G. (1997) 'Theta-alignment and the *by*-phrase', *Proceedings of the Chicago Linguistics Society* 33: 129–139.

Green, L. (1998) 'Semantic and syntactic patterns in African American English', ms., University of Massachusetts.

Green, M. (2007) *Focus in Hausa*, Blackwell, Oxford.

Grice, H. P. (1975) 'Logic and conversation', in P. Cole & J. Morgan (eds), *Syntax and Semantics 3: Speech Acts*, Academic Press, New York, pp. 41–58.

Grimshaw, J. (1993) 'Minimal Projection, Heads, and Optimality', draft manuscript, Rutgers University.

Groat, E. (1995) 'English expletives: A minimalist approach', *Linguistic Inquiry* 26: 354–365.

Groat, E. & O'Neil, J. (1996) 'Spell-out at the LF interface', in W. Abraham, S. D. Epstein, H. Thráinsson & C. J.-W. Zwart (eds), *Minimal Ideas*, Benjamins, Amsterdam, pp. 113–139.

Groefsema, M. (1995) 'Understood arguments: A semantic/pragmatic approach', *Lingua* 96: 139–161.

Grohmann, K. K. (2003) *Prolific Domains*, John Benjamins, Amsterdam.

(2006) 'Top issues in questions: Topics – Topicalization – Topicalizability', in Cheng and Corver (eds), pp. 249–288.

Grohmann, K. K., Drury, J. & Castillo, J. C. (2000) 'No more EPP', *Proceedings of the West Coast Conference on Formal Linguistics* 19: 153–166.

Grohmann, K. K. & Haegeman, L. (2002) 'Resuming reflexives', *Proceedings of the 19th Scandinavian Conference in Linguistics*, Tromsø, Norway, 46–62.

Grosu, A. & Horvath, J. (2006) 'Reply to Bhatt and Pancheva's "Late Merger of Degree Clauses": The irrelevance of (non)conservativity', *Linguistic Inquiry* 37: 457–483.

Gruber, J. S. (1965) 'Studies in lexical relations', PhD diss., MIT.

(1976) *Lexical Structures in Syntax and Semantics*, North-Holland, Amsterdam.

Gualmini, A. & Crain, S. (2005) 'The structure of children's linguistic knowledge', *Linguistic Inquiry* 36: 463–474.

Guasti, M. T. (2002) *Language Acquisition: The Growth of Grammar*, Bradford Books, MIT Press, Cambridge Mass.

Guilfoyle, E. (1994) 'VNPs, finiteness and external arguments', *Proceedings of NELS* 24: 141–155.

Guilfoyle, E., Hung, H. & Travis, L. (1992) 'Spec of IP and spec of VP: Two subjects in Austronesian languages', *Natural Language and Linguistic Theory* 10: 375–414.

Haddican, B. (2007) 'The structural deficiency of verbal pro-forms', *Linguistic Inquiry* 38: 539–547.

Haeberli, E. (2003) 'Categorial features as the source of EPP and abstract Case phenomena', in E. Brandner & H. Zinsmeister (eds), *New Perspectives on Case Theory*, CSLI publications, Stanford, Calif., pp. 89–126.

Haegeman, L. (1990) 'Non-overt subjects in diary contexts', in J. Mascaró and M. Nespor (eds), *Grammar In Progress*, Foris, Dordrecht, pp. 167–179.

(1992) *Theory and Description in Generative Syntax: A Case Study of West Flemish*, Cambridge University Press, Cambridge.

(1994, 2nd edition) *Introduction to Government and Binding Theory*, Blackwell, Oxford.

(1995) *The Syntax of Negation*, Cambridge University Press, Cambridge.

(2000) 'Inversion, non-adjacent inversion and adjuncts in CP', in *Transactions of the Philological Society* 98: 121–160.

(2006) 'Clitic climbing and the dual status of *sembrare*', *Linguistic Inquiry* 37: 484–501.

Hale, K. & Keyser, S. J. (1991) *On the Syntax of Argument Structure*, Lexicon Project Working Papers, MIT, Center for Cognitive Science, Cambridge Mass.

(1993a) 'On argument structure and the lexical expression of semantic relations', in Hale & Keyser (eds), pp. 53–109.

(1993b) (eds) *The View from Building 20*, MIT Press, Cambridge Mass.

(1994) 'Constraints on argument structure', in B. Lust, M. Suñer & J. Whitman (eds), *Heads, Projections and Learnability*, Erlbaum, Hillsdale, New Jersey, vol. 1, pp. 53–71.

Halle, M. & Marantz, A. (1993) 'Distributed morphology and the pieces of inflection', in Hale & Keyser (eds), pp.111–176.

Han, C.-H. (2001) 'Force, negation and imperatives', *The Linguistic Review*, 18: 289–325.

Han, H.-S. (2004) '*There* as an existential operator', *Language Research* 40: 451–464 (published by Language Research Institute, Seoul National University).

Hankamer, J. (1971) 'Constraints on deletion in syntax', PhD diss., Yale University.

Hankamer, J. & Sag, I. (1976) 'Deep and surface anaphora', *Linguistic Inquiry* 7: 391–428.

Hardt, D. (1993) 'Verb phrase ellipsis: Form, meaning and processing', PhD diss., University of Pennsylvania.

Hauser, M. D., Chomsky, N. & Fitch, W. T. (2002) 'The faculty of language: What is it, who has it, and how did it evolve? *Science* 298: 1569–1579.

Hawkins, J. A. (2001) 'Why are categories adjacent?', *Journal of Linguistics*, 37: 1–34.

Hazout, I. (2004a) 'Long-distance agreement and the syntax of *for-to* infinitives', *Linguistic Inquiry* 35: 338–343.

(2004b) 'The syntax of existential constructions', *Linguistic Inquiry* 35: 393–430.

Heck, F. (2004) 'A theory of pied-piping', PhD diss., Universität Tübingen.

Henderson, B. (2006) 'Multiple agreement and inversion in Bantu', *Syntax* 9: 275–289.

Hendrick, R. (1991) 'The morphosyntax of aspect', *Lingua* 85: 171–210.

Henry, A. (1995) *Belfast English and Standard English: Dialect Variation and Parameter-Setting*, Oxford University Press, Oxford.

Herdan, S. & Sharvit, Y. (2006) 'Definite and non-definite superlatives and NPI licensing', *Syntax* 9: 1–31.

Hiemstra, I. (1986) 'Some aspects of wh-questions in Frisian', *North-Western European Language Evolution (NOWELE)* 8: 97–110.

Hiraira, K. (2001) 'Multiple agree and the Defective Intervention Constraint', *MIT Working Papers in Linguistics* 40: 67–80.

(2005) 'Dimensions of symmetry in syntax: Agreement and clausal architecture', PhD diss., MIT.

Hiramatsu, K. (2003) 'Children's judgments on negative questions', *Language Acquisition* 11: 99–126.

Hoge, K. (1998) 'The Yiddish double verb construction', *Oxford University Working Papers in Linguistics, Philology and Phonetics* 2: 85–97.

Holmberg, A. (1999) 'Remarks on Holmberg's generalization', *Studia Linguistica* 53: 1–39.

(2000a) 'Am I unscientific? A reply to Lappin, Levine and Johnson', *Natural Language and Linguistic Theory* 18: 837–842.

(2000b) 'Scandinavian stylistic fronting: How any category can become an expletive', *Linguistic Inquiry* 31: 445–483.

(2005) 'Is there a little pro? Evidence from Finnish', *Linguistic Inquiry* 36: 533–564.

Hong, S.-H. (2005) 'Aspects of the syntax of questions in English and Korean', PhD diss., University of Essex.

Hornstein, N. (1995) *Logical Form: From GB to Minimalism*, Blackwell, Oxford.

(1999) 'Movement and control', *Linguistic Inquiry* 30: 69–96.

(2001) *Move: A Minimalist Theory of Construal*, Blackwell, Oxford.

(2003) 'On Control', in R. Hendrick (ed.), *Minimalist Syntax*, Blackwell, Oxford, pp. 6–81.

(2007) 'A very short note on existential constructions', *Linguistic Inquiry* 38: 410–411.

Huang, C.-T. J. (1982) 'Logical relations in Chinese and the theory of grammar', PhD diss., MIT.

(1984) 'On the distribution and reference of empty pronouns', *Linguistic Inquiry* 15: 531–574.

(1991) 'Remarks on the status of the null object', in R. Freidin (ed.), *Principles and Parameters in Comparative Grammar*, MIT Press, Cambridge Mass., pp. 56–76.

(1993) 'Reconstruction and the structure of VP: Some theoretical consequences', *Linguistic Inquiry* 24: 103–38.

Huddleston, R. (1994) 'The contrast between interrogatives and questions', *Journal of Linguistics* 30: 411–439.

Hurford, J. (1991) 'The evolution of the critical period for language acquisition', *Cognition* 40: 159–201.

Hyams, N. (1986) *Language Acquisition and the Theory of Parameters*, Reidel, Dordrecht.

(1992) 'A reanalysis of null subjects in child language', in J. Weissenborn, H. Goodluck & T. Roeper (eds), *Theoretical Issues in Language Acquisition*, Erlbaum, London, pp. 249–267.

Iatridou, S. (1990) 'About Agr(P)', *Linguistic Inquiry* 21: 766–772.

Ingham, R. (2000) 'Negation and OV order in Late Middle English', *Journal of Linguistics* 36: 13–38.

(2002) 'Negated Subjects and Objects in 15th century non-literary English', *Language Variation and Change* 14: 291–322.

(2007) 'A structural constraint on negation in Late Middle and Early Modern English', in M. Krygier & L. Siworska (eds), *Medieval English Mirror 3: To make his Englissh Sweete upon his Tonge*, Peter Lang, Frankfurt am Mein.

Isac, D. (2006) 'In defense of a quantificational account of definite DPs', *Linguistic Inquiry* 37: 275–288.

Ishii, T. (2006a) 'On the relaxation of intervention effects', in Cheng & Corver (eds), pp. 217–246.

(2006b) 'A uniform/nonuniform analysis of overt wh-movement', *Linguistic Inquiry* 37: 155–167.

Jackendoff, R. S. (1972) *Semantic Interpretation in Generative Grammar*, MIT Press, Cambridge Mass.

(1974) *Introduction to the X-bar Convention*, Indiana University Linguistics Club.

(1977a) *X-bar Syntax: A Study of Phrase Structure*, MIT Press, Cambridge Mass.

(1977b) 'Constraints on phrase structure rules', in Culicover *et al.* (eds) pp. 249–283.

Jackendoff, R. S. & Culicover, P. W. (2003) 'The semantic basis of control in English', *Language* 79: 517–556.

Jaeggli, O. (1982) *Topics in Romance Syntax*, Foris, Dordrecht.

(1984) 'Subject extraction and the null subject parameter', *NELS* 14: 132–153.

(1986) 'Passive', *Linguistic Inquiry* 17: 587–622.

Jaeggli, O. & Safir, K. (1989) *The Null Subject Parameter*, Kluwer, Dordrecht.

Jenkins, L. (1975) *The English Existential*, Narr, Tübingen.

Jespersen, O. (1937) *Analytic Syntax*, George Allen and Unwin, London (reprinted in 1969 by Holt, Rinehart and Winston, New York).

Jiménez, Á. (2000a) 'The interpretation of tense and aspect in argument small clauses', *Revista Canaria de Estudios Ingleses* 40: 279–298.

(2000b) 'The aspectual morpheme *as* and feature movement in argument small clauses', *Generative Linguistics in Poland* 1: 59–69.

Johnson, K. (2000) 'Few dogs like Whiskas or cats Alpo', *University of Massachusetts Occasional Papers* 23: 59–82.

Jones, M. A. (1994) *Sardinian Syntax*, Routledge, London.

Julien, M. (2001) 'The syntax of complex tenses', *The Linguistic Review* 18: 125–167.

Kato, M. A. (1999) 'Strong pronouns and weak pronominals in the null subject parameter', *Probus* 11: 1–37.

(2000) 'The partial *pro-drop* nature and the restricted VS order in Brazilian Portuguese', in M. A. Kato & E. V. Negrão (eds), *The Null Subject Parameter in Brazilian Portuguese*, Vervuert-IberoAmericana, Madrid, pp. 223–258.

Katz, J. J. & Postal P. M. (1964) *An Integrated Theory of Linguistic Descriptions*, MIT Press, Cambridge Mass.

Kayne, R. S. (1984) *Connectedness and Binary Branching*, Foris, Dordrect.

(1989) 'Facets of Romance past participle agreement', in P. Benincà (ed.) *Dialect Variation and the Theory of Grammar*, Foris, Dordrecht, pp. 85–103.

(1994) *The Antisymmetry of Syntax*, MIT Press, Cambridge Mass.

(2005) 'Some notes on comparative syntax, with special reference to English and French', in Cinque and Kayne (eds), pp. 3–69.

Kayne, R. S. & Pollock, J.-Y. (1978) 'Stylistic inversion, successive cyclicity, and Move NP in French', *Linguistic Inquiry* 9: 595–621.

Kennedy, C. (2002) 'Comparative deletion and optimality in syntax', *Natural Language and Linguistic Theory* 20: 553–621.

(2003) 'Ellipsis and syntactic representation', in K. Schwabe & S. Winkler (eds) *The Syntax–Semantics Interface: Interpreting (Omitted) Structure*, John Benjamins, Amsterdam.

Kennedy, C. & Merchant, J. (2000), 'Attributive comparative deletion', *Natural Language and Linguistic Theory* 18: 89–146.

Keyser, S. J. & Roeper, T. (1992) 'Re: the abstract clitic hypothesis', *Linguistic Inquiry* 23: 89–125.

Kimball, J. & Aissen, J. (1971) 'I think, you think, he think', *Linguistic Inquiry* 2: 241–246.

Kishimoto, H. (2006) 'On the existence of null complementisers in syntax', *Linguistic Inquiry* 37: 339–345.

Kiss, É. K. (2001) 'The EPP in a topic-prominent language', in P. Svenonius (ed.) *Subjects, Expletives and the EPP*, Oxford University Press, Oxford, pp. 107–124.

Kitagawa, Y. (1986) 'Subjects in English and Japanese', PhD diss., University of Massachusetts.

Klima, E. S. (1964) 'Negation in English' in J. A. Fodor & J. J. Katz (eds) *The Structure of Language*, Prentice-Hall, Englewood Cliffs, N.J., pp. 246–323.

Koizumi, M. (1993) 'Object agreement phrases and the split VP hypothesis', *MIT Working Papers in Linguistics*, 18: 99–148.

(1995) 'Phrase Structure in Minimalist Syntax', PhD diss., MIT.

Koopman, H. (1984) *The Syntax of Verbs: From Verb Movement Rules in the Kru Languages to Universal Grammar*, Foris, Dordrecht.

Koopman, H. & Sportiche, D. (1991) 'The position of subjects', *Lingua* 85: 211–58.

Kornfilt, J. (2004) 'Unmasking covert complementiser agreement', unpublished paper presented at LSA conference, Boston Mass., January 2004.

Koster, J. (1978) 'Why subject sentences don't exist', in S. J. Keyser (ed.) *Recent Transformational Studies in European Languages*, MIT Press, Cambridge Mass., pp. 53–64.

Kratzer, A. (1993) 'On external arguments', *University of Massachusetts Occasional Papers in Linguistics* 17: 103–130.

(1995) 'Stage-level and individual-level predicates', in G. Carlson and F. J. Pelletier (eds) *The Generic Book*, Chicago University Press, Chicago, pp. 125–175.

(1996) 'Severing the external argument from its verb', in. J. Rooryck & L. Zaring (eds) *Phrase Structure and the Lexicon*, Kluwer, Dordrecht, pp. 109–137.

Kroch, A. (2001) 'Syntactic Change', in Baltin and Collins (eds), pp. 699–729.

Kuno, S. (1981) 'Functional Syntax', *Syntax and Semantics* 13: 117–135.

Kural, M. (2005) 'Tree traversal and word order', *Linguistic Inquiry* 36: 367–387.

Kuroda, Y. (1988) 'Whether we agree or not', *Lingvisticae Investigationes* 12: 1–47.

Ladusaw, W. (1979) 'Polarity sensitivity as inherent scope relations', PhD diss., University of Texas, Austin.

Lahiri, U. (1998) 'Focus and negative polarity in Hindi', *Natural Language Semantics* 6: 57–123.

Laka, M. I. (1990) 'Negation in syntax: On the nature of functional categories and projections', PhD diss., MIT.

Landau, I. (1999) 'Elements of control', PhD diss., MIT.

(2001) 'Control and Extraposition: The case of Super-Equi', *Natural Language and Linguistic Theory* 19: 109–152.

(2002) '(Un)interpretable Neg in Comp', *Linguistic Inquiry* 33: 465–492.

(2003) 'Movement out of control', *Linguistic Inquiry* 34: 471–498.

(2004) 'The scale of finiteness and the calculus of Control', *Natural Language and Linguistic Theory* 22: 811–877.

(2006a) 'Severing the distribution of PRO from case', *Syntax* 9: 153–170.

(2006b) 'Chain resolution in Hebrew V(P) fronting', *Syntax* 9: 32–66.

(2007) 'EPP extensions', *Linguistic Inquiry* 38: 485–523.

Lappin, S., Levine, R. D. & Johnson, D. E. (2000a) Topic . . . Comment: The structure of unscientific revolutions', *Natural Language and Linguistic Theory* 18: 665–671.

(2000b) 'The revolution confused: A response to our critics', *Natural Language and Linguistic Theory* 18: 873–890.

(2001) 'The revolution maximally confused', *Natural Language and Linguistic Theory* 19: 901–919.

Lappin, S. & Shieber, S. (2007), 'Machine learning theory and practice as a source of insight into universal grammar', *Journal of Linguistics* 43, 393–427.

Larson, R. (1988) 'On the double object construction', *Linguistic Inquiry* 19: 335–391.

(1990) 'Double objects revisited: Reply to Jackendoff', *Linguistic Inquiry* 21: 589–632.

(1991) '*Promise* and the theory of control', *Linguistic Inquiry* 2: 103–139.

Larson, R. & Lefebvre, C. (1991) 'Predicate cleft in Haitian Creole', *North Eastern Linguistics Society* 21: 247–261.

Lasnik, H. (1992) 'Case and expletives: Notes toward a parametric account', *Linguistic Inquiry* 23: 381–405.

(1995a) 'Verbal Morphology: *Syntactic Structures* meets the Minimalist Program', in H. Campos and P. Kempchinsky (eds) *Evolution and Revolution in Linguistic Theory*, Georgetown University Press, Georgetown, pp. 251–275.

(1995b) 'Case and expletives revisited: On Greed and other human failings', *Linguistic Inquiry* 26: 615–633.

(1998) 'Some reconstruction riddles', in *Penn Working Papers in Linguistics* 5: 83–98, Penn Linguistics Circle, University of Pennsylvania, Philadelphia.

(1999) 'Chains of arguments', in S. D. Epstein & N. Hornstein (eds) *Working Minimalism*, MIT Press, Cambridge Mass., pp. 189–215.

(2000) *Syntactic Structures Revisited: Contemporary Lectures on Classic Transformational Theory*, MIT Press, Cambridge Mass. (with Depiante, M. & Stepanov, A.).

(2003) *Minimalist Investigations in Linguistic Theory*, Routledge, London.

(2006) 'Conceptions of the cycle', in L. Cheng & N. Corver (eds), pp. 197–216.

Lasnik, H. & Uriagereka, J. (2002) 'On the poverty of the challenge', *The Linguistic Review* 19: 147–150.

Lebeaux, D. (1991) 'Relative clauses, licensing and the nature of derivation', in S. Rothstein (ed.) *Syntax and Semantics 25: Perspectives on Phrase Structure*, Academic Press, New York, pp. 209–239.

(1995) 'Where does Binding Theory apply?', in *University of Maryland Working Papers in Linguistics* 3: 63–88.

Lechner, W. (2001) 'Reduced and phrasal comparatives', *Natural Language and Linguistic Theory* 19: 683–735.

Legate, J. A. & Yang, C. D. (2002) 'Empirical re-assessment of stimulus poverty arguments', *The Linguistic Review* 19: 151–162.

Lema, J. & Rivero, M. L. (1990) 'Long head movement: ECP vs. HMC', *Proceedings of NELS* 28: 219–245.

Lenneberg, E. (1967) *Biological Foundations of Language*, Wiley, New York.

Levin, B. & Rappaport Hovav, M. (1995) *Unaccusativity at the Syntax-Lexical Semantic Interface*, MIT Press, Cambridge Mass.

Lewis, J. & Elman, J. (2002) 'Learnability and the statistical study of language: Poverty of stimulus arguments revisited', in B. Skarabela, S. Fish & A. Do (eds) *Proceedings of the 26th Annual Boston University Conference on Language Development*, Cascadilla Press, Somerville Mass., pp. 359–370.

Lightfoot, D. (1976) 'The theoretical implications of Subject Raising', *Foundations of Language* 14: 257–286.

(1999) *The Development of Language: Acquisition, Change and Evolution*, Blackwell, Oxford.

Lightfoot, D. & Hornstein, N. (eds) (1994) *Verb Movement*, Cambridge University Press, Cambridge.

Linebarger, M. (1987) 'Negative polarity and grammatical representation', *Linguistics and Philosophy* 10: 325–387.

Lobeck, A. (1995) *Ellipsis: Functional Heads, Licensing and Identification*, Oxford University Press, Oxford.

Löbel, E. (1989) 'Q as a functional category', in C. Bhatt, E. Löbel & C. Schmidt (eds) *Syntactic Phrase Structure Phenomena*, John Benjamins, Amsterdam.

Longobardi, G. (1994) 'Reference and proper names', *Linguistic Inquiry* 25: 609–666.

(1996) 'The syntax of N-raising: A minimalist theory', OTS Working Papers no 5, Research Institute for Language and Speech, Utrecht.

(2001) 'The structure of DPs: Some principles, parameters and problems', in Baltin and Collins (eds), pp. 562–603.

Los, B. (2005) *The Rise of the To-Infinitive*, Oxford University Press, Oxford.

Lust, B. (2006) *Child Language: Acquisition and Growth*, Cambridge, Cambridge University Press.

Lutz, U., Müller, G. and von Stechow, A. (eds) (2000) *Wh-Scope Marking*, Benjamins, Amsterdam.

MacWhinney, B. (1995). *The CHILDES project: Tools for analyzing talk* (2nd ed.), Hillsdale, N.J.: LEA.

McCawley, J. D. (1993) 'Gapping with shared operators', *Berkeley Linguistics Society* 19: 245–254.

McCloskey, J. (1997) 'Subjecthood and subject positions', in L. Haegeman (ed.) *Elements of Grammar*, Kluwer, Dordrecht, pp. 197–235.

(2000) 'Quantifier Float and *Wh*-Movement in an Irish English', *Linguistic Inquiry* 31: 57–84.

(2001) 'The morphosyntax of WH-extraction in Irish', *Journal of Linguistics* 37: 67–100.

(2002) 'Resumption, successive cyclicity, and the locality of operations', in S. D. Epstein & T. D. Seeley (eds) *Derivation and Explanation in the Minimalist Program*, Blackwell, Oxford, pp. 184–226.

McDaniel, D. (1986) 'Conditions on Wh-chains', doctoral dissertation, City University of New York.

(1989) 'Partial and multiple wh-movement', *Natural Language and Linguistic Theory* 7: 565–604.

McGinnis, M. (2004) 'Lethal ambiguity', *Linguistic Inquiry* 35: 47–95.

McGinnis, M. & Richards, N. (eds) (2005) *Perspectives on Phases*, MIT Working Papers in Linguistics, 49.

McNally, L. (1992) 'VP-coordination and the VP-internal subject hypothesis', *Linguistic Inquiry* 23: 336–41.

McNeill, D. (1966) 'Developmental psycholinguistics', in F. Smith & G. A. Miller (eds) *The Genesis of Language*, MIT Press, Cambridge Mass., pp. 15–84.

Maekawa, T. (2007) 'The English left periphery in linearisation-based HPSG', PhD diss., University of Essex.

Mahajan, A. (1994) 'Active passives', *Proceedings of the West Coast Conference on Formal Linguistics* 23: 286–301.

Manzini, M. R. (1994) 'Locality, Minimalism and parasitic gaps', *Linguistic Inquiry* 25: 481–508.

Manzini, M. R. & Roussou, A. (2000) 'A Minimalist approach to A-movement and control', *Lingua* 110: 409–447.

Manzini, M. R. & Wexler, K. (1987) 'Parameters, binding theory and learnability', *Linguistic Inquiry* 18: 413–444.

Marcus, G. F. (1993) 'Negative evidence in language acquisition', *Cognition* 46: 53–85.

Martin, R. (1996) 'A Minimalist theory of PRO and Control', PhD diss., University of Connecticut, Storrs.

(2001) 'Null case and the distribution of PRO', *Linguistic Inquiry* 32: 141–166.

Matushansky, O. (2006) 'Head movement in linguistic theory', *Linguistic Inquiry* 37: 69–109.

Merchant, J. (2001) *The Syntax of Silence: Sluicing, Islands and Identity in Ellipsis*, Oxford University Press, Oxford.

(2005) 'Fragments and ellipsis', *Linguistics and Philosophy* 27: 661–738.

Milsark, G. (1974) *Existential Sentences in English*, Indiana University Linguistics Club, Bloomington, Indiana.

(1977) 'Peculiarities of the existential construction in English', *Linguistic Analysis* 3: 1–29.

Miyagawa, S. (2005) 'On the EPP', *MIT Working Papers in Linguistics* 49: 201–236.

(2006) 'Moving to the edge', in *Proceedings of the 2006 KALS-KASELL International Conference on English and Linguistics*, Pusan National University, Busan, Korea, 3–18.

Montalbetti, M. (1984) 'After binding', PhD diss., MIT.

Morgan, J. L. & Travis, L. (1989) 'Limits on negative information in language input', *Journal of Child Language* 16: 531–552.

Moro, A. (1997) *The Raising of Predicates*, Cambridge University Press, Cambridge.

Müller, G. & Sternefeld, W. (1993) 'Improper movement and unambiguous binding', *Linguistic Inquiry* 24: 461–507.

Nakajima, H. (2001) 'Verbs in locative constructions and the generative lexicon', *The Linguistic Review* 18: 43–67.

(2006) 'Adverbial cognate objects', *Linguistic Inquiry* 37: 674–684.

Neeleman, A. & Szendrői, K. (2004) 'Superman sentences', *Linguistic Inquiry* 35: 149–159.

(2005) 'Pro Drop and Pronouns', in J. Alderete *et al.* (eds) *Proceedings of the 24th West Coast Conference on Formal Linguistics*, Cascadilla Press, Somerville Mass., pp. 299–307.

Newmeyer, F. J. (2004) 'Against a parameter-setting approach to language variation', *Linguistic Variation Yearbook*, 4: 181–234.

(2005) 'On split CPs, uninterpretable features and the "perfectness" of language', *Zentrum für allgemeine Sprachwissentshaft Papers in Linguistics* 35: 399–422.

(2006) 'A rejoinder to "On the role of parameters in Universal Grammar: a reply to Newmeyer" by Ian Roberts and Anders Holmberg', ms., University of Washington.

Nkemnji, M. (1995) 'Heavy pied-piping in Nweh', PhD diss., University of California, Los Angeles.

Nomura, T. (2006) *ModalP and Subjunctive Present*, Hituzi Syobo, Tokyo.

Nunes, J. (1999) 'Linearization of chains and phonetic realisation of chain links', in S. D. Epstein & N. Hornstein (eds) *Working Minimalism*, MIT Press, Cambridge Mass., pp. 217–249.

(2001) 'Sideward movement', *Linguistic Inquiry* 32: 303–344.

(2004) *Linearization of Chains and Sideward Movement*, MIT Press, Cambridge Mass.

Nunes, J. & Uriagereka, J. (2000) 'Cyclicity and extraction domains', *Syntax* 3: 20–43.

Ochi, M. (1999) 'Multiple spell-out and PF-adjacency', *Proceedings of the North-Eastern Linguistic Society* 29: 293–306.

O'Neil, J. (1995) 'Out of control', *Proceedings of NorthEastern Linguistics Society* (NELS) 25: 361–371.

Ormazabal, J. (1995) 'The syntax of complementation', PhD diss., University of Connecticut.

Ortiz de Urbina, J. (1989) *Parameters in the Grammar of Basque*, Foris, Dordrecht.

Ouhalla, J. (1990) 'Sentential negation, relativized minimality and the aspectual status of auxiliaries', *The Linguistic Review* 7: 183–231.

Oya, T. (2002) 'Reflexives and resultatives: Some differences between English and German', *Linguistics* 40: 961–986.

Perlmutter, D. (1970) 'The two verbs *begin*', in R. A. Jacobs & P. S. Rosenbaum (eds) *Readings in English Transformational Grammar*, Ginn, Waltham Mass., pp. 107–119.

Pesetsky, D. (1982) 'Complementiser-trace phenomena and the Nominative Island Condition', *Linguistic Review* 1: 297–343.

(1987) '*Wh*-in-situ: Movement and unselective binding', in E. J. Reuland and A. G. B. ter Meulen (eds) *The Representation of (In)definiteness*, MIT Press, Cambridge Mass., pp. 98–129.

(1995) *Zero Syntax: Experiencers and Cascades*, MIT Press, Cambridge Mass.

(1997) 'Optimality Theory and syntax: Movement and pronunciation', in D. Archangeli & D. T. Langendoen (eds) *Optimality Theory: An Overview*, Blackwell, Oxford, pp. 134–170.

(1998) 'Some optimality principles of sentence pronunciation', in P. Barbosa, D. Fox, P. Hagstrom, M. McGinnis & D. Pesetsky (eds) *Is the Best Good Enough?* MIT Press, Cambridge Mass., pp. 337–383.

(2000) *Phrasal Movement and Its Kin*, MIT Press, Cambridge Mass.

Pesetsky, D. & Torrego, E. (2001) 'T-to-C movement: Causes and consequences', in M. Kenstowicz (ed.) *Ken Hale: A Life in Language*, MIT Press, Cambridge Mass., pp. 355–426.

(2007) 'The syntax of valuation and the interpretability of features', in S. Karimi, V. Samiian & W. Wilkins (eds) *Phrasal and Clausal Architecture: Syntactic Derivation and Interpretation*, John Benjamins, Amsterdam, pp. 262–294.

Phillips, C. (2003) 'Linear order and constituency', *Linguistic Inquiry* 34: 37–90.

Piattelli-Palmarini, M. (2000) 'The metric of open-mindedness', *Natural Language and Linguistic Theory*, 18: 859–862.

Poletto, C. & Benincà, P. (2004) 'Topic, Focus and V2: Defining the CP sublayers', in L. Rizzi. (ed.) *The Structure of IP and CP: The Cartography of Syntactic Structures*, vol. 2, Oxford University Press, Oxford.

Polinsky, M. & Potsdam, E. (2001) 'Long-distance agreement and Topic in Tsez', *Natural Language and Linguistic Theory* 19: 583–646.

(2006) 'Expanding the scope of control and raising', *Syntax* 9: 171–192.

Pollard, C. & Sag, I. A. (1994) *Head-Driven Phrase Structure Grammar*, CSLI Publications, Chicago.

Pollock, J.-Y. (1989) 'Verb movement, Universal Grammar, and the structure of IP', *Linguistic Inquiry* 20: 365–424.

Postal, P. M. (1966) 'On so-called pronouns in English', in F. Dinneen (ed.) *Nineteenth Monograph on Language and Linguistics*, Georgetown University Press, Washington DC (reprinted in D. Reibel & S. Schane (eds) (1969) *Modern Studies in English*, Prentice-Hall, Englewood Cliff N.J., pp. 201–224).

(1974) *On Raising: One Rule of English Grammar and Its Theoretical Implications*, MIT Press, Cambridge Mass.

(1998) *Three Investigations of Extraction*, MIT Press, Cambridge Mass.

Potsdam, E. (1997) 'NegP and Subjunctive', *Linguistic Inquiry* 28: 533–541.

(1998) *Syntactic Issues in the English Imperative*, Garland, New York.

Potts, C. (2002) 'The syntax and semantics of *as*-parentheticals', *Natural Language and Linguistic Theory* 20: 623–689.

Pullum, G. K. & Scholz, B. C. (2002) 'Empirical assessment of stimulus poverty arguments', *The Linguistic Review* 19: 9–50.

Rackowski, A. & Richards, N. (2005) 'Phase edge and extraction: A Tagalog case study', *Linguistic Inquiry* 36: 565–599.

Radford, A. (1981) *Transformational Syntax*, Cambridge University Press, Cambridge.

(1988) *Transformational Grammar: A First Course*, Cambridge University Press, Cambridge.

(1992) 'The acquisition of the morphosyntax of finite verbs in English', in J. M. Meisel (ed.), *The Acquisition of Verb Placement*, Kluwer, Dordrecht, pp. 23–62.

(1993) 'Head-hunting: On the trail of the nominal Janus', in G. Corbett, N. M. Fraser & S. McGlashan (eds) *Heads in Grammatical Theory*, Cambridge University Press, Cambridge, pp. 73–111.

(1997a) *Syntactic Theory and the Structure of English*, Cambridge University Press, London.

(1997b) *Syntax: A Minimalist Introduction*, Cambridge University Press, London.

(2004a) *Minimalist Syntax: Exploring the Structure of English*, Cambridge University Press, Cambridge.

(2004b) *English Syntax: An Introduction*, Cambridge University Press, Cambridge.

(2007) 'Split projections, percolation, syncretism and interrogative auxiliary inversion', *Research Reports in Linguistics* 53: 157–191, University of Essex.

Radford, A., Atkinson, M., Britain, D., Clahsen, H. & Spencer, A. (1999) *Linguistics: An Introduction*, Cambridge University Press, Cambridge.

Radford, A. & Vincent, M. (2007) 'On past participle agreement in transitive clauses in French', paper presented to *XXXIII Incontro di Grammatica Generativa*, available at http://amsacta.cib.unibo.it/archive/00002397/01/PROCEEDINGS_IGG33.pdf

Ramchand, G. (1996) 'Two subject positions in Scottish Gaelic: The syntax-semantics interface', *Natural Language Semantics* 4: 165–191.

Raposo, E. (1986) 'On the null object in European Portuguese', in O. Jaeggli & C. Silva-Corvalan (eds) *Studies in Romance Linguistics*, Foris, Dordrecht, pp. 373–390.

Reinhart, T. (1998) '*Wh*-in-situ in the framework of the Minimalist Program', *Natural Language Semantics* 6: 29–56.

Reintges, C. H., LeSourd, P. & Chung, S. (2002) 'Movement, wh-agreement and apparent wh-in-situ', paper presented to Workshop on Wh-Movement, University of Leiden, December 2002.

(2006) 'Movement, *wh*-agreement and apparent *wh*-in-situ', in Cheng and Corver (eds), pp. 165–194.

Reuland, E. (2000) 'Revolution, discovery and an elementary principle of logic', *Natural Language and Linguistic Theory* 18: 843–848.

(2001a) 'Primitives of Binding', *Linguistic Inquiry* 32: 439–492.

(2001b) 'Confusion compounded', *Natural Language and Linguistic Theory* 19: 879–885.

Reuland, E. & Everaert, M. (2001) 'Deconstructing Binding', in Baltin & Collins (eds), pp. 634–670.

Rezac, M. (2003) 'The fine structure of cyclic Agree', *Syntax* 6: 156–182.

(2006) 'The interaction of Th/Ex and Locative Inversion', *Linguistic Inquiry* 37: 685–697.

Richards, M. D. (2007) 'On feature inheritance: An argument from the Phase Impenetrability Condition', *Linguistic Inquiry* 38: 563–572.

Richards, N. (1997) 'What moves where when in which language?', PhD diss., MIT. (A published version appeared as Richards 2001.)

(2001) *Movement in Language: Interactions and Architectures*, Oxford University Press, Oxford.

(2004) 'Against bans on lowering', *Linguistic Inquiry* 35: 453–463.

Rizzi, L. (1982) *Issues in Italian Syntax*, Foris, Dordrecht.

(1986) 'Null objects in Italian and the theory of *pro*', *Linguistic Inquiry* 17: 501–557.

(1990) *Relativised Minimality*, MIT Press, Cambridge Mass.

(1997) 'The fine structure of the left periphery', in L. Haegeman (ed.) *Elements of Grammar*, Kluwer, Dordrecht, pp. 281–337.

(2000) 'Remarks on early null subjects', in M.-A. Freidemann & L. Rizzi (eds) *The Acquisition of Syntax*, Longman, London, pp. 269–292.

(2001a) 'Relativized minimality effects', in Baltin & Collins, pp. 89–110.

(2001b) 'On the position "Int(errogative)" in the left periphery of the clause', in G. Cinque and G. Salvi (eds) *Current Issues in Italian Syntax*, Elsevier, Amsterdam, pp. 287–296.

(2004) 'Locality and Left Periphery', in A. Belletti (ed.) *Structures and Beyond: The Cartography of Syntactic Structures*, vol.3, Oxford University Press, pp. 223–251.

(2006) 'On the form of chains: Criterial positions and ECP effects', in Cheng & Corver (eds), pp. 97–133.

Rizzi, L. & Shlonsky, U. (2005) 'Strategies of subject extraction', ms., Universities of Siena and Geneva.

Roberts, I. (1987) *The Representation of Implicit and Dethematized Subjects*, Foris, Dordrecht.

(1993) *Verbs and Diachronic Syntax*, Kluwer, Dordrecht.

(1994) 'Two types of head movement in Romance', in Lightfoot & Hornstein (eds), pp. 207–242.

(1997) 'Restructuring, head movement and locality', *Linguistic Inquiry* 28: 423–460.

(1998) '*Have/Be* Raising, Move F and Procrastinate', *Linguistic Inquiry* 29: 113–125.

(2000) 'Caricaturing dissent', *Natural Language and Linguistic Theory* 18: 849–857.

(2001a) 'Who has confused what? More on Lappin, Levine and Johnson', *Natural Language and Linguistic Theory* 19: 887–890.

(2001b) 'Head Movement', in Baltin and Collins (eds), pp. 113–147.

Roberts, I. & Holmberg, A. (2006) 'On the role of parameters in Universal Grammar: A reply to Newmeyer', ms., University of Cambridge.

Roberts, I. & Roussou, A. (2002) 'The Extended Projection Principle as a condition on the tense dependency', in P. Svenonius (ed.) *Subjects, Expletives and the EPP*, Oxford University Press, Oxford, pp. 125–155.

Romero, M. (1997) 'The correlation between scope reconstruction and connectivity effects', in E. Curtiss, J. Lyle and G. Webster (eds) *Proceedings of the XVI West Coast Conference in Formal Linguistics*, CLSI, Stanford, pp. 351–365.

Rosen, S. T. (1990) *Argument Structure and Complex Predicates*, Garland, New York.

Rosenbaum, P. S. (1965) 'The grammar of English predicate complement constructions', PhD diss., MIT (published as Rosenbaum 1967).

(1967) *The Grammar of English Predicate Complement Constructions*, MIT Press, Cambridge Mass.

Rosengren, I. (2002) 'A syntactic device in the service of semantics', *Studia Linguistica* 56: 145–190.

Ross, J. R. (1967) 'Constraints on variables in syntax', PhD diss., MIT (published as *Infinite Syntax!* by Ablex Publishing Corporation, Norwood, New Jersey, 1986).

(1970) 'On declarative sentences', in R. A. Jacobs & P. S. Rosenbaum (eds) *Readings in English Transformational Grammar*, Ginn, Waltham, Mass. pp. 222–272.

Rothstein, S. D. (1983) 'The syntactic form of predication', PhD diss., MIT.

Rudin, C. (1988) 'On multiple questions and multiple *wh*-fronting', *Natural Language and Linguistic Theory* 6: 445–501.

Runner, J. (1998) *Noun Phrase Licensing and Interpretation*, Garland, New York.

(2006) 'Lingering challenges to the raising-to-object and object-control constructions', *Syntax* 9: 193–219.

Rupp, L. (2003) *The Syntax of Imperatives in English and Germanic: Word Order Variation in the Minimalist Framework*, Palgrave Macmillan, New York.

Rymer, R. (1993) *Genie: A Scientific Tragedy*, Harper Perennial, New York.

Sabel, J. (2002) 'A minimalist analysis of syntactic islands', *The Linguistic Review* 19: 271–315.

Saddy, D. (1991) 'Wh scope mechanisms in Bahasa Indonesia', in L. Cheng & H. Demirdache (eds) *MIT Working Papers in Linguistics* 15: 183–218.

Sadler, L. & Arnold, D. J. (1994) 'Prenominal adjectives and the phrasal/lexical distinction', *Journal of Linguistics* 30: 187–226.

Safir, K. (1984) 'Missing subjects in German', in I. Toman (ed.) *Studies in German Grammar*, Foris, Dordrecht, pp.193–230.

(1986) *Syntactic Chains*, Cambridge University Press, Cambridge.

Sag, I. (1980) *Deletion and Logical Form*, Garland, New York.

(1997) 'English relative clause constructions', *Journal of Linguistics* 33: 431–483.

Sampson, G. (2002) 'Exploring the richness of the stimulus', *The Linguistic Review* 19: 73–104.

(2005) *The Language Instinct Debate*, Continuum International Publishing Group, London.

Sauerland, U. (1998) 'The meaning of chains', PhD diss., MIT.

Sauerland, U. & Elbourne, P. (2002) 'Total reconstruction, PF movement and derivational order', *Linguistic Inquiry* 33: 283–319.

Sawada, H. (1995) *Studies in English and Japanese Auxiliaries: A Multi-stratal Approach*, Hituzi Syobo, Tokyo.

Scholz, B. C. & Pullum, G. K. (2002) 'Searching for arguments to support linguistic nativism', *The Linguistic Review* 19: 185–223.

Schütze, C. (1999) 'English expletive constructions are not infected', *Linguistic Inquiry* 30: 467–484.

(2004) 'Synchronic and diachronic microvariation in English *do*', *Lingua* 114: 495–516.

Schwarz, B. (1999) 'On the syntax of *either . . . or*', *Natural Language and Linguistic Theory* 17: 339–370.

(2000) *Topics in Ellipsis*, GLSA Publications, Amherst Mass.

Seppänen, A. & Trotta, J. (2000) 'The *wh+that* pattern in present-day English', in J. M. Kirk. (ed.) *Corpora Galore: Analyses and Techniques in Describing English*, Rodopi, Amsterdam, pp. 161–175.

Shlonsky, U. (1991) 'Quantifiers as functional heads: A study of quantifier float in Hebrew', *Lingua* 84: 159–180.

Sigurðsson, H. Á. (1996) 'Icelandic finite verb agreement', *Working Papers in Scandinavian Syntax* 57: 1–46.

(2006) 'The nominative puzzle and the Low Nominative Hypothesis', *Linguistic Inquiry* 37: 289–308.

Smith, N. (1998) 'Jackdaws, sex and language acquisition', *Glot International* 3, 7: 7.

(2004, 2nd edition) *Chomsky: Ideas and Ideals*, Cambridge University Press, Cambridge.

Smith, N. & Cormack, A. (2002) 'Indeterminacy, inference, iconicity and interpretation: Aspects of the grammar-pragmatics interface', in M. Makri-Tsilipakou (ed.) *Selected Papers on Theoretical and Applied Linguistics*, Aristotle University of Thessaloniki, pp. 38–53.

Sobin, N. (1997) 'Agreement, default rules and grammatical viruses', *Linguistic Inquiry* 28: 318–343.

(2003) 'Negative inversion as non-movement', *Syntax* 6: 183–212.

(2004) 'Expletive constructions are not "lower right corner" movement constructions', *Linguistic Inquiry* 35: 503–508.

Sorace, A. (2000) 'Gradients in auxiliary selection with intransitive verbs', *Language* 76: 859–890.

Speas, P. (1986) 'Adjunction and projections in syntax', PhD diss., MIT, Cambridge Mass.

Spencer, A. J. (1991) *Morphological Theory*, Blackwell, Oxford.

Spinillo, M. G. (2004) 'Reconceptualising the English determiner class', PhD diss., University College London.

Sportiche, D. (1988) 'A theory of floating quantifiers and its corollaries for constituent structure', *Linguistic Inquiry* 19: 425–49.

(1998) 'Movement, agreement and case', in *Partitions and Atoms of Clause Structure*, Routledge, London, pp. 88–243.

Sprouse, J. (2007) 'Rhetorical questions and wh-movement', *Linguistic Inquiry* 38: 572–580.

Stepanov, A. (2001) 'Late adjunction and minimalist phrase structure', *Syntax* 4: 94–125.

Stockwell, R., Schachter, P. & Partee, B. (1973) *The Major Syntactic Structures of English*, Holt, Rinehart and Winston, New York.

Stowell, T. (1981) 'Origins of phrase structure', PhD diss., MIT.

(1982) 'The tense of infinitives', *Linguistic Inquiry* 13: 561–570.

Stroik, T. (2001) 'On the light verb hypothesis', *Linguistic Inquiry* 32: 362–369.

Suñer, M. (1984) 'Controlled *pro*', in P. Baldi (ed.) *Papers from the XIIth Linguistic Symposium on Romance Languages*, University Park Press, Baltimore, pp. 254–273.

Surányi, B. (2006) 'Mechanisms of wh-saturation and interpretation in multiple wh-movement', in Cheng and Corver (eds), pp. 288–318.

Svenonius, P. (2002a) 'Case is uninterpretable aspect', http://www.hum.uit.no/a/svenonius/paperspage.html.

(2002b) 'Icelandic case and the structure of events', http://www.hum.uit.no/a/svenonius/paperspage.html.

Tallerman, M. O. (1993) 'Case assignment and the order of functional projections in Welsh', in A. Siewierska (ed.) *Eurotyp Working Papers*, Programme in Language Typology, European Science Foundation, Berlin, pp. 1–41.

Tamburelli, M. (2006) 'Remarks on richness', *UCL Working Papers in Linguistics*, 18: 1–17.

(2007) 'The role of lexical acquisition in simultaneous bilingualism', PhD diss., University College London.

Ten Hacken, P. (2001) Review of Radford (1997a,b), *Natural Language Engineering*, 7(1): 87–97.

Tenny, C. (1987) 'Grammaticalizing aspect and affectedness', PhD diss., MIT.

Thomas, M. (2002) 'Development of the concept of "the poverty of stimulus"', *The Linguistic Review* 19: 51–71.

Thompson, E. (2006) 'The structure of bounded events', *Linguistic Inquiry* 37: 211–228.

Thornton, R. (1995) 'Referentiality and *Wh*-Movement in Child English: Juvenile *D-Link*uency', *Language Acquisition* 4: 139–175.

Ticio, M. E. (2003) 'On the structure of DPs', PhD diss., University of Connecticut.

(2005) 'Locality and anti-locality in Spanish DPs', *Syntax* 8: 229–286.

Tieken-Boon van Ostade, I. (1988) 'The origins and development of periphrastic auxiliary *do*: a case of destigmatisation', *Dutch Working Papers in English Language and Linguistics* 3: 1–30.

Toda, T. (2007) '*So*-inversion revisited', *Linguistic Inquiry* 38: 188–195.

Torrego, E. (1984) 'On inversion in Spanish and some of its effects', *Linguistic Inquiry* 15: 103–129.

Toyoshima, T. (2000) 'Heading for their own places', *MIT Working Papers in Linguistics* 36: 93–108.

Travis, L. (1984) 'Parameters and effects of word order variation', PhD diss., MIT.

Uchibori, A. (2000) 'The syntax of subjunctive complements: Evidence from Japanese', unpublished dissertation, University of Connecticut.

Ura, H. (1993) 'On feature-checking for *wh*-traces', *MIT Working Papers in Linguistics* 18: 243–280.

(2001) 'Local economy and generalized pied-piping', *The Linguistic Review* 18: 169–191.

Uriagereka, J. (1988) 'On Government', PhD diss., University of Connecticut.

(1998) *Rhyme and Reason*, MIT Press, Cambridge Mass.

(2000) 'On the emptiness of "design" polemics', *Natural Language and Linguistic Theory*, 18: 863–871.

(2001) 'Cutting derivational options', *Natural Language and Linguistic Theory*, 19: 891–900.

Vainikka, A. & Levy, Y. (1999) 'Empty subjects in Finnish and Hebrew', *Natural Language and Linguistic Theory* 17: 613–671.

van Craenenbroeck, J. & den Dicken, M. (2006) 'Ellipsis and EPP repair', *Linguistic Inquiry* 37: 653–664.

van Eynde, F. (2006) 'NP-internal agreement and the structure of the noun phrase', *Journal of Linguistics* 42: 139–186.

van Gelderen, E. (2004) *Grammaticalization as Economy*, John Benjamins, Amsterdam.

van Langendonck, W. (1994) 'Determiners as heads?', *Cognitive Linguistics* 5: 243–259.

van Riemsdijk, H. (1989) 'Movement and regeneration', in P. Benincà (ed.) *Dialectal Variation and the Theory of Grammar*, Foris, Dordrecht, pp. 105–136.

Verkuyl, H. J., de Swart, H. & van Hout, A. (eds) (2005) *Perspectives on Aspect*, Springer, Dordrecht.

von Fintel, K. (1999) 'NPI licensing, Strawson entailment and context dependency', *Journal of Semantics* 16: 97–148.

Watanabe, A. (2001) '*Wh*-in-situ languages', in Baltin & Collins, pp. 203–225.

(2004) 'The genesis of negative concord: Syntax and morphology of negative doubling', *Linguistic Inquiry* 35: 559–612.

(2006) 'The pied-piper feature', in Cheng & Corver, pp. 47–70.

Wexler, K. (1994) 'Optional Infinitives, Head Movement and the Economy of Derivations', in Lightfoot & Hornstein (eds), pp. 305–350.

(1998) 'Very early parameter-setting and the unique checking constraint: A new explanation of the optional infinitive stage', *Lingua* 106: 23–79.

Williams, E. (1980) 'Predication', *Linguistic Inquiry* 11: 203–238.

(2006) 'The subject-predicate theory of *there*', *Linguistic Inquiry* 36: 648–651.

Willis, D. (2000) 'On the distribution of resumptive pronouns and *wh*-trace in Welsh', *Journal of Linguistics* 36: 531–73.

Wiltschko, M. (1998) 'On the syntax and semantics of (relative) pronouns and determiners', *Journal of Comparative Germanic Linguistics* 2: 143–181.

(2001) 'The syntax of pronouns: Evidence from Halkomelem Salish', *Natural Language and Linguistic Theory* 20: 157–195.

Woolford, E. (1991) 'VP-internal subjects in VSO and nonconfigurational languages', *Linguistic Inquiry* 22: 503–40.

Yang, C. D. (1999) 'Unordered Merge and its linearization', *Syntax* 1: 38–64.

Yang, H. (2006) 'On overt and covert wh- and relative movement in Hindi and Punjabi', in Cheng & Corver (eds), pp. 135–164.

Zagona, K. (1987) *Verb Phrase Syntax*, Kluwer, Dordrecht.

Zamparelli, R. (2000) *Layers in the Determiner Phrase*, Garland, New York.

Zanuttini, R. (1991) 'Syntactic properties of sentential negation: A comparative study of Romance languages', PhD diss., University of Pennsylvania.

Zlatić, L. (1997) 'The structure of the Serbian Noun Phrase', PhD diss., University of Texas, Austin.

Zwart, C. J.-W. (2001) 'Syntactic and phonological verb movement', *Syntax* 4: 34–62.

Zwicky, A. (2002) 'I wonder what kind of construction that this kind of example illustrates', in D. Beaver, L. D. Casillas Martínez, B. Z. Clark & S. Kaufmann (eds) *The Construction of Meaning*, CSLI Publications, Stanford, pp. 219–248.

Index